"...and the

Mille Lacs

who have no reservation..."*

*A history of the Chippewa Indians in
Mille Lacs County, Minnesota up to 1934*

Clarence Ralph Fitz, BS, DVM

VOLUME 1

*April 20, 1892 letter from Commissioner of Indian Affairs T.J. Morgan to Secretary of the Interior John W. Noble, RG75, NAKC, Dept. of Interior, Office of Indian Affairs, White Earth Agency, Letters received from the Office of Indian Affairs 1889 — 1900, Box 49, NAID:7479717, HM:2014.

Copyright © 2016 by Clarence Ralph Fitz

All rights reserved.

No part of this book may be reproduced or transmitted in any form or by any means, electronic or mechanical, including photocopying, recording or by any information storage and retrieval system, without the written permission of the author, except where permitted by law.

ISBN: 978-1-60414-938-8

FIRST EDITION

Published by
Fideli Publishing Inc.
119 W. Morgan St.
Martinsville, IN 46151

www.FideliPublishing.com

Cover art: http://www.123rf.com/profile_skvoor

This Book is Dedicated to:

- The Love of my life, my late wife Donna, who was my inspiration for this work and was my companion in this struggle for just short of 50 years.

- Our three wonderful children, our son-in-laws and our granddaughters, who all have graciously listened to me discuss and vent about these issues.

- To my dear friend Verna, who has given me insight into the issues from a different perspective.

A Note of Gratitude...

to Lana Marcussen, who by example taught me how to navigate the National Archives and for her help in my understanding of federal Indian policy,

to Nancy Schumann for her encouragement and guidance in the early stages of my book,

to Elaine Willman and Lauralee O'Neil for their editing and suggestions with the final draft and to Lauralee for designing the cover,

to the staff at The UPS Store #2820 for their help,

to my daughter for solving a Windows 8 issue, and

to Karrie Roeschlein, city clerk of Wahkon, MN, for referring a message to me from a FOIA representative that resulted in a face-to-face meeting at the Bureau of Indian Affairs in Washington, D.C. and ultimately to my finding the briefs to SCOTUS on the 1913 case.

Prologue

My late wife Donna and I were both born and raised in Iowa. We moved to Minnesota in 1964, started a veterinary practice there and began spending our summer vacations at Lake Mille Lacs. We had the entrepreneurial spirit so common in the 1960's and saw Mille Lacs Lake—the Walleye capital of the world—as fertile ground. Inspired, we purchased a small run-down housekeeping resort, the kind common at that time, and spent many loving hours and hard-earned dollars in refurbishing. Under my wife's management families would come for a few days at a time, cook their own meals and play in the lake, all at affordable cost. Neither in casual conversation with friends nor in professional dealings did we get any inkling that the land and property we had purchased was considered by some to be located on an Indian reservation.

Not until the early 1990's, when the Mille Lacs tribal government attempted to make a behind the scenes agreement with the State of Minnesota to divide Lake Mille Lacs into a tribal zone and a non-tribal zone, did we get concerned. Even more importantly, we found out that the same agreement would have **forced** the State of Minnesota to recognize the land we had purchased and the surrounding 61,000 acres as being part of an Indian reservation.

Admittedly naive in the beginning, I thought that conversation at the negotiation table could resolve these issues, but I came to find out that it was not that simple. The opinions on both sides of the dispute are so deep-seated that it will undoubtedly require litigation to settle the question. Thousands of dollars—donor and taxpayer dollars—have already been spent in that endeavor, but to no avail. The litigation efforts were not productive and the disagreement lives on.

To state it simply, the federal government, primarily through the Department of the Interior—of which the Bureau of Indian Affairs is a part—the Mille Lacs tribal government and some Mille Lacs County citizens claim that the Mille Lacs Indian reservation, which was established in 1855, still exists. In contrast, the State of Minnesota and Mille Lacs County, as well as a portion of its cities, townships and citizens, believe that the 1855 reservation was sold and disestablished years ago.

As you travel around the United States you will notice that highway signs usually announce Indian reservations. In Mille Lacs County we are confused by the presence of highway signs at the borders of trust lands, purchased by the United States government for the use of the Mille Lac Indians—Indians who were classified by the government at the time as the "homeless non-removal Mille Lacs." There are no highway signs on the borders of the 61,000 acres saying "Now entering Mille Lacs Indian Reservation."

The goal of my research has been to uncover the historical facts that play into the situation. Most certainly in the settling of this country we had technologically advanced immigrants with skills they brought with them from Europe. These immigrants were clashing with the Indians, who were in large part living off the land—hunting, fishing and gathering on land that they defended and enlarged by warfare. As an example, the east coast settlers were living in well-built permanent structures and people like Benjamin Franklin were inventing devices to make life easier. At the same time, the Chippewa Indians of Minnesota were living in birch bark huts and battling with the Sioux at Mille Lacs for territory. At the time the United States government defined "civilization" as the progression of the Indian from nomadic hunting, fishing and gathering to a stable existence on a defined piece of land where they were expected to grow crops to feed their families. Additionally, there were major differences in how these tribal societies governed themselves. And thus there were struggles; some honest, some devious and yes, some criminal.

I have chosen to limit this work to a study beginning with the arrival of the Chippewa in Minnesota through 1934. The advent of the Indian Reorganization Act in 1934 completely changed the governmental structure for the Indians, for the United States government and for us all.

The primary questions I hope readers will be able to answer for themselves are:

1) Does the 1855 Mille Lacs Indian Reservation still exist?
2) Is there an Indian reservation in Mille Lacs County, Minnesota?
3) Was the Mille Lacs band a recognized band at the time of the passage of the 1934 Indian Reorganization Act? And
4) Did our federal Government create a massive fraud which still haunts the citizens of Mille Lacs County, Minnesota, in the twenty-first century?

In order to answer these questions, we need to answer even more basic questions:
1) Can the provision in the 1855 treaty that created the Mille Lacs Reservation and gave the Indians this reservation as their permanent home, survive the sale of that reservation?
2) When the Indians sold the reservation in the treaties of 1863-64, what did the proviso granting them the right of occupancy mean?

3) Because the Indians relinquished that right of occupancy in 1889, can the reservation still exist? And
4) If the reservation still existed after the 1889 Nelson Act, why did the Mille Lacs band ask the United States Court of Claims and ultimately the United States Supreme Court to be paid for the reservation land?

Some of the general topics in the first few chapters are necessary because they delve into concepts and conditions that influenced the events that followed. They helped me gain a deeper understanding, and I hope they will also assist the reader. I have endeavored to give the reader a feel for the people and the times in which they lived, using actual quotes when I felt they were helpful for comprehending the realities of the day. Also included are a few anecdotes because I found them interesting, and hope you do so as well.

I have chosen to use the term "Indians" for the people who were living in this country at the time the Europeans arrived, and to call the Indian tribe about which I write "Chippewa", because that is the terminology used in the many archival documents which I studied for the writing of the book.

In conclusion, my original goal was to be completely objective in writing this book, but what I have discovered is that no author can be completely objective. Even deciding what to include becomes subjective. However, I have done my best to remain unbiased because I wish you, the reader, to come to your own conclusions. My opinions will surface at times, but the facts are there for your use in deciding whether to agree, or not.

This has been a massive undertaking, and I have thoroughly enjoyed the researching and writing of this book. Most significantly, my understanding of the subject has substantially mushroomed. There were times that I experienced empathy for the Chippewa people, and certainly times that I shared the fears of the isolated settlers. But most of all, I sincerely hope that the reader will find reading this book interesting, provocative and, above all, accurate.

Clarence Ralph Fitz,
B.S., D.V.M.

Table of Contents

Dedication iii

A Note of Gratitude v

Prologue vii

Chapter 1	Early Migration 1
Chapter 2	Savages? 3
Chapter 3	The "Doctrine of Discovery" And "Manifest Destiny" 5
Chapter 4	The Doctrine of Discovery in Action 7
Chapter 5	So Who Was John Tanner? 12
Chapter 6	Hole-in-the-Day 16
Chapter 7	Minnesota — A Poster Child for Corruption in the Indian System in the Nineteenth Century? 27
Chapter 8	The 1837 Treaty 34
Chapter 9	The 1855 Treaty 42
Chapter 10	1862 - The Sioux Uprising 64
Chapter 11	Chippewa Involvement — 1862 Uprising 79
Chapter 12	1863 — 1864 Treaties 83
Chapter 13	Treaties in Action 95
Chapter 14	The 1870s 98
Chapter 15	The 1880s 108
Chapter 16	Chippewa Approve the Nelson Act 129
Chapter 17	Early 1900s 156
Chapter 18	One Last Effort 160
Chapter 19	*The Mille Lac Band of Chippewa Indians vs The United States* — 1913 168

Chapter 20	The Homeless Non-Removal Mille Lacs	175
Chapter 21	White Earth and the Nelson Act	211
Chapter 22	The Saga of Shaw vosh Kung's land	225
Chapter 23	Henry Mower Rice, 1816–1894	229
Chapter 24	John Collier's Dream	234
	Epilogue	237
	Notes	245

Appendix

	Maps	257
	Treaty with the Chippewa — 1837	263
	Treaty with the Chippewa — 1855	267
	Treaty with the Chippewa of the Mississippi and the Pillager and Lake Winnibigoshish Bands — 1863	275
	Treaty with the Chippewa, Mississippi, and Pillager and Lake Winnibigoshish Bands —1864	280
	An act for the relief and civilization of the Chippewa Indians in the State of Minnesota, (Nelson Act)	285
	Mille Lac Band Brief - SCOTUS No. 736 — Oct. 1912	362
	United States Brief - SCOTUS No. 736 — Oct. 1912	293
	U.S. Supreme Court Decision - No. 736 (229 U.S. 498) — June 9, 1913	409
	Reply to request from Senator Thomas	418
	Index	427

CHAPTER 1

Early Migration

The early history of the Ojibwe tribe of Indians in North America is recorded only by oral accounts of events as told and retold down through the generations, and consequently contradiction and exaggeration is common. We know, however, that the Ojibwe originally inhabited the area on the east coast, on the Atlantic Ocean in the vicinity of the gulf of the St. Lawrence River. How they got there we will leave to others. At this point we can either accept the legend that their ancestors spontaneously emerged from the waters of the ocean[1] or we can leave that determination to the archeologist who presently is being thwarted by the Native American Graves and Repatriation Act (Public Law 101-601, 101st Congress).

For whatever reason, the Ojibwe began a gradual migration westward to their final destination near the center of the North American continent in what is now the state of Minnesota. In a movement likely extending over a period of about two hundred years, the band would establish a community for a period of time and then move on. Traveling down the St. Lawrence River, they located for a time on the river bank near Montreal, and after some years moved on to Sault St. Marie on the St. Mary's River where Lake Superior flows into Lake Huron. Whether they were searching for more plentiful food sources, or, as the legend has it, seeking the land where food grows on water (wild rice), or whether their constant battles with the Six Nations of New York (the Iroquois) were taking their toll, we do not know. What we do know is that the Ojibwe lived in a primitive state at this time, and by necessity much emphasis must be placed on skirmishes with surrounding tribes.[2]

After a number of years they left Sault St. Marie. However, it was apparently at this point that the migration split. One group traveled along the north shore of Lake Superior into Canada. The second group traveled the south coast and camped for a time on a sandy point on the shore of Lake Superior. However, after constant harassment from the Fox and the Dakota tribes into whose territory they had intruded, the tribe opted for the protection afforded by the water and eventually established their camp on the Island of La Pointe (now called Madeline Island) in Lake Superior. Here they stayed for some years, subsisting on fish, moose, deer, elk, bear and other smaller animals and birds, and gardens of primarily Indian corn and pumpkins.

While both the Dakota and the Fox tribes occasionally traveled to the island in birch bark canoes for the purpose of attack, the Ojibwe, with their superior canoes designed for Lake Superior and their advantage of location, were able to exact revenge. Thus the attacks against them were few and of relatively small consequence.

The Ojibwe at the La Pointe village seemed to be living fairly well at this time, what with sufficient food sources and relative security from their enemies. This period was likely from around 1715 to 1775.[3] However, as you will read in subsequent chapters, the elder 'Hole in the Day' was allegedly born on Madeline Island in about 1800, and the Ojibwe reportedly drove the Dakota away from Mille Lac in about 1750, so exact or even approximate dates are suspect.

One must ask why the La Pointe settlement was eventually abandoned, with some of the Ojibwe retracing their migratory path and returning to areas previously occupied, while others pushed further westward to establish their village at Fond du Lac, located near the cities of Cloquet and Duluth in present day Minnesota. Was it because food became scarce due to crop failure or lack of game? Or perhaps it was due to threats and pressures from their enemies. Or was it as William W. Warren suggests (and as reluctantly told him by elder members of the Ojibwe tribe) that the religious practice of cannibalism, promoted by medicine men of the time, eventually haunted them into abandoning La Point?[4] At any rate, it was from this settlement at Fond du Lac that the tribe fanned out to occupy what would eventually become the State of Minnesota.

CHAPTER 2

Savages?

The Declaration of Independence was passed by the Second Continental Congress on July 4, 1776. The main body of the document passed by the original thirteen colonies enumerates the perceived wrongs endured by the colonies at the hands of the King of Great Britain. One of those 'wrongs' reads, "HE has excited domestic Insurrection amongst us, and has endeavored to bring on the Inhabitants of our Frontiers, the merciless Indian Savages, whose known Rule of Warfare, is an undistinguished Destruction, of all Ages, Sexes and Conditions."

Remembering that the British under King George had a relationship with the Indians as they colonized North America, it is reasonable to believe that the British, and also the Loyalists who were faithful to King George, might have been responsible for riling up the Indians. This relationship survived well past the Declaration and even the establishment of the United States of America.

What does history tell us? Were the Ojibwe and other Indian tribes in fact "merciless savages?" In order to properly understand how the colonists came to the conclusion prompting the description Indian Savages, several common practices used by the Indians in warfare must be examined.

First was the practice of scalping. Scalping was a ritual that had multiple significances. Initially one must understand that warfare was an almost constant pastime for the Ojibwe, and most often with the Dakota. While there were periods when the two tribes were friendly even to the point of living together, intermarrying and mixing blood lines, sooner or later an incident would occur that set them back on the warpath. Revenge was one of their methods of "covering the dead," and so they were constantly going back and forth seeking to revenge a killing. The act of scalping brought as much if not more honor to the young brave Indian as the actual slaying. Scalps were brought back to the village, at which point the religious or spiritual aspect of scalping took over. The scalp would be attached to the end of a stick and a ceremony or celebration would be performed, complete with dancing and feasting. Tribal members believed that these ceremonies released the spirit of the avenged into the spirit world. Not to be scalped following death in battle was seen as contempt: if one died in battle it was an honor to be scalped.[1]

Whether for revenge or for enlargement of territory it was not unusual in the heat of battle for whole villages to be killed, women and children included. Bows and arrows, knives and war clubs were used in earlier times, followed later by firearms.[2] Sometimes in the passion of revenge or in haste the entire head was removed and carried off; other times the scalping was done before the victim was slain. One such incident describes a child who came crawling back to its mother missing its scalp.[3]

Torture by fire was a technique practiced by the Fox tribe, as well as other tribes. This technique was apparently learned by the Ojibwe from the Fox. There are tales of prisoners being tied so close to the campfire that their skin blistered and burned, of flaming fat laden animal skins being draped on naked bodies, and of prisoners being tied up in animal skins and suspended above the fire until they cooked to death. However the method used, the prisoner was tied close enough to the campfire to cause him to roast until dead. William Warren writes about such incidents in his book *History of the Ojibway People*, as does David Price in his book *Love and Hate at Jamestown*.

Methods of warfare also differed greatly. While the colonists were familiar with the British technique where battles were fought in formation, the Ojibwe and their archenemy, the Dakota, used surprise to their advantage. Especially for revenge, small hunting parties might be chanced upon, killed and scalped. On other occasions entire encampments or villages were surrounded and everyone, including women and children, were massacred. Only occasionally would a captive, particularly a woman or a child, be taken back to their village.

Given the above referenced torture and mayhem it is easy to understand how the Indians could be described as "merciless savages" in our day, where techniques such as water boarding are hotly debated as to whether or not they are indeed torture.

In all fairness we must keep in mind that, at the same time that the Indians were scalping and torturing by fire, colonists were performing lynchings in the town square and whipping negro slaves, sometimes unto death.[4] Even as late as 1893, when Henry Smith was accused of murdering the three year old daughter of a white police officer in Paris, Texas, some 10,000 spectators turned out to see him tortured and burned in the village square.[5] And even today, while certainly less public, there occur acts of brutality and torture— including beheadings— in some countries including the United States.

In light of the above one might consider then that the writers of the Declaration of Independence were pointing out that the King was 'inciting' these actions against the settlers and that words such as "merciless savages" were used to embellish the charge of incitement.

CHAPTER 3

The "Doctrine of Discovery" and "Manifest Destiny"

Any student of federal Indian policy will eventually run into the concepts of the "Doctrine of Discovery" and "Manifest Destiny," both of which were instrumental in the creation of the United States of America and, at least in the case of the Doctrine of Discovery, remain as a viable doctrine of law. What follows is a brief discussion of these two concepts as I understand them.

The Doctrine of Discovery: In 1452, Catholic Pope Nicholas V released an order that authorized the Christian nations to establish ownership to any lands that they encountered or discovered that were not already inhabited and claimed by other Christian rulers, and to take possession of the land, and property, and the non-Christian inhabitants (called pagans or heathens) of that land. This order is referred to as the "papal bull" which simply means an order from the pope. Thus there was authorization from the highest religious leader of the day to take possession of any lands and peoples that they encountered who were not Christian, claiming ownership of said lands and peoples, usually for the leader of the nation that they served, and all done under the umbrella of Christendom.

Manifest Destiny: And so, using the Doctrine of Discovery as a foundation, it is easy to understand how settlers in the 1800's believed, rightly or wrongly, that it was their manifest destiny to push westward all the way to the Pacific, taking possession of and settling the land and saving souls by converting the Indians to Christendom, while at the same time using whatever method they deemed necessary to move the Indians out of the way so settlement could continue unimpeded. They were simply doing what God, through the church that spoke for God, had asked them to do.

While the pioneers were settling the land, the churches were sending missionaries into the frontier country to work with the Indians in order to introduce and convert them to Christianity. In Minnesota it was primarily the Catholic Church who sent

Bishop Henry Benjamin Whipple

missionaries into Chippewa country, and to a lesser extent the Episcopal Church, followed to a far lesser extent by the Methodist Church.

Bishop Henry Benjamin Whipple, the first Episcopalian Bishop of Minnesota, played a major role in the history of the fledgling state in the mid-1800's as Minnesota struggled to become a state, and as it dealt with the Indian population of first the territory and then the state.

In 1823 it was Chief Justice John Marshall who made the Doctrine of Discovery part of the United States law by his opinion in the case of *Johnson v. M'Intosh*, the first of the Marshall trilogy. In his opinion he explained that the European nations gained title to the newly discovered lands as a result of the Doctrine of Discovery and that title had passed down to the United States when it gained its independence in 1776.

This legal doctrine has survived the test of time as evidenced by the opinion of the court delivered by Justice Powell in 1985 in *Oneida County v. Oneida Indian Nation*. Justice Powell said, "The 'doctrine of discovery' provided, however, that discovering nations held fee title to these lands, subject to the Indians' right of occupancy and use."

Even more recently, the opinion in *Oneida County v. Oneida Indian Nation* was cited in a footnote to the 2005 case, *City of Sherrill v. Oneida Indian Nation of New York* in an opinion written by Justice Ginsberg, saying, "fee title to the lands occupied by Indians when the colonists arrived became vested in the sovereign—first the discovering European nation and later the original States and the United States."

CHAPTER 4

The Doctrine of Discovery in Action

We now flash back to the 1400's in Europe in order to better understand the motivation behind the exploration across the expansive ocean that was beginning to occur. Because it was difficult and expensive finding trade routes across land to the East (India, China and Japan) efforts were made to find an ocean route to those regions. Most seafaring explorers had plans to sail east until they discovered a route, but Christopher Columbus thought he could sail west to find a trade route. He obviously was unaware that the American continent lay in his path, let alone that there was no water route across that landmass.

Columbus was born in Italy and his father was a weaver. After working for his father as a youth, Columbus decided at age 14 to go to sea, gaining experience as a sailor. As his proficiency grew he began dreaming of fame and fortune. Perhaps he thought that by sailing west he could be the one to discover that long sought after water route to the East. After several rejections he finally found favor with Ferdinand II and Isabella, the monarchs of Spain, who agreed to finance his exploration. They named him "admiral of the Ocean Seas" and governor of any lands that he might discover. And in return Columbus promised to spread the Christian faith to the people he encountered and to return with riches: gold, silver and spices.

And so it was that in the fall of 1492, Columbus set sail with three ships; the *Nina*, the *Pinta*, and the *Santa Maria*. After a harrowing voyage and near mutiny land was finally discovered. It is likely true that Columbus thought he had landed on outlying islands in the region of India. But, since this land was inhabited by natives, he laid claim to their lands and declared the natives as subjects of the monarch he served. After all, Columbus served the monarchs of a Christian nation and this was what the Pope had decreed. Columbus called the inhabitants he encountered 'Indians' because he thought he was in India.

Another Italian explorer named Amerigo Vespucci is credited with discovering that the islands Columbus landed on were not outlying regions of India but were, in fact, part of an entirely separate continent, and it is for him that America got its name.

Who really did discover America? Was it Columbus? Or was it the Norseman Leif Erickson? Or was it the Chinese? Or was it the Irish monks? And did America even need discovering? After all, there were people already living there.

Whatever the answer, in my view there is no denying that Columbus put the Doctrine of Discovery into motion, opening the way for many European voyages to the American continent and including colonization of what was to become the United States of America.

It took a century though (1607) for an English concern—the Virginia Company of London—to attempt colonization and settlement in North America. Three small ships, the *Susan Constant*, the *Godspeed* and the *Discovery*, landed in what would become Virginia and established the colony at Jamestown. Organized as a communal system, Jamestown soon floundered until Captain John Smith took charge and transformed the system to one based on hard work instead of equality for all.[1]

In 1620 the *Mayflower* set out from England carrying the Pilgrims. While they had intended to land in northern Virginia, they got off course and landed at Plymouth Rock in what would become Massachusetts.[2]

Ten years later, 1630 marked the arrival of the Puritans who desired freedom of religion without the influence of the Catholic Church. Their colony thrived and Boston soon became the largest city in America.[3] The Puritans were very strict in their religion and that prompted Rev. Roger Williams and his followers to break away in 1644 and start a colony called Providence at Narragansett Bay in what is now Rhode Island.[4]

Another dissenting group resulted in Maryland being colonized as a refuge for Catholics.[5]

The Dutch also played a part in colonization of the North American continent. Henry Hudson, an Englishman and navigator employed by the Dutch East India Company of the Netherlands, sailed in 1609, and it is for him that the Hudson River is named. The Dutch settled New Netherlands on the Hudson River with New Amsterdam as their capital. Located on Manhattan Island, this area was purchased, so the story goes, from the Canarsie Indians for $23.70. An interesting tidbit is that after Hudson's death, Peter Stuyvesant became the governor of the colony of New Netherlands and it is he that is credited with building a wall to help defend lower Manhattan—the street that ran along the wall being named Wall Street.[6]

It was at about this same time that William Penn, having converted to the Quaker religion, was able—through a convoluted series of events—to establish a Quaker colony in what later became the State of Pennsylvania.[7]

It is interesting to recount the early colonization of what would become the United States, especially in light of the modern day attempt to paint the United States as a sectarian nation. It certainly was not sectarian in those formative years. While the profit and power motives, as well as the order from the Pope, were likely the reasons the European monarchs helped finance early colonization, it was undoubtedly freedom of religion in the hearts of the people that dared them to risk all to flee from religious persecution.

The French explorers apparently could not convince their monarchs to provide them financial backing and so, while they had pushed into the interior of North America, it was principally because of the fur trade, rather than a desire for land to colonize. They were primarily in what is now Canada. Because of this difference in objectives, the French developed more of a friendship with the Indians than did the English. The Indians needed the French to secure the goods that they desired, while the English were looked upon more as competitors. This also resulted in more intermarrying between the Indians and the French, which in turn strengthened their relationship.

I relate the above proceedings to set the time frame for events in what would become the state of Minnesota, and especially occurrences in the Mille Lacs Lake area. While the Atlantic coast region was being colonized, the area west of the Mississippi River—the future Minnesota—was pretty much wilderness and Indian country with only an occasional Catholic priest or a trader venturing into the area occupied by the Indians.

The Dakota (Sioux) Indians were in possession of the Mille Lacs area at the time colonization was occurring on the Atlantic coast. Some even believe, due to archeological evidence, that the ancestors of those who would become the Sioux Nation lived in the vicinity of the outlet of Mille Lacs Lake at least some 800 years ago.[8] The archeologic history of the Mille Lacs area, particularly the formative years of Mille Lacs Lake, is noteworthy. As quoted in the Petaga Point Archeological Site website:

> *"10,000 years ago central Minnesota was a spruce and tundra landscape at the edge of melting glacial lobes. Glacial ice remained at the southern end of Ogechie Lake, so Ogechie was a bay of a larger and deeper Mille Lacs Lake, rather than a lake unto itself. As the climate warmed about 8,000 years ago, water found its way through the ice blockage at Petaga Point, which became the headwaters of the Rum River as we know it today."* [9]

Evidence that people were present in this area is dated to about 9,000 years ago and that people actually lived on the peninsula between the Rum River and Ogechie Lake about 3500 years ago.[10] Whether or not these inhabitants were Dakota ancestors is only conjecture.

While dates are elusive with only scant written records, we know that Father Hennepin stayed with the Mdewakanton Dakota at Mille Lacs from May to September, 1680, and that he was captured and taken prisoner by the Dakota that same year.[11]

The previous year Daniel Greysolon, Seiur Du Lhut (now spelled Duluth) visited Mille Lac and noted in his memoirs, "On the second of July, 1679, I had the honor to set up the arms of his Majesty in the great village of Nadouecioux [Sioux] called Izatys, where no Frenchman had ever been."[12]

Evidence shows that the Sioux had three villages at Mille Lac by 1750. There were two large villages, one at Cormorant (Shaw vosh Kung) Point which is the area now inhabited by the Mille Lac Band's government center, and one at the mouth of the Rum River somewhere in the vicinity of the stone monument commemorating the battle between the Ojibwe and the Sioux. A third smaller village was at the south point of Ogechie Lake.[13][14]

So how did this area, long occupied and controlled by the Sioux, become the home of the Mille Lacs Ojibwe? The scenario is recounted from oral history and generally substantiated by written records, and is recorded in William W. Warren's book, *History of the Ojibway People*. Other accounts vary in some details but in general are in agreement. First we must remember that the Ojibwe were relative newcomers to this area west of the Mississippi. As the need arose to expand their hunting grounds the Ojibwe were often in clashes with the Sioux, who were little by little being pushed to the west. There were also periods lasting for some years when the two tribes lived in peace, even to the point of allowing intermarrying. The incident I am about to describe happened after a period of several years of peace between the two tribes.

As the story goes, the first incident involved a love triangle. A Dakota woman who lived at Mille Lacs was being courted by both a Dakota man and an Ojibwe man. She favored the attention of the Ojibwe and as a result, the Dakota man murdered the Ojibwe man. Nothing more happened for a time.

Now there was an Ojibwe man from Fond du Lac who had four sons, all of whom frequently visited the Dakota women at Mille Lacs with their father's blessings. A short time after the first episode and during a visit to Mille Lacs, one of the brothers was murdered. Only three returned. The father was forgiving, and later gave the remaining three sons permission to once again visit the Dakota women at Mille Lacs. This time two more brothers were murdered and only one returned. While the father was very saddened, he still gave the remaining son permission to go to Mille Lacs to visit the graves of his dead brothers. After waiting for a month for his remaining son to return, the father concluded that he, too, had been killed.

As was the Ojibwe custom, revenge was in order. The Fond du Lac father spent two years accumulating the weapons and supplies that he would need and rallying his friends to accompany him in avenging his four son's deaths.

The first battle occurred early in the morning at Cormorant Point with only a few Dakota escaping with their lives, using canoes to travel on Mille Lacs Lake to the second and larger village at the mouth of the Rum River. The Ojibwe followed and, after struggling to defend themselves with bows and arrows, the Sioux took refuge in their earthen lodges. The Ojibwe proceeded to throw bags of gun powder down the chimney openings into the open fire below, causing a devastating ball of fire resulting in death and destruction. One account describes the Ojibwe clubbing the blinded

Sioux to death as they ran out of their dwellings. A few Sioux, not being familiar with gun powder, thought it the work of the spirits, and gave up the fight. A small number escaped during the night, making their way down the Rum River to the smaller village on Ogechie Lake only to be attacked again the morning of the second day. On the morning of the third day the Ojibwe discovered that the remaining few had escaped down the Rum River during the night and that the village was now deserted.

This was a battle for revenge, and not a battle for territory. The Ojibwe probably did not occupy the Mille Lacs area for some undetermined time after this occurrence. So while Benjamin Franklin was busy discovering electricity (1749) by flying his kite in a thunderstorm in the bustling economy of Philadelphia, the Ojibwe and the Dakota were living an exceedingly primitive life in the area that would become Minnesota.

CHAPTER 5

So Who Was John Tanner?

John Tanner, of English descent, was born around 1780. His mother died when he was about two years old. His father, an immigrant from Virginia, lived on the Kentucky River some distance from the Ohio River. When young John Tanner was eight or nine years old his family consisted of his father and stepmother, two sisters, a baby brother and an older brother. It was at about this time that the family packed up their belongings, including their Negro slaves, and moved deeper into unsettled territory, relocating at the mouth of the Great Miami River in southwest Ohio. There they assumed ownership of cabins and some cleared land that had presumably been abandoned by previous settlers because of the threat of Indian attack.

John Tanner - Portrait in A narrative of the captivity and adventures of John Tanner, by Edwin James, London, 1830

While his father, older brother and the Negro slaves were busy in the fields planting the corn crop, young John, having been forbidden to leave the house, slipped out anyway and cautiously made his way to the wooded area. Taking care not to be observed by his father, who was standing guard with rifle in hand against Indian attack, John began filling his hat with walnuts. Suddenly two Indians seized young John from behind and dragged him off into the forest.

Apparently these Indians had been sent by a Shawnee woman, wife of the older of the two, to steal a son for her to replace the son who had recently died. John Tanner, having disobeyed his father and being in the wrong place at the wrong time, was the chosen one. And so began Tanner's thirty year experience living life as an Indian.

Young John's first couple of years with the Indians were filled with hard work, almost daily beatings, humiliation, and what seemed like near starvation by his Shawnee Indian mother's husband and family. John was led to believe that the rest of his family had been killed by war parties from the Shawnee camp.

After approximately two years an offer was made by another Indian woman to purchase him to (here we go again!) replace her own son who had died. This second woman, although a female, was considered a chief. Tanner's adoptive mother initially refused; however, after much whiskey and feasting she agreed, and John Tanner was taken away to live with the Ojibway (Chippewa) people.

I recount John Tanner's story in order to give the reader a feel for what Indian life was like for the Ojibway, who were just becoming established in what would become Minnesota. John's new Ojibway father claimed the Red River as home; probably in the area further north that is now southern Canada. Tanner and his family frequented the area from Lake Superior over to Rainey Lake, around Lake of the Woods and on toward the Red River.

As a young man Tanner spent a good deal of time developing his hunting and trapping skills. Because he was white he was often ridiculed by the Indian boys his same age, which gave him further incentive to hone his skills. His first attempt at hunting resulted in a dead pigeon and a bruised and bloodied face. But since he had brought a pigeon home (any game they killed, they ate) he was then given a proper firearm by his family for hunting. On another occasion his Ojibway father taught him how to make proper traps so he could keep up with the Indian boys.

The Indian men spent most of their time either hunting and trapping or heading out on the warpath. There were frequent war parties setting off to kill whites or the Sioux; most often not all of the same tribe. Any young male Indian looking for excitement or revenge would be welcomed into a war party. These were dangerous times for young Tanner, as he was obviously white, and enraged young Indian warriors were not particular which white person they killed. His Ojibway mother would often take pains to have him hidden and cared for while the Indian family journeyed to where they might encounter war parties or white people.

By this time the Indians had grown accustomed to the goods they could get through trade with the French and English dealers. Traders would fill their canoes with firearms, gun powder, cloth items, trinkets and other items—including whiskey—and make their way into Indian country where they would trade their wares for the animal pelts that the Indians had accumulated for that purpose. In some cases permanent trading houses were established that the Indians could visit, and even purchase on credit, as needed.

Much time was spent by the Indian men trapping animals for pelts, such as fox, mink, martin, muskrat and the prized beaver, which they accumulated until they had enough to visit the trader to either buy goods or pay off their debts. Pelts were like money to the Indian, and inevitably a return from the trader meant that the whole camp was drunk until the whiskey was gone.

These Indians grew some crops such as corn, harvested berries and roots and made maple sugar, but their main food source was game: birds, bear, moose, elk, buffalo, and even porcupine. As the game population was depleted, hunting parties had to range farther and farther from home. After a bear or a buffalo or moose was killed, the women of the tribe were brought to the spot of the kill to process and dry the meat. Smaller animals might be carried or dragged back to camp for processing. While success on the hunt usually meant food for the entire camp, it wasn't always like that. There were times when jealousies and quarrels would result in depriving someone or some family from partaking in the feast. This would also occur if an able-bodied fellow was perceived as a slacker, not contributing his share of effort.

Tanner relates one incident while hunting buffalo, when he shot a fat buffalo cow. But the bull that had been following the cow charged Tanner, who escaped into the woods. There he waited all day for the bull to leave the dead cow's carcass so that he could retrieve his kill, eventually having to abandon the meat he had so hoped to take back to camp.

When hunting and trapping became difficult due to depletion of the animal populations, the camp, often comprised of one extended family, would dismantle their dwelling, pack up their belongings and move in search of more abundant game. But then, as they pushed further into the territory of other tribes—primarily Dakota or Sioux—the danger of encountering resistance from war parties was greater. Winter was a time for hunting and trapping; for survival. Summer was the time for war parties to push the Sioux back and gain more territory for hunting.

Tanner's tales seem to describe a people who were not motivated to hunt for food, especially in winter, until hunger and near starvation were advanced. This resulted in much suffering, death or near fatalities if the hunting was difficult due to scarcity of game or the distance was great. As a result, a motivated and successful hunter was not always willing to share with those who were not contributing. Tempers would flare and grudges would be held. Combine that with the fact that life was cheap; death or injury due to a tomahawk chop to the head or death by gunshot was a frequent occurrence, and you get a feel for how fragile life was. Tanner's second mother-in-law even hired a hitman in an unsuccessful attempt to have him shot. But then at a later time she lived in the same camp with him and the rest of the family.

Life was harsh, especially in the wintertime. Staying nourished and avoiding starvation. Keeping warm or trying to keep from freezing to death. All was a challenge, keeping in mind that housing was a tent-like structure built with bent branches and covered with animal skins, while living in the harsh climes of northern Minnesota and southern Canada.

Medical care, of course, was non-existent. Tanner tells the story of a hunter who was accidently shot in the elbow. The elbow joint was shattered and steadily worsened instead of healing. The hunter could not convince anyone to amputate his arm so one day when he was alone he took matters into his own hands. Taking two knives, one of which he had fashioned into a saw, and using his right hand and arm, he sawed off his own left arm. This poor man was later found in a pool of blood, but somehow survived the ordeal; his amputated limb healed and he again was able to hunt.

Tanner also describes at least two severe injuries that he himself recovered from. One was a tomahawk chop to the skull by a disgruntled family member and the other the result of a fall from a horse. Tincture of time seemed to be the treatment of choice but he relates several stories of life-threatening illnesses and the efforts to transport the patient to a place to die.

Although most often walking, the Indians would occasionally purchase a horse with pelts, or they would steal one. Theft of a horse would then bring on revenge, with the other tribes either stealing the horse back—or worse.

Men frequently had more than one wife. A father might approach an eligible young man and offer to sell his daughter. Daughters were considered a saleable commodity and a virgin would bring the highest price. John Tanner had two Indian wives. The first one at least apparently chose herself as there is no talk of him having to purchase her. He fathered several children during his thirty years living with the Indians.

After the war of 1812 was over, Tanner started thinking about abandoning his Indian ways and returning to Kentucky to see if any of his white family was still alive and whether he could find them. His second wife accompanied him for a time, but shortly returned to Indian country. Tanner ultimately found at least one family member, and eventually married a white woman. But try as he may, Tanner could not fit into the white culture after his thirty years of life as an Indian, and he never did get used to sleeping inside a building.[1]

CHAPTER 6

Hole-in-the-Day

While neither Hole-in-the-Day the Elder nor Hole-in-the-Day the Younger ever lived at Mille Lacs, they were extremely influential and important in the history of the Ojibwe Indians, and especially the Mille Lacs Band history. The actions of Hole-in-the-Day the Younger continue to haunt relations between the Mille Lacs Band and the surrounding community to this day. This chapter has been drawn almost exclusively from the excellent, impartial and well-documented book written by Anton Treuer, T*he Assassination of Hole-in-the-Day.*

Hole-in-the-Day the Elder

While Hole-in-the-Day the Elder was not a Mille Lacs Ojibwe, his life is important in Mille Lacs history. In order to avoid confusion, we need to know that there were at least four Ojibwe Indians named Hole-in-the-Day in the 1800's. In addition to Hole-in-the-Day the Elder and Hole-in-the-Day the Younger—about whom we are concerned—there was a Red Lake Ojibwe Indian named Hole-in-the-Day who was involved with the 1889 Nelson Act. There was also a Leech Lake Ojibwe Indian named Hole-in-the-Day who was involved with the battle at Sugar Point in 1898.

Hole-in-the-Day the Elder was born sometime around 1800 on Madeline Island in Lake Superior near La Pointe, Wisconsin. His father was an ordinary fellow named Smoke, and thus Hole-in-the-Day the Elder was born a common man. This is important to note because the traditional Ojibwe culture would prevent a common man from becoming a chief.

Hole-in-the-Day the Elder moved to the village at Sandy Lake in the year 1820. In his youth this young man killed a Dakota man and earned himself an eagle feather and a seat on the war council at Sandy Lake. Alfred Brunson, a Methodist missionary, described Hole-in-the-Day the Elder: "He was distinguished for his eloquence, wisdom, and force of argument. His daring exploits on the war path, the chase, and in personal encounters, as well as his boldness and force in council, naturally drew around him the young men of his tribe ... who acknowledged him as a leader."[1]

And so it was that Curly Head, head chief at Sandy Lake with no children of his own, chose Hole-in-the-Day the Elder to assist him in his chiefly duties. Hole-in-the-Day the Elder further solidified his position as a rising young leader by marrying a daughter of Broken Tooth, another prominent Sandy Lake chief, as well as marrying the daughter of Flat Mouth, a highly respected Leech Lake chief. This was a common practice, whether for love or increase of power.

Also in 1820 Hole-in-the-Day the Elder accompanied Curly Head to Sault Ste. Marie. Alfred Brunson described the events that took place there something like this: After the War of 1812, the British continued to pay annuities to the Indians—as agreed in treaties—in order to maintain the allegiance of the Indians. Lewis Cass, the superintendent of Indian Affairs for the Northwest, led a group to intercept a British trade shipment. When Cass arrived he found 2,000 to 3,000 Ojibwe, including the Sandy Lake delegation, waiting for their annuities. These Indians were flying the British flag, which Cass immediately tore down and replaced with the American flag. Cass then demanded that any Indians who were loyal to the United States should step up and assist in the defense of the United States flag. Understanding that most Ojibwe had sided with the British in the War of 1812, Cass was taking quite a risk.

Now Curly Head and Hole-in-the-Day the Elder had noticed Cass's canoes heavily laden with trade goods, and they also were fully aware of the power of the United States. So it was that Curly Head and Hole-in-the-Day the Elder, along with about one hundred Ojibwe, rushed to support the Americans. As a result the British canoes were not allowed to land. It is further recounted that Cass rewarded the Sandy Lakers handsomely. These deeds elevated the status of the Sandy Lakers with the Americans and their fellow Ojibwe alike.

Author Anton Treuer doubts the veracity of Brunson's account when Brunson says, "Discovering that Hole-in-the-Day was not a regular or hereditary chief, and feeling that his daring, bravery and evident influence over the tribe demanded recognition and reward, Cass elevated him to that rank and dignity and gave him a flag and a medal in the presence of all."

Whether truth or myth, "years later Hole-in-the-Day would proudly display the medal and flag given the Sandy Lake delegation."[2]

In an effort to establish a trade zone in the un-ceded area that had been a stronghold of British trade since the Revolutionary War, the United States gained permission from the Dakota tribe to establish Fort Snelling. Fort Snelling was begun in 1819 under the direction of Lt. Colonel Henry Leavenworth, completed in 1825 under direction of Colonel Josiah Snelling, and then staffed with Major Lawrence Taliaferro as Indian Agent.

Taliaferro tried valiantly, although not always wisely, to achieve peace between the Ojibwe and the Dakota. Hopeful that peace between the two tribes would improve trade issues, a council was called at Prairie du Chien in 1825 in an effort to delineate which area would be considered Dakota land and which Ojibwe land. Treaty Commissioner Lewis Cass and Commissioner of Indian Affairs William Clark negotiated the treaty.

Sandy Lake chief Broken Tooth wanted the boundary drawn such that the Ojibwe would occupy the land north of a line from Fort Snelling to Minot, North Dakota. Cass reportedly asked what right the Ojibwe had to such a large area. Treuer relates that Hole-in-the-Day the Elder rose to his feet and said, "My father! We claim it upon the same ground that you claim this country from the British King — by conquest. We drove them from the country by force of arms, and have since occupied it; and they cannot, and dare not, try to dispossess us of our habitation."

Cass reportedly replied, "Then you have a right to it."[3]

During the return journey home from the treaty negotiations many of the Ojibwe became dreadfully sick from apparent food poisoning. Both Hole-in-the-Day the Elder's father and one of his wives fell ill and died *en route*. Of significant historic impact, however, was the terminal illness of Curly Head. Having no children upon which to pass his chieftainship, he asked Hole-in-the-Day the Elder to watch over his people after his death. Thus the incidents at Sault Ste. Marie and Prairie du Chien launched Hole-in-the-Day the Elder into his quest to become a legitimate chief.

While American principals viewed Hole-in-the-Day the Elders rise to authority as an opportunity for beneficial negotiations, tribal heads viewed it differently. The leaders at Mille Lacs reportedly began to resent Hole-in-the-Day the Elders rise to power because he did not have the traditional Ojibwe right to chieftainship. Back home at Sandy Lake there was not total agreement that Hole-in-the-Day the Elder was their chief. Other Sandy Lake chiefs saw this as Hole-in-the-Day the Elder usurping the power that should have been theirs.

As Chief, Hole-in-the-Day vacillated between promoting peace between the Ojibwe and the Dakota and reverting back to covering the dead or revenge. At the same time the American government concluded that using Fort Snelling as the approved meeting place for official business with the two tribes was not working. Their solution was to transfer Ojibwe business to Sault Ste. Marie.

Allegedly Hole-in-the-Day the Elder developed a mental depression at around this same time, likely due to the deaths of his first wife and his father, as well as the loss of his daughter from mortal wounds incurred during a Dakota attack at Fort Snelling. In any event Hole-in-the-Day the Elder did not recover from his melancholy until the birth of his son; the boy who would become Hole-in-the-Day the Younger.

After the loss of an uncle and two cousins, slain by the Dakota, Hole-in-the-Day the Elder temporarily abandoned his quest for peace and joined a war party against the Dakota. During the battles he slew and scalped a Dakota warrior; however, instead of continuing on the war-path Hole-in-the-Day the Elder traveled to Fort Snelling intending to turn himself in to authorities for his deed. Agent Taliaferro reportedly empathized with the young man's desire for revenge after the tragic loss of a wife, father, daughter, uncle and two cousins, following which Taliaferro sent Hole-in-the-Day the Elder back home. These actions increased Hole-in-the-Day the Elder's authority and esteem in the eyes of both his own people and the Americans.

As a side note, Hole-in-the-Day the Elder's brother was not wholly convinced that peace with the Dakota was the solution when a party of Sandy Lakers was led to attack the Dakota at Long Prairie—the only large battle of the 1830's.

In 1836, Hole-in-the-Day the Elder moved to Gull Lake and established a village in the area known today as Brainerd, Minnesota. In this new home he could be the undisputed chief of his village and exert uncontested influence in the surrounding area. To capitalize on Hole-in-the-Day the Elders move, white traders established a settlement at Crow Wing just a few miles south of the new Ojibwe encampment.

The new settlement was very near the line established by the Prairie du Chien treaty, and thus was a dangerous location, particularly during the summer when Ojibwe-Dakota feuds were most common. To avoid this peril many members of Hole-in-the-Day the Elder's band spent summers at Sandy Lake, Leech Lake or Mille Lacs. And although still advocating for peace, Hole-in-the-Day the Elder continued to advance the band's encampments deeper into the territory held by the Dakotas. Meanwhile William Aitkin and Joseph Renville Sr., who were fierce trading competitors, seized every opportunity to stir up tribal hostilities that might damage the others business and aide their own.

Although Hole-in-the-Day the Elder was not a principal speaker at the treaty of 1837, his diplomatic skills made him a principal player in the treaty outcome by objecting to Aitkin's and Warren's inflated claims on the annuity payment. Both traders were guilty of playing both ends against the middle. Since they both had mixed blood families, they would accept annuity payments as Indians while presenting overblown claims on the payment as non-Indian traders.

The Prairie du Chien treaty did not turn out as the Indians had hoped. Since Hole-in-the-Day the Elder had been central in convincing the other chiefs to accept it, he was the one blamed, although the United States officials continued to champion him. Adding to the problems was the fact that the Dakota's were displeased with the increase of white settlers as a result of the treaty. The Dakota and Ojibwe battles continued in 1837 and 1838; neither tribe could be trusted and the Americans were unable to control hostilities.

Then in the summer of 1839 the Dakota—Ojibwe tensions reached a tipping point at Fort Snelling. Hole-in-the-Day the Elder and his brother led a large delegation of Mississippi Ojibwe to Fort Snelling. Included in the delegation were Gull Lake, Crow Wing, Sandy Lake, Mille Lacs and St. Croix Ojibwe—all villages included in the 1837 treaty. Many Dakota Indians came as well, and all proceeded without incident.

The Ojibwe thought they were to receive their annuities at Fort Snelling only to find out that they would get them at La Pointe, so Hole-in-the-Day the Elder's delegation headed home. However, two of his band remained behind, intent on seeking revenge against the Dakota for the killing of two Ojibwe. This they accomplished near Lake Calhoun, killing two Dakota. Ironically, Agent Taliaferro had earlier given the Dakota permission to attack the Ojibwe if any Dakota were killed, and that they set out to accomplish. A large force of Dakota followed the Ojibwe on their journey home. Both the Mille Lacs group and the St Croix group were attacked, with seventy Ojibwe reportedly killed. Most of those slain were women and children. Agent Taliaferro was upset with the occurrence but he had, after all, authorized it himself. In 1840 Taliaferro gave up, resigned his post and returned to Pennsylvania leaving his Dakota wife and mixed-blood children behind in Minnesota.

Indian-white relations continued to deteriorate. Government officials tried withholding annuity payments in the early 1840's to ensure peace between the Dakota and the Ojibwe but that only made matters worse.

In 1841 Hole-in-the-Day the Elder led a war party intent on attacking Little Crow's village, but during the journey all but two of his warriors deserted. The three remaining continued on, attacking the village and killing the son of one of the chiefs. On the one hand this desertion demonstrated a lack of confidence in his leadership; however, the fact that only three accomplished the strike enhanced Hole-in-the-Day the Elder's supremacy due to his bravery.

Anton Treuer describes Hole-in-the-Day the Elder's power this way: "Hole-in-the-Day was powerful because he was perceived to be powerful. His influence stemmed from his skills at persuasion and instilling fear more than control or love. As his power and influence grew, he began to proclaim himself head chief of all the Ojibwe, even though no such position existed."[4]

The Mille Lacs band strongly repudiated Hole-in-the-Day the Elder's claim to head chieftainship, yet at times they continued to follow his lead. He was a brilliant politician and manipulator. He would gain favor with missionaries, giving the impression that he would follow their ways when he, in fact, had no intention of doing so.

Making an already complicated and seemingly unmanageable situation worse, traders like William Aitkin and others used alcohol as a means of doing business. Many Indians developed alcoholism as a result of their despair. Hole-in-the-Day the Elder and his brother both succumbed to the effects of alcohol. His brother died of alcohol poisoning in 1845, leaving Hole-in-the-Day the Elder to lead alone.

Unsuccessful at all their other attempts, the U.S. government came up with a strategy to separate the Dakota and Ojibwe by moving the Ho Chunk (Winnebagoes) and the Menominee from Wisconsin into a buffer zone between the Dakota and the Ojibwe. This plan would open up prized areas of Wisconsin to settlement by whites as well. But first a treaty had to be negotiated for the purchase of the land for the relocation of the Wisconsin Indians. Hole-in-the-Day the Elder, still promoting his agenda of peace rather than for financial gain, endorsed the treaty. Treaties to accomplish this goal were scheduled in May 1847. Hole-in-the-Day the Elder visited Ho Chunk leaders in Wisconsin to persuade them to accept the relocation.

Anton Treuer relates the events of Hole-in-the-Day the Elder's return trip: "On his way back to Gull Lake from Wisconsin, Hole-in-the-Day stopped at the Falls of St. Anthony to visit traders there and drink several shots of whiskey. Sometime later, as his horse-drawn cart crossed the Mississippi River at Little Falls, one hundred miles away, he fell out of the wagon in a stupor. The wheel ran over his chest, aggravating the spinal wounds incurred in 1827 at the hands of the Dakota at Fort Snelling. He was brought to the home of an Ojibwe family nearby and died a few hours later."[5]

"As the chief lay dying, he summoned his son…to his side and told him, 'Take the tribe by the hand. Show them how to walk.' At age nineteen, Hole-in-the-Day the Younger thus inherited his father's role as principal leader for the Gull Lake Ojibwe."[6]

Hole-in-the-Day the Younger

Upon the death of his father the teenager assumed the status of chief. His father had groomed him for this position and he assumed the name Hole-in-the-Day.

Claude Beaulieu, a local trader, described young Hole-in-the-Day as "a man of distinguished appearance and native courtliness of manner. His voice was musical and magnetic, and with these qualities he had a subtle brain, a logical mind, and quite a remarkable gift of oratory. In speech he was not impassioned, but clear and convincing, and held fast the attention of his hearers."[7]

Missionary Alfred Brunson went on to say, "No one strutted, or seemed to feel his consequence, more than he did."[8]

Hole-in-the-Day the Younger's first real opportunity to test his skills as a chief came with the Treaty of 1847 at Fond du Lac. Numerous chiefs were present and apparently ready to negotiate, but as the meeting opened Hole-in-the-Day the Younger arose and said to those assembled, "Our Great Father instructed you to come here, for the purpose of asking us to sell a large piece of land, lying on and west of the Mississippi River. To accomplish this you have called together all the chiefs and headmen of the nation, who to the number of hundreds are within hearing of my voice; that was useless, for they do not own the land; it belongs to me.

"My father, by his bravery, took it from the Sioux. He died a few moons ago, and what belonged to him became mine. He, by his courage and perseverance, became head chief of all the Chippewas, and when he died I took his place, and am consequently chief over all the nation. To this position I am doubly entitled, for I am as brave as my father was, and through my mother I am by descent legal heir to the position.

Hole-in-the-Day 1858

PHOTO FROM THE SMITHSONIAN INSTITUTE'S NATIONAL ANTHROPOLOGICAL ARCHIVES

"Now, if I say sell, our Great Father will obtain the land; if I say no, you will tell him he cannot have it. The Indians assembled here have nothing to say; they can but do my bidding."[9]

While the Mille Lacs chiefs, along with other chiefs, did not support Hole-in-the-Day's claim, they did nothing about it during the negotiations. After the treaty was negotiated Resting Feather, chief of the Mille Lacs, wrote to President Polk and objected to Hole-in-the-Day the Younger's claim that he represented all of the Chippewa. But the damage was done; they signed the treaty negotiated in large part by Hole-in-the-Day the Younger, selling a million acres of the land they had controlled.

With the confidence gained at Fond du Lac, Hole-in-the-Day the Younger began solidifying his power over Gull Lake and neighboring villages. Charles Cleland described it this way:

"Hole-in-the-Day's rise to a position of leadership and influence was part of a pattern of larger change. With the cooling of hostility between the Dakota and the Chippewa and the advent of American settlement in the 1840s, war chiefs began to lose influence. This was also in part due to the decline in the fur market, which not only increased the importance of annuities but also enhanced the position of civil chiefs who were able to secure more annuities by consolidating their followers and accommodating American demands. In this situation the government tried to manipulate Ojibwe politics by channeling treaty-stipulated goods and services to 'cooperative' chiefs. The result was that those chiefs who could acquire more goods for their people built their prestige."[10]

Hole-in-the-Day the Younger was politically savvy and saw a personal opportunity with a government hungry for land and eager to reward those who helped. The young chief cultivated friendships with missionaries and traders, which helped to elevate his status. He even added some traders to the tribal rolls, thereby allowing them to double-dip at annuity payment time. Often these actions with traders were rewarded with free drinks from the whiskey bottle.

Anton Treuer reports that Hole-in-the-Day the Younger "became a U.S. citizen before any of his constituents by special act of the Minnesota State Legislature."[11]

He used diplomacy to benefit his people while never forgetting to line his own pockets. In the 1847 treaty Hole-in-the-Day the Younger successfully negotiated an article that would have guaranteed annuity payments at nearby Crow Wing, only to have it stricken by the Senate.

Around 1850 Hole-in-the-Day the Younger was advocating for a peace conference to deal with the warfare between the Ojibwe and the Dakota, and to discuss the location of the annuity pay station. The constant fighting between the Dakota and the Ojibwe was upsetting to everyone, but Hole-in-the-Day the Younger was conflicted on the issue. Like his father before him, he was advocating for peace at the same time as engaging in revenge warfare. Governor Ramsey assented and, on June 9, 1850 a peace conference assembled. Once again Hole-in-the-Day the Younger seized the moment and demanded a financial settlement from the Dakotas for being the aggressors. Governor Ramsey appeared to agree.

Starting with the Fond du Lac treaty and the peace conference Hole-in-the-Day the Younger was honing his negotiating skills and solidifying his position— real or not—as head chief of the Mississippi Ojibwe. For the next twenty years he would play a principal role in nearly all Ojibwe treaties.

The treaty of 1854 divided the arrowhead region of Minnesota between the Mississippi Ojibwe and the Lake Superior Ojibwe and ceded most of northeastern Minnesota to the government. Hole-in-the-Day the Younger signed this treaty with the words "Head Chief" after his name.

In 1855 Hole-in-the-Day the Younger led a delegation to Washington, D.C. The administration wanted the Mississippi Ojibwe, the Pillager Ojibwe and the Winnibegoshish Ojibwe to cede all of their lands in Minnesota and Wisconsin to the government. Anton Treuer says that Hole-in-the-Day the Younger was largely responsible for the Ojibwe retaining a portion of their homeland in the form of eleven reservations, but he also negotiated a cash payment for himself—which was later stricken by Congress—and a land grant of 640 acres which he received.

While the Ojibwe were losing land and resources and power, Hole-in-the-Day the Younger gained personal benefit. He was slowly losing the trust and confidence of his followers and he knew it. According to Treuer, "After the 1855 treaty signing, Major H. Day wrote to Commissioner Manypenny, '[Hole-in-the-Day] often passed a sleepless night ... from the mortification of being accused of betraying or sacrificing the interests of his nation.' "[12]

After receiving his 640 acre land grant negotiated in the 1855 treaty, Hole-in-the-Day the Younger decided to build his own house on his own private land and live apart from his Gull Lake followers. This land was located across the river from Crow Wing. After the move Hole-in-the-Day the Younger no longer claimed to be village chief but rather chief of the whole Gull Lake region, including the villages at Crow

Wing, Gull Lake and Rabbit Lake. He started farming and, in addition to supplying his own needs, was able to grow and sell excess produce. Treuer reports that he told his followers, "This my brethren is the result of my farming. While you have been wandering, pursuing the uncertain chase, I have been laboring; you are poor, I am rich; I have no fears with winter, as I have sufficient food to carry me through; profit by my example."[13]

These words angered and alienated those of his followers who thought he was profiting from their displacement and land loss. It was becoming more and more difficult for the Ojibwe to live in the traditional way, and they resented the loss of freedom to live where and how they chose.

By 1862 tensions were growing, not only among the Dakota but the Ojibwe as well. In response to the white settlements encroaching around Fort Ripley, the Ojibwe were fighting back. The Ojibwe had destroyed white churches, trading posts and personal homes around Leech Lake, Crow Wing and Ottertail City, and had taken white prisoners. Indians greatly outnumbered the whites; settlers lived in fear of Indian attacks. A number of cattle were killed without retaliation, but when a white man was killed the local sheriff was overwhelmed by a posse of settlers and the Indians responsible for the killing were hanged.

Reverend Manney, the chaplain at Fort Ripley, wrote in his journal, "We may now expect personal violence, and murders, and destruction of property on the ceded lands, and all along the frontier."[14]

And he was right. Hole-in-the-Day the Younger and Little Crow had been talking about joining their two nations in opposition to the whites. Reverend Manney's journal writings were prophetic, but probably not in the way he, Hole-in-the-Day the Younger or Little Crow thought.

On March 23, 1861, Lucius C. Walker became the Indian Agent for the Ojibwe under the fraudulent Indian system inherited by the new Lincoln administration, answering to Agency Superintendent Clark Thompson—likely also part of the fraudulent system. Most traders and many government officials profited handsomely from the annuity economy to the detriment of the Indians. Between 1855 and 1862 several government warehouses and annuity stations were burned in response. Hole-in-the-Day the Younger complained to both St. Paul and Washington, D.C. about this fraud. William P. Dole, Commissioner of Indian Affairs, agreed to investigate, but not much happened, perhaps because he was part of the system.

Hole-in-the-Day the Younger was angry, not only at the fraudulent system but also at Agent Walker because the agent would not cooperate with Hole-in-the-Day the Younger's usual habit of insisting on a chief's bonus above and beyond what the other Indians received. Hole-in-the-Day the Younger was losing his influence with the government because he was running out of land to sell, which was the basis of his affluence, so it was personal.

All of the above history is background for Hole-in-the-Day the Younger's plan to join Little Crow against the whites. While the Sioux uprising was started by accident, the Ojibwe's portion was calculated by Hole-in-the-Day the Younger. Bishop Whipple said, "This outbreak among the Ojibwe was entirely due to a personal grievance of Hole-in-the-Day."[15]

By September of 1862, with the Sioux uprising ended, a council was scheduled for September 10, 1862. Commissioner Dole had agreed to council with the Ojibwe, and had suggested Fort Ripley as the site for negotiation. However, Hole-in-the-Day the Younger objected and Crow Wing was chosen. Commissioner Dole had agreed to come unarmed but Hole-in-the-Day the Younger was skeptical, and rightfully so; Dole had secretly planned to capture and imprison him. The background of the council was contentious. Most Ojibwe leaders from Leech Lake, Sandy Lake and Mille Lacs were upset because Hole-in-the-Day the Younger had lied to them. Government officials wanted him arrested or killed because of his role in the uprising. John Johnson just wanted Hole-in-the-Day the Younger dead because he blamed him for the death of two of his children and because Hole-in-the-Day the Younger had tried to have Johnson killed. According to Treuer, both Bad Boy and John Johnson wrote to Commissioner of Indian Affairs Dole that there would never be peace in Minnesota "until he is dispose [sic] of."[16]

Commissioner Dole came to the council unarmed as promised, which made it simple for Hole-in-the-Day the Younger to get the upper hand by surrounding the council with his braves. Dole spoke to the council first and Hole-in-the Day the Younger followed with a scathing speech and concluded by saying, "Are you the smartest man the Great Father could send in a trying time like this? Because, if you are the smartest man the Great Father has got, I pity our Great Father: You have been talking to me as if I was a child. I am not a little child. I have grey hairs on my head ... [Y]our talk sounds to me like baby talk ... you say the treaty reads so and so. Now that is a lie and you know it."[17]

The council did not turn out the way Commissioner Dole had planned. Hole-in-the-Day the Younger walked away still a free man and Commissioner Dole returned immediately to Washington. Crow Wing postmaster Ashley Morrill was interim special Indian Agent after Walker's suicide, so he was left with the problem.

Tensions increased the next day when two Crow Wing residents burned down Hole-in-the-Day the Younger's house. Hole-in-the-Day the Younger held the government responsible and demanded payment for his destroyed house, at the same time blaming the government for the theft of annuities by government Indian system officials. He threatened to attack Crow Wing but was convinced by other chiefs not to carry out his threat.

His threats worked, however. On September 15, 1862, Henry M. Rice and Governor Alexander Ramsey met with Hole-in-the-Day the Younger and negotiated a treaty, agreeing to pay overdue annuities within thirty days. Because no land was involved the treaty was not presented for ratification but the payments were made on October 27, 1862, and Hole-in-the Day the Younger and other Ojibwe leaders were officially exonerated from their crimes. Once again Hole-in-the-day the Younger had gained the upper hand, although his respect by both whites and many Ojibwe had suffered. In the treaty of 1864, Hole-in-the-Day the Younger was awarded five thousand dollars for the burning of his house.

Mille Lacs leaders tried to distance themselves from Hole-in-the-Day the Younger. They sent a petition—signed by a number of chiefs—to the government which read, "We the undersigned chiefs of the Mille [Lacs] Lake Band wish to express hereby our mind, that we don't agree in any way with the plans of [Hole-in-the-Day]."[18]

Ojibwe—Dakota warfare finally ended in 1862 and was solidified by the presenting of the Big Drum to the Ojibwe by the Dakota.

As a result of 1862, most whites and half-breeds feared **all** Indians in Minnesota.

On a treaty negotiating trip to Washington, D.C. sometime around 1859—1860 Hole-in-the-Day the Younger met a young white chambermaid named Ellen McCarty who had asked to interview him for a paper she was writing. The meeting resulted in romance and they were married in St. Paul.

In 1867 a new treaty was negotiated, reducing the size of the Leech Lake reservation and creating the large White Earth reservation. It also specified that the Ojibwe would move there only after the government constructed roads, a saw mill, a gristmill, and a house for each Ojibwe family. All Mississippi Ojibwe were to move there.

Hole-in-the-Day the Younger was content to wait for the government to build the roads and houses and other facilities as required by the treaty. Other chiefs thought their only future was to move onto the reservation immediately. According to Treuer, Hole-in-the-Day the Younger knew that if there was a mass exodus to White Earth, his power as a diplomat and leader would evaporate. He decided to once again visit Washington, D.C. to make sure the treaty would be fulfilled.

On June 27, 1868, Hole-in-the-Day the Younger and his cousin started for Washington, D.C., stopping first in Crow Wing to arrange financing for their trip. After completing their business in Crow Wing they set out for St Paul. From there they would take the train to Washington, D.C. Just outside Crow Wing near the annuity agency Hole-in-the-Day the Younger was accosted by twelve men and assassinated. He was 40 years old.

Thus ended the saga of father and son Hole-in-the-Day. None of their descendants have risen to influential leadership like their two legendary ancestors.

CHAPTER 7

Minnesota: A Poster Child for Corruption in the Indian System in the Nineteenth Century?

Bishop Henry Whipple is quoted as saying "that the Indian Department was the most corrupt in our government." The Department, he said, was "characterized by inefficiency and fraud."[1] On the floor of the U.S. Senate Oregon Senator James Nesmith stated it this way: "If there is any one department of our Government worse managed than another it is that which relates to our Indian affairs. Mismanagement, bad faith, fraud, speculation and downright robbery have been its great distinguishing features."[2]

This was the situation facing Minnesota as it struggled to become a state in 1858. Minnesota was on the edge of the frontier—further to the west only Texas (in 1845) and California (in 1850) had already been admitted to the Union. A portion of what was to become the State of Minnesota was included in the Northwest Territory which was created by the Continental Congress in 1787 and signed into law by President George Washington in 1789. The Louisiana Purchase from France in 1803 added most of the remainder of what would become Minnesota and the remainder was a British cession in 1818.

The Northwest Ordinance, created at the same time as the Northwest Territory by the Continental Congress, established guidelines by which the federal government would be sovereign and would expand westward with the admission of new states. Two articles in the Northwest Ordinance mention Indians[3]:

> "The utmost good faith shall always be observed towards the Indians; their lands and property shall never be taken from them without their consent; and, in their property, rights, and liberty, they shall never be invaded or disturbed, unless in just and lawful wars authorized by

> *Congress; but laws founded in justice and humanity, shall from time to time be made for preventing wrongs being done to them, and for preserving peace and friendship with them."*

and,

> *"the governor shall make proper divisions thereof ... to lay out the parts of the district in which the Indian titles shall have been extinguished, into counties and townships."*

How was this lofty objective to be accomplished? Using the Doctrine of Discovery as authorization, the monarchs of Europe laid claim to most of the North American continent. Great Britain, France, Spain and Russia were the major players. The British had used treaties to acquire land for their colonies and to move the Indians out of their way. Right or wrong, the young United States adopted this same practice. To this Bishop Whipple opined that "it was based on a 'falsehood,' the idea of treating Indians as independent nations with whom treaties could be made."[4]

As treaties became more numerous and more and more land was settled, the process of administering it all became a huge challenge. This was the birth of the Indian System to which Whipple referred. The first Office of Indian Affairs was established in 1824 by the Secretary of War, but in 1832 the Office was moved to the Department of the Interior under the direction of the Secretary of the Interior. The chain of command descended from the President, who shared his power with Congress, to the Secretary of the Interior, to the Commissioner of Indian Affairs, to the regional superintendents, to the agent attached to a particular tribe or reservation. In addition, the General Land Office was involved in the disposition of lands acquired by treaty, the Interior Department was involved in railroad and mineral development which often involved Indians and their lands, and the War Department was often called upon to mediate Indian—white conflicts or to supervise removal of Indians. Once a territory became a state the congressmen

Bishop Henry Benjamin Whipple

that represented that state became involved. They not only made recommendation to the President for the appointees they favored for the Indian system positions, but they also approved the treaties and acts of Congress that provided the money and the jobs to make the system work. In addition, Congressmen acted as conduits for claims of all sorts, for special interest requests and for job seekers.

There was money to be made in the Indian System and three major groups accounted for most of the profits: Claimants, Contractors and Traders.

The system was comprised of hundreds of people: a formidable management task!

Many claims were made to the government for damages caused by Indians. Most were settled in favor of the claimant: Indians did not vote and congressional courtesy prevailed.

Contracting was big business. The government contracted for services and supplies involved with the management of the Indian system: food, supplies, buildings, printing, removal and transportation, and even vaccination for such things as Smallpox. There were government school teachers, superintendents, janitors, seamstresses, cooks, doctors, nurses, hospital personnel, blacksmiths, millers and more.

The seldom told truth is that, while money for all these entities was appropriated by Congress, much if not all of it came from the Indian trust fund that was created by purchase of the Indian's land and timber, etc. through the negotiation of treaties and agreements. The Indian trust fund was money supposedly belonging to the Indians, but it was all under government management, used by the government to finance the Indian system, which in turn manipulated the Indian people to the advantage of the governmental purposes.

Then there were the traders, licensed by the government, who often had a close relationship with the agent on whose reservation they frequently held a monopoly.[5]

At the age of 17 Henry Hastings Sibley started working as a clerk in a mercantile house in Sault Ste. Marie. The following year—and for the next five years—Sibley worked as a purchasing agent at the American Fur Company at Mackinac owned by John Jacob Astor. In 1834 Sibley became a partner in the company and moved to their headquarters in St. Peter's, Minnesota—now called Mendota. In 1836 Sibley built the first stone house in Minnesota. Composed of limestone, it sits overlooking the Mississippi River and Fort Snelling and is today maintained as an historic site. Sibley lived here as a bachelor until his common law marriage to Red Blanket Woman, the granddaughter of an Mdewankonton Dakota chief. The couple parented a daughter but within a couple of years both went on to other relationships. Sibley married Sarah Jane Steele in 1843. Sarah Jane was the daughter of General James Steele, commander of Fort Snelling.

At about this time the American Fur Company was reorganized into two business groups. The Western Outfit covered the territory from southern Wisconsin to Iowa. It was headquartered at Prairie du Chien under the leadership of Joseph Ralette,

Henry Hastings Sibley (Feb 20, 1811-Feb 18, 1891)

PUBLISHED IN THE US BEFORE 1923 AND PUBLIC DOMAIN IN THE US

Hercules Dousman and Henry Sibley. The Northern Outfit operated out of La Pointe under the leadership of William Aitkin and Lyman Warren. Warren ran the operation at La Pointe and Aitkin managed the operation at Fond du Lac. The Northern Outfit covered the territory from Lake Superior to the Red River Valley.

William Aitkin was born in Scotland and arrived in Upper Mississippi country in the early 1800's. It is recorded that he complained that the British traders had an advantage over the American traders because they were permitted to supply liquor to the Indians. Aitkin apparently had at least two marriages but he and his wife, Striped Cloud, parented seven children. It is reported in one source that he also was married to Gingioncumigoke. Apparently he was prolific; in one account he is said to have fathered twenty five children. Both Aitkin County and the city of Aitkin in Minnesota were named for William Aitkin.

Lyman Warren was married to his Ojibwe—French wife Mary and they lived on Madeline Island in Lake Superior where Lyman was a fur trader at the time their oldest son William was born, moving to La Point in about 1832. William was the author of *History of the Ojibway People*, a work often quoted in this book.

Quoting from *Faith in Paper* by Charles E. Cleland: "In 1837 there was a great financial crisis in the American economy as a result of unsecured land speculation in the Old Northwest. The traders of both the Northern Outfit and the Western Outfit were saved from financial ruin only by the Chippewa, Sioux and Winnebago treaties negotiated that year, which provided a huge windfall of $325,000 in the combined payment of trade debts. As a result of the panic of 1837, the Northern Outfit was reorganized, and both Warren and Aitkin were fired and replaced by Dr. Charles Borup, who operated out of La Pointe. Dr. Borup was born in Copenhagen, Denmark in 1806. Borup had founded the Isle Royale and Lake Superior Mining Company and along with a Mr. Oakes started a bank in St. Paul. William Aitkin, however, soon returned as the company trader at Sandy Lake."[6]

Over the years, Ramsey Crooks had become a part of Astor's American Fur Company and in 1842 Crooks sold the company's share in the Western Outfit to the Pierre Chouteau Company of St. Louis. "Chouteau now joined Sibley and Dousman in a new arrangement called the Upper Mississippi Outfit, which negotiated a non-interference compact with the Northern Outfit, now owned and operated by Ramsey Crooks under the American Fur Company name ... Traders of both outfits haunted the annual treaty payments, where they managed to get the lion's share of annuity money paid to Indians, by offering goods in trade and by collecting debts."[7]

In 1846, Dousman retired and his place was taken by Bernard Bresbois of Prairie du Chien and Henry Rice of Ohio. (Charles Cleland says Henry Rice was from Ohio but other sources say he was already in Minnesota in 1839, having migrated to Michigan in about 1835 to work surveying the canal route between Lakes Superior and Huron.) Rice cultivated the Chippewa and Winnebago trade and was able to manipulate their affairs to his own advantage. Rice cited an earlier arrangement between Dousman and Aitkin, claiming a monopoly on the fur trade of the upper Mississippi region to the detriment of the American Fur Company. He hired away the best traders from Dr. Borup's Northern Outfit, and was then able to compete in the upper Mississippi Valley with goods supplied by himself and Henry Sibley.

Rice then organized the Chippewa Outfit along with Pierre Chouteau. Chouteau held interests in the Winnebago and Sioux trades and collectively they were known as the Northern Outfit of the Chouteau Company. The old Northern Outfit of the American Fur Company continued to operate from La Pointe as the Northern Fur Company and Rice was able to bring that company into the Chippewa Outfit. But, during the summer of 1849, Dr. Borup, who owned the Northern Fur Company, replaced Rice and moved the newly consolidated business from La Pointe to St. Paul.

Charles E. Cleland, in his book *Faith in Paper*, summarizes the situation as follows:

> "In 1849 a consortium of traders, merchants, and politicians was actively promoting St. Paul as the main commercial center of the Upper Mississippi Valley. Henry Sibley and Henry Rice were central in this effort, since, as major Indian traders, they both had investments in the Chouteau Company of St Louis. Between the two, they had already cornered the Sioux, Winnebago, and southern Chippewa trade. Rice and Sibley were also involved in a real estate venture in St Paul with the brother of Governor Alexander Ramsey. When Sibley went to Washington as the Minnesota territorial delegate in 1849, he was able to establish a working relationship with Thomas Ewing, Secretary of the newly created Department of the Interior. Ewing personally managed the office of Indian Affairs and was notorious for authorizing payment of dubious trader claims ... Ambitious trading interests in Minnesota had not just the support of the governor but also that of the Secretary of the Interior."[8]

Caleb B. Smith from Indiana was the Secretary of the Interior from March of 1861 to December of 1862. He had been appointed by Lincoln as a reward for his work on behalf of Lincoln during the presidential campaign. In his 1861 report Smith was very critical of the traders. He reported that the money paid to the Indians went immediately to the traders, leaving the Indians continually in debt. Smith is quoted as saying, "Witnesses are produced, who establish the debts by evidence, which cannot be contradicted by any available proof, sufficient to absorb most of the proceeds of their [the Indians] lands." He estimated that licensed traders charged a profit margin ranging anywhere "from one to three or four thousand per cent."[9]

David Nichols, in his book *Lincoln and the Indians*, relates the following story: "In May 1862, the Indian Committee of the Senate requested $15,000 to negotiate a new treaty with the Chippewas of Minnesota. Fessenden [Senator from Maine] opposed the appropriation and informed the Senate that he knew a man who had been offered a bribe to promote this bill. The committee opposed Fessenden, insisting the treaty and the funds were necessary. Sen. Morton Wilkinson of Minnesota was especially outspoken in defense of the treaty that was to be negotiated in his home state. Suddenly Sen. John Sherman of Ohio inquired whether 'there was not an appropriation for this very project last year?' Senator Wilkinson answered, 'A wicked and corrupt Administration appointed an incompetent man, Goddard Bailey, and he squandered the whole of it.' Asked what had become of Bailey, Wilkinson replied that the agent had been arrested for stealing $870,000 in bonds out of a safe in the Interior Department. Wilkinson quickly assured his colleagues that such corruption ended with the election of Abraham Lincoln and the new administration appointed only 'honest men'. Thus reassured, the senators passed the appropriation."

Goddard Bailey, a clerk in the Land Office, had gone to his friends Senator Henry Rice and Secretary of the Interior Thompson and confessed that he had embezzled $870,000 in state funds from the Indian Trust Fund. He had loaned the money to military contractor William H. Russell and had hoped that he would be repaid and could replace the bonds before anyone found out they were missing. Apparently, once Russell found out where the money came from and how easy it was to come by, he blackmailed Bailey into continuing to steal money until the original $150,000 loan grew to $870,000.

"Henry Hastings Sibley of Minnesota provides a clear example of how the System could be a 'pathway to power' for a clever man. Sibley was born in Michigan. At the age of 23, he became a manager for the American Fur Company in the Minnesota region. Sibley entered politics in 1848 and in 1849 was elected a territorial delegate to Congress. He continued in the fur trade and represented the traders at the Sioux treaty negotiations of 1851. That treaty promised the Santee Sioux $475,000 in exchange for land. Henry Sibley succeeded in claiming $145,000 of that amount, due him for the 'overpayment' to the Sioux for furs! The Sioux objected to this obvious fraud, but the claim was approved by agent Alexander Ramsey. Henry Sibley became a rich man and in 1856 was commissioned a major general in the militia. He became the first governor of the state of Minnesota in 1858. His successor as governor was, not surprisingly, Alexander Ramsey. Sibley was later commissioned as a brigadier general for his service in the Indian War of 1862. The Indian System served Sibley well, as it did many other ambitious men."[10]

The Indian System had become well developed and "well oiled" by the time Minnesota became the 32nd state to be admitted to the Union in 1858. Only the year before the U.S. Supreme Court, under Chief Justice Roger Taney, had ruled in the *Dred Scott* case that Negroes were property and could never become citizens of the United States. In that United States Supreme Court case Chief Justice Taney included Indians in the same category as Negroes but left the door ajar, saying that Indians could become full citizens once they were civilized. Indians were not held in high regard.

There were a few who knew that the system was corrupt and abusive. One such person was Henry Benjamin Whipple. Born in New York in 1822, Whipple entered the Episcopalian ministry and, after serving parishes in Rome, New York and Chicago, Illinois was elected as the first bishop in the new state of Minnesota in 1859.

Bishop Henry Whipple was clearly troubled by the dishonesty rampant in the Indian System and waged a never-ending campaign for reform of the system. In 1862 he traveled to Washington to consult with President Lincoln regarding the issue. Lincoln heard him, but obviously the president's main concern at the time was winning the Civil War and preserving the Union. However, as a result of Whipple's description of the fraudulent activity, Lincoln, according to Bishop Whipple, was clearly moved. Bishop Whipple reported Lincoln's response as, "If we get through this war, and I live, the Indian System shall be reformed."[11]

The North did win the Civil War and the Union was preserved, but John Wilkes Booth ended any chance of President Abraham Lincoln fulfilling his assurance to Bishop Whipple.

Even as late as 1907, as described in Chapter 19, traders such as Charles Malone—who operated a store in Isle, Minnesota—were playing "loose" with the Indian's money.

CHAPTER 8

The 1837 Treaty

Citizens of the Wisconsin Territory were desirous of legal access[1] to the bountiful pine that the Territory offered. It is reported that Wisconsin territorial delegate George W. Jones convinced Congress that the Winnebago's and Chippewa were asking Governor Dodge to "enable them to dispose of their lands." (Jones 1836)

Indian Affairs was still a part of the Department of War in 1837, so it was President Van Buren's Secretary of War, Lewis Cass, who laid out the main objectives of the treaty negotiations. This was the first treaty that actually involved the area inhabited by the Mille Lac Chippewa. These objectives that Secretary Cass enumerated were to gain access to the bountiful stands of pine for lumber harvesting, with a secondary objective of eventually having land to sell to settlers. As the frontier continued to spread westward the expense of shipping lumber from the east for building projects grew, and thus the desire for lumbering was the primary goal of the treaty. In addition, Secretary Cass seemed to think that, since it was more or less a border land between the Chippewa and the Sioux, the territory was quite unimportant to either tribe and that allowing an American settlement between the two warring tribes would feasibly create a buffer zone.

It seems obvious in reading the treaty and the negotiations leading up to it that there were other objectives. Most often the traders viewed

Governor Henry Dodge
PUBLISHED IN THE US BEFORE 1923 AND PUBLIC DOMAIN IN THE US

treaties as a way to collect on unpaid debts from the Indians. There apparently was also a monopoly of sawmill sites and lumbering rights that had developed through pacts made between tribal chiefs and traders of influence because of having married Chippewa wives. The government apparently was desirous of breaking up this monopoly. There was also fear of bloodshed as the settlers—desirous of timber—and the Indians clashed. There was also concern about British influence on the Indians since the northern border of the United States was not yet settled, and realizing that the Chippewa fought on the side of the British in the Revolutionary War. All of these concerns, whether real or not, contributed to the decision to negotiate a treaty.

Henry Dodge was the Wisconsin territorial governor at the time, and he and General W.R. Smith were appointed treaty commissioners. General Smith, however, did not show up to participate in the treaty negotiations. Ver Planck Van Antwerp was the treaty secretary and it is from his diary that we glean much of the information about the treaty council. All of the different bands of Chippewa were invited, and most of the Chippewa tribes were represented—Mississippi Chippewa, Lake Superior Chippewa and Pillager Chippewa[2]—so there were attendees from Leech Lake, Gull Lake, Swan Lake, Mille Lacs Lake, Sandy Lake, Snake River, St. Croix River, Fond du Lac, La Pointe, Lac du Flambeau and Lac Courte Oreilles. Many of the Indians who attended did not live on the lands that would be affected by the cessions in the treaty.

Van Antwerp's journal is written in English; all statements made by the Indians are translations. There were two official translators of English to Chippewa—Steven Bonga and Patrick Quinn—and two translators of Chippewa to English—Scott Campbell and Jean Baptiste Dubay, and, as one might expect, interpretations were not perfect.

Treaty negotiations were held at the St. Peters Agency—present day Mendota, MN—located on property owned by the military near Fort Snelling. Governor Dodge opened negotiations on July 20, 1837, even though most of the Wisconsin Indians—those who would be most impacted by the outcome of the treaty—had yet to arrive. Dodge seized upon the opportunity to perhaps make progress toward his goal without waiting for the other invitees. The Indians assembled were mostly from Minnesota and they steadfastly refused to discuss it until the Wisconsin Indians arrived. After waiting for two days for the Wisconsin tribes to arrive Dodge reportedly grew impatient and pushed for answers from those assembled, regardless of the fact that the interior Wisconsin Indians had not yet arrived.

Flat Mouth from Leech Lake, who apparently had considerable influence among the chiefs, reminded Dodge that there was no chief who was head of the entire Chippewa people. Flat Mouth warned against proceeding until the Wisconsin invitees arrived. The council journal records Pillager Chief Flat Mouth's comments this way: "My Father, I shall say but little to you at this time. I am called a chief. I am not the chief of the whole nation, but only of my people or tribe. I speak to you now only because I see nobody else ready to do so. I do not wish to take any fur-

*Aysh-ke-bah-ke-ko-zhay
Chief Flat Mouth, a Chippewa Chief*

ther steps about what you have proposed to us until the other people arrive who have been expected here. They have not yet come, and to do so before their arrival might be considered an improper interference, and unfair towards them. The residence of my band is outside of the country which you wish to buy from us. After the people who live in that country shall have told you their minds I will speak. If the lands you wish to buy were occupied by my band, I would immediately have given you my opinion. After listening to the people who we are expecting and who will speak to you, I will abide by what they say, and say more to you myself."

While proceedings were held up due to the Wisconsin Indians tardiness, the Mille Lacs Chief Washaskkoone (translated as 'Muskrat's Liver') made it clear that land occupied by the Mille Lacs was also involved in treaty negotiations. The chief told Dodge, "We are talking about the land you have come for. I have tread all over it with my war club in my hand. My ancestors and those of Pagoonakeezhig [Hole-in-the-Day] were the chiefs and protectors of that country and drove the bad Indians [Sioux] away from it."

Finally, after five days word came that the Wisconsin Indians, together with subagent Bushnell and trader Lyman M. Warren, were approaching. Finally reaching the Agency on July 25th meant that negotiations could proceed in earnest.

Council convened the next day, July 26th with all of the Chippewa present. Once more Governor Dodge explained his proposal for purchase of a specified portion of their territory. After the council had been in session for 6 days Dodge attempted to close the deal by urging the Indian delegates to reach a decision by the next morning. Dodge further suggested to the assembled Indians that he would like to have them choose two spokesmen to speak for the group.

The next morning—July 27th —when the council convened Dodge again explained the proposal and the map depicting the territory in question. He asked if the Indians were satisfied with the explanation and if they had chosen their spokesmen. The Indians indicated their satisfaction with Dodge's explanation and specified those they had chosen to speak for them: Latrappe, a warrior from Leech Lake, and Hole-in-the-Day from Gull Lake.

After Latrappe and Hole-in-the-Day had spoken at length in their own language to the assembled Indians, Latrappe told Dodge that they were prepared to sell the land in question to Dodge, but with conditions, saying "My Father, Listen to me. Of all the country that we grant you we wish to hold on to a tree where we get our living, and to reserve the streams where we drink the waters that give us life."

Secretary Van Antwep wrote in the margin of his journal: "This of course is nonsense — but is given literally as rendered by the Interpreters, who are unfit to act in that capacity. I presume it to mean that the Indians wish to reserve the privilege of hunting & fishing on the lands and making sugar from the Maple."

Latrappe next asked Dodge what he was willing to pay for this land. Dodge replied that he wanted the Indians to tell him how much they wanted. Latrappe answered that they wanted an annuity for 60 years and that they wanted the "half breeds" included in the payment. He went on to say that his people accept the proposition but that they wanted a place selected for the "half breeds" to live, saying, "If I have rightly understood you, we can remain on the land and hunt there." Latrappe then asked all the chiefs who agree to selling this land to stand; thirty or more stood up.

Latrappe then took Governor Dodge by the hand and said, "My Father, I will not let go your hand 'till I count the number of villages. The Great Spirit first made the Earth thin, but now it is much heavier. We do not wish to disappoint you and our Great Father [the President of the United States] in the object you had in coming here. We therefor grant you the country, which you want from us; and your Children, the Chiefs that represent all the villages within its limits are now present. The number of villages [Nineteen] is marked on this paper, and I present it to you in acknowledgement that we grant you the land. This piece [retaining in his hand another piece of paper] we will keep, because we wish to say something more, on it. At the conclusion of this treaty you will ask us to touch the quill, but no doubt you will grant what we ask, before we do so. At the end of the treaty, I will respect what the Chiefs have to say to you and keep this paper for that purpose. My Father The Great Spirit has given us a clear sky together today. We must now rest awhile, and when we meet again, we will speak further."

Addressing the council, Governor Dodge then explained that the Great Father never buys land for a term of years; on behalf of the President he would only agree that they would have free use of the rivers and hunting privileges on the lands that they sold to the United States, <u>during his pleasure</u>.

Dodge agreed that the "half breeds" should be provided for, but in money and not land, and that the payment for the land could be both in goods and money.

Dodge then suggested—for their consideration—that part of their payment be designated for providing:

- Teachers to educate your children & make them wise like those of the white people
- Farmers and Instructors in Agricultural pursuits, for agricultural implements, and seed to plant in the earth

- provisions and salt
- tobacco
- Blacksmiths, Iron & Steel
- Mills and Millers to grind your corn and other grain

Dodge then adjourned the council saying, "…let me know the amount you wish me to pay you for your land; and I will be glad to meet you in council … tomorrow morning."

On Friday July 28th, Governor Dodge opened the council by asking whether the Indians had made up their minds about the proposition he had made the day before and who would speak for them that day. Flat Mouth, a chief from Leech Lake, came forward together with many of the other chiefs. After they had all shaken hands, Flat Mouth spoke saying, "…your children are willing to let you have their lands, but they wish to reserve the privilege of making sugar from the trees, and getting their living from the Lakes and Rivers … and of remaining in this country. It is hard to give up the lands. They will remain, and can not be destroyed — but you may cut down the trees, and others will grow up. You know we cannot live, deprived of our Lakes and Rivers …"

No other chief came forward to speak, so Governor Dodge replied, " … I will make known to your Great Father, your request to be permitted to make sugar, on the lands; and you will be allowed, during his pleasure, to hunt and fish on them. It will probably be many years, before your Great Father will want all these lands for the use of his white children. As you have asked me what I will give you for the country which I wish to buy from you, I offer you the sum of Eight Hundred Thousand Dollars ($800,000). I propose to give you an annuity for Twenty years, of $20,000 … a year, in goods and money, one half in each — or all in goods, if you choose; …"

He went on to suggest an amount to be paid to the 'half breeds' and to pay their creditors.

Flat Mouth then spoke again saying that the chiefs thought the government should pay the amounts owed to the traders and that payments should be made to the Indians so they could decide for themselves how they wanted to spend it. He went on to say, "If it was my land you was buying [sic], I would, instead of an annuity for only 20 years — demand one from you, as long as the ground lasted. You know that without the lands, and the Rivers and Lakes, we could not live …"

Dodge said that he was only suggesting; it was their decision as to how the payment was to be used.

Flat Mouth appeared to get upset, saying that had he known that the subject of debts owed to traders would come up, he would not have attended the council. Flat

Mouth seemed to think that the traders had already been paid with the fish they had taken from the lakes and the wood they had burned, etc.

Adjourning the council Governor Dodge said that he hoped all would be ready to finish their business the next day.

On Saturday morning July 29th, Governor Dodge opened the council and announced that the sub-agents had agreed that the amount he was offering for the land was a fair price and that they approved of his proposal for payments. Dodge went on to say, "There is one subject which it is necessary for you now to determine upon. It is, whether you will make any donation to your "half breed" relatives, & if so, how it shall be paid to them."

The chiefs had just sat down to discuss this issue when a large number of warriors in full combat regalia approached the council, singing and dancing, war flag flying—but unarmed. The Little Six, a "half-breed" chief from Snake River, came forward to speak. "… The braves of the different bands have smoked and talked together … They have not come here to undo what our chiefs have done — but ask a favor of you … they are afraid to return home, if their traders are not paid. They fear they should not survive during the winter without their aid. It is the wish of the Braves that you should pay the traders; but they do not want to undo what the chiefs have done … You now come to buy our lands from us; and why do you offer us so little for them. The speaker who told you that we ought to be paid for sixty years, expressed our opinions."

The Little Six then said they would sign the treaty if Dodge could comply with their wishes.

Governor Dodge asked The Little Six if $70,000 paid to the traders would satisfy them After some discussion they agreed that it would. Governor Dodge then addressed the chiefs saying that he had heard the request of the Braves and he wanted them to be happy—**all** of them to be happy—so he was willing to pay $70,000 to satisfy the debts of the traders in addition to what he had already offered. He asked for their comments.

Hole-in-the-Day then spoke with a great deal of passion and animation, saying first to the chiefs, "Chiefs what we agreed and determined upon yesterday; shall consent to undo, when my head is severed from my body and my life no more — we must abide by it firmly.

Braves! There are many of you — but none of you have done what I have — nor are any of you my equals!! — Our Father wishes to go home in peace."

Turning to the Governor he then said, "My Father, listen to me — my words shall be few. What the braves have come and told you must be true, and should be listened to … yesterday in council the chiefs told you what they would do. They are perfectly content with that arrangement … We agree to what has just been done, and are satisfied with it …"

Following opinions voiced by several others, Governor Dodge recessed the council so that the treaty could be prepared for signing and copies made. Upon completion the treaty was read to the council:

Article 1. The Chippewa Nation cede to the United States all that tract of country within the following boundaries: [see copy of actual treaty for legal description].

Article 2. In consideration of the cession aforesaid the United States agree to make to the Chippewa nation annually for the term of twenty years, from the date of the ratification of this treaty, the following payments.

> $9,500 to be paid in money.
> $19,000 to be delivered in goods.
> $3,000 for establishing three black smiths shops, supporting the black smiths, and furnishing them with iron and steel.
> $1,000 for farmers, and for supplying them and the Indians, with implements of labor, with grain or seed; & whatever else may be necessary to enable them to carry on their agricultural pursuits.
> $2,000 in provisions.
> $500 in tobacco.

The provisions and tobacco to be delivered at the same time with the goods and money to be paid, which time or times, as well as the place or places where they are to be delivered, shall be fixed upon under the direction of the President of the United States.

The blacksmiths shops to be placed at such points in the Chippewa country as shall be designated by the Superintendent of Indian Affairs, or under his direction.

If at the expiration of one or more years, the Indians should prefer to receive goods, instead of the $9,000, agreed to be paid to them in money, they shall be at liberty to do so. Or, should they conclude to appropriate a portion of that annuity to the establishment of school, or schools among them, this shall be granted them.

Article 3. The sum of $100,000 shall be paid by the United States to the "half breeds" of the Chippewa nation under the direction of the President. It is the wish of the Indians that their two sub-agents Daniel P. Bushnell and Miles M. Vineyard superintend the distribution of this money among their "half breed" relations.

Article 4. The sum of $70,000 shall be applied to the payment by the United States of certain claims against the Indians; of which amount $28,000 shall at their request be paid to William A. Aitkin; $25,000 to Lyman M. Warren, & the balance applied to liquidation of other just demands against them — which they acknowledge to be the case with regard to that presented by Hercules L. Dousman, & they request that it be paid.

Article 5. The privilege of hunting, fishing & gathering the wild rice, upon the lands, the rivers and the lakes, included in the territory ceded, is guaranteed to the Indians, during the pleasure of the United States.

Article 6. This treaty shall be obligatory from and after its ratification by the President and the Senate of the United States.

Done at St. Peters in the Territory of Wisconsin the 29th day of July, 1837.

 Governor Dodge was the first to sign the treaty. He then addressed the council, saying that since they had not chosen a chief to receive their copy of the treaty for safe keeping, he would hand it to the first to give it his signature. Hole-in-the-Day did so promptly, offered his signature and received the copy of the treaty.
 After some closing comments Governor Dodge said to the council, "The treaty which we have now made will bring us oftener together hereafter, and I hope always, as friends."
 And with that, the council was adjourned. [3] [4]

CHAPTER 9

The 1855 Treaty

It was on a Monday evening, February 12, 1855 that a delegation of Chippewa chiefs assembled in the office of Commissioner of Indian Affairs George Manypenny in Washington, D.C. They had been invited there by the Commissioner for the purpose of making a treaty for the purchase of Chippewa land in Minnesota.

Manypenny, appointed to the position of Commissioner of Indian Affairs by President Franklin Pierce, served the same four year term as the President. During Pierce's term in office the economy seemed to be progressing nicely, while President Pierce's principal aim seemed to focus on the prevention of a crisis over the issue of slavery.

Colonel George W. Manypenny

Commissioner Manypenny objected to the removal of Indians without the land being ceded by treaty. As a matter of fact in his 1856 report to Congress he is quoted as saying, "Since the 4th of March, 1853, fifty-two treaties with various Indian tribes have been entered into ... the quantity of land acquired by these treaties ... is about one hundred and seventy-four millions of acres ... in no former equal period of our history have so many treaties been made, or such vast accessions of land obtained."

Consequently Manypenny was an experienced treaty-maker as he met with the delegation representing the Mississippi Chippewa and the Pillager Chippewa of Minnesota.

The delegation that assembled in Manypenny's office that February evening consisted of Chief Hole-in-the-Day, 'Croping Sky', 'Crowfeathers', 'Bad Boy', 'Coming Home Following' and 'One Who Knows'. Chief Hole-in-the-Day (the Younger) was considered—at least by the government—to be the principal chief of the Chippewa, a role Hole-in-the-Day accepted without hesitation. The delegation was accompanied by their agent, Maj. David J. Herriman, U.S. Interpreter Truman A. Warren and Paul H. Beaulieu.

It is obvious in reading the transcript of the first gathering that it was Manypenny's intent that it simply be a get acquainted meeting and an opportunity for him to acquaint himself with any possible opposition. While the Indians may have been told prior to the meeting why they had been invited there, they nevertheless appeared to be suspicious. There was concern that perhaps they had been invited to Washington only to be imprisoned.

Only Manypenny and Hole-in-the-Day spoke at this first meeting. Manypenny wanted the Chippewa to be impressed by the white man's way of life and spent the evening courteously sparing with Hole-in-the-Day over his desire for the Indians to learn to live and work as the whites.

When asked what he thought about the train ride to Washington, the transcript records Hole-in-the-Day's response as "he liked it very much and admired the wisdom of the white man which enabled them to accomplish such works. Although his color was different from that of the Commissioner, he knew that the same Great Spirit made both, and felt as an American at heart, and took great pleasure and satisfaction in noticing the wonderful increase and progress of the whites in improvements. These things he intimated were natural to the whites, as the habits, customs and pursuits of the red man were to them, and each should adhere to their own way of life."

The Commissioner disagreed that each should live in their own way, replying to Hole-in-the-Day thusly; "So long as the red man relies upon the subsistence afforded by the chace [sic] [hunting, fishing & gathering], so long will he remain ignorant of the advantages of industry and civilization—so long will the Indian decrease and diminish in numbers. Let them but once learn to depend upon the cultivation of the earth for their support, and education, improvement and independence will follow…"

Manypenny's prophetic reply to Hole-in-the-Day substantiated the government's aim for the future.

The remainder of the meeting mainly built upon these first two statements by Manypenny and Hole-in-the-Day. Hole-in-the-Day said the Indians wanted to be like the whites if they only knew how to accomplish it. But what could they accomplish on only $4 each per year?

Manypenny replied that he had no doubt that the Indian had the capacity to achieve their goal, declaring that the white man had accumulated their wealth through hard work and cultivating the soil.

Acting the victim, Hole-in-the-Day asked what his people could do; they are but savages. How could men with their traditions and ideas acquire wealth? They had not been educated by their ancestors, like the whites had been, because they were savages. It takes time to change from the old customs, habits and superstitions. The red men will always live in poverty.

Then giving a glimmer of hope Hole-in-the-Day said that, if only my people, the Chippewas, could follow your advice [the Commissioners] it would be in their best interest.

Following Manypenny's words of encouragement, Hole-in-the-Day replied by recounting the words of his father, spoken on his death bed. "My Son, I charge you to take care of the Chippewa nation. Take the tribe by the hand, show them how to walk, and light them to fame, as it were, and make them resemble the whites."

After some minutes Hole-in-the-Day had had enough of the chit-chat, and asked that they come to the point of the meeting. He wanted to know why they had been sent for, to which Manypenny replied that he wanted to buy from them a portion of their lands, and went on to say that once the Chippewas become cultivators of the soil they would no longer need all of that land.

Hole-in-the-Day declared that he interpreted Manypenny's assertion as "I want to buy your land" and was offended by this curt statement. After some mild sparring the meeting ended with only Manypenny and Hole-in-the-Day having spoken.

By Thursday evening the Pillager and Winnibigoshish bands had arrived and another council was convened. Additional attendees were Mr. J.W. Lyon and trader and interpreter Peter Roy along with Eskebee (Flatmouth), Rejeke (Buffalo), Naba na osh (Young-man's son), Magejabo, Magizzy (Eagle) and Cobnubby. Manypenny opened the meeting much as a continuation of the previous meeting's line of conversation. However, Manypenny gave the impression that they had all gathered because the Chippewa had requested the meeting. He went on to say that a nomadic life is not productive of good, asserting that the red man should change his ways and conform to the times and the spirit of the current age.

Stating that everyone who had been expected had arrived, Manypenny said they should now talk about business. He said he was satisfied that the Chippewa should confine themselves to a smaller extent of territory, using every means in their power to induce their young men to abandon their present mode of living and turn their attention to the farming.

Flatmouth, head chief of the Pillager band, spoke first, saying that he was deaf and heard very little but what he did hear was that Manypenny wanted land and he, Flatmouth, wanted time to think about it.

Manypenny gently made fun of Flatmouth replying that if Flatmouth fully understood, why was he asking for time to think. Manypenny summarized his understanding of Flatmouth's thoughts this way: that the Indians have more land than they needed but needed more money, while the government has more money than it needs and wants land—both would be solved by reaching an agreement.

The Commissioner then scolded Buffalo for being there wearing a head-dress of feathers and having a painted face. Buffalo replied that it was a badge of honor. The Commissioner then asked if he had a farm, a house, stock and other comforts, and Buffalo replied that he had none of those. Manypenny responded, "While you, my friend, have been spending your time and money in painting your face, how many of your white brethren have started without a dollar in the world, and acquired all those things mentioned so necessary for your comfort and independent support. The paint, with the exception of what is now on my friend's face, has disappeared but the white persons to whom I allude by way of contrast, are surrounded by all the comforts of life, the legitimate fruits of their well-directed industry. This illustrates the difference between civilized and savage life and the importance of our red brethren changing their habits and pursuits for those of the whites."

The Indians talked among themselves. Hole-in-the-Day then said that he thought he should be quiet and the Pillagers should talk. Manypenny disagreed and said his remarks were for all the Chippewas.

Buffalo added that the Pillagers lived in far more remote areas than the others and had less means of understanding and so needed more time to think. Manypenny then bade the Pillagers not to take too much time if there was to be an agreement reached in time for ratification before Congress adjourned.

Buffalo asked whether the Commissioner was trying to unify the Chippewa into one nation. Manypenny said he had no desire to interfere in their internal affairs, but only wanted to attain a treaty with the whole Chippewa tribe. The Indians appeared firmly convinced that they were not all one nation, nor did they want to be.

Next Commissioner Manypenny urged the bands to define each of their tribal boundaries so that he could make them an offer. Hole-in-the-Day replied that there was no use looking at boundaries, stating, "Make your proposition, say what you want, and what you will give, and we will consider it. There is no use making child's play of the matter. It can be expressed in a few short words."

After further exchange between Manypenny and Flatmouth, the Commissioner declared that "the Pillagers and the Mississippi bands must determine the lines of their respective interests. He wishes [interpreter speaking] them to define, among themselves, their boundaries, and to say what quantity of land they wish reserved and where." He said that thenceforth he could make them an offer.

Hole-in-the-Day criticized the Commissioner for not being more explicit, to which Manypenny replied that he did not have the necessary information to be more specific. Manypenny summarized by adding that when the Pillagers and the Mississippi bands shall have settled their things among themselves and stated the extent of the reservations which they desire, he will then be able to act understandingly, and will render a proposal.

Hole-in-the-Day and Manypenny argued politely, followed by Hole-in-the-Day declaring, "I may have uttered some words, father, which you do not like; and you

Hole-in-the-Day 1858

BY JOEL EMMONS WHITNEY (1822-1886)
MINNESOTA HISTORICAL SOCIETY

may have said some things which we do not like. Both should act within a forgiving spirit, and if such words have been the case, let those unpleasant words pass without bad feeling … we all fully understand what you want, and now is the time for consultation and reflection."

On Saturday morning February 17th, Commissioner Manypenny met with only the Pillager and Winnibigoshish bands. They represented the 2200 or so Chippewa—exclusive of Red Lake—who lived in the northern part of Minnesota. Manypenny explained that they were assembled in order to make a treaty for the sale of their Chippewa lands to the United States. After consulting amongst themselves Flatmouth said, "My father and friend, I am glad you have come right to the point. My reason yesterday in pointing out the limits of our boundaries was to show you the country which you ought to have, and not to state precisely what our bands claim as a right. We are not like the whites. We differ among ourselves in respect to our boundaries. Our ideas, owing to our ignorance, are conflicting. We intended to designate what we want to cede. If we sell, we do not want to part with all. We want reserves to live upon at Lake Winnibigoshish, Cass Lake and Leech Lake. We feel that as we have yet the control and possession of our own lands, we should not part with them without reserving a home. We had better not be in existence than not to have a place we can call our own."

The Commissioner then asked if reservations at those places would be satisfactory, to which the bands responded Yes! He also inquired if the bands desired a reserve at Otter Tail Lake, and they replied that they should have mentioned it but that they did want indeed a reserve in that location.

At last the Commissioner said he was ready to make an offer: $20,000 a year for 30 years to be paid in cash, or part goods and part cash, whichever the President might judge best for their interests; to furnish them with two blacksmiths plus tools, iron, steel, etc. for ten years; to erect a saw mill with portable grist mill attached and to furnish them with a miller for ten years; to give them—at the first payment—a gift of $10,000 in guns, traps, blankets, etc. Manypenny added that at the end of ten years the bands should have trained millers and blacksmiths of their own.

The Commissioner went on to explain why he wished to reserve to the President the decision on how the annuity would be paid. Manypenny said he himself preferred the annuity be paid in money as soon as they knew how properly to take care of and appropriate it, because the sooner they are given control over their own resources, the better for them. Until that time however, the President would be in control. Manypenny also informed them that he would reserve the right to survey the land and divide it among them like the whites.

The Indians in attendance said they understood the matter fully and signified agreement.

Manypenny next asked what the Indians thought of his proposition.

After again emphasizing how old he was, Flatmouth responded, "We came here to act not for myself alone, but for my associates, and my people at home. You desire to purchase our land—our homes—it is an important matter to us; and I therefore desire time for reflection until Monday morning."

Manypenny answered that he was willing to give them time but hoped they could decide before Monday morning because Congress would only be in session for another twelve working days. Manypenny added that he had no objection to the bands consulting a friend. And with that the session ended.

Later that same day, at 2:30 in the afternoon, Commissioner Manypenny met with the Mississippi Chippewa. A map of the country owned by the Mississippi Chippewa and drawn by Capt. Eastman was brought forward and examined. Then a letter from the Rev. Mr. Breck, an Episcopal missionary at Long Prairie, was handed to the Commissioner and read aloud. The letter spoke in glowing terms of the character and conduct of Bad Boy, one member of the delegation. Their Agent, Maj. Harriman said, notwithstanding Bad Boy's name, there was not a better Indian in the tribe.

Commissioner Manypenny then explained to Hole-in-the-Day the number of acres in the tract that he wanted to purchase. Paul H. Beaulieu, who was the interpreter, added that it was difficult to make the delegates understand owing to the large quantity of acres, but by dividing the numbers he finally succeeded.

The Commissioner then asked the Chippewa, What land did you wish to reserve if you sell your country?

After thoughtfully pondering the question, Hole-in-the-Day said, "Father, you ask us where we want our reserves set apart. This question implies that you want to buy our land. Do I understand you?"

Manypenny replied, "Certainly, but I want you to have a home."

Hole-in-the-Day responded, "We did partially understand, but now we understand fully what you want. Before we commence to trade further, let us lay dignity aside. Will you allow me to look at you as a trader? As you want to buy my land, I must be excused if I look upon both of us as speculators. I decline to act on this matter as a business man, and lay all dignity aside. You have just now told me the number of acres I own, and, of course, when men trade for land they are in the habit of asking or offering so much per acre. Now, what are you willing to give per acre?"

Commissioner Manypenny then inquired, "The statement as to the number of acres in the limits of your reserve, refers to the water as well as the land? How much water is there on it—how many lakes?"

Hole-in-the-Day answered, "Although, father, there is a good deal of water, there are a great many fine sights upon our rivers and lakes. I do not know how many lakes, but there is not too much water for the land, or for the convenience of those who may settle upon it hereafter. You need have no kind of fear that the water will run short, or that there will not be always sufficient to cook by or wash with. I think the water upon the land is well proportioned. There is plenty of fish in the country, and you know father, fish must have water to live. They couldn't get along without it."

The Commissioner then advised, "I propose to make a round offer of a certain sum, to be paid in a given number of years."

Hole-in-the-Day came back with, "I have a general idea of the way the whites do business. I want to know how much the country we occupy is worth in your estimation."

Manypenny reply, "It is worth, in yearly payments, say from $250 to 300,000 or 250 boxes of a thousand in a box."

This response seemed to perturb Hole-in-the-Day and he responded, "Do not joke with me, my friend. I wish you to be serious, and I want a fair understanding—I want to ask you should we be thrown out of our possessions, and you should take all the land—take all the water—take the graves of our fathers, is $250,000 all the land is worth?"

The Commissioner said, "Yes, I think so."

Changing the course of the exchange Hole-in-the-Day said, "Leaving business aside, and viewing it as one of natural feelings, everyone knows that there is not an Indian tribe in America but what calls you their 'father'. This being the case, what should you do in dealing with your red children? The natural feeling of a father is to try and help his children, and to leave them a legacy enough to save them from want, and enable them to live after him. See the Indians here — we all have fathers, but you are the only human living who we call father in common. It is in this view of the case, that we appeal to your liberality, and good feeling on behalf of your red children."

"If you were my own children, I would not think it an advantage to give you more than you could manage and judiciously use," Manypenny responded. "Labor, after all, my friend, is what makes the man. It is no advantage to leave children a large unproductive estate."

"Father, it is true: every word you have uttered is true," replied Hole-in-the-Day. "It is not often advantageous or profitable to leave children a large estate, but is not money—is not means—necessary to the civilization of those who have everything to learn?"

The Commissioner answered, "Labor is the great thing to make men prosperous and rich."

Hole-in-the-Day came back with, "Father, it is very true labor is the main thing. Everything shows it that we have too much land; but those destitute of means ought to get enough to start on. Nothing can be done without money. Our father told us we had land which was of no use to us — more than we want. Why, then, not act liberally and give us out of his surplus means plenty of money for our land?"

"It is true, my friend has land which he don't work, and is therefore of no use to him," agreed Manypenny. "I want to buy a part from him and pay a fair price for it. It will be in his interest to sell, and the more money he gets, the worse it will be for the future of his tribe. Because nothing but necessity will drive them to work."

Hole-in-the-Day then declared, "We want to dress like whites. We envy them their comfortable clothing. We want to adopt their habits and customs and desire to have the means to accomplish it."

Pleased, the Commissioner responded, "I am glad to hear my friend say so. I feel confident the Indian can adopt and imitate successfully the habits, manners, and customs of their white brethren, and I am anxious to do all in my power to aid them."

"Very true," Hole-in-the-Day agreed. "Father, you can see by our past and present conduct what we think of our Great Father. Whenever commissioners have been sent by him into our country to treat with us, we have invariably sold him portions of our land. We now want to sell the residue to our Great Father, that he may be satisfied, but we must be satisfied too. Our whole conduct shows our affection for our Great Father."

At this point the Indians and other attendees gathered to confer among themselves, following which Hole-in-the-Day resumed the discussion. "Father the words I have expressed are just my view. I have said a good deal ... I am like a man traveling through snow, who clears it away with his stick ..."

Commissioner Manypenny asked, "Have you got the snow cleared away yet?"

"Pretty nearly, but I now want to hear the Commissioners views," the chief replied.

Manypenny said, "In addition to what I have indicated, I am willing to furnish a blacksmith and blacksmith shop and a mill and miller, and to support them for a few years, but I want the Indians to be their own blacksmith and millers after a while. I want them to learn every useful trade and avocation like the whites, and to do their own labor."

Hole-in-the-Day then explained, "Father, the reason why I desire to hear you speak is, because I want to get a general idea of matters and things so that after hearing your views, we may retire and deliberate among ourselves."

The Commissioner then clarified the nature of his proposition: he proposed to give them for their land a quarter of a million dollars, run out into a series of annual payments, and a mill, miller, blacksmith shop, blacksmith, iron and tools for ten years, and besides breaking up some land, say 3 or 400 acres of land. "The first year," he explained, "I shall provide for an additional present of $10,000, to be expended in guns, traps, etc. I think at the end of ten years, the Chippewas will have some blacksmiths and millers among themselves, and that is the reason why I deem it inappropriate to provide for their employment any longer. No one will work as long as he can get somebody else to work for him. Do you understand these propositions?"

The delegates answered, "We do, every one of us."

Manypenny went on to say, "I have no objection to your advising and consulting a friend, if you choose, in reference to these negotiations; but outsiders should not be made acquainted or permitted to interfere with them while they are pending."

"I understand," Hole-in-the-Day declared. "One trader has one mind, and another another. People will differ about such matters."

The Commissioner reiterated, "As I said before, I have no objection to your consulting a particular friend in whom you have confidence."

"Father, we will not be influenced by anybody," Hole-in-the-Day announced. Pointing to the delegates present he added, "Here are the people who are to be consulted. When they are pleased, that is enough."

In answer the Commissioner said, "I did not suppose you were so influenced. There are a great many curious people in the world, who try to find out everybody's business, and my object in saying what I did, was to put you on your guard against such persons. I would like to know when I may expect a final answer. The Great Council of the Nation [Congress] has only twelve working days more left, and, whatever is done, should be done in time to enable Congress to act upon it."

"We will give a final answer on Monday next," the chief promised, adding, "I would like to know how the Commissioner has got along with the Pillagers."

Manypenny responded, "They, also, will give me an answer on Monday. I presume there will be no difficulty in so arranging it that both parties can get a hearing on that day. I will get my scribes to work on both treaties, should we be successful in making them, so as to avoid delays."

Hole-in-the-Day then raised the issue of payment, saying, "Father, I understand that the value of gold is not now what it was in former days, owing to the great quantity discovered all over the west and that white money, being scarcer, is more in demand. As you will probably pay us in gold, you should therefore give us a good price."

"What you say is very true, with the discovery of gold," Manypenny agreed, "but it is not all coined into money. It is so plentifully used for ear rings, breast pins, etc. that there is no danger of its falling in value. This being the case, my friend need have no fears on that account."

Hole-in-the-Day retorted, "Father, what you say is very true. I had no idea at one time that gold was a mark of distinction among the white and that all those who wear it were great people. I have lately found out, however, that those who wear the most gold on their persons were the least thought of."

"Hole-in-the-Day has said what is very true," the Commissioner replied. "Those who wear the most gold are seldom our greatest people. Great people prefer simplicity of dress. On this account, I want my red children to abandon their foolish ornaments and live and dress like sensible white people."

Hole-in-the-Day agreed. "That is the reason why we want means. We desire to quit wearing blankets, which, when they blow open, expose our purses and everything we wear. If we had clothes like white people, we could hide away our money in our pockets."

Commissioner Manypenny expounded. "The best way to keep money in the pocket, is to open farms, cultivate the land, and sell the produce. The white man gets wealthy by labor, by the legal or medical profession, or by the mechanic arts and industry. That is the way the white man makes money to support himself and family, besides putting money in his strong box. That is the way, and the Indian should follow his example."

The sparring over, the delegates shook hands and departed.

At 7:00 p.m. that same evening the Pillager and Winnebigoshish bands assembled for another meeting, well prepared to bargain and announce the results of their deliberations.

Flatmouth spoke first with a rather eloquent speech. He said he desired to tell his father what he has been, what he now is, and how he has been looked upon by the Indians and whites.

"You see me here before you, father, and it would be useless for me to attempt to hide my age. My old head and grey hairs tell for themselves. I have seen a great many snows and rains. It is many years father, since I first became acquainted with the Long-knives. White men. A little before the war with Great Britain, I met them, and they hugged me and kissed me with kindness, and promised to be my friend. They were also kind to my people. Before that time, I was a British subject. From this kind of treatment of me, maybe dates my first connection with the Americans. Since then, my father, I have been their steady and fast friend." While these words were uttering, Flatmouth was seated, but he then rose, and, in a more animated manner, addressed the Commissioner.

"Now to the point, my father, as I must call you, although, from the difference of our ages, I might call you my son — I will speak to you plainly. I am not afraid to talk to a white man, because, when I look back upon my life, I can see no black stain on my [life] …, which should make me ashamed to look you in the face. I do not speak with forked tongue either, although, being an old man, when I talk, my thoughts may take a different direction from what I intended. We came here this morning, we had a friendly talk; you gave us further time to consider your propositions, and said, if we had a friend in whom we placed confidence, we might consult him. We have consulted a friend whom we have known long and well and with whom we have had many transactions in the past; and he has, at our request, put our thoughts on paper.

We heard your proposition this morning. We know and fully understand the nature and amounts of your offer. I do not wish to withhold from you what you want. You made us a proposition to suit yourself, but if we put in a little more, you must not think hard of us on that account. You must not feel angry because you may have to humor us. Do you see me, father? When I say a word I stick to it. If my name is not recorded in the annals of history according to the whites, I feel that I am a big man with my tribe. They have witnessed my actions and know me. You can see, my father, from my looks and from the manner in which I address you, what I think of you. I call you father, a name which we as a people give to none among our tribe. We look up to you for protection. If I were traveling and met a person, and that person should be a spirit, I should ask that spirit for what I wanted. If I beg of you a little more money to cloth and provide for my children which I have left back, I hope you will excuse me. They are poor and in want, and expect me to protect their interests and provide for them. This morning when I spoke, I had my head down, because I did not know what I was about. Since then, I went to my friend, he opened my eyes, and I now feel confidence. If I ask more than you offered, it is because I know you are rich, and I have left children behind me who are poor. When I left home, father, I did not know for what purpose I left. Since I came here, I have found out what you want, and am now coming to show you what I propose having done. Even if your heart was made of rock, father, if you would accompany me when I return to my home on the beautiful lake where I reside, and see my people coming nearly naked to meet me and ascertain what their Great Father has done to relieve their wants, it would move you to pity, and you would excuse me for asking, on their behalf, a little more than was offered this morning. You see, my father, I am taking a great deal of pains to explain, because I am about to part with the graves of my fathers, and sell my birth-right, as it were if I agree to what you offer. I want you to concede something also to my request, so as to lighten my burden, and justify me in the eyes of my people. I had no idea, when I left home, you were so rich, but on my way I have been surprised at the fine houses and great wealth of the whites, and if you give a few cents more to relieve the necessities of your red children, you will never miss it from your abundance.

"I am afraid, father, I am consuming your time, but you must bear with me, and listen to the wailings of an old man who has but a few short days to live. He speaks on behalf of his tribe, and hopes you will listen to his words. I am getting through, my father, with my little speech. If you agree to its requests, when you see the Northern lights running this way along the firmament, after we reach our homes, they will convey to you the shouts and salutations of the Pillager band of Chippewas, in gratitude for your kindness."

American Eagle spoke next, saying, "… our views are just like those of the old man [Flatmouth], and if you do as he asks, we will let you have our land …"

Winneshiek followed next, asserting, "If you send us back, father, without accepting our proposition, we will not think the worse of you on that account. But, if you accept, then the bargain is made ..."

Buffalo then spoke. "... You have told us that, if we would gain wealth and comfort, we must work with our hands, feet and toes. We have worked, and have property, but don't by rejecting our requests, scatter the fruits of our labor to the winds ..."

North Star was the last to speak, proclaiming "... We have put our proposition on paper, and have given it to our friend, in whom we have confidence ... If you accept it, father, the bargain is made."

The Honorable Henry M. Rice then handed the memorandum to the Commissioner.

"I have done thinking," the Commissioner announced, "and I will have to close the bargain on the proposition of my old friend. I cannot get over the moving eloquence of the old gentleman's speech, and therefore can only answer it by saying that I accept his offer."

On Monday the 19th the proposition was put into appropriate form, signed and witnessed.

At 10:00 that same morning, Monday February 19th, 1855, the Mississippi Chippewa arrived for an additional meeting. The first speaker was Hole-in-the-Day:

"Father, we have not yet spoken to you frankly, although we have had some very good talks: Father, we have made up our minds to one thing: your offer is too small. The payments you propose will not be sufficient to give us a start, and enable us to support ourselves while preparing to live like the whites. A great many of our children are so young that they can never receive any benefit from the payments which you propose. The only difference between us is that you do not offer us enough. You see, father, how we all are situated. We want to change our habits and customs and live like whites. How can we do this without the means to start upon and carry out your views? My father, it is with no ill feeling that we differ from you in this matter; but we must look out for our young. You want us to work, to change our habits, and live like the whites, and I see the benefit of your advice, and so do the Chiefs. I appreciate every word you say from the bottom of my heart, but if we begin a task so difficult, we should have enough to start upon to prevent failure hereafter. You will see my friend, by summing up closely our numbers, and considering the various purpose to which the proposed annuities must be applied, that they are entirely inadequate. If you would change our habit, you must not withhold the means necessary for its accomplishment. You must give us enough for a fair start. We do not want money to squander upon paint, or ornaments, or other trifling objects, but to purchase articles of necessity to give us a fair start. We will leave it to yourself, father, as to what is right.

We know you have a good heart. We are not so ignorant but that we know those who are our friends; but the means you offer are too limited to enable us to carry out your benevolent intentions. This is what we object to. The way we argue the matter is this: The thing we are about to do will make us either happy or wretches forever. It is therefore a subject which should be fully understood. You want us to be civilized — to adopt the manners and customs of the whites, but before these changes can be effected there must be a good many things provided. Had we had experience in cultivating the soil, and some acquaintance with the arts of the whites, then industry might do, but as we have had no such experience, nothing but means can insure success. This is all I have to say for the present."

After listening to Hole-in-the-Day's words the Commissioner replied that it was a poor reliance to place confidence in money to produce civilization—or anything else. "Give me plenty of money and I will not work," he said. "No one will labor until necessitated to do so. Still I understand and appreciate the motives of Hole-in-the-Day. The Indians have great ideas of annuity payments. With them it is annuities, annuities, annuities, all the time. It is doubtful, so far as their civilization is concerned, if it would not have been better for the Indians if they had no annuities."

The delegates requested time for discussion, and at their bidding all were asked to leave the room except for the delegates and the Commissioner. Following deliberations, and first shaking hands, Hole-in-the-Day spoke.

"I call upon the Master of Life to hear the words I am about to utter. I am about to talk respecting the property which I own. The Master of Life, who has made this world, has put us here. He has made everything we own for our benefit, that we may profit by it. Every man living may thank the Master of Life that he has placed him here, and given to him the means of making his support by his own exertions. Father, you now shall hear me upon the subject of the sale of my land; I am now coming to the point. Father, I am but poor and ignorant in my own estimation; have not the power to express myself — I cannot over estimate myself. When I look all around me to the four corners of the earth, and look at everything within my sight, and reflecting upon what we are and have been, and what the whites are, I cannot but feel that a good weight of responsibility rests upon me in what I shall say and do on the present occasion. It is seven years ago since I first took my present position in my nation; it is seven years ago since I first headed the band here; It is seven years ago since I first began to exert myself for my people's advancement. In this, I have had the assistance of some annuities, and assistance and advice of the whites. In thinking over the matters delegated to us, we have brought them, like mechanics, to perfection. We know the wants of the Chippewa nation — no one knows them better than ourselves, and we cannot be blamed if we look after and take care of our own interests. In looking away further back — considering the Indian habit of living — you must admit that we know our wants better than anyone else. You see, my father, I have taken a great deal of pains to explain what our situation is. We desire to convey to you our ideas.

My father, your name is the Long-Knife. We call you father, because we look up to you for protection. Now, listen to what I shall say. You see us here — we the Chippewa Indians. We want you to be friendly. We do not want a mock show. Do not look upon us as you would upon the English. We are your children. We do not live outside, but within your nation. We are your friends. Why then look upon us as a foreign nation? My father, we want your friendship. No use of making us a mock show as a separate nation. We want to give ourselves up to your government. We want to cease to be Indians, and become Americans. We want to be citizens, and to have the right to vote. All we desire is to imitate the whites, and to follow their example. We want to live as they do. You should look upon us as your children. A thick veil hides us from your view. Remove that veil, and see if we are not as good Americans as the whites."

Hole-in-the-Day consulted with the other delegates and then continued: "Father, we want to be citizens, and treated like the whites; and if you grant our request, and you should have a fight with any other nation, you can call upon us, and we will form a portion of your militia. We know how to fight and will stand by you. We want the right of suffrage, the right to vote, to be subject to your laws, and have set our hearts upon it. Grant our requests, and you will find that we will be up to our words. We might talk until we died — we might speak a hundred years, but we can plainly see that we can never be anybody until we become American citizens. I hope, father, you now understand my views."

Commissioner Manypenny answered. "I understand them very well, and are happy to learn that the chiefs have turned their thoughts that way. They desire to be made white men and citizens by their Great Father; but the matter of making voters does not belong to Congress; that is a thing which must be done by the States or the Territories. Minnesota can, if she chooses, make the Chippewas citizens, and as soon as they understand their rights and duties, and the obligations which citizenship imposes, they doubtless will do it. I will do all in my power however to prepare you for that purpose by imparting to you a knowledge of their duties and of the acts of civilized life."

Hole-in-the-Day then spoke privately to Paul Beaulieu, and, disagreeing with Manypenny and having consulted with Beaulieu, said, "The Great Council [Congress] can enact such laws as will bring that about hereafter — the right of voting."

After some chit-chat the Commissioner asked all except the negotiators (the delegates) to leave the room.

Hole-in-the-Day then specified that he wanted a claim put in the treaty providing for the Chippewa becoming citizens, adding that they should be governed by the laws of the United States.

Manypenny said he would prepare an article with that objective in mind.

It was agreed to meet again at 4:00 p.m. that same day, and again at 9:15 that night they gathered to continue negotiations. Hole-in-the Day spoke:

"The time has arrived, my friend, when your red children are perfectly at a loss what to do— ... there [is] something which deters their acting with promptness. I am an Indian of very little understanding but I know what my people want. Father, look at your red children — give them time to reflect. Those who have had experience know that, all they can do is to bow down their heads. You can see my father; what point we have come to. When we look upon these cities, these fine buildings and the numbers and wealth of the whites, and reflect upon what the Indians have been, and of what the whites have come to, we must have time to reflect, for meditation is everything with an Indian. When we view the past, and reflect upon the fact that the Indians once owned the land covered with these cities — when we think of our former treaties and past transactions with you — we understand what was your object in sending for us, and what you intend to do with us. When, in view of all this, we come to make a new treaty, for the sale of all that is left of our land, and to change our habits of life, we ask will it be our ruin or will it not? Under these circumstances, we are compelled to reflect. Father, be patient with your red children. Let us take time to consider, and have a full understanding. We look at everything. We are not near so ignorant as white men think us to be. When we view the country owned by the Indians, we feel like a wild beast driven into a hollow tree where he can't get away. That is the way, father, we now feel. You may think, my father, from our hesitation and plainness of speech we have not a proper respect for you. This, however, is not the case. The matter is important to us, and, if we cannot come to a conclusion, give us a little more time. It is for these reasons that I have uttered what I said just now. It is twenty years past since we made the first treaty. Since then we have made several others, in which we have parted with most of our land. We have not been well treated, and experience shows that we should be very careful before we make another, for the final disposition of our land. We don't hold the land now from you. We therefore have it in our control and before we give up our rights, we should be careful. We do not mean to intimate, father, that your intentions toward us are not good — that you do not mean to do right by us. As I said before, which teaches us to ponder well before we act. You cannot then blame us if we do not come right to the point."

Following Hole-in-the-Days speech the assembly was recessed until the following morning at 9:00 a.m.

At 2:00 p.m. when the Chippewa finally appeared Commissioner Manypenny opened the meeting by stating that he had been waiting for their arrival since 9:00 a.m. that morning.

After consulting among themselves the Mississippi Chippewa delegates requested that the Hon. Henry M. Rice, Senator from Minnesota, speak for them. What follows are the words of Henry M. Rice.

"They were the first Indians of the North who had expressed a desire to have such measures taken as to induce them to become white men. They were convinced that this was the only thing which can save or satisfy the tribe. They wish to have their means in their own hands like the whites. They desire to become white men, and felt satisfied that they would succeed in a few years, if at all. If at the end of that time, they don't succeed, they think it would be useless for the government to attempt to do anything for them. They wish, in the first place, as far as that can be done here, to be placed upon the same footing as a white man, and leave the balance with the Legislature of the Territory of Minnesota, as to the proper time to make them citizens and enable them to enjoy its benefits. In order to accomplish that object, at Lake Superior, last summer, they [decided?] to give up all their rights to the country; and they wish to have their farming, [urged?] upon them for their compensation; They want the present system done away with. It is true, the system costs the government a good deal; but farmers, blacksmiths, and other employees have their favorites among the Indians. Those they like, they will do everything for, and for those they don't, they will do nothing. They want it fixed, so that mechanics and others who choose, may go and establish themselves on this reserve. Their annuities will soon cease, and this is the last treaty they will have to make with the government. As this, then is their last chance, they hope you will help to lift them out of the mire and place them on high ground. They desire to make farms, buy cattle and stock, and they want the means to do it. In order to carry out their object and explain their view, they have put down on paper, what they think will do. They hope you will not be limited in this matter by what you may think the value of their land, but will consider what is necessary to enable them to change their habits and make them good Christians. They wish to have conferred upon them the right of citizenship, so far as you can do it, and the Territorial Legislature can finish it."

Mr. Rice finished by explaining the specific details of the requested items.

On Wednesday evening the 21st of February, both the Pillager and the Mississippi bands met with the Commissioner to consider the documents that had been prepared as a result of negotiations. Hole-in-the-Day found fault with the government employing blacksmiths, laborers, schoolmasters and farmers, explaining, "We have been constantly paying money out of our annuities to these persons, without ever having received any benefit. It is a useless waste of money, that could better [be used] for the same objects under our own direction."

Manypenny said he was willing to compromise on that matter with all but the teachers, to which Hole-in-the-Day responded, "The teachers who have been sent among us have never done us any good. They seem to care about nothing but their salaries."

Senator Rice agreed that was a literal truth, adding that he did not know a single Indian who had been educated by them, notwithstanding the large sums expended out of their annuities.

Hole-in-the-Day summarized by saying, "Listen, father, to me one minute, and I will make you understand what I mean. In all our treaties, there are provisions made for laborers, blacksmiths, teachers, etc. and we have expended a goodly amount for them. It has done us no good. It is very essential that the Indians shall be thrown on their own resources. The country is getting scarce of game, and we cannot get along without changing our habits. We have tried the old system and found it wanting. We should therefore try a new one. Under the old system we were sinking into ignorance worse than we ever were before. You can see the reason of this. Our people are getting to know the use of money, and when they see a person working for them for pay they say, there is no use in our doing anything for ourselves. They say, here is our servant, here is our slave — we pay him to labor — why then shall we work when he works for us? With the exception that it does not do away with this practice under former treaties, I have no objection to the articles of the proposed treaty. I have studied its provisions. The Indians have given away all, and leave themselves no alternative, but to work. They know under the proposed arrangement they must work or starve."

Still Manypenny was unwilling to compromise on the education provision.

Once again Hole-in-the-Day recapped. "Father, it is twenty years since we began to receive annuities. Refer back, and you will find those stipulations for the employment of laborers, teachers, etc. They have done us no good. We have remained in ignorance, depending upon others, and we now want to try and do something for ourselves. You will see that for twenty years that money was appropriated for education, but what good has it done us?"

Manypenny asked, "How can you educate your children, without some such provision is made for the purpose?"

"In looking back, father, on the past," Hole-in-the-Day continued, "I can see nothing to blur the view which I have expressed. So long as we feel confidence in annuities, we think we have nothing to fear; but under the proposed treaty, the Indian will know he has something to fear, because he will soon have nothing to expect, except from his own industry. This transaction here is calculated to make an Indian think. If he looks ahead, and looks back twenty years, he will then see what he has profited by the annuities, and what he may expect from the future. It will teach him a good lesson. The little pieces of land we get by this treaty, will, in twenty years, be our only resource, and then we will improve and beautify by our own exertions. In twenty years our annuities will cease and then we will have nothing to rely upon but our own labors. Emigrants are coming among us. They won't be satisfied with the land now open for entry, and we cannot resist their encroachments, if we would. We should therefore prepare for a state of things which we cannot avert, and settle down like whites. Father, as to education, I am in favor of it as much as anyone. I know its value, and feel it's want; but, if I wish to educate my children, I can take my own money, and employ my own teacher. I want to educate my children, father. The reason why I have said so much, is that I am anxious to explain my motives. I want a good pile of money to start upon. A good start is an important point. We are all fond of our children. We know and feel the necessity of education; to effect this we must have means. A lot of us can get together, and we say our children ought to be educated. To effect this, all know we must have a teacher. We employ such a one as we think will suit. We will then have him under our control, because there is no other influence to operate with him. There is a schoolmaster in our country, but I want the privilege, if I don't like him, to employ another. Your poor red children understand well, from experience, what they want; and to explain this has been my object. Do you understand me father?"

"I understand you fully," was the Commissioner's reply.

Hole-in-the-Day resumed, "We have traders in our part of the country. They generally come from New York. They show us their goods, and we buy them if we like them and want them. We desire to have the same privilege with regard to teachers. If we like them and we want them, we will employ them, and if not otherwise."

Here the Hon. Henry Rice chimed in, adding, "The half-breeds among these Northern Indians are generally educated men, but not one of them is indebted for it to government schools. This shows the necessity of trying the voluntary system, as Hole-in-the-Day suggests."

Manypenny then responded by saying, "I agree to all your propositions in the main, but I cannot consent that you shall have the right to apply all your funds, without any reservation whatever for education. You talked about working, Hole-in-the-Day! Why, I felt your hand just now, and I find it as soft as any lady's hand in Washington. I, however, admire your ideas about the necessity of working, and I hope you will stick to them. It is a good resolution. I have no objection to you hiring your own teachers, but there must be a fund reserved applicable to that purpose. Go home, my friends, and consider it."

"Father, you must not misunderstand us," Hole-in-the-Day responded. "We have no objection to education. I told you we wanted to have our children educated. We also want school houses, but, as to teachers, such as we have had, we know too much about them. We object to having teachers, whom we don't like, forced upon us. They come, not to teach, but to get money and have their ease."

Relenting a bit the Commissioner offered, "We will try and have the evil referred to corrected. Suppose, however, we set apart the fund, and let the Indians employ their own teachers. How would that do?"

Henry Rice responded, "I think that is a good idea and will be acceptable."

Hole-in-the-Day threw in one last barb. "Father, if you want to have us educated so bad, why don't you take some of your own money, instead of ours; and sacrifice it in upholding the present system?"

With that the meeting ended.

At 7:00 p.m. the next day, February 22, 1855—George Washington's birthday—both the Pillager and the Mississippi bands of Minnesota Chippewa met with Commissioner Manypenny to finalize the treaty that had been read to them the night before. While it was being transcribed the attendees conversed; word was that apparently a number of Indians had gotten drunk the night before, causing a disturbance. When Manypenny asked whether any of the rowdies were Chippewa the attendees all denied any involvement. Following some story-telling and entertainment the treaty was read—sentence by sentence—by the interpreter.

Still hesitant about the provision providing for the employment of teachers, Hole-in-the-Day said that he hoped it would be stricken from the agreement.

After concluding comments the session ended and the treaty was finished.

The Chippewa delegation was still in Washington when, on March 8th they met with Commissioner Manypenny to discuss the provisions of the treaty.

The third article of the treaty provided for $50,000 to be appropriated by Congress for the purpose of settling the debts of the Mississippi band. The Indians had submitted a list of debts to be paid totaling $35,000. Commissioner Manypenny tried valiantly to make them understand that, without any evidence there was no way of justifying the claims. The Indians simply wanted their claims to be paid, regardless of whether or not said claims were correct and could be substantiated. At one point Hole-in-the-Day said, "We don't think we owe the traders that much, but we want to give them that much."

"The difficulty is," the Commissioner explained, "I am not prepared to sanction such wholesale transactions as these trading claims, although I have no special reason to doubt their correctness. I want the Indians to pay their debts, but I would like to be certain that they justly owed whatever they paid. I will, however, submit the matter for the decision of the Secretary of the Interior." It was for Manypenny to decide whether—under the treaty—an exhibit of the books and accounts upon which these claims were founded should be made.

That afternoon the Pillager band met with the Commissioner, submitting claims totaling $30,000. The outcome of the meeting was similar to the earlier Mississippi band meeting.

The next day both the Mississippi and the Pillager bands met yet again with Commissioner Manypenny. The Commissioner read both articles of agreement which also listed debts to be paid. "The Mississippi band appropriates $35,000 and the Pillager band $30,000 for payment of their traders, and $4,000 each for their half-breeds and $6,000 each for the chiefs of their respective bands."

The Commissioner explained that, although the bands were ready to sign the agreements, the Secretary of the Interior had final say as to what would, and would not be paid. After further brief discussion they adjourned.

The Chippewa delegation had been in Washington for about a month when, on March 10th they had their final conference with Commissioner Manypenny. They had previously met with President Pierce and first briefly discussed that event.

After having been chastised by Commissioner Manypenny the day before, the Pillager Chief Flatmouth said, "Father, we have come to tell you our wants. What you shall hear, will be the truth, and will be nothing but what we want. I am sorry father, we Indians cannot manage our own affairs the way we desire, but we have fathers [agents] who manage them for us, and we want to bring our business to a close. We have expressed ourselves very often that we didn't understand figures. We have to count them on our fingers. We told you that we wanted $10,000 to buy goods and presents for our people at home. We desire that sum to be placed in the hands of our friend [Agent Herriman] for that purpose. We want him to purchase for us what we want to take home to our people. We have faith in our agent; he knows what will suit, and how and when goods can be bought. He can satisfy us — I speak only for the Pillagers. I don't know what the other bands want. They can speak for themselves. Father, it is very essential that we should take something home to our young men, to please those we have left behind. Many of our people are poor, and they will expect something from us on our return and will be disappointed if they don't get it. It will satisfy them. It has pleased you, father, to make the promise, and we expect you to comply with your word. We, the delegates, have had everything we wanted since we have been here — we have been well provided for — although not a dime in money, and now we want something to take home with us. I want to state a circumstance connected with a piece of land which was bought from us before. According to articles in the first treaty, it is all correct — Mr. Rice and the Winnebago agent found everything right. I want to throw blame on no man's character, but it is very surprising how the money which we were to get for the piece of land referred to, did go. The third payment was made at Sandy Lake; we saw only a few goods there — not as much as the two previous years. There was something wrong about these payments; and for that reason, father, I want a copy of the late treaty, and also a copy of the invoices every year, so that we may know what we get, and judge for ourselves, as to whether all is right."

The Commissioner agreed with Flatmouth, saying, "I am glad, my friend you are satisfied, but, as to your getting nothing but enough to supply your wants to a limited extent. I hope you have had plenty to eat, and that you have been comfortably lodged and provided. If so, that is all I intended you should have....In all my treaties with the Indians (and I have had many) I have given my red children what they could eat, and no more, during the ... negotiations. The reason is, I did not wish to influence them by largesse or presents. You must, my friends, get your young men out of the idea of asking or taking presents. It is bad policy...."

Then turning to Hole-in-the-Day he asked, "What requests have you to make for the Mississippi band?"

Hole-in-the-Day responded, "Father, there is one thing very essential for the Indians to know—that is, the day when they may expect their payments hereafter. They should be made, so that the Indians may not be detained long at the Agency. There should be a fixed day, say the first of September. After that, we have to put away our crops and attend to our fisheries in the Fall, so to be prepared for the Winter."

The Commissioner had no objection.

Hole-in the Day continued, "Out of the $10,000 to which we are entitled, it is only necessary to get $9,000 worth in goods. The other $1,000 we will want to take home, to get such articles as we may want for our young men, or to be divided out among them. Such a course will give great satisfaction to all parties, and I hope it will be adopted."

"In respect to that," the Commissioner pushed back, "I will see what can be done. The treaty expressly provides the way the $10,000 shall be expended, and, of course, it will have to be carried out. This shows the importance of putting nothing in a treaty which we don't want."

Agent Herriman came to the aid of the Indians, stating that, "The treaty says $10,000 to be expended in 'goods and other useful articles.'"

"With $1000, they can buy a good many useful articles for their young men at home," Paul H. Beaulieu then chimed, adding, "They want to know about the time the payment will be made."

Commissioner Manypenny addressed the issue of traders preying on the payment sites. "I am in favor of early payments, but would not like now to fix upon a day, but when it has been decided upon, I will notify your father, the Agent, for your information. Suppose I was to ask you for a company of light horsemen to attend the payments — could I organize such a force? I want Indians to make payments like the whites, and to allow no trader to get his pay at the payment table. This will operate as an inducement to the traders to make the Indians honest and punctual in their dealings."

Hole-in-the-Day declared, "We formed such a company the payment before last. If our father thinks anything, the Indians cannot go contrary. They must do as he says."

Agent Herriman added, "If instructed to raise a company, or to keep traders away from the payment table, I will carry out my instructions."

"I would be very thankful, father," Hole-in-the-Day responded, "if you would carry out the idea, and exclude traders from the pay table."

Agent Herriman replied, "The Commissioner will so instruct me, and then the traders will have to be careful who they trust."

After summarizing the conversation Commissioner Manypenny issued a threat. "Your father says you are going home out of debt, and I rejoice at the fact, and hope you will always try and keep [it] that way. Keep out of debt; never buy what you don't want. Quit buying such useless articles as beads, paint, trinkets, firewater, etc. or I will stop the annuity of every Chippewa who will not do so. I have nothing more to say. Hole-in-the-Day, did I understand you as saying that you wanted to buy articles at St Paul with the $1000?"

The chief answered, "The young men have spoken to me about the $1000. Father, it is hard to be in a country, where they see things they want, without money to buy them. Our expenses are paid, to be sure; but we want a little money in our pockets."

The Commissioner said he would see what he could do.

Flatmouth made one final statement. "Father, my words shall be but few, but I want them to have their weight. The promises and considerations named in the treaty, we expect to be fulfilled. The people — our children whom we have left at home, expect it. Father, it is a pity I don't hear plain — I am getting very deaf, and can't understand, but I used to talk since when I had my understanding. Father, I have listened to your advice — it is very sound and good. When I was a child, I used to like good advice, but I am not too old yet to take advice you have given us. Your advice, as far as liquor is concerned, is the greatest advice ever given to Indians. Firewater makes Indians poor, and it makes white men poor also. When our money runs out, we take our guns, take our blankets — we give all, for liquor. It ruins us; and the reason I like to see the payments at our doors is this. Liquor is within reach at the Agency, but in my country there is none to tempt the appetite of the Indian. Father, although old, I have never had much to do with liquor; it never tempted me. I therefore insist that payments shall be made where the Indian cannot get it."

With that and a few additional minor comments the last session between the Chippewa Indians and the Commissioner was adjourned. The 1855 Treaty had been passed and ratified. Apparently negotiations regarding exactly what areas would comprise the reservations—referred to in the treaty—were done in private, likely with Senator Henry Rice. We can see from the above iterated negotiations with the Commissioner that the Indians were asked where they wanted to have reservations, but regardless of how it was decided the Mille Lac Indian Reservation had now come into existence.[1]

> As a side note, four Mille Lac chiefs were apparently among the delegates that visited Washington D.C.: Pedudense (Muskrat's Liver), Menomenkeshin (Rice Maker), Kay g way dash (The Attempter) and Sho baushkum (He That Passes Under Everything).[2] However, the only evidence we have is names on the list of treaty signers. Apparently none of them spoke during treaty negotiations. All of the negotiating for the Mississippi bands was left to the Gull Lake chief Hole-in-the-Day. The only words recorded by any of these four Mille Lac chiefs was during the session on claims to be paid when Rice Maker said, "I do not know anything about the paper. I have not seen it."

CHAPTER 10

1862 — The Sioux Uprising

We may never know what was discussed at the meetings of the Soldiers Lodge. Was there a plan in motion to eliminate the whites from Minnesota? We do know that a dance—a war dance?—took place near Fort Ridgely on August 4th, 1862, and we know that the Sioux had requested that they be allowed to have the dance on the parade grounds within the fort and that, although the request was denied the dance still took place nearby. What with the tense atmosphere between the Indians and the government does it seem logical that this request would even have been made? Was this a foiled plot to take over the fort from the inside? Whatever the case was, it seems unquestioned that the events at Acton on August 17, 1862 were spontaneous. On that day several Sioux from Red Middle Voice's village went to the Big Woods, either to hunt or look for Chippewa.

Four of the Sioux party separated from the rest; Brown Wing (Sungigodan), Breaking Up (Kaom-de-i-ye-ye-dan), Killing Ghost (Nagi-wi-cak-te) and Runs Against Something When Crawling, (Pa-zo-i-yo-pa). These four ultimately advanced on the home of a settler in Acton, located in Meeker County and today an unincorporated village located about 14 miles west of Litchfield or 4 miles south of Grove City.

Advancing onto the settler's acreage the Sioux foursome came upon a hen's nest full of eggs. One of the four, being hungry, picked up the eggs, but was cautioned by another of the party that he should not take them because they belonged to a white man and it would get them in trouble. In anger the hungry young man smashed the eggs on the ground and called the other a coward. The two debated about who was the bravest and was not afraid of white men. Alexander Berghold, in his book *The Indians' Revenge* says that at this point one of them shot and killed a heifer to prove his bravery. The argument continued as they taunted one another—which was brave enough to kill a white man?—and they approached the house of Robinson Jones.

Now Mr. Robinson Jones had filed a preemption claim on this property after the Preemption Act of 1841, which allowed settlers to claim land before the area was officially opened for settlement. Jones and his neighbor Howard Baker had filed their preemption claims in 1857. Both men farmed and provided lodging; Jones had a small general store and was also the postmaster. Mr. Jones had married Howard Baker's mother, and the couple had two adopted children. A Mr. and Mrs. Webster, immigrants from Michigan (Berghold says they were from Wisconsin) were staying at Baker's house while they searched for a place to settle.

Details of the story vary, but it is known that all seven of these pioneers ended up at the Baker home where the Indian party initiated conversation with Jones and Baker over a gun that Baker had for sale. Feigning interest in purchasing the gun, the foursome engaged in target practice. When both Jones and Baker had fired their guns and found themselves with unloaded guns, the Indians opened fire. Soon five of the seven settlers lay dead or dying. Mrs. Baker escaped death only because she fainted with a child in her arms and fell through the open cellar door into the cellar.

The four Sioux young men had proven that they were brave enough to kill a white man; the damage was done. The four headed home to their village at Rice Creek to inform their chief Red Middle Voice of the event and seek his counsel. Understanding that Rice Creek is the location where the Soldiers Lodge had held their meetings, it was not a coincidence that Red Middle Voice's warriors were among the most militant of the Sioux bands. Upon listening to the tale from the four Sioux, Red Middle Voice saw at once that his small band was in trouble. Red Middle Voice went first to counsel with Chief Shakopee because many of Shakopee's warriors had also attended meetings of the Soldiers Lodge. However, even with the two bands together they were not large enough to take on the whites. Little Crow was the answer.

Who was this Chief Little Crow? Little Crow's band was the Mdewakanton Sioux. His biographer wrote that Little Crow had an "insatiable personal hunger for power". He was a skilled orator and he liked being the center of attention. Little Crow's father was a Mdewakanton chief and, as the first born, Little Crow expected to be designated as chief upon his father's death. However, the wild ways of his youth altered his fortune.

Little Crow's father accidently shot himself and the wound proved fatal. Upon his death bed the old chief named a younger half-brother of Little Crows as chief. Little

Little Crow, circa 1862

PHOTOPRINT BY WHITNEY

Crow believed that he was entitled to be chief since marrying four wives—all of whom were sisters—giving up his wild ways and settling down as a family man. The river was still frozen when Little Crow learned of his father's death and that he had been passed over as chief, so it wasn't until the river opened in the spring that he could head down the river to his father's Mdewakanton village to reclaim his birthright. Accompanied by some of his followers, the young man stepped ashore to be met by a hostile crowd of his half-brothers supporters. Taunts were thrown and shouting ensued, telling him that he was not welcome in the village. But Little Crow pushed his way through the crowd to confront the new chief, his half-brother. One brother shouted that he was not wanted here. Little Crow boldly folded his arms across his chest, daring his brothers to shoot him. Someone fired and the bullet crushed the wrists of both of Little Crow's folded arms. Falling into the arms of his own supporters the wounded young man was carried back to the river and on to Fort Snelling where the army surgeon advised amputation of both hands in an attempt to save his life. Little Crow refused. He was taken back to his own village and medicine man. Little Crow survived but would always have severely deformed forearms.

Upon his recovery the Mdewakanton elders decided to support Little Crow for chief, partly because he had shown such courage before his enemies—perhaps too because they believed that the Great Spirit had spared Little Crow's life to become chief of the Mdewakanton. Little Crow's brothers were soon killed and he was firmly in possession of the title Chief Little Crow.

Little Crow was a man torn between two worlds. While he lived in a two story house instead of a deerskin lodge and often dressed like a white man, he still wore his hair long, ate and slept like an Indian and rejected the white man's religion. In contrast to his wild youth, as chief Little Crow advocated abstinence and hard work and even arranged to acquire missionaries for his people.

However, in the late 1850's some of Little Crow's people thought he was catering too much to the white man's government and had given up too much by signing the treaties. One important position in the tribe was that of speaker, and when the old speaker died—in the spring of 1862—Little Crow assumed that he would be elected to the job. Instead a farmer Indian by the name of Traveling Hail was elected. After years of trying to cater to both worlds, Little Crow was being rejected.

Little Crow then decided, that if a farmer Indian was favored, he himself would embrace farming. He cut off his long hair, started wearing shirts and trousers, and began attending church. He even went so far as to order a stove and proper furniture for his house and did some tilling of the soil with his bare hands.

Soon, however, Little Crow was bidden to forsake all of his white man's ways and join the blanket Indians in war. Upon awakening one morning he found his house filled with Indians. As these warriors presented their case for going to war Little Crow took note of the fact that many of these Indians were ones who had vetoed his election as speaker. Asking why the warriors were seeking his counsel, Little Crow suggested that they should go to the man they had chosen as speaker and seek his advice.

When Little Crow queried the group about their objectives he was told by Red Middle Voice that they wanted to kill all the whites; they wanted to drive all the whites out and reclaim their land. They emphasized the fraud that was being perpetrated against them and listed the other tribes that they supposed would join them in their war party, adding perhaps even the British. Many arguments ensued between Little Crow and the warriors until finally Red Middle Voice called Little Crow a coward.

Hearing this taunt Little Crow seized control of the gathering. Grabbing Red Middle Voice's headdress he threw it to the floor, and, using all of his skills as an orator made an impassioned speech. And while speaking he had also to be reasoning and pondering. Quite likely his thoughts ran like this: war was inevitable—defeat was inevitable—the end of the Sioux was inevitable. However, aloud he declared, Little Crow is not a coward—he will die with you! The entire group erupted with, "Kill the Whites!"

The stage was now set for a bloodbath that would rock a young nation that was already struggling for its very existence.

The bloodbath was about to begin at the Lower Sioux Agency. Recall that the northern part of the non-existent reservation had been sold in 1858; the Upper Agency—called Yellow Medicine—was still active and inhabited by one Maj. Galbraith. The massacre began at the Lower Agency, with the inhabitants at the Upper Agency completely unaware until around noon on the first day of battle.

The Lower Agency—sometimes referred to as the Redwood Agency—is located at Morton, Minnesota, twenty eight miles northwest of New Ulm, and is the site of the present day Jackpot Junction Casino. The Lower Agency was about twelve miles upstream from Fort Ridgely on the opposite side of the river. Little Crow's village was about two miles from the agency. The stone agency building still stands as an historic site managed by the Lower Sioux Indian Community.

The agency village was basically unsuspecting of the imminent massacre. The appearance of Sioux Indians dressed and painted for war was not unusual since the Sioux were often prepared for war when searching for Chippewa. The traders, many of whom had trading posts located at the Lower Agency and had refused the Sioux credit, were the first targets of the incensed Sioux warriors, but soon all the agency buildings were surrounded. The slaughter was without plan; some whites spared due to their friendship with certain Indians. But no one was safe.

Duane Schultz, in his book *Over the Earth I Come*, recounts an encounter between the warriors and Philander Prescott, who was on his way to Fort Ridgely when he was surrounded. Prescott was an old man who had lived and worked with the Sioux for years as an interpreter. Prescott reportedly said, "I am an old man. I have lived with you now forty-five years, about half a century. My wife and children are among you, of your own blood. I have never done you any harm, and have been your true friend

"Attack on New Ulm" 1904 oil on canvas painting by Anton Gag

PUBLISHED IN THE US BEFORE 1923 AND PUBLIC DOMAIN IN THE US

in all your troubles. Why should you wish to kill me?" Medicine Bottle reportedly answered, "We would save your life if we could, but the white man must die. We cannot spare your life. Our orders are to kill all white men. We cannot spare you." And with that Prescott was shot and killed.

History books are filled with many similar stories, and we have to wonder about the accuracy of such reports. Obviously the best source for the encounter mentioned above, Philander Prescott, was dead. So how did these quotes come to find their way into the printed accounts of the massacre? The only likely source would be the statements from the warriors who committed these violent acts.

We do, however, know that Philander Prescott had been an advocate for the plight of the Indians. In a report to the Bureau of Indian Affairs in 1856 he stated, "Estimates and requisitions have annually been made from the Sioux agency office for all the funds due the Sioux by treaty stipulations. To the honor of the president and congress these funds to the full extent have been annually appropriated. And when it was represented a few years ago that an earlier payment of the annuities would be desirable these appropriations have been since made one year in advance. Have the officers under the president applied these funds, so appropriated in the manner stipulated by the treaties? I can distinctly say no! The treaties say these funds shall be annually expended, whereas large amounts have been kept back and are now in arrears after repeated applications to have them expended. These arrears are not mere petty sums, surpluses or remnants of funds remaining unexpended but large amounts thousands and tens of thousands- and in some cases the whole fund appropriated for a special purpose." But Prescott was killed because he was white.

Yet Reverend Samuel Hinman, whose sermon Little Crow had heard the day before, was apparently allowed to escape and thereby spared, likely a deliberate choice by Little Crow.

With the ferry soon permanently moored on the opposite side of the river and the horses stolen by the Indians, the whites—and in many cases the half-breeds—had no choice but to run as best they could, abandoning all of their worldly possessions. According to Berghold many of the whites at the agency were killed in this first attack, totaling some forty or fifty men. When the slaughter had ended the Indians looted the buildings, taking all of the contents they could carry with them on the stolen settler's wagons, and then set each building on fire.

The Sioux warriors then traveled up the Minnesota River from the Lower Agency, bringing death, torture and devastation to the many homesteads along their way. Clusters of homesteads around the several streams were encountered and the settlers and property destroyed: Birch Coulee, Beaver Creek, Smith Creek, Middle Creek, Timms Creek, Sacred Heart Creek, all in turn. The Indians behaved as though crazed with wrath.

Duane Schultz in *Over the Earth I Come* describes one incident: "A warrior snatched up the Henderson girl and beat her about the face and head with a violin case taken from the wagon. In moments, the child's features were obliterated. He swung her by the feet, slamming her against a wagon wheel again and again, and threw the battered body to her mother. Helen watched as another Indian grabbed the Henderson baby, and, holding her by one foot, head downwards, deliberately hacked her body, limb from limb, with his tomahawk, throwing the pieces at the head of Mrs. Henderson. Some of the Indians made a big fire and when it was burning fiercely, they lifted the feather bed on which Mrs. Henderson lay, and tossed bed and woman and the mangled portions of her children into the flames." Details of other atrocities—as well as names of the families destroyed—can be found in the references cited as my sources of information for this chapter.

While the warriors brought death and destruction to the homesteads north of the Lower Agency, escapees were beginning to straggle into Fort Ridgely. Fort Ridgely, established in 1853 to keep an eye on the Sioux, was not much of a fort as forts go, being simply a group of buildings surrounding a parade ground. The only defendable buildings were a two-story stone structure used as a barracks for the troops and a one-story stone commissary. Company B of the Fifth Minnesota Infantry—seventy six soldiers and two officers to deal with 7000 angry Sioux—greeted the refugees as they began arriving. By sundown more than 200 refugees had arrived at the fort.

Captain John Marsh, who had fought at Bull Run, was in charge of Fort Ridgely. Capt. Marsh's first action was to send a courier to catch up with the Civil War enlistees who had passed through Fort Ridgely the day before on their way to Fort Ripley. The courier carried the following message, "It is absolutely necessary that you should return with your command immediately to this post. The Indians are raising hell at the Lower Agency."

Capt. Marsh then took forty seven of his troops and headed for the Lower Agency, leaving nineteen year old Lt. Thomas Gere in charge of the Fort. The Captain encountered additional refugees along the way, including the Rev. Hinman, who warned him that he would be badly outnumbered. Undeterred, Marsh and his troops continued on toward the Redwood ferry. When the soldiers arrived at the ferry they were greeted with an ambush, during which Marsh drowned trying to cross the river and twenty four of his men were killed. Sgt. Bishop then led the fifteen survivors back to Fort Ridgely, with an additional eight stragglers showing up later.

Ironically, at the same time that Capt. Marsh's men were being ambushed a shipment of gold—gold to pay the long awaited annuity—arrived at Fort Ridgely. Lt. Gere wisely kept the gold's arrival secret. However, worry prompted him to draft a memo to the commanding officer at Fort Snelling: "Capt. Marsh left this post at 10½ this morning to prevent depredations at the Lower Agency. Some of the men have returned and from them I have learned that Capt. Marsh is killed and only thirteen of the company are remaining. The Indians are killing the settlers and plundering the country. Send reinforcements without delay." He then added to the memo, "Please hand this to Gov. Ramsey immediately."

One Pvt. Sturgis set out on horseback to deliver the message. But on his way he was directed to go by way of St. Peter and notify the Renville Rangers, a company of Civil War volunteers who were on their way to Fort Snelling. It took Sturgis eighteen hours in the saddle to complete his mission.[1]

By mid-morning on Monday—about the same time the refugees started arriving at Fort Ridgely from the Lower Agency—news was arriving at the Upper Agency, the Yellow Medicine Agency. The Sioux from the Upper Agency went into council. The Sissetons wanted to kill all the whites and take their property. The Wahpetons just wanted to take the white's property without killing them. It soon became evident, though, that the Wahpetons would join the others in the massacre and the slaughter began.

Once again the traders were the first target; traders were slain and the trading posts raided of goods. John Otherday, a Christian Sioux, sent word to two missionaries about the massacre: Dr. Thomas Williamson and Reverend Stephen Riggs. During that night, while the trading posts were being raided, John Otherday led sixty-two men, women and children, including Agent Galbraith's wife and three children, to the river crossing and safety. Once the slaughter ended at the agency the warriors attacked the surrounding homesteads much as they had done on their journey from the Lower Agency.

Both Williamson and Riggs, at first doubting the seriousness of the situation, reluctantly but separately led their followers on a harrowing trek toward Fort Ridgely. Upon arrival they found the Fort bulging with refugees and elected to move on to safety at Henderson.

The two agencies and the surrounding homesteads had been devastated and Little Crow now wanted to attack Fort Ridgely while it was vulnerable. He was aware that there were very few soldiers defending the Fort. But the other young warriors had their sights set on New Ulm. While they debated and dithered, Lt. Sheehan and his fifty men arrived at Fort Ridgely. Soon after their arrival the Renville Rangers, composed of another fifty soldiers appeared, plus a group of volunteers from St Peter. Fort Ridgely's defenses quickly grew from twenty-two armed men to about one hundred eighty. Their mission was to guard the three hundred refugees and two boxes of gold. When Little Crow's followers learned of the reinforcements at the Fort, they were disheartened and returned home. The remaining militant warriors headed for New Ulm.

While the previous settlements had been caught pretty much by surprise, the news had filtered into New Ulm and most residents were busy fortifying their village. But there were still many who couldn't believe that what was coming their way was happening, was real, and that fact—plus a reluctance to leave the settlement they had worked so hard to establish—caused them to delay until the last minute. There are numerous harrowing tales of settlers rushing for the safety of New Ulm while Sioux warriors were killing as many as possible. In the afternoon of August 19th, while about half of the warriors were busy raiding and wasting scattered settlements, the other half launched an unorganized attack against New Ulm. Fortunately for residents of New Ulm the resistance of the people, aided by a sudden rainstorm, ended the attack with minimal damage. Only one thirteen year old girl was killed when she disobeyed orders and stepped outside the building to see what was happening.

The following day, August 20th, the warriors turned their attention toward Fort Ridgely. While they managed a fairly organized attack they had no means to counter the artillery—five canons—and after about five hours the Sioux combatants withdrew. Several soldiers and settlers were killed during the attack on the Fort and more were injured but they held on until the Sioux retreated. The flaming arrows and the Sioux muskets were no match for the canons. Heavy rain that night and the next day gave everyone a chance to regroup.

While burning arrows were being exchanged in battle against cannon balls at Fort Ridgely and the people of New Ulm were huddled together wondering what would come next, the Sisseton band was terrorizing southwestern Minnesota in the area centered near Lake Shetek. Lake Shetek, about six miles north of present day Slayton, in Murray County, was a beautiful and placid place to settle and many had done so by 1862. But terror reigned that week of August 17, 1862. Adults were slaughtered, babies were left to fend for themselves in abandoned houses and a six year old girl was "...nailed up to the side of the house, naked, arms and limbs extended, and large nails driven through hands and feet"[2]. The body of a new enlistee by the name of Pvt. Joseph Gilfillin was discovered with a bullet through his chest, his head cut off and smashed[3]. Settlers hiding in the tall grass of a swamp just west of Lake Shetek were shot one by one as they dared to attempt escape. Little wonder it was thereafter called Slaughter Slough.

Kandiyohi County—to the northwest of the agencies—was not to be spared from marauding bands of Sioux. Within a few days virtually the entire population of the county was either dead or dying; others fleeing for their lives, some never to return.

After the attacks were deterred at Fort Ridgely and New Ulm, chief Little Crow was nervous that the tide of the war might be turning. He knew the army would soon be sending reinforcements—bad news for his band. Apparently he had forgotten his pledge made in his bedroom: "Little Crow is not a coward—he will die with you!" He decided it would be safer if he moved his settlement away from the Lower Agency and reestablish the village at the Upper Agency. But when he arrived, together with all the loot from previous raids and including several hundred prisoners, Little Crow was not welcomed by the chiefs of the Upper Agency and was not allowed to camp there.

While Little Crow was entertaining ideas of reaching out to Governor Ramsey in an effort to secure a peaceful conclusion, his mutinous warriors—under the leadership of other than Little Crow—had their eyes set on plundering Forest City and Hutchinson. On their journey there this mutinous band encountered a company of soldiers whom they overwhelmed without much difficulty. Encouraged, they marched on toward Forest City and Hutchinson.

By now word of the massacres had spread throughout the state and villages such as Maine Prairie, St. Joseph, St. Cloud, Sauk Center and Little Falls were feverishly building defenses of one kind or another. For those who refused to take the obvious threat to heart their fate was the same as the other isolated settlements. Terror, death and destruction as the Sioux continued from target to target.

The people of Forest City and Hutchinson were well barricaded by the time the bloodthirsty band reached their villages and thus escaped widespread death. The shops and houses were raided, however, and the buildings burned. Little Crow's band returned to their temporary headquarters with even more contraband.

Upon arrival Little Crow received a letter from Henry Hastings Sibley offering to talk peace. Sibley wrote, "If Little Crow has any proposition to make, let him send a half-breed to me and he shall be protected in and out of camp."[4]

Sibley had been assigned the task of taking care of the Sioux uprising as best he could by Governor Ramsey.[5] Sibley was in no hurry to assume his post. Admittedly he had no military experience and he spent time complaining to Governor Ramsey about the equipment he was issued. Most of the available military equipment was already in use in the Civil War. While it took courier Sturgis only 18 hours to deliver the request for reinforcements to Fort Snelling, it took Sibley and his 225 troops eight days to reach Fort Ridgely. Even when word reached Sibley on August 20th that the Fort had been attacked and partly burned, Sibley did nothing to increase his speed nor did he send word to Gen. Grant, who was to join him at the Fort. It took him two and a half days to reach St. Peter, while most could make the same journey in one long day. While at St. Peter Sibley learned from his half-breed friend, Jack Frazer, that there were seven thousand Sioux and fifteen hundred well-armed warriors to contend with. Sibley promptly sent word to Gov. Ramsey requesting five hundred more troops and more and better equipment. He made no effort to check the accuracy of Frazer's information. While at St. Peter Sibley got word that New Ulm was under attack, but rather than rushing to their aid he waited at St Peter for his requested reinforcements to arrive. His request was fulfilled with the arrival of fifteen hundred well-armed men plus a cavalry. Now Sibley was ready to move on but—ever concerned about his image—he first sent off a request to Gov. Ramsey for copies of recent newspapers. At last he was finally ready to proceed to Fort Ridgely, arriving two days later on August 27th. When Sibley's requested newspapers arrived he could not have been pleased when he read what was written regarding his qualifications for the job that was assigned him nor his dithering and delaying in assuming it.

The next morning, after the first attempt by the Sioux to take Fort Ridgely, it was dark with threat of rain. Fort Ridgely was low on water, having no water source at the Fort, a column of soldiers was dispatched to a nearby spring along with the water wagon, only to find the tank destroyed and the water poisoned. A second spring was similarly destroyed. Badly in need of water soldiers had no choice but to dig a well on the fort grounds. This they accomplished—using shovels—by about 2:30 the next morning, just in time to prepare for the second Sioux assault on the fort. So while Colonel Sibley delayed at St. Peter waiting reinforcements, the Sioux warriors attacked, using the same battle plan that had failed two days earlier. And once again they were beaten back, largely because of the canon fire.

It was obvious that the colonists were regaining the offensive and that the doubters were growing fewer. But the offensive had been gained mainly by the actions of the settlers themselves. Colonel Sibley—with help from Governor Ramsey—was still on his way. Secretary of War Stanton had been asked for help and while all available troops were occupied with fighting the confederates, Stanton authorized the use of the 3rd Regiment of Minnesota Volunteers. This entire regiment had surrendered to Confederate troops in Tennessee and were then part of a prisoner exchange, meaning that they could not be used to fight Confederates, but nothing prevented them from fighting the Indians. However, the arrival of the regiment would take time.

It was Saturday August 23rd and the anticipated second attack of New Ulm was imminent. But this time New Ulm was better prepared. Volunteers had arrived from St. Peter and LeSeuer County and from Mankato and Garden City—an estimated

325 to 500 more volunteers than were there for the first attack. In addition there were from 1200 to 1500 residents and refugees hunkered down in town. Five doctors were ready to tend the wounded and sick, including one Dr. William Mayo.

Upon hearing rumors that the Winnebagos were joining the fight and were planning attacks on Mankato and South Bend, about 75 of the volunteers left New Ulm to defend their own towns. For unknown reasons a contingent of defenders was sent across the river; a mistake as it turned out, because it further reduced the number left to defend New Ulm.

So it was that on Saturday morning New Ulm was surrounded by approximately 600 Sioux warriors. The volunteers fought bravely—while Colonel Sibley waited in St. Peter for more soldiers and weapons—and ultimately prevailed; the Sioux gave up the fight and withdrew. However, during the attack some 25 New Ulm defenders were killed and another 80 were wounded, some 200 buildings were burned with only about 30 remaining, and roughly 2000 people were hunkered in unbearably unsanitary conditions. Ammunition was short, there was little food and the surrounding farms and crops were mostly destroyed.

The decision was made to evacuate the town and on August 25th a caravan of refugees from New Ulm and the surrounding area arrived in Mankato hoping for at least a good meal and a good night's sleep before deciding, 'What next?'

The attacks on Fort Ridgely and New Ulm did not go particularly well for the warriors but that did not deter them from raiding and murdering the more isolated homesteads in Brown County, Nicollet County, Jackson County, the upper Red River Valley and the town of Breckenridge. The settlers that were not murdered fled by whatever means available including running and hiding. And after a week of terrorizing an area 120 miles wide—west to east—and 200 miles long—north to south—the Sioux stopped pursuing the fleeing settlers. The warriors packed up their village and headed north and west, leaving thousands of square miles of territory nearly devoid of human population. But there were still a few battles to come.

How many settlers were murdered? The newsman Marion P. Satterlee says 447, Governor Ramsey said 500 and Bishop Whipple in his memoirs says 800. At any rate it was rather easy pickings for the Sioux warriors. According to author Gregory F. Michno in *Dakota Dawn* most of the settlers did not even own a firearm—at least one capable of warfare. They had grown accustomed to being at least outwardly neighborly with the Indians who frequented their area and as a result made no effort to fight until it was too late.

The fledgling state of Minnesota was in shock. Colonel Sibley wrote in a letter to Governor Ramsey, "Don't think there is exaggeration in the horrible pictures given by individuals. They fall short of the dreadful reality".[6]

The war was essentially over but there was still skirmishing to do, and Colonel Sibley was nearly prepared. He continued to train his troops at Fort Ridgely and finally welcomed 270 more troops from the paroled 3rd Minnesota Regiment.

On September 2nd an advance force under the direction of Capt. Hiram P. Grant was attacked by Sioux warriors at Birch Coulee. His command was nearly destroyed in this 2 day battle before help came.

The next day, September 3rd, Capt. Richard Strout and his command encountered a skirmish near Hutchinson, and that same day—and again on the 6th —Sioux warriors attacked Fort Abercrombie on the Red River.

Sibley was at last prepared to move up the Minnesota River by September 15th but it rained that day so Sibley delayed two days and finally left Fort Ridgely with 600 plus troops on September 17th.

The largest conflict occurred on September 23rd near Wood Lake just below the Upper Agency. Sibley's forces defeated Little Crow's warriors, probably as a result of the canon fire, and Chief Mankato was killed.

The Christian chiefs at the Upper Agency were growing more and more displeased with Little Crow and his followers; while Little Crow was away the Christian Chiefs took control of the hostages and moved them to the Upper Agency.

This was pretty much the last gasp of the uprising. All of the losses demoralized Little Crow and his warriors. Hank H. Cox describes the scene: "But the warriors returned defeated and, perhaps more important, realized that the insurrection was all but over. Little Crow announced his intent to flee with his people. Wabasha said he would stay, hoping to trade the hostages still alive for leniency. When the Sioux warriors arrived at the Upper Agency and learned the captives had been moved, they made no effort to retrieve them. Little Crow went to his camp to spend his last night in the Minnesota River Valley. The next morning he ordered his wagons loaded with his possessions for a long trek to the west and summoned his people for a final statement. 'I am ashamed to call myself a Dakota [Sioux],' he said. 'Seven hundred of our best warriors were whipped yesterday by the whites. Now we had all better run away and scatter out over the plains like buffalo and wolves. To be sure, the whites had wagon-guns and better arms than we, and there were many more of them. But that is no reason why we should not have whipped them, for we are brave Dakotas and the whites are cowardly women. I cannot account for the disgraceful defeat. It must be the work of traitors in our midst.' Little Crow, along with about one hundred of his people, set out for the west along with other groups led by Shakopee, Red Middle Voice, and the four young warriors who had initiated the uprising with the killings at Acton. Not all of the Sioux who were most active in the killings fled, but most of them did."[7]

Sibley reached the Upper Agency on September 26th. While he was taking his time the raping of the hostages continued. When Sibley arrived he called for a council. After all parties had a chance to make their speeches the Indians asked for mercy and Sibley asked for the hostages. Ninety one white women and children and one hundred fifty half-breeds were released and put in Sibley's custody at what had been named Camp Release close to present day Montevideo. The following week seventeen hundred Sioux, both innocent and guilty, gave themselves up.

Sibley thought his job was done and once again asked to be relieved of duty. Instead, he was promoted to brigadier general.

With the hostages at last rescued Sibley busied himself with getting the Sioux under lock and key. His intent was to set up a court and try the Indians who were in his custody. He set up a military court of sorts with five of his officers as judges. St. Paul attorney Isaac V.D. Heard acted as court recorder. Rev. Stephan Riggs, who had led his followers out of harm's way during the uprising, acted pretty much as a grand jury and decided which Indians would be put on trial. No defense counsel was provided for the accused Sioux Indians. In a little more than a month, 392 prisoners were tried and 303 were sentenced to hang, with some trials lasting no longer than ten to fifteen minutes.

Trials now done Sibley wrote to Pope, "They will be forthwith executed. Perhaps it will be a stretch of my authority. If so, necessity must be my justification."[8]

Pope replied to Sibley, "It is my purpose to utterly exterminate the Sioux. They are to be treated as maniacs or wild beasts."[9]

President Lincoln was disturbed with Pope's apparent eagerness to initiate the hangings.

Who was this man John Pope? A graduate of the U.S. Military Academy in 1842, Pope had worked his way up to the rank of general. His success in the west prompted Lincoln to involve him in the Civil War. At the Second Battle of Bull Run the Union forces were defeated and General Pope blamed the defeat on General McClellan. Lincoln had a problem. Two of his generals were arguing with each other and the Union army was suffering because of it, or so Lincoln thought. John Pope was a friend of both Secretary of War Stanton and Lincoln's wife Mary Todd Lincoln, so that complicated his dilemma. He couldn't just relieve Pope of duty.

Lincoln's solution was to relieve Pope of duty in the Civil War, create a Department of the Northwest and appoint Pope to command it. Pope was not happy with the President's decision. Secretary Stanton tried to smooth it over with a memo to Pope, stating, "The Indian hostilities ... require the attention of some military officer of high rank, in whose ability and vigor the government has confidence".[10]

Thus the bickering generals were separated and the President had someone to deal with affairs in Minnesota.

But now that the war was over General Pope and Governor Ramsey were calling for retribution—and Lincoln was uneasy. The President sent Assistant Secretary of the Interior John Usher to Minnesota to

President Abraham Lincoln

make sure no hangings took place without his approval, asking Henry Rice to assist Usher.

Pope informed Sibley, "The President directs that no executions be made without his sanction."[11] Lincoln had telegraphed Pope, "Please forward, as soon as possible, the full and complete record of these convictions."[12]

The names and court records of 303 Sioux condemned to hang were sent to both President Lincoln and to Governor Ramsey.

In his reply to President Lincoln Pope penned, "The only distinction between the culprits is as to which of them murdered most people or violated most young girls." He warned that the people of Minnesota "are exasperated to the last degree, and if the guilty are not all executed I think it nearly impossible to prevent the indiscriminate massacre of all the Indians—old men, women and children."[13]

General John Pope

To the Governor Pope wrote, "The Sioux prisoners will be executed unless the President forbids it, which I am sure he will not do."

Governor Ramsey chimed in with a message to the President, "I hope the execution of every Sioux Indian condemned by the military court will be at once ordered. It would be wrong upon principal and policy to refuse this" lest "private revenge would on all this border take the place of official judgment on these Indians."[14]

Emotions ran hot—perhaps rightfully so—but President Lincoln was not about to let passion cloud sound judgment. He knew he needed Minnesota votes and the support of the Minnesota electorate, but he could not trade blood for votes. In his annual message to Congress Lincoln reported on the Minnesota war and the toll it had taken on its settlers, adding that the people of Minnesota wanted the Indians removed. He even introduced to Congress the notion that the Indian system was in need of remodeling. But he said nothing about the 303 Sioux who had been sentenced to hang and whose fate he held in his hands.[15]

After reviewing all the court records President Lincoln reached the decision that 39 of the worst offenders would be hung. The rest would be pardoned. But the sad truth is that the worst offenders had already left Minnesota before Sibley had any prisoners in custody and were now somewhere in Dakota Territory, perhaps even in Canada.

Thus it was that on the day after Christmas, December 26, 1862, 39 Sioux Indian men were hanged at Mankato before a cheering crowd of onlookers.

Execution of the thirty-eight Sioux Indians at Mankato, Minnesota, December 26, 1862 by W.H. Childs

ORIGINALLY PUBLISHED ON FRANK LESLIE'S ILLUSTRATED NEWSPAPER, JANUARY 24, 1863, PAGE 285

CHAPTER 11

Chippewa Involvement — 1862 Sioux Uprising

Ojibwe involvement in the 1862 Sioux uprising played an important role in the subsequent events, and continues to do so today. One could make the case that Little Crow—a Sioux, and Hole-in-the-Day—an Ojibwe, had some sort of a mutual understanding. There were periods in history when the Sioux and the Ojibwe were mortal enemies. After all, the Ojibwe were pushing the Sioux farther and farther west as they found need for additional hunting grounds. But there were also interludes when the two tribes lived in harmony with one another.

Both Hole-in-the-Day and Little Crow vacillated between adopting the ways of the white man and living as they had for years, likely dependent upon which mode was personally most advantageous at a given time.

Anton Treuer states from his research that Hole-in-the-Day went to St. Paul quite often to meet with the Sioux, especially Little Crow.[1]

The Gull Lake chief Bad Boy relates that Hole-in-the-Day made plans with the Sioux in the summer of 1861 to jointly wage war against the whites. Bad Boy is quoted as saying, "Hole-in-the-Day's headman came to me and told me that Hole-in-the-Day was about to make a treaty with the Sioux and that they were to fight the whites together ... Afterward, I met Hole-in-the-Day and had a talk with him. He said ... 'I want your assistance in my undertaking.' He told me we were going to kill all the Indians that join the whites ... he also told me they were going to attack the fort [Ripley] and then fall back to the British possessions, and then get the Indians up there to help us."[2]

It was in Little Crow's sleeping quarters that a militant Sioux from Red Middle Voice's band claimed that they could count on support for war against the whites from other tribes and perhaps even support from the British. One must wonder if Red Middle Voice participated in the talks with Hole-in-the-Day.

In his memoirs, Bishop Whipple says that Little Crow had sent a letter marked "immediate" to Hole-in-the-Day, warning him of a Sioux warrior's intent to attack the Chippewa. The letter read, "Your young men have killed one of my people—a farmer Indian. I have tried to keep my soldiers at home. They have gone for scalps. Look out." It was signed, Little Crow.[3] According to Whipple, this was just a few days before the incident at Acton that started the uprising. This rather indicates some sort of friendly relationship between the two chiefs.

Apparently Hole-in-the-Day had planned a massacre farther north at the same time, according to Whipple, as the Sioux were raiding farther south. There are obviously some holes in the story. If Little Crow and Hole-in-the-Day had some previously arranged plan, why then did Little Crow have to be convinced by Red Middle Voice to join the massacre? Could it be that the unquestionably unplanned actions of the four warriors at Acton altered the master plan? Indian history on these questions is murky.

At any rate, Hole-in-the-Day was up to mischief. Hole-in-the-Day was not fond of Emmegahbowh, and had threatened Emmegahbowh's life a few years earlier.[4] Emmegahbowh and other missionaries were imprisoned briefly on August 17th, 1862. Chief Crossing Sky of Rabbit Lake had told Emmegahbowh, "I am come to advise you to prepare to flee away to Fort Ripley. Hole-in-the-Day is going to march with his warriors to the Agency in two days from today."[5]

Bishop Whipple writes that Emmegahbowh sent a message that night to the Mille Lacs band urging them to send warriors to protect Fort Ripley—a fort much the equivalent to Fort Ridgely and located in the same geographic area as present day Camp Ripley. Built in 1848, it was just a few short miles from Hole-in-the-Day's village at Gull Lake, and at this time Fort Ripley was sheltering a goodly number of terrified settlers who had received word of the raiding further south.

At the urging of Emmegahbowh the Mille Lacs band did indeed send 100 warriors, encircling the fort and thwarting any attempt by Hole-in-the-Day and his forces to initiate their planned raid. Emmegahbowh believed that because of his having alerted the Mille Lacs, he would be blamed and his family would be in danger. Emmegahbowh walked all night with his wife and children to make sure the fort was warned and to move his family to safety.

Who was this man Emmegahbowh? Emmegahbowh (who's conversion name was John Johnson) was an Ottawa Indian from Canada. The Ottawa were a tribe relative too, but separate from the Ojibwe. Trained as a young man in the Grand Medicine Lodge, Emmegahbowh was at some point convinced by missionaries to become a Christian. In 1841 he married a niece of Hole-in-the-Day the elder named Iron Sky Woman, and spent much of his early years in northern Minnesota and southern Canada, and sometimes talked of John Tanner—who we met in an earlier chapter. He had lived in Hole-in-the-Day's village for a year, so he knew of the ways of his wife's uncle. Emmegahbowh is credited with alerting the Mille Lacs band and saving Fort Ripley from devastation, and perhaps even preventing the Ojibwe from joining the

Emmegahbowh (left) with Rev. James Lloyd Breck (right) and Isaac Manitowab (center)

PUBLISHED IN THE US BEFORE 1923 AND PUBLIC DOMAIN IN THE US

Sioux in their endeavor to rid Minnesota of white people. Emmegahbowh went on to become the first American Indian Episcopal priest in 1867.

Meanwhile, the federal government was already in the process of planning treaties in order to move the Ojibwe out of the way of advancing civilization. Both John Nicolay, President Lincoln's personal secretary, and Commissioner of Indian Affairs William P. Dole were in Minnesota to observe these treaty negotiations with the Chippewa when the 1862 uprising began. They sent the following wire to Washington: "We are in the midst of a most terrible and exciting Indian war. Thus far the massacre of innocent white settlers has been fearful. A wild panic prevails in nearly one-half of the state."[6] And again, the uprising occurred at the same time as the federal government was designing treaties to relocate the Ojibwe who stood in the way of U.S. expansion.

As news of the devastation reached settlements further north some 200 refugees gathered at Fort Ripley for protection. Meanwhile, Hole-in-the-Day—employing bold tactics—was occupied in his push for the Ojibwe to unite with him in a joint massacre with the Sioux. The Mille Lacs chiefs refused to accept Hole-in-the-Day's manipulations.[7] When they were warned by Emmegahbowh, Chief Migizi (Eagle) and Niigaanigwaneb (First Seated Feather) put together a force of warriors to protect Fort Ripley from attack.[8]

Among those that were barricaded at Fort Ripley were Commissioner of Indian Affairs William P. Dole, President Lincoln's personal secretary John Nicolay, Lucius Walker, who had previously been the Indian Agent for the Ojibwe and—despite his having embezzled large amounts of Indian funds—was now a Minnesota legislator, and most likely also Minnesota Senator Morton S. Wilkinson.

The actions of Hole-in-the-Day and the standoff at Fort Ripley had profound ramifications for the future.

Bad Boy, a Gull Lake Chief, moved to Mille Lacs, probably because of his warnings to Emmegahbowh resulting in the Mille Lacs warriors protecting the Fort against the wishes of Hole-in-the-Day.[9]

Lucius Walker, an Indian Agent and current Minnesota legislator who had embezzled Indian funds and had ordered the arrest of Hole-in-the-Day had a mental breakdown, sent his family ahead to St. Paul, and then committed suicide.[10]

Commissioner of Indian Affairs, and the other government officials who were present at the Fort at the time of the aborted attack, promised the Mille Lac chiefs that in return for their support of the government they would not be removed.[11]

Anton Treuer capsulated it very well when he wrote, "The Mille Lacs chiefs could not have gained favor with the United States if Hole-in-the-Day had not directly opposed the government."[12]

In a report to his Board of Missions Bishop Henry Whipple wrote the following: "The Chippewa history is no whit brighter. They have been from the earliest settlement of this country our friends. They have borne outrage and wrong with unparalleled patience. In 1862 their head chief organized his band to commence a war upon the whites. Had it not been for Emmegahbowh, Bad Boy, Shaboshkung, and Buffalo, we should have had another desolated border. Emmegahbowh travelled all night in the storm, with his wife and children, to warn the garrison at Fort Ripley. Two of his children died in consequence of the night's journey. The Commissioner of Indian Affairs, the Secretary of the Interior, and a Committee of the legislature of Minnesota, pledged these friendly chiefs that for this act of fidelity they should never be removed. This pledge was incorporated in two separate treaties, and ratified by the United States Senate, and signed by the President. In violation of this solemn pledge of the nation, these men have been forced into a treaty, and will be compelled to remove."[13]

CHAPTER 12

1863–1864 Treaties

As 1863 dawned in Minnesota, the hanging of the condemned Sioux was over, and most of the remaining Minnesota Sioux were in custody at Fort Snelling. Commissioner Dole had returned to Washington after visiting Minnesota with the intent of attending to treaty negotiations with the Chippewa, but by accident of timing was there when the Sioux massacre started. He probably accomplished little more than escaping with his life and developing a bond of gratitude toward the Mille Lac Chippewa as a result of their having prevented Hole-in-the-Day from attacking Fort Ripley.

On the morning of February 25, 1863, representatives from the Mississippi Chippewa, Red Lake Chippewa and the Winnebago band met with Commissioner of Indian Affairs Dole in Washington. Commissioner Dole stated that he understood that they were gathered that morning to pay their respects to him, but that their primary purpose for visiting Washington was to review the treaty between the bands and the United States government.

Mille Lacs chief Sho-bos-cum spoke first, sharing his recollection of how they had met the previous summer during the Sioux uprising. He stated that they had asked permission to visit Washington because they were not able to resolve their problems through their agent.

Commissioner Dole praised the way the Mille Lacs had responded during the Sioux uprising. He recognized the presence of the Pillager chief who had followed Hole-in-the-Day during the uprising, adding that he hoped they could all depart Washington as friends.

The Winnebago chief Raw-be-mow expressed a genuine description of the emotions in Minnesota at the time, saying, "We want [you] … to understand, that it is a matter of life and death to us, our visit here. I know the feeling of the people in the state of Minnesota is intense against us and for the purpose of relieving ourselves from any wrong that may be imputed to us is the cause of our visit here also."

John Palmer Usher

That evening the delegation met with Secretary of the Interior John P. Usher. Secretary Usher welcomed them with a statement about the power and wealth of the United States and a wish that they would get to meet President Lincoln. Usher had apparently visited the Chippewa the previous December, stating that the President had sent him to attend to their welfare. He went on to say that President Lincoln, "will be very glad to see you and particularly to see you so well dressed, like white men. He wants you to be like white men. In order that you may be like white men he finds it necessary and important that you should be nearer together ... He has heard about the Millacs and the Sandy Lakes—that they did nothing that was ugly or bad to his commissioner when he sent him out to Leech Lake and he is very glad of that. He believes that all the Chippewa are very sorry for the difficulty they got into last summer, and thinks they want to live together peacefully and happily, and have no difficulties with the whites."

During his visit the previous December, Secretary Usher had presented a treaty, the execution of which he left to the Chippewa upon payment of the annuity at Leech Lake and Gull Lake. He opined that they were all willing to sign, but could not because the Indians from Millac and Sandy Lake were not present.

Usher went on to say, "We expected at the time the Millacs would be reluctant to agree to this treaty, because they had a good home where they were, and were peaceable and have done no harm. Your Great Father has no complaint to make against you. You are good Chippewas and good men. But what we say about it, we think, is for their good. We have heard, and believe it is true, that there is danger of their rice being cut off by damming the river, or the flood, there is no security of their having rice there year after year, owing to the whites going up there for lumber. We know that is not fair to you, yet your Great Father cannot always help that. It will always make trouble, and the trouble will be increased from this time on. Because the Sioux (not the Leech Lake Indians) were so wicked and exasperated the whites so that they hardly know how to distinguish between one and the other and they will be in danger down there."

Describing the removal plan in general, Usher stated, "You could all live there happily together."

The Secretary continued, "It was not the intention to wrong or take anything from you to make you as good homes up there as those you left—and indeed better because when you are all together you can so much more enjoy your benefits. ... If you have farms there on Millacs or on Sandy Lake you would not be compelled to leave them this summer. ... if you were up there you would have all that country towards Rainy Lake and Lake of the Woods where the whites would scarcely ever get between you and that country."

Usher added that it was important to do this now due to the Sioux uprising and the war to be fought the next summer, and because of the difficulties with Hole-in-the-Day and the Leech Lake Indians.

Usher told the Millacs, "to you who have behaved so well, the Millacs and others, he would try to oblige you in any way he could, allow you to select your new places for farms, and try to make your houses and fix up your gardens; so that you can live like white men."

"Now you have come here to see him [the President], and he is sure you have come to take his advice." He continued by urging haste in their deliberations, as the Senate would be adjourning in a few days.

Shaw-bus-com suggested that, since another Millac chief would be arriving that evening it would be best to wait until another day for further discussion of the treaty, adding also "that there was a great many things on that paper that did not meet our views."

The session closed with a comment by another Mille Lac chief, Mon-o-min-a-ga-shee, who said, "When we heard that paper read, there were some sections I don't know whether they were there or not. They said if we did not touch the pen [sign it] and put our names on the paper we should never receive annuities, because we would not be under the protection of the government."

Two days later, on the 27th of February, the chiefs representing the Mississippi Chippewa again met with Secretary of the Interior Usher. The Secretary opened the meeting declaring that he had said his piece two days ago and now it was the Indian's turn to talk.

After first shaking hands with Secretary of the Interior Usher and Commissioner of Indian Affairs Dole, Shaw-bus-cum spoke. He explained that the agent was attempting to intimidate the Indians into accepting the treaty, adding that they had decided to go through the proper channels and get permission to visit Washington. They had been informed that they could not leave the reservation without permission. Shaw-bus-cum declared that his people wanted to visit with their superintendent in St Paul, which would necessitate leaving the reservation. They had requested permission in person, but their agent said not a word. Since that didn't work they next sent a letter to the agent requesting permission to leave the reservation to visit the superintendent. The request was denied. It was then decided that they hire their own teams, go to St Paul, and ask permission from the superintendent to visit with you here. "Knowing that we were undeservedly classed with the Sioux which was very degrading to us, and that the whites of Minnesota were not kindly disposed to us on that account, we felt it was our duty to come here, where redress could be found." He concluded by saying that he wished their two senators were present.

The Secretary responded that the senators were engaged in Congressional session, although they had certainly been invited. Growing a bit snappish the Secretary added, "We want you to attend to business and to make a new bargain—one that will be best for you. ... I thought you came here to talk about that."

Commissioner Dole gently defended Shaw-bus-cum, at which point Shaw-bus-cum continued, "I understand very well the time is short and that you want to hear our objections. When we left our section of country we thought we had picked out the best interpreters we had, but we have a complaint to enter against them. We have thought that they have not moral courage enough. We are afraid that whenever we extend views that will not meet yours they will not say them to you. At the time the negotiations were pending at the Chippewa agency all the chiefs that are here were present, with the exception of three—the last delegation that came from Millac. The treaty was given to us and we understood it fully. It was interpreted not only once but day after day until we understood the whole purport of the treaty. There were a great many things that we did not like in the treaty and for that purpose we are here today. We are willing to acquiesce with the views of the government. They call us their friends and we call the government our father. They have treated us as such theretofore. We have been under the care of our great father ever since we were born. At the present time we are in a situation that is deplorable not only on account of our women and children, but on account of all the persons that are residing amongst us at the homes we reside on. We are coupled with guilty parties. We are very sorry to leave our present homes. I think we can live at peace all the time with our brothers. The proposed country you intend to remove us to you have been very much misinformed about. We do not think that number of Indians could subsist there, even with the utmost exertions on agricultural pursuits, for two years, because the land will not allow it. We are very well acquainted with that country. There is hardly one Indian of our tribe but what has been over it. I know that it is a country of starvation. It is nothing but sand barrens and swamps. There is a little strip along the lakes that may do for a few families but what is that for the subsistence of all these? I do not know where is the best place to remove us to, but the place you propose, I candidly say it is a place of starvation. We always like to adhere to the wishes of the government, but in adhering to the wishes of the government we always like to know that we shall have a subsistence on certain portions of land where they intend to remove us to. At the place you propose you cannot cultivate corn enough to winter a squirrel during the winter, let alone feed several bands of Indians. You know my objections now to removing there."

The proposed land was chosen by some of the Chippewas and by the traders, Commissioner Dole asserted, adding that there was as much good land at the new site as the Indians currently had at Millac. Dole again explained that the government wanted to concentrate the Chippewa so it would be less expensive for the government to provide doctors and blacksmiths and such. He said, "We want you to get together. You all might go down to Millac, but you will be in the way of the whites there, or they will be in your way. That is the trouble." He opined that if there was enough land at Millac it might be possible to concentrate the Chippewa in two areas. The government desired that all the currently scattered villages be relocated to one region.

Neb-a-wash, a Pillager, declared, "... A portion of our tribe was included in the late raid last summer. The punishment that was inflicted on our bands pecuniarily [sic] was very heavily felt. The poverty that is existing in our band cannot be told ... We have nothing to complain about that. ... We know the section where you wish to remove our fellow Chippewas. It is not a country where we can live all together. ... The rice fields are thin. I am very sorry to say that whoever gave you the information—whether he is an Indian—or whether he is a trader ... that he is very much mistaken. He must have done it from a matter of interest. I know that there is a great many living amongst us that will sacrifice not only the lives of one, but of all the tribe, if they can only put something into their own pockets. ... We are afraid that much of my band will starve before we get home. ... I am considered a good hunter ... I have only killed one deer in that section in ten years. ... Whenever there is a rise in the water our rice fields are destroyed."

Cobmubbi, a Winnibigoshish spoke up. "The person you met in your travels misinformed you. ... When we came down to see our Great Father in 1855 we knew enough to reserve the best portion of our country. ... There is no place around us where any other bands can live."

Secretary Usher asked, "Do you know of any place where they could all be got together? Our chief desire is to locate them so that the agent can be with them."

"The Mississippi bands could be concentrated at Millacs," Shaw-bus-com replied. "There would be sufficient land for all the Mississippi to be concentrated there, provided the reservations extended around the lake."

"Who are the Mississippi bands?" asked Secretary Usher.

The interpreter answered, "The Gull Lake bands, the Rabbit Lake bands, the Sandy Lake band, the Poughkagemies, the Rice Lake bands and the Millacs."

Secretary Usher next inquired, "Are there any white settlers east of the Millac?"

Shaw-bus-com responded, "There is only a white man settled thereon. There were some white men settled upon it but they abandoned it. They stayed there about a year ... there have been none since on the East and North of the lake."

"I want to understand now that I shall be a party to no arrangement that will starve you," Usher reassured. "I want you to keep together for the reasons that we can take care of you. Your sugar camps will not last many years. The trees will die from cutting so much. You must try to get a living some other way."

"That is very true," Shaw-bus-com agreed,

Secretary Usher continued, "The white people ... get their living by working the soil — none of them live by hunting. You say all the Mississippi Indians could live around Millac. What do the Sandy Lake, Gull Lake and Poughkagemies say?"

Shaw-bus-com stated, "They are all here and can talk for themselves."

Cross-in-the-Sky—from Gull Lake—responded, "All I will have to do will be to tumble over in my bed and roll into the middle of them — I am so near them."

Speaking for Sandy Lake was a chief of the Rice Lake band. He said, "I want to state fact to you although I am not the head chief. ... The chief of Sandy Lake told me to act in concert with Shaw bus com. ... I have only ten wigwams under my control. Those ten wigwams shall remove to Millac. ... During the raid of the Chippewa he [Commissioner Dole] told us to remain quiet, and go back to our reservations and we should have the payment at Millac. That promise was faithfully fulfilled and we are very much obliged to him for that. All the persons that represented the different reservations there at Millac, had an understanding at the time that should the commissioner wish them to remove there or remain at Millac they should remain. That idea is not changed now. We are all willing to remove to that place and make it our home."

"I want to say a word to these chiefs," Commissioner Dole explained. "The object that the Secretary has laid before them of getting them together is only one of the great objects that we have in view. There is another great object and that is where shall we place these chiefs far enough away from the white settlement to prevent them getting into difficulty with them again. We want them distinctly to understand [;] have these chiefs and their people to agree in relation to a location but that we have to satisfy the people of Minnesota—so that they will not take the law into their own hands and make war upon these people. Now while it may be true—and probably is true that there is sufficient good land about Millac for the whole of the Mississippi bands, yet it is known to these chiefs that the land is sold upon the adjoining lake to the government—that it has been surveyed for settlement, and the question arises whether we can take that land which has been sold to the government and put into market and get it for the Indians allowing them to move there from Poughkagemie and Sandy Lake. Let us meet this question fairly in the face. The remark of Shaw bus com was a good one—that it was better to have the Senators and representatives of Minnesota here in these councils. The further we progress in these councils the more I am convinced of the necessity of doing that thing, because when they go home to their people they will be called upon to know why it is we have not removed these people from their midst, or from their border. I have not forgotten the councils that I held with the chiefs here from Millac. I have not forgotten all my promises to them but they remember that the question of their removal was not thought of at that time, and therefore I made no promises to them on that subject. I sent for them when the country there was in great difficulty. There was a question in the minds of the whites there whether they were not joining with the other part of the Mississippi band in the raid. They came and promised to keep the peace, they did so, and I am determined to be their friend in all their troubles; but I cannot promise but what it may be necessary that the government should use its power for their removal and the only question now is, where can they go for a home where they can make a living. It may be barely possible that the people of Minnesota will consent to the Indians now living at Millac, to remain there for the present. They may consent in the future for them to remain there forever if they will become good citizens. But I am sure that we will not give satisfaction to the people of Minnesota, however much it may be desired by the Indians. If we remove them all to Millac my view of it is that at least the Gull Lake Indians will have to remove further north."

Superintendent Clark W. Thompson closed the days' meeting saying, "I have come down here with you, have an interest in your welfare, and therefore I want to say a few words. You are aware of the difficulties that exist up in Minnesota, and of the feeling of the people of Minnesota towards you. You are also aware of the fact that the country is filled with soldiers under the control of a different department from this and you also know that there has been trouble there and these men have been sent to put them back on the reservations. I want you to look at the business before you seriously and not to make a proposition to stay where you know you cannot stay without trouble."

On March 5, 1863, the Mississippi bands of Chippewa Indians once again met with Commissioner of Indian Affairs William P. Dole. Commissioner Dole opened the meeting with the following statement: "Brothers, we must make good use of our time—it is short. I have had several councils with you, on the subject of a treaty. You have been no doubt thinking on the subject and preparing your minds to tell me what your conclusions are in relation to it. Before you left home you must have all been well satisfied that you could not remain on your present reservations—that the difficulties that the Sioux have had with the whites—together with the difficulty that some of you have had with the settlement, render it necessary that you should have a new treaty with the government. I appreciate fully the difficulties that you labor under. Your love for your homes—the anxiety that you have to remain at your present reserve—and I understand that some of you are deserving of the right from the government to remain there but we must look at the difficulties that have arisen between the whites and the tribe of Chippewa as a whole. We cannot separate a part of you from the balance. I know of two, or perhaps three of the bands of the Chippewas near Crow Wing where we had our difficulties that remained true friends of the white man. I remember well that you came to me while at Fort Ripley, gave me your hand, and continued our friends. In consequences of that you can remain so near the white settlements. The whites, it seems, demand their removal on account of the recent difficulties. I am sure that we will be able to make no treaty by which we can separate the Millac band and

Poughkagemies, and the Sandy Lake bands from the Mississippi band. I myself am inclined to do so. The Millac band have earned this from the government that they ought to be allowed to remain where they are for the present. But I believe at the same time that it will be absolutely necessary for your reserve at Gull Lake agency to be abandoned. I have not the least idea that you can remain there at peace with the white people, but wish to say this, that if any part of your people are removed—if you have to leave any part of your reserve—that your Great Father, the President, will be inclined to pay the full value of that reserve and to place you in as good or better condition in your new homes than you are now at this present location. So far as the Millacs reserve is concerned, in consequence of the Indians belonging to that band having behaved so nobly during our difficulties last fall, it can be arranged that they might remain there a year or two until they themselves shall seek out a new home to their satisfaction. I shall be glad. They are aware however, that the white people are already settling near them, that the lands are surveyed and put into market, on one side of the lake, and with the bitter feeling that exists in Minnesota between the white man and the Indian, I doubt very much if it is not better for them to make haste in their removal. I want now to hear what the chiefs have to say. You are an intelligent people; you have advanced far in civilization; you understand well what I am talking about. I do not wish to confine you to the treaty that has been read before you. I wish you to say to me now what change you ask in that writing. If there is any part of that treaty drawn up by the Secretary of the Interior that you do not like, speak frankly and freely—say wherein it displeases you. You can remain here but a few days longer. It is necessary to your people that you should return to them. Difficulties may arise in your absence which if you were at home, you might have prevented, and it is therefore necessary that you speak frankly and freely in relation to the treaty which you wish to make."

Shaw-bus-com replied, "It seems to me that I am not mistaken in looking at you. You are the person we met here at Fort Ripley last summer and my superintendent [Clark W. Thompson] was there at the time, but there was one man there also who I do not see here. I think if I remember right he was the Secretary [John Nicolay] of our Great Father. I have not forgotten the words that were spoken at the time we met in council. All those words were treasured by us. We heard them and they were very pleasant. We were very glad to accept them and treasure them in our hearts and also in our minds. We are very sorry to hear that there is one who has been the instigator of all the transactions of which we have to bear the blunt. He would not be the proper one to listen to all the complaints made by the government. We are very sorry too, that we could not have the Senators here from our State, at this council. When we met you there at Fort Ripley, the very same words that we were given to understand when we were in Washington heretofore; you made us understand and the very same words. Whatever stipulations there has been made in the treaty heretofore made, we have it at heart all the time. There is not one stipulation but what we still adhere to. We know all the stipulations and what has been promised us. When we wake up in the morning we have nothing to think of but those stipulations. How can it be possible to abandon our reservations when we were told to seize [?] every inch of the land with the exception of the land for the Reserves [?] If it is not good enough for an Indian to live upon [,] how can it be good enough for a white man to live on, where we are living now [?] We demand that we should be allowed to live on our Reserves."

"I must answer a few words that the chief has spoken," Commissioner Dole responded. "I have not forgotten the council that we held at Fort Ripley. I have not forgotten the promises made there. But the chief who has spoken will remember well that the subject of the removal of the Indians from their present Reserves was not a subject of conversation or of council. When Hole-in-the-Day in the wickedness of his heart called the Chippewas to Gull Lake, that they might make war upon the White people, I sent to Millac for this chief and those under him to come to me at the Fort. He came with some fifty of his chiefs and promised anew that they would keep the peace with the Whites and with the Great Father and their government and that they would not join in the raid against the settlement. And they kept their promise well. I promised on the part of the government, that the Millac, the Sandy Lake and the Poughkagemie bands of Indians should receive their full annuities in goods and money, payable at their reserves, which had never been done before and that they should not be liable to the payment of damages committed by the balance of the tribe, and I kept my word in that respect. That is, I believe all the promises made on their side, other than the general promise that these Indians should keep good faith in their treaties with the government of the United States and I promising on the part of the government that we would keep good faith with them. That we still propose to do. With the Gull Lake band no council was held other than the one that was held at the point of the bayonet, armed on both sides—where bad faith was kept by taking prisoners on the council ground. With them we made no promises, and are under no obligation to them, as they have forfeited their rights under the treaty. But I wish to say that the government has no revengeful spirit toward that tribe. Our object is to have peace and good will and while we are willing to forgive their depredations we at the same time ask them, for their own good, to remove from that reservation to the reserve sixty miles north, that they may be at a distance from the white men they have had trouble with, and avoid further difficulty with them. I see Bad Boy here. I met him at the Fort. His tribe had driven him from home. But I believe there are chiefs here who were against the government. Here is Mr. Johnson, who they took prisoner at the time. I know not for what reason unless it was that he was an educated Indian and might be a friend of the whites. I do not mention these things to create bad faith but to show you that I fully understand the case, and that altho [sic] you were enemies to us then you are friends now and the treaty we wish to make is not that we wish to punish you but you have had trouble with the whites and you cannot live at peace with them and we now ask you to fix some terms by which you can remove from contact with them, and desire that you may live at peace. I too am anxious that the Senators and members of Congress from Minnesota should be at our councils, and they have been invited to be present at every one of them. I am more anxious they should be with us because of this difficulty with the Chippewa Indians and the government of the United States and when we adjourn this council we will adjourn to meet at such time when we can have them with us. The chief who was the most friendly to us in our difficulties is put forward here to make the speeches on all occasions for the whole tribe. Now while I am very glad to hear that chief—he is a fine orator and possesses judgment and intelligence—I want to hear from that tribe who have had the trouble with the United States. I want to hear something they have to say."

"… So far as I am concerned I am very tired of speaking for the rest of the bands and wish they would speak for themselves," Shaw-bus-cum declared. "Let the guilty culprits come forward and speak for themselves."

Bad Boy, chief at Gull Lake—Hole-in-the-Day's band—took up the challenge. He began by asserting, "I would state this circumstance that the Reserves he [Commissioner Dole] is touching upon today I still own." This was in reference to the land they had chosen as their reserve while in private discussion with Senator Rice during the Treaty of 1855 negotiations. "Hole-in-the-Day is spoiling everything that has been done in our country."

At Bad Boy's request the Commissioner then called a recess until the next day, hoping that a Gull Lake chief—who was unable to attend that day due to illness—might arrive by the following day.

In spite of the call for recess Bad Boy continued, speaking of his own actions during the proposed raid on Fort Ripley. Apparently siding with the whites, Bad Boy wanted the Commissioner—and perhaps others in the room—to understand his conduct was not because he feared his fellow Indians, but instead was a product of his loyalty toward the whites because the whites had been his support as long as he could remember.

The next day, March 6th, the Mississippi band delegates once again convened. Senator Rice was now present.

Secretary Usher opened the meeting. "My brothers, you have been here a good many days and I do not see that much has been done. I suppose you are tired of staying here and that you want to go home to your women, your young men and your children. The business which you came to attend to required a good deal of reflection and consideration, and I am not much surprised that you have not been enabled to make up your minds yet. I know you have been detained because Senator Rice, who is your friend, has been engaged in the councils of the nation, and could not give you his attention until now. He has consented to act as your friend. He has known you a long time, and he knows what is for your interest. I advise you to listen to what he tells you and to take his advice for this reason that he has had a great deal of experience in the world, that he knows much more than you do and will give you any advice that is for your good. You can tell him everything you want and he will tell us, and then we will see if we can agree. It is necessary for you to be in a hurry about this because it is not profitable for you to remain here much longer and his time will not permit him to devote much more of it to you. I told you before, and I tell you now, that your Great Father wants no advantage of you. He wants to do for your good, and if you consult with your friend he knows what is for your good and he knows what is good for the whites — what is best for both, and your Great Father will be inclined to take his advice when he tells him what he had better do for you. Your Great Father has confidence in him as you have, and knows that he will do nothing to harm you, and nothing to harm his white children."

With that negotiations were turned over to Senator Rice.

"It is not necessary for me to say anything to you now," Senator Rice countered. "We have talked so frequently that we understand each other and I am ready to meet them anytime."

"We are willing to meet with the Senator at any time," Shaw-bus-cum concurred.

Records indicate that, just as had happened during negotiations for the Treaty of 1855, this meeting next moved from public to private discussion. "[T]he Indians … held a private consultation with Senator Rice at the office of the Secretary of the Interior." Previous negotiations had been conducted through the Commissioner of Indian Affairs.

The treaty was signed on March 11, 1863 by Commissioner Dole, Superintendent Thompson and Henry Rice, in addition to the chiefs from the Gull Lake band, the Mille Lac band, the Leech Lake band, the Winnebegoshish band and the Cass Lake band. The completed treaty ceded the Gull Lake, Mille Lac, Sandy Lake, Rabbit Lake, Pokagomin Lake and Rice Lake reservations to the United States. The Indians were all to remove to the new reservation provided, with the exception of the Mille Lacs—who could remain as long as they behaved themselves.

It is noteworthy that, while Hole-in-the-Day or his father had been key figures in all the previous treaties involving the Mille Lacs, in 1863 he was absent. One can only wonder why. After all, Hole-in-the-Day was the self-proclaimed chief of all the Chippewa. Only a year earlier he had endeavored to align the Chippewa with the Sioux effort to massacre all the whites in Minnesota, and perhaps it gave him pause to realize that the Sioux he had hoped to join had all been either hanged or imprisoned, or had fled—as fugitives—to hide in the Dakotas.

However, by 1864 Hole-in-the-Day had apparently regained courage and—along with Sandy Lake Chief Mis-qua-dace—was able to secure permission to re-negotiate the 1863 treaty. It is easy to convince one's self that the Sandy Lake band was displeased that the Mille Lacs were not required to relocate while the Sandy Lakers were thus obliged. After all, Sandy Lake had also refrained from joining Hole-in-the-Day's massacre plans. And so it was that the two bands re-negotiated the treaty with Commissioner of Indian Affairs Dole.

The only significant difference in the 1864 treaty as compared to 1863 is the increased amounts of money to be expended for the benefit of the Indians. As usual, however, chief Hole-in-the-Day was looking out for himself. The treaty included money specific for rebuilding Hole-in-the-day's house that had burned, as well as one section of land each—in fee-simple—for himself, Sandy Lake chief Mis-qua-dace and Mille Lac chief Shaw-vosh-Kung. In addition, the Sandy Lake band would not be required to remove until so directed by the President.

The final article of the treaty stated that the 1864 treaty would replace the 1863 treaty.

CHAPTER 13

Treaties in Action

The following chapter is intended to give the reader a feel for the type of negotiations that were taking place between the tribes and the government during the 1862 to 1864 time period. While the negotiations did involve the Mille Lac band, the issues and influences on tribes were of a broader nature.

Treaty after treaty was being negotiated and signed, some involving all of the Chippewa and others involving only particular bands. At least twenty-eight treaties were negotiated with—and signed by the Chippewa Tribe, or bands within the Chippewa tribe. Keeping it all straight and, more importantly, parties to the treaties understanding how they were being administered, was becoming a problem; not to mention that the Civil War was a constant drain on government funds.

During the same time period that the Mississippi bands were negotiating what would later become the 1863 Treaty, the Chippewa Indians from Lake Superior met with Commissioner of Indian Affairs Dole. Commissioner Dole opened the meeting on March 3, 1863, saying that he was there to listen to the tribes concerns and then would furnish the papers for their examination in response to their previous request to be allowed to examine their (financial) accounts.

At least as far back as June 10, 1862, the various chiefs had been attempting to determine whether they were being paid as promised. Chief Hole-in-the-Day had met briefly with Commissioner Dole that day and was told that if they would put their requests down on paper he, Dole, would have the requests examined.

On February 16th the following year Dole again met with Chippewa chiefs, including some from Mille Lac, Sandy Lake and Snake River. The chiefs complained about unequal treaty payments and asked for an accounting of the funds due them; funds they believed they had not received. Another complaint was that they had been promised government employees in the treaties, but that these employees had sometimes not been provided or had remained for less than the agreed upon number of years. And at times these government employees—although provided—accomplished little or none of the work assigned to them.

Several chiefs complained about the government moving the location where annuity payments were disbursed. According to Anton Treuer, Hole-in-the-Day may have had a part in convincing the government to move the treaty payments from LaPointe to Sandy Lake.[1] The move made it better for the Mississippi bands but disastrous for the Michigan and Wisconsin bands. In 1850 President Zachary Taylor had signed an executive order which required the removal of Chippewa Indians from Wisconsin and from the Upper Peninsula of Michigan to Minnesota.[2] The first step was to move the station for annuity payments from Wisconsin at LaPointe to Sandy Lake, Minnesota. That appeared to be a reasonable move, introducing the Wisconsin and Michigan Chippewa to their future home. The government set the date for the first payment at Sandy Lake late in the fall. Thousands of Chippewa made their way to Sandy Lake—but no money or goods showed up. The Chippewa waited for three weeks as winter set in, while the government reportedly provided moldy flour and spoiled meat. Major food poisoning—as well as a measles outbreak—took its toll. 150 Chippewa died at Sandy Lake and another 450 perished on the journey home.[3]

The plan obviously backfired and President Taylor's order to remove the Wisconsin and Michigan Chippewa to Minnesota was retracted in 1851.[4]

The meeting on February 16, 1863, concluded with Commissioner of Indian Affairs Dole saying, "It is not possible for me to make them any regular answer to the speeches they have just made as I informed them the other day. [Obviously talking to the interpreter] I will at once examine into the charges that they make against the government and say how much is true and how much we can show them is in error. ... [T]hat you have some cause of complaint I have no doubt. I have no doubt some agents of the government have dealt unjustly by you. This cannot always be avoided. It is your right however, to inquire into these matters ... If it is found on this examination that the government has failed to pay you the money that they have promised you ... I shall recommend to Congress that they make up any loss ..."

The next day the Commissioner again met with a delegation led by the same chiefs as the previous day. Commissioner Dole reported that the government had determined that approximately one fifth of the whole Chippewa tribe was the band in Michigan, so one fifth of the payment had been delivered to their agent and four fifths to the other bands. Apparently some of the chiefs thought there should be only one paymaster; however the Commissioner assured them that the result would be the same. One of the chiefs then described how well civilized his band was becoming and that they wanted patents issued for their land. The Commissioner replied that he was sure the President would approve the issuing of patents "just so soon as you are capable of taking care of the land."

One chief then expressed his band's desire to be able to hunt anywhere—on or off the reservation—as long as the Indians did not trespass upon a white man's land or on anybody else's property. He concluded by saying that "at the time of the treaty I was promised that I should have a patent for my reservation, and now I see that it is only written here on the paper. It says that they should be issued only for 80 acres—that every individual should have 80 acres of land, but I was promised that I should have one for my reservation."

Commissioner Dole replied, "In relation to the patent that the chief speaks of … it must have been this: - that the commissioner who made the treaty to them promised him that his reservation should be reserved and entered of Records, so that the government would not sell it."

Coming back to individual patents for their individual 80 acres of land, the Commissioner specified that the treaty [of Sept. 10, 1854] says that, "the principle of which is that you be able to manage your own affairs and take care of your own property." He went on to say that he was glad the chiefs had attained the position where they were able to manage their own affairs intelligently. "And yet I doubt whether there is not a large proportion of your tribe who do not know how to manage their affairs and would fool the money away on trinkets if they were allowed to sell their lands."

On March 6, 1863, Commissioner Dole again met with the Lake Superior Chippewa delegates. They apparently were planning to leave Washington and return home and were wrapping up, or summarizing their negotiations. Commissioner Dole stated that he understood that the chiefs wanted $1500 to purchase presents for themselves and their people. Dole agreed to meet with them in New York and arrange for the purchase of the presents. The chiefs again asked for an accounting of how much money they were owed from the treaties, again emphasizing their desire to have schools and to receive patents on their individual parcels of land. The Commissioner responded, "I will give you today in writing, the amount of money and goods due them under each treaty, so they may know what amount of money and goods we place in the hands of their agent."

Addressing the issue of possible fraud, the Commissioner declared, "It is very wrong for you to undertake to transact your business with parties who have no authority from the government. You surely get into trouble when you do so. If upon any occasion you come to the conclusion that your agent is not doing his duty—that he is wasting your funds—it is entirely proper that you call a council, and that you there in his presence, give notice to the agent and send your letter here giving your opinion and belief in relation to it and your Great Father will authorize an investigation and look into the facts at once and see that justice is done to you."

One must wonder, is this the government fraud that Bishop Whipple and others spoke of? It would typically require much prior deliberation before accusing the person who was in charge of your welfare—even your life—with fraud. And ponder, too, that the men who might gather in council to consider such moves had wives and children to consider, as well as themselves.

CHAPTER 14

The 1870s

The year was 1870. Minnesota had only been a state for a little over ten years. Many Minnesotans who had survived the Sioux uprising in 1862 were still nervous about the Indians, regardless to which tribe they belonged. Mille Lacs County residents, mostly in the southern part of the county, were no exception. Princeton, located on the southern edge of the county, had only had a permanent resident since about 1854.

Civil War hero and Republican Ulysses S. Grant had been elected President in 1869. As a soldier Grant had depended a great deal on the assistance of Ely Parker, a Seneca Indian and Grant's friend, and upon his election Grant installed Parker as head of the Bureau of Indian Affairs. As President, Grant endeavored to foster peaceful relations with the Indians. Parker favored assimilation of the Indians and supported Grant's attempt at peaceable interaction with the tribes. This approach, however, was not popular with the administration's adversaries in Washington. Parker was accused of defrauding the government in various dealings with Indian tribes, and—although cleared of any wrongdoing—resigned his position in July of 1871 believing that he could no longer be effective as Commissioner of Indian Affairs. In his letter of resignation, effective August 1, 1871, he wrote, "The effect of the Congressional legislation ... has been to almost wholly divest the Indian Bureau of all its original importance, duties and proper responsibilities. The Commissioner of Indian Affairs, under the present arrangements, is merely a supernumerary officer of the Government, his principle duties being simply those of a clerk to a Board of Indian Commissioners, operating wholly outside of and almost independent of the Indian Bureau. I would gladly and willingly do

Ely S. Parker

anything in my power to aid in forwarding and promoting to a successful issue the President's wise and beneficent Indian policy, but I cannot, in justice to myself, longer continue to hold the ambiguous position of Commissioner of Indian Affairs." Thus began a 'revolving door' in the office of Commissioner of Indian Affairs; following Parker there were three more commissioners before the end of Grant's eight years as President ending in 1877.

But back to Mille Lacs County! The treaties of 1863 and 1864 had been signed just a bit over five years earlier, ceding the Mille Lacs Reservation to the United States. The Mille Lacs Indians had, just the year before, opposed Hole-in-the-Day's attempt to convince the Chippewa to join the Sioux in seeking to rid Minnesota of "white" people. At one point the Mille Lacs had apparently surrounded Fort Ripley, siding with the United States in protecting the fort from attack. Bishop Whipple is quoted as saying, "More than a hundred Mille Lacs warriors went at once to the fort and before Hole-in-the-Day could begin war the massacre was averted."[1] Commissioner of Indian Affairs Dole commented, "I feel confident that this diversion of nearly one-half the followers upon whom Hole-in-the-Day doubtless relied, went far in enabling us finally to effect a settlement of the Chippewa difficulties without a resort to arms."[2]

At the time that Commissioner Dole was at Fort Ripley under threat of attack by Hole-in-the-Day's warriors, with the Mille Lac warriors coming to the defense of the fort, Dole had made a promise to the Mille Lacs. Whatever Dole's words were, Chief Shaw vosh kung did not forget them. And although final negotiation for the treaty of 1863 was done in private, we can be fairly certain that it was Shaw vosh kung who insisted on Article 12—even though Dole was trying to weasel out of it.

Article 12 said, "that owing to the heretofore good conduct of the Mille Lac Indians they shall not be compelled to remove so long as they shall not in any way interfere with or in any manner molest the persons or property of the whites." The language in Article 12 created the confusion that existed for the next 150 years and continues as of this writing.

In the 1864 treaty Chief Shaw vosh kung was given 640 acres of land in fee simple in an area now occupied by a casino and tribal buildings in Vineland. So it is no surprise that the chief influenced his followers not to do anything to trigger their removal.

United States policy was such that all Minnesota Chippewa were to be removed to the White Earth and Red Lake Reservations. One must wonder, then, what the commissioners had in mind with the Article 12 clause clearly stating, "shall not be required to remove". Did it mean that the Mille Lacs could remain only until the white settlers wanted or needed the land? During the public portion of the 1863 treaty negotiations Commissioner Dole had held that they could likely arrange for the Mille Lacs to remain at Mille Lac for a year or two. In the 1837 treaty Governor Dodge had said to the Chippewa assembled, "… you will be allowed, during his pleasure [the

President's], to hunt and fish on them. It will probably be many years before your Great Father will want all these lands for the use of his white children."

Or did they have in mind that the Mille Lacs would be allowed to acquire land in fee simple, like they seemed to be favoring by awarding one of the seven chiefs and headmen who signed the 1863 treaty with 640 acres in fee simple? Or did they assume by some method, the Mille Lacs would be convinced or forced to remove to White Earth? Evidence exists that many officials in high positions as well as ordinary folks favored elimination of all Indians from Minnesota except the Chippewa, or maybe including the Chippewa, who were to be concentrated on the White Earth and Red Lake Reservations. Even Bishop Whipple, who spent his life trying to reform the fraudulent federal Indian system, favored removal of the Chippewa to the White Earth and Red Lake Reservations.

Probably with removal of the Mille Lacs as a motive, there was local effort to accuse the Mille Lac Indians of violating Article 12. George Wheeler, from Princeton, wrote in 1870 to Indian Agent Atcheson, complaining of the sale of whiskey to the Indians. He said, "[T]he Indians are very well behaved when they can get no whiskey."[3] That same year Joseph Roberts, from St. Paul, wrote the agent intimating that he had been sent to find out if the Mille Lacs were willing to leave the former reservation. He is quoted as saying, "[T]hey are now just as much opposed to leave the reservation as they were in the year 1866 ... they claim the right under the treaty of 1863 or 4 that they should be allowed to remain at that reservation or the country they had occupied before, for four hundred years, providing they would commit no depredations which they claim they did not ..." .[4] Charles Peltier, who lived near Little Falls, also wrote to the agent saying, "We have in our neighborhood ... a lot of Chip. Indians numbering perhaps twenty and they are getting to be quite troublesome to myself and several of my neighbors. We are but a few settlers here and cause us a good deal of fear for our lives & property ... we are in fear day and night of them."[5]

Apparently complaints about the Indians were so numerous that George Atcheson, Indian Agent at the Chippewa Agency, was asked in mid-1870 by Commissioner Parker to report on the situation. Parker reported on June 30 that, "during the early part of last March I visited the town of Princeton ... where most of the adverse reports derive their origin ... the prime desire for the removal of the Indians on the part of the inhabitants would seem to arise from the fact that so long as the former [Indians] are permitted to abide near the towns and to roam at will over adjacent country, encamp in the vicinity of the farms, drink whiskey, carouse, gamble, and make hideous noises, the settlements labor under great disadvantage ... The nearness of the settlements to the ceded Mille Lacs Reservation retards their growth, depreciates the value of their lands, and deters many desirable emigrants from establishing themselves in that quarter.

"The inveterate begging propensities of the Indians is another annoyance of which the settlers complain. Wandering over the country, whether on a journey for liquor, or to obtain food by the chase [hunting], they usually stop at the isolated farm houses by the way and make demands for food on the inmates, occasionally women and children, which latter through fear of imagining results think they dare not refuse. In this manner houses have now been rendered destitute of food … The citizens of Princeton have been advised in case the Indians had interfered with or molested the persons or property of the whites that satisfactory proof of such interference or molestation should be furnished this office within a reasonable time. As yet nothing positive touching the matter has been received by me."

Atcheson also related having consulted with three of the Mille Lacs Chiefs on the matter; Shaw-bah-skung, Be-dud-dunce and Shaw-ne-yaw. Shaw-bah-skung was apparently the major chief of the Mille Lacs at this time, evidenced by the fact that only he and Hole-in-the-Day from Gull Lake were awarded lands in the treaty of 1864. According to Atcheson, Shaw-bah-skung really didn't want to talk about removing to White Earth, blaming complaints by Princeton area residents on one chief, Mo-zo-eno-nay and his roughly one hundred followers. Shaw-bah-skung is quoted as saying, "[T]he Chief Mo-zo-eno-nay and his band numbering about one hundred have just gone down the country by way of Mille Lacs … to sore amongst the white settlements. This is what they always do and what they always intend to do and the whole Mille Lacs Indians must share the blame. I have endeavored to dissuade them from going down but it is of no use. They listen to no one, even if the Great Spirit should say to them, 'do not go' they would continue on. Mo-zo-eno-nay is the only chief who sores amongst the whites. We three remain here and can always be found."

Atcheson concluded his report to Commissioner Ely Parker by saying, "The Mille Lacs appear to be very much attached to what they believe to be their country and doubtless could not be persuaded to remove voluntarily without heavy expense to the Government and possibly without resorting to compulsion in a few instances."[6]

About a year later (March 1871) Edw. P. Smith, U.S. Agent at St. Paul, reported to Commissioner Ely Parker regarding trouble between the Mille Lacs Indians and the settlers in Becker and Isanti Counties. He recounted that, "the marauding complained of in Isanti County is done by them. They are yet living according to treaty stipulation upon the reservation, which they ceded to the government on the condition that they should be permitted upon their old ground during their good behavior or the pleasure of the President. They have been ordered to remove by the Department and hitherto no provision has been made according to the treaty stipulation for their removal to White Earth. Meanwhile the settlers have crowded upon them. Their lumber is being cut, the game is driven off & they really have but little chance for life except as they take a much larger range for hunting than the lines of the Mille Lac Reservation will allow."

General Hancock had reported that he, too, found little evidence of harm caused by the Indians. He thought that the settlers were "unacquainted with the habits of the Indians," causing fear, not only for themselves but for future settlement of the county.

In response to appeals by the settlers, Governor Austin had authorized the organization of a county militia and had issued arms "with instructions and authority to prevent Indians from coming among the settlements." Agent Smith was fearful of bloodshed and advised the Governor that United States forces could more easily calm the situation without the fear of bloodshed. Agent Smith was able to exact a promise from General Howard of "troops to be sent into the county if it was found that they were needed to keep the peace." Governor Austin acquiesced to Agent Smith's plan but kept the door open for use of the county militia if the U.S. troops were not "at hand when needed." Agent Smith concluded his report by saying, "I would respectfully suggest the expediency of giving them [the Indians] formal notice to leave the Reservation and settle at White Earth within two years from next May."[7]

Again in May of 1871 Agent Smith reported to Commissioner Ely Parker on the "trouble between the Mille Lacs and the settlers." He said that though the reservation had been ceded to the government, it should not yet be subject to entry by settlers because the Mille Lacs had not been ordered to leave, and that according to their treaty were still entitled to all rights on the ceded reservation. He related that, in violation of those rights a man named O.E. Garretson had sent men in and cut from 2 to 3 million feet of pine logs on the ceded reservation. Agent Smith reminded the Commissioner that it was the custom of the Surveyor General's Office to collect stumpage in such cases, and that this process had begun. He then requested, "on behalf of the Mille Lacs, that whatsoever stumpage may be collected from this lumber shall be turned over to the agency for the benefit of the Mille Lacs in their removal to White Earth and establishment in homes."

"The Indians," Smith went on to say, "clearly have possessory rights on the Reservation until they shall have received formal and sufficient notice to leave. ... There is, however, a question back of this, which, I learn from the Register of the land office, has been referred to the General Land Commissioner at Washington, viz.- Whether the lands of the Mille Lacs Reservation are properly subject to entry. They have been surveyed and the plats returned to the Register, so that on the face of things there is no barrier to the taking up of all those lands by homestead or preemption." On behalf of the Mille Lacs Agent Smith requested, "that their lands be not thrown open to entry, of any kind, so long as they remain, and that they be permitted to receive, as compensation for the timber cut unlawfully upon their reservation, whatever stumpage may be awarded by the Surveyor." He went on to say, again on behalf of the Mille Lacs, "that, up to this time, there has been no adequate provision made for their removal or beginning to live at White Earth ... under the terms of the treaty."

Concluding his report Smith said that, until suitable appropriation can be made for the Indians to be removed to White Earth, he respectfully requested on behalf of the Mille Lacs that "their lands be not open to settlement by any process whatever."[8]

In a letter to Secretary Delano a couple of weeks later Bishop George Whipple added his opinion to the report made by Agent Smith. "It seems to me that two things should be done in their [the Mille Lacs] behalf. 1st. They should receive the formal notice to leave, which their treaty seems to require, and should be furnished with the means of removing and of beginning to live at White Earth, but 2. As this cannot be done this year, there being no adequate appropriation, they should be protected in their rights at Mille Lac until sufficient notice has been given and the means provided for them to go to White Earth. If their lands are opened to settlement by a decision of the Land Commissioner, they will be reduced to a pitiable condition. If their lands can be held as they are for two years more and Congress will appropriate funds for their removal next year, notice being given to them at once to that effect, it will afford an easy solution of the difficulty.

"The other course of not removing them, and bringing settlers upon their lands they now hold, will be so apparently unjust as to bring bad feeling and hinder the work of bringing Indians to live in a civilized way. They will say if that is civilization we like the Indian way better."[9]

In July of 1871, Indian Agent Smith visited the Land Office in Taylors Falls on business and reported his findings to the attention of Commissioner of Indian Affairs Ely Parker and Secretary of the Interior Delano. He informed them that, "The Indians [still have] treaty possessory rights, in that Reservation, never having been notified to leave, and no adequate provision for their removal having been made. But I find that their whole reservation has been covered since April 5th with scrip and preemptive claims filed in the Taylors Falls Office. I also find that there has been no order from the Gen. Land Office making this reservation subject to entry, but that these entries have been filed under color of law as follows; - The late Surveyor General for Minnesota ordered the survey of this Reservation last year under his discretionary power of surveying lands between certain parallels.

"When the surveyor's bill for services was allowed at the Department it was considered an authorization of the survey. The plat was then filed in the land office at Taylors Falls and that is considered authority to open these lands for public entry.

"In this way, without permission of any sort from the Department, settlers and lumber men are taking possession of this Indian reserve. The consequence is a double wrong. (1) The Indians are dispossessed without being removed, and (2) an injustice is done the public in not being allowed an equal opportunity to enter these lands. The very few men who in some way had knowledge of the time when entries would be received having been ready to take the land. About one fourth of these lands are taken by scrip which will be shown to be largely fraudulent. The other entries are under preemptive claims for lumbering purposes and preparations are making for extensive lumbering next winter.

"In the name of these Indians I respectfully ask that all these entries may be cancelled as without authority of law. And that I may be authorized to protect the Reservation from any encroachment until the Indians are removed."[10]

Willis Drummond — by Louis Weisner

One can then assume that, as a result of this discovery, the Register and Receiver at Taylors Falls received a letter from Commissioner Willis Drummond of the General Land Office in Washington, that read in part, "You are now informed that these lands are still occupied by the Indians and are not subject to disposal, and you are requested to give public notice by advertisement in a newspaper of general circulation in that neighborhood of the above fact and also that all settlements and entries thereon are illegal and will not be recognized by this office. You are also requested to transmit an abstract of all filings or locations you may have allowed for said lands and report why you permitted the same." In a post script to the letter the Commissioner added, "You will allow no entries on these lands until so ordered by this office –"[11]

On the same day—September 1— that Commissioner Drummond ordered all filings on the ceded reservation to be illegal, Agent Smith wrote Commissioner of Indian Affairs H.R. Clum (apparently acting in that capacity as a result of Ely Parker's resignation) informing him that several parties had hired men to stay on the reservation and within a few days would be ready to prove up their claims and receive duplicates, "and then will be settlers in possession and it will be much more difficult to dislodge them." He suggests a telegram to the Taylors Falls Office forbidding them to issue duplicates. Smith continued, "I furthermore respectfully regret that the U.S. District Attorney at St Paul be instructed to prosecute any parties found trespassing on the Mille Lacs Reservation."[12]

Ten days later U.S. Attorney General Akerman wrote to acting Secretary of the Interior B. R. Cowen as follows: "I have received your letter of the 8th instant, requesting that the District Attorney of Minnesota be directed to prosecute any persons who may be found trespassing upon the Mille Lac Reservation, and have the honor to inform you that the District Attorney of Minnesota has been directed to prosecute accordingly."[13]

On September 21, 1871, acting Commissioner of the General Land Office in Washington informed the Commissioner of Indian Affairs that, "Certain tracts in T43N, R27W, lying within the limits of the Mille Lac Reservation were patented to the State of Minnesota as swamp lands May 13, 1871. The Governor of said State has this day been requested to execute a relinquishment of the State's claim to said lands."[14] Then on September 24th Governor Austin informed the General Land Office that he had referred the matter to the Minnesota Attorney General for his opinion as to whether the State is not entitled to Swamp Lands on the so called Mille Lac Reservation.[15]

Indian Agent Smith, in mid-November 1871, reported to the Secretary of the Interior through acting Commissioner of Indian Affairs Clum that a number of settlers on the Mille Lacs Reservation had retained Ira H. Pierce as their attorney. They were claiming that they had gone upon the reservation in good faith for the purpose of making homes and had now been compelled to leave their homes and crops and were now waiting outside the lines of the reservation, some of them in poverty and suffering. Agent Smith stated that he had called a council of the Mille Lacs Indians, with Mr. Pierce in attendance, and told them of the condition of these settlers and explained to them the mistake that had allowed settlement upon their lands. During that council Smith had asked the Mille Lacs if they would relinquish their right of occupancy in one township for these settlers. Smith said that the Indians doubted the facts, declaring that the so-called settlers had only come to cut timber and put up a few shanties—which could not be intended for homes. The Indians had told Smith that they had not seen any families on the reservation but if, on examination, they found "settlers had come on by mistake and were suffering in being driven off, they would consent to relinquish their right of occupancy to one township, provided it did not in any way necessitate their removal from the Reservation. In those conditions they were willing to leave the adjustment of the case with me." (Emphasis in original)

Reporting that he was unable to determine the facts without going on the reservation, Agent Smith made a tour of inspection accompanied by J.F. Stock, a special agent sent by Commissioner Drummond. The two spoke with traders and lumbermen in the vicinity, visited some fifteen claims on the reservation and examined the improvements that had been made. They concluded that (1) "A large part of the three fractional townships that constitute the Mille Lacs Reserve, has been entered either by Chippewa half-breed Scrip or pre-emption claims. (2) In all cases the claims selected are upon the pine lands in preference to the hardwood lands which are better adapted to agriculture. (3) Nearly all the half-breed scrip, by reference to the report lately made by the Commissioner, will be found to have been fraudulently obtained," and "(4) the entries by pre-emption have been largely made by parties who were employed and paid by the day, and sent up in gangs of from 6 to 35 men to make improvements, prove up at the Land Office, and then transfer their titles to their employers."

Agent Smith came to the conclusion "that the entries on the reserve have been made for the purpose of securing the pine timber and not for making actual settlements. I therefore respectfully request that no trespassing be permitted upon this reservation, and that the entries already allowed at Taylor Falls Land Office be cancelled."[16]

Five years later, in 1876, the Surveyor General in St. Paul, J.H. Baker, inquired of the General Land Office in Washington whether some 300,000 feet of timber cut on what is known as the Mille Lacs Reservation was government land held as a reservation or State land held as school land. Baker declared, "I am unable ... to find from any record in this office, that they are to be considered as other than ceded lands, and subject to the same jurisdiction as other public lands."[17] The reply received stated that the lands in question were still under the jurisdiction of the Commissioner of Indian Affairs and the cutting of timber should be considered trespass.[18]

On January 27, 1877, Zachariah Chandler, Secretary of the Interior, wrote a short, to the point letter to John Q. Smith, Commissioner of Indian Affairs. "Sir: I have the honor to request that you inform me why the tract of land heretofore known as the 'Mille Lac Indian Reservation' in the State of Minnesota, and ceded to the United States by the treaty of March 3rd, 1863 is still held as an Indian Reservation."[19]

Three days before the new President, Rutherford B. Hayes, was inaugurated, Secretary of the Interior Zachariah Chandler, in opining on an appeal of Frank W. Folsom's preemptive filing and entry, made the following decision. He stated that the decision to deny Folsom's entry was made by the Commissioner of the General Land Office, "based on the ground that the tracts were within the Mille Lac Indian Reservation." He went on to recount the details of the 1863 and 1864 treaties and then stated, "[T]he sums of money required by said treaty have been appropriated by Congrefs [sic] from time to time, and a full compliance with its terms have been made or tendered by the United States. A part of said band has been removed to White Earth Reservation, and a part still remains at Mille Lac, although they have been repeatedly solicited to remove, and ample preparations were long since made on the former reservation for their permanent location thereon. All of the conditions of said treaties having been complied with by the United States, the titles of said lands now rests absolutely in the United States. In your communication of the 30th ultimo, you state that 'the reason said lands have been suspended from sale or other disposition is that, on the 22nd of August 1871, a request was made by the Indian Office that no part of said reservation be considered as subject to entry or sale as public lands until notification by the General Land Office that the lands comprising the reservation were no longer needed for Indian purposes.'

"This request of the Indian Office, from the communication of the Commissioner of Indian Affairs of the 29th ultimo, appears to have been made upon a construction given to the proviso to the 12th Article of the treaty aforesaid: 'That owing to the heretofore good conduct of the Mille Lac Indians, they shall not be compelled to remove, so long as they shall not in any way interfere with, or in any manner molest the persons or property of the whites.'

"Under this proviso, it is true that, so long as said Indians do not interfere with the persons or property of the whites, they cannot be compelled to remove; but it by no means gives them an exclusive right to the lands, nor does it, in my judgment, exclude said lands from sale and disposal by the United States.

"It was anticipated that these lands would be settled upon by white persons, that they would take with them their property and effects, and it was provided that as long as the Indians did not interfere with white persons, they might remain, not because they had any right to the land, but simply as a matter of favor.

"But in view of the fact that there is now a part of said band of Indians upon said tract of lands, and also that there is no appropriation available for their immediate removal to the White Earth Reservation, you are hereby instructed to suspend the execution of this decision, and to direct the local officers to allow no filings or entries upon any of said lands included in the Mille Lac Reservation until the close of the next regular session of Congrefs [sic], unless said Indians shall voluntarily remove therefrom prior to that date, and I further direct that, in the meantime, all existing claims on any of said lands, if any there be, remain in status quo."[20] (Emphasis in original)

The 1870's ended and Rutherford B. Hayes became the President with the status of the ceded Mille Lacs Reservation still in question. With the meaning of Article 12 still in limbo and political corruption still rampant in the Indian system, the decade ended.

CHAPTER 15

The 1880s

During the 1880's the United States had five different presidents; Hayes, Garfield, Arthur, Cleveland and Harrison. The decade opened with President Rutherford B. Hayes in office. The 19th President and a Republican, Hayes was inaugurated March 4, 1877 and served until March 4, 1881. President Hayes believed in assimilation and ignoring the impeding racial barriers, appointing Carl Schurz, who supported those views, as Secretary of the Interior. The Hayes administration was committed to bettering the treatment of Indians and thought that could best be accomplished by breaking up Indian reservations into individually owned plots—likely the forerunner of the Dawes Act—and dissolving tribal governments, which were thought to hamper assimilation.

Apparently, however, Hayes did not object to reservations, perhaps because reservations gave tribes—who were being stressed—their own place to live. In any event Hayes created several reservations by executive order during his presidency, all located in the southwest: Arizona, Nevada, California and New Mexico. Secretary of the Interior Schurz made significant gains in eliminating—or at least decreasing—the fraud which was rampant in the Indian Bureau.

In January of 1880, some of the Mille Lacs chiefs asked Joseph Roberts of St. Paul to write to Secretary Schurz on their behalf, request permission to come to Washington, D.C. Roberts wrote, "They claim that efforts have been made to defraud them out of their lands; that they have been and are being robbed of their pine timber; that they are misrepresented — that their reservation rights are disregarded, etc."[1] The treaties of 1863 and 1864 were obviously being disregarded.

Apparently the request for a meeting in Washington, D.C. did not occur because on March 22, 1880 seven Mille Lacs chiefs and one brave again appealed to Washington, this time directly to President Hayes. They apologized for not going through channels but said their agent would not listen to them and they feared he was working against them. They asked for the President's help "so that we shall not be driven from our homes without having done any rong [sic] to our white neighbors."

The Indians reminded the President that "the great and good men with him who ruled this great nation made us a promise that we should inherit our home on beautiful and to us lovely Mille Lac forever ..." adding that false charges of wrongdoing were being made against them and asking for an investigation. If the charges proved true, they said, they would take their punishment, but if not, "we shall ask for a new treaty or that the one we now have be made more definite and perfect ..." Once again asking for a meeting in Washington, D.C., the Indians added that, if it be denied, at least they requested that attention be paid to their grievances.[2]

Citizens in Morrison County were also getting involved. In March of 1880 a committee of three, appointed at a meeting of citizens of Morrison County, drafted a petition that was subsequently circulated among Morrison County citizens. The cover letter on the petition was on a Little Falls trader's letterhead: "Leon Houde, dealer in General Merchandise, Little Falls, Minn. — Specialties: Hides, Furs & Venison." The first three signatures on the petition are those of N. Richardson, Leon Houde and J. Simmons —the three who made up the appointed committee. The petition recounted how the Mille Lac Indians thwarted Hole-in-the-Day's war plans and probably saved their lives and possessions. The petition went on to explain that the charges of wrongdoing against the Mille Lac Indians were instigated by what were called "pine thieves" and were unfounded. The plea further suggested that, if efforts to remove them continued it would likely lead to violence. Therefore, the petition stated, "in behalf of said Indians and the people living in the surrounding country that the proper authorities take immediate steps to secure to said Indians their reservation and home at Mille Lac."

The petition was signed by eighty four persons and delivered to Secretary of the Interior Carl Schurz. The Morrison County residents were obviously thankful that the Mille Lacs had stopped Hole-in-the-Day and one must also wonder if the traders were fearful of losing their lucrative customers if the Mille Lacs were removed.[3]

President James A. Garfield, the 20th President of the United States, was inaugurated on March 4, 1881. Garfield became the Republican candidate for President at the 1880 Republican convention as a compromise candidate when the nomination became deadlocked. President Garfield appointed Samuel J. Kirkwood of Iowa as his Secretary of the Interior and Hiram Price, also from Iowa, as his Commissioner of Indian Affairs.

In office for just over six months, Garfield was shot by a disgruntled office seeker named Charles Guiteau. It was effortless for Guiteau to walk up to Garfield at the train station and shoot him twice since—even following Abraham Lincoln's assassination— the government had not seen the need for providing protection for the President. Although initially surviving the gunshot wounds, Garfield died from infection, likely due to attempts to remove the bullet with ungloved fingers and possibly contaminated instruments; sterility had not yet been embraced by all medical practitioners.

Meanwhile, Article 12 was still haunting Mille Lacs County. In 1871, Commissioner Drummond had ordered all entries on the Mille Lacs Reservation cancelled. Instead of dealing with the meaning of Article 12, it is obvious that pressure was continuing to try to convince the Mille Lacs Indians to remove.

So it was on December 30, 1881, to Commissioner of Indian Affairs Hiram Price, the Garfield appointee, that Commissioner McFarland of the General Land Office in Washington made his report concerning entries appearing on his office records for lands within the Mille Lacs Reservation. Commissioner Drummond had directed that all entries be cancelled and the General Land Office had apparently been asked by Commissioner Price to furnish him a list of entries on the books. McFarland's report shows the following:

- 155 acres as a cash entry by Frank W. Folsom — SE4 NW4 and Lots 1,2 & 3 of Sec. 6, T43,R27

- 665 acres by reason of the Treaty of 1864 to Shaw-bosh-Kung — Fractional Sec. 16, 21 & 22, Lots 1 & 2, Sec 27, N2 NE4 & N2 NW4 of Sec. 28, T43, R27

- 154 acres homesteaded by Shar-Vash-King — SW4 NW4 & Lot 5, Sec. 27, SE4 NE & Lot 1, Sec. 28, T43, R27 under consideration

- 701 acres claimed by the State of Minnesota as swamp land — Lot 7, Sec. 18 and SE4 NE4 Sec. 20. T43, R27

- Acreage patented to State of Minnesota under swamp land acts — Lots 2 & 3, Sec. 18; Lot 4, Sec. 21; NE4 NW4, SW4 SW4 and Lot 4 and SE4 SE4 Sec. 32 and NW4 NW4, Sec 33, T43, R27

All other entries had been cancelled.[4]

By this time, Chester A. Arthur, vice-president under Garfield, had assumed the presidency and with him came a renewed emphasis on dealing with "the Indian problem." In a speech reportedly delivered to Congress—in 1884 by one source and 1881 from another, and incomplete from both sources—we get some idea of Arthur's thoughts on solving the Indian issue. It could be that the documents this author located were simply an unfinished draft; at any rate they give us an insight into the opinions of President Arthur.

Arthur says in this document, "First, I recommend the passage of an act making the laws of various states and territories applicable to Indian reservations within their borders ... the Indian should receive the protection of the law. He should be allowed to maintain in court the rights of person and property ... Second, permitting the allotment in severalty to Indians of a reasonable quantity of land secured to them by patent, and for their own protection made inalienable for twenty or twenty five years."

His belief was that this would persuade Indians to sever tribal relations and take up farming. And third, pass appropriation to fund Indian schools.

While the Dawes Act did not come into existence until 1887 under President Grover Cleveland, President Arthur was obviously leaning in that direction.

On April 5, 1882, Secretary of the Interior Kirkwood wrote to Commissioner of Indian Affairs Price with a request for "such history of the Mille Lacs Indian Reservation ... as shall give its present status and the condition of the Indians thereon, their rights in said lands, and also your views as to the disposal of said lands, with a citation of any pending legislation now under consideration in your office in relation thereto."[5] Apparently this letter was sent less than two weeks before Henry Teller replaced Kirkwood as Secretary of the Interior.

The answer to Secretary Kirkwood's request, written to his successor Secretary Teller, is dated April 26, 1883—more than a year after the initial request—so one wonders if it could actually have been 1882 instead of 1883. Then again, perhaps not since his reply is exhaustive. Commissioner of Indian Affairs Hiram Price's historical reply is reprinted here:

> Sir:
>
> In reply to letter of your predecessor of the 5th instant, calling for such history of the Mille Lac Indian Reservation, in the State of Minnesota, as shall give its present status and the condition of the Indians thereon, their rights in the lands embraced therein, as also the views of this office as to the disposal of said lands, and a citation of any pending legislation now under consideration regarding the same, I have the honor to submit the following statement of facts, with my views and recommendations thereon, which it is respectfully suggested may be considered also as a reply to Department reference of a "Statement of Mille Lac entries", March 7, 1882, herewith returned.
>
> The Mille Lac Indian Reservation in Minnesota was created by treaty concluded February 22, 1855, (Stats. 10. 1165). It embraces three fractional townships and three small islands in the southern part of Mille Lac Lake. It was set apart for the <u>permanent home</u> of the Mille Lac Chippewas, and to that end allotments in severalty and patents were expressly provided for in said treaty. (Art. 11). However, on March 11, 1863, by another treaty with the various bands of Chippewas (including the Mille Lac) said reservation, with five others established under the provisions of the first mentioned treaty was ceded by the Indians to the United States (Stats. 12. P. 1249).
>
> In consideration of the above cessions, the United States agreed, among other things, to set apart, and did set apart for the future homes of the Chippewas of the Mississippi other lands described in said treaty:

to extend the annuities of said bands ten years beyond the periods mentioned in existing treaties; to pay certain sums of money for certain purposes therein mentioned; to clean, stump, break and grub, upon the reservation set apart for said Chippewas a certain number of acres for each of said bands; to build houses for their chiefs, and to furnish them with teams and farming utensils etc. for the period of ten years.

By the terms of said treaty it is expressly provided (in the XII Article), that "It shall not be obligatory upon the Indians, parties to this treaty, to remove from their present reservations until the United States shall have first complied with the stipulation of Article IV and VI of this treaty, where the United States shall furnish them with all necessary transportation and subsistence to their new homes, and subsistence for six months thereafter; provided that owing to the heretofore good conduct of the <u>Mille Lac Indians, they shall not be compelled to remove so long as they shall not in any way interfere with or in any manner molest the persons or property of the Whites.</u>"

[The stipulations of Articles IV and VI referred to above, relate to clearing lands, building houses for chiefs, and removing the sawmill from Gull Lake Reservation].

On May 7, 1864, still another treaty was entered into, (Stats. 13.P. 695) by which in consideration of the cession aforesaid other and additional lands were set apart for these bands of Chippewas, and the sums of money to be expended by the United States for the objects therein mentioned, were <u>particularly stated.</u>

It must be admitted that the obligations of the United States have been fulfilled as regards the <u>treaty aforesaid. The money required has been appropriated and a full compliance with the terms</u> of the treaty has been made or tendered by the government.

But as regards the Mille Lac band, the question arises — Have they forfeited their right of occupancy as guaranteed them by the XII Article of said treaty?

<u>Interference in any way with, or molestation</u> in any manner of the <u>persons or property of the whites,</u> would it is presumed constitute a forfeiture of such right.

The precise language of the article has just been stated. By its terms the Indians of the several ceded reservations were not to be obliged to remove from reservations then occupied by them <u>"until"</u> certain conditions, as set out in articles 4 and 5 had been complied with on the part of the government, <u>"when"</u> it was agreed the United States would furnish them the means of transportation and subsistence to their new homes. But it was provided, in the case of those with whom we are more especially concerned, that owing to the heretofore good conduct of the *Mille Lac Indians, they* shall not be compelled to remove so long as they shall not in any way interfere with, or in any manner molest the persons or property of the whites. Here was a special provision in the nature of and intended as a separate and additional immunity or franchise, conferred evidently for some signal good conduct on the part of this particular band of the Chippewas — the Mille Lacs. The other bands were to remove as soon as the government had fulfilled certain promises, (analogous to the case of a merchant who agrees to deliver merchandise *when paid for*).

They had ceded *their lands* for a valuable consideration and agreed to vacate upon compliance with the terms of cession. So the Mille Lacs had ceded the title to their lands, but their removal therefrom was not required as in the case of others, but was made dependent upon their continued good conduct.

At the time of the outbreak of the Chippewas in 1862, under the famous Hole-in-the-Day, resulting from the efforts of Southern cession agents operating through Canadian Indians and fur-traders, when the devastation of the whole country there was threatened, and the massacre of the entire population the Mille Lac bands being urged to join Hole-in-the-Day, *positively refused*, and not only remained loyal to the Government but assisted so far as they found it within their power, to prevent a general Indian war. This it is understood was the "good conduct" for which they were to be remembered. Not only were they to receive their share of the pecuniary and other common benefits, but "so long as they shall not in any way interfere with or in any manner molest the persons or property of the whites" they were not to be compelled to remove from their reservation.

The questions that naturally arise are: "Who were the whites to whom reference was intended", and What would constitute interference with or molestation of the persons or property of the whites?"

Manifestly, I think, reference was intended to the white settlers occupying the surrounding country, their neighbors especially, for there could have been no whites lawfully living upon the reservation at that time, and it was hardly intended in anticipation of the entry and settlement of whites upon the reservation and with a view to the protection; for the Indians being in occupation, the introduction of whites would be quite impossible. The Indians were there, and until they were removed either by their own consent or by reason of the forfeiture of their right of occupancy, the whites manifestly must keep out.

It does not matter that the lands embraced within the reservation were surveyed and plat filed with the local land office, as in the case of other public lands;- the rights of the Indians could not be affected thereby. (The public surveys were extended over the Mille Lac Reservation — Town 43 N. Range 27 W in 1870), and in this connection I will state that as soon as it became known, through their agent, that such surveys had been completed, this office, seeing the impropriety of permitting white settlers to go upon the reservation while the Indians were still in occupation, at once addressed a communication to the Department (August 22, 1871), requesting that no part of said reservation should be considered as subject to entry or sale as public lands and that the local land officers for the district embracing said reserve, be notified accordingly. Whereupon (Sept. 1, 1871) the General Land Office instructed the local land officers at Taylor's Falls, Minn. to give public notice that settlements on the Mille Lac Reservation were illegal and would not be recognized, and on Sept. 11th, immediately following request having been made to that end, the Honorable Attorney General informed the Department that he had instructed the U.S. District Attorney to prosecute trespassers on the Mille Lac Reservation. Furthermore on September 21st following, the General Land Office preferred a request to the Governor of Minnesota to execute a relinquishment of the State's claim to certain tracts lying within the reservation that had been patented to the State as swamp lands on the 13th of May previous (1871). I am informally advised by the General Land Office that the relinquishment asked for has not, however, been obtained.

Settlers were at once moved off the reservation by Agent Smith, who made report to this Bureau under date of November 13th, 1871, as follows, "Upon the representation of Ira H. Pierce, Attorney for a certain number of these settlers, that a large number of these settlers had gone upon the reservation in good faith for the purpose of making homes, and that by notice of warning they had been compelled to leave their homes and crops, and were now waiting outside the lines of the reserve (some of these in poverty and suffering), I was induced to call a council of the Mille Lac Indians at which, Mr. Pierce being present, I told them the condition of the settlers and explained to them as well as I could, the mistake under which settlements had been allowed upon their lands, and asked that they would relinquish to their Great Father the right of occupancy in <u>one township</u> for these settlers. The Indians doubted the facts, that any such settlers were or had been on the reservation. They said that parties had only <u>come to cut timber</u> and put up a few log shanties, which <u>could not be intended for homes</u>; that they had not seen any families upon the reservation, but on examination if I found settlers had come on by mistake, and were suffering by being driven off they would consent to relinquish their right of occupancy to <u>one</u> township, <u>provided it did not in any way necessitate their removal from the reservation.</u> On these conditions they were willing to leave the adjustment of the case with me.

On my return to St Paul I found it impossible to determine the exact state of the case without going upon the reservation, and have just returned from a tour of inspection in company with J.F. Stock, Special Agent, sent by Commissioner Drummond, to investigate the facts of the Mille Lac Reservation.

We made diligent inquiry of all parties on the way and of the Indians and lumbermen in the vicinity, and visited some fifteen claims upon the reserve and examined the improvements made. Our observation led to the following conclusion as to the facts in the case:

1st, A large part of the three fractional townships that constitute the Mille Lac reserve, has been entered either by half breed scrip or pre-emption claimed.

2nd. In all cases the claims selected are upon the <u>pine lands</u> in preference to the hardwood lands which are better adapted to agriculture.

3rd, Nearly all the half-breed scrip, by reference to the report lately by the Commissioner will be found to have been fraudulently obtained.

4th, The entries by pre-emption <u>have been largely made by parties who were employed and paid by the day and sent up in gangs of from 6 to 35 men to make improvements, prove up</u> at the Land Office, and then <u>transfer</u> their titles to their employers.

Mr. Stock has reported specifically upon some of these facts, giving dates and names and numbers of the parties thus employed, and also giving descriptions of the actual improvements found upon a large number of claims verified by the affidavits of three citizens of Princeton.

I respectfully refer to the statement and affidavits of that report as furnishing the basis, together with my personal observations, for the decision which I have reached, viz: that the entries on the reserve have been made for the purpose of securing the pine timber and not for making actual settlement. I therefore respectfully request that no trespassing be permitted upon the reservation, and that the entries already allowed at Taylor's Falls be cancelled."

In returning to the consideration of the questions — who were "the whites" to whom reference was intended in the 12th Article, and what would constitute _interference_ with or _molestation_ of their persons or property:-

If it is conceded that the white settlers occupying the country surrounding or adjacent to the reservation were the object of the intended protection (which is clear in my mind), then it would certainly be unnecessary to discuss the question as to what would constitute interference with or molestation of the persons or property of such. If on the other hand, it be denied and contended, as it is by some, that the word "whites" was employed in anticipation of the speedy settlement of whites upon these lands, who would bring with them property and effects, and with a view to the protection of such persons in their persons and property, then it is important to know what was meant by the language "any way interfere with, or in any manner molest the persons or property" (of whites).

For the sake of argument let us suppose that the language of the proviso was intended to apply to settlers coming upon the reservation. Then the Indians, if they would not work a forfeiture of their right of occupancy, must not _interfere_ with or _molest_ either the _persons_ or _property_ of such. Surely nothing more. It does not provide that they shall make way for, or vacate or abandon any improvements or shelter they have, or land to these people. It is only required that they shall not _interfere with_ or _molest_ either their _persons_ or _property._ These words (interfere and molest) when employed in such connection, in respect of the conduct or action of _Indians_, are, I think, to be interpreted in their _worst sense_. And when it is remembered that only a few months before the treaty was made, the whole country there had been thrown into a state of the greatest alarm on account of the uprising of the Indians of that section, it is clear in my mind that the framers of the treaty intended that they should be interpreted in no other way.

In examining the evidence we have as showing what the conduct of these Indians has been during the past ten or twelve years, we shall see not only that their agents and the citizens of the neighboring country as well, claimed for the Indians the right of occupancy during good behavior, but that the people residing in the section of the country contiguous to the reservation (presumably as much interested in getting rid of the Indians as any body) acknowledged and believed that nothing short of interference with or molestation of the persons or property of themselves or others outside the limits of the reservation, would constitute a rightful forfeiture of such right.

Let us look at the evidence we have in the premises:

In his annual report for 1870, Lieut. Geo. Atcheson, of the Army, says: "In the month of February last, certain accusations were made against the Mille Lac band of Chippewa by white settlers, residing contiguous to the ceded reservation upon which this band is yet allowed to remain: Complaints alleging their roving propensities, drunkenness, and general misconduct, detrimental to themselves and annoying to the whites, who, for this reason, desired their removal. In compliance with instructions from the Department I investigated the subject and found that these complaints of general misconduct were not without foundation, but in no case was evidence produced to show actual interference with or molestation of the persons or property of the whites, which alone under the treaty, would be just cause of their removal.

In accordance with this showing I made report to the Department." *(An examination of the report shows it to be of above tenor.)*

Agent, afterwards Commissioner of Indian Affairs, E.P. Smith, in his annual report for 1871, being then in charge of the Chippewa Agency, says "The Mille Lac bands of Mississippi Chippewas still reside on their original reservation, the title to which they ceded in 1863, reserving the right of occupancy during good conduct toward the whites. There have been from time to time individual complaints made against them for trespassing in the adjoining country. For the most part this trespass has been a violation of the game laws of the State. Unfortunately for these Indians their reservation is rich in pine lands, which makes them prey of lumber dealers, and a strong pressure is kept up on all sides to secure their early removal": *In his report for the following year (1873) Agent Smith stated that* "of Mille Lac band of Mississippi Chippewas only about twenty five have been persuaded as yet to remove to White Earth."

In 1873, Agent Douglas being in charge of the Agency, in his annual report says: "nothing whatever is being done to improve the condition of that portion of the Mille Lac Indians still residing in the vicinity of the lake bearing that name. No class of Indians under my charge appear more manly and noble than these, and I am profoundly impressed with the moral obligation of the Government to adapt immediate measures for their education and civilization. They hold their present territory by the most feeble tenure."

The Commissioner of Indian Affairs (Hon. E.P.Smith) in his report for 1874 says: "The Mille Lacs are located around a lake of the same name on lands ceded in 1863, reserving the right of occupation during good behavior. Nothing has been done for them beyond the payment of their annuities in cash and goods which payment is in itself a source of demoralization, leading directly to indolence and intoxication. Nothing can be done for them until they are removed to White Earth, or until the fee of the Mille Lac is restored to them ... All efforts to induce them to remove to White Earth have as yet been of no avail."

Agent C.A. Ruffee, late Agent for the Chippewas, in his annual report for 1878, says: "The larger proportion of the Mississippi bands still remaining on the White Oak Point reservation and at Mille Lac are in deplorable condition and subjects of annoyance to the white people surrounding them": And in his report for the year following (1879) he says, speaking of the Mille Lacs, "Those residing at Mille Lac should be removed as speedily as possible without an infraction of existing treaties."

This brings us down to 1880. On May 26, 1880, this Office by Department reference of the 25th of same month, received a petition numerously signed by citizens of Morrison County, Minnesota, (a county bordering on the Mille Lac Reservation), commending the Mille Lac Indians in the highest terms for their uniform good conduct, and appealing for protection in their behalf, on the matter of their reservation lands. The petitioners deny that the Indians have ever committed depredations upon the whites: on the contrary they protest that they are a peaceful inoffensive people, and that the charges that have been made against them are unjust, and have been instigated by designing people who wish to secure the valuable timber with which their reservation abounds.

Of the character and standing of the petitioners I am not informed.

Thus it would appear from the above evidence, if the grounds I have taken are correct, that these people have never violated the conditions upon which their continued occupancy of the lands in question solely depends. That their position, however, since the cession of their reservation in 1863, has been a matter of concern not only to the Indians, but to this Bureau as well. The feeble tenure by which they have held their lands has been a great obstacle to their advancement, and but little has been done for their improvement. The attention of the Department and of Congress has, from time to time been called to their condition with a view to securing their removal, or in case of their remaining where they are now, such legislation as shall secure to them a proper share of the reservation in severalty. A Bill was prepared in this Office and presented to the last Congress, (S. 1630, 46th Cong. 2nd Sess.) authorizing negotiations with these Indians (as well as numerous other bands) for their removal to and consolidation with the Indians residing upon White Earth Reservation. It never, however, became a law.

To allow this condition of things to continue, is in the highest degree demoralizing to these Indians. Either they should be removed (with their consent), or lastly lands in severalty should be allotted to them where they are, at the earliest practicable moment. They have ever manifested the strongest objection to removal, and it is not known whether their free consent could be obtained to quit their old homes for the White Earth or any other reservation. Possibly a liberal reward would induce them to yield and the effort should be made. Their present reservation being rich in pine lands, is the envy of lumber men, and as long as the Indians occupy their present anomalous position with respect to these lands, the pressure for their removal will continue, and it is to be feared that the evil influences that have heretofore been brought to bear upon them to effect a forfeiture of their rights will also continue, until they are reduced to a state of utter depravity and helplessness.

In a letter to the Commissioner of the General Land Office, dated March 1, 1877, I find that the then Secretary of the Interior, (Hon. Z. Chandler), decided in the case of the appeal of Frank W. Folsom from the decision of the said Commissioner of May 27, 1876, affirming the action of the register and receiver in rejecting his D.S. dated May 1st, 1876, for the SE ¼ of NW ¼ and Lots 1,2 and 3, of Section 6, T.48, R.27. Taylor's Falls Land district, Minnesota — that the Indians occupying the reservation in question, have not an exclusive right to the lands, but that, on the contrary, they are subject to sale and disposal by the United States. He says: "Under the proviso (referring to proviso 12th art. of the Treaty of 1863), it is true that so long as said Indians do not interfere with the persons or property of the whites, they cannot be compelled to remove; but it by no means gives them an exclusive right to lands, nor does it, in my judgment, exclude said lands from sale and disposal by the United States."

"It was anticipated evidently that these lands would be settled upon by white persons, that they would take with them their property and effects, and it was provided that so long as the Indians did not interfere with such white persons or their property, they might remain, not because they had any right to the lands, but simply as a matter of favor.

In this view of the case, and I am satisfied that this is the proper construction of said proviso, said lands are now and were at the time Folsom offered to file his D.S., subject to preemption, filing and entry."

However, in view of the fact that the Indians were in occupation of the lands and that there were no funds available for their removal to the White Earth Reservation, the Secretary directed the suspension of the execution of the decision above quoted, and directed the Commissioner of the General Land Office to allow no filings or entries upon any of said lands included in the Mille Lac Reservation until the close of the next regular session of Congress (45*th* Congress) unless said Indians shall voluntarily remove therefrom prior to that date", and he further directed "that in the meantime, all existing claims on any of the said lands, if any there be, remain in status quo."

It appears that at the expiration of the limit of time placed by Secretary Chandler, Folsom's entry was allowed, and in due time patent was issued for the tract entered. The local land officers also allowed entries to the extent of over 23,000 acres, which were subsequently cancelled by direction of Secretary Schurz, of May 19, 1879.

I enclose herewith a copy of a letter from the Commissioner of the General Land Office dated December 30*th*, 1881, by which it will be seen that all additional homestead entries, locations under Chippewa treaty of May 7, 1864, and preemption entries made from time to time embraced within the Mille Lac Reservation have been cancelled save such few as there are therein indicated and described. The correspondence in respect to these entries (including Department decisions and instructions) which has been somewhat extended, has been had with the General Land Office, of which no information is afforded from the records of this Office.

However, it is understood that the status of all these entries remains unchanged since the date of the General Land Office letter above referenced.

The Indians have continued in occupation of the reservation since the cession of 1863 — nearly twenty years. The Department has seen the importance of protecting them in their right of occupancy as guaranteed to them by said treaty, and to that end has refused to allow settlements to be made in their midst. Undoubtedly it has been hoped and expected that the Indians would in time yield to the pressure for their removal and take homes upon the White Earth. Appropriations have been made from time to time (as has been stated) for their removal (Stats. Vol. 13 P. 560.-561: Vol. 15, p. 204; Vol. 17. P. 189), but only a few have been persuaded to remove. As a band they have ever manifested the strongest desire to remain where they are. It is known that the deplorable condition into which they have fallen is attributable largely to the uncertainty which has been felt, as regards the tenure by which they hold their lands.

Nothing could be done or can be done towards opening farms and establishing them in the pursuits of agricultural life so long as this uncertainty continues. The strong pressure from the outside has, no doubt, increased their opposition to removal, and it would seem that their chief ambition and effort has been simply to avoid a forfeiture of their rights by any overt act.

In conclusion I will state that it is not claimed by the Bureau that the Indians have any title or fee in the lands, nor am I prepared to say that the lands are, by the terms of the treaty, excluded from sale and disposal by the United States; but it is clear to my mind, that the government is bound to protect the Indians in the continued occupancy thereof, so long as they shall refuse to remove therefrom, unless they shall work a forfeiture of their right by reason of future misconduct.

Clearly this condition of affairs should not be allowed to continue, and steps should be taken to remedy the evil without further delay.

A Bill is now pending before Congress which provides for the removal and consolidation of the various bands of Chippewas in Minnesota, upon the White Earth Reservation. The Mille Lac Indians are included and for the purpose of the Act, their reservation is declared to belong to them, (H. R. 3862, 47th Cong. 1st Sess.)

The Bill provides, among numerous things, that any Indian, 21 years of age, having valuable improvements upon any of the reservations vacated under the Act, may under certain conditions, select 160 acres for himself and receive patent therefore. The proceeds of the sale of the several reservations, after payment of expenses of survey, appraisement, etc etc is by the terms of the Bill to be placed in the Treasury for the benefit of the Indians so removed and consolidated upon the White Earth.

It is very doubtful, however, if this Bill will become law at the present session of Congress, and as I think it important that an early adjustment of the case be had. I would respectfully suggest whether it would not be well to ask Congress (by special Bill) for authority to negotiate with these Indians for the relinquishment of their right of occupancy to the lands in question and for their removal to White Earth for a specified sum of money.

Very respectfully,
Commissioner of Indian
Affairs
Hiram Price
(Emphasis in original)

Hiram Price

Secretary Teller responded to the Commissioner's letter, saying that he was inclined to agree with the decision made by his predecessor, Zachariah Chandler, that proviso 12 of the 1863 treaty gave the Mille Lac band "the right to remain on the reservation until they should voluntarily remove therefrom." He made the point that at the time the treaty was signed, there were a large number of other Indians living on the Mille Lac reservation and they were to be removed. He went on to say, "It has been insisted that the proviso allowing the Mille Lac Indians to remain, gave them exclusive permission to occupy the entire reservation to the exclusion of white settlers. By the act of July 2, 1855, it was provided in Article 2, that the President might at any time he considered it advisable, assign to each head of a family, or singly, 80 acres of land for his or their separate use. It does not appear that this was done, and it is to be presumed that whatever portion of the Mille Lac reservation was occupied by the Mille Lac Indians at the time of the making of the treaty of 1863, was occupied in common and not held in severalty. Whatever title they had passed by this treaty to the United States; nothing remained in the Indians, but the Government saw fit to say that they need not remove therefrom until they were ready to do so. It was undoubtedly understood by the Government and the Indians that the Indians would ultimately remove therefrom to White Earth, as provided in the treaty; but they have refused so to do, and still refuse. The interests of the Indians undoubtedly require their removal; but this cannot be done by the Department except with their consent, unless the Indians by disturbing the whites have forfeited their right; this, however has been denied. No provision is made in the treaty for determining a controversy on this point and it ought not to be adjudged against the Indians except on the clearest proof."

In an effort to determine the area actually inhabited by the Mille Lac Indians, Secretary Teller sent Inspector George M. Chapman to Mille Lacs to examine the area and report his findings. Teller's report starts with a recommendation that the Mille Lac Indians be removed to White Earth. He found 6+7/8 acres cultivated, 6+3/4 acres fenced and living quarters of 7 log houses and 20 wigwams. He advocated a reservation for these Indians of 7436 acres, in two plots not adjoining. Teller reported an Indian population of 944 with 400 of them living on the Snake River, most of whom, he stated, have no fixed habitation with many scattered about the country in a radius of thirty to forty miles. The report concludes by saying, "These Indians do not cultivate the soil, but live on wild rice, fish and game. They have no teams, oxen, wagons or any farming utensils and under present management with no one to look after them, nothing can be expected but 'drunkenness, wretchedness and poverty.'"

Here it behooves the reader to recall that one of the stated motives for wanting all Chippewa to move to White Earth and Red Lake was to make it easier for the Indian agents to deal with issues, and to help the Chippewa in acclimating to a new way of life.

Apparently in response to Inspector Chapman's report, a group of Mille Lac chiefs again wrote to Washington asking to be allowed to visit. They had heard that there was a plan afoot to steal their land. In addition, they reported, white men had built a dam which was flooding their hay and damaging their rice crop. They say that they have stopped the flooding, but gave no details. Emphasizing that the Chippewa considered this their land, they state that Inspector Chapman visited their land and that they have heard that Chapman had reported that they were willing to leave their homes. Stating that they had not spoken with Chapman, the Chippewa would rather the Government kill them than have them leave their homes. They concluded by stating that for two years they had been requesting a meeting and had been refused each time, and were now asking again, adding that they only see their Indian Agent about five days a year.

Commissioner Price, too, was searching for first hand reporting on conditions at Mille Lac so that he could report to Secretary Teller. Special Agent John A. Wright had apparently been charged by Commissioner Price with the task of gathering the information asked for by Secretary Teller, and on June 27, 1883, he submitted his report.

Reporting that he visited every village on the Mille Lac reservation and nearly every scattered house not in the villages, Agent Wright stated that the Indians were very poor, with few comforts and barely anything to eat except fish caught by means of traps. They live mostly in birch-bark tepees, he said, though there are a few log houses in tolerable condition. He observed no oxen and but few ponies or plows and so their garden patches are small and poorly cultivated. Any ground that is broken is done with a shovel and spade. Wright stated, "As a rule the men were lying idly around the lodges while even the labor of taking fish from the nets and bringing wood and water was imposed upon the women." The Indians, he reported, at proper seasons of the year gather wild-rice, cranberries, blue berries etc. and hunt deer, rabbits, and other animals when they can be found, but are often in want because of relying on such resources instead of making personal effort toward advancement by way of manual labor. I have failed to devise any plan by which their interests can be permanently promoted in their present location. The majority of the males, adults, are the victims of the low grade rum sellers by whom they are apparently hemmed in and as there is no check on this traffic the Indians boldly carry whiskey to their homes, sometimes in five gallon kegs.

The reserve is mostly of good quality pine, Wright reported, and the pressure is great by the whites to get access to the pine. He said no less than fifty pretended settlers are now living among the pine hoping to gain title to the lands. "The idea of people settling in the woods," he said, "with the intention of making homes by agriculture or by any other means is simply absurd."

"The Indians are well aware of the hollow pretense of these people and are greatly irritated by their presence, claiming to a man that their reserve was ceded to the government by the deception of the interpreters who were present when the treaty of 1863 was made, that under no circumstances, would their chiefs have signed the treaty had they known its purport. I have not overdrawn the picture and the remark made by Bishop Whipple of the Protestant Episcopal Church in conversation today that this state of affairs is comparable to a magazine and a lighted match in close proximity, is but too true. Drunken Indians looking at these matters from such a standpoint are liable to do desperate deeds. I was told by D.H. Robbins, a surveyor, whom I found on an island in the lake, that the Indians had ordered some of these settlers off the reserve and that through fear of their lives they had obeyed the mandates of the Indians. Mr. Robbins is engaged in exploring the pine lands on the reserve in the interest of capitalists at Minneapolis and elsewhere, and I do not believe he would falsely make such a representation for the reason that it has a tendency to work to the detriment of his employers. These white persons appear to have entered on these lands within the past few months and have removed from their homes into the woods since the close of last winter. Nah-gua-na-be', a chief whose face was bloated with whiskey, deliberately asked me what the Indians should do with these settlers.

"I speak thus plainly in order to lay the true state of affairs at Mille Lac fully before you. I do not know one of these settlers and have no reason whatever to do them an injustice. It would be inconsistent with my duty to conceal facts so plainly visible.

"Of the five hundred (500) Indians accredited to Mille Lac I found not exceeding two hundred and seventy (270) on the reservation, the balance are on Snake River and in the adjacent country.

"Of these two hundred seventy (270) Indians, the best disposed, sixty seven (67) in number under chief Sha-bosh-chung live in township 43N. Range 27W and the worst element, under chiefs Nah-gus-na-be' and Mo-so-ma-na in Township No. 42N Range 26W.

"All the Indian lodges are near the shores of the lake, hence with the aid of a plat of 43-27 purchased of D.E. Garrison, a civil engineer who surveyed the reservation in 1865 and 1870; plats of Town 42, Ranges 25, 26 and 27 borrowed from other sources; a large rowboat with two pairs of oars; and information obtained from the Indians I had no difficulty in reaching the villages and separate lodges in person and am therefore enabled to speak from personal observation.

"I regret my inability to definitely locate the portions of the reserve occupied by the Indians twenty (20) years ago, when the treaty was made: none but the older Indians could give any information and their statements were so much in variance with each other that after considerable effort I concluded further attempts useless. I am sure however that the lands now occupied by them embrace two-thirds (2/3) if not three-fourths (3/4) of those occupied in 1863. (See enclosure No. 1), and the balance so far as the Indians are concerned, no particular importance is attached to them.

"The expression that 'the best interests of the Mille Lac Band demand that they be removed to White Earth' has been so often made that it is superfluous for me to repeat it, but their removal is not only the best but the only solution of the Mille Lac problem."

Following receipt of the inconclusive report from Inspector Chapman and the more thorough report from John Wright, Commissioner Price wrote to Secretary Teller with his conclusions. The Secretary had asked him to determine how much land the Mille Lacs now occupied and how much more they needed for their support, in order that the remainder of the land could be opened up to settlers. Price's conclusion was that the Mille Lacs are in deplorable condition and the only way to save them is to remove them to White Earth.[4]

At this same time Congressman Knute Nelson was getting wind that Indian Agent Luse was stealing money from the annuities. Nelson wrote to Charles N. Beaulieu in an effort to learn what was going on, and Bieulieu replied, "It may probably be best to await a week or so to give the Indian Inspector Gardner time to make his report to the Secretary of the Interior before calling the latter's attention to Indian Agent Luse's 'crookedness.'" He was afraid Gardner would try to protect Luse. Apparently Beaulieu was in possession of the testimony of two witnesses that some five persons on payrolls [at Mille Lac] were marked paid when these five persons were not even present. Beaulieu states that Gardner reportedly said he did not think Luse stole much.[5]

Knute Nelson, a Republican, was elected to Congress and served in the House of Representatives from March 4, 1883 to March 3, 1889. Choosing not to run for another term Nelson instead was elected Governor of Minnesota. He resigned during his second term as governor and was next elected to the United States Senate—in 1895—where he served until his death in 1923. While serving in Congress Nelson took an interest in the above proceedings since both the White Earth Reservation and the former Mille Lac Reservation were in his district.

In a letter to Secretary Teller dated July 21, 1883, responding to an article which appeared in the Pioneer Press Nelson wrote that he essentially agreed with the newspaper article. The article began by reporting that, "The report on the condition of the Indians on the Mille Lacs Reservation disclosed again the same old story that has been told as often as any tribes were to be found occupying land that was coveted by the settler. All that is said of the deplorable condition of the Indians and the hopelessness of remedying it as long as they remain where they are may be true, and it may be for their best interests to be transferred to White Earth. Still, the hunger of private capitalists for their pine lands is not to be omitted from a consideration of the case, and if their present reservation contained nothing more valuable than scrub oak there would be a less deep and affectionate interest in their welfare. … It is for the Department to determine whether or not the Indians should be removed to White Earth; whether a part of their reservation should be set aside for their use and the remainder thrown open to settlement, or whether things should be let as they are."[6]

Just a few days earlier Knute Nelson had written Secretary Teller regarding another newspaper article—what paper contained the article is not stated but I would presume it was a Washington paper. In his letter Nelson wrote, "I see from today's paper that the Indian Bureau are recommending and urging removal of the Mille Lac Indians to the White Earth reservation on the ground that the Mille Lac Reservation is wanted for settlement, etc. Against this removal I leave to enter my most earnest objection and protest ... aside from the pine this land is of no account for white men, but is food enough for the Indians to live on as they live mainly by hunting, berrying and fishing. The White Earth Reservation, on the other hand, contains the choicest agricultural prairie and timberland of the State and that land, if any, should be thrown open to white settlers ... Neither the Indians in the White Earth reservation nor the white people in any of the surrounding country want the Mille Lac Indians on this reservation. If there are any more lands in the White Earth reservation than are required for the Indians now on it, these lands should be devoted to white settlements, and not to shiftless, lazy, and annuity consuming Indians."[7]

This gives one a fairly candid view of the sentiment of the United States representative from Minnesota toward the Mille Lac Indians—a Congressman whose name would appear on a significant act of Congress to be passed in 1889.

Grover Cleveland, a conservative Democrat, was the President at the time that both the Dawes Act and the Nelson Act were passed and approved. The Republican Party pretty much dominated the political scene during and after the Civil War—from 1861 to 1933—but Cleveland was able to garner enough votes to become President during a Republican era. In three successive elections he received more popular votes than his opponent, but in the 1888 election Benjamin Harrison, a Republican, received more electoral votes. So while Grover Cleveland served as President for two terms, there was a four year interval between the two.

Cleveland was of the opinion that Indians were wards of the federal government. In his first inaugural address he declared, "[T]his guardianship involves, on our part, efforts for the improvement of their condition and enforcement of their rights." He pushed for passage of the Dawes Act, opining that the passage of this act would help raise the Indians out of poverty and encourage assimilation. He apparently thought the ward-ship was temporary and that the Dawes Act would eliminate it.

Henry L. Dawes was a Senator from Massachusetts from 1875 to 1893, and chairman of the Senate Indian Affairs committee. Dawes objective was to convince tribes to eliminate the communal ownership of land, abandon the system of tribal government, and become part of the United States as assimilated citizens. While they undoubtedly had not thought it out in much detail, this is—in concept—what the Chippewa had asked for thirty some years earlier when Hole-in-the-Day, as their spokesman, said to Commissioner Manypenny, "We want to cease to be Indians, and become American. We want to be citizens and have the right to vote ... All we desire is to imitate the whites ... we want to live as they do."

Ownership of property was and is the bedrock of the American Dream, and so the General Allotment Act of 1887—called the Dawes Act—was passed. As we shall see in subsequent years, Manypenny was right, regardless of his motive. The Indians had apparently not been schooled in the concept of property ownership as it was imposed upon them, but rather had increased their ownership of property at the point of a gun instead of a pencil.

The Dawes Act gave the President the authority—at his option—to allot a certain number of acres on each reservation to each head of family or single person, in severalty. The United States would own the allotments for a period of twenty five years and at that time the ownership would pass to the allottees as fee land, and the owners would become full citizens of the United States with all its privileges and responsibilities.

Minnesota Senator Knute Nelson was a member of the Senate Indian Affairs Committee that was chaired by Senator Dawes. Nelson undoubtedly knew that the Dawes Act would not work for the Mille Lac Chippewa. For over twenty years pressure had been brought to bear on the Mille Lacs to remove to White Earth, which the Mille Lac Chippewa steadfastly refused to do. And they were within their right to refuse because of Article 12 in the 1864 treaty. The basis of the Dawes Act was the allotment of reservation lands to each individual Indian, and that wouldn't work at Mille Lac because there was no reservation to allot. The reservation had been ceded to the United States in 1863-1864.

It is quite clear in the treaty of 1863—negotiated by Mille Lac chief Shaw-vosh-Kung with Secretary of the Interior Usher and Commissioner of Indian Affairs Dole—that the Mille Lac Indian Reservation (created by the Treaty of 1855) had been ceded to the government. To quote the treaty: "The reservations known as Gull Lake, Mille Lac, Sandy Lake, Rabbit Lake, Pokagomin Lake and Rice Lake, as described in the second clause of the second article of the treaty with the Chippewas of the 22d February, 1855, are hereby ceded to the United States ..." The treaty was signed by Mille Lacs chief Shaw-vosh-Kung and six other Mille Lac chiefs, in addition to many others.

Again in 1864, in the treaty negotiated by Gull Lake chief Hole-in–the-Day and Sandy Lake chief Mis-qua-dace, with Commissioner of Indian Affairs Dole and superintendent of Indian Affairs Clark Thompson, the identical language was agreed upon, ceding the same six reservations—including Mille Lac. This treaty was signed by the above named four individuals.

Thus, the Mille Lac Reservation clearly had been ceded to the government and the Mille Lac Indians clearly retained no title.

Apparently Senator Nelson was the primary proponent and author of a bill with many of the same objectives as the Dawes Act but specific to the Minnesota Chippewa and the Mille Lacs Chippewa in particular. That bill in its original form did not pass Congress in 1887. It was not until 1889, with some amendments to the original, that the act entitled "An act for the relief and civilization of the Chippewa Indians in the State of Minnesota" and known as the Nelson Act passed and was signed into law. Containing the same objectives as the Dawes Act, the two acts were to work together.

The Nelson Act provided that the President would appoint a commission to gain approval from the Chippewa Indians for the Nelson Act. (See Chapter 16) By now Republican Benjamin Harrison had been inaugurated as the 23rd president of the United States, assuming office on March 4, 1889. Even though Grover Cleveland had received more popular votes, Benjamin Harrison received more electoral votes. President Harrison believed in assimilation of the Indians and supported the Dawes Act, even though it was during the Harrison administration that the Battle of Wounded Knee—in South Dakota—occurred as the result of the Lakota Sioux's spiritual movement called the Ghost Dance.

Negotiations with the Chippewa bands for approval of the Nelson Act were not even completed but the opinions of the Commissioner of Indian Affairs, T.J. Morgan, were clearly in support of a change of direction for Indian affairs. In his annual report to the Secretary of the Interior Morgan said, in part, "…the reservation system belongs to a 'vanishing state of things' and must soon cease to exist. The logic of events demands the absorption of the Indians into our national life, not as Indians, but as American citizens. As soon as a wise conservatism will warrant it, the relations of the Indians to the Government must solely depend upon the full recognition of their individuality. Each Indian must be treated as a man, be allowed a man's rights and privileges, and be held to the performance of a man's obligations. Each Indian is entitled to his proper share of the inherited wealth of the tribe, and to the protection of the courts in his 'life, liberty, and pursuit of happiness.' He is not entitled to be supported in idleness. …"

The decade ended with the Chippewa bands having clearly approved the agreement that would set the Nelson Act in motion. During the first few days of March President Harrison signed the agreements, and by July the original Commission had been re-appointed to put the Nelson Act into action.

CHAPTER 16

Chippewa Approve the Nelson Act

In these supposedly enlightened times it may be difficult for us to understand the mindset of the settlers and their government representatives during the last quarter of the eighteen hundreds, but allow me to recount some events that may assist. Remember that the Declaration of Independence clearly states that "all Men are created equal." Perhaps we should also recall that the Chippewa supported the British in the Revolutionary War, and many fought with the British in the War of 1812 as well. However, they were not part of the peace agreements. Bear in mind, too, that the very first law George Washington signed as the first President of the United States was the Northwest Ordinance, which stated that Indians would not be deprived of their land—except by purchase—unless it was an act of war. Remember, too, that the Dredd Scott decision by the United States Supreme Court in 1857 had not only relegated black people to the status of property, with no chance of becoming citizens of the United States, but also created a state of pupilage whereby Indians could become citizens once they were civilized.

Minnesota white settlers had been slaughtered by the hundreds during 1862, mostly by the Sioux but to a smaller extent by the Chippewa. Now put yourself in the shoes of the Commissioner of Indian Affairs Dole, who had traveled to Minnesota to visit with the Chippewa regarding future treaties, only to find his life in imminent danger as the Chippewa—under the leadership of Hole-in-the-Day—approached Fort Ripley. Imagine how—and why—he might have promised Shaw vosh Kung that his people would not be forced to leave Mille Lac against their will if they could only prevent an attack on Fort Ripley.

Next we must reflect that capitalism was the economic basis of the United States, but more importantly capitalism was irregular and turbulent—often times even brutal—in those days since enforcement of law had not adequately developed to the degree that the Indians felt secure, and to some extent settlers as well. Businessmen, mainly lumbermen, were exerting constant pressure on the Chippewa at Mille Lac and throughout the area where there was pine to harvest for a handsome profit. Factor into the equation the corruption in the Indian system that, although slowly improving, still continued.

Still capitalist but with a different viewpoint were the traders, desiring to keep the Indians in their particular trading district. After all, the Indians were their customers. And then there were the missionaries who, out of doctrine, feared that the Indians were not being treated according to God's will.

The viewpoints of settlers and the Government were most likely influenced by economics, by basic commitments, by conscience and by protection of the Indians in addition to an element of racism and of fear.

Signer of both the Dawes Act and the Nelson Act, President Grover Cleveland stated in his inaugural address, "Our relations with the Indians located within our border impose upon us responsibilities we cannot escape. Humanity and consistency require us to treat them with forbearance and in our dealings with them to honestly and considerately regard their rights and interests. Every effort should be made to lead them, through the paths of civilization, to self-supporting and independent citizenship. In the meantime, as the nation's wards, they should be promptly defended against the cupidity of designing men and shielded from every influence or temptation that retards their advancement."

Massachusetts Senator Henry Dawes was the author of the Dawes Act and chairman of the Senate Indian Affairs Committee. Minnesota Senator Knute Nelson was the author of the Nelson Act and an active member of that same committee.

The primary goal of the Dawes Act of 1887—likely with honorable intentions—was to civilize the Indians by granting them individually owned land. Land ownership was the bedrock of this new nation and fulfillment of the "pursuit of happiness." Owning and farming one's own land and providing a good life for one's family was the most common way settlers had of achieving that "happiness." So it was natural to believe that, through land ownership the Government could provide a path for the Indians to achieve civilization and that same "pursuit of happiness".

In 1776 the founders of what would become the United States of America proclaimed "that all Men are created equal." However, in order to achieve that stated goal, compromise was necessary. Slavery was allowed to continue until the Civil War and Abraham Lincoln. But even President Lincoln did not wholeheartedly believe that black people and white people could live together. Bishop Whipple, a man who spent his life advocating for the Indians of Minnesota, believed in creating reservations where Indians could be kept separate from the white people. Was it fear? Was it racism? Was it an honest belief that separation was best for the Indians? Was it the basis for attempting to aid Indians in achieving civilization and the pursuit of happiness? Separate but equal?

But what about those Mille Lac Chippewa who had refused to remove to the White Earth Reservation earlier? Recall that the Mille Lac Reservation had been sold to the United States in the Treaty of 1864. Thus the Dawes Act would not work for the Mille Lac Chippewa since they had no reservation on which to allot them land.

But what, then, about Article 12 of the Treaty of 1864? Article 12 gave the Mille Lacs permission to remain as long as they behaved themselves. To not remove is obviously the right of occupancy, but occupancy of what? They had no place to occupy and the treaty was silent on what or where they were allowed to occupy. That is the question that still haunts Mille Lacs County.

In 1889 the Nelson Act, "An Act for the Relief and Civilization of the Chippewa Indians in the State of Minnesota," was passed by Congress. The Nelson Act provided that the President was to appoint a commission of three to negotiate with the Chippewa Indians of Minnesota for the complete relinquishment of all their reservations—except the White Earth and Red Lake Reservations. Each Indian was to be allotted a parcel of land on those two reservations and any excess land would be sold and opened for settlement. President Cleveland appointed Henry M. Rice, Bishop Martin Marty and Joseph B. Whiting to the Commission, but by the time they were able to assume their duties they were serving under President Benjamin Harrison.

The Nelson Act directed that a census be conducted of each tribe or band, and that the Act would have to be agreed to in writing by at least two thirds of the adult (at least eighteen years of age) male Chippewa Indians, and then must be approved by the President for the Act to take effect. Considering that women in the United States had not yet gained suffrage, it is understandable why only males were to vote.

The above named three commissioners set out on what would be a five month journey conducting negotiations with each Chippewa band, one after another, in an effort to gain approval of the Nelson Act. Remember that in 1871 the Government had ended treaty making with Indian tribes. Hence, this was an agreement, authorized by an act of Congress; a transition not completely internalized by either the commissioners or the Indians, as evidenced by the verbiage used in negotiation sessions.

What was it that the Chippewa Indians were being given an opportunity to agree to?

- That they would cede all the Chippewa reservations in the State of Minnesota to the United States, except that portion of the Red Lake and White Earth Reservations necessary for allotment to the Indians,
- that no Indian who already had an allotment in severalty would be disturbed,
- that all Chippewa Indians, except those on the Red Lake Reservation, not already living at White Earth, would remove to White Earth and be allotted lands there, except that any Indian who preferred to be allotted land where he now lived could do so,
- that allotments in severalty were to be made to each Chippewa Indian according to the provisions established by the Dawes Act of 1887,

- that the ceded reservation lands would be surveyed and be divided into forty acre plots, with each forty acre plot being classified as either pine land or agricultural land, and in case of pine land the pine would be estimated as to quantity and quality and the cash value of each plot estimated according to guidelines established,
- that an auction would be advertised widely and an auction held to dispose of the pine lands,
- that the agricultural lands after advertisement would be opened to homesteading by settlers under the provisions of the homestead law,
- that any parcel of land on any of these reservations that had on it a valid pre-emption or homestead entry would not be disturbed,
- that the funds from the sale of these ceded lands would be deposited in the United States Treasury as a fund for the benefit of all the Chippewa in Minnesota, would draw interest at five per cent per year, interest to be paid to the Chippewa yearly. At the end of fifty years the entire fund would be divided among the living Chippewa. Each year one-fourth of the interest would be devoted to schools for Chippewa Indian children. Congress however had the right to draw money from the principal fund to promote civilization and self-support amongst the Chippewa,
- that in anticipation of interest to be earned, the United States would advance $90,000 yearly as a loan until the principal fund was large enough (three million dollars) to repay the loan and be self-supporting.

First was the Red Lake Chippewa, which began with the first council on June 29 and ended with the seventh and final council on July 6, 1889. Indian Agent Shuler introduced commission chairman Rice, following which each commissioner expounded on the purpose of the Commission. They each commented on the burned and burning pine on the reservation, using this as a reason to accept the act. The commissioners explained that the land was lying useless, and that the Government's aim was to give each Indian a parcel of land and the implements needed to farm it, in addition to a house for each family. They explained that the pine would be sold before it all burned, and the proceeds from the sale put in a fund for the Chippewa. Commissioner Whiting then read the Act while interpreter Paul H. Beaulieu translated for the Chippewa. The Act was further explained at the second council, and again at a third council on July 3rd.

Chairman Rice opened this third council by gently scolding the Indians for setting the meeting time and then not showing up. Chief Ne-gaun-ah-quod next stated that he had been chosen to be the spokesman and stated that the Commission's mission there was a failure. He opined that they never sign an instrument in which they had no voice, which was an obvious reference to previous treaty negotiations. Chairman Rice countered by reminding the Chippewa that they had shared their opinion three years earlier and that those opinions had been taken into consideration by the President in constructing the Act. The Commissioner again commented on the burning pine and how it was driving all the game away, thus stressing the importance that the Indian become self-sufficient by farming their own piece of land. The Commissioner emphasized the fact that each person should be allowed to speak because each would have to make up their mind as to whether or not to sign approval of the Act. The same speaker who claimed to be the spokesman pointed out that it was whites who were burning the pine, not the Indians, and that the Indians had to get a pass from the agent to leave the reservation, yet whites were coming onto the reservation and harvesting pine and setting fires.

Commissioner Rice then voiced his surprise at the opinion of the Indians, saying that he was sure the President would not be pleased. Bishop Marty then gave a simplified version of the Act and requested that others share their views. He went on to state that the Chiefs had no right to speak for everyone, because each individual would be asked to vote. Chief May-dway-gon-on-ind avowed that he would never consent to the allotment plan, saying, "I wish to lay out a Reservation here, where we can remain with our bands forever." Bishop Marty responded that that was what the Government also wanted, so they were in agreement. After one last comment by an Indian opposing the idea of a consolidated annuity fund with all Chippewa sharing, the council was adjourned until the next day.

The fourth council met on July 4th. After brief introductory remarks Chief May-dway-gon-on-ind voiced his dislike for Senator Nelson—calling him the "Ground Squirrel"—because he felt that Nelson did not advocate for the best interests of the Chippewa. He went on to object to the consolidation of Chippewa funds into one combined fund, objecting also to the allotment plan.

Chairman Rice then gave an account of the Nelson Act. "In regard to the Act to which you refer, I will try to explain why this misunderstanding has arisen. That bill was introduced two years ago, into Congress. [At the same time as the Dawes Act?] The bill was amended in the committee and was reported and examined. It went to the Senate, and was by it, referred to the Committee upon Indian Affairs; Mr. Dawes, of whom you have heard, and who visited White Earth two years ago, was Chairman. The Senate amended the bill; it went back with those amendments to the House; the House refused to accede to some of them; the House returned it to the Senate and asked for a conference committee, and an agreement was arrived at by the joint committee, after which the House and the Senate also agreed. The bill then went to the President, and he, in connection with his cabinet, examined it; they examined it in every part, concluded that every interest you had was properly guarded, and the President approved it. I mention this, that you may see the great time taken to consider this bill, and the great care with which it was perfected. Now if the Great Council of the nation and the President would consume so much time in considering what was best for you, we think that you can devote a little time also, in investigating what they did."

Rice continued with some comments on each reservation. His comment on Mille Lac is especially relevant here: "The Mille Lac Reservation has large and valuable tracts of pine upon it, but I do not wish to say anything about that, for there is controversy, as to its termination we have no knowledge."

Bishop Marty opined that the Commissioners are friends of the Indians and are not being directed by Mr. Nelson. He continued by scolding the Red Lake Indians for not wanting to help one-another, to which the chief voiced disagreement.

The council moved on discussing their low opinion of the Pillagers; perhaps the reason they were opposed to sharing funds.

The conversation then turned to money and the bleak outlook, should the band reject the annuity plan and allotment plan proposed by the commissioners. Several comments were put forth regarding suspected fraud when dealing with the Government. Agreeing to further deliberate on these issues, the council then adjourned.

The fifth council continued in the same vein after veering off the subject at hand and at one point questioning the validity of the Commission since they served under a different President than had appointed them. The council ended with the announcement that the Commission would give the Indians one more day to deliberate and decide.

On July 6th the largest council to date convened, opening with statements from several new voices. This was followed by Chief May-dway-gon-on-ind stating that the Red Lake Chippewa were generally in favor of the agreement, with the condition that enough land be reserved and that there be no consolidation of funds. Chairman Rice then explained the consolidation plan, and discussion ensued regarding the decision on just how much land to reserve. The tone of the council had obviously changed, and the meeting was adjourned in order that details could be discussed before the afternoon session.

The afternoon session was spent initially in selecting specific areas for each chief and his followers. It was pointed out by Bishop Marty that the Act has already been voted upon by Congress—and approved—and the Indians had only to agree for the Act to take effect.

Next came the actual signing of the agreement by 247 signatory. The secretary reported, "[A] large majority of the Indians present signed." In a reconciliation report of total votes it is related that there were 386 male adult Red Lake and Pembina Chippewa, with 324 of them assenting to the agreement. That figure would include the 247 at Red Lake and 77 Pembinas who occupied one township on the White Earth Reservation.

This first series of councils at Red Lake was an apparent success for the Government and the Commission, and next to come were councils at White Earth.

The first assembly at White Earth convened on July 17; the first of nine councils ending on July 29, 1889. As before, the Commission was introduced by Agent Shuler and the Nelson Act was read and interpreted. Next Commissioner Rice explained that the Act had already been approved by Congress and signed by the President, and—contrary to treaties—all the Indians had to do was concur for the Act to be accomplished. It was explained that the provisions of the Dawes Act passed two years earlier would apply to allotments made under the Nelson Act, and thus the two acts would work together.

John H. Beaulieu expressed concern that there would not be land enough on the reservation to allot to every one entitled to an allotment, especially mentioning all the Indians at Mille Lac and White Oak Point.

A good deal of time was spent, especially by Chief White Cloud, emphasizing that the Government was not living up to its' previous agreements, and not paying debts owed them and desperately needed. White Cloud said they had not received the previously approved compensation for damages due to flooding of their reservation and rice fields by construction of a dam, nor had they received stumpage due them from timber harvested. He stated that they were hesitant to make further agreements with the Government because the Government did not keep its promises.

Joseph Charette said, "We think we should come to an understanding about this old debt before entering upon any new and complicated arrangement." The Commissioners responded by saying they had no authority to deal with past debts but were instructed to listen and forward any concerns to Washington, which they would do. Bishop Marty explained it this way, "[T]he reason, payments are delayed, is that it is said in Congress that the money sent here does not do any good ... Congress is waiting for evidence that you are able and willing to make good use of it, which evidence you can furnish by carrying out the provisions of this Act." The chiefs countered saying that they needed money to get their farming operations going, followed by Bishop Marty advising that they not turn down new money because they have not received old money. Bishop Marty also commented that the Indians would no longer be wards of the Government after the Nelson Act was enacted. Charette commented that he wasn't sure they were ready for citizenship, and especially for the white man's law. He continued voicing dislike for the pooling of Chippewa money.

Commissioner Whiting made the point that this Act was probably the last chance for the Indians to be saved from the unscrupulous whites, saying he envisioned an independent and prosperous Indian community under the Nelson Act.

The White Earth chiefs had employed two well educated men, John H. Beaulieu and Gustav H. Beaulieu, to act as a committee to study the provisions of the Act and then advise them. Gustav Beaulieu questioned whether the Gull Lake Indians would be covered under this Act. Commissioner Rice responded saying, "[T]he Indians who come within the purview of this Act and to whom the proposed negotiations are to be extended are those of the following reservations: White Earth; Red Lake; Leech

Lake; Cass Lake; Lake Winnebagoshish; White Oak Point; Mille Lac; Fond du Lac; Grand Portage; Bois Forte and Deer Creek; and also scattered bands of non-reservation Indians throughout the State."

John Beaulieu next asked about the interpretation of the provision in the bill, stating "that in no case where an allotment has been made in severalty, the holder shall be deprived thereof or disturbed therein." Commissioner Rice replied, "That is capable of two constructions: some believe that it has relation to Mille Lac lands; if you should cede a portion of your lands upon which an Indian has settled, that provision protects him under the Dawes bill."

John Beaulieu requested clarification as to how the Indian would be affected by the civil and criminal laws of the white man. Commissioner Rice replied that he thought they would come under the same rules as officers on a military reservation.

Gustav Beaulieu inquired as to the status of the Mille Lac Indians and Commissioner Rice simply stated that, "In 1863 and 1864 the Mille Lac Indians ceded their reservation, but reserved the right of occupancy so long as they do not molest the persons or property of the white man."

Gustav Beaulieu voiced concern that there would not be enough land on the reservation to allot all those entitled to allotments. He related that, "[T]he evident intent of this bill is to consolidate all the Indians in Minnesota upon this reservation, except the Red Lake and Pembina bands ..." He continued, "[T]here are quite a number of Indians who belong to no reservation, and are still entitled to the same rights as we: the Gull Lakers, for instance, and there are quite a number of mixed bloods at Mille Lac and around Snake River and in that vicinity besides other scattered bands of whom we do not know." He was uneasy over the selling of a portion of the reservation and wondered whether those portions sold would become part of an adjoining county and the Indians living there would come under county law.

Gustav Beaulieu addressed the assembled Indians saying, "I have asked them whether the reservation will be kept intact or not ... I think that the intention is to dispose of a part of this reservation, because they say that whatever pine may not be reserved for the use of the Indians here shall be sold ... Now they say they cannot allot lands except agricultural or grazing lands ... I want to say this much before closing, that if one foot of this reservation is disposed of, - that it is the intention of the Commission, to dispose of a single foot of this reservation, I will not sign the bill; I want to be placed on record as to that. I refuse to sign it; I refuse to sign it."

Chief Nay-tow-aush rose to share his opinion, concluding by stating that he would sign the agreement.

Another chief by the name of Me-zhake-ge-shig commented, asserting that they had hired the committee to interpret the bill, but they each still retained the right to their own opinions.

The Nelson Act creates a great benefit for future generations, Commissioner Rice remarked, because they will be able to inherit the allotments of their ancestors. He further reminded the Indians that under this Act their status would be the same as the white man.

John Johnson, one of the spiritual advisors to the Indians, related that he liked the Act and would sign it.

The Reverend Charles Wright opined that "[A] good man need not be afraid of the law …"

Due to the evident fear of the white man's laws, Commissioner Rice instructed, "Your lands cannot be taken from you, nor your farming implements, even for debt … your land cannot be taxed, because the President holds this land in trust for you." He continued by opining that they should have their own separate county.

The senior chief, White Cloud, said, "We now wish to understand what portion of this reservation the Commissioners think best to cut off, and why it should be done. When we come to that understanding, we see no impediment to an agreement …" Commissioner Rice responded that they had determined that they should dispose of four townships.

Bishop Marty suggested that if the Indians "are anxious to have your young men take up lands and cultivate them. If you sell the pine, you do not need, you will obtain the means to improve your farms."

From time to time during both negotiations at Red Lake and those at White Earth, reference was made to negotiations held three years earlier. That was apparently referring to the Northwest Commission, which attempted to consolidate all the Indians of the State—including the Red Lakers—at White Earth. Negotiations had occurred first at White Earth where agreement was secured, but later at Red Lake negotiators had met with complete opposition to being moved to White Earth. That plan was then apparently abandoned, and—according to Chief White Cloud—the Commission returned to Washington without even informing the White Earth band that the Red Lakers had refused. This experience is most likely the reason the Commission appointed to secure approval of the Nelson Act went to Red Lake first.

As one studies this history one finds reference to lands being held communally, but there is question as to whether the Indians considered it such. I relate this exchange between Chief White Cloud and Commissioner Rice.

Chief White Cloud: "When you visit the other reservations occupied by the Chippewas of the Mississippi, if they should say to you that the White Earth Reservation belongs to us in common, what answer will you make to them? If you want to cut off a portion of this reservation, your answer will naturally be, We have given the people of White Earth Reservation what we thought was a sufficiency for their use; we have cut off a portion because we did not think they needed it."

Commissioner Rice: "The answer will be an easy one. Three years ago they refused to come here. They have always refused, and even treated the Commissioners' proposition with indifference. They said that that was their reservation, and that this was yours…"

Chief White Cloud: "... At that time I uttered these words; 'I shall not touch the pen for my consideration, ceding lands which I have no right to cede, and I have no right to cede any of the Red Lake lands.'"

Chief White Cloud obviously was optimistic that this Act would provide a great future for the Chippewa. He said to the assembled Indians, "We wish you all to think over this matter, and follow the example of the chiefs, because we think it is for the good of all ... the white man is withdrawing his guardianship over you, and you must carry out the policy of the government in that respect."

John Johnson made perhaps the most profound statement, "We sign this agreement to conquer poverty by out exertions."

One by one the chiefs and male adults signed the agreement; 273 White Earth signers and 54 Gull Lake signers. Chief White Cloud, in his final comments, asked the Indians of his reservation to take advantage of the allotments and above all, to see to it that their children were educated.

The council at White Earth was concluded on July 29th and on August 5th council was opened at Gull Lake. The Gull Lake Indians were obviously prepared to remove to White Earth, and after the Nelson Act was explained by Mr. Rice, Chief Wah-de-nah, son of deceased Bad Boy, stated, "Everything done by the White Earth people with whom we are in interest, we are in accord with, and we accept the whole thing." Every male adult Gull Lake Indian signed the agreement and the council was adjourned later that same day.

Three days later, August 8th what would prove to be the longest and most difficult council was opened at Leech Lake. When advance notice had reached Leech Lake that Henry Rice and his Commission was scheduled to visit, hopes apparently ran high that old, unfinished business with the Government was about to be dealt with.

Some forty years earlier it had been the plan of the Government to move the Menomenies from Wisconsin to Minnesota. The Menomenies and the Pillagers were apparently friends and the Government thought that by positioning the Menomenies as a buffer between the Pillagers and the Sioux, warfare between the two could be curtailed. The Pillagers agreed to a minimal price for the land, with the understanding that this land was to be given to the Menomenies. But after considering the move the Menomenies decided it was not a good idea to be located in between two warring factions, and so refused to remove to Minnesota and instead took a smaller area of land in Wisconsin. Subsequently the Government sold the land to settlers and the Pillagers had never been compensated further.

To make matters worse, the Government had built dams, which created reservoirs, which then destroyed much of the wild rice fields that the Pillagers relied on for food. Negotiations had been held in an attempt to determine the damages owed the Pillagers, but the Pillagers had never been compensated. Henry Rice was aware of the situation and had repeatedly advised the Pillagers to remain calm because justice would be done. Thus when Henry Rice arrived as Chairman of the Commission the Pillagers, living in extreme poverty, had high hopes that these old matters would finally be settled.

As Henry Rice opened the council at Leech Lake, the Leech Lake Pillagers were optimistic. Rice had had many dealings with the Leech Lake band during his career, often with Chief Flat Mouth—who was now deceased—but represented by his daughter Ruth Flat Mouth, who sat at the head of a line of chiefs.

As they had done at previous councils, the Commission read the Nelson Act and Chairman Rice explained it fully. Rice offered to have the band provide their own interpreter and they accepted that offer, selecting two full blood Chippewas. Rice reminded them that in negotiations three years earlier they had refused to leave Leech Lake; now the Government was saying the band could remain where they were or move to White Earth. The choice was theirs. So now it was half way through the third council and the Pillagers had essentially said nothing regarding the arrangement. Finally Chairman Rice said, "If you do not see fit to talk, all that is left for us to do, is to pack up and leave."

The speakers talked about how happy they were to hear Mr. Rice reminisce about their departed ancestors.

The Pillagers had chosen speakers to share the views of the entire band, and at last, finally during the third council, one of the speakers summarized council proceedings up to that point when he said, "The only stumbling block there is to the arrangement you now bring and lay before us is, the adjustment of those old dues, which now belong to us ... when this Act is now read to me, having been treated as I have ... I am afraid of getting my foot in the trap again ..."

Agreeing, Chairman Rice knew they were right because he had been the Government representative when the land was essentially donated—paying only one and one half cent an acre—for the use of the Menomenies. It was also Rice who had encouraged them to remain calm and wait for Government compensation for the damage caused by the dams.

It was obvious that the speakers were adamant in their desire for a settlement on past broken promises before considering any new agreement. They claimed to have signed an agreement with the Pillager Indians at Cass Lake, Lake Winnebagoshish and Pine Point, to stand fast until the old issues were solved, but perhaps this was wishful thinking. They essentially threatened any who might sign the new agreement with punishment. The speakers then brought up the fact that, although they were not part of the 1862 uprising, yet money had been taken from money due them to pay damages caused by the raiders.

Chairman Rice and the Commission could not disagree. Attempting to explain, Rice said, "It was not long after Flat Mouth was in Washington, that there came a change in the administration, and then, or soon after, came the great war [Civil War], when everything else was laid aside, and it has taken nearly all the time since, to settle questions that were raised by the war, - paying the great debt incurred, taking care of four million blacks who were thrown upon our hands; of the widows and orphans of the soldiers killed in battle, and of the soldiers who were wounded during the war.

"You can also imagine the business your Great Father had on hand, when a million men were under arms, and every ship we had was armed and at sea. It is as if the storm was but just over and the ship had just arrived safely at anchor. These matters with the other pressing business of the Government, have taken up all its time, and it is no surprise that many matters of small importance to your Great Father, but of Great importance to you, should have been laid aside, or overlooked."

It appears that Henry Rice felt that they were at an impasse. He said to the Indians assembled, "We have opened our hearts to you, leaving the result with you and your decision will be final. We have our opinion as to what is best, but no two or three men can decide for a band. The interests at stake are your interests, not ours, and we hope that whatever you do will be for the best. We have made no promises, and given you no advice, save to keep together."

As the council was about to take a break for dinner Rice added, "It is for you to say whether you wish to see us again." Mah-ge-gah-bow said, "If we think of anything we will let you know this afternoon."

"I suppose that if you do not think of anything else, we will prepare to go home," Rice responded.

Mah-ge-gah-bow asked, "At what time will you meet us?" A standoff was thus averted and the council resumed at 3:00 that afternoon.

The afternoon discussions, however, generated much of the same debates, including threats toward anyone who weakened and decided to sign the agreement. So the fourth council ended as the previous three had, with no movement toward accepting the Nelson Act.

On August 13th the Indians spent most of the day in deliberation, and not until 5:30 PM did they ask to meet with the Commission. Once assembled the band informed the Commission that they did not want this Act of Congress and did not want to accept the proposition offered them.

Pointing out that thus far none of the chiefs had spoken during the councils, Chairman Rice stated, "We are taking back to the Great Father [the President] from the Pillagers no message but insults. One man gets up and says he speaks for the Pillagers. He says he speaks for the chiefs, the head men and the young men, and you send through him, word to the Great Father that you will throw the first man who touches the pen [signs] into the Lake. You say that the man who attempts to touch the pen will be brushed away and that if it had not been for me, you would have destroyed the reservoir dams. What words are these for us to take to Washington? Threats and insults!" He added that the Government was trying to prevent what was happening to the Mille Lacs from happening to them. Clearly frustrated, Rice said, "I received word this afternoon that the chiefs wished to meet us at nine o'clock tomorrow morning. Perhaps you wish to withdraw that request. If so, do it."

Chief O-ge-mah arose. Breaking the impasse he said that the chiefs and many of the young men had decided that they should at least consider the proposition presented by the Commission. The Chief then confirmed the nine o'clock council for the next morning.

An Otter Tail Pillager from Pine Point declared that his band had gone home to attend to their crops; they accepted the proposal presented by the Commission but did not have time to take part in the wrangles of the Leech Lakers. The tone of the council appeared to be changing.

As the sixth council opened on August 14, Chief O-ge-mah stood and said to the largely friendly Indians who were assembled that they must ask questions so that they could fully understand the proposal. At this point the more hostile group entered with a noisy demonstration—apparently intended to intimidate those who wanted to consider the agreement. But the protestors were not effective and the assembly soon quieted.

Ruth Flat Mouth, an exceedingly religious woman, brought the views of God into the council. She made known that she had asked for God's guidance, with the purpose of asking the Indians to seriously consider the proposal, and then asking the other chiefs to speak after her.

The Pillagers then spoke of apparent rumors they had heard that greatly concerned them, one being that they were to be removed. These rumors were soon debunked by the Commission and the discussion moved on to the long term benefits of owning your own land—land that one could use to generate a living for your family. While much attention was paid to the current proposal, comments kept returning to the unfulfilled promises of the Government.

Bishop Marty explained that under this proposal they would hold their land exactly like the whites except that no white man would be allowed to buy their land from them for twenty five years and during that time there would be no taxes on the land.

Chairman Rice assured them that the Commissioners would do their best to urge Congress to address the issues that were uppermost in the minds of the Pillagers.

Again at the ninth council Ruth Flat Mouth expressed support for the Act.

A Cass lake Indian asked if the Commission planned to stop at Cass Lake for a council and Rice responded that their intent was to go to Cass Lake next.

During the ninth council an exchange occurred regarding the Mille Lac situation that is interesting to note.

> "Kay-ke-now-aus-e-kung: If I should not sign would I be allowed to go to Washington?
>
> "Mr. Rice: that is a question that I could not answer. Indians are not, however, allowed to go to Washington. I suppose you mean

a delegation. The reason is, that Indians have gone there and sold their land, making agreements of which their people knew nothing.

"Kay-ke-now-aus-e-kung: That is the truth.

"Mr. Rice: Your Great Father is determined that no transaction with a band of Indians shall take place hereafter without all of them knowing about it.

"Kay-ke-now-aus-e-kung: That is right.

"Mr. Rice: A great deal of trouble arose from Indians going there and transacting business, which they did not understand after they got home. The trouble at Mille Lac has been brought on by that very thing."

Ruth Flat Mouth then signed the agreement and others followed, with the chiefs signing first.

On August 20, 1889, the eleventh council wrapped up affairs at Leech Lake. 466 Pillager Indians signed the agreement from Leech Lake, Cass Lake and Lake Winnebagoshish.

Three days later, August 23rd, the first of three councils at Cass Lake convened. The council was opened by Rev. John Coleman, a Chippewa Episcopal clergyman. As customary, the Commission was introduced by Agent Shuler. This council must have seemed like a piece of cake to the commissioners after the Leech Lake council, much of which was controlled by the young more militant band members. At Cass Lake the chiefs controlled the tone of the council.

Most of the discussion remained on topic—the Nelson Act—with only a few comments concerning broken government promises. The participants appeared sincere in wanting to understand the proposal that the Commission was presenting, asking three times that the Act be explained again. By the third day, August 26th, the Cass lake Chippewas signed the agreement.

The first council at Lake Winnebagoshish was held late in the afternoon on August 31st around the campfire, due to the late arrival of the Indians. The Nelson Act was fully explained.

The second council was held September 2nd, and again at the request of the Indians the Act was fully explained. Commissioner Whiting emphasized that White Earth was a beautiful place, but that the Act would allow the Indians to remain where they were if that be their desire. From there the comments turned to the damage that the dams had caused to the rice crop, gardens and burial grounds. The Indians complained that Government promises had previously been made but not kept. As they signed the agreement the council continued, adjourning later in the day only to resume again around the campfire for further discussion.

The Commission next moved on to Payment Point for a council with the White Oak Point Indians on September 4th. The meetings with the White Oak Point Indians included scattered bands from near White Oak Point, Payment Point, Rabbit Lake, Trout Lake and Sandy Lake.

Since there was no settlement at Payment Point, this first council was convened out of doors. Henry Rice explained the Act of Congress passed January 14, 1889, as well as the Dawes Act. First to speak was Way-me-tig-ozhence, saying, "I have been tampered with so often that when a white man says anything to me I don't know what to believe."

Perhaps Commissioner Whiting exaggerated a bit when he replied, "If you accept this proposition, and your young men take hold of it and do the best they can, in a few years they will be the richest farmers in the State of Minnesota."

The Indians were nervous about spending too much time in council because it was wild rice harvest season and each days delay meant less rice harvested. There were a few comments made about not wanting to move to White Earth, and also about the Government's broken promises. The Indians then suggested that the Commission delay a few days, but Henry Rice was also getting nervous about how long the negotiations were taking. After considerable hesitation, nearly all the chiefs and other men signed the agreement.

The Commission moved on to White Oak Point and were surprised to find that Sturgeon Man and some of the other more militant members of the Leech Lake Band—who had not signed the agreement—had followed them to White Oak Point. Requesting an interview with the Commission, on September 6th Sturgeon Man sort of apologized for the happenings at Leech Lake, saying he would return to Leech Lake and use his influence to unite the band, and then proceeded to sign the agreement.

The council at White Oak Point was held the evening of September 6th. Everybody seemed in a hurry; the Indians to get back to the rice fields and the Commission because of how long these councils negotiations were taking. There was some jealous talk about the White Earth band getting favors while those at White Oak Point got none. But before the evening was over all those who had not previously signed at Payment Point had signed the agreement.

The next day, September 7th, the third council was held near Grand Rapids with the Indians of Trout Lake. The Indians present signed the agreement with very little discussion.

The Commission moved on down the river to where they had notified some of the White Oak Point Indians to assemble at Sandy Lake, only to be told by the messenger that the Indians were busy gathering wild rice. The rice was very ripe and the wind would blow it away if not harvested promptly.

The Commission then sent messengers out in various directions asking the Sandy Lake Indians—part of the White Oak Point Reservation band—to meet with them at Kimberley. So on September 19th the fourth council held an informal evening meeting, and as usual the situation was explained. By September 21st most of the Indians or their representatives were present and the first formal session began and the Act of Congress was explained.

First to speak was O-ge-mah-woub, jealously stating, "At White Earth they had seats. Here we have to sit on the ground." There was talk about the same broken Government promises that were discussed at the other councils, and some thoughtful questions regarding the Act. By that evening the Indians had voiced their satisfaction with the Act of Congress and appeared hopeful that this time promises would be kept. Commissioner Rice responded saying, "The President has never meant to be unjust to you. The injustice has been done by others. He has been deceived and you have been wronged."

At the next council on Monday September 23rd, more discussion ensued with one participant stating what had apparently endeared many to the proposal, saying, "I do not wish to go to White Earth. I wish to live and die in the land of my fathers. Most of my people feel as I do." The provision in the Act allowing them to receive allotments where they currently lived was important in their acceptance. Before the day was over all 172 participants signed the agreement but one, who declared that he supported the agreement, but since the failed treaty of three years ago he had pledged to the Great Spirit that he would never sign another treaty.

Next the Commission traveled to Mille Lac where the first council was convened on October 2nd in the woods by the shore of Lake Mille Lac. After an introduction by Agent Shuler, Commissioner Rice and Commissioner Whiting led the council. Commissioner Whiting acknowledged that the Mille Lacs had been having troubles and recognized the assistance they had given the Government during the 1862 uprising. He went on to say that people had described the Mille Lacs as unfriendly, but that he was pleased to find that this was untrue. After the Act was read to the Indians assembled, Commissioner Rice spoke, apologizing or at least acknowledging what had happened to the Mille Lacs since 1864. Rice indicated that the previous events were the result of men who cared more for themselves than for the Indians, attempting to drive them off. Rice added, "Here is the acknowledgement of the Government that you were right, that 'you have not forfeited your right to occupy the reservation'. We want to correct all mistakes that have been made so far as we can."

During the afternoon session Commissioner Rice reminded the Mille Lac Indians that they—along with the other Chippewa—had taken this land from the Sioux and that the toughest battle was at Mille Lac before the Sioux were finally driven out. He said that after the Sioux were driven out, the Chippewa owned the country, and as they had taken it in common with most Chippewa tribes and bands participating at some level, that the land now belonged to them in common. Rice then described in some detail the provisions of the Nelson Act and referred to some of the provisions of the Dawes Act. He assured the Indians that the commissioners were there to listen and answer questions and would give them as much time as they needed to reach a decision. The council concluded so the Indians could talk amongst themselves.

At the second council on October 3rd the head chief of the Mille Lacs—Way-we-yay-cumig—asked that the commissioners repeat what they had said the day before because some of them had not understood. He thanked the commissioners for meeting with them "here on what used to be called my father's reservation." The commissioners again explained the agreement in detail and the council adjourned.

The third council met on October 4th and the head chief suggested that the day be devoted to questions, and the next day they would take action. Shob-aush-Kung suggested that they might not get all their questions answered in one day, requesting to look at a map so he could see the size of their reservation. A map was produced for them all to study. Pointing to the map, Commissioner Rice explained, "[T]here is the Mille Lacs Reservation, containing three islands in the southern part of the Lake—three in all—although only two are shown on the map ... This is your reservation north of Leech Lake."

Upon critical study of Rice's written explanation of the map, this author must state that, while Rice did not declare anything that is untrue, he did make statements in such a way that they could easily be misconstrued. It would also seem so because the Indians complained that the map, with part of the Mille Lacs Reservation not shown, was not what they were led to believe it was. They spoke of the reservation extending to the mouth of a river or creek. Apparently the contested area was Township 41, Range 28, Section 3, Lots 1 & 2 on the west side of the Lake, which a Mr. Dinwiddie now owned and was cultivating. Thus the line was 3 miles south of where the Indians say they were told it was, and that Indian treaty money was used to cultivate the land so that now they had lost both the money and the land. Rice said that apparently a mistake was made and they would try to correct it in some way, but that they could not take the land back once it had been sold.

Shob-aush-kung then declared that he was present for the treaty negotiations where it was understood "that the water was not counted in as land at all." Rice explained that this was a navigable lake and that the Indians have the right to use the lake the same as the whites. Shob-aush-kung went on to make the point that Mr. Dinwiddie's farm is the only land on the reservation that the Government had plowed, as provided in the treaty and overseen by Indian Agent Harriman. Muh-eng-aunce, another chief, expressed the opinion that although the commissioners had explained that anyone who wanted to move to White Earth could do so, the Indians wanted to take their allotments at Mille Lac instead.

Rice was asked to explain the allotments, and the Indians were told that they could select lands—called farming lands—and that nothing would be done with the lands until the Indians had their allotments. He explained that they could choose farm land, hay land, hard wood lands or sugar bush and that each member of the family might want to choose whichever they preferred.

The Indians asked how their future children would be provided for and Rice replied that by that time they should be able to buy more land. He explained what a great deal they were getting; that regardless of how many children a white man had, he was only given 160 acres, but Indians would be given 40 acres for **each** member of the family.

The Indians then asked if they would get a saw-mill, a blacksmith, someone to teach them how to farm, a school master and an overseer. Rice answered that the Commissioners would recommend these things, and that it was his expectation that the Indians would get them.

At the afternoon session on October 4th, Rice began by explaining that the law provided land for the missionaries' use, where schools would be established, and also that money would be provided for the school children's education and clothing.

Muh-eng-aunce then voiced his concerns and asked several questions. He spoke of the dams being built that destroy their wild rice crops. He asked how the Indians would be compensated for the hay that had been stolen by the white people, and wanted to know what the final result would be of the pine that had been cut. He asked whether Indians would be allowed to hunt deer off the reservation in hunting season, and how was the Government going to get rid of the white people that are on the reservation. Muh-eng-aunce complained that when the whites come onto their land they steal things.

Commissioner Rice addressed the dam issue first, saying that it was a state issue and that soon there should be a reply on the matter. With regard to the hay and timber question, Rice said, the Indian agent would probably deal with that issue. On the matter of settlers on the reservation Rice told the Indians that it was a matter to be settled in Washington and more would be said about it at a later date. Rice did indicate that he did not think any more settlers would come on the reservation and perhaps those already on the reservation would leave, adding that whatever was right would be done.

As for hunting deer, Rice told them it was up to the state legislature to determine, but that they would have the same hunting rights as the whites. He added a warning that if any man's property was harmed, there would be punishment.

Indian Agent Shuler then assured the Indians that if any hay or timber had been cut by a white man, the offending white man was liable for prosecution and the hay or pine would be seized and sold with the proceeds credited to the Indians. He asked to be notified if and when this wrongdoing occurred and was immediately handed the name of one such offender.

The subject of mixed blood people then came up, and Rice's explanation was that any mixed-blood person who lived on the reservation and was enrolled would be treated the same as a full-blood Indian, with any other cases needing to be decided in Washington. Rice emphasized that only enrolled members would be allotted land.

It was explained that Indians could take their allotment on the reservation or they could homestead land—like anyone else could—off the reservation. Either way, the Indians would still receive annuities as long as they were enrolled tribal members. Moreover, additional land could be purchased without affecting annuities.

Once more the subject of whites cutting timber was mentioned, avowing that whites had been cutting timber for 15 years.

The fourth council began on October 5th with Chief Muh-eng-aunce encouraging his fellow tribal members to accept the deal offered by the Government. The chief said the agreement would provide resolution for past difficulties, reminding the Indians of the assurance that they could remain on their land forever. In closing Muh-eng-aunce asked if the Indians would be given cattle and farm machinery.

Commissioner Rice explained that first the allotments would be made, and that some of the $90,000 loan from the Government could be used for improvements. Rice reminded the Indians that they would not have any money until they sold their pine. It might be, he added, that the Government would advance some money, but that his comment did not constitute a promise.

When the Indians inquired about prior annuities that had never been received, Rice agreed that—from the treaty at La Pointe in 1854—money was due, adding that there had been ongoing study of the issue until the war began [Civil War] and then everything came to a halt. Rice then rather blamed the tribes for not getting their payment because of their "unsettled condition".

Another tribal member then raised the issue of the dams once again. He spoke of the damage done to the rice crops, saying that it had been 30 years since the dams were built and each year their rice crop was destroyed. This tribal member also talked about the problem of white men cutting the Indians' pine. Commissioner Rice promised to take all of these concerns to Washington.

At the afternoon session one of the chiefs asked whether allotments could be taken on land after the pine was removed and he was told that the pine and land go together; when a white man buys the pine, the land goes with it. The question of whether persons who did not receive their annuities in the past could still get them was asked, and agent Shuler said he had been too busy to check into that but that he would do so.

Shob-aush-kung wondered where the message the commissioners had brought to this council had come from and he was told that it came only from the President. Shob-aush-kung went on to say that the commissioners "have acknowledged in the name of the Government that it owes these Indians, and have made the explanation. The Government has borrowed that money from us and is keeping it." The assembled Indians cheered in agreement. Shob-aush-kung then asked that these issues be given the attention of the Government, and Rice replied, "[W]e will do all that we can to benefit you …"

Another of the Indians said, the Mille Lac Indians "wish to know positively that the whites will be removed immediately, that is what we wish."

Rice once more emphasized that this was an issue to be determined in Washington and that the Indians should simply wait for the reply. "If there is anything wrong he will correct it; he will not permit you to do so. The law has come to stay … its decisions will be made in the interests of justice without regard to preference" ... of race or station in life.

Shob-aush-kung and others then made closing remarks indicating that they understood that they would get allotments at Mille Lac and could remain on their land, and that they were happy with the agreement. The Commissioners and all of the chiefs and male tribal members over 18 years of age—a total of 189—signed the agreement.

At the conclusion of the final council with the Fond du Lac band, Henry Rice forwarded a copy of the proceedings of the councils to T.J. Morgan, Commissioner of Indian Affairs on December 18, 1889. On December 28th, 1889, the Commission sent a report to the Commissioner of Indian Affairs summarizing in detail the activities of the Commission since its inception.

Specific to Mille Lac they reported:

> "On the second of October we met the Mille Lac Indians, and were with them until the close of the 5th, and almost constantly in council.
>
> "Contrary to the general opinion, we found them intelligent, cleanly and well behaved. Their neighboring white settlers gave them a good name. Some who had been on these borders for many years said they had never been molested in person or property by them. Upon this reservation there are a large number of whites, who have made claims thereon, and many of these testified to the harmless conduct of the Indians. Their principal fault seems to lie in possessing lands that the white man wants.
>
> "This reservation was set aside for their use by treaty of February 22, 1855, and was guaranteed as their permanent home. By this treaty land was to be ploughed and prepared for cultivation. "As a sample of injustice to them we were told that the land had been ploughed several miles North of their reservation, and not a foot for their use thereon. To satisfy ourselves of this, we visited the place designated, (Lots 1 & 2, Sec. 13, Town. 44, Range 23, West) and ascertained from the then occupant, a very respectable citizen by the name of Dinwiddie, that his farm embraced the improvement mentioned, which had been made before he purchased.
>
> "By the treaty of March 11, 1863, this reservation was ceded to the United States, but by a proviso in article 12, it was stipulated 'That owing to the heretofore good conduct of the Mille Lac Indians, they shall not be compelled to remove so long as they shall not in any way interfere with or in any manner molest the persons or property of the whites.'

"By article 4 of same treaty, it was agreed that the United States should clear and stump and grub, and break for the Mille Lac band, upon said reservation, seventy (70) acres of land, which confirmed the belief that they were not only permanently located, but had the sole occupancy of the reservation.

"In the treaty of May 7th, 1864, which was intended to supercede [sic] the one last alluded to, article 4 makes the same stipulation as to the breaking of seventy acres of land, and by article 12,- a proviso as to their living thereon,- the same as provided by the treaty of March 11, 1863.

The Interior Department now holds that, 'The Mille Lac Indians, have never forfeited their right of occupancy, and still reside on the reservation.'

"But, notwithstanding this, white men have been permitted to rob them of their pine, and for years to settle upon their agricultural lands, and there to remain in quiet possession, to this day, to the great injury and fear of the Indians. Some of the whites had the shameless audacity to take from the Indians, land the latter had, with much labor and perseverance put into cultivation. Squatters are now settling upon this reservation, and the interest of the Indians ignored.

"There are many persons upon the Mille Lac Reservation who went there believing that they had a right to do so. They were induced to believe so by the action of persons who not only sought the rich pine forests thereon, but actually secured, as is believed, patent to many acres thereof. It is possible matters can be so arranged as to give in some way protection to the well intentioned but misled whites who have made homes upon this tract, but be that as it may, the question of right should be settled at the earliest possible moment, for the greater the delay the more difficult will be its adjustment.

All present assented to the agreement and signed the same.'"

In a report from Secretary of the Interior John Noble to President Benjamin Harrison, the Secretary said, "The Indians at Mille Lac were found to be intelligent, cleanly and well behaved, and of good reputation among the neighboring whites. White men unfortunately have been permitted to rob them of their pine, and for years to settle upon their agricultural lands to the great injury and fear of the Indians. Squatters are now settling upon this reservation, as the Commissioners report. The question of right should be settled at the earliest possible moment, for the greater the delay the more difficult will be the adjustment. All signed the agreement at this place.

"The rights of the Indians upon this reservation has been a vexed question, full of difficulties and embarrassments, but it is hoped that this agreement will furnish a basis for its early and final solution."

The Commission reported that all the Indians present at the Mille Lacs Council signed the agreement. Following is the agreement that 189 Mille Lac Chippewa signed:

We the undersigned being male adult Indians over eighteen years of age of the Mille Lac band of Chippewas of the Mississippi, occupying and belonging to the Mille Lac Reservation, under and by virtue of a clause in the twelfth article of the treaty of May 7, 1864 (13 Stat., p. 693), do hereby certify and declare that we have heard read, interpreted and thoroughly explained to our understanding the act of Congress, approved, January 14, 1889, entitled "An Act for the relief and civilization of the Chippewa Indians, in the State of Minnesota" (Public No. 13), which said act is embodied in the foregoing instrument, and after such explanation and understanding have consented and agreed to said act, and have accepted and ratified the same, and do hereby accept and consent to and ratify said act, and each and all of the provisions thereof, and do hereby grant, cede, relinquish and convey to the United States all our rights, title, and interest in and to all and so much of the White Earth Reservation, as is not required and reserved under and in accordance with the provisions of said act to make and fill the allotments in quantity and manner as therein provided for the purpose and upon the terms stated in said act; and we do also hereby grant, cede, and relinquish to the United States for the purposes and upon the terms stated in said act, all our right, title and interest in and to the lands reserved by us and described in the first article (ending with the words "to the place of beginning"), of the treaty with the Chippewas of the Mississippi, proclaimed, April 18, 1867 (16 Stat., p. 719), and also, to the aforesaid Executive addition thereto made and described in an Executive Order, dated October 19, 1878; and we do also hereby cede, and relinquish to the United States, all our right, title and interest in and to all and so much of the Red Lake Reservation, as is not required and reserved under and in accordance with the provisions of said act, to make and fill the allotments to the Red Lake Indians, in quantity and manner as therein provided; and we do also hereby forever relinquish to the United States, the right of occupancy on the Mille Lac Reservation, reserved to us by the twelfth article of the treaty of May 7, 1864 (13 Stat., p. 693).

Witness our hands and seals hereto subscribed and affixed at Mille Lac in the State of Minnesota, this fifth day of October, 1889.

(signed) Henry M. Rice
Joseph B. Whiting
Commissioners

The above document was signed by 189 Mille Lac Chippewa including the following eleven chiefs: Wah-we-yay-cumig; Shah-baush-kung; Mah-eeng-annce; Aay-gwon-ay-be #1; Aay-gwon-ay-be #2; Pug-gwon-ay-ge-shig; Me-zee-gun; Mah-ge-ke-wis; Nah-bah-nay-aush; Mooze-o-mah-nay; and In-zahn.

****

We hereby certify that the foregoing instrument was fully interpreted and explained to the Indians whose names are subscribed and affixed thereto, and that we were present and witnessed the signature of each.

(Signed)	C.H. Beaulieu	P.H. Beaulieu
	Allen R. Jourdan	Interpreter to the Commission
	Interpreters.	

At Mille Lac, Minnesota,
October fifth, 1889.

****

We hereby certify that we were present and witnessed the signatures of the above named Indians to the foregoing instrument.

(Signed)	C.H. Beaulieu	B.P. Shuler
	G.A. Morison	U.S. Indian Agt.
	Theo. H. Beaulieu	W.C. Hubbell
		Secretary to Commission

Mille Lac October fifth, 1889.

****

EXECUTIVE MANSION

March 4th 1890.

This instrument in writing negotiated with the MILLE LAC band of Chippewa Indians in the State of Minnesota, under and in pursuance of the Act of Congress of January fourteenth, eighteen hundred and eighty-nine, entitled "An Act for the Relief and

Civilization of the Chippewa Indians in the State of Minnesota," wherein it is also provided "That all agreements therefor shall be approved by the President of the United States before taking effect," is hereby approved.

(Signed) Benjamin Harrison

∻

From Mille Lac the Commission traveled to Grand Marias—apparently by boat—and there met a small group of Grand Portage Chippewa on October 20th. After the Commission spent the day explaining the proposition the Indians suggested that they all proceed to the Grand Portage reservation where they could all discuss the proposal. Apparently Henry Rice was not present during this particular council as Bishop Marty and Commissioner Whiting did all the speaking for the Commission.

It was then on October 23rd that the Indians and members of the Commission assembled in a Government school house at Grand Portage. Most of the discussion concerned the Nelson Act, with only a few comments about the Government's broken promises. The general tone of the council was that they were very pleased to be offered this opportunity. May-dway-aush said it well when he commented, "You may represent to the President and Congress that the hatchet is buried forever, and that the civilization you extend to us we accept with open arms. Many a day and many a year have I waited for this day to appear ... The words I have spoken express the feelings of the people of Grand Portage, and we accept fully the propositions you have made to us."

Commissioner Whiting responded, "I expected to meet a band of ragged, half-frozen people. But when I come here, I find you men: men like men everywhere: resembling the laboring men I meet in my city." The council adjourned on October 25th after 72 Grand Portage Chippewa had signed the agreement.

From Grand Portage the Commission moved on to the Bois Forts Reservation at Vermillion, where — on November 9th — the first council was held on the second floor of the Government warehouse. Again Chairman Rice was not a participant.

The Nelson Act was read and explained in the morning, and the afternoon session started with a complaint about the size of Bois Forts Reservation. Ay-dah-wah-ne-kway-be-naos, who had been present in Washington, D.C. when the 1865 treaty was signed, had understood that the reservation would be 20 miles square, and now he was told that it was only 12 miles square. He said, "... the Government at Washington promised a tract of land twenty miles square. We were told that the law-makers had fixed it in that way. We were disappointed, and that is the way the white man generally does, -- lies to us." He continued, "We were told in Washington, 'You are never to talk about this reservation or your lands again, because this is put in the treaty as a perpetual thing for you.'"

"This land does belong to you," Bishop Marty replied. "We did not come to take it away, but to make it secure for you. Each man is to get a patent for his own land."

A complaint was put forth about a few Indians going to Washington and selling land that did not belong to them, and it was agreed that it was good that the Commission was talking to the whole band.

There seemed to be a sense among these Indians that they could trust Bishop Marty because he was a religious man — a man of the church. On Sunday morning Marty had conducted a Divine service to which they had all been invited.

As the council progressed the Indians emphasized that they did not want to move to White Earth; that they wanted the English language taught in their schools; and that they wanted no liquor on their reservation. Commissioner Whiting encouraged them to have some of their young men trained to do the carpentry and blacksmithing and such so that they would not have to rely on the Government.

By the fourth council they were ready to sign the agreement. Tay-bway-waindung signed first, followed by 210 chiefs and other band members from the Bois Forts band — which included Deer Creek.

Fond du Lac was the eleventh and final Chippewa band with which Congress had authorized the Commission to negotiate. The first council there was held on November 18th. Captain M.A. Leahy, Indian Agent, introduced all three commissioners and the Nelson Act was read by Commissioner Whiting.

The next day during the second council Henry Rice spent time recounting the history of exactly how the boundary line was established — at the treaty of La Pointe in 1854 — to separate the lands of the Lake Superior Chippewa and the Mississippi Chippewa. He followed with a review of the negotiation sessions of the Commission thus far. At the afternoon session the Indians asked to have their own interpreter, choosing Frank Blatchford, a U.S. Interpreter at the La Pointe Agency.

The head chief of the Fond du Lac band was Nah-gah-nup, a man said to be over ninety years old with a keen mind for facts, although verbalization was sometimes challenging for him. The chief was concerned about a strip of land about one mile wide that he believed had never been ceded by the tribe. His contention was probably true, and had likely occurred at the time that the border line between Wisconsin and Minnesota was established.

Henry Rice was apparently well versed on the history of this band, and how treaties had been made to secure minerals — copper and such — near Lake Superior in 1842. At the third council Rice reiterated how the Indians had been cheated by the Government and how he personally had worked to get a reservation restored to them. At one point he stated, "Our mission here now, is to tender you proposals which will give you homes, for yourselves and your children and your grand children; homes from which you cannot be removed and in which you cannot be disturbed."

As the third council continued more complaints surfaced, but all were stated in a business-like manner, and the elderly chief again talked in detail about border lines as well as other issues.

During the fourth council on November 21st one of the mixed blood Chippewa, Michael Dufauld, voiced the opinion that he tended to believe the promises of the Commission because a man of the church, Bishop Marty, was one of the commissioners. He said, "I for one, have considered the bill you have presented to us. That bill shows that it is well intended for our good ... I shall hold on to the proposition, and accept it."

"Elderly chief Nah-gah-nup, in addressing the band, gave Bishop Marty the impression that Nah-gah-nup thought his young men would be leaving this reservation and the chief confirmed that that was exactly what he had been thinking. Bishop Marty said, "That is entirely false." Marty then again read the section of the Nelson Act which allowed the band to remain on their present reservation if they so desired.

The old chief again gave a lengthy speech and afterward signed the agreement. He was followed by 122 Fond du Lac band members, and the final council adjourned.

The Commission, Chairman Henry Rice, Martin Marty and Joseph Whiting, must have left this council with light hearts after having spent nearly half a year in almost constant — and most notably successful — negotiation with the various bands of Minnesota Chippewa. While the record does not indicate such, I am sure they made haste to join their families for Thanksgiving and much needed sleep in their own beds.

Following their brief respite the Commission headed off to the office to formulate the required reports to the Government, reports that would then end up on the desk of the President to be signed. In their report the Commission stated that the census showed 8,304 Chippewa Indians in Minnesota, of which 2,178 were adult males, with 1,884 having signed the agreement — clearly well over the two-thirds majority required to enact the agreement.

President Benjamin Harrison signed all eleven agreements on March 4, 1890 and the Nelson Act was ratified.

Much has been written about how disastrous the Dawes Act was. This author believes that the Nelson Act was part of the Dawes Act, only made necessary by the fiasco at Mille Lac. And as it turned out it was a disaster for the Indians and, one might argue, for the people of the United States as well. As I have gone word for word through the abstracts of the negotiation sessions I am firmly convinced that:

- The Indians were not coerced in any way to accept this agreement. To be sure there were times when Chairman Rice became frustrated by certain Indians insisting on complaining about past events — events that Rice had no power to remedy — rather than discussing the issues at hand, but Rice always simply said it was their choice as to whether they signed the agreement or not.

- Most of the Indians saw this agreement as an immense opportunity to become self-supporting, to gain full citizenship, and to break the umbilical cord binding them to the Government. And truly, on its face it was a great opportunity for the Indians — to farm their own land with implements and livestock of their own, together with a comfortable house in which to raise their family.

So what happened? Was it too soon? Were the Indians not ready for this step? Was the Indian Service at fault? True — the Government had put safeguards in place, but they failed. Why? Was it the Burke Act or the Clapp Act? Were the Indians not ready for these measures? Was there some sinister plot behind the Burke and Clapp Acts? It is my sincere hope that many of the answers to the above questions may be found in this book.[1]

CHAPTER 17

Early 1900s

A new century dawned, with the 19th century experiencing two presidents having been assassinated while in office, the Louisiana Purchase—which brought much of the land which would become Minnesota into the possession of the United States, a civil war fought and won by the Union, and a rather systematic method of dealing with the inhabitants of the land that the United States claimed.

For the most part Indian policy originated with Thomas Jefferson, who apparently believed that Indians—as individuals—could be assimilated as citizens of the United States; but failing that, should be removed so that further settlement could continue. It is my belief that Jefferson's hope was that once these removed Indians became accustomed to agricultural pursuits and thereby, civilized, they could become a part of the citizenry of the United States, but as individuals, not as a tribe. Perhaps that was an easy out for a country that was struggling with its conscience after declaring in its founding documents that all men are created equal while accepting slavery as a compromise.

However, in this new century Negro slaves had been freed, slavery had been abolished and the United States had survived a brutal war over secession and enslavement. Not all of the issues, however, surrounding the Negro inhabitants of the United States were solved by Lincoln's accomplishments, as is well known.

One crucial occurrence dealing with the status of freed slaves, and a significant event affecting the future of Indian policy, was the Dredd Scott case. In the process of explaining why Negro inhabitants of this United States could never become citizens the court compared them to the Indian inhabitants. The Dredd Scott decision was admittedly one of the worst decisions made by our U.S. Supreme Court. Chief Justice Taney wrote in his opinion, "They [the Indians] may without doubt, like the subjects of any foreign government, be naturalized by the authority of Congress, and become citizens of a state, and of the United States; and if an individual should leave his nation or tribe, and take up his abode among the white population, he would be entitled to all the rights and privileges which would belong to an immigrant from any other foreign people."

Taney apparently ignored Chief Justice Marshall's prior opinion—at least in part—that the Indian tribes inhabiting this country were fierce savages whose occupation was war, and whose subsistence was drawn chiefly from the forest. "To leave them in possession of their country, was to leave the country a wilderness; to govern them as a distinct people, was impossible …"

Taney argued that Negroes were "a subordinate and inferior class of beings, who had been subjugated by the dominant race … and had no rights or privileges but such as those who held the power and the Government might choose to grant them."[1]

Even Thomas Jefferson became hard-nosed during the War of 1812, when most tribes allied themselves with the British against the United States. Jefferson opined that the most humane response for the United States was to force the Indians to leave our country—which simply meant pushing them westward. However, Jefferson did leave the door open for individual Indians to assimilate once they were 'civilized.'

In 1901 President McKinley had succumbed to gunshot wounds about six months into his second term and Theodore Roosevelt was sworn in as President. While born into wealth and having led a privileged childhood, Teddy Roosevelt is well known for his successful efforts in breaking the strangle hold that Wall Street had on the United States economy. While Roosevelt knew about the problems involving Indians, these issues were not one of his major interests. Roosevelt is reported to have made the statement in 1901 that, "In my judgment the time has arrived when we should definitely make up our minds to recognize the Indian as an individual and not as a member of a tribe. The General Allotment Act [Dawes Act] is a mighty pulverizing engine to break up the tribal mass."

With that as a backdrop, we now look at what had been occurring in Minnesota—particularly in Mille Lacs County. It is fact that the Mille Lac Indian Reservation was created in 1855 and was comprised of 61,000 acres. And although we know of the negotiations leading up to the 1855 treaty, the treaty itself was ostensibly finalized and signed in private in an office with Minnesota Senator Rice.

The Mille Lac Reservation existed for nine years before being sold by the treaty of 1863. The treaty of 1863 was negotiated by head chief Shaw vosh kung, but once again was finalized and signed in private—again with Senator Henry Rice. In Article 12 of that treaty the Mille Lacs were guaranteed occupancy on the former reservation. What exactly did that mean? It certainly could not mean possession of the area itself because that had been sold and was no longer theirs to possess.

Did the Government intend that the Mille Lacs would be given allotments on that former reservation? Nowhere has an explanation of the meaning of Article 12 surfaced, and remains so today. The Government vacillated between essentially saying that no sale had occurred to opening the former reservation to settlement as public land, while at the same time paying the Indians for the land as promised.

The treaty of 1864 was rather a farce because Hole-in-the-Day was displeased that Shaw vosh kung handled the negotiations while Hole-in-the-Day thought he was head chief of the Chippewa. The Sandy Lake band was apparently unhappy because their band was required to remove, while the Mille Lacs band was not compelled to do so. So Hole-in-the-Day and Sandy Lake chief Mis-qua-dace negotiated a new treaty in Washington with Commissioner of Indian Affairs Dole. Regardless, that new treaty made no changes to the status of the former Mille Lac Reservation, but true to form, Hole-in-the-Day negotiated a section of land for himself in addition to land for Mis-qua-dace and Shaw vosh kung. The last article of the 1864 treaty states that it is in lieu of the 1863 treaty.

By agreeing to the Nelson Act the Mille Lac band gave up their claim of occupancy on the former Mille Lac Reservation. The supposed intent of the Nelson Act was to concentrate all the Chippewa at White Earth and Red Lake, but the Government torpedoed that goal by essentially telling the Indians that they did not have to move to White Earth unless they chose to do so. And of course the Indians did not want to relocate if they were already comfortably situated. Did the Mille Lacs agree to give up the privilege awarded them by the treaty of 1864 to remain on the former reservation because that same privilege was now granted to all the bands?

By the time Congress got around to opening up the former Mille Lac Reservation to settlement in 1898, it had all been claimed, with the exception of perhaps 2,000 acres. Thus the Mille Lac Indians, who had been promised occupancy, had no land to occupy.

In a Joint Resolution passed by Congress in 1898, a tract of land had been reserved as a burial place for the Mille Lac Indians. A part of this reserve was Lot 4, Sec. 28, T 43N, R. 27W, which—it turned out—was patented to the State of Minnesota as swamp land and subsequently sold to the Lake Superior and Mississippi Railroad Company, which by 1901 was part of the Northern Pacific Railway.

A letter from Agent Michelet on January 19, 1903, reporting to Commissioner of Indian Affairs Jones, stated that the area chosen as a burial ground for the Mille Lac Indians was mostly meadow land, with graves located on the higher knolls and the lower area unused. Agent Michelet wrote that, on Lot 4 "there are about forty graves with little houses built over them, and about forty or more which have been destroyed." He went on to state that, "on Lots 1 and 2 there are about fifty graves in sight and 7 or 8 acres where Indians have been buried but the evidence from the surface destroyed." Agent Michelet noted, "[T]he Mille Lac Indians feel that the Government has promised them these tracts as a burial ground and insist on having them. The Mille Lac Indians claim many grievances against the Government for the unfilled promises, and it is very difficult for them to understand why the Government cannot give them these tracts of land for burial grounds when they were promised them by Act of Congress," adding, "In connection with this I wish to say that in view of the fact that the Government is to remove the Mille Lac Indians from the former Mille Lac Reservation it is not, at this time, very desirable to advise them that the

Government cannot comply with their promise to give them the tracts mentioned as burial grounds."[2]

On May 27, 1902, Congress passed an act (32 Stat. L. 268) which appropriated $40,000 for payment to the Indians occupying the Mille Lac Reservation for improvements made by the Indians on lands they occupied, on the condition that they remove from the Mille Lac Reservation. The 1902 council held at Lawrence [See Chapter 18] was basically the final active effort to convince the Mille Lac Chippewa to remove from Mille Lac.

CHAPTER 18

One Last Effort

On May 27, 1902, thirteen years after the passage of the Nelson Act, Congress passed an act entitled, "An Act making appropriations for the current and contingent expenses of the Indian Department and for fulfilling treaty stipulations with various Indian tribes for the fiscal year ending June thirtieth, nineteen hundred and three, and for other purposes."

The last paragraph of that act reads as follows:

> "For payment to the Indians occupying the Mille Lac Indian Reservation, in the State of Minnesota, the sum of forty thousand dollars, or so much thereof as may be necessary, to pay said Indians for improvements made by them, or any of them upon lands occupied by them on said Mille Lac Indian Reservation, said payment to be made upon investigation, examination, and appraisement by the Secretary of the Interior, upon condition of said Indians removing from said Mille Lac Reservation: Provided, That any Indian who has leased or purchased any Government Subdivision of land within said Mille Lac Reservation from or through a person having the title to said land from the Government of the United States shall not be required to move from said reservation; but shall be entitled to the benefits of said appropriation to all intents and purposes as though they had removed from said reservation; And provided further, That this appropriation shall be paid only after said Indians shall, by proper council proceedings, have accepted the provisions hereof and declared the manner in which they wish the money disbursed; and said Indians upon removing from said Mille Lac Reservation shall be permitted to take up their residence and obtain allotments in severalty either on the White Earth Reservation or on any of the

ceded Indian reservations in the State of Minnesota on which allotments are made to Indians."

At a council that began on August 19, 1902, held at Lawrence, Minnesota, (now the western portion of Wahkon) U.S. Indian Inspector James McLaughlin and U.S. Indian Agent Simon Michelet met with about sixty Mille Lac Chippewa Indians. Donald S. Morrison and Louis Manypenny were the interpreters and Fred Dennis the stenographer. The purpose of the council was to explain the May 27, 1902 act of Congress to the Mille Lac Indians and secure their agreement.

After being introduced by Michelet, Inspector McLaughlin addressed the council. He acknowledged that for many years conditions had been unsettled at Mille Lac, and the Mille Lacs had grievances. He went on to say that this recent act of Congress should "bring this matter to a satisfactory conclusion." McLaughlin then read the paragraph from the act that pertained to the Mille Lacs, after which he stated, "[Y]ou have no claim to the lands upon this reservation; you have ceded all that by your agreement of 1889." He explained that the band could "acquire good homes" on the White Earth Reservation "or upon any other ceded reservation in Minnesota upon which allotments can be made to yourselves and your children, and thus you have something that you cannot secure here." (Here we must keep in mind that, under the Nelson Act the Indians could only take their allotment on the reservation where they dwelt if they chose not to move to White Earth).

Inspector McLaughlin continued, stating that "every man, woman and child is entitled to eighty acres of land under the Allotment Act," emphasizing that they were there to tell the Indians the truth, and wanted "to inform you fully in all matters pertaining to your removal from this reservation."

"Now the question before you is," McLaughlin posed, "are you willing to accept a fair appraisement for improvements that you have made upon certain locations here, and remove from the former Mille Lac Reservation?"

"Bear in mind that you have lost all rights to lands here," McLaughlin reminded the band, "you have no rights to lands here now, and you can acquire none here," unless it is land that you have acquired from parties having legal title thereto. He told them there was no reason why they should drift around this country working for other people when they could have homes on other reservations and become independent. He then assured them that if they accepted the offer being made by Congress then discussions could turn to the items that would be furnished to the Indians in order to help them establish homes on their new allotments.

Wah we yay cum ig, a Mille Lac chief, stated that he had spoken to four different representatives of the government, "and not one of them have yet told me the truth."

McLaughlin addressed the issue by stating that they were not authorized to discuss past grievances, but that he knew they had not always been dealt with fairly and that their condition at present was deplorable and pitiful. He said, "[Y]ou have no homes here upon your old reservation, your landed rights have gone and it is now the desire of the Government to reimburse you ... for the improvements that you may have had upon this reservation." He then suggested that they should, "confine our discussions, negotiations and talks ... to this one subject, that is, your removal from the Mille Lac Reservation and compensation for the improvements that you had thereon," and "also to secure for yourselves and your children homes upon lands to which the title can be in yourselves. ... I can assure you, my friends, that whatever we agree to will be carried out in full to the letter." And finally, McLaughlin cautioned the Indians not to drink any liquor that evening so that they could discuss matters the following day with clear heads.

The next day the Indians asked that the proposal be read again so that they could be certain that they understood. It was read once again, following which McLaughlin read from a letter of instructions from the office of Indian Affairs, as follows:

1) That the Indians by proper council proceedings shall accept the provisions of the act, and shall declare the manner in which they wish the money to be dispersed.

2) That the Indians shall consent to remove from the so-called Mille Lac Reservation. And after such consent they are permitted to remove to either the White Earth Reservation or to some reservation in Minnesota where allotments may be made to them.

3) The investigation, examination and appraisement of the damages sustained by the Indians.

4) That after removal, allotments shall be made to them, respectively, upon the reservation to which they shall remove, under the provision of the act of Congress of January 14, 1889 (25 Stats. 642).

5) That after the acceptance of the provisions of this act, the declaration of the manner in which they wish the money to be dispersed, and their actual removal from the so-called Mille Lac Reservation (except the excepted classes), the appraisal damages shall be paid in accordance with the provision of the act and the council proceedings to them.

McLaughlin explained that any Indian who held title to land on the former Mille Lac Reservation would still get the benefit of the appraisement of damages but would not be required to remove, but **ALL** the other Indians must remove from said reservation. He again emphasized, "none of you people have any landed rights within the so-called Mille Lac Reservation, that is, you ceded in 1889 all claims that you had to these lands. ... If we reach an agreement by which you people consent to remove from the reservation we shall endeavor to make a very equitable and just appraisement of your improvements ..."

Wah we yay cum ig again spoke, concluding with, "If all the wrongs that have been done by the white people on this reservation were ascertained there is no scale that is large enough to weigh the losses we have sustained. Formerly the white residents used to stick themselves under the grass and now they are afraid to move around for fear of soiling the nice clothes they now wear which they have bought from the money they have made off our land."

"That is something that we have nothing to do with," McLaughlin replied, in part. "It is not under discussion in this council ... Nothing that you can do, or that we can do, will bring back the timber that stood upon the reservation, and it is now for us to make the best out of the conditions as they actually are ... these grievances must not be considered ... look only at the present and what is going to be best for the future ... you have no home on this reservation ... you are ... trespassing upon white man's property, and you can acquire no landed rights here, unless you purchase them ..." He then read from a telegram he had received from the Secretary [of the Interior]. "Each of you who take allotments as recommended will be provided with a comfortable dwelling, one yoke of oxen or equivalent, a cook stove, wagon, plow and other necessary farming implements and subsistence actually required until able to support yourselves by your own labor."

McLaughlin then chastised the Indians for playing cards and dancing the night before when they should have been discussing this proposal.

The next morning the Indians asked to have the Nelson Act read once again, calling it the Rice Treaty! After the Act was read McLaughlin reminded them that, "There was an article prepared for the Indians of each reservation to sign when ratifying the act, by which they relinquished all right to the land outside of the tracts reserved on the White Earth and Red Lake Reservations. You will understand, my friends, that by this act you ceded everything that you had on this Mille Lac Reservation. No right whatever is reserved to you here and you ... ceded everything that you had any claim to under former treaties, except a right to take allotments upon the White Earth Reservation ... Allotments were not made here for the reason that there was no land that could be allotted. There was no vacant land here, it had all been appropriated by white men prior to that time." ... "It is for your good to understand this, and it is not in our power to change it, you have no rights here whatever, you have ceded them entirely to the United States." "After you relocate, there are certain payments that you would be entitled to that you are not receiving a share of now ..."

McLaughlin then counseled the Indians that, "The more that we try to explain these treaties to you, my friends, the more confusing it will be to you. It is sufficient for you to know ... that you have ceded your rights to this reservation and that you have no rights here whatever ... I am here to negotiate an agreement with you by which you will remove from the Mille Lac Reservation ... I can understand, my friends, how you are opposed to your leaving here where you were born and raised and where your children have been born and grown up, that it is very natural, and if I had the power to leave you here in this country I would gladly do it. But you cannot acquire any rights to lands here except by purchase." He told them that they might be able to contest the white man's claims but that it wouldn't be worth the risk in the long run.

Michelet then took over and explained that while the Indians may have been told some lies, this is what they actually brought upon themselves through the act of 1889.

> 1st they agreed to cede any land on the White Earth Reservation not needed for Indian allotment.
>
> 2nd they ceded to the United States all interest in the lands reserved to them by the first article of the treaty with the Chippewa of the Mississippi, signed April 18, 1867, which was all the reservation lands in Minnesota except for White Earth and Red Lake.
>
> 3rd they ceded any land on the Red Lake reservation not needed for allotments for the Indians.
>
> 4th they forever relinquished to the United States the right of occupancy on the Mille Lacs Reservation reserved to them by the twelfth article of the treaty signed May 7, 1864.

"Now my friends, under the act of May 7, 1864," Michelet concluded, "you had the right of occupancy of this Mille Lac Reservation. If you had any right to take allotments on the Mille Lac Reservation before the act of 1889 then by this act you have given up that right. As I said before if lies were told you at the time you made this treaty we cannot pass judgment upon that, but you signed this agreement and signed away all your land, consequently you cannot have rights upon this reservation ... I advise you to accept the benefits that the government is now offering. Every year Congress passes acts opening Indian reservations all over the country. I think that it is best for you to take allotments on some reservation and assure yourselves that you have land for yourselves and your children. I see this beautiful lake here and do not blame you for not wanting to leave it ... I want to say in regard to commencing lawsuits here against the white men in possession of the land, such might be decided in your favor, but I do not think it will ... and after you have spent a lot of money it may end in disappointment, and if you should finally win it would already have cost you more than the land is worth."

Responding to Michelet's explanation of the Nelson Act, Wah we yay cum ig recounted how Commissioner Rice had said that he had been sent there by the Great Father at Washington [President Harrison]. He described how Rice had made promises. "He pointed to the different directions defining our reservation and said that it would come to pass that this land would be allotted to us, and if there is not sufficient land on this reservation to allot us there was plenty of Government land upon which we might locate. He said that our Great Father at Washington desires to secure the pine trees upon the reservation, and then followed the consent of my people to let our Great Father have our pine timber. I told the commissioner that I did not desire to let the roots and tops of the trees go, that we would let them have the body of the tree and not the roots nor branches. In answer Mr. Rice said that we would have a payment of $10.00 in the fall … It was this promise that the Indians recognized as being a good thing for them … We did not say anything relative to removing to the White Earth Reservation. He said that we would commence to notice the movement of the white men from our territory immediately upon the acceptance of the treaty. I have not realized any of the promises that were made to me, neither do I recognize this act that you have read to me today as the one that was presented and ratified at the time Mr. Rice was here to treat with us."

Ain dus o geeshig spoke next, saying, "This reservation was to be ours from our Great Father, it was promised to us. Mr. Rice said that sometime in the future we would see that we had been good people and that is what these people here have been going by. The promise which was made to us was, that all the lands here belonged to us and there was no way that the white man could come and take the land from us."

Ko gee then added, "[A]t the time Mr. Rice visited us, nothing was said in regard to the land at that time — the only thing that was spoken of by Mr. Rice for us to relinquish and let go, was the pine timber … If any mention had been made of taking our land at that time the agreement that was read to us today would never have been ratified by us … this talk about our having ceded this land to the government is something that is news to us … this matter that we are speaking of is simply a mistake that has been made in writing … As it is it appears that Mr. Rice himself made this treaty without our knowledge or consent … we did not say at the time that Mr. Rice was here that we were willing to let our land go, we simply talked about pine, and nothing was said about the land … what is the reason why the white men wish my removal from these parts so much? What have I done to incur the enmity of the white men? They appear to be so anxious to have me removed from my native soil. I wish you to tell us…"

U.S. Indian Inspector James McLaughlin addressed these issues, stating, "… the persons desiring the Indians removed from this tract of country are not the whites of this locality, but the Department officials for the welfare of the Indians. The government is very anxious to find homes for them … I think he [Mr. Rice] must have misunderstood the act and did not interpret it properly … I see that Mr. Rice promised you that you could take allotments on this reservation, as it is shown in his own words, but the facts did not justify him in making that statement … we feel for you very much and would if we could help you out of the difficulty, but it is not in our power to do so. The best thing for you now is to accept the proposition which we have presented."

The third day of council began when Chief Wah we yay cum ig declared that he was surprised that the facts they had previously conveyed as true were now said to be untrue. The chief suggested that the government representatives should tour the reservation and see the property that belonged to the Mille Lacs that had been burned and otherwise destroyed.

McLaughlin countered that they wanted the Indians to first agree to remove. Otherwise surveying the damage would be a waste of time. He emphasized that the reason they were gathered was to obtain consent from the Indians that they would indeed remove.

The chief replied that the Indians were not yet ready to agree to remove.

Speaking next, Ko de Quah ko jeence emphasized that the Indians had only sold the timber in previous agreements, not the land. He said that the Mille Lacs—who had moved to White Earth—were sent there as punishment for supporting Hole-in-the-Day in his desire to get involved in the 1862 uprising. Ko de Quah ko jeence added that the Mille Lacs who still reside at Mille Lac did not sign any treaties ceding the land, suggesting that Commissioner Rice had changed the treaty after the signing.

McLaughlin explained that the treaty was a written document that governs. He went on to say that the only way the Indians could receive the $40,000 that Congress had authorized was to agree to remove to White Earth; that was the sole purpose of this council. Once again McLaughlin emphasized that they were not authorized to deal with previous claims, stating that it was therefore fruitless to talk about these claims.

The day ended with a discussion of the stumpage fee that the government was paying the Indians for timber removal from the reservations. However, it was emphasized that only those Indians who had removed from the Mille Lac Reservation would be allowed to receive a portion of that fee.

The following day Wah we yay cum ig again spoke. "I am pretty well along in age now and I have never heard my people at any time consent to the cession of this territory we claim as our own." He reported that the Indians had decided that they wanted the inspector to appraise the damage to their property, to pay them for the damages, and that only then would they confer further. The Indians had been lied to in the past, he added, and thus were very skeptical.

Ain dus o gee Shig declared that when he had visited Washington he was led to believe that they could take allotments on the Mille Lac Reservation, adding that they wanted to be paid for damages and also to be allowed to remain.

Once more McLaughlin declared that the Indians must agree to remove before they could proceed any further. Then relenting a bit he added that perhaps the Indians could receive payment for damages before removing as long as they did, in fact, agree to remove.

Ain dus o gee Shig then requested that $10,000 of the $40,000 be set aside for them to buy land at Mille Lacs, but McLaughlin answered that they were not authorized to commit to that request.

After listening to a few more speakers the council appeared stuck on which would come first; the inspector's appraisals or Indians' agreement to remove.

Ain dus o gee Shig rather issued an ultimatum. The Indians wanted the appraisals done first so that they could purchase some land in their present location. That way anyone who removed would have a place to return to if they so desired. He said that if the government would accept his proposal, the Indians would accept the government's proposition. If not, it was useless to continue.

Agent Michelet said they could not make that promise. After the $40,000 was paid to individuals, the government no longer had any control of its use.

McLaughlin emphasized that payment of the money was contingent upon their removing from the Mille Lac Reservation.

Michelet again reminded the Indians that each man, woman and child would get 80 acres of land, and have a house built for them and furnished with farming equipment, and, "by taking these allotments you become citizens of the United States." He added that if the Indians wanted to purchase land around Lake Mille Lac, no one could stop them.

McLaughlin reminded the council that he must make a report to the Interior Department for their approval, and this report must clearly confirm the Indians' consent to remove before the $40,000 would be paid.

On the afternoon of the fifth day of the council, Wah we yay cum ig announced, "At our council we have fully decided what we are going to do as regards the proposition you have made to us. We have decided to accept the proposition as submitted to us by you …"

McLaughlin and Michelet bid the Indians send two representatives of their choosing to accompany them during the appraisal of the damages to their improvements. It took the appraisal crew a week to tour the reservation, moving from place to place by steam launch. At the conclusion the council re-convened August 30, 1902.

The appraisal results were accepted and signed by both government officials and Mille Lac Indian representatives, approving $40,000 in payments for improvements "… which were appropriated or destroyed by white men, who took possession of and forced the Indian occupants off their respective locations …"

The agreement was then signed by U.S. Indian Inspector James McLaughlin, U.S. Indian Agent Simon Michelet, and 74 male adult Indians occupying the Mille Lac Indian Reservation.

The agreement stated, "… that … by act of Congress … approved May 27, 1902, there was appropriated … ($40,000) … for payment to the Indians occupying the Mille Lacs Indian Reservation … for improvements made by them … upon condition of said Indians removing from said Mille Lac Reservation …the said Indians … accept the appraisement … as full compensation … and agree to remove from said Mille Lac Indian Reservation … upon payment to them of the … sum of … ($40,000) … as soon thereafter as notified by the proper authorities that the necessary arrangements have been made for them upon the White Earth Reservation…"

CHAPTER 19

The Mille Lac Band of Chippewa Indians
vs
The United States
1913

In previous chapters of this book we have discussed the progression of events as the Chippewa Indians sold more and more of their land to the United States, how those land sales were accomplished and the motivations on both the part of the Indians and of the Government.

It is obvious that many of the Indians had little or no interest in becoming farmers like the Government was promoting, yet they needed money for food, especially with their former means of livelihood disappearing as settlement progressed ever westward.

One gets the impression (at least this author does) that the Indian chiefs were shrewd negotiators but that the everyday needs of the people they represented often overshadowed good judgment.

Perhaps the two most troubling situations, in the opinion of this author, encountered to this point were (1) Article 12 of the 1863-64 treaties with its completely inadequate detail and (2) Commissioner Henry Rice's woefully inadequate and often misleading explanation of the Nelson Act to the Mille Lac council delegation. While a large majority of the Mille Lacs had relocated to White Earth by 1889—as desired by the Government—or lived outside the contested area on the Snake River or in Pine County, Article 12 was responsible for the hold-outs. And those few hold-outs were the ones who agreed to the Nelson Act.

But be all that as it may, the treaties were in large part written in plain and understandable language, and whether it was wise or not, the Mille Lacs assented to and signed them, thereby making them the law.

By the early 1900's it apparently became evident to the Mille Lacs that they had misunderstood the Nelson Act. In response, Congress was apparently attempting to mediate the disagreement by turning the matter over to the courts. This they did by passing the act of February 15, 1909 (35 Stat. at L. 619, chap. 126). That act authorized the Court of Claims "to hear and determine a suit or suits to be brought by and on behalf of the Mille Lac band of Chippewa Indians in the state of Minnesota against the United States, on account of losses sustained by them or the Chippewas of Minnesota by reason of the opening of the Mille Lac Reservation ... to public settlement under the general land laws of the United States."

On May 28, 1909 the Mille Lac Band filed suit in the United States Court of Claims. They alleged:

— that they sustained great harm by the United States opening the 1855 reservation to settlement,

— that the 1855 treaty stipulated that the lands of the reservation would eventually be allotted to them, that they were fully capable of managing their own affairs, but the allotment was not done,

— that in the 1863-64 treaties communal ownership was abandoned and the other bands gave the Mille Lacs complete ownership of the Mille Lac Reservation,

— that the Nelson Act said any Chippewa instead of removing to White Earth could be allotted on the reservation where he now lived, and

— that instead the Mille Lac Reservation had been opened to public settlement depriving the Mille Lacs of the value of the pine lands on the Mille Lac Reservation.

The Mille Lac Band asked that the court confirm that they were the rightful owners of the Mille Lac Reservation and they asked for a three million dollar judgment in return for the pine lands that had been opened to settlement.

Attorneys for the Mille Lac band argued that by the treaties of 1863-64, "the United States ... entered into a treaty with the Chippewas of the Mississippi, the Pillager and Winnibigoshish bands of Indians. By each of said treaties, *all* the said six reservations so reserved and set apart for the Chippewas of the Mississippi under the treaty of 1855, *except the Mille Lac Reservation*, were ceded back to the United States.

"By each of these two treaties the Gull Lake, Sandy Lake, Rabbit Lake, Pokagomin Lake and Rice Lake bands of Chippewa of the Mississippi, with the consent, and at the suggestion, of the United States, *in effect*, ceded all their right and interest in the Mille Lac Reservation to the Mille Lac band; such Mille Lac Reservation was by the terms of each of such treaties *reserved* to the Mille Lac band and made the separate and sole property of the Mille Lac band, to be occupied by such band as an Indian Reservation so long as the Mille Lac band of Indians in no way interfered with the persons or property of the whites.

"In other words, the Mille Lacs by each of the treaties of 1863 and 1864 became possessed of the Indian title in and to the Mille Lac Reservation."

On that basis attorneys for the Mille Lacs concluded that "the Mille Lac band of Indians understood and believed that by the treaties of 1863 and 1864 they were reserving to themselves the Mille Lac Reservation as a permanent home to be occupied by them so long as they should not molest the persons or property of the whites." And that "On October 5, 1889 ... they ceded and relinquished their rights in the other reservations in Minnesota, and relinquished their right of occupancy in the Mille Lac Reservation, believing and understanding and having been informed, that such reservation came under the act of 1889 ... that it would be classified into 'pine lands' and 'agricultural lands' and disposed of in the same manner as the other reservations ... and that they had the right of allotment upon the Mille Lac Reservation, if they should so elect."

(Article 1. of the 1864 treaty reads, "The reservations known as Gull Lake, Mille Lac, Sandy Lake, Rabbit Lake, Pokagomin Lake, and Rice Lake, as described in the second clause of the second article of the treaty with the Chippewas of the twenty-second of February, 1855, are hereby ceded to the United States...")

George B. Edgerton, attorney for the Mille Lac band further concluded, "The Mille Lac band of Indians understood and believed that the proviso to article 12 secured to them the Mille Lac Reservation for a permanent home, and they continued to occupy such reservation in that belief, giving notice to the whole world that they were the owners of such reservation, until the act of January 14, 1889, was passed. Then the commissioners appointed by the President to secure the cession and relinquishment of all the reservations of the Chippewas of Minnesota went to their reservation, and, after several meetings in council with the head men and members of the Mille Lac band, the Mille Lac band finally relinquished to the United States the Mille Lac Reservation, as they believed and understood, and as they were informed by the commissioners under and in accordance with the provisions of the act of January 14, 1889.

"The United States accepted such relinquishment under such act; and the cession and relinquishment of the Mille Lac band was approved by President Harrison."

The Mille Lacs band therefore was asking for the judgment of three million dollars by the Court of Claims.

Attorneys for the United States Government argued that the Indians ceded the Mille Lac Reservation to the United States in the treaties of 1863-64 and the tract became public land open to settlement, but that Article 12 stated that the Mille Lacs would not be compelled to remove under certain conditions: that the reservation was opened to settlement in 1871 and by 1889 nine-tenths of it had been entered; that entries were confirmed by Congress in 1893 and 1898 and the entire tract opened to settlement.

They argued that the Nelson Act of 1889—and the subsequent act of 1902—offered gratuities to the Indians if they would remove to White Earth.

The Government attorneys pointed out that of the six reservations created by the treaty of 1855, only the Mille Lac Reservation was created out of lands ceded to the United States in 1837, and that the other provisions of the treaty clearly show the intention that the Indians would turn to agricultural pursuits.

They argued that in the treaties of 1863-64 the intent of the Government was to concentrate the Indians in the interest of making it easier to care for them.

The Government attorneys stressed the fact that most of the Mille Lacs had already moved to White Earth by 1889, and that in so doing they abandoned any claim to the reservation.

They argued that the jurisdictional act does not mean that something is due the Mille Lacs but only authorizes adjudication of their claim.

The United States attorneys went on to argue that by accepting the conditions and benefits of the acts of 1889 and 1902, the Indians abandoned all claim to the Mille Lac tract; that by accepting the terms of the Nelson Act and agreeing to remove to White Earth they gave up any right of occupancy of the Mille Lac tract.

The United States attorneys argued and expanded on the Nelson Act by saying that, "If the Mille Lac Reservation be considered one of the reservations ceded by the Indians under the Nelson Act of 1889, their measure of damages is found in that statute. Section 6 excludes from sale under the act every tract on which there was a subsisting valid preemption or homestead entry. Such subsisting entries covered over 55,000 acres of the Mille Lac tract; only the remaining 5,000 acres could therefore be sold under the Nelson Act."

But if the Nelson Act is not applicable, "the loss sustained by the Indians is merely the value of their right of occupancy, and not the fee-simple value of the land."

The decision by the Court of Claims was made on May 29, 1911 with judgment in favor of the Mille Lac band of $764,210.89. The decision was by a slim majority with Chief Justice Peelle and Judge Howry dissenting.

As authorized by the act of February 15, 1909, the United States appealed to the United States Supreme Court and on June 9, 1913, the Supreme Court—with Justice McKenna and Justice Day dissenting—reversed the judgment of the Court of Claims and remanded the case for further proceedings in conformity with their opinion, which stated in part that "Whatever might be said of its merits, it is apparent that there was a real controversy between the Mille Lacs and the government in respect of the rights of the former under article 12 of the treaty of 1864, and that the controversy was still subsisting when the act of 1889 was passed by Congress and assented to by the Indians. And we think it also is apparent that this controversy was intended to be and was thereby adjusted and composed. A manifest purpose of the act was to bring about the removal to the White Earth Reservation of all the scattered bands residing elsewhere than on the Red Lake Reservation, the Mille Lacs as well as the others; and this was to be accomplished, not through the exertion of the plenary power of Congress, but through negotiations with and the assent of the Indians. The provision in 6 for perfecting subsisting preemption and homestead entries, if found regular and valid, pointed most persuasively to a [229 U.S. 498, 507] purpose to extend the negotiations to the Mille Lac Reservation. The commission, the Secretary of the Interior, and the President, in seeking, obtaining, and approving the relinquishment of that reservation, all treated it as within the purview of the act, and the Mille Lacs did the same. Then, too, Congress recognized by the act of 1890, shortly following the approval of the agreement, that the Indians had come to have an interest in the disposal of the lands in that reservation.

"But while the government thus waived its earlier position respecting the status of the reservation and consented to recognize the contention of the Indians, this was done upon the express condition stated in the proviso to 6, 'that nothing in this act shall be held to authorize the sale or other disposal under its provision of any tract upon which there is a subsisting, valid pre-emption or homestead entry, but any such entry shall be proceeded with under the regulations and decisions in force at the time of its allowance, and if found regular and valid, patents shall issue thereon.' In other words, the controversy was intended to be and was adjusted and composed by concessions on both sides, whereby the lands in the Mille Lac Reservation were put in the same category, and were to be disposed of for the benefit of the Indians in the same manner, as the lands in the other reservations relinquished under the act, but subject to the condition and qualification that all subsisting bona fide pre-emption and homestead entries should be carried to completion and patent under the regulations and decisions in force at the time of their allowance.

"True, it is said on behalf of the Indians that they did not understand that existing entries could be thus carried to patent. But of this it is enough to observe that the language of the proviso to 6 is plain and unambiguous; that the agreement recites that the Mille Lacs 'do hereby accept and consent to and [229 U.S. 498, 508] ratify the said act, and each and all of the provisions thereof,' and that the Indians, no less than the United States, are bound by the plain import of the language of the act and agreement. Not only so, but the act conferred upon the Mille Lacs many very substantial advantages which doubtless constituted the inducement to the adjustment and composition to which they assented. Among other advantages, it enabled them to share in the proceeds of the disposal of a vast acreage of lands in which they otherwise would have had no interest.

"On behalf of the Indians it also is said that the proviso was limited to 'regular and valid' preemption and homestead entries, and that no entry of lands within the Indian reservation could come within that limitation. But this assumes the existence of the Mille Lac Reservation at the time of the entries, which was the very matter in dispute. Besides, the interpretation suggested could not be accepted without wholly rejecting the proviso, for if it was inapplicable to entries in the Mille Lac tract, it was equally inapplicable to any of the other tracts relinquished under the act. In saying this we do not indicate that there were other entries, for the reports of the Land and Indian Offices, which were before Congress when the act of 1889 was passed, disclosed the entries in the Mille Lac tract and did not show any others. Of course the proviso cannot be rejected. It had an office to perform and must be given effect. It meant, as its terms plainly show, that entries made in accordance with existing regulations and decisions could, if bona fide, be carried to completion and patent in the usual way; and the phrase 'if found regular and valid' was evidently used with special reference to the charge that some of the entries were fraudulent, and with the purpose of eliminating such as were of that character.

"We are accordingly of the opinion that the act of 1889, to which the Indians fully assented, contemplated and [229 U.S. 498, 509] authorized the completion, and the issuing of patents on, all existing pre-emption and homestead entries in the Mille Lac tract which, in the course of the proceedings in the Land Department, should be found to be within the terms of the proviso of 6, and therefore that no rights of the Indians were infringed in so disposing of lands embraced in such entries. And we think the evident purpose of the proviso requires that it be held to include entries of that class theretofore passed to patent, of which there were some instances during the early period of the controversy.

"As respects other lands in that tract, that is, such as were not within the terms of the proviso, we are of opinion that they came within the general provisions of the act, and were to be disposed of thereunder for the benefit of the Indians, in like manner as were the ceded lands in the other reservations, of which it was said in *Minnesota v. Hitchcock*, 185 U.S. 373, 394, 46 S.L. 3e. 954, 965, 22 Sup. Ct. Rep. 650: 'The cession was not to the United States absolutely, but in trust. It was a cession of all of the unallotted lands. The trust was to be executed by the sale of the ceded lands and a deposit of the proceeds in the Treasury of the United States, to the credit of the Indians, such sum to draw interest at 5 per cent.'

"As before stated, the lands not within the proviso were disposed of, not under the act of 1889, but under the general land laws; not for the benefit of the Indians, but in disregard of their rights. This was clearly in violation of the trust before described, and the Indians are entitled to recover for the resulting loss. In principle it is as if the lands had been disposed of conformably to the act of 1889, and the net proceeds placed in the trust fund created by 7, and the government then had used the money, not for the benefit of the Indians, but for some wholly different purpose. The wrongful disposal was in obedience to directions given in two resolutions of Congress does not make it any the less a violation of the trust. The resolu-[229 U.S. 498, 510]tions, unlike the legislation sustained in *Cherokee Nation v. Hitchcock*, 187 U.S. 294, 307, 47 S.L. ed.

183, 190, 23 Sup. Ct. Rep. 115, and *Lone Wolf v. Hitchcock,* 187 U.S. 553, 564, 568 S., 47 L., ed. 299, 305, 307, 23 Sup. Ct. Rep. 216, were not adopted in the exercise of the administrative power of Congress over the property and affairs of dependent Indian wards, but were intended to assert, an unqualified power of disposal over the lands as the absolute property of the government. Doubtless this was because there was a misapprehension of the true relation of the government to the lands, but that does not alter the result.

"The Court of Claims gave no effect to the proviso to 6, and the findings afford no basis for separating the damages rightly recoverable from those erroneously assessed on account of lands disposed of under pre-emption and homestead entries allowed prior to the act of 1889. The case must be remanded for a reassessment of the damages."

CHAPTER 20

The Homeless Non-Removal Mille Lacs

On October 5, 1889, the Chippewa Indians living in the Mille Lacs area—or at least those claiming to be Mille Lacs—signed away their last vestige of interest in the 1855 Mille Lac Reservation. There is no doubt in the mind of this writer that the Mille Lacs were misled—and likely lied to—during the Nelson Act negotiations. That said, they did sign the document, and also had their day in court—first through the Court of Claims and ultimately through the United States Supreme Court. Consequently they were homeless, with a desire to remain at Mille Lac but without the legal right to remain.

It is abundantly clear that the goal of the Government was to concentrate the Chippewa Indians in one place, since it was becoming a monumental task to administer the Indian Service with Indians scattered all over, not to mention the additional expenses of duplicating services. The ultimate goal was to "civilize" the Indians, by which the Government meant convincing them to abandon subsistent living—hunting, fishing and gathering—and take up farming like the settlers. This goal could, of course, best be accomplished if the Indians were all in one locale.

There was a problem with that plan, however. Firstly, the Red Lake Chippewa had no interest in being a part of a consolidated Chippewa group. And even more troublesome was Article 12 of the 1863-1864 Treaty. True, the Mille Lac Reservation had been sold to the United States. On the other hand, because of the promise made by Commissioner of Indian Affairs Dole—a promise that the Mille Lacs did not forget—and due to the off the record final negotiations of the 1863 treaty by Senator Henry Rice the Mille Lacs retained the right of occupancy on the former reservation. Nonetheless, by signing the document agreeing to the Nelson Act, the Mille Lacs were now homeless.

Large amounts of the Chippewa trust fund monies belonging to the Chippewa had been spent in attempting to convince the Mille Lacs to move to White Earth. And some Chippewa did move.

A letter from Indian Agent Luse to U.S. Indian Inspector Chapman of August 21, 1882, reported a population of 912 Mille Lac Chippewa—with some 400 living on Snake River near Mora. An 1891 report states that 156 Mille Lacs had relocated to White Earth. An 1891 annual report maintains that there were about 800 Mille Lacs yet to be removed.[1] The 1889 census taken in connection with the agreement to the Nelson Act said that there were 895 Mille Lacs, of which 213 were adult males, of which 189 had signed the agreement to accept the Nelson Act.[2] This gives one a feel for how successful the Government effort was to remove the Mille Lacs to White Earth—up to the end of the 1800's.

As stated in Chapter 18, the 1902 council held at Lawrence was the last concentrated effort to convince the Mille Lac Chippewa to remove to White Earth. And until 1914 it appears that the remaining Mille Lacs were basically left to fend for themselves and live wherever they could. The Government must have been encouraged when, on November 24, 1903, they received word from Gus Beaulieu that Chief Wah-we-yea-cumig, the very chief who had announced at the Lawrence council the previous year that the band had decided to accept the agreement offered by the Government, was now requesting that arrangements be made—for himself, four other adults and two children—to remove to White Earth as soon as possible.[3]

For the very first time in my research, in a letter of January 11, 1904, from Commissioner of Indian Affairs Jones to Agent Michelet, I find the Mille Lac Indians referred to as "Non-Removal Mille Lacs" and "Removal Mille Lacs."[4]

On May 23, 1904, Congressman Bede from the 8th District of Minnesota reported to the Acting Commissioner of Indian Affairs that citizens of his district were telling him that the U.S. Indian Agent had been to the area repeatedly to induce the Indians to move, but the Agent had only been successful in removing one chief and a family of seven, and that "there are about 400 remaining in the different camps who say they will not remove." Bede reported that his constituents said that "the Indians with the exception of about four families, do not pretend to do anything but hunt, fish and pillage; that payments are being made to them there instead of at White Earth, thus making it unnecessary for them to remove."[5]

Acting Commissioner of Indian Affairs A.C. Tanner again funneled a complaint to Agent Michelet in June of 1904, which Tanner had received from Rev. J.A. Gilfillan of Washington, D.C., who had then relayed it from Rev. Mark Hart, an Indian clergyman at Beaulieu, Minnesota. Rev. Hart charged that, "[W]hen the Mille Lac Removal Indians arrive at White Earth they are not shown their allotments by the Indian Agent, but that one Frank Porter shows them their land, which in most instances, they think is poorly adapted to agricultural pursuits."[6]

Then on the 28th of June Agent Michelet was notified by Acting Commissioner of Indian Affairs Tanner that Secretary of the Interior Ethan Hitchcock had directed, "that the act of Congress of January 14, 1889 [Nelson Act] … under which allotments have been made to the Indians residing on the White Earth Reservation, imposes no condition of residence by the allottee on his allotted land or yet on the reservation as a right to draw annuities or tribal funds; that such allottee does not forfeit his right to an allotment which has <u>legally and rightfully</u> been made him by residing off the reservation."[7] (Emphasis in original)

Tanner communicated to Agent Michelet on July 2, 1904, stating that he had received from Minnesota Senator Clapp a message from a Mr. L.H. Schnabel, dated at Sandstone, Minnesota on June 18, 1904, "complaining of annoyances by a band of Indians said to belong to the Mille Lac tribe (about 100 in number) who have established a village on Sec. 29, T. 42, R. 17 in Pine County …" located about 50 miles east of the Mille Lac Reservation. Mr. Schnabel continued, "[T]he Indians remain in the village throughout the year, their numbers being greatly increased during the fall and spring by Indians who come from other localities; and that the band exists entirely by foraging on the surrounding country."[8]

On July 11, 1904, Agent Michelet was scolded by Acting Commissioner Tanner. Tanner had received a letter from I-ta-tso-yi-jig and Mi-gi-di—two Mille Lacs chiefs—complaining that they, together with 19 other Mille Lac Indians, had arrived at White Earth to select lands in preparation for moving to White Earth, at which point they were told that they could return to Mille Lacs until their houses were built. However, now they are told that there is no authority to pay for their return trip. The chiefs, Tanner said, were recommending that only heads of families should make the trip to select sites, and then return with their families after the houses were built.

Tanner said to Michelet, "[T]he office desires to know what representations were made either by yourself or your representative in order to induce the 19 Mille Lac Indians referred to to come to the White Earth Reservation. The office adds that Indian Agents and others who have to do with Indians should be very sure that the promises could be carried out before they are made."[9]

A letter dated October 22, 1906, from Theo. H. Beaulieu, Removal Clerk at White Earth, to Agent Michelet reports on a group of Mille Lacs being removed to White Earth. Beaulieu related that, "No. 182, Nay-tum-gwon-a after having reached Mora, Minnesota, and being furnished with a pair of shoes, pants, hose and having been transported from Lawrence, furnished supper, lodging and breakfast left the party … and returned to Mille Lacs." Beaulieu suggested that the cost of these items be deducted from Nay-tum-gwon-a's annuity.

On June 25, 1907, the following notice was sent by Agent Michelet to all Mille Lac Chippewa under instruction from the Commissioner of Indian Affairs. It is noteworthy that the Mille Lac council was held at White Earth, not at Lake Mille Lac.

> "NOTICE is hereby given that in compliance with instructions from the Honorable Commissioner of Indian Affairs, dated June 5, 1907, a General Council of all Mille Lac Bands of Chippewa Indians in Minnesota will be held at the White Earth Agency, Minnesota, on MONDAY, the 15th day of July, 1907, for the purpose of determining what Indians are entitled to participate in the distribution of the $5,600, deposited by Gus H. Beaulieu in the Merchant's National Bank of St. Cloud, Minnesota, in settlement of a suit between himself and the Mille Lacs Indians; said sum of $5,600 being a part of the amount secured for the Mille Lacs Chippewas by the agreement of August 30, 1902."

But it was not that simple. As stated in the notice, the $5,600 was only part of the amount Gus Beaulieu had agreed to pay the Mille Lacs. Apparently $2,380 had already been sent to Mille Lacs Lake by mistake, as evidenced by the following letter of March 27, 1908, from Minneapolis Attorney Alexander M. Harrison to Agent Michelet:

> "My dear friend:
>
> "I have just returned from St. Cloud where I have succeeded in making arrangements with the bank to send you to-day a cashier's check or a draft payable to your order for $2380, the amount of money due the 272 Indians which are upon the White Earth Reservation.
>
> "There was a mistake in issuing the checks which went to Mille Lacs Lake, one being issued in duplicate so that it makes one short in the list that I sent you. There are 273 names in that list and the amount sent lacks one of being $8.75 for each of them. I have written to Mille Lacs Lake to have that one check returned and if it is returned, I will send it to you.
>
> "The list which I enclose are [sic] the members of the band whose checks were not sent to Mille Lacs Lake and I would be glad if you would take receipts from each one of the Indians to whom you pay the $6.90. You can forward me check for my proportion as soon as you see fit to do so.
>
> "Yours truly,
>
> "P.S. I also enclose you the authority to retain from each share $1.85, for my services and expenses."

Of course the attorney received his share—amounting to $1.85 per share—of the $8.75 per Indian, leaving $6.90 for each of the Mille Lacs. In addition, Michelet was apparently no longer the agent at White Earth. The person taking Agent Michelet's place is identified only as the Superintendent and Disbursing Agent—probably J.R. Howard. The Government had apparently eliminated one position of authority. J.R. Howard stated in a letter on February 3, 1909, that he had the cashier's check in his possession for the some $2,300. But, he reported, he had no record of payment to the Indians living at Mille Lacs of the balance of this money. The $5,600 had been deposited in the Merchant's National Bank of St. Cloud on April 10, 1907. Apparently suit was being threatened against the Merchant's National Bank of St. Cloud to force distribution of the $5,600.

On February 3, 1909, the Superintendent & Disbursing Agent of the White Earth Agency sent the following letter to Charles Malone of Isle:

> "Dear Sir:
>
> "I have been requested by the Indian Office to report on the manner of disposing of some $5600 deposited in the Merchants Nat'l Bank, St. Cloud, Minn. to the credit of the Mille Lac Indians April 10th, 1907, and as the records of this Office are not altogether clear on the matter, and as I understand you were connected in some way with the distribution of this money to these Indians living at Mille Lac I have the honor to apply to you for advice in the premises. It seems that these Indians had a council, or several of them, and I wish you would give me the dates, if possible, together with a statement of the action taken in relation to the funds above referred to.
>
> "Any information that you can give me will be very much appreciated.
>
> "Very respectfully,"

He also that same day wrote the Merchants National Bank of St Cloud:

> "Gentlemen:
>
> "I have been requested by the Indian Office to report the manner of disposing of the matter of some $5600 deposited with you by Gus H. Beaulieu, April 10th, 1907, and as the records of this Office are somewhat incomplete I have the honor to request that you advise me.
>
> "I understand that the Mille Lac Indians had one or more councils and I shall be glad if you will give me the dates of these councils and anything that was done in relation to the matter above referred to. I have in my possession your Cashier's check for some $2388.75, representing, I understand, a part of this Beaulieu money, the same having been left by Simon Michelet, my predecessor. I have no

record, however of how payment was made to the Non-Removal Indians living at Mille Lac.

"Any information that you can give me in the premises will be greatly appreciated.

"Very respectfully."

That same day, February 3rd, Howard wrote Attorney A.M. Harrison as follows:

"Dear Sir:-

"I have been requested by the Indian Office to make a report on the manner of the disposition of some $5600 deposited in the Merchant's National Bank, St. Cloud, Apr. 10. 1907, and as the records of this Office are somewhat incomplete, and as I understand that you had some connection with the matter at the time I have the honor to request that you advise me.

"I have in my possession a Cashier's check for some $2300, which was left here by Mr. Michelet, my predecessor, which I understand represents a part of the amount above referred to. I have no record of the payment of the balance of this money to the Indians living at Mille Lac, and I shall greatly appreciate the favor if you will advise me fully as to whether they have been paid, and if so how, and by what authority.

"Thanking you in advance for a prompt reply, I am.

"Yours very truly,"

To finish his inquiry that day, Howard wrote to Simon Michelet, the former Agent:

"Dear Mr. Michelet:

"I am in receipt of a communication from the Indian Office in which I am requested to report on the distribution of the funds placed in the Merchants Nat'l Bank, St. Cloud, Minn., April 10, 1907, amounting to some $5600, by Gus H, Beaulieu, for Mille Lac Indians.

"I have in my possession Cashiers checks amounting to some $2388.75, the same being payable to your order, and endorsed by you in my favor, which amount, I understand, belongs to the Removal Mille Lac Indians residing on this reservation. I have also a list, which purports to show the parties who are entitled to share in the distribution of this fund. I fail to find, however, authority by which this money was turned over to you, and I fail to find, also, record of the disposition of the balance of this $5600. I have been told, however, that the balance of this money was turned over to one Charles Malone, for distribution to the Indians living at Mille Lac Lake. Please advise me whether this is true, and cite the authority of the bank for disposing of it, if possible, and state whether Malone has distributed the funds. I have been told that Malone retained the money and distributed to the Indians entitled to receive it certain due bills, good for merchandise at his store in Isle, Minn. If you know anything about this I wish you would advise me.

"Any information which you are able to give me in relation to this matter will be greatly appreciated.

"Very respectfully,"

Then Superintendent Howard received a letter written February 11, 1909, from Attorney Brower under letterhead of Law Offices of Stewart & Brower, St. Cloud, Minn:

"Friend Howard:-

"This cashier's check for $2388.75 to which we have referred in the letter enclosed herewith is a cashier's check concerning which we wrote you some two or three months ago. Charles Malone of Isle had helped these Indians a great deal. Without him they would never have gotten any of this money and as stated in our letter he claims a certain amount out of this check and desires that no distribution of the proceeds of it be made until he has an opportunity to present his claim.

"Yours very truly,"

Just what was going on here? The court had apparently made an agreement—sometime prior to June 25, 1907—to settle a lawsuit against Gus Beaulieu brought by the Mille Lac Indians. Mr. Beaulieu had made good on the agreement, but what was going on at the Mille Lac end? Eight months had gone by and the Indians still had not been given their share. A cashier's check for $2388.75 was sitting in the Agent's office; an agent who was no longer employed there. But what happened to the other $5600? You decide!

While probably not critical to this historical review, the above sequence of events points out some important aspects of this time period. First, the Federal Government chain of command was flowing through the White Earth Reservation to the Non-Removal Mille Lacs, and not directly to the Non-Removal Mille Lacs. Second, we are given population figures of Removal and Non-Removal Mille Lacs. Third, we can note the rather shady business dealings occurring at that time. And lastly, we have an example of how excruciatingly slow business dealings must have been compared to our current mode of nearly instant communication.

As mentioned earlier in Chapter 18, the 1902 council at Lawrence was the last real effort to get the remaining Mille Lacs to remove to White Earth. And—until 1914—those who refused to remove were basically left to fend for themselves without a real place to call their own.

In 1909, however, Congress passed a resolution authorizing the Mille Lac band to bring suit against the United States for any damages done to them by opening the former Mille Lacs Reservation to settlement. [See Chapter 19]

Sometime in January of 1914, Mille Lac Chiefs Me-ge-zee and Ne-gon-e-binase met with Commissioner of Indian Affairs Cato Sells in Washington. These two Mille Lacs were filing a claim on behalf of the Non-Removal Mille Lacs for lands, houses, stock, etc. On January 21 of that year Commissioner Sells responded that he had consulted with the Superintendent of the White Earth School and they had decided that, since the 90 or so Non-Removal Mille Lacs had no land on which to place houses and farming equipment, that decision would have to be delayed, adding that he, Sells, was requesting Congress to include $20,000 in the next Indians appropriation bill for the purchase of lands for the "homeless, Non-removal Mille Lacs Indians," and once they had land the Government would provide houses, etc.

Commissioner Sells and the Superintendent of the White Earth School had apparently been asked for schools and churches, also. But, with no land they were perhaps only able to provide temporary facilities.

The chiefs had also complained that the Government had disposed of land and timber belonging to them "contrary to the understanding of the Indians," and were told that he, Sells, would look into the matter.

The two Mille Lac chiefs also asked that land be purchased adjoining the allotments of Chief Me-ge-zee [there is no explanation as to how this chief had an allotment] which of course could not be done until funds were appropriated—and then only if that land was available. Additionally, the chiefs complained that various persons had "entered upon Indian lands around Mille Lac Lake, and burned the homes of the Indians, destroyed their grains, etc."

The Indians and the government were obviously not operating with the same fact base.

Commissioner Sells concluded his letter to the Indians saying, "[T]he Office cannot take final action toward locating you on lands where you now reside, until it obtains the appropriation mentioned from Congress, nor would it be wise to issue stock, farming implements, etc., until you shall have been permanently located. As soon as the lands shall have been purchased, the matter of establishing you in homes, providing permanent school and church facilities, etc., will then be pushed promptly, to the end that your wants may be relieved and suitable homes provided."

The 2nd session of the 63rd Congress, on August 1, 1914, passed an act making appropriations for the expenses of the Indian Bureau.

> *"Be it enacted by the Senate and House of Representatives of the United States of America in Congress assembled,* That the following sums be, and they are hereby, appropriated, out of any money in the Treasury, not otherwise appropriated ... The Secretary of the Interior is hereby authorized to withdraw from the Treasury of the United States, at his discretion, the Sum of $205,000, or so much thereof as may be necessary, of the principal sum on deposit to the credit of the Chippewa Indians in the State of Minnesota, arising under section seven of the 'Act for the relief and civilization of the Chippewa Indians in the State of Minnesota,' and to use the same for the purpose of promoting civilization and self-support among said Indians in manner and for purposes provided for in said Act: *Provided,* That not to exceed $40,000 of this amount may be used in the purchase of lands for the homeless non-removal Mille Lacs Indians, to whom allotments have not heretofore been made, to be immediately available and to remain available until expended, said lands to be held in trust and may be allotted to said Indians, subject to the provisions of the Act of February eighth, eighteen hundred and eighty-seven (Twenty-fourth Statutes at large, page three hundred and eighty-eight, as amended): provided further, That not to exceed $5,000 of the amount herein appropriated may be expended in the removal of Chippewa Indian bodies from the burial grounds and suitable burial and marking of the graves of Indian bodies at Mille Lacs ..."[10] (Emphasis in original)

It is vastly apparent in researching the relationship between the Federal Government and the Mille Lac Chippewa from 1863 until 1934 that those Mille Lacs who had refused to remove to White Earth were still considered a part of White Earth.

There were no allotments made at Mille Lac until land was purchased for them— and even then not until 1925. There was no Indian Agent assigned to Mille Lacs. They were made the jurisdiction of the agent at White Earth. There was no school provided for Mille Lac children until well into the twentieth century. They received no houses, no farm implements, no churches, and no livestock, unlike the recognized bands who were receiving these things.

It was obvious, too, that health care and subsistence was administered through the White Earth Reservation. Government offices were housed at the White Earth Indian School and the Superintendent's annual report for the year 1914 recounts expenditures for contracted health care for the Lake Shore Mille Lacs. The population of the Chippewa was reported as 1152 Removal Mille Lac Mississippi Chippewa and 276 Non-Removal Mille Lac Chippewa; that they all wear modern attire but only the mixed-blood Indians were citizens of the United States and voted.[11]

The following receipt was furnished to Superintendent John R. Howard of the White Earth Agency on May 12, 1915:

> "Dear Sir,
> "Please find here enclosed my receipt for check #11185 in full payment for land to the Mille Lacs homeless Indians as was bought by the government Oct. last.
> "Very respectfully,
> "Nils B. Berg
> "Isle, Minn."

In his annual report for 1916, Superintendent John Howard of the White Earth Agency reports—regarding the number of allotments, "Neither does this number include the homeless Non-Removal Mille Lac Indians for whom lands are being provided under the Act of August 1, 1914, which contains an item of $40,000 for the purchase of lands for said Indians."

As mentioned previously, the Non-Removal Mille Lac Indians were being provided a contract physician for their health care. In 1916 this physician was Dr. O.M. Roadman. In a January 18th letter of that year Dr. Roadman stated that he cares for Mille Lac Indian patients at Vineland, Cove, Isle, Wahkon and Onamia, and wonders if the Government will pay his livery bills.[12]

On June 13, 1917, Mr. D.H. Robbins of Vineland had written the Commissioner of Indian Affairs complaining that the Indians in the vicinity of Vineland were dancing day and night and refusing the offer of good paying jobs. This complaint was funneled to Superintendent Hinton at White Earth, who responded, "[T]hey are more than 200 miles, by rail, from this agency, and it is impossible to communicate with them personally, except by visit at considerable expense."[13]

The population of the White Earth Reservation, under the section on schools in the 1918 annual report, was recorded as 6555—of which 1236 were Removal Mille Lacs and 290 were Non-Removal Mille Lacs. It is obvious that the Non-Removal Mille Lacs were considered part of the White Earth Reservation. The report states that 6555 wear modern attire, 6300 can speak English, an estimated 2700 can read and write, 1494 are voters of the State and 6300 are citizens of the United States.[14]

The minutes of the General Council of all Chippewa Indians of Minnesota, which met July 9, 1918 at the Elko Theatre in Bemidji, Minnesota, are quite revealing as to the status of the Non-Removal Mille Lac Indians and their claimed reservation—claimed, at least, by some of the Chippewa leadership. James Coffey was the president of the General Council and led the meeting. Delegates and chiefs were from White Earth, Fond du Lac, Winnibegoshish, Leech Lake, White Oak Point, Cass Lake and Bois Fort reservations. Executive committeemen were elected; two from White Earth and one from each of the other reservations in Minnesota, namely White Earth Reservation, Cass Lake Reservation, Winnibegoshish Reservation, Leech Lake Reservation, Bois Fort Reservation and Fond du Lac Reservation. Resolution 17—passed by the council—did, however, involve the Non-Removal Mille Lacs. It reads as follows:

> "RESOLUTION 17
>
> "Whereas, that on the 12th day of June 1915, a meeting was held at White Earth, Minnesota, by Gus H. Beaulieu, Ben L. Fairbanks, Frank D. Beaulieu, Henry W. Warren, Eugene J. Warren, George A. Berry, John G. Morrison, Jr., William Potter and Nay-she-kay-we-gaj-bow, who have about one-half Indian blood.
>
> "Of the said meeting the Chippewa Indians of Minnesota had no knowledge until during the session of the General council on July 12th, 1917, two years and one month after the said meeting, a part of their acts at said meeting became known to the Chippewa Indians of Minnesota, to-wit:-
>
> "That said meeting was held and participated in by the above named persons only. That Gus H. Beaulieu and Ben L. Fairbanks were the instigators of said meeting, that the meeting was called for the purpose of promoting a scheme to obtain a particular sum of money approximating one hundred and eight thousand dollars of the funds belonging to the Chippewa Indians of Minnesota, purporting to be based upon a claim for compensation for services in the prosecution of the so called Mille Lacs case, *United States v. Mille Lacs Chippewas,* 229 U.S. 458, at 509, 510, and expenses incurred by Gus H. Beaulieu for some individual Indians and for money loaned Gus H. Beaulieu by said Ben L. Fairbanks, and for other purposes,
>
> "Therefore, the said mixed-bloods, at said meeting adopted a resolution which they numbered No. 9, of date of June 12th, 1915, purporting the authorization by the Chippewa Indians of Minnesota, the payment of said claim for the sum of approximating $108,000, out of the common funds of said Indians to the said Gus H. Beaulieu, Ben L. Fairbanks and others.
>
> "That John G. Morrison, Jr., presided over said meeting, and certified to the resolution in his capacity as the President of the General Council of the Chippewa Indians of Minnesota, and that Paul H. Beaulieu, attested to the said resolution in his capacity as

the Secretary of the General Council of the Chippewa Indians of Minnesota, the same being done for the purpose of giving effect to said resolution for the purpose of obtaining the payment of said sum of money out of said funds belonging to the Chippewa Indians of Minnesota, without the knowledge of, or previous authority having been given by said Chippewa Indians of Minnesota in any manner.

"That the said claim was compiled and printed and bound in pamphlet form which included the said resolution No. 9, said resolution purporting to be the act of the Chippewa Indians of Minnesota, in their General Council, for the purpose of distribution among the members of the Congress of the United States, that the said Gus H. Beaulieu and Ben L. Fairbanks, or their agents procured the draft of a BILL, which to all intents and purposes contained every provision necessary in the draft of a BILL for introduction in either house of Congress provided for enactment of law, said BILL to provide for the payment of a said sum of money out of the funds of the Chippewa Indians of Minnesota, to said Gus H. Beaulieu and to Ben L. Fairbanks and others, as provided in said resolution No. 9, adopted at said meeting and certified to and attested to by John G. Morrison, Jr., and Paul H. Beaulieu, in their official capacity as President and Secretary of the General Council of the Chippewa Indians of Minnesota.

"That said BILL was taken to Representative Charles A. Lindbergh of Minnesota, by said Gus H. Beaulieu and Ben L. Fairbanks or their agent, and made request of Chas. A. Lindbergh to introduce said BILL or have it introduced in Congress of the United States for the purpose of enactment into law, the evident purpose being that the said Gus H. Beaulieu and Ben L. Fairbanks and their interested friends should be paid the sum named therein out of the funds belonging to the Chippewa Indians of Minnesota deposited in the Treasury of the United States.

"While Representative Lindbergh received the BILL from said parties, he held the same for some time hesitating to carry into effect the request of said Gus H. Beaulieu and Ben L. Fairbanks (so-called mix-bloods) for the reason given by Mr. Lindbergh that he had not been satisfied as to the validity of the claim therein alleged and the responsibility of the men promoting the enactment of the bill into law, which Representative Lindbergh told James I. Coffey who was then in Washington looking after the affairs of the Chippewa Indians of Minnesota as a member of the legislative committee of the General Council.

"Mr. Coffey, then told Representative Lindbergh that the claim was not known to the Chippewa Indians of Minnesota, and the payment of said claim had not been authorized by said Indians, then Lindbergh advised Mr. Coffey that the interests of the Chippewa would be protected."

In an August 2, 1918 letter from Assistant Secretary of the Interior, S.G. Hopkins, Superintendent Hinton is authorized as follows:

"Dear Mr. Hinton:

"Authorization hereby granted for you to expend the sum of $880 from 'Chippewa in Minnesota Fund, (Purchase of Lands for Homeless Mille Lacs)' in making payment to Sheridan Greig and wife of the consideration named in a certain deed from them to the United States for the E2 of the SE4 of Section 10, Twp. 41 North, Range 16 West of the 4th P.M. in Minnesota, containing 80 acres, purchased under the Act of August 1, 1914 (38 Stats. L. 591), providing for the expenditure of not to exceed $40,000 in the purchase of land for the homeless non-removal Mille Lac Indians."[15]

Four days later the Assistant Secretary authorized Superintendent Hinton further:

"Dear Mr. Hinton:

"Pursuant to the Act of August 1, 1914 (38 Stat. L., 591) making an appropriation for the current and contingent expenditures of the Bureau of Indian Affairs, etc., for the fiscal year ending June 30, 1915, containing an item providing for the expenditure of not to exceed $40,000 for the purchase of lands for the homeless non-removal Mille Lacs Indians, to whom allotments have not heretofore been made, such appropriation to be available until expended, authority is hereby granted for the payment of the sum of $4200 to James M. Rait, for the S/2 NE/4 and S/2 NW/4 Sec. 2 and N/2 SE/4 and SE/4 NW/4 Sec. 3, T. 41 N., R. 17 W., of the 4th Principal Meridian, Pine County, Minnesota, containing 280 acres for allotment to the above Indians. Payment to be made from the fund, 'Chippewas in Minnesota Fund, purchase of Land for Non-removal, Mille Lac Indians.'

"The use of the above authority is contingent upon your faithful compliance with the requirements of Indian Office letter of July 18, 1918, on this subject."[16]

A third authorization arrived on Superintendent Hinton's desk written September 3, 1918 from Assistant Secretary of the Interior Hopkins:

"Dear Mr. Hinton:

"Pursuant to the Act of August 1, 1914 (38 Stat. L., 591), making an appropriation for the current and contingent expenditures of the Bureau of Indian Affairs, etc., for the fiscal year ending June 30, 1915, containing an item providing for the expenditure of not to exceed $40,000, for the purchase of lands for the homeless, Non-removal, Mille lacs Indians, to whom allotments have not heretofore been made, such appropriation to be available until expended, authority is hereby granted for the payment of the sum of $1935 to J.C. Cloyd and wife and R.L. Cragg and wife, for the following described lands for allotment to the above Indians.

"The fractional W/2 of NW/4, Section 18, Township 41 North, Range 17 West, of the 4th P.M. in Pine County, Minnesota, except that part of Section 18 lying south of the center line of Crooked Creek, containing 100 acres, more or less, for the compensation of $1075.00.

"The E/2 of NW/4 Section 6, Township 41 North, Range 17 West, of the 4th P.M. in Pine County, Minnesota, containing 80 acres for a consideration of $860.00.

"Payment to be made from the fund 'Chippewas in Minnesota Fund, Purchase of Land for Non-removal, Mille Lacs Indians.'"[17]

In a letter dated February 3, 1920, from E.B. Meritt, Assistant Commissioner of Indian Affairs to Chief Me-ge-zee, chairman and F.H. Pequette, secretary of the Mille Lacs band, reference is made to a resolution passed by a general council of the Mille Lac band of Chippewa Indians held at Vineland, regarding the affairs of the band and the lands purchased for allotment to the members.

Meritt reiterated that Congress had appropriated $40,000 for the purchase of lands for the "homeless nonremoval Mille Lacs Indians" and that it had been done.

Meritt stated that allotment of these lands would soon be done and trust patents issued as requested. He pointed out, however, that the Mille Lacs who were allotted on the White Earth Reservation and had sold their allotments and returned to Vineland, were not eligible for an additional allotment.

The buildings, Meritt related, that were located on the tract purchased from D.H. Robbins would suffice for a school and the proposed sub-agency.

In answer to the suggestion that White Earth allottees currently living at Vineland be allowed to sell their White Earth allotment and buy land near Vineland, the Commissioner had no objection if individuals so desired.

It is obvious that not all government officials were supportive of re-creating a reservation at Mille Lacs as evidenced by a February 14, 1920 letter from Congressman Thomas D. Schall to Commissioner of Indian Affairs Cato Sells. The letter asked whether it was possible to move certain Mille Lac Indians to White Earth. Schall was, of course, told that Congress had authorized purchasing lands for the homeless Non-Removal Mille Lac Indians.

In a May 10, 1920 letter from the Supervisor in charge of the White Earth Indians Agency (probably P.R. Wadsworth) to the Commissioner of Indian Affairs, the Supervisor relates that he spent 3 days at Vineland and that the lands purchased near Vineland and Isle for the homeless Non-Removal Mille Lac Indians be promptly allotted as suggested by the Commissioner in his February 3, 1920 letter to chief Me-ge-zee. Not until the Indians knew where their allotment would be, he wrote, could they begin developing their home.

However, on July 8, 1920, the Assistant Commissioner of Indian Affairs wrote that allotment could not begin until the lands at Vineland, Isle and pine County were surveyed and there were no funds available for that purpose in the fiscal year 1921. Therefore, progress in the matter was on hold.

Pressures were coming to bear in the spring of 1922, concerning the Indian burial grounds at Mille Lac. In response to the concern of some of his constituents Congressman Harold Knutson became involved. The land in question was Lots 1 and 2 in Section 33, T. 43, R. 27. Knutson was under the impression that these lots were part of the "perpetual reserve" established by the joint resolution of Congress No. 40 of March 28, 1898 (30 Stat. 745) and that when the Mille Lacs were re-established in this area they would again use these lots as burial grounds. The Congressman was apparently getting pressure from his white constituents, however, who were anxious to acquire these desirable lakeshore lots.

In an annual report for 1923 from the White Earth Agency, White Earth Reservation, it is reported that there was a day school at Mille Lacs with a total enrollment of 38 pupils and an average attendance of 19. The total population of the White Earth Reservation that year (1923) was 7635 with 1424 of them being Removal Mille Lacs and 294 being Non-Removal Mille Lacs.[18]

On March 16, 1923 the Superintendent of the Consolidated Chippewa Agency (presumably Wadsworth) wrote to the Commissioner of Indian Affairs, "… you state that about seventy-five members of the Mille Lac country have signed a petition for the removal of Harry Ayer as licensed trader at Vineland.

"You direct me to make an investigation and report in this matter. If there is no good reasons for not doing so, I will be pleased if you will mail me a full list of the Indians who have signed this petition.

"If you can do so I will be pleased if you will send me the original petition with signatures to me. This will be helpful in making the investigation."

There was obviously much confusion regarding which lands were under Government jurisdiction and which lands the Indians—or part-Indians—were allowed to administrate on their own, owing primarily to the Clapp Act.

Assistant Commissioner of Indian Affairs E.B. Meritt wrote, on July 13, 1923, to Superintendent Wadsworth as follows:

> "My dear Mr. Wadsworth:
> "The following letter has been received from Tom Hill, Onamia, Minnesota.
> " 'The white people on Mo-so-ma-ni Point are digging up the graves of the Indians, for relics and other things that are laid in the coffin of the dead, and after they do that they just let the bones lay around on the ground. Can anything be done?'
> "This matter is refereed to you for investigation and report. Please give same your prompt attention and furnish such information as will be necessary in replying to the communication received from Mr. Hill.
> "Very truly yours,"

And on July 17th the Superintendent replied:

> "... I wish to report that the Indian grave-yard on Mo-so-ma-ni Point is not located on Indian land. Therefore I know of nothing that can be done to prevent people from digging up the graves of the Indians on that Point, other than taking the matter up with County authorities, and endeavoring to get some action from the county authorities.
> "Mo-so-ma-ni Point is owned by white people, and several Indians are living on this Point, without apparent authority from any source.
> "Very respectfully,"

Regarding claims of Chief Wadena, C.F. Hauke, Chief Clerk of the Washington Office of Indian Affairs, wrote the following letter to superintendent Wadsworth of the Consolidated Chippewa Agency on July 18, 1923:

> "My dear Mr. Wadsworth:
> "Reference is made to your letter of July 2, 1923, relating the case of Chief Wadena.
> "The Act of Congress of January 14, 1889 (25 Stats. L. 642), provides for the removal of all Chippewa Indians in Minnesota to the White Earth Reservation and their allotment, after removal on that reservation. The act further provides that Chippewa Indians

of Minnesota could be allotted on the reservation on which they reside. It does not appear that Chief Wadena ever selected land on the Mille Lac, or any other reservation, as an allotment.

"The Mille Lacs band of Chippewa Indians brought suit in the Court of Claims against the United States. This case is reported in 47 Ct. Cl. 415. The Court awarded the Indians $827,589. 72 for their claim to the Mille Lac Reservation. The case was carried to the Supreme Court of the United States and was finally determined in the case of the United States vs. Mille Lac Band of Chippewa Indians in the State of Minnesota (229 U.S. 498) and remanded for reconsideration of the amount to be awarded.

"In view of the fact that title of the Chippewa Indians in the Mille Lac Reservation has been extinguished by appropriate acts of Congress, and that they have had their day in Court, the only tracts to which they can now lay claim are some that have been purchased for your use. Section 16 on which the land in dispute is located, passed to the State under its school land grant, and the State has a right to dispose of it by sale to Mr. Guy C. Johnson or any other party. Chief Wadena has no right on the land that the United States can recognize or defend, and you should so inform him. You may also inform the United States District Attorney and the attorneys for Johnson.

"Very truly yours,"

A reply to Chief Wadena soon followed from the Acting Superintendent of the Consolidated Chippewa Agency:

"Dear Sir:
"Please be advised that the Washington Office has informed me that you have no right on the land that you are now occupying, and the United States cannot defend you. You should make arrangements as soon as possible to move from the land you are now occupying to the land that was bought by the Government for the Mille Lac Indians.

"Very respectfully,"

Notice was given on August 27, 1923, by the Superintendent of the Consolidated Chippewa Agency, that an annuity payment of $13.30 each would be distributed at various places including Vineland.[19]

It had been at least five years since land had been purchased for the homeless Non-Removal Mille Lac Indians and still only tentative allotments had been accomplished. Chief Me-ge-Zee was instructed by the Superintendent of the Consolidated Chippewa Agency:

> "My dear friend,
>
> "Now that tendative [sic] allotments have been made to the Mille Lac Band of Chippewa Indians, and that I have good reason to believe that they will cut, remove and otherwise destroy timber from these lands, wither(sic) for personal use or for commercial purposes, and that trespassing will be of frequent occurrence among them and also some of them will be building homes on lands that do not belong to them causing considerable trouble and confusion among the Indians themselves as well as this office. Therefore, in view of the above, I will ask you to read this letter to the Indians and try to have them understand what I want to say to them.
>
> "These tracts of land that have been selected for your band, are only tendative [sic] allotments and are subject to modification before their final approval by the department at Washington. Plats will have to be prepared showing all these allotments and same approved by the Department. The allotment schedule likewise will have to be approved. And it is also my opinion, trust patents covering a certain period will be issued for each allotment as has been done on all other Indian reservations, making these allotments trust allotments and will be so held until a fee simple are issued. During the time these allotments will be held in trust, no timber other than dead and down should be removed without the permission of the officer in charge, and that these lands will be inalienable during the trust period without the consent of the secretary of the interior.
>
> "Therefore, in view of the fact that the allotments to the Mille Lacs band of Chippewa Indians have not been fully approved by the Department at Washington, I will ask every Indian at Mille Lacs to see that no one cuts green living timber, or destroy it otherwise, either from lands tendatively [sic] allotted to them or to others.
>
> "I do not have any objection, and do not see any material damage that can be done, if some of the Indians want to cut dead and down timber from lands tendatively [sic] allotted to them for wood to use in their homes, provided they do not trespass on other lands.
>
> "In regard to the building of homes, especially by those persons that build on lands not tendatively [sic] allotted to them, any one who does so will do so at his own risk. In order to avoid trouble developing later on this account I ask that this practice be discour-

aged. In some instances this was done in other reservations and always trouble is the result.

"As I stated before, please tell the Indians about what is said in this letter, and that in order to avoid confusion and trouble, I am asking all of them to help us.

"Yours respectfully,"

The census rolls at Vineland and Isle had been closed on October 24th, 1923, and the allotment schedule had been prepared by December 4th of that year—except for inserting land descriptions.

The 1924 annual report for the White Earth Reservation listed the population of Removal Mille Lacs as 1450 and Non-Removal Mille Lacs as 289. By 1925 that number had increased to 1470 Removal Mille Lacs and 292 Non-Removal Mille lacs. The number for the entire White Earth Reservation had increased from 7806 to 8000.[19]

A March 5, 1924 letter from Superintendent Wadsworth to Commissioner Burke would make current environmentalists cringe:

"Sir:

"Answering your letter initialed as above, will say that after giving consideration to the question raised by you as to whether it would be advisable to install a cesspool in connection with indoor toilets for the Mille Lacs Day School, will say that I find it not advisable to drain these cesspools directly into the soil. I find that in this particular locality, there is a hard sand below the surface, from two to four feet, and it is probable that the seepage would be carried over quite a wide territory, making it possible to penetrate to some water bearing strata. Therefore, it would be advisable to either put in a pump or have the cesspool drained by putting in a line for about 400 ft., which would then take care of this matter, by draining it into a lake.

"Very respectfully,"

White Earth Superintendent Wadsworth, in an April 12, 1924 letter to the Club Women of Minnesota, reflected on the status of the Non-Removal Mille Lacs with respect to health care.

"We have eight government physicians under the Cass Lake Agency. Their names and locations are as follows:

"Dr. Frank Hicks, residing at Grand Marias, Minnesota, is the physician for the Indians living at and around Grand Marias and Grand Portage.

"Dr. Wilfred McKechnie, residing in Cook, Minnesota, is the physician for the Nett Lake Indians and the surrounding country.

"Dr. Franklin S. Raiter, residing at Cloquet, Minnesota, is the physician for the Fond du Lac Indians.

"Dr. Z.E. House, residing at Cass Lake, Minnesota, is the physician for the Indians living at and around Cass Lake.

"Dr. Peter A. Slattery, residing in Onigum, Minnesota, is the physician for the Leech Lake Indians.

"Dr. Thomas F. Rodwell, residing at Mahnomen and Naytahwash, Minnesota, is the physician for the White Earth Indians living in Mahnomen and Clearwater County.

"Dr. Ira M. Roadman, residing at Ponsford, Minnesota, is the physician for the White Earth Indians residing at and around Ponsford.

"Dr. Wm. Abbott, residing at White Earth, Minnesota, is the physician for the White Earth Indians residing at and around White Earth.

"All the services rendered by these physicians, including all medicines, for the Indians are without any individual costs to them. Conveyances are furnished to these physicians and they make trips to the houses of Indians and give treatments. Examinations are made and medicines dispensed at their offices."

Obviously the health care for the Removal Mille Lacs was included in the above list, but no mention is made of health care for the Non-Removal Mille Lacs. Therefore a contract physician was provided at times, as previously noted.

Superintendent Wadsworth also reported that, "The boarding schools in the Indian country in Minnesota were closed because Congress cut off appropriations for their support, and this was brought about by the action of leading Indians who opposed the appropriation of their funds for maintaining the schools. This is the reason why the different boarding schools are vacant at the present time."

But, Wadsworth added, "We have government schools under the Cass Lake Agency at Grand Portage, Nett Lake, Mille Lac Lake and Ponsford. There is one teacher at Grand Portage, two at Nett Lake, one at Mille Lac Lake and two at Ponsford. The Ponsford school is on the White Earth Reservation. A hot noon-day meal is given to the children at the schools at Nett lake and Ponsford and clothing is furnished for the school children at Ponsford. These schools are all in government buildings, and all equipment is furnished by the government."

Apparently the Mille Lac Indians were not doing a good job keeping their horses and cattle confined, which resulted in a letter of complaint from a Mr. A.P. Jorgenson of Onamia. In response Superintendent Wadsworth wrote to the teacher at the Indian school at Vineland—Wesley R. Mezian—on May 5, 1924, asking him to talk to the Indians about keeping their livestock off of other persons' lands.

By May 13, 1925, the government was ready to submit for approval a schedule of allotments for the 282 Non-Removal Mille Lacs; allotments of from 5 to 15 acres each, with 13.11 acres reserved for a park and 5 acres reserved for a cemetery. The submission was approved by Assistant Secretary of the Interior John H. Edwards and by the General Land Office.

In his annual report for the Consolidated Chippewa Agency for 1925, Superintendent Wadsworth related that there were five reservations under the jurisdiction of the Consolidated Chippewa Indian Agency, named as follows: White Earth Reservation, Leech Lake Reservation, Fond du Lac Reservation, Grand Portage Reservation and Nett Lake or Bois Fort Reservation.[20]

Wadsworth's 1926 annual report shows a population of 1515 Removal Mille Lacs Chippewa and 294 Non-Removal Mille Lac Chippewas.[21]

A letter from Commissioner of Indian Affairs Chas. H, Burke to U.S. Senator Thomas D. Schall is reflective of the goings-on at Mille Lacs:

"Jan. 7, 1926

"My dear Senator:

"Reference is made to your letter of December 15, 1925, with enclosure from Mr. E.E. Dinwiddie, of Wigwam Bay, Minnesota, concerning taxation of lands in Mille Lacs County, Minnesota.

"Mr. Dinwiddie states that previous to purchase of lands in Mille Lacs County by the Government for Indians the town of Kathio had issued bonds in the sum of $12,000 for road purposes; that the bonds are maturing at the rate of $2000 per annum; that the purchased lands, within the town are not taxed, therefore to pay the bonds, excessive rates of taxation are imposed upon the other lands.

"Without full knowledge of the conditions under which the bonds were issued and of the pledges made in connection therewith, this Office could not properly suggest any plan for the relief of the tax payers. However, Mr. Dinwiddie's letter has been referred to the Superintendent of the Consolidated Chippewa Agency at Cass Lake, Minnesota, for investigation and report. When his report has been received the Office will be glad to take up with you further. The purchased lands have been allotted in severalty to the Indians and patents containing the usual 25 year trust clauses issued to them individually.

"Mr. Dinwiddie's letter will be returned to you when the further reply is made.

"Cordially,"

At last, on February 11, 1926, allotments were finalized to the 282 Non-Removal Mille Lac Indians.

The Superintendent of the Consolidated Chippewa Agency was now E.A. Allen, who concluded his 1926 annual report with observation made during his visit to Mille Lac.

"At the time of the annuity payment last fall, I went in the evening to the Indian village at 'Mille Lacs Lake where a pagan dance was in progress in the 'round house'. Just outside the door, before entering, I found a fifteen year old mixed blood boy in a state of beastly intoxication and a young man of twenty-one years or so, also a mixed-blood, reeling about the premises. The day school inspector, one of the clerks and I took the boy to his sister's home to be cared for and relieved the young man mentioned of a quart jar with a little moonshine still in it. We chased him away and then entered the dance hall. Everything there was being conducted decorously with about all the full bloods of the village in attendance. We were given a cordial welcome and the leader of the dance delivered an address of welcome in which he deplored the drinking being done by the boys and assured us of the strong disapproval of all those present in the room. Both the drunken fellows had been ejected from the room shortly before my arrival. The dance then proceeded, both men and women engaging in it but all dancing without physical contact. It broke up at eleven P.M. and all participants went quietly to their homes.

"It seems that these pagan dances are perfectly innocent in themselves but are made the occasion for indulgence in immoral practices. They are much more innocent than the average road house dances and productive of less harm. Whatever influence would break up the prevalent camps of idleness, would put a pause to Indian dances and substitute therefor participation by the young in those of the neighborhoods, with exposure to the attendant vices."[22]

Superintendent Allen reported on the state of affairs regarding the allotments made to the Chippewa. As of 1926, 9020 allotments had been made to various Chippewa Indians. He reports as follows:

"There are included in this agency about 12,600 Indians. Most of this number are landless. About 9,020 allotments in all have been made to various allottees belonging to the present Consolidated jurisdiction but by reason of expiration of the trust period and, to a very great extent, by reason of the granting of Patents-in-fee in advance of the arrival of such time of expiration, the number of allotments still in Indian ownership is sadly reduced. In the granting of a patents-in-fee in the past, the tests of competency made were in great measure farcical. Hundreds of those judged competent, who have received patents and have sold their lands are among the most helpless persons in the jurisdiction. ... As a general proposition an Indian patent-in-fee is a certain precursor of a sale and the allottee usually has knowledge of who the next owner will be before his restrictions have been removed. Ownership of land to him is merely a sign of enslavement to one spot and bondage to drudgery; both abhorrent to him

— so he removes the sign and frees himself from the bondage at the earliest possible opportunity.

"Of the 2,613 restricted allotments 282 are those diminutive ones made two or three years ago by Dr. Wooster of your office, to the Mille Lac Chippewas. Not to exceed a half dozen of the Mille Lac allottees are occupying their newly acquired tracts and there exists considerable opposition among them to the urging of this office that they abandon their village and open small farms and make improvements on their allotments. The conditions are most unfavorable to such removal. Marshes and cut-over land or land covered with stumps and granite boulders will appal [sic] the most hardy white pioneer and the Indian, untutored without capital and with no inclination to persistent, arduous labor, with rewards uncertain and long deferred recoils from the task involved in building a home upon and wresting a livelihood from a tract of from five to seven and one half acres. These allottees are now asking the Government to finance the building of houses, etc., but I have been able to give them no encouragement, as from the standpoint of likelihood of repayments such reimbursable agreements would not be desirable securities. The Indians, it should be further observed, have not asked for loans but for donations sufficient for the making of such improvements."[23]

Much had been made—indeed was still being made—as to the competency of the Chippewa Indians, which, to the Government at this time, meant the ability to manage money and property. There is no doubt that such considerations were foreign to the Chippewa prior to the white man's arrival. The Government had attempted to control the situation by placing restrictions on the land that was allotted to the Chippewa, but by 1926 that system had considerably broken down.

Superintendent Allen, in his 1926 annual report, opined:

"Individual Indian money, of which we have nearly four hundred thousand dollars, is paid out under office regulations. If we did not apply the brakes somewhat relentlessly, most of the Indians would spend all their funds as soon as placed to their credit — even before, if they could get them. They are constantly endeavoring to anticipate credits and are most insistent in their demands for any money to their credit to be used immediately for living expenses. It is difficult to induce even those who have considerable money to apply it on home improvements. An appropriate illustration is furnished in the case of Chief Wah-we-yay-cumig. Last year Congress appropriated five thousand dollars to pay him for alleged services in behalf of the Mille Lac Chippewas. The money was sent to him in a treasury warrant in May 1925, and by June 30, the same year, or in two months, four thousand three hundred dollars had disappeared without his even having a good suit of clothes. When I assumed charge of the agency July 1, the last seven hundred dollars was on deposit in the First National Bank of Cass Lake. This was not in my care but was deposited in such a manner that the cashier would not permit the Chippewa to draw without the approval of the

Superintendent. By refusing to go with him to the bank as often as he wished me to the seven hundred dollars was made to last until the first of June this year.

"However, during the eleven months, it was necessary for me to stand off an attorney and to explain to a congressman, whose aid had been solicited by the Indians. You will understand of course, that this five thousand dollars was not restricted money and that the Superintendent sustained only an advisory relation, otherwise it would have been made to last longer. It indicates how quickly such Indians will go through their money if there exists no control outside of themselves."[24]

Regarding the allotments—which had finally been accomplished—Superintendent Allen stated in his 1927 annual report that, "At Mille Lac Lake about a dozen of the 198 allottees are living upon the lands given them. Of course about half of the 298 are minors and as husband and wife and children all received allotments, in most cases, there are fewer than 100 families. We are still pressing these people to go on their lands but in some cases we have had little argument to back our insistence. For example, I find that the land allotted in one township is practically all sand upon which no person, Indian or white, could hope to make a living."[25]

Superintendent Allen's 1927 annual report lists the population of the White Earth Reservation as including 1529 Removal Mille Lacs and 291 Non-Removal Mille Lacs.[26] However, in that same report folder is a "NOTATION OF ERROR IN STATISTICAL REPORT" which reads as follows:

> "Reservation areas: Your letter of February 18th indicates that you have combined the White Oak Point Reservation data with the data for the Leech Lake Reservation, and we are assuming that you have also combined the data for the Deer Creek Reservation with the Bois Fort Reservation data. Inasmuch as we are working up data for all reservations separately, you are requested to submit new pages 18 and 19 for the several separate reservations mentioned above, including the Mille Lac Reservation. Blanks enclosed."[27]

By this change in data collection and reporting it makes it appear that the former Mille Lac Reservation still exists, when in reality it is simply land purchased and placed in trust for this remnant of Mille Lacs who refused to remove to White Earth—as agreed. The narrative section of that same 1927 annual report says,

> "The Consolidated Chippewa Agency at Cass Lake, Minnesota was formed July 1, 1922 by consolidating the White Earth, Leech Lake, Fond du Lac, Nett Lake and Grand Portage reservations. The jurisdiction extends 400 miles from East to West and about 250 miles from North to South. To visit all the principal settlements, which does not include many small villages scattered about the

area mentioned, requires a travel of about 1500 miles. In this territory would be included our population of 12,766 were all residing within the former reservations. But not more than half can be found there, the remainder being scattered with 2301 making their homes outside the State."[28]

This narrative clearly indicates that the few Mille Lacs still remaining at Mille Lacs were never the less considered part of the White Earth Reservation.

In the 1928 annual report of the Consolidated Chippewa Agency the introductory paragraph reads as follows:

"The Consolidated Chippewa Agency at Cass Lake has been in existence since July 1, 1922, having at that time been formed by uniting the White Earth, Leech Lake, Fond du Lac, Nett Lake and Grand Portage jurisdictions. On our rolls are all Minnesota Chippewa Indians, save those of the unallotted Red Lake reservation. Sub-agencies and other settlements are scattered over the State from Grand Portage on the north-east to White Earth on the south-west, from Nett and Vermillion lakes on the north to Minneapolis and St. Paul on the south. A visit to the principal settlements, excluding all the many minor ones, involves not less than 1,500 miles by automobile. A trip to the stations at Cloquet, Grand Portage and Nett Lake requires covering 700 miles; to Ponsford, White Earth, Onigum and Naytahwaush, 300 miles; to Mille Lacs and St. Paul, 480 miles, and to Bena, Ball Club and Inger and Squaw Lake, 140 miles. Covering this mileage would still leave unvisited a multitude of smaller settlements, extending to the Canadian border."[29]

Superintendent Allen concluded this 1928 report with the following commentary:

"In fairness to the Tribe it should be said that thousands of its members have left the reservations and they, with a few still within reservation borders, have taken an honorable place in society, not only bearing their own burdens but also contributing their share to the general welfare of the communities in which they live. The forgoing discussion has been devoted almost entirely to those comparatively unambitious members of the Tribe who remain in the vicinity of the old reservations, for whose benefit it is deemed necessary to continue the activities of the Federal Government."[30]

John Arrowood of Isle had apparently been visited by a delegation of Chippewa Indians who had asked him to write to Senator Henrick Shipstead on their behalf. On February 20, 1928, he wrote:

> "Dear Sir:
>
> "Yesterday a delegation of Chippewa's Indians called on me and wanted me to write you in regard to a Treaty made with the Chippewas Indians in 1837 to find out if that treaty had ever been canceled or any other been made in its place. Chief Wadena claimed he had a copy of 1837 which reads as follows White man can take white pine and Norway pine and but can no take any Birch for that is my house and my no Oak and Indian alwas [sic] can hunt Deere and Bear for that is his meat Indian can always gather wild rice for that is his bread, Indian can always trap in lake or stream for all kind's [sic] of fur. Chief Wadena says Indian never sold any pulp wood or R.R. ties and now white man don't want Indian to cut firewood. Also Indian never sold any Maple for that is his sugar & Molassel [sic]. Indian don't like Indian Agent at Cass lake no good for Indians. Better get another good Agent at Cass Lake.
>
> "Now Mr. Shipstead will you please write letter for publication in the St. Paul Daily — news favoring the Indian Hope you will see this letter gets in committee
>
> "John Arrowood"

Senator Shipstead forwarded the Arrowood letter to Chas. H. Burke, Commissioner of Indian Affairs. Commissioner Burke responded saying,

> "My dear Senator:
>
> "The receipt is acknowledged of your letter of February 25, 1928, enclosing a communication to you from Mr. John Arrowood of Isle, Minnesota, in regard to a treaty alleged to have been made between the United States and the Chippewa Indians in 1837.
>
> "This matter will be looked into and you will be informed."

Obviously the Commissioner of Indian Affairs funneled the matter to Superintendent Allen of the Consolidated Chippewa Agency, who in turn inquired of John Jekey, also of Isle, as to who this man John Arrowood was. On March 12, 1928, John Jekey replied,

> "My Dear Sir-
>
> "I have your favor of March 10 asking who this man John Arrowood is. He is a man that come here about two years ago he has no thing [sic] to do with the Indians it seem to me that he is just

trying to agetate [sic] something so that he will get paid from us for his so-called work for us we do not want this man to be recognized he is not helping us and firther [sic] more do not listen to anything that Wa-de-na writes about he is allways [sic] trying to do something that will detain us to get what we should get so please do not listen to any letters that he has any one write for him."

Superintendent Allen reported on March 13, 1928 to Commissioner Burke saying,

"Sir:

"... In order to find out who this man Arrowood is I wrote to Mr. John Jekey of Isle, Minnesota, who is a leader of the Indians of that neighborhood. Jekey is a man who stands well with all the Indians and his qualities are such that he also has the respect of the white people in the neighborhood. ...

"Several times, Wadena, who is a leader of a little group of Indians, has been insisting that the Government under the Treaty of 1837 should build houses for all the Mille Lac Chippewas on the allotments made to them by Dr. Wooster. I tried to explain to him that there is no provision by which such houses can be constructed; that while an arrangement was made for building houses on the White Earth Reservation for such Mille Lac Chippewas as would go to that reservation at the time allotments were being made, that arrangement was discontinued years ago, there being no longer funds for the purpose and that such arrangement was never contemplated for the Mille Lac Chippewas on the Wooster allotments. Wadena is firmly convinced, regardless of all I have told him, that such houses could be built were it not for the fact that the present Superintendent is obstructing the carrying out of the provision of the Treaty of 1837.

"Wadena has also been told that settlement was made with the Indians not only for the pine timber but also for the hardwoods. He has further been advised that there is no treaty in force by virtue of which the Indians can hunt and fish in violation of the State law. Notwithstanding the many patient explanations that have been made, he is convinced that the Superintendent is not only wrong but acts adversely to the desires and rights of Indians of his class."

In his 1929 annual report Superintendent Allen made the following summary regarding allotments:

"Allotment to all the bands except Red Lake was completed years ago. Some of the Mille Lac Chippewas who failed to take advantage of the opportunity for getting lands then were the last ones to receive allotments. It was necessary, in order to give them small parcels, to purchase some land around Mille Lac Lake and Markville [Pine County], Minnesota. These allotments, of from two and a half to five acres, were made in 1924. No allotments have been made since except some in lieu selections to take the place of tracts that were classified as State swamp land, the ownership of which was confirmed in the State of Minnesota by the United States Supreme Court a couple of years ago. ..."[31]

In his introductory remarks of his 1930 annual report Superintendent Allen seems to be promoting the winding down of federal involvement with the Indians and encouraging the transfer of unfinished business to the States. Allen says,

"Previous annual reports submitted by me have begun with a brief historical sketch, dealing with the consolidation of five jurisdictions into the one at Cass Lake, the closing of several boarding and day schools, the discontinuance of a number of farmers and other positions, and the taking of other measures looking to a contracting of Government activities, in response to the clamor of leading Chippewa political agitators, and in pursuance of the policy of the Department to relinquish to the State responsibility for this class of citizens. It was believed — and it appears to me as sane philosophy, justified by existing conditions — that when the Federal Government had discharged its remaining legal obligations to the Chippewas of this jurisdiction, assumed through early treaties and the Rice agreement of 1889, it should no longer consider them a special charge." Later in his report he wrote, "My belief is that the earlier program of decreasing paternalism, looking to a not long deferred withdrawal of the Federal Government from the position of special guardian and wet nurse is the sane one." In a later section he made the observation that. "The Government has wasted much time and money in attempting the impossible project of making farmers of these Chippewas. Both by nature and by situation they are precluded from such career. ... At this time, our Indians, in most cases, even if they have land of any sort, possess neither, Capital, courage, inclination nor business ability to engage in farming, successful prosecution of which, in this day, requires all four items of equipment."[32]

By 1931 M.L. Burns was the superintendent of the Consolidated Chippewa Agency. In the population section of Burns' 1931 annual report were listed five reservations as part of the Consolidated Chippewa Agency, namely; White Earth, Leech lake, Fond du Lac, Nett Lake and Grand Portage. The Non-Removal Mille Lacs were not mentioned by name in the report, but obviously they were included as part of White Earth as evidenced by reference made to an excellent 4H Club at Mille Lacs, and also by mention that the handicraft work of Mille Lac Indian women contributed much to the income of their families. Superintendent Burns also declared that Mille Lacs trader Harry D. Ayer employed a crew of all Indians in his boat factory and employed Mille Lac Indians during the maple sugar and fishing seasons.[33]

Subsequent to a trip to Mille Lacs to follow up on an elderly Indian woman's request for help, White Earth Field Clerk John Morrison made an observation in a July 17, 1931 letter to Superintendent Burns at Cass Lake. "While rambling around over the little reservation there it appears to me that some attention should be given these Indians. They are very backward and are far from doing as well as they should do. Their little gardens are, in the main, sadly neglected; there seems to be absolutely no ambition, on their part, to make any advancement towards self support [sic] .

"If it meets with your approval I should be glad to make periodical trips there and see if some method could be found whereby these Indians could do more for themselves than they are doing now."

Here again is an indication that these Indians were considered a part of White Earth.

On October 5, 1931, White Earth Field Clerk Morrison reported to Consolidated Chippewa Agency Superintendent Burns saying, "In the Mille Lacs Lake and Danbury country the Indians are very backward, but it is fully believed that their lagging interest in things agricultural could be revived by frequent visits of a Field man who would try leading rather than driving."[34]

Apparently in 1931 government rations were being furnished to the Non-Removal Mille Lacs through White Earth, and that—at least in the Vineland area—Trader H.D. Ayer was involved in distribution.[35] The Indians in the Isle area also would appeal to White Earth when in need of food or other help.[36]

Businesses at Mille Lac, it appears, were not above taking advantage of the Indians as evidenced by this letter from White Earth Field Clerk John Morrison to Consolidated Chippewa Agency Superintendent Burns on December 3, 1931:

> "Dear Mr. Burns,
>
> "Complying with your instructions, dated the 2nd, ultimo, I called on Mr. Joseph M. Eagle, Vineland Lodge, Onamia, Minn., in reference to his letter to you relative to the sale of his land and timber and the recovery from Mr. H.D. Ayer of money collected

from Eagle for the payment of the hospital and operation expenses of Mee gee zee's.

"I found Mr. Eagle living in a tarred paper house near the Vineland Lodge, which is operated by Lewis Garvey and the man who wants to buy a portion of Eagle's land and timber. Eagle did not know how much Garvey wanted to buy and there had been no price agreed upon.

"The office had, I gather from Eagle's letter to you, turned down the proposed sale and this phase of his letter was settled, but at his earnest solicitation I went over the tract with him and found that he had a most desirable piece of property and it was a most fortunate thing for Eagle that the office did not accede to his request and allow him to sell his land, or even part of it, under existing conditions.

"Eagle was much concerned over the method employed by Mr. Ayer in collecting the bill of Mee gee zee, mentioned above, in the sum of $300.00.

"Eagle claims that he was working for Mr. Ayer and Ayer held out $1.00 each day from the wages of Eagle to apply on this bill, and in addition to this, Eagle claims that Mr. Ayer rented out maple trees on Eagle's property, collected the rent and applied it on the $300 bill. Mee gee zee, by the way, was the father of Eagle and willed him the larger portion of his property at his death.

"Mr. Ayer was incapacitated to the extent that his side of the story could not be obtained. It does seem queer that Eagle would permit such high handed methods to be employed in the collection of a debt unless he had, in some manner, guaranteed the payment of it.

"I cannot reconcile Eagle's story with the high handed method said to have been employed by Mr. Ayer, and it is believed that the proper thing to do would be to get these two men together and ascertain all the facts in the case.

"In reciting the foregoing I am assuming, of course, that Eagle is a restricted member of the tribe.

"In the absence of instructions to the contrary it is my intention to make an effort to get these two men together on my next trip to Mille Lac Lake."[37]

White Earth Field Clerk Morrison purchased needed supplies for the Mille Lac Non-Removal Indians from H.S. Nyquist in Isle, who operated the Time O Day Store, Chas. Domit of Danbury, Wisconsin, and H.D. Ayer of Onamia who managed the Mille Lacs Indian Trading Post, and apparently also from Dahlgren Brothers in Onamia. Indians in need of groceries would make their needs known to the merchants and those requests would be relayed to White Earth.[38]

It is abundantly clear in reviewing the business dealings of the Non-Removal Mille Lacs that there was no official contact point at Mille Lacs or Pine County, and that all business dealings were being accomplished through the White Earth Reservation—again a clear indication that they were still considered a part of the White Earth Reservation in the early 1930's.[39]

It is interesting to note that great care was being taken in 1933 to determine whether a particular incident occurred on federal land or state land. Billy Bedausky had allegedly taken a shot at a deputy game warden on the so-called Mille Lac Indian Reservation. The issue was whether or not the incident occurred on Indian land.

Another incident involved trapping by Joe Bush, Sr. and Jack Uran—in violation of state game laws. In both of these incidents there was the question of whether state law or federal law applied.

As of the writing of this book there is still major disagreement amongst involved parties as to whether or not the Mille Lacs Band of the 21st century was a **recognized** band at the time that the Indian Reorganization Act was passed on June 18, 1934.

There is no doubt that the goal of the Nelson Act of 1889—to concentrate all of the Chippewa at White Earth—had failed by 1934. What resulted was a closed reservation at Red Lake and a Consolidated Chippewa tribe composed of five open reservations; White Earth, Leech Lake, Fond du Lac, Nett Lake and Grand Portage reservations, plus numerous small settlements throughout the area from Minneapolis — St. Paul to the Canadian border. Mille Lacs, which itself was composed of three even smaller villages—Vineland, Isle and Pine County—was one of those settlements, and was administered through White Earth.

At the urging of the Washington statisticians with the Bureau of Indian Affairs, some of these smaller settlements were separated out for statistical purposes. Mille Lac was one of those separated, and became known in annual reports as the "homeless Non-removal Mille Lacs on purchased land." The first time they were listed as a Mille Lac Reservation was in the annual report of the Consolidated Chippewa Agency submitted on December 31, 1935, but even in that report they are also categorized as "NON-REMOVAL MILLE LAC — PURCHASED LANDS."

In archival records was found an undated and unsigned document entitled "Proposals for Provisions of the Constitution of the Minnesota Chippewa Tribe." It reads, "The jurisdiction of the Minnesota Chippewa Tribe shall extend to all allotted or tribal land within the original boundaries of the following reservation sites: - White Earth, Nett Lake, Leach Lake, Grand Portage, Fond du Lac and Mille Lac, and to such other tribal lands or lands held in trust by the United States for the tribe or for any of its members as have been or may hereafter be acquired." Attached to this document is another document entitled: "Considerations affecting the method of organizing the Minnesota Chippewa Indians."

Section II of that document reads as follows: "There is serious question whether any of the old reservations except Red Lake and White Earth still exist in contemplation of the law. Under the act of 1889 the various bands of the Chippewa agreed to 'cede' all the reservations except White Earth and Red Lake and remove to White Earth Reservation except for those individual Indians who preferred allotments where they were. Moreover, those remaining on the old reservation sites are only individual remnants of the old recognized bands and it is doubtful whether these remnants could now be recognized as a band."

While not official, clearly someone involved with preparing a proposed constitution for the Minnesota Chippewa Tribe was having similar thoughts about the legality of what they were contemplating, as have I.

The Indian Reorganization Act had been passed into law on June 18, 1934. On March 12, 1937, Senator Elmer Thomas, Chairman of the Senate Committee on Indian Affairs, requested a list of Indian tribes under the Indian Reorganization Act. On March 18, 1937, the following list was supplied to Senator Thomas by John Collier, Commissioner of Indian Affairs and author of the Howard-Wheeler Act—which became the Indian Reorganization Act.

INDIAN TRIBES UNDER THE I.R.A.				
STATE	AGENCY OR SCHOOL	RESERVATION OR RANCHERA	TRIBE	TOTAL POPULATION (ESTIMATED)
Minnesota	Con. Chippewa	White Earth	Chippewa (Minn.)	8,059
		Leech Lake	" "	2,076
		Fond du Lac	" "	1,298
		Bois Fort	" "	627
		Grand Portage	" "	377

Obviously the Non-Removal portion of the Mille Lac band located on purchased land was not considered a reservation but was included under the White Earth Reservation—as it had been since 1889.[40]

Following the passage of the Indian Reorganization Act, Assistant Commissioner Zimmerman wrote on, August 7, 1934, to Superintendent Burns of the Consolidated Chippewa Agency saying, "In accordance with the provisions of the Wheeler-Howard Act, it is planned to proceed with the organization of at least one of the groups or bands under your jurisdiction at an early date. Some of the elements which should be considered in determining which band should be selected first are: enthusiasm and previous thought of tribe, absence of land difficulties, geography and type of tribe, and simplicity."

Superintendent Burns replied to Commissioner Collier on August 27, 1934, stating, "Receipt is acknowledged of Office letter dated August 7, and the same is answered herein in regard to the organizing of our Indians under the provisions of the Wheeler-Howard Act. There are listed herein the order these Indians or groups of them that have expressed their assent to organize or otherwise accept the provisions of the above act should be organized, with some information or comments made in this connection by us.

"First: Leech Lake

"Second: Mille Lac

"These Indians accepted the principles of the Wheeler-Howard Act at the Hayward meeting in April. They were allotted on land which was purchased for this band, allotments consisting of approximately 2 to 10 acres, no sales or patents in fee have been issued and thus remain intact which removes to a large extent land difficulties. ... It is my opinion that when one or more of the reservations under this jurisdiction have organized corporate communities some of those more reluctant will swing their way. It must be noted that there is no recognized or authentic tribal organization of the Indians, without which in my opinion they can not [sic] hope to do justice to themselves as there is so much that can be accomplished in unity that cannot be otherwise. ..."

On November 5, 1934, John Collier, Commissioner of Indian Affairs, wrote to the Indians of the White Earth Reservation. "Superintendent Burns advises me that by your vote on October 27 you have unquestionably decided to accept the Indian Reorganization Act ... Secretary Ickes and I are highly gratified at the action taken, and we wish to congratulate you upon the wisdom shown and the interest displayed by your people in casting the ballots of so large a portion of the entire voting population. ... This letter gives formal notice that the Indians of the White Earth jurisdiction have accepted the Indian Reorganization Act."

Superintendent Burns wrote on December 6, 1934, again to John Collier regarding Collier's insistence that a separate form be filed giving information on the tribal organization on each reservation under his jurisdiction. Burns penned, "Further, wish to advise that there is no tribal organization of the Chippewas in this jurisdiction that can be properly recognized as a representative organization of the tribe, while there are one or two local councils they are merely community councils members being of the local communities where they exist and not truly representative of the entire reservation or tribe, and not the proper councils that should be incorporated under the Wheeler-Howard Law."

A rather interesting letter was written to a Miss Annie O'Brien on February 23, 1935 from Superintendent Burns. Miss O'Brien had apparently been a former teacher in one of the Indian schools. Burns explained that the Chippewa Agency was moved to Cass Lake in 1920 or 1921 and that this move had been made because of the fact that there had been five distinct agencies, which were now covered by the Consolidated Chippewa Agency. Burns explained that the status of the White Earth Indians at that time was that fully 95 per cent of them had no land and many of them were without homes. He continued that, "[I]t is my belief that there is not a full blood in Minnesota let alone White Earth, Minnesota though in mode of living and habits they are like old-time Indians. There is much drinking and immorality among them, but no more so than in white communities similarly situated." He went on to say, "The number of Indian children from White Earth attending non-reservation schools is not very large by reason of the fact that the quantum of Indian blood is taken into consideration when the question of eligibility is decided and a very large number of the children of White Earth are not eligible by reason of the fact that the amount of Indian blood is considered insufficient."

In the 1936 annual report of the Consolidated Chippewa Agency the Mille Lacs were still categorized as "Non-Removal Mille Lac—Purchased Land". There was very meager data included except that the population as of January 1, 1936, was listed as 358 with only 6 being classified as full blood.[41]

On April 29, 1936, Assistant Solicitor Charlotte T. Westwood wrote to the Land Division of the Indian Office. She stated that the proposed constitution for the Minnesota Chippewa talked about 6 reservations: Fond du Lac, Grand Portage, Leech Lake, Mille Lac, Nett Lake and White Earth. Westwood said, "The Mille Lac Reservation is frequently officially referred to as 'Purchased Lands' rather than a reservation. The lands involved were purchased under the act of August 1, 1914 (38 Stat. 591), for the homeless non-removal members of the Mille Lac Band. Is it proper to refer to these lands as a reservation?"

J.M. Stewart, Director of Lands, replied to Assistant Solicitor Westwood on May 1, 1936, explaining that the Treaty of 1855 set aside a reservation for the Mississippi Band of Chippewa and the Mille Lac Band was a part of that. He continued that, by the Treaty of 1864, the lands of the reservation were ceded to the United States, clarifying that the remaining Mille Lacs were referred to as "non-removal Mille Lac Indians" because of Article 12 of the 1864 treaty. The Act of August 1, 1914 (38 Stat. 591), he said, provided for the use of not to exceed $40,000 to purchase lands for these homeless Indians who had never received allotments. These purchased lands would be held in trust and allotted to the Indians. "These purchased lands may be considered as the reservation of the non-removal Mille Lac Indians."

Director Stewart's explanation up to his last sentence is essentially correct, but one must ask, by what authority can he consider purchased land as being a reservation?

Obviously Assistant Commissioner of Indian Affairs Wm. Zimmerman was not convinced by Director Stewart's opinion—or was he? On May 20, 1936, Zimmerman wrote to Secretary of the Interior Harold Ickes saying that the Chippewa, under the jurisdiction of the Consolidated Chippewa Agency, are calling for an election to approve a constitution and by-laws. The Tribe, he stated, was officially called the "Chippewa Indians in the State of Minnesota" and consisted of all the bands that had reservations at the time of the 1889 Nelson Act. All of the reservations in Minnesota—except Red Lake—were placed under the Consolidated Chippewa Agency, Zimmerman added, and that only six of the old reservations were still recognized administratively as reservations, namely: 1) Bois Fort (or Nett Lake), 2) Fond du Lac, 3) Grand Portage, 4) Leech Lake, 5) The purchased lands for the Non-Removal Mille Lacs, and 6) White Earth. Zimmerman explained that there was a great deal of conflict between Red Lake and the others, and Red Lake had decided not to join the Minnesota Chippewa of the Consolidated Agency. As a result the Minnesota Chippewa Tribe, he said, consisted of all the Minnesota Chippewa except Red Lake. The Act of 1889 (Nelson Act) tried to physically relocate all Chippewa to White Earth, Zimmerman said, but that did not transpire, but that currently the organization of the Minnesota Chippewa tribe brought them all together organizationally. Cases cited were:

> *United States v. Minnesota*, 270 U.S. 181
>
> *United States v. Mille Lac Band*, 229 U.S. 498
>
> *Minnesota v. Hitchcock*, 185 U.S. 373
>
> *Chippewa Indians of Minnesota v. United States*, 80 Ct.Cl. 410, Cert. den. Oct 14, 1935

On May 22, 1936, Secretary of Interior Harold Ickes called for the election.

On June 27, 1936, Superintendent of the Consolidated Chippewa Agency Burns wrote to Fred Daiker, Assistant Commissioner of Indian Affairs, reporting on how successful the election to accept the constitution was. In that communication Burns refers to White Earth, Leech Lake, Fond du Lac, Nett Lake (Bois Fort) and Grand Portage as reservations, but calls Mille Lacs "the Mille Lacs District."

The constitution of the Minnesota Chippewa Tribe was approved July 24, 1936, and ratified November 13, 1937.

In the annual report of the Consolidated Chippewa Agency for 1937, the Mille Lacs account is entitled, "Non Removal Mille Lac (Purchased Lands) Reservation". This seems a clear indication that Mille Lac was not a reservation—but they wanted it to be.[42]

There was some disagreement as to whether or not the vote to accept the constitution was done legally, and Commissioner Collier responded to that question by stating that it was simply a misunderstanding of the law. There were 6662 eligible voters, with 2082 favorable votes cast—over 30%.

In the 1938 Consolidated Chippewa Agency annual report the Mille Lacs are entitled, Non Removal Mille Lac Reservation (Purchased Lands). The population was listed on January 1, 1938 as 378.[43]

In 1939 through 1943 the annual report titles the Mille Lacs as, "Non Removal Mille Lac (Purchased Lands) Reservation." The population increased by one to 379 in 1939 and had increased to 415 by January 1, 1943.[44]

By September of 1939 there was discussion about purchasing the Weide and Haverstock property for the Mille Lac Indians. These properties were located a mile to a mile and a half north of Vineland. There apparently were 70 taxpaying homeowners in Isle—residing in Eastside Township—who were protesting the purchase of any land in Isle for the Indians. These Isle residents wanted the Indians moved to some other location.

Superintendent Burns had spoken with the Indians about moving, and seven or eight families had agreed to move to Vineland. Burns declared that there was no opportunity for the Indians to achieve economic independence in Isle, while Vineland offered good schools, good roads and other features not available in Isle. The Weide and Haverstock property contained 5 houses, three of which were large enough for two families each. This seemed like a perfect solution to a problem that had caused serious difficulties for a number of years.

In 2009, the United States Supreme Court, in *Carcieri v. Salazar* (555 U.S. 397), ruled that the Indian Reorganization Act applied only to those tribes "under federal jurisdiction" at the time of its passage. Unfortunately the Court did not define "under federal jurisdiction."

In 2010, Monroe Skinaway, chairman of the Sandy Lake Band of Ojibwe, reportedly wrote that he was well aware that the Minnesota Chippewa Tribe was organized under the Wheeler, Howard, Indian Reorganization Act of 1934. Skinaway said that it was his understanding that five reservations were originally restored or recognized, which were White Earth, Leech Lake, Boise Forte, Fond-du-lac, and Grand Portage, and that the Mille Lacs Band was added later by the Bureau of Indian Affairs (BIA) administratively. The recreated Mille Lacs Band, he wrote, was to consist of Vineland, Isle, Danbury, East Lake communities and the Sandy Lake Indian Reservation. The Government record seems to substantiate in large part chairman Skinaway's perception.

At the time of this writing, 2016, the Mille Lacs Band calls themselves officially the Non-removable Mille Lacs Band. The first time I found this term used in the archival records was in regard to the Isle Indians. And in a December 6, 1939 letter to Land Field Agent A.L. Hook, Assistant Commissioner of Indian Affairs Wm. Zimmerman refers to the Isle group of Indians as the "group of non-removable Mille Lacs Indians."

CHAPTER 21

White Earth and the Nelson Act

By 1889 the Government's plan to concentrate all the Minnesota Chippewa—except for Red Lake—into one area at White Earth Reservation was accepted as official policy. The Nelson Act, or what we might look at as the Dawes Act adapted to Minnesota, was a further step toward assisting the Chippewa Indian people into becoming more self-sufficient, and to assimilate the Indians into the citizenry of the United States—as full citizens—with all the same privileges and duties.

That was the basis of the Nelson Act: to provide each Indian family with land of their own, a house and implements needed to establish themselves as farmers, instructional guidance on how to become farmers, and a path to becoming full citizens.

The Chippewa had never truly had a unified governmental structure up until White Earth was established. Hole-in-the-Day the elder and Hole-in-the-Day the younger had claimed some central Chippewa structure, but their idea disappeared at their deaths and nonetheless was never widely accepted.

The Nelson Act had been approved by President Benjamin Harrison on March 4, 1890, following acceptance by all eleven Chippewa bands in Minnesota. On April 12th of that year the same Commission—Rice, Marty and Whiting—had been appointed to place the Nelson Act into effect, but only Henry Rice was actively engaged in the effort. Marty and Whiting were in reserve, to be called to duty only as needed. The assignment of the commission was to remove all the Chippewa to White Earth—those who were entitled and desired to remove—and then to allot all those residing there.

The task of deciding which Chippewa were entitled to be covered under the Nelson Act was not a simple job. The promise of free land and homes was enticing to unqualified claimants, and untangling the issue consumed a good deal of the Commission's time. While some Chippewa were trying to move to White Earth although they were not entitled to do so, a great amount of effort was still being expended in an effort to get the remaining Mille Lacs to remove.

On July 6, 1891, Chairman Henry Rice resigned his position and was replaced by Chairman Darwin Hall. In short order Chairman Hall ran into difficulties in attempting to accomplish the task assigned him because, at least in his view and likely true, the Indian Agent at White Earth did not agree with the way the program was being implemented and, instead of assisting, was obstructing the process. For example, Agent Shuler controlled the saw mill and Commissioner Hall had difficulties procuring enough lumber to erect the required houses because little or no lumber was being produced.

The task before the Chippewa Commission was daunting. In the annual report for 1891, the statement is made, "There are about 5,000 Indians whose names appear upon the census rolls of the various bands of Chippewas in the State of Minnesota who are privileged under the act to remove to the White Earth Reservation if they so desire, present removals being included. All of them however, have the privilege, if they so elect, of taking their allotments upon the reservations where they now live, except the Mille Lacs who have under the decision of Secretary Noble of date January 9, 1891, no reservation, although previous to that opinion, their right to take allotments on the Mille Lac reservation was conceded."[1]

It was reported that during the last half of 1891, a total of 33 Chippewa had been removed to White Earth. Also 396 persons were being supplied with rations and 45 had been removed from the ration list because they had become self-sufficient. Two hundred acres of land had been broken for farming that season and 47 houses were built.

This was the work of the Commission summarized by Agent Campbell, saying, "I take pleasure in saying that the Indians who have already been removed to this reservation, while at first somewhat discontented are, on the whole, well satisfied with the change and are now beginning to appreciate the benefits arising from the possession of a home and the means of gaining a livelihood, and should they have any degree of success on their farms in the coming year, they will be able to more plainly see the advantage of civilized life over their former lives, and will be anxious to do their best toward civilization and self-support."[2]

By the beginning of 1892, allotments were beginning to be made at White Earth, but many were refusing to take 80 acres, claiming they had been promised 160 acres. Apparently Agent Shuler was promoting this disagreement. Under the treaty of 1867 the Indians had been promised up to 160 acres under certain conditions—that of putting the land under cultivation—and that was the cause of the disagreement.[3]

Matters were made worse by promises that Henry Rice had made. The record showed Henry Rice stating during the Nelson Act negotiations, "Now, we will go back to the treaty of 1867. This land was reserved under certain conditions, of which you are well aware, it being provided that you could have no land until you had complied with the conditions in regard to making improvements. Although twenty years have passed since that treaty was concluded, I am informed that a great many of you have not yet taken allotments. Under the present act, as soon as these negotiations shall have received the approval of the President, we are authorized to give to every man, woman and child 160 acres of land as an allotment …"

Remembering Rice's statement it was no wonder that the Indians were refusing the offered 80 acres. The law would have to be changed in order for Commissioner Rice's promise to be kept.

Assistant Attorney General George H. Shields opined, "The Commissioners had no authority to promise the Indians a larger allotment than the law prescribed, and any such promises would not bind the United States. 106 U.S. 196, 230.

"I am therefore of the opinion and so advise you, that under the proper construction of said acts, there cannot be allotted to each Indian one hundred and sixty acres of land.

"The representations of the Commissioners were undoubtedly made in good faith and under a construction of the law which in my view is erroneous. There is abundance of land reserved according to the letter of the Indian Commissioner to give these Indians 160 acres as promised and it would seem to be equity and justice that additional legislation be had granting the right to allot the Indians 160 acres without conditions."[4]

In an October 18, 1892 letter the Chippewa Commission reported that over 1300 Indians had been allotted at White Earth and that they were about half done.[5]

By December of 1892, 83 houses had been built at White Earth. By that time allotments had been made to about 2,000. The process of allotment at White Earth was in fact progressing, but apparently the Commissioner of Indian Affairs had visited White Earth and was not entirely pleased with what he saw, especially considering how much money had been spent in the effort.[6]

It is interesting to note that the headquarters of the Chippewa Commission which housed Commissioner Hall's office was in Detroit [now known as Detroit Lakes] while Agent Flint ran the operation at White Earth. So in a time when communication was slow anyway, this separation slowed interaction even more.

In a 1892 report made to Commissioner Hall, Agent Flint summarized the success at White Earth this way: "The first formal application for an allotment was taken Dec. 9, 1891, but the progress made for several months was slow by reason of an unfortunate disagreement between the Indians and the Department in regard to the proper interpretation of that part of the act of January 14, 1889, relating to allotments … The Indians maintain that an allotment of 160 acres was promised to each Indian of the Mississippi bands of Chippewa, in open council, by the commissioners during the negotiation of the agreement and they cite the printed proceedings of the council in proof of their claim. … To empower the Department to lawfully fulfill the promise made by the Commissioners, a bill was introduced in the Senate, May 20, 1892, by Hon. H.L. Dawes, chairman of the committee on Indian Affairs, (S. 3, 184) 'To provide for allotments to Indians on White Earth reservation in Minnesota', the purpose of which is to give each Indian of the bands referred to 160 acres.

"In order to remove the dead-lock and enable the Commission to go on with the allotment this prospective action by Congress was made the basis of an arrangement between the Commission and the principle chiefs and headmen at White Earth, by which the Indians were to take an allotment of 80 acres, provided they be permitted to select an additional 80 acres to be held in reserve; and in the event of favorable action by Congress, the 80 acres so reserved to each Indian to then be made a part of his allotment. ...

"There have been built during the past year 82 houses for Removal Indians ... they are substantially built of hewed or sawed logs and roofs shingled. As a rule they are 16 x 18 feet. ... Many of the houses built by Indians for their own use under Commissioner Campbell and reported by him I have found to be mere log huts or board shanties that must soon be replaced by permanent buildings. Some of these have been rebuilt this year. ...

"The progress made in farm operations during the past season is encouraging and in general the removal Indians have taken much interest in their work. Many of the mixed-bloods have opened good farms and are now in condition to provide for the subsistence of their families.

Monthly rations have been issued to Removal Indians who were not in a condition to support themselves ... November 1st a number of families considered able to support themselves, were dropped comprising 87 persons."[7]

On June 14, 1893, William M. Campbell was notified that he had been appointed to replace Darwin Hall as Chairman of the Chippewa Commission. The assignment given him was as follows:

"The work remaining for the Commission to accomplish consists in securing removal to the White Earth reservation of such remaining Indians belonging to the other reservations embraced within the act as elect to remove thereto and take their allotments of land thereon, (particularly to secure the removal of the Mille Lac band to the White Earth reservation), in completing the allotments in severalty to the Indians of the Fond du Lac and White Earth reservations, and in making allotments to the Indians of the Red Lake reservation, and of the other reservations embraced within the act who refuse to remove to the White Earth reservation."[8]

However, by July of 1894, the emphasis on removing more Chippewa to White Earth was being relaxed by the Washington Office. Orders came to Chippewa Commission Chairman Campbell on July 10th stating, "I am directed by the Secretary of the Interior ... to instruct the Chippewa Commission ... that on and after October 1, 1894, further efforts looking to the removal of Chippewa Indians to White Earth reservation ... shall cease. ... After October 1, 1894, the Commission should devote their entire time and energy to making allotments in severalty to the Chippewa Indians ..."[9]

It is therefore apparent that the Commission was urged to complete its work, and that the amount of money that had been spent was not commensurate with the progress made. Commissioner of Indian Affairs Browning wrote to the Secretary of the Interior saying, "I shall not however, feel satisfied to continue this work in the unsatisfactory way in which it was carried on in its earlier stages <u>and unless it is shortly made apparent that the entire business, contemplated in the law, will be completed within a reasonable time.</u>"[10] (Emphasis in original)

By January of 1895 the Washington Office was becoming more directly involved with the Commission's work and cost cutting measures were being put in place.[11]

The Commission's annual report for 1894 told of having removed 205 Chippewa to White Earth during the year, totaling 967 removals since the Commission came into existence. They reported that 628 allotments had been made at White Earth that year, making a total of 2960 to date. The Commission reported that there were still some hold-outs waiting for Congress to authorize the promised 160 acres each.[12]

Once again there was a change in Commission Chairman. William Campbell resigned on November 30, 1894, and on March 8, 1895 Melvin R. Baldwin received word that he had been appointed to replace Campbell.[13]

Upon assuming office Chairman Baldwin recognized the strategic difficulties of locating his office in Detroit, and immediately abolished the office at Detroit and established it at White Earth. Baldwin requested that the deadline for removals be extended to September 1st and told the Commissioner of Indian Affairs that he thought the work of removals and allotments—except for Red Lake—could be completed by January 1, 1896. He also commented on how little respect the Commission was receiving from the Indians.[14]

Following a visit to Washington by Commissioner Baldwin, the Commissioner of Indian Affairs and Secretary of the Interior issued further instructions:

- removals could continue until May 1, 1896

- a tract of land could be set aside at White Earth for the Mille Lacs who refused to remove

- assistance to mixed-blood removals curtailed

- authorized allotting "pine lands" at White Earth if the land was not chiefly valuable for the pine.[15]

By mid-1896, Congress had reduced the Chippewa Commission to only one Commissioner, leaving only Chairman Baldwin.[16]

By June 30, 1897, 3634 allotments had been made on the White Earth reservation.[17]

On July 20, 1897, Melvin Baldwin was asked to resign his position as a Chippewa Commissioner.[18] He did not go quietly, claiming that it was pressure from the "pine-ring"—with whom he had had disagreements over fairness to the Indians—that was causing his termination.[19] At any rate, former Commissioner Darwin Hall was then named to replace Baldwin.[20]

Commissioner Hall received word from the Acting Secretary of the Interior on August 17, 1899, that the Chippewa Commission would be dissolved in sixty days, and that any remaining work on allotments at White Earth would be done by the Indian Agent.

And so, it appears that the allotting authorized by the Nelson Act was essentially as done as it was going to get. Red Lake would never be allotted.

The law evidently allowed only minors, widows, orphans, and disabled Chippewa to lease their land. This law, however, was being abused and able-bodied Indians were often cheated by their renters without recourse.[21] Obviously the Government was controlling the use of the allottee's lands—or at least attempting to do so.

On April 28, 1904, an act was passed by Congress known as the Steenerson Act. This act authorized to each Chippewa Indian entitled, an allotment on White Earth Reservation of 160 acres—as promised by Commissioner Henry Rice.

The Dawes Act and its Minnesota version, the Nelson Act, made allotments to Indians that were under the complete control of the United States Government for twenty five years or until the allottee was declared competent. Once the allottee was granted a patent in fee simple, they became full citizens of the United States. In order to clarify the issue the Burke Act was passed:

> "*Be it enacted by the Senate and House of Representatives of the United States in Congress assembled.* That section six of an Act approved February eighth, eighteen hundred and eighty-seven, entitled 'An Act to provide for the allotment of lands in severalty to Indians on various reservations, and to extend the protection of the laws of the United States and Territories over the Indians, and for other purposes,' shall be amended to read as follows:
>
> " 'SEC. 6. That at the expiration of the trust period and when the lands have been conveyed to the Indians by patent in fee, as provided in section five of this Act, then each and every allottee shall have the benefit of and be subject to the laws, both civil and criminal, of the State or Territory in which they may reside: and no Territory shall pass or enforce any law denying any such Indian within its jurisdiction the equal protection of the law. And every Indian born within the territorial limits of the United States to whom allotments shall have been made and who has received a patent in fee simple under the provisions of this Act, or under any law or treaty, and every Indian born within the territorial limits of the United States who has voluntarily taken up within said limits his residence, separate and apart from any tribe of Indians therein,

and has adopted the habits of civilized life, is hereby declared to be a citizen of the United States, and is entitled to all the rights, privileges, and immunities of such citizens, whether said Indian has been or not, by birth or otherwise, a member of any tribe of Indians within the territorial limits of the United States without in any manner impairing or otherwise affecting the right of any such Indian to tribal or other property: *Provided* That the Secretary of the Interior may, in his discretion, and he is hereby authorized, whenever he shall be satisfied that an Indian allottee is competent and capable of managing his or her own affairs at any time to cause to be issued to such allottee a patent in fee simple, and thereafter all restrictions as to sale, incumbrance [sic], or taxation of said land shall be removed and said land shall not be liable to the satisfaction of any debt contracted prior to the issuing of such patent: *Provided further*, That until the issuance of fee-simple patents all allottees to whom trust patents shall hereafter be issued shall be subject to the exclusive jurisdiction of the United States: *And provided further*, That the provisions of this Act shall not extend to any Indians in the Indian Territory.'

"That hereafter when an allotment of land is made to any Indian, and any such Indian dies before the expiration of the trust period, such allotments shall be cancelled and the land shall revert to the United States, and the Secretary of the Interior shall ascertain the legal heirs of such Indian, and shall cause to be issued to said heir and in their names, a patent in fee simple for said land, or he may cause the land to be sold as provided by law and issue a patent therefor to the purchaser or purchasers, and pay the net proceeds to the heirs, or their legal representatives, of any deceased Indian. The action of the Secretary of the Interior in determining the legal heirs of any deceased Indian, as provided herein, shall in all respects be conclusive and final."

This action of Congress made it perfectly clear that once an allottee was issued a patent in fee simple for his allotment he was a full citizen of the United States.

Then in the Indian Bureau appropriations legislation approved June 21, 1906, the Congress agreed,

"That all restrictions as to the sale, incumbrance [sic], or taxation for allotments within the White Earth Reservation in the State of Minnesota, now or hereafter held by adult mixed-blood Indians upon application shall be entitled to receive a patent in fee simple for such allotments; and as to full-bloods, said restrictions shall be removed when the Secretary of the Interior is satisfied that said adult full-blood Indians are competent to handle their own affairs, and in such case the Secretary of the Interior shall issue to such Indian allottee a patent in fee simple upon application."

This action of Congress was known as the Clapp Act, and since most of the Indian allottees at White Earth were mixed-bloods it effectively removed the safeguard—which Congress had initially thought was important—in an effort to help the Indians transformation from communal ownership to individual ownership.

In the 1914 annual report of the White Earth Agency mention is made of the great amount of litigation on the reservation requiring the presence of the Department of Justice.[22]

Already by 1914 it was reported that "about three-fourths of the adult allottees have received patents in fee to their land under the Clapp Act ... Practically all of the Indians on the Reservation are held to be citizens, and are subject to the laws of the State ... Law violators should properly be dealt with by State authority. These officers, however, are quite reluctant to exercise their authority over the Indian or within the boundaries of the Indian Reservation. Consequently the liquor traffic on the Reservation has grown ... With the lack of federal authority on the one side and the indifference of State Officials on the other, the situation in regard to the liquor traffic among the Indians of this Reservation seems almost hopeless ..."[24]

The Government had been closing some of the boarding schools, and by 1914 there were only one boarding school and four day schools on the White Earth Reservation.

The Government plan to convince the Chippewa to become farmers had obviously failed, in large part because by 1914 it was reported that, "Farming operations on the White Earth Reservation are confined almost exclusively to small tracts of land. About 90% of the allotments on the Reservation have been sold to White men and the remaining 10% belongs to either full-blood or minor Indians ..." The 1914 report goes on to state that those Indians that still had their allotments were encouraged to—at the very least—raise a garden and some livestock. The report goes on to say that, "The abundant supply of fish and wild game on the Reservation furnishes a number of Indians with meat during the year. Blueberries, Raspberries and Wild Rice which are found in abundance also afford a number of Indians with subsistence." Not exactly what Congress had in mind when they passed the Nelson Act.

Apparently there continued to be a great deal of animosity existing between the mixed-blood and full-blood Chippewa, making any cooperative effort difficult.

The 1914 situation on the White Earth Reservation was summarized by the Superintendent when he said, "The so called Clapp Act passed in 1906, removed the restrictions on the allotments of all adult mixed bloods on the Reservation. These

Indians immediately disposed of their allotments and the money received, which in most cases was a small fraction of the actual value, was squandered, and the Indians did not receive any beneficial return for the same. In the vast majority of cases the money was spent in riotous living. As fast as the minor mixed blood Indians become of age they immediately proceed to dispose of their allotment and to squander the proceeds. Some action should be taken by Congress to amend the Clapp Act and make it ineffective so far as Indians who are now minors are concerned. During the past year several sales of minor's land have been made through this office after it was found that the minor or the minor's parents had illegally entered into a contract for the sale of the land. In each of these cases a great deal more was received for the land that the purchaser had originally offered."[22]

Thus in a period of approximately twenty years the Chippewa had each been allotted land, and most had sold their land, thereby becoming landless.

In the 1916 annual report the allotment issue was described this way: "These lands have very often been sold for only a small percentage of their actual market value. The Chippewa Indian of this reservation makes a notoriously poor salesman of his land. Very often he has not seen his allotment, knows little or nothing as to the kind of soil, timber if any, amount of agricultural land on the allotments or their market value. The Indian's ignorance as to his allotments, together with his idle habits and consequent poverty, places him at a great disadvantage in bargaining for the sale of his land, and in order to continue in idleness and to save himself and those dependent upon him for support from want and suffering, he is forced to dispose of his allotments at a sacrifice.

"A part of the proceeds from his allotment, the Indian expends for food, clothing and the betterment of home surroundings and part is expended for teams which are much used in traveling about the reservation, visiting relatives and friends and attending Indian dances and councils. Another part is expended for useless articles of all kinds, the chief item of extravagance being the purchase of automobiles for pleasure purposes. A large part of the funds realized from the sale of lands by the Indian owner have, until the past two years, been spent for intoxicants, but thanks to the rigid enforcement of the Indian Treaty of 1855, which makes this reservation and a considerable area outside of the reservation dry territory, this evil has been almost wholly suppressed."[23]

In that same report the Superintendent writes about another issue facing the Government. "It is impossible to tell the number of deceased Indians whose estates are to be probated under the jurisdiction of the Indian Office, for the reason that the blood status of the deceased Indian allottees has never been determined, so that it is not known which of said decedents were full bloods and which mixed bloods."

The opinion of the solicitor for the Interior Department, dated August 2, 1915, D-29636 held that where the allottee (deceased) was an adult mixed-blood there was no authority for the determination of the heirs by the Secretary of the Interior.[24]

In a belated effort to curtail the rapid deterioration of at least one of the very purposes of the allotments, the Indian Office directed that the following clause be made a part of every deed to non-competent Indians:

> "Subject to the condition that, while the title is in the grantee or heirs, no deed, mortgage, power of attorney, contract to sell, or other instrument affecting the land herein described, or the title thereto, shall be of any force or effect or capable of confirmation or ratification unless approved by the Secretary of the Interior.
>
> "In addition to the foregoing, where the deeds cover lands previously unrestricted there should be indorsed on the back of each deed the following:
>
> "The consideration for the within deed is paid with funds held in trust by the United States for the relief of the grantee."[25]

By these clauses the Indian Office was administratively putting some degree of restriction on the Act of Congress—the Clapp Act.

By 1917 Woodrow Wilson was the President, and the United States was beginning to engage in World War I. Wilson's Commissioner of Indian Affairs, Cato Sells, issued a new "Declaration of Policy in the Administration of Indian Affairs." The underlying principle was summarized by Commissioner Sells this way: "The time has come for discontinuing guardianship of all competent Indians and giving even closer attention to the incompetent that they may more speedily achieve competency." He continued, "Broadly speaking, a policy of greater liberalism will henceforth prevail in Indian administration to the end that every Indian, as soon as he has been determined to be as competent to transact his own business as the average white man, shall be given full control of his property and have all his lands and moneys turned over to him. After which he will no longer be a ward of the Government. ... This is a new and far reaching declaration of policy. It means the dawn of a new era in Indian administration. It means that the competent Indian will no longer be treated as half ward and half citizen. It means reduced appropriations by the Government and more self-respect and independence for the Indian. It means the ultimate absorption of the Indian race into the body politic of the Nation. It means, in short, the beginning of the end of the Indian problem."

It is obvious that management of Indian monies, the question of competency and guardianship of Indian children—all things that the Government was trying to control—was becoming almost unmanageable at the local level. A one-size-fits-all program was not suitable when there were Indian people in all stages of transition from ward to citizen. For example, the superintendent of the White Earth Agency wrote in a letter to Commissioner Sells, "Most of these people have received two allotments of eighty acres each. In case, therefore, of a family the husband and wife have had 320 acres, their full land inheritance. They have had also their pro rata share of the one-fourth trust fund payment. Where such people have retained their allotments, or if sold, have reinvested the money in lands or other property of value, and can show that they have conserved or added to their inheritance, and also properly used their one-fourth trust fund, it seems to me that other things being equal, such persons should be appointed guardians of their minor children.

"But where the husband and wife have sold and disposed of all their lands and expended their pro rata trust fund payment, and have nothing to show for it, it would appear that they do not meet the standard indicated, and that they are not entitled to be appointed guardians of their minor children, and especially so if they are spendthrifts, or have been guilty of 'boozing' or 'boot-legging.'"[26]

By October 1918, the Office of Indian Affairs had simplified the clause to be added to the deeds of all non-competent Indians to read,

> "Subject to the condition that while the title is in the grantee or heirs, the land herein described shall not be alienated or incumbered [sic] without the consent of the Secretary of the Interior."

For minors of less than one-half Indian blood, the clause was to read,

> "Subject to the condition that while the title is in the grantee, no alienation or incumbrance [sic] of the land described herein shall be valid until he (or she) reaches his (or her) majority, as determined by the laws of the State wherein the land is situated, without approval of the Secretary of the Interior."[27]

The White Earth Agency reported a need for more office staff in 1919, stating, "At the present time the agency force seems adequate, except that there is needed an additional clerk in the office. This agency has an enrollment of 6794 Indians; we have nearly five thousand individual Indian bank accounts. This entails an enormous amount of clerical work. There is one annuity payment each year. Under the agency there are one boarding school, four day schools, one hospital, and two old folks homes. We have in addition to this a great deal of clerical work involved in the White Earth Land Suit Settlement Cases. These suits and settlements effect White Earth allotments, and while the litigation is carried on, and the settlement made by the Department of Justice, yet all complaints originate at the agency office, and the final settlements adjudicated, deeds prepared, and funds dispersed through the agency office. It is estimated at this time, that settlements have been made which will cause a million and a half dollars to be distributed and paid out under rules and regulations of the Department, through this office.

"While it is anticipated that the White Earth Boarding School will be discontinued the coming year, it is expected that other work will arise which will more than offset the clerical work incident to the supervision of the school. The Office is aware that there have been many complaints made against the agency; correspondence has not been promptly answered, and unnecessary delay has been caused in paying out individual Indian funds and negotiating land settlement suits. This has been due to the lack of clerical force, and this office is in need of an additional clerical position; such position should carry a salary of $1400 or $1500 per year, as it would require a knowledge of the law and exceptional clerical ability."[28]

The 1919 annual report states that "The Indians of the White Earth Reservation are largely of the mixed blood; self supporting [sic], and are to be found in all professions and industrial occupations ... tribal matters and leadership fall into the hands of the mixed bloods. Seventy-five percent of these Indians in my estimation should be 'turned loose' from the Government supervision; their tribal funds should be pro rated [sic] and paid to them, and they should be made to assume all the responsibilities of citizenship at the earliest practicable date ... the remaining 25 percent of these people are not altogether incompetent; in fact, many of the full bloods and near full bloods are making good livings. There is a percentage of incompetent Indians, old and indigent; widows and orphans that must be cared for, and are being cared for."[29]

In regard to the land the 1919 report states, "Generally, the allotments of this reservation have passed into the hands of White speculators through the provisions of the so-called Clapp Act. Many of the full bloods have made deeds, and these allotments are now in suit, instigated through the Department of Justice in its endeavors to straighten out titles and conditions brought about through unfortunate legislation, which has proven to be such a grave menace to the welfare of the allottees."[30]

Prohibition in the United States was a 1920—1933 plan to rid the country of intoxicating liquors, and White Earth Reservation did not escape the effects. The Chippewa Agency superintendent reported to Commissioner of Indian Affairs Burke that, "The Indians are in the habit of getting together in camps in certain localities and drinking certain drinks that are made by themselves or sold to them that are intoxicating and I consider it an absolute impossibility to stop this entirely." Nevertheless Liquor Officers were at work chasing and arresting bootleggers.

In 1923 the White Earth Agency reported that "The enrollment of Indians on the White Earth reservation is 7635 of which 92% are classified as mixed bloods whose real estate and personal property is subject to taxation for the reason that they are full fledged [sic] citizens caused by the Act of Congress known as the 'Clapp Act' (34 Stat., 352 Ante. 220)"[31]

By 1926 the Consolidated Chippewa Agency had been formed, combining White Earth, Leech Lake, Fond du Lac, Nett Lake and Grand Portage agencies into one—headquartered at Cass Lake. The annual report that year states that while the Indians are willing to be governed by the laws of Minnesota, "the white tax paying people do not wish to incur the expense of setting their tribunals in motion for the protection of a non-tax-paying Indian or to admonish him so long as he is molesting only another Indian."[32]

The 1927 annual report of the Consolidated Chippewa Agency stated, "We have a population of 12,766. Most of this number are landless … The granting of so many patents in fee in advance of the arrival of the expiration of the trust period was a great misfortune."[33]

In 1929 the Superintendent of the Consolidated Chippewa Agency held that, "A number of applications for patents-in-fee have been made during the year but the granting of such patents is not looked upon with favor, as the Indians have already parted with much of their real estate and squandered the money. Whenever an application is made for patent-in-fee, we know of a certainty that the completion of the plan includes the sale of the tract, for which application is made, at a grossly inadequate price and the immediate dissipation of the money. Even though the allottees are not making beneficial use of their land, it appears to me that it is best to require them to keep it as it furnishes a reserve for future emergencies. Not one Indian, living on the reservation, in fifty ever has a bank account or any reserve fund against the time of trouble. Then, too, if the allottee himself does not wish to make use of his land it may be that his heirs at sometime [sic] in the future will take a more enlightened view of the opportunity.

"I reported last year that the number of sales being made is practically negligible. There is no demand for northern Minnesota real estate, generally speaking, unless it be lake shore property suitable for summer resort purposes … Most of the land belonging to the Chippewas, as heretofore described, is cut-over stuff that usually requires an expenditure of more than the land is worth to put it under plow … In the past, millions of dollars have been realized by and for the Indians of this jurisdiction, as proceeds of the sale of land and timber, aside from the ceded lands. Some of the White Earth Chippewas realized as high as $25,000.00 for timber sold on a single allotment. It was not many years ago that all of the White Earth Chippewas … were living at a rapid pace from the proceeds of the sale of their timber …Many of those who are now seeking aid from the appropriation for the relief of indigents are men who spent their thousands only a few years ago with no thought of tomorrow. Very little of the money was used for beneficial purposes as is shown by the poor houses, poor improvements, in short the extremely unsatisfactory economic condition of the majority of those who wasted their money in the recent past. The result is a discontented people living in the memory of the easy money of the past and now looking to the Court of Claims for more easy money to be spent in the same way that it was squandered by themselves or their ancestors in the past."[34]

By 1930 the Superintendent of the Consolidated Chippewa Agency was of the opinion that "the earlier program of a decreasing paternalism, looking to a not long deferred withdrawal of the Federal Government from the position of special guardian and wet nurse is the sane one."[35]

The Field Clerk at White Earth obviously had a rather different viewpoint than Superintendent Burns of the Consolidated Chippewa Agency. The Field Clerk reported to Burns, "These Indians are willing workers, they crave a chance to earn money, and with the country wide depression engulfing us, these men find it extremely difficult to provide the necessities of life for their families. Nearly a year at this station now I have found the large majority of the men ever on the alert for a job, no matter how menial, wherein an honest dollar could be earned ... It would appear that the Department must come to see the point that some activity must be started on the White Earth reservation which would give employment, even at part time, for the people remaining here. Annuity and per capita payments and the issuance of rations offer, at best, only temporary relief, and I am satisfied that, as a whole, are not conducive to advancement."[36]

In this chapter I have endeavored to outline the goings-on at White Earth where a large majority—roughly 1500—of Mille Lac Chippewa dwelt by 1934, and to contrast it with those few—around 300—who had refused to remove and only recently had been allotted on purchased lands at Mille Lac.

CHAPTER 22

The Saga of Shaw-vosh-Kung's Land

Shaw-vosh-Kung was born in about 1817, and was destined to become a respected Chief of the Mille Lac Chippewa.

Chief Shaw-vosh-Kung, also known as "He who Passeth Under Everything" or "Passes Under Everything," was a signer of the 1855 treaty that established the Mille Lacs Indian Reservation together with 12 other chiefs and delegates of the Mississippi band of Chippewa.

Shaw-vosh-Kung was the primary negotiator and one of 7 chiefs and headmen from the Mille Lacs band who signed the Treaty of 1863. That treaty sold the Gull Lake, Mille Lac, Sandy Lake, Rabbit Lake, Pokagomin Lake and Rice Lake Reservations to the United States.

The following year (1864) Gull Lake Chief Hole-in-the-Day the younger and Sandy Lake Chief Mis-qua-dace were granted permission to renegotiate the treaty of 1863. That new treaty replaced the 1863 treaty and was signed on May 7, 1864 by Chief Hole-in-the-Day and Chief Mis-qua-dace as representatives of the Mississippi Chippewa and the Pillager and Lake Winnebagoshish bands of Chippewa. The Treaty of 1864 provided that one section of land was to be awarded in fee simple to each of the three chiefs—Chief Hole-in-the-Day at Gull Lake, Mis-qua-dace at Sandy Lake and Shaw-vosh-Kung at Mille Lacs—and that the Secretary of the Interior would locate the land.

On January 16, 1867, a patent for the following land was awarded to Shaw-vosh-Kung by President Andrew Johnson:

Fractional Section 16 — 195 55/100 acres
Fractional Section 21 -233 65/100 acres
Fractional Section 22 — ½ acre
Lots 1 and 2 in Section 27 — 62 65/100 acres
N1/2 of NE1/4 of Section 28 — 80 acres
N1/2 of NW1/4 of Section 28 — 80 acres
All in Twp43N, Range 27W

The total acreage was 652 and 35/100 acres. Note that this land is now all part of the trust lands that are home to the Mille Lacs band government center and casino.

On December 2, 1886, Chief Shaw-vosh-Kung and his wife, Way-She-ye-Shic-go-gua, sold the pine timber on all their land to a Mr. James L. Lochren for $5, plus $2 per 1000 feet of the timber.

Note that the Dawes Act was passed by Congress in 1887 and the Nelson Act in 1889.

On November 22, 1889, Chief Shaw-vosh-Kung and his wife gave power of attorney to Nathan Richardson—an attorney from Morrison County that we met earlier in this book—with authorization to execute deeds and make contracts for the sale of their lands at such price as he shall deem reasonable. (Courthouse records do not reveal what was going on in the chief's life at the time, but we do know that the chief, his wife and at least 5 of his children signed documents with an 'X', indicating that they probably could not read and write.) On the same day the chief and his wife mortgaged the 195 55/100 acres in Sec 16, twp43, R27 to Peter W. Blake for $250.

Apparently at some point between November 22, 1889, and February 9, 1891, Chief Shaw-vosh-Kung died.

The chief's wife and children sold 195 55/100 acres (the NW1/4 of SW1/4 and Lots 1, 2, 3, 4, & 5 in Sec 16, T43, R27) on Feb 9, 1891, to Francis M. Campbell and Annie C. Warren for $650. There was a mortgage held by Peter W. Blake for $250. The buyer was to assume the back taxes. It is my guess that that is the explanation for why, on February 24, 1891, due to not having paid their taxes, 195 acres (Lots 1, 2, 3, 4 & 5 and the NW1/4 of SW1/4 of Sec. 16) owned by Chief Shaw-vosh-Kung and his wife were offered for sale by the county. There being no bidders at auction, the property was sold to the State of Minnesota for taxes due—$30.37. The State in turn sold the property to Francis M. Campbell for $162.43.

On May 14, 1891, a mortgage foreclosure sale notice was filed for default of $288.52 from the mortgage that Chief Shaw-vosh-Kung and his wife had executed on November 22, 1889 with Peter W. Blake and apparently had not paid. Peter Blake had assigned the mortgage to Reuben F. McClellan, who then was filing for foreclosure. For reasons I do not comprehend, the entire 652 35/100 acres was to be offered for sale on the courthouse steps, even though only 195 55/100 acres had been mortgaged. The first notice of sale was to be June 29, 1891.

On June 16, 1892, the chiefs widow, 2 daughters and one son—Way-she-ge-skie-go-gua, widow, Quay ransh, daughter and her husband, Ne-be-da-gonce, daughter and her husband, and Way-ke-ge-ke-shie (Eagle), son and his wife—sold the entire 652 35/100 acres to Charles Wallblom for $1650.

On December 31, 1892, one daughter—Ah-nank-me-ance—and one son—Pin-de-ga-ge-Shie—both of whom had removed to the White Earth Reservation, sold their interests in the 652 35/100 acres to Charles Wallblom for $355.

On November 27, 1893, Charles Wallblom had apparently declared bankruptcy, and on September 8, 1894, the bankruptcy court oversaw the sale of the entire 652 35/100 acres to John M. Carlson for $125.

It is difficult to understand the confusing scenario, but, even though Ah-nah-me-ance and her husband and Pindr Ga ge Shie and his wife—now living at White Earth—had sold their interest in the 652 35/100 acres to Charles Wallblom before he went bankrupt, they sold the same property to one John M. Carlson for $100 on August 22, 1900.

Apparently, in order to clarify ownership, John M. Carlson filed suit on Sept 27, 1900, in District Court, 7th Judicial District, against the known heirs and any unknown heirs of Chief Shaw-vosh-Kung. The court found that he was the rightful owner of the 652 35/100 acres.

However, adding to the confusion, on March 14, 1903, John Carlson settled with Wa Boose, daughter of deceased Ka-cheu and granddaughter of Chief Shaw-vosh-Kung, for $50 for her interest in the 652 35/100 acres.

On March 15, 1912, Marie and Charles Keith of Princeton sold—for $2600—to "The Agency", a corporation, the following property:

Lots 3 & 4, Sec 27, T43, R27
NW1/4 of SE1/4, Sec 35, T42, R27
Lot 1, Sec 36, T42, R27
SE1/4 of SE1/4, Sec26, T42, R25
SW1/4 of NW1/4 and NE1/4 of SW1/4, Sec35, T43, R27
NW1/4 of NE1/4 and NE1/4 of NW1/4, Sec 13, T39, R26
SW1/4 of SE1/4, Sec 28, T38, R27

While it is incomprehensible how it came back into their possession, Mathilda Wallblom and Charles Wallblom, who had previously lost the property due to bankruptcy, sold on a contract for deed for $1575 on July 12, 1917, Lot 1, Sec22 and Lots 1 & 2, Sec 27, Twp43, R 27, comprising 63 15/100 acres, to a Mr. William Anderson.

On July 31, 1920, William Anderson sold to Harry D. Ayer for $5367.75 the following:

Lot 1, Sec 22, and
Lots 1 & 2, Sec 27, Twp 43, R 27
Total of 63 15/100 acres

On June 1, 1938, the estate of Eugene A. Cooper deeded this property to the United States in trust for the Minnesota Chippewa Indians. Apparently the land was forfeited for failure to pay taxes and was purchased by the United States in trust for the Minnesota Chippewa tribe:

Lot 5 and Sec 21 and N1/2 of NE1/4, Sec28, T43, R27

The United States filed a lawsuit on August 18, 1939, against the State of Minnesota, Mille Lacs County, The Agency and any others claiming any interest in: Lots 3 & 4, Sec27, T43, R27W comprising 80.9 acres. The court ordered that all taxes levied and assessed, be abated and cancelled and taxation of these lands be declared illegal and void and that Mille Lacs records be amended and corrected.

On Feb 19, 1940, Millie M. Weide sold Lots 1, 2, 3 Sec16, T43, R27W to the United States in trust for the Minnesota Chippewa Tribe for $7000.

On Feb 21, 1940, Catherine B. Haverstock and Henry W. Haverstock sold the following to the United States in trust for the Minnesota Chippewa Tribe for $7000:

Lot 4
NW1/4 of SW1/4, Sec16, Twp43, R27W

And then, on April 30, 1959, Harry D. Ayer and his wife Jeannette O. Ayer sold to the Minnesota Historical Society:

Fraction of Sec28, T43, R27 (lakeshore), about 1 acre, and
Lot 8, Sec28, T43, R27W and Lots 1 & 2, Sec27. T43, R27, about 63 15/100 acres, and
SW1/4 of NE1/4, Sec28, T43N, R27W except a 5 acre plot for cemetery, 35 acres.

Details regarding events affecting Shaw-vosh-Kung's section of land are meager except for the legal records on file at the Mille Lacs County Courthouse. It is obvious that unpaid taxes became an issue as they apparently did for other land owners as well. Chief Shaw-vosh-Kung or his family maintained some interest in at least parts of the land awarded him in 1864 until the last granddaughter sold her interest in 1903.

CHAPTER 23

Henry Mower Rice, 1816–1894

Henry Mower Rice was born in Vermont on November 29, 1816, of Welsh ancestry. His father died at an early age and following his death the family moved to Kalamazoo, Michigan where young Henry attended common schools and academies. He later moved to Detroit and became involved with the first canal survey at Sault Ste. Marie. In 1839 he went to Fort Snelling and became the sutler (one who sells provisions to an army) for the United States Army for Fort Atkinson and the Iowa Territory. It was as a sutler that Rice probably got his initial training as a trader. Rice went on to become an integral part of the fur trading industry in about 1846 as part of the American Fur Company, in the area that would later become Minnesota and the surrounding area. Rice was apparently a fierce competitor in this cutthroat industry, and while his speculation and the actions of his competitors made business difficult at times, he obviously fared pretty well. Rice used the "Indian system" to his advantage, making sure that one of his traders was present to represent him during all annuity payments with plenty of goods to exchange for the money the Indians had just been given. Apparently Rice and Henry Sibley had fairly well solidified the trade of the Winnebago's, Sioux and southern Chippewa.

In addition to his trading business Rice was part of a real estate venture in St. Paul where he had settled in 1848. His home in St Paul was probably 285 Summit Avenue, an eloquent and massive structure, still standing and occupied, within walking distance of the St Paul Cathedral and the James J. Hill mansion. In 1853 he was elected as a delegate to Congress for the Minnesota Territory. When Minnesota was admitted to the Union on May 11, 1858, Henry Rice was elected as a Democrat to the United States Senate and served as a U.S. Senator from May 11, 1858 to March 3, 1863. He did not run for reelection in 1862. In 1865 he ran for election as the Governor of Minnesota but was defeated. Obviously held in rather high regard, he served as president of the State historical society, president of the board of public works and Treasurer of Ramsey County.

Henry Rice was also a primary negotiator in many treaties with the Indians; Winnebago, Sioux and Chippewa. He was primarily responsible for the treaties with both the Sioux and the Chippewa which ceded the lands—to which both tribes claimed ownership—to the United States.

Of particular importance to the subject of this book is first with Rice's involvement in the treaty of 1855. One must wonder what was said during the finalization of this treaty since we have no records of same, and the final treaty was done in private without a secretary present. What possible reason could there have been for holding such an important portion in private?

In the 1863 treaty with the Chippewa, then Senator Rice once again negotiated the final treaty in private. Rice was looked upon as a friend of the Indians, but was he, in fact, their friend? Commissioner of Indian Affairs Dole promoted Rice as a friend to the Indians, and the Chippewa took the bait. But what truly were Henry Rice's thoughts in agreeing to Article 12 as an open ended right of occupancy of the lands that he, Rice, had at the same time purchased in the name of the United States government. Where were the Indians to occupy?

For the next 35 years the government struggled with that question. How easy it would have been to clarify and expand on that article, leaving no question as to its meaning. Did Rice secretly think the Mille Lacs could somehow be convinced to remove to White Earth? In fairness we have to remember that eventually most of the Mille Lacs did remove, and perhaps they all would have if the Nelson Act had not come into play—followed by the purchase of lands by the United States—because there was none to allot the Mille Lacs like Rice had promised. But we must ask how many thousands of dollars had been spent in trying to convince the Mille Lacs to remove? And even worse, we need to realize that while the United States Congress was appropriating money for this effort, the monies used were coming from the Chippewa

Fund that was established in the United States Treasury by the purchase of Chippewa lands—as well as from other sources—and so in reality the Government was using the Indians own money to try to remove them to White Earth.

On January 14, 1889, the Nelson Act had been passed by Congress and Henry Rice was named as one of three commissioners charged with gaining agreement to the Nelson Act through negotiation with each of the eleven bands of Minnesota Chippewa. Rice was an accomplished negotiator with the Indians and was probably a logical choice to negotiate this Act. But when Rice and Whiting reached Mille Lac the Article 12 provision in the treaty of 1863 would come back to haunt negotiations. It is obvious that Rice was well versed on the struggles between the Mille Lac Chippewa and the United States Government, caused by the very article which he himself had obviously had a part in inserting in the 1863 treaty. So what was he thinking as he negotiated with the Mille Lacs? Was he actually a wolf in sheep's clothing? Was he sick? Was he becoming senile?

We know from the record that Commissioner Whiting had thanked the Mille Lacs for traveling to that location (probably near present day Garrison) so that Commissioner Rice didn't have to come to them. We also know that Commissioner Rice had just been through 38 days of fairly intense negotiation stretched over a three month period. Add to that Rice was now 73 years old in an era when life expectancy for men was, at most, about 80. And we know that while he had participated in all the negotiations up to and including Mille lacs, he did not participate in the next two, Grand Portage and Bois Fort.

Henry Rice obviously knew that the Mille Lac Reservation had been ceded to the United States in 1863 because he helped write the treaty. And he obviously knew how much difficulty and distress that treaty had caused. He said as much to the Mille Lacs. He said to them, "I wish to refer to an old matter that has given you a great deal of trouble, a great deal of uneasiness. That is the treaty made at Washington some twenty five years ago. I was there, and know all about it. That was a wise treaty, and if it had been properly carried out, you would have escaped all the trouble that has befallen you. Men who cared more for themselves than they did for you, thought they had found a hole in it and that they would take advantage of that and deprive you of your rights."

Rice was obviously passing on the blame to someone else for the problems created by a treaty provision so poorly written—under his supervision—and so ambiguous that it was still being debated 35 years later.

Rice continued to the Indians, "Here is the acknowledgement of the Government that you were right, — that you were right all the time: that you have <u>not</u> forfeited your right to occupy the reservation. ... We have not come here to tell you that you have forfeited your rights; that soldiers will be sent to remove you, or that you will be disturbed; your Great Father says that you have not forfeited your rights. Some mistakes have been made during this long period. We wish now to see if we cannot now correct them so that no one should be wronged. We want to correct all mistakes that have been made so far as we can, and to start out for a new life, without any heart-burning. No honest man, no matter who he may be, feeling that he has been wronged either by the Government or by you." (Emphasis in original)

What was Henry Rice saying? Had he forgotten the purpose for which he was there? Did he realize that if the Mille Lacs rejected the Nelson Act he would have failed on his pledge to the United States Government—a pledge he had accepted as Commissioner? Or did he actually believe that the United States Government would eject the white settlers from the former reservation in opposition to the very agreement that he was promoting so that the allotments that he was promising the Mille Lacs at Mille Lac could proceed?

Whatever his thoughts, he continued his double talk when chief Shaw vosh kung asked to see a map of their reservation and a map was produced. Rice pointed to the map and said, "[T]here is the Mille Lacs Reservation, containing three islands in the southern part of the Lake — three in all — although only two are shown on the map ... This is your reservation north of Leech lake." Certainly this was not an understandable explanation, although nothing specific was said that was incorrect regarding the map. It is obvious that the Indians were misled because they continued making corrections to the map of the Mille Lac Reservation, at least as they understood it.

As negotiations continued it was as if the Mille Lacs were convincing Henry Rice that they would be getting allotments on the former Mille Lac reservation. Mah-eng-aunce then rose to say, "Our friend, White Rice, I have understood everything that you have put before us for our consideration. You say that whoever wishes to go to White Earth or elsewhere as he pleases, shall be allowed to do so. We make known to you that as the Government speaks so kindly and as you have uttered the words of the law, stating that an Indian can take his allotment on the reservation where he resides — we make known to you that we wish to take our allotments on this reservation, and not be removed to White Earth."

Henry Rice did not correct him, but continued by stating that, "You are entitled to select for your allotments on the lands called farming lands, - all that can be used as such, — we do not ask you to dispose of a foot of that. And there will be nothing done with the lands until you have all gotten your allotments. You will not only have your farming lands and sugar bush and all the hardwoods. ..."

It is clear that either Henry Rice believed that in fact the Mille Lac Reservation would be allotted to the Mille Lac Indians, or he was promoting a massive fraud as a representative of the United States Government.

However, whichever it was, Commissioner Rice and Commissioner Whiting convinced the Mille Lac Indians to sign the agreement accepting the Nelson Act—which essentially negated the hopes of the Mille Lac Indians and kept the successful negotiations of the Nelson Act proceeding as Congress had desired.

With the 'successful' conclusion of the Nelson Act negotiations, Henry Rice was again selected to be a part of the commission to put the Nelson Act into practice, but after a relatively short time—July 6, 1891—Rice resigned and returned to his home in St Paul. Three years later, while on a visit to San Antonio, Texas, Henry Mower Rice became ill and died.[1 & 2 & 3]

CHAPTER 24

John Collier's Dream

It was in April of 1933 that John Collier was sworn in as Indian Commissioner, became a part of the FDR administration and the beginning of the establishment of the Indian "New Deal". Collier's previous endeavors had focused on the social problems of the time. He was greatly influenced by his study of the works of the Russian anarchist, Peter Kropotkin, who rejected the ideas of competition and survival of the fittest and favored a classless society based on mutual aid between its members. Collier was also greatly influenced by the fact that his lawyer/banker father had been involved in a financial scandal that resulted in his father's suicide and his mother, very distressed over her husband's scandal, died as a result of addiction to relaxants. This led Collier to reject the system that had led to his parent's downfall and

John Collier

influenced the rest of his life. Kenneth Philp, in his book on the life of John Collier, states that "[Collier] vowed not to seek 'any success in the society' that had led to his parent's downfall."

It was a natural then that Collier became involved in social work with the Peoples Institute in New York City where he worked with recent immigrants to the United States. He came to the conclusion that capitalism—that focused on the creation of wealth—was destroying the fabric of society. His attempts to mold the immigrants he worked with—guiding their leisure in the direction he thought was correct—was greatly influenced by his admiration of the methods the Bolsheviks used to influence the peasants. Author Philp makes the statement that, "Collier favored censorship and municipal ownership of amusement places so films would concentrate on the universal strivings of mankind, thus raising the level of the working class…Collier believed that the Bolsheviks 'had provided the most important single sociological experiment of our time' in their effort to revive community life…"

Statements such as these, at a time when nationwide fear of Communism was mounting, resulted in Collier coming under the surveillance of the Justice Department, leading eventually to his departure for the wilderness of Mexico. En route, however, Collier wound up in Taos, New Mexico, became enthralled with the Pueblo culture and Indian life in general, and abandoned his plan to escape to Mexico.

In his association with the Taos Pueblo culture Collier saw in practice what he had come to believe—that an association in which individuals are oriented to the large association, as much if not more than to their own self-interest, is superior to an association in which the individual is more important than the association of which he is a part. Philp states that, "Collier concluded that Pueblo culture, and tribal life in general, must survive, not only in justice to the Indian but in service to the white."

So it was with this background that Collier accepted the appointment, for which he had campaigned, as Indian Commissioner. He realized, however, that the Dawes Land Allotment Act was in direct opposition to his dream of the communal system that he envisioned and that he hoped would become a model that all of America would eventually adopt.

Collier set the wheels in motion to write an omnibus bill that would replace the Dawes Act and accomplish his dream of re-establishing the tribal way of life. The resulting bill was introduced in mid-February of 1934 by Congressman Edgar Howard of Nebraska and Senator Burton Wheeler of Montana, and became known as the Wheeler-Howard Bill.

Expecting general approval, Collier was no doubt disappointed by the opposition to his romantic plan. His plan was opposed not only by many Congressmen and missionaries but also by some of the Interior Department staff. Perhaps most dismaying to Collier was the lack of approval by many Indian tribes, who for various reasons opposed his plan. While there is no doubt that many Indians lost their allotments, due either to shrewd and/or sometimes unscrupulous business deals, others were happy with their allotments and proud to be land owners—part of the melting-pot philosophy of this new nation.

Collier ignored the warnings and was undeterred in the promotion of his social experiment. Even after many amendments, cross-country meetings to explain the bill, requesting and receiving the support of President Roosevelt, threats of dismissal to staff members and even opposition to some parts of the bill by its original sponsors, the bill, now only 10 pages of the original 48, was passed by Congress and signed into law by President Roosevelt on June 18, 1934, and became known as the Indian Reorganization Act (IRA).

The IRA, which in current times is claimed to be the authorization for the fee-to-trust process, at least until recently, solved some problems with Indian policy but created even more, just as Senator Wheeler had feared. It paved the way for the American Indian Movement (AIM)—an American Indian advocacy group founded in 1968—to become a force in federal Indian policy, and also allowed the Nixon administration to make changes that continue to divide rather than unite our nation.

Philp, in summarizing his study of the life and crusade of John Collier, makes the statement that, "the Indian Reorganization Act was a flawed product that failed to meet the needs of a diversified population."[1]

But, we are getting ahead of ourselves. While the Nelson Act—Minnesota's version of the Dawes Act—was not turning out the result Congress had intended, Collier and Congress were about to authorize an almost completely opposite approach to what had been termed "the Indian problem." As the Indian Reorganization Act was put into practice, the Chippewa tribal organization, including Mille Lacs, was about to change dramatically.

Epilogue

It is 2016, and so why are this book and the research that led up to it important? At the current time and for several years previous to 2016, the United States federal government, primarily through the Department of the Interior of which the Bureau of Indian Affairs is a part, and all under the Executive branch, have been actively engaged in recreating the Mille Lac Indian Reservation as it was formed by treaty on February 22, 1855.

Why is that important? Tribal government structure as initiated by John Collier and his Indian Reorganization Act, does not allow non-tribal citizens of that area claimed as under tribal jurisdiction, to have a voice in the government under which they find themselves. That is in direct violation of the Constitution of the United States. That is exactly what caused the Revolutionary War, the break away from British rule and the creation of the United States. King George was imposing duties upon the colonists and they had no voice in the government that imposed those duties.

So how has the utopia envisioned by John Collier worked out for those who are tribal members living on Indian reservations? The sad truth is that due to the manipulations of governments, the tribal people who live on Indian reservations find themselves **not** covered by the United States Constitution. And thus freedom of speech, freedom of assembly, due process of law—and on and on—that are so essential to us as United States citizens, are not guaranteed to tribal members living on Indian reservations. On Indian reservations sovereignty rests not with the people but with the tribal government. An excellent example is that of the Indian Child Welfare Act which gives the tribal government precedence over that of the parents regarding care of children.

Why do Indian reservations still exist? Is that also not a violation of the United States Constitution; the formation of a state within a state? That is a question for another study. But first, how did we get to where we are in Mille Lacs County?

In this study I have tried to give the reader a feel for what life was like for the Indians who inhabited what would become Mille Lacs County when the white man first arrived. I think that we can conclude that their daily existence was one of securing food and shelter, which meant defending and enlarging their domain as resources became depleted—not so very different in purpose from today, but certainly different in method.

In their quest for the things that the traders offered that the Indians wanted for themselves, the most ready resource, animal pelts, was becoming scarce. So when government influence expanded westward, all the Indians had left to bargain with was timber and land. Thus the money and supplies offered by the government were enticing.

When the treaty of 1837 was negotiated, the Mille Lac area was involved pretty much by default. It is important to remember that by 1837 the Mille Lac Chippewa had inhabited the Mille Lac area for less than 100 years, having driven the Sioux out of the area sometime around 1750. They had not been there since "time immemorial" as one of the judges stated in the litigation that led up to the 1913 Supreme Court case.

In 1837 the area which is now Mille Lacs County was part of Wisconsin Territory. The Government negotiators, I believe, had no real interest in Mille Lac Lake. They wanted the pine timber primarily in what is now Wisconsin because it had great value to the expanding settlement. Nor did they care much about the land, at least for the time being, as evidenced by Governor Dodge's statement to the Chippewa to the effect that it would probably be quite a while before the President would want the land for his white children. And so it is ironic that this treaty has had such an impact on the Mille Lacs Lake area, arguably threating to destroy the industry which has grown up in the area because of the Mille Lacs Lake fishery. What possible justification could there be for authorizing both Wisconsin Indians and Minnesota Indians to harvest spawning Walleyes with 100 foot long gill nets? This is a practice that arguably is destroying the fishery for other citizens. I believe this to be quite a stretch from the intent of the 1837 treaty. This treaty (and others) and the negotiations leading up to it are included for the readers study so you may decide for yourself.

The first treaty that directly involved the Mille Lac Chippewa was the treaty of 1855. This treaty involved both the Pillager bands and the Mississippi bands but separate negotiations were held and separate treaties were signed. In present times much has been made of the first sentence in Article 2 of the 1855 treaty. It reads in part, "there shall be, and hereby is, reserved and set apart, a sufficient quantity of land for the permanent homes of the said Indians …" Because the final treaty was done in private with Henry Rice, we have no record of what was said. Consequently, let us examine the other provisions of the treaty for clues.

We know that the Chippewa were rather a nomadic people, moving to the area where food was available at various times of the year: to the blueberry patches at picking time; to the rice fields during rice harvest; to the sugar bush during the sap run in the spring. We know that the treaty talks included patenting of up to 80 acres of land to the head of each family, and that government assistance would be available to help them get established in farming. Was this what the sentence regarding permanent homes referred to—a sufficient quantity of land for permanent homes? A home established on a specific parcel of land where food would be produced, eliminating the nomadic life of moving from place to place to hunt and gather sustenance? We must recognize that no parcel of land was ever given to each family as the treaty describes. In defense of the government, however, the treaty did include what I would call a 'weasel clause' by stating that land would be assigned "at all such time or times as the President may deem it advisable for the interests and welfare of said Indians …"

So no land was assigned by the government and no soil was ploughed by the government in preparation for farming. Neither party lived up to the agreement of the treaty.

Before moving on it is worth emphasizing that the Chippewa were apparently desirous of becoming full citizens and a part of the United States—even as early as 1855. Chief Hole-in-the-Day in negotiations with Commissioner Manypenny, and apparently with the assent of the other chiefs, had lobbied hard for becoming full citizens. In any case, that did not happen either. Nor, I would argue, has it fully occurred today. But be that as it may, the permanency of the Mille Lac Reservation disappeared just nine years later—in 1863—when Mille Lac Chief Shaw-vosh-Kung led the delegation of Mississippi Chippewa to Washington and negotiated the sale of the Mille Lac Reservation to the United States.

Or did it? By reading this book you have learned of the circumstances surrounding Minnesota in 1863 and you know that the Mille Lac Chippewa prevented even further devastation. You know that Commissioner Dole made some sort of promise to the Mille Lacs which they did not forget. Henry Rice claimed to have written the 1863 treaty, so what was his thinking regarding the actual wording of article twelve? Was the thought behind the wording that the Indians would be assigned parcels of land there as the 1855 treaty had suggested? If that was the intention, why in God's name was it not clearly so stated? And why would the sale of the Mille Lac Reservation even have occurred? Or did they actually think they could eventually convince all the Mille Lacs to move to White Earth? And, if that was their thinking, then the article was complete injustice to the Indians. Did the Senate even read the treaty before it was ratified? They must have, because Henry Rice commented at one point that he was unhappy with the changes the Senate had made in the treaty as he had written it.

Whatever the case, the treaty was negotiated, signed by both the government and the Chippewa, ratified by the Senate and became law. A law so devoid of intent and detail that the government vacillated from one extreme to the other for another twenty five years, and the effects are still being felt today by generations of citizens who had no involvement in the cause and can only read about the details.

Under a law that was so unclear it was impossible to know if it was being followed or not. Sometimes the area was the exclusive domain of the Mille Lac Indians and other times it was open to settlement by the public. In no way was justice served to either party.

Leading up to 1887, Congress was considering a plan to finally bring the Indian people into the mainstream of civilization. In spite of what happened, I am still of the opinion that the Dawes Act was a notable attempt by the Government to assimilate the Indians into society and give them the same opportunities and obligations as other citizens. But the former ineptness of the Government made the Dawes Act unworkable at Mille Lac. To state it simply, you cannot allot lands on a reservation that doesn't exist, and that was the situation at Mille Lac.

The only answer to the dilemma was to do something different for Minnesota, and so Congress passed the Nelson Act in 1889. The Nelson Act required all the Chippewa in Minnesota to move to White Earth where they would be allotted land, but it gave them the option of being allotted land where they now lived if they didn't want to remove to White Earth. A three member Commission was appointed to secure the agreement of the Nelson Act by the eleven Chippewa bands in Minnesota. One of the three-member team—ironically the one they appointed as the chairman—was the very same person who had written the 1863 treaty that was the cause of all the trouble at Mille Lac: Henry Rice. What could he have been thinking when, as spokesman for the United Stated, he negotiated with the Mille Lac Chippewa? Why would Rice mislead the Indians into thinking that they would be allotted land on the former Mille Lac Reservation? He certainly knew what the 1863 treaty said. He also knew that as a result of the 1863 treaty much—if not most—of the land on the former reservation had already been claimed. And if he had read the Act (which we know that he did) he knew that those bona fide claims could not be allotted to the Indians. Rice understood the proviso that stated that legitimate claims would not be disturbed because he intimated such during the Red Lake negotiations. In his reports to his superiors following the negotiations Rice made definite observations and recommendations regarding Mille Lac. Once again it had been Henry Mower Rice, a spokesman for the federal government, who set up the problems now surfacing in 2016.

We cannot blame the few Mille Lac Chippewa who still remained at Mille Lac for being distressed when the truth surfaced and they learned that Henry Rice had lied to them. Nor can we blame the Indians for complaining—a complaint that Congress heard.

Congress passed an act authorizing the Mille Lacs to file suit in the Court of Claims for any losses they may have suffered as a result of the federal government having opened up the former Mille Lac Reservation to settlement. In that suit the Mille Lacs argued that they had not sold the Mille Lac Reservation in 1863, but rather had retained ownership as a result of Article 12, until they sold their right of occupancy in 1889. The Court of Claims sided with the Mille Lacs and awarded them not the three million dollars they had sought but some eight hundred thousand dollars for the value of the land of the Mille Lacs Reservation, using the Nelson Act as a guide.

The legislation that had authorized the suit had cleared the way for an appeal to the United States Supreme Court by either party. The United States appealed the decision of the Court of Claims to the Supreme Court, essentially saying that the Mille Lacs had sold the Mille Lac Reservation in 1863 so had nothing to sell now. The United States Supreme Court concluded, somewhat by compromise I believe, that the Mille Lacs band had not sold the Mille Lac Reservation until 1889, but that under the provisions of the Nelson Act all but about 5000 acres of land was exempt from sale because of previous bona fide claims. They therefore reversed the decision and remanded the case back to the Court of Claims to re-calculate the amount due the Mille Lacs for the sale of the Mille Lac Reservation, which was only the 5,000 or so acres not already claimed and confirmed by Proviso 6 as not being part of the acreage available for sale for the benefit of the Chippewa Indians of Minnesota.

There were less than three hundred Mille Lacs who had not removed to White Earth and were still living at Mille Lac. Land had been reserved for them at White Earth, and some had actually been allotted land at White Earth but then moved back to Mille Lac.

The Government must have realized by now that their attempts to remove that last vestige of the Mille Lacs band had failed and that the whole situation had been handled so poorly that the only way to do justice to these "homeless non-removal Mille Lacs" was to purchase land on which they could be allotted as had been promised. So money was appropriated to purchase land at Mille Lac; money incidentally that came from the Chippewa Indian fund. While those Mille Lacs still living at Mille Lac would have been allotted 160 acres each if they had removed to White Earth, thirty five years later—in about 1925—the homeless non-removal Mille Lacs were allotted plots ranging from two to ten acres each.

These are the facts that have caused me to conclude, as Commissioner of Indian Affairs T.J. Morgan did back in 1892, that there is no Indian Reservation in Mille Lacs County. And if there is no Indian reservation, how can there be reservation boundaries—those same boundaries that are claimed as being the basis for fee-to-trust applications, as well as other requests for additional tribal jurisdiction?

The Mille Lac Tribal government claims that they were a recognized band on June 18, 1934, when the Indian Reorganization Act was passed, making them eligible for the benefits of that Act. Were they?

Between 1863 and 1889 and continuing even thereafter, the Government had been trying to convince the Mille Lac Indians to remove to White Earth as the 1863-64 treaty required. In order to keep track of this progress the Government tabulated them as Removal Mille Lacs and Non-Removal Mille Lacs. Meager progress was made during those twenty five or so years, however, and by 1912 the record shows 912 Mille Lac Indians still living at Mille Lac with 400 of those 912 living near Mora on the Snake River and only 156 having removed to White Earth.

The intent of the Government was to shepherd these Indians on the path to civilization which was done through a central agency at White Earth and another at Red Lake. There was no agent at Mille Lac. Any attention the Indians at Mille Lac got was administered through White Earth. They were clearly considered part of the White Earth Reservation. Even as late as 1937 that fact was substantiated vividly by a letter from the Superintendent of the Consolidated Chippewa Agency J.S. Monks to J.M. Stewart, Director of Lands at the Office of Indian Affairs in Washington. In this letter Monks is recommending that the federal government purchase a piece of land on Swamp Lake in Aitkin County for the creation of a permanent wild rice camp for the use of the Chippewa in the area, including those at Mille Lac. The first paragraph of that letter reads, "The Consolidated Chippewa Agency and <u>the Indians at Mille Lac, which are part of the White Earth Band</u>, recommend the purchase of a permanent wild rice camp on Swamp Lake ..."[1] [emphasis added]

The Nelson Act, however, had promised these Indians 80 acre allotments each—later amended to 160 acres each—at White Earth and all the benefits that went with it and so removals slowly increased until by 1914 there were 1152 Mille Lacs living at White Earth and only 276 still living at Mille Lac. It was becoming obvious to Congress that the remaining few were probably not going to remove. After they had essentially been lied to by the Commissioners who negotiated the Nelson Act, and having promised all the Minnesota Chippewa an allotment, Congress in 1914 appropriated $40,000 to buy land on which to allot these remaining Mille Lacs.

By 1925 when allotments actually started happening at Mille Lac there were 1470 Mille Lac Indians living at White Earth and 292 living at Mille Lac. One might ask which group was the real Mille Lac band. The Consolidated Chippewa Agency in 1925 was made up of five reservations: White Earth, Leech Lake, Fond du Lac, Grand Portage and Bois Fort. The Non-Removal Mille Lacs were clearly part of the White Earth Reservation. There was no point of contact at Mille Lac with even the rations furnished the Indians by the Government being administered through White Earth.

At the urging of Washington statisticians with the Bureau of Indian Affairs, these smaller settlements were separated out for statistical purposes. Mille Lac was one of these settlements and they became known in the records as "the homeless Non-Removal Mille Lacs on Purchased Land."

The first time in the annual reports that I found Mille Lac listed as a reservation was in the 1935 report, and even then they were categorized as "Non-Removal Mille Lacs — Purchased lands."

The Mille Lacs located at Mille Lac were clearly not recognized as a band or as a reservation on June 18, 1934. That was confirmed by Commissioner of Indian Affairs John Collier in 1937. Senator Elmer Thomas, who was the Chairman of the Senate Committee on Indian Affairs, requested that Collier provide a list of tribes covered under the Indian Reorganization Act. The list John Collier provided to the Senator enumerated the Minnesota Consolidated tribe as being made up of five reservations: White Earth, Leech Lake, Fond du Lac, Bois Fort and Grand Portage.

After the Indian Reorganization Act was passed and the Minnesota Chippewa were working on a constitution in 1936, their proposal listed six reservations: the list John Collier had provided plus Mille Lac. One of the attorneys with the Bureau of Indian Affairs questioned whether the Mille Lacs should be referred to as a reservation since they were referred to in the records as "purchased land" and not a reservation. The Director of Lands replied to the solicitor that "these purchased lands <u>may be considered</u> as the reservation of the non-removal Mille Lac Indians." [emphasis added]

So by 1937 they were listed in the annual report as "Non-Removal Mille Lac (Purchased Land) Reservation.

And by 1938 it was "Non-removal Mille Lac Reservation (purchased lands).

Clearly this play on words was in the process of re-creating the Mille Lac Reservation.

I trust that you will conclude, as I have, that the Indians were treated very unfairly by many of the local people during this period in history. That was probably caused in large part by the panic experienced during the 1862 uprising. That we can't change. But that certainly is not motivation for the federal Government to continue to treat them unfairly, and in so doing, involve non-Indians as well. All, I would contend, caused by the lust for power centered in our federal Government, of which tribal government is a part.

Yes, tribal governments operate under the charade of self-determination but in reality all they do is under the thumb of the federal Government and authorized by the War Powers that—contrary to President Lincoln's wishes—have survived since the reconstruction days of the Civil War. It is time for the Indian people to be made full citizens of the United States with the full protection of the United States Constitution.

I would add one last point in regarding current 2016 happenings in Mille Lacs County. We need to recognize that when more and more land is removed from the county tax base—going all the way back to 1915—and placed under federal control, and when laws such as the Tribal Law and Order Act are authorized for Mille Lacs County, all under the erroneous assumption that the 1855 Mille Lac Reservation still exists, then the "justifiable expectations" of the non-tribal residents are upset. The United States Supreme Court said just that in *The City of Sherill v. Oneida Indian Nation*, 544 U.S. 197 (2005) stating that restoring tribal interests in mostly non-tribal areas upsets the "justifiable expectations" of the property owners and citizens of that area.

As I am completing this epilogue (March 2016) Susan Rice, spokesperson for President Obama, is on TV explaining that the President believes that the people of Cuba deserve genuine democracy. If that is true, and I believe that it is, then no less the Indians of the United States deserve genuine democracy in republic form by including them under the protection of the United States Constitution. Only in so doing, I believe, can we all achieve equality.

As I have researched, studied and written in preparation for this book I have been struck by the extreme patience exhibited by the federal government in early times when dealing with the Chippewa Indians. Week after week in negotiations—weeks at a time the Indian representatives were housed and fed in Washington, D.C. while negotiations progressed. Hour after hour in discussion and interpreting, often repetitive, as the government representatives endeavored to explain things to the delegations in a manner that the Indians could fully understand.

I was also struck by the willingness of the Indians to sell their timber and their land. They seemed to have a genuine desire to please their "Great Father" and to become an equal part of this new nation—at times almost begging to become full citizens.

In 2016 we see almost the exact opposite.

What happened?

Notes

Chapter 1: **Early Migration**

1. *History of the Ojibway People* (1885), William W. Warren — pg. 27 — (literally translated "an-ish-in-aub-ag" means spontaneous man. However, the Fond du Lac website says that the word Anishinabe means "the people."
2. *History of the Ojibway People* (1885), William W. Warren - "…these movements were made while they were living in their primitive state, when they possessed nothing but the bow and arrow, sharpened stones and bones of animals to kill game and fight their enemies. During this period they were surrounded by inveterate foes and war was their chief pastime."
3. *History of the Ojibway People* (1885), William W. Warren — footnote pg. 70.
4. *History of the Ojibway People* (1885), William W. Warren, — pgs. 67-70.

Chapter 2: **Savages?**

1. *The Assassination of Hole in the Day,* Anton Treuer - pgs. 30-34.
2. *History of the Ojibway People,* (1885) William W. Warren.
3. Ibid.
4. *Uncle Tom's Cabin,* Harriet Beecher Stowe.
5. *America's peculiar and horrifying tradition of Vigilante Justice,* Reed Karaim - pgs. 50-55 (Feb. 2012) issue of American History magazine.

Chapter 3: ***The Doctrine of Discovery* and *Manifest Destiny***

Chapter 4: **The *Doctrine of Discovery* in Action**

1. *America The Last Best Hope, Vol. 1, From Age of discovery to a World at War*, William J. Bennett, pgs. 33-36.
2. Ibid. pgs. 37-40.
3. Ibid. pgs. 40-42.
4. Ibid. pg. 42.
5. Ibid. pgs. 42-43.
6. Ibid. pg. 43.
7. Ibid. pgs. 45-46.
8. Petaga Point Archeological Site website.
9. Ibid.
10. Ibid.
11. Ibid.
12. Ibid.
13. *History of the Ojibway People* (1885), William W. Warren — pgs. 107-108.
14. In 1922 John and Judith Moore established their home and farmed the area on the peninsula formed where the Rum River exits Ogechie Lake. Their farm most likely included the former smaller village of the Sioux. They had a son named Hugh whose nickname was Buck. Therefore, the Buck More Dam.

Chapter 5: **So Who Was John Tanner?**

1. *A Narrative of the Captivity and Adventures of John Tanner during Thirty Years Residence Among the Indians in the Interior of North America—1830*, Edwin James

Chapter 6: **The 1837 Treaty**

1. The Indian Trade and Intercourse Acts had been passed by Congress to give the federal government the authority to regulate trade with the Indians, so cutting timber on Indian lands was prohibited without special permission.
2. Governor Dodge called the invitees the "Chippewa Nation of Indians" when in fact no such entity existed, at least as a governing entity.
3. *Chippewa Treaty Rights*, Ronald N. Satz.
4. *Fish in the Lakes, Wild Rice, and Game in Abundance: Testimony on Behalf of Mille Lacs Ojibwe Hunting and Fishing Rights*, Charles E. Cleland; Thomas Lund; John D. Nichols; Helen Tanner; Bruce White; James M. McClurken

Chapter 7: **The 1855 Treaty**

1. Documents relating to the negotiation of ratified and unratified treaties with various Indian tribes 1801 - 1869, NAChi, Records of BIA, RG75, T 494, Roll 5, Ratified Treaty No. 287, Documents Relating to the Negotiation of the Treaty of February 22, 1855, with Mississippi, Pillager, Lake Winnebagoshish bands of Chippewa Indians.
2. *Faith in Paper - The Ethnohistory and Litigation of Upper Great Lakes Indian treaties (Ethnohistory of the Mille Lacs Reservation Boundary),* Charles E. Cleland, Michigan State University.

Chapter 8: **1862 — The Sioux Uprising**

1. *Lincoln and the Sioux Uprising of 1862,* Hank H. Cox — pgs. 67-70.
2. *Dakota Dawn,* Gregory F. Michno — pg. 257.
3. Ibid. pg. 265.
4. *Lincoln and the Sioux Uprising of 1862,* Hank H. Cox — pgs. 122-123.
5. Ibid. pg. 123.
6. *Dakota Dawn,* Gregory F. Michno — pg. 393.
7. *Lincoln and the Sioux Uprising of 1862,* Hank H. Cos — pgs. 148-149.
8. Ibid. pg. 154.
9. Ibid. pg. 154.
10. *Lincoln and the Indians,* David A. Nichols - pg. 85.
11. *Lincoln and the Sioux Uprising of 1862,* Hank H. Cox - pg. 171.
12. Ibid. pg.175.
13. Ibid. pgs. 175-176.
14. Ibid. pg. 176.
15. *Lincoln and the Indians,* David A. Nichols - pg. 107.

Chapter 9: **Chippewa Involvement — 1862 Sioux Uprising**

1. *The Assassination of Hole in the Day,* Anton Treuer — pg. 128.
2. Ibid.
3. *Lights and Shadows of a Long Episcopate,* Henry Benjamin Whipple — pg. 107.
4. *The Assassination of Hole in the Day,* Anton Treuer — pg. 135.
5. Ibid.
6. *Dakota Dawn,* Gregory F. Michno - pg. 389 and *Lincoln and the Sioux Uprising of 1862,* Hank H. Cox — pg. 56.

7. *The Assassination of Hole in the Day*, Anton Treuer — pg. 134.
8. Ibid.
9. Ibid. pg.128.
10. Ibid. pgs. 135 and 137.
11. *Lights and Shadows of a long Episcopate*, Henry Benjamin Whipple — pg. 529.
12. *The Assassination of Hole in the Day*, Anton Treuer — pg. 134.
13. *Lights and Shadows of a Long Episcopate*, Henry Benjamin Whipple — pg. 529.

Chapter 10: **Hole-in-the-Day**

1. *The Assassination of Hole in the Day*, Anton Treuer - pg. 37.
2. Ibid. pg. 40.
3. Ibid. pg. 42.
4. Ibid. pg. 76.
5. Ibid. pg. 81.
6. Ibid.
7. Ibid. pg. 85.
8. Ibid. pg. 87.
9. Ibid. pg. 89.
10. Ibid. pg. 93.
11. Ibid. pg. 95.
12. Ibid. pg. 113.
13. Ibid. pg. 114.
14. Ibid. pg. 125.
15. Ibid. pg. 131.
16. Ibid. pg. 137.
17. Ibid. pg. 138.
18. Ibid. pg. 141.

Chapter 11: **Minnesota — A poster child for Corruption in the Indian System in the Nineteenth Century?**

1. *Lincoln and the Indians*, David A. Nichols — pgs. 6-7.
2. Ibid. pg. 7.
3. Wikipedia, the free encyclopedia with the footnote as "Transcript of the Northwest Ordinance — 1787."

4. *Lincoln and the Indians*, David A. Nichols — pg. 7.
5. For the foregoing description of the Indian System I have relied heavily on the coverage of that subject by David A. Nichols in his book, *Lincoln and the Indians*.
6. *Faith in Paper*, Charles E. Cleland — pg. 119 and MN Historical Society, Henry Mower Rice papers, corresp. & other 1824-1893, P439, Box 1.
7. Ibid.
8. *Lincoln and the Indians*, David A. Nichols — pg. 14.
9. Ibid. pgs. 17 & 18.
10. Ibid. pg. 19.
11. Ibid. pg. 141.

Chapter 12: **1863 — 1864 Treaties**
1. RG75, NAChi, Records of BIA, Documents relating to the negotiation of ratified and unratified treaties with various Indian tribes 1801-1869, Ratified treaty No. 322, Documents relating to the negotiation of the treaty of March 11, 1863, with the Mississippi, Pillager, and Lake Winnebagoshish bands of Chippewa Indians, T494, Roll 6.

Chapter 13: **Treaties in Action**
1. *The Assassination of Hole in the Day*, Anton Treuer - pg. 100.
2. Ibid. pg. 101.
3. Ibid.
4. Ibid. pg. 106.

Chapter 14: **The 1870s**
1. *The Assassination of Hole in the Day*, Anton Treuer - pg. 134.
2. Ibid.
3. Letter from George A. Wheeler (Princeton resident) to Indian Agent George Atcheson, Feb. 14, 1870.
4. Letter from Joseph Roberts of St. Paul to Cap. George Atcheson, May 12, 1870.
5. Letter from Charles Peltier (Little Falls resident) to Indian Agent Atcheson, June 27, 1870.
6. Letter from Bat. Capt. George Atcheson, U.S. Indian Agent Chippewa Agency to Commissioner of Indian Affairs Ely S. Parker, June 30, 1870.

7. Letter from Edw. P. Smith, Indian Agent at St Paul to Commissioner of Indian Affairs Ely Parker, Mar. 31, 1871.
8. Letter from Indian Agent Edw. P. Smith to Commissioner of Indian Affairs Ely Parker, May 1, 1871.
9. Letter from Bishop George Whipple to Sec. of the Interior Columbus Delano, May 13, 1871.
10. Letter from Indian Agent Edw. P. Smith to Commissioner of Indian Affairs Ely Parker, July 17, 1871.
11. Letter from Willis Drummond, Commissioner of General Land Office in Washington to Register & Receiver in Taylors Falls, Minnesota, Sept. 1, 1871.
12. Letter from Indian Agent Edw. P. Smith to H.R. Clum, Commissioner of Indian Affairs, Sept. 1, 1871.
13. Letter from U.S. Attorney General Akerman to B.R, Cowen, acting Secretary of the interior, Sept. 11, 1871.
14. Letter from W.W. Curtis, acting Commissioner of General Land Office in Washington to Commissioner of Indian Affairs, Sept. 21, 1871.
15. Letter from Minnesota Governor Austin to Commissioner of General Land Office in Washington, Sept. 24, 1871.
16. Letter from Indian Agent Edw. P. Smith to acting Commissioner of Indian Affairs Clum, Nov. 13, 1871.
17. Letter from Surveyor General Baker, St Paul to J.A. Williamson, General Land Office, Washington, July 1, 1876.
18. Letter from J.A. Williamson, General Land Office to Surveyor General Baker, July 13, 1876.
19. Letter from Sec. of Int. Zachariah Chandler to Commissioner of Indian Affairs John Q. Smith, Jan. 27, 1877.
20. Letter from Secretary of Interior Zachariah Chandler to the Commissioner of the General Land Office, Mar. 1, 1877.

Chapter 15: **The 1880s**

1. Letter from Joseph Roberts to Sec. Carl Schurz, Jan 15, 1880, RG75, Entry 102, Box 80, Sp. Case 109, NA.
2. Letter from Mille Lac chiefs to President Hayes, Mar. 22, 1880, RG75, Entry 102, Box 80, Sp. Case 109, NA.
3. Morrison County Petition, RG75, Entry 102, Box 80, Sp. Case 109, NA.

4. Letter from Commissioner of Indian Affairs Hiram Price to Secretary of Interior Henry Teller, July 7, 1883.
5. Letter from Chas. N. Beaulieu to Congressman Knute Nelson, July 16, 1883.
6. Letter from Congressman Knute Nelson to DOI Secretary Teller, July 24, 1883.
7. Letter from Congressman Knute Nelson, Minnesota 5th to Secretary of Interior Henry Teller, July 21, 1883.

Chapter 16: **The Nelson Act**

This entire chapter except for the transcript of the Mille Lac negotiations can be found in RG75, Records of the BIA, NADC, Recs. Land Dev., Gen. Rec., Box 60, PL 163, Entry 310, item #104. The Mille Lac transcript is missing from this file at NADC but can be found at RG75, Dept. of Int., Off. Ind. Aff., WE Agency, Minutes of councils called to accept Act of 1889, Box 50, NAID: 7479718, HM:2014, NAKC.

Chapter 17: **Early 1900s**

1. Frederick E. Hoxie, *What was Taney Thinking — American Indian Citizenship in the Era of Dredd Scott.* 82, Chi.-Kent. L. Rev. 329 (2007).
2. RG75, DOI, Off.Ind.Aff., Wht Earth Agy., correspondence, 1/30/1901-3/2/1909, Fin. 1908, Land, Jan. 1905, Box 4, NAID 7479707, Hm:2014, NAKC.

Chapter 18: **One Last Effort**

1. RG75, Dept. of Int., Off. Ind. Aff., WE Agency, Agency Central Subject File 1/31.1895 — 7/1922, Box 39, NAID: 7479714, HM:2014, NAKC.

Chapter 19: **The Mille Lac Band of Chippewa Indians vs The United States — 1913**

1. Law Library, University of Minnesota Law Center, 220 - 19th Ave. S., Minneapolis, MN 55455

Chapter 20: **The Homeless Non-Removal Mille Lacs**

1. RG75, DOI, Off. Ind. Aff., WE Agency, Annual Reports & Corr. 6/1910 — 6/1922, NAID:7479715, Corr. Chip. Comm. 1888-1900, NAID:7479716, Box 47, HM:2014, NAKC.
2. RG75, Rec. BIA, Rec. Land Div., Gen. Rec., Box 60, PL163, Entry 310, item#104, NADC.
3. RG75, DOI, Off.Ind.Aff. correspondence, Finance 1908, Land Jan. 1905, Box 4, NAID: 7479707, Hm:2014, NAKC.

4. RG75, DOI, Off.Ind.Aff., WE Agency, correspondence 1/30/1902-3/2/1909, Finance 1908, Land: Jan.1905, Box 4, NAID:7479707, Hm:2014, NAKC.
5. Ibid.
6. Ibid.
7. Ibid.
8. Ibid.
9. Ibid.
10. Statutes at Large, 63rd Congress, Session 2, Chap. 222.
11. RG75, DOI, Off.Ind.Aff., WE Agency, annual reports 6/1910-6/19221, NAID:7479715, correspondence 1888-1900, NAID:7479716, Box 47, Hm:23014,
12. NAKC.
13. RG75, DOI, Off.Ind.Aff., correspondence 1/10/1910-6/12/1922, 1916-Mar. 1920, Box 7, NAID:7479708, Hm:2014, NAKC.
14. Ibid.
15. RG75, Off.Ind.Aff., WE Agency, annual reports and correspondence, 6/1910-6/1922, NAID:7479715, correspondence Chip. Comm.. 1888-1900, NAID:7479716, Box 47, Hm:2014, NAKC.
16. RG75, DOI, Off.Ind.Aff., correspondence 1/10/1910-6/12/1922, 1916-Mar. 1920, Box 7, NAID:7479708, Hm. 2014, NAKC.
17. Ibid.
18. Ibid.
19. RG75, BIA, Cons.Chip.Agency, Cass Lake, Minn., annual reports 1922-1925, Box 341, Hm:1989, NAKC.
20. Ibid.
21. Ibid.
22. Ibid.
23. RG75, Records of BIA, Cons.Chip.Agency., Cass Lake, Minn., Annual Reports 1925-1930, Hm:1989, Box 342, NAKC.
24. Ibid.
25. Ibid.
26. Ibid.
27. Ibid.
28. Ibid.
29. Ibid.

30. Ibid.
31. Ibid.
32. Ibid.
33. Ibid.
34. RG75, Records of BIA, Cons.Chip.Agency, Cass Lake, Minn., annual reports 1931-1936, Box 343, Hn:1989, NAKC.
35. Ibid.
36. RG75, BIA, John Morrison correspondence, Box 1, Pl163, Entry 1026, NAChi.
37. Ibid.
38. Ibid.
39. Ibid.
40. Ibid.
41. RG75, NADC.
42. RG75, Records of BIA, Cons.Chip.Agency, Cass Lake, Minn., Annual Reports 1931-1936, Box 343, Hm:1989, NAKC.
43. RG75, Records of BIA, Cons.Chip. Agency, Cass Lake, Minn., annual reports 1937-1941, Box 344, HM:1989, NAKC.
44. Ibid.
45. Ibid and annual reports, 1942-1946, Box 345, HM:1989, NAKC.

Chapter 21: **White Earth and the Nelson Act**

1. RG75, DOI, Off.Ind.Aff., WE Agency, annual reports & corresp. 6/1910 — 6/1922, NAID: 7479715 & Corres. Chip. Comm. 1888-1900, NAID:7479716, Box 47, HM:2014, NAKC.
2. Ibid.
3. RG75, DOI, Off.Ind.Aff., WE Agency, letters fr. Ind. Aff. 1888-1900, Box 49, NAID:7479717, HM:2014, NAKC.
4. RG75, DOI, Off.Ind.Aff., WE Agency, Corres. Chip. Comm. 1888-1900, NAID:7479716, HM:2014, Box 48, NAKC.
5. RG75, BIA, Letters fr. Comm. Chr. To Sec. Int. May-Dec 1892, Box 1, Pl 136, Entry 1300, NAChi.
6. RG75, BIA, Letters sent by Chr., Box 1 of 3, Pl 136, Entry 1298, NAChi.
7. RG75, DOI, Off. Ind. Aff., WE Agency, Corres. Chip, Comm. 1888-1900, Box 48, NAID:7479716, Hm:2014, NAKC.

8. RG75, DOI, Off.Ind.Aff., WE Agency, Letters fr. Off. Ind. Aff. 1889-1900, NAID:7479717, Hm:2014, Box 49, NAKC.
    1. RG75, BIA, Letters sent by Chr., Box 1 of 3, Pl 136, Entry 1298, NAChi.
9. RG75, DOI, Off.Ind.Aff., WE Agency, Letters recd fr Off.Ind.Aff. 1889-1900, Box 49, NAID:7479717, Hm:2014, NAKC.
10. Ibid.
11. RG75, DOI, Of.Ind.Aff., WE Agency, corres. Chip.Comm.1888-1900, Box48, NAID:7479716, Hm:2014, NAKC.
12. RG75, DOI, Off.Ind.Aff. , WE Agency, letters recd fr Ind.Aff. 1889-1900, NAID:7479717,Hm:2014, Box 49, NAKC.
13. RG75, BIA, Letters sent by Chr., Box 2 & 3 of 3, Pl 136, Entry 1298, NAChi.
14. RG75, BIA, Letters sent by Chr. Box 1 of 3, Pl 136, Entry 1298, NAChi.
15. RG75, records of Chip. Comm. — correspondence, Box 1, Row 301, Entry 1297, NAChi.
16. RG75, BIA, Letters sent by Chr., Box 2 & 3 of 3, Pl 136, Entry 1298, NAChi.
17. Ibid.
18. Ibid.
19. Ibid.
20. RG75, DOI, Off.Ind.Aff., WE Agency, Corres. Of Com. Ind.Aff. 1/30/1901-3/2/1909, Finance:1908-Land:Jan 1905, Box 4, NAID:7479707, HM:2014, NAKC.
21. RG75, DOI, Off.Ind.Aff., WE Agency, Annual reports & corresp. 6/1910-6/1922, NAID:7479715, NAKC.
22. Ibid.
23. RG75, DOI, Off.Ind.Aff., WE Agency, Annual reports & corres. 6/191—6/1922, NAID:7479725 & corres.chip.comm.1888-1900, NAID:7479716, Box 47, Hm:2014, NAKC.
24. Ibid.
25. RG75, DOI, Off.Ind.Aff., corres.comm. Ind.Aff. 1/10/1910-6/12/1922, 1916-Mar.1920, Box 7, NAID:7479708, Hm:2014, NAKC.
26. Ibid.
27. Ibid.

28. RG75, DOI, Off.Ind.Aff., WE Agency, Annual reports & corres. 6/1910-6/1922, NAID:7479715, Corres. Chip Comm. 1888-1900, NAID:7479716, Box 47, Hm:2014, NAKC.
29. Ibid.
30. Ibid.
31. RG75, BIA, Cons.Chip.Agency, Cass Lake, annual reports 1922-1925, Box 341, Hm:1989, NAKC.
32. RG75, BIA, Cons.Chip. Agency, Cass Lake, annual reports 1925-1930, Box 342, Hm:1989, NAKC.
33. Ibid.
34. Ibid.
35. Ibid.
36. RG75, BIA, Cons.Chip.Agency, Cass Lake, annual reports 1931-1936, Box 343, Hm:1989, NAKC.

Chapter 22: **The Saga of Shaw-vosh-Kung's Land**
1. Mille Lacs County courthouse property records

Chapter 23: **Henry Mower Rice, 1816 - 1894**
1. Nelson Act negotiations. NAKC.
2. MN Hist. Soc., Henry Rice papers, P439, Box 5.
3. Ibid., Box 1, Correspondence & other, 1824 — 1893.

Chapter 24: **John Collier's Dream**
1. *John Collier's Crusade for Indian Reform*, Kenneth R. Philp.

Epilogue
1. RG75, BIA Records, Cons.Chip.Agency, Mille Lacs Exp. Land Acquisition Program, Box 544, HM:1990, NAKC.

Maps
1928 — Dept. of Interior files, Washington, D.C.
1930 — Mille Lacs County Map file, National Archives, College Park, MN.
1936 — Ibid.
1950 — Ibid.
1967 — Ibid.

Appendix

Treaty with the Chippewa 1837

Treaty with the Chippewa 1855

Treaty with the Chippewa of the Mississippi and the Pillager and Lake Winnibigoshish Bands 1863

Treaty with the Chippewa, Mississippi, and Pillager and Lake Winnibigoshish Bands, 1864

An act for the relief and civilization of the Chippewa Indians in the State of Minnesota

Supreme Court of the United States, 1912, No. 736, Brief for the United States.

Supreme Court of the United States, No. 735, 1912, Brief for the Mille Lacs Band of Chippewa Indians in the State of Minnesota.

United States Supreme Court decision, No. 736, June 9, 1913.

1937 reply to letter from Senator Elmer Thomas to Commissioner John Collier requesting list of Indian tribes under the I.R.A.

Indian tribes under the I.R.A. by John Collier.

Acknowledgement by Senator Thomas.

Maps

1928

UNITED STATES
DEPARTMENT OF THE INTERIOR
HUBERT WORK, SECRETARY

GENERAL LAND OFFICE
WILLIAM SPRY, COMMISSIONER

STATE OF MINNESOTA

Compiled from the official Records of the General Land Office and other sources

1928

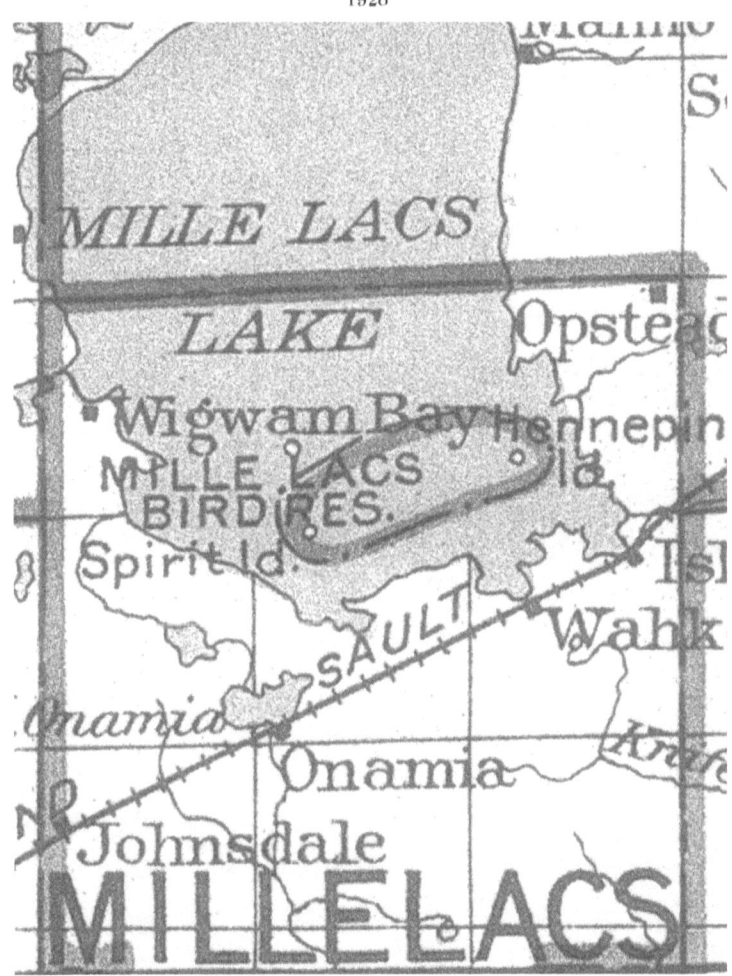

Author's note: This map of the State of Minnesota shows only the White Earth Reservation and the Red Lake Reservation.

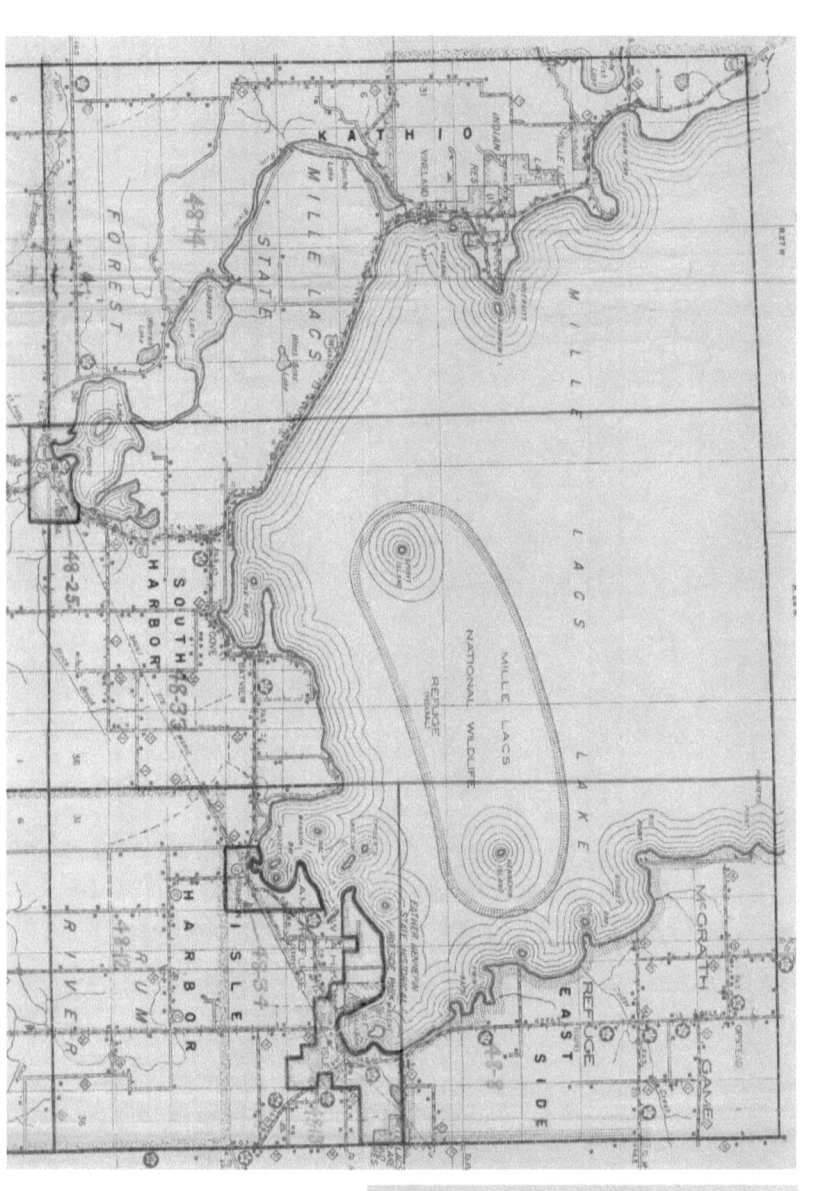

Author's note: This map shows scattered areas of land purchased for the homeless Mille Lac Indians and labels them as "Mille Lacs Lake Indian Reservation."

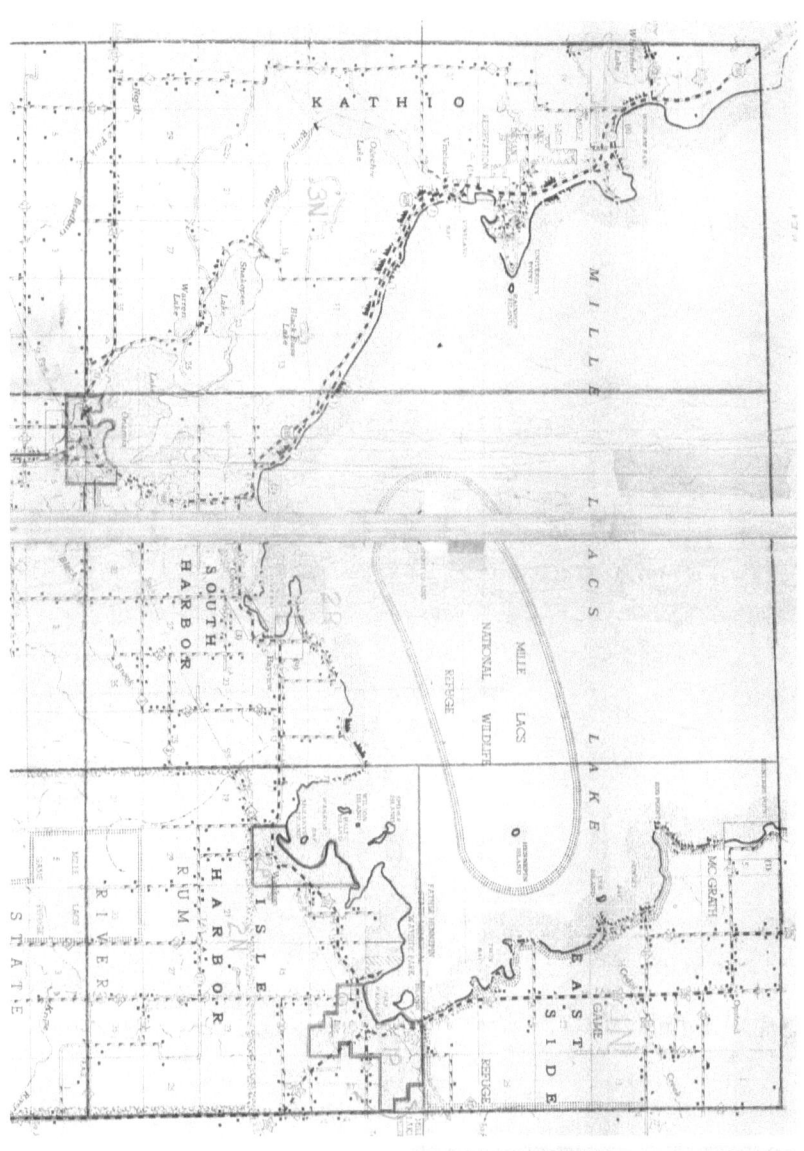

1950

Author's Note: This map shows the purchased lands as "Mille Lacs Lake Indian Reservation."

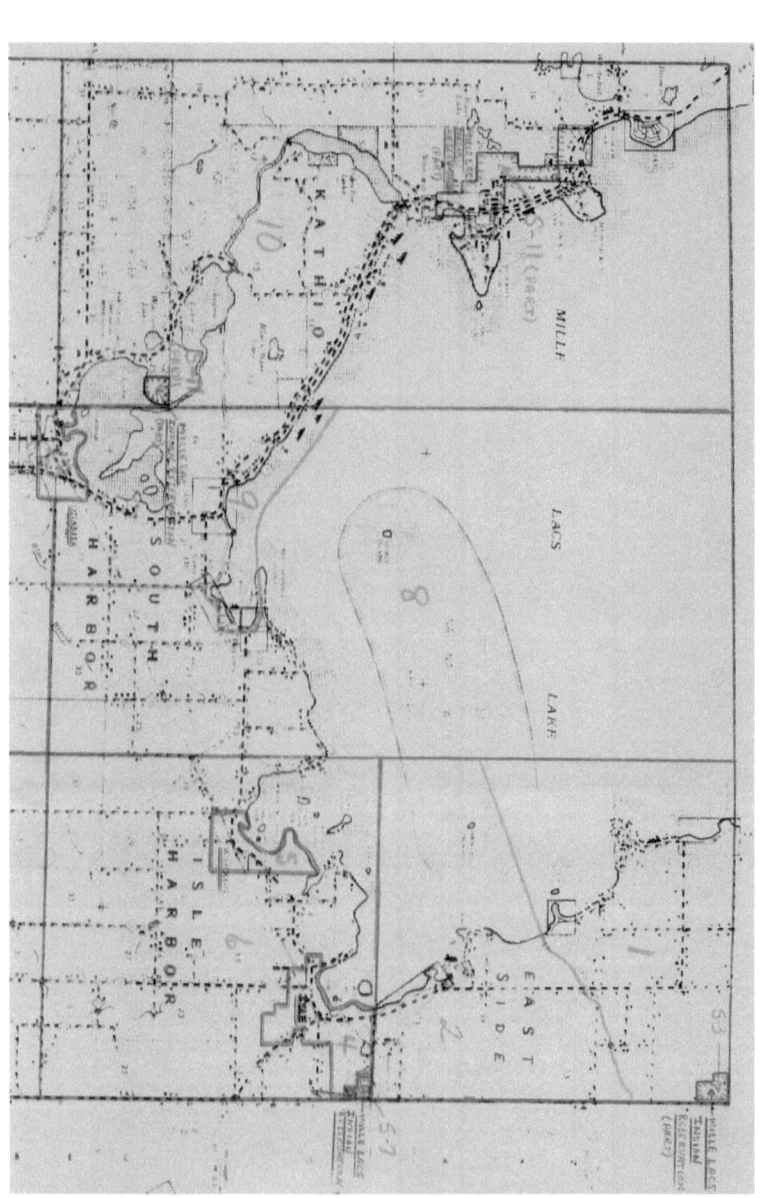

GENERAL HIGHWAY MAP
MILLE LACS COUNTY
MINNESOTA

1967

Author's Note: This map shows purchased land as "Mille Lac Indian Reservation" at one location and "Mille Lacs Indian Reservation" in another.

APPENDIX

Treaty with the Chippewa, 1837

Articles of a treaty made and concluded at St. Peters (the confluence of the St. Peters and Mississippi rivers) in the Territory of Wisconsin, between the United States of America, by their commissioner, Henry Dodge, Governor of said Territory, and the Chippewa nation of Indians, by their chiefs and headmen.

Article 1.

The said Chippewa nation cede to the United States all that tract of country included within the following boundaries:

Beginning at the junction of the Crow Wing and Mississippi rivers, between twenty and thirty miles above where the Mississippi is crossed by the forty-sixth parallel of north latitude, and running thence to the north point of Lake St. Croix, one of the sources of the St. Croix river; thence to and along the dividing ridge between the waters of Lake Superior and those of the Mississippi, to the sources of the Ocha-sua-sepe a tributary of the Chippewa river; thence to a point on the Chippewa river, twenty miles below the outlet of Lake De Flambeau; thence to the junction of the Wisconsin and Pelican rivers; thence on an east course twenty-five miles; thence southerly, on a course parallel with that of the Wisconsin river, to the line dividing the territories of the Chippewas and Menomomies; thence to the Plover Portage; thence along the southern boundary of the Chippewa country, to the commencement of the boundary line dividing it from that of the Sioux, half a days march below the falls of the Chippewa river; thence with said boundary line to the mouth of Wah-tap river, at its junction with the Mississippi; and thence up the Mississippi to the place of beginning.

Article 2.

In consideration of the cession aforesaid, the United States agree to make to the Chippewa nation, annually, for the term of twenty years, from the date of the ratification of this treaty, the following payments.

1. Nine thousand five hundred dollars, to be paid in money.

2. Nineteen thousand dollars, to be delivered in goods.
3. Three thousand dollars for establishing three blacksmiths shops, supporting the blacksmiths, and furnishing them with iron and steel.
4. One thousand dollars for farmers, and for supplying them and the Indians, with implements of labor, with grain or seed; and whatever else may be necessary to enable them to carry on their agricultural pursuits.
5. Two thousand dollars in provisions.
6. Five hundred dollars in tobacco.

The provisions and tobacco to be delivered at the same time with the goods, and the money to be paid; which time or times, as well as the place or places where they are to be delivered, shall be fixed upon under the direction of the President of the United States.

The blacksmiths shops to be placed at such points in the Chippewa country as shall be designated by the Superintendent of Indian Affairs, or under his direction. If at the expiration of one or more years the Indians should prefer to receive goods, instead of the nine thousand dollars agreed to be paid to them in money, they shall be at liberty to do so. Or, should they conclude to appropriate a portion of that annuity to the establishment and support of a school or schools among them, this shall be granted them.

Article 3.

The sum of one hundred thousand dollars shall be paid by the United States, to the half-breeds of the Chippewa nation, under the direction of the President. It is the wish of the Indians that their two sub-agents Daniel P. Bushnell, and Miles M. Vineyard, superintend the distribution of this money among their half-breed relations.

Article 4.

The sum of seventy thousand dollars shall be applied to the payment, by the United States, of certain claims against the Indians; of which amount twenty-eight thousand dollars shall, at their request, be paid to William A. Aitkin, twenty-five thousand to Lyman M. Warren, and the balance applied to the liquidation of other just demands against them — which they acknowledge to be the case with regard to that presented by Hercules L. Dousman, for the sum of five thousand dollars; and they request that it be paid.

Article 5.

The privilege of hunting, fishing, and gathering the wild rice, upon the lands, the rivers and the lakes included in the territory ceded, is guaranteed to the Indians, during the pleasure of the President of the United States.

Article 6.

This treaty shall be obligatory from and after its ratification by the President and Senate of the United States.

Done at St. Peters in the Territory of Wisconsin the twenty-ninth day of July eighteen hundred and thirty-seven.

Henry Dodge, Commissioner.

From Leech lake:
Chiefs:
Aish-ke-bo-ge-koshe, or Flat Mouth.
R-che-o-sau-ya, or the Elder Brother.
Warriors:
Pe-zhe-kins, the Young Buffalo,
Ma-ghe-ga-bo, or La Trappe,
O-be-gwa-dans, the Chief of the Earth,
Wa-bose, or the Rabbit,
Che-a-na-quos, or the Big Cloud.

From Gull Lake and Swan river:
Chiefs:
Pa-goo-na-kee-zhig, or the Hole-in-the-Day,
Songa-ko-mig, or the Strong Ground.
Warriors:
Wa-boo-jig, or the White Fisher,
Ma-cou-da, or the Bear's Heart.

From St. Croix river:
Chiefs:
Pe-zhe-ke, or the Buffalo,
Ka-be-ma-be, or the Wet Month.
Warriors:
Pa-ga-we-we-wetung, Coming Home Hollowing,
Ya-banse, or the Young Buck,
Kis-ke-ta-wak, or the Cut Ear.

From Lake Courteoville:
Chief:
Pa-qua-a-mo, or the Wood Pecker.

From Lac De Flambeau:
Chiefs:
Pish-ka-ga-ghe, or the White Crow,
Na-wa-ge-wa, or the Knee,
O-ge-ma-ga, or the Dandy,
Pa-se-quam-jis, or the Commissioner,
Wa-be-ne-me, or the White Thunder.

From La Pointe, (on Lake Superior):
Chiefs:
Pe-zhe-kr, or the Buffalo,
Ta-qua-ga-na, or Two Lodges Meeting,
Cha-che-que-o.

From Mille Lac:
Chiefs:
Wa-shask-ko-kone, or Rats Liver,
Wen-ghe-ge-she-guk, or the First Day.
Warriors:
Ada-we-ge-shik, or Both Ends of the Sky,
Ka-ka-quap, or the Sparrow.

From Sandy Lake:
Chiefs:
Ka-nan-da-wa-win-zo, or Le Brocheux,
We-we-shan-shis, the Bad Boy, or Big Mouth,
Ke-che-wa-me-te-go, or the Big Frenchman.
Warriors:
Na-ta-me-ga-bo, the Man that stands First,
Sa-ga-ta-gun, or Spunk.

From Snake river:
Chiefs:
Naudin, or the Wind,
Sha-go-bai, or the Little Six,
Pay-ajik, or the Lone Man,
Na-qua-na-bie, or the Feather.
Warriors:
Ha-tau-wa,

Wa-me-te-go-zhins, the Little
　　Frenchman,
Sho-ne-a, or Silver.

From Fond du Lac, (on Lake Superior):
　Chiefs:
　　Mang-go-sit, or the Loons Foot,
　　Shing-go-be, or the Spruce.

From Red Cedar Lake:
　Mont-so-mo, or the Murdering Yell.

From Red Lake:
　Francois Goumean (a half breed).

From Leech Lake:
　Warriors:
　　Sha-wa-ghe-zhig, or the Sounding Sky,
　　Wa-zau-ko-ni-a, or Yellow Robe.

Signed in the presence of—

Verplanck Van Antwerp,
　Secretary to the Commissioner.
M.M. Vineyard,
　U.S. Sub-Indian Agent.
Daniel P. Bushnell.
Law. Taliaferro,
　Indian Agent at St. Peters.
Martin Scott,
　Captain, Fifth Regiment Infantry.
J. Emerson,
　Assistant Surgeon, U.S. Army.
H.H. Sibley.

H.L. Dousman.
S.C. Stambaugh.
E. Lockwood.
Lyman M. Warren. J.
N. Nicollet.
Harman Van Antwerp.
Wm. H. Forbes.
Jean Baptiste Dubay, Interpreter.
Peter Quinn, Interpreter.
S. Campbell, U.S. Interpreter.
Stephen Bonga, Interpreter.
Wm. W. Coriell.

(To the Indian names are subjoined a mark and seal.)

Treaty with the Chippewa, 1855

Articles of agreement and convention made and concluded at the city of Washington, this twenty-second day of February, one thousand eight hundred and fifty-five, by George W. Manypenny, commissioner, on the part of the United States, and the following-named chiefs and delegates, representing the Mississippi bands of Chippewa Indians, viz: Pug-o-na-ke-shick, or Hole-in-the-Day; Que-we-sans-ish, or Bad Boy; Wand-e-kaw, or Little Hill; l-awe-showe-we-ke-shig, or Crossing Sky; Petud-dunce, or Rat's Liver; Mun-o-min-e-kay-shein, or Rice-Maker; Mah-yah-ge-way-we-durg, or the Chorister; Kay-gwa-daush, or the Attempter; Caw-caug-e-we-goon, or Crow Feather; and Show-baush-king, or He that passes under Everything, and the following-named chiefs and delegates representing the Pillager and Lake Winnibigoshish bands of Chippewa Indians, viz: Aish-ke-bug-e-koshe, or Flat Mouth; Be-sheck-kee, or Buffalo; Nay-bun-a-caush, or Young Man's Son; Mauge-gaw-bow, or Stepping Ahead; Mi-gi-si, or Eagle; and Kaw-be-mub-bee, or North Star, they being thereto duly authorized by the said bands of Indians respectively.

Article 1.

The Mississippi, Pillager, and Lake Winnibigoshish bands of Chippewa Indians hereby cede, sell, and convey to the United States all their right, title, and interest in, and to, the lands now owned and claimed by them, in the Territory of Minnesota, and included within the following boundaries, viz: Beginning at a point where the east branch of Snake River crosses the southern boundary-line of the Chippewa country, east of the Mississippi River, as established by the treaty of July twenty-ninth, one thousand eight hundred and thirty-seven, running thence, up the said branch, to its source; thence, nearly north in a straight line, to the mouth of East Savannah River; thence, up the St. Louis River, to the mouth of East Swan River; thence, up said river, to its source; thence, in a straight line, to the most westwardly bend of Vermillion River; thence, northwestwardly, in a straight line, to the first and most considerable bend in the Big Fork River; thence, down said river, to its mouth; thence, down Rainy

Lake River, to the mouth of Black River; thence, up that river, to its source; thence, in a straight line, to the northern extremity of Turtle Lake; thence, in a straight line, to the mouth of Wild Rice River; thence, up Red River of the North, to the mouth of Buffalo River; thence, in a straight line, to the southwestern extremity of Otter-Tail Lake; thence, through said lake, to the source of Leaf River; thence down said river, to its junction with Crow Wing River; thence down Crow Wing River, to its junction with the Mississippi River; thence to the commencement on said river of the southern boundary-line of the Chippewa country, as established by the treaty of July twenty-ninth, one thousand eight hundred and thirty-seven; and thence, along said line, to the place of beginning. And the said Indians do further fully and entirely relinquish and convey to the United States, any and all right, title, and interest, of whatsoever nature the same may be, which they may now have in, and to any other lands in the Territory of Minnesota or elsewhere.

Article 2.

There shall be, and hereby is, reserved and set apart, a sufficient quantity of land for the permanent homes of the said Indians; the lands so reserved and set apart, to be in separate tracts, as follows, viz:

For the Mississippi bands of Chippewa Indians: The first to embrace the following fractional townships, viz: forty-two north, of range twenty-five west; forty-two north, of range twenty-six west; and forty-two and forty-three north, of range twenty-seven west; and, also, the three small islands in the southern part of Mille Lac. Second, beginning at a point half a mile east of Rabbit Lake; thence south three miles; thence westwardly, in a straight line, to a point three miles south of the mouth of Rabbit River; thence north to the mouth of said river; thence up the Mississippi River to a point directly north of the place of beginning; thence south to the place of beginning. Third, beginning at a point half a mile southwest from the most southwestwardly point of Gull Lake; thence due south to Crow Wing River; thence down said river, to the Mississippi River; thence up said river to Long Lake Portage; thence, in a straight line, to the head of Gull Lake; thence in a southwestwardly direction, as nearly in a direct line as practicable, but at no point thereof, at a less distance than half a mile from said lake, to the place of beginning. Fourth, the boundaries to be, as nearly as practicable, at right angles, and so as to embrace within them Pokagomon Lake; but nowhere to approach nearer said lake than half a mile therefrom. Fifth, beginning at the mouth of Sandy Lake River; thence South, to a point on an east and west line, two mile south of the most southern point of Sandy Lake; thence east, to a point due south from the mouth of West Savannah River; thence north, to the mouth of said river; thence north to a point on an east and west line, one mile north of the most northern point of Sandy Lake; thence west, to Little Rice River; thence down said river to Sandy Lake River; and thence down said river to the place of beginning. Sixth, to include all the islands in Rice Lake, and also half a section of land on said lake, to include the present gardens of the Indians. Seventh, one section of land for Pug-o-na-ke-shick, or Hole-in-the-Day, to include his house and farm; and for which he shall receive a patent in fee-simple. For the Pillager and Winnibigoshish bands, to be in three tracts, to be located and bounded as follows, viz: First, beginning at mouth of Little Boy River; thence up said river to Lake Hassler; thence through the center of said lake to its western extremity; thence in a direct line to the most southern point of Leech lake; and thence through said lake, so as to include all the islands therein, to the place of beginning. Second, beginning at the point where the Mississippi River leaves Lake Winnibigoshish; thence north, to the head of the first river; thence west, by the head of the next river, to the head of the third river, emptying into said lake; thence down the latter to said lake; and thence in a direct line to the place of beginning. Third, beginning at the mouth of Turtle River; thence up said river to the first lake; thence east, four miles; thence southwardly, in a line parallel with Turtle River, to Cass Lake; and thence, so as to include all the islands in said lake, to the place of beginning; all of which said tracts shall be distinctly designated on the plats of the public surveys. And at all such time or times as the President may deem it advisable for the interests and welfare of said Indians, or any of them, he shall cause the said reservation, or such portion or portions thereof as may be necessary, to be surveyed; and assign to each head of a family, or single person over twenty-one years of age, a reasonable quantity of land, in one body, not to exceed eighty acres in any case, for his or their separate use; and he may, at his discretion, as the occupants thereof become capable of managing their business and affairs, issue patents to them for the tracts so assigned to them, respectively; said tracts to be exempt from taxation, levy, sale, or feature; and not to be aliened or leased for a longer period than two years, at one time, until otherwise provided by the legislature of the State in which they may be situate, with the assent of Congress. They shall not be sold, or alienated in fee, for a period of five years after the date of the patents; and not then without the assent of the President of the United States being first obtained. Prior to the issue of patents, the President shall make such rules and regulations as he may deem necessary and expedient, respecting the disposition of any of said tracts in case of the death of the person or persons to whom they may be assigned, so that the same shall be secured to the families of such deceased person; and should any of the Indians to whom tracts may be assigned thereafter abandon them, the President may make such rules and regulations, in relation to such abandoned tracts, as in his judgment may be necessary and proper.

Article 3.

In consideration of, and in full compensation for, the cessions made by the said Mississippi, Pillager, and Lake Winnibigoshish bands of Chippewa Indians, in the first article of this agreement, the United States hereby agree and stipulate to pay, expend, and make provision for, the said bands of Indians, as follows, viz: For the Mississippi bands:

Ten thousand dollars ($10,000) in goods, and other useful articles, as soon as practicable after the ratification of this instrument, and after an appropriation shall be made by Congress therefor, to be turned over to the delegates and chiefs for distribution among their people.

Fifty thousand dollars ($50,000) to enable them to adjust and settle their present engagements, so far as the same, on an examination thereof, may be found and decided to be valid and just by the chiefs, subject to the approval of the Secretary of the Interior; and any balance remaining from said sum not required for the above-mentioned purpose shall be paid over to said Indians in the same manner as their annuity money, and in such instalments as the said Secretary may determine; Provided, That an amount not exceeding ten thousand dollars ($10,000) of the above sum shall be paid to such full and mixed bloods as the chiefs may direct, for services rendered heretofore to their bands.

Twenty thousand dollars ($20,000) per annum, in money, for twenty years, provided, that two thousand dollars ($2,000) per annum of that sum, shall be paid or expended, as the chiefs may request, for purposes of utility connected with the improvement and welfare of said Indians, subject to the approval of the Secretary of the Interior.

Five thousand dollars ($5,000) for the construction of a road from the mouth of Rum River to Mille Lac, to be expended under the direction of the Commissioner of Indian Affairs.

A reasonable quantity of land, to be determined by the Commissioner of Indian Affairs, to be ploughed and prepared for cultivation in suitable fields, at each of the reservations of the said bands, not exceeding, in the aggregate, three hundred acres for all the reservations, the Indians to make the rails and inclose the fields themselves.

For the Pillager and Lake Winnibigoshish bands:

Ten thousand dollars ($10,000) in goods, and other useful articles, as soon as practicable, after the ratification of this agreement, and an appropriation shall be made by Congress therefor, to be turned over to the chiefs and delegates for distribution among their people.

Forty thousand dollars ($40,000) to enable them to adjust and settle their present engagements, so far as the same, on an examination thereof, may be found and decided to be valid and just by the chiefs, subject to the approval of the Secretary of the Interior, and any balance remaining of said sum, not required for that purpose, shall be paid over to said Indians, in the same manner as their annuity money, and in such instalments as the said Secretary may determine; provided that an amount, not exceeding ten thousand dollars ($10,000) of the above sum, shall be paid to such mixed-bloods as the chiefs may direct, for services heretofore rendered to their bands.

Ten thousand six hundred and sixty-six dollars and sixty-six cents ($10,666.66) per annum, in money, for thirty years.

Eight thousand dollars ($8,000) per annum, for thirty years, in such goods as may be requested by the chiefs, and as may be suitable for the Indians, according to their condition and circumstances.

Four thousand dollars ($4,000) per annum, for thirty years, to be paid or expended, as the chiefs may request, for purposes of utility connected with the improvement and welfare of said Indians; subject to the approval of the Secretary of the Interior; Provided, That an amount not exceeding two thousand dollars thereof, shall, for a limited number of years, be expended under the direction of the Commissioner of Indian Affairs, for provisions, seeds, and such other articles or things as may be useful in agricultural pursuits.

Such sum as can be usefully and beneficially applied by the United States, annually, for twenty years, and not to exceed three thousand dollars, in any one year, for purposes of education; to be expended under the direction of the Secretary of the Interior.

Three hundred dollars' ($300) worth of powder, per annum, for five years.

One hundred dollars' ($100) worth shot and lead, per annum, for five years.

One hundred dollars' ($100) of gilling twine, per annum, for five years.

One hundred dollars' ($100) worth of tobacco, per annum, for five years.

Hire of three laborers at Leech Lake, of two at Lake Winnibigoshish, and on one at Cass Lake, for five years.

Expense of two blacksmiths, with the necessary shop, iron, steel, and tools, for fifteen years.

Two hundred dollars ($200) in grubbing-hoes and tools, the present year.

Fifteen thousand dollars ($15,000) for opening a road from Crow Wing to Leech Lake; to be expended under the direction of the Commissioner of Indian Affairs.

To have ploughed and prepared for cultivation, two hundred acres of land, in ten or more lots, within the reservation at Leech Lake; fifty acres, in four or more lots within the reservation at Lake Winnibigoshish; and twenty-five acres, in two or more lots within the reservation at Cass Lake: Provided, That the Indians shall make the rails and inclose the lots themselves.

A saw-mill, with a portable grist-mill attached thereto, to be established whenever the same shall be deemed necessary and advisable by the Commissioner of Indian Affairs, at such point as he shall think best; and which, together, with the expense of a proper person to take charge of and operate them, shall be continued during ten years: Provided, That the cost of all the requisite repairs of the said mills shall be paid by the Indians, out of their own funds.

Article 4.

The Mississippi bands have expressed a desire to be permitted to employ their own farmers, mechanics, and teachers; and it is therefore agreed that the amounts to which they are now entitled, under former treaties, for purposes of education, for blacksmiths and assistants, shops, tools, iron and steel, and for the employment of farmers and carpenters, shall be paid over to them as their annuities are paid:

Provided, however, That whenever, in the opinion of the Commissioner of Indian Affairs, they fail to make proper provision for the above-named purposes, he may retain said amounts, and appropriate them according to his discretion, for their education and improvement.

Article 5.

The foregoing annuities, in money and goods, shall be paid and distributed as follows: Those due the Mississippi bands, at one of their reservations; and those due the Pillager and Lake Winnibigoshish bands, at Leech Lake; and no part of the said annuities shall ever be taken or applied, in any manner, to or for the payment of the debts or obligations of Indians contracted in their private dealings, as individuals, whether to traders or other persons. And should any of said Indians become intemperate or abandoned, and waste their property, the President may withhold any moneys or goods, due and payable to such, and cause the same to be expended, applied, or distributed, so as to insure the benefit thereof to their families. If, at any time, before the said annuities in money and goods of either of the Indian parties to this convention shall expire, the interests and welfare of said Indians shall, in the opinion of the President, require a different arrangement, he shall have the power to cause the said annuities, instead of being paid over and distributed to the Indians, to be expended or applied to such purposes or objects as may be best calculated to promote their improvement and civilization.

Article 6.

The missionaries and such other persons as are now, by authority of law, residing in the country ceded by the first article of this agreement, shall each have the privilege of entering one hundred and sixty acres of the said ceded lands, at one dollar and twenty-five cents per acre; said entries not to be made so as to interfere, in any manner, with the laying off of the several reservations herein provided for. And such of the mixed bloods as are heads of families, and now have actual residences and improvements in the ceded country, shall have granted to them, in fee, eighty acres of land, to include their respective improvements.

Article 7.

The laws which have been or may be enacted by Congress, regulating trade and intercourse with the Indian tribes, to continue to be in force within the several reservations provided for herein; and those portions of said laws which prohibit the introduction, manufacture, use of, and traffic in, ardent spirits, wines, or other liquors, in the Indian country, shall continue and be in force, within the entire boundaries of the country herein ceded to the United States, until otherwise provided by Congress.

Article 8.

All roads and highways, authorized by law, the lines of which shall be laid through any of the reservations provided for in this convention, shall have the right of way through the same; the fair and just value of such right being paid to the Indians therefore; to be assessed and determined according to the laws in force for the appropriation of lands for such purposes.

Article 9.

The said bands of Indians, jointly and severally, obligate and bind themselves not to commit any depredations or wrong upon other Indians, or upon citizens of the United States; to conduct themselves at all times in a peaceable and orderly manner; to submit all difficulties between them and other Indians to the President, and to abide by his decision in regard to the same, and to respect and observe the laws of the United States, so far as the same are to them applicable. And they also stipulate that they will settle down in the peaceful pursuits of life, commence the cultivation of the soil, and appropriate their means to the erection of houses, opening farms, the education of their children, and such other objects of improvement and convenience, as are incident to well-regulated society; and that they will abstain from the use of intoxicating drinks and other vices to which they have been addicted.

Article 10.

This instrument shall be obligatory on the contracting parties as soon as the same shall be ratified by the President and the Senate of the United States.

In testimony whereof the said George W. Manypenny, commissioner as aforesaid, and the said chiefs and delegates of the Mississippi, Pillager and Lake Winnibigoshish bands of Chippewa

Indians have hereunto set their hands and seals, at the place and on the day and year hereinbefore written.

George W. Manypenny,
    commissioner. [L.S.]
Tug-o-na-ke-shick, or Hole in the Day,
    his x mark. [L.S.]
Que-we-sans-ish, or Bad Boy,
    his x mark. [L.S.]
Waud-e-kaw, or Little Hill,
    his x mark. [L.S.]
l-awe-showe-we-ke-shig, or Crossing Sky,
    his x mark. [L.S.]
Petud-dunce, or Rat's Liver,
    his x mark. [L.S.]

Mun-o-min-e-kay-shein, or Rice Maker,
    his x mark. [L.S.]
Aish-ke-bug-e-koshe, or Flat Mouth,
    his x mark. [L.S.]
Be- sheck-kee, or Buffalo,
    his x mark. [L.S.]
Nay-bun-a-caush, or Young Man's Son,
    his x mark. [L.S.]
Mah-yah-ge-way-we-durg, or The Chorister,
    his x mark. [L.S.]
Kay-gwa-daush, or the Attempter,
    his x mark. [L.S.]

Caw- cang-e-we-gwan, or Crow Feather, his x mark. [L.S.]

Show-baush-king, or He that Passeth Under Everything, his x mark. [L.S.]

Chief delegates of the Mississippi bands.

Maug-e-gaw-bow, or Stepping Ahead, his x mark. [L.S.]

Mi-gi-si, or Eagle, his x mark. [L.S.]

Kaw-be-mub-bee, or North Star, his x mark. [L.S.]

Chiefs and delegates of the Pillager and Lake Winnibigoshish bands.

Executed in the presence of—

Henry M. Rice.
Geo. Culver.
D.B. Herriman, Indian agent.
J.E. Fletcher.
John Dowling.
T.A. Warren, United States interpreter.

Paul H. Beaulieu, interpreter.
Edward Ashman, interpreter.
C.H. Beaulieu, interpreter.
Peter Roy, interpreter.
Will P. Ross, Cherokee Nation.
Riley Keys.

Treaty with the Chippewa of the Mississippi and the Pillager and Lake Winnibigoshish Bands, 1863

Articles of agreement and convention, made and concluded at the city of Washington, this eleventh day of March, A.D. one thousand eight hundred and sixty-three, between William P. Dole, Commissioner of Indian Affairs, and Clark W. Thompson, superintendent of Indian affairs of the northern superintendency, on the part of the United States, and Henry M. Rice, of Minnesota, for and on behalf of the Chippewas of the Mississippi and the Pillager and Lake Winnibigoshish bands of Chippewa Indians in Minnesota.

Article 1.

The reservations known as Gull Lake, Mille Lac, Sandy Lake, Rabbit Lake, Pokagomin Lake, and Rice Lake as described in the second clause of the second article of the treaty with the Chippewas of the 22d February, 1855, are hereby ceded to the United States, excepting one-half section of land, including the mission-buildings at Gull Lake, which is hereby granted in fee simple to the Reverend John Johnson, missionary.

Article 2.

In consideration of the foregoing cession, the United States agree to set apart for the future homes of the Chippewas of the Mississippi, all the lands embraced within the following-described boundaries, excepting the reservations made and described in the third clause of the second article of the said treaty of February 22, 1855, for the Pillager and Lake Winnibigoshish bands; that is to say, beginning at a point one mile south of the most southerly point of Leech Lake, and running thence in an easterly course to a point one mile south of the most southerly point of Goose Lake; thence due east to a point due south from the intersection of the Pokagomin reservation and the Mississippi River; thence on the dividing-line between "Deer River and Lakes" and "Mashkorden's River and Lakes," until a point is reached north of the first-named river and lakes; thence in a direct line north westwardly to the outlet of "Two-Routes Lake;" thence in a southwesterly direction to "Karbekaun" River; thence down said river to the lake of the same name; thence due south to a point due west from the beginning; thence to the place of beginning.

Article 3.

In consideration of the foregoing cession to the United States, and the valuable improvements thereon, the United States further agree: 1st. To extend the present annuities of the Indians, parties to this treaty, for ten years beyond the periods respectively named in existing treaties; 2nd. And to pay toward the settlement of the claims for depredations committed by said Indians in 1862, the sum of twenty thousand dollars, or so much thereof as may be necessary, provided that no money shall be paid under this item, except upon claims which have been duly adjudicated and found to be due under existing treaties, from said Indians, and allowed by the Secretary of the Interior, or under his direction; 4th. To the chiefs of the Chippewas of the Mississippi, sixteen thousand dollars, (provided they shall pay to the chiefs of the Pillager and Lake Winnibigoshish bands one thousand dollars,) to be paid upon the signing of this treaty, out of the arrearages due under the 9th article of the treaty concluded at La Pointe, in the State of Wisconsin, on the 30th of September, 1854; 5th. And to pay the expenses incurred by the legislature of the State of Minnesota in the month of September, 1862, in sending commissioners to visit the Chippewa Indians, amounting to thirteen hundred and thirty-eight dollars and seventy-five cents.

Article 4.

The United States further agree to clear, stump, grub, and break in, the reservation hereby set apart for the Chippewas of the Mississippi, in lots of not less than ten acres each, at such point or points as the chiefs of each band may select, as follows, viz: For the Gull Lake band, seventy acres; for the Mille Lac band, seventy acres; for the Sandy Lake band, fifty acres; for the Pokagomin band, fifty acres; for the Rabbit Lake band, forty acres; for the Rice Lake band, twenty acres; and to build for the chiefs of said bands one house each, of the following description: to be constructed of hewn logs: to be sixteen by twenty feet each, and two stories high; to be roofed with good shaved pine shingles; the floors to be of seasoned pine-plank, jointed; stone or brick fire-places and chimneys; three windows in lower story and two in the upper story, with good substantial shutters to each, and suitable doors; said houses to be pointed with lime mortar; provided, that the amount expended under this article shall not exceed the sum of three thousand six hundred dollars.

The United States agree to furnish to said Indians, parties to this treaty, ten yoke of good, steady, work oxen, and twenty log-chains, annually, for ten years, provided the Indians shall take proper care of, and make proper use of the same; also, for the same period, annually, two hundred grubbing-hoes, ten ploughs, ten grindstones, one hundred axes, handled, not to exceed in weight three and one-half pounds each; twenty spades. Also two carpenters and two blacksmiths, and four farm laborers, and one physician — not exceeding, in the aggregate, one thousand dollars.

Article 6.

The United States further agree to remove the saw-mill from Gull Lake reservation, to such point on the new reservation hereby set apart as may be selected by the agent, and to keep the same in good running order, and to employ a competent sawyer, so long as the President of the United States may deem it necessary; and to extend the road between Gull Lake and Leech Lake, from the last-named lake to the junction, or as near thereto as practicable; but not more than three thousand dollars shall be expended for this purpose.

Article 7.

The President shall appoint a board of visitors, to consist of not less than two nor more than three persons, to be selected from such Christian denominations as he may designate, whose duty it shall be to attend the annuity payments to the Indians, and to inspect the fields and other improvements of the Indians, and to report annually thereon, on or before the first of November; and also as to the qualifications and moral deportment of all persons residing upon the reservation under the authority of law; and they shall receive for their services five dollars per day for the time actually employed, and ten cents per mile for travelling expenses: Provided, That no one shall be paid in any one year for more than twenty days' service, or for more than three hundred miles' travel.

Article 8.

No person shall be recognized as a chief whose band numbers less than fifty persons; and to encourage and aid the said chiefs in preserving order, and inducing by their example and advice the members of their respective bands to adopt the pursuits of civilized life, there shall be paid to each of said chiefs, annually, out of the annuities of said bands, a sum not exceeding one hundred and fifty dollars, to be determined by the Commissioner of Indian Affairs, according to their respective merits.

Article 9.

To improve the morals and industrial habits of said Indians, it is agreed that no agent, teacher, interpreter, traders, or their employees, shall be employed, appointed, licensed, or permitted to reside within the reservations belonging to the Indians, parties to this treaty, missionaries excepted, who shall not have a lawful wife residing with them at their respective places of employment or trade within the agency, and no person of full or mixed blood, educated or partially educated, whose fitness, morally or otherwise, is not conducive to the welfare of said Indians, shall receive any benefits from this or any former treaties.

Article 10.

All annuities under this or former treaties shall be paid as the chiefs in council may request, with the approval of the Secretary of the Interior, until otherwise altered or amended: Provided, That not less than one-half of said annuities shall be paid in necessary clothing, provisions, and other necessary and useful articles.

Article 11.

Whenever the services of laborers are required upon the reservation, preference shall be given to full or mixed bloods, if they shall be found competent to perform them.

Article 12.

It shall not be obligatory upon the Indians, parties to this treaty, to remove from their present reservations until the United States shall have first complied with the stipulations of Articles 4 and 6 of this treaty, when the United States shall furnish them with all necessary transportation and subsistence to their new homes, and subsistence for six months thereafter: Provided, That owing to the heretofore good conduct of the Mille Lac Indians, they shall not be compelled to remove so long as they shall not in any way interfere with or in any manner molest the persons or property of the whites.

Article 13.

Female members of the family of any Government employe residing on the reservation, who shall teach Indian girls domestic economy, shall be allowed and paid a sum not exceeding ten dollars per month while so engaged: Provided, That not more than one thousand dollars shall be so expended during any one year, and that the President of the United States may suspend or annul this article whenever he may deem it expedient to do so.

Article 14.

It is distinctly understood and agreed that the clearing and breaking of land for the Chippewas of the Mississippi, as provided for in the fourth article of this treaty, shall be in lieu of all former engagements of the United States as to the breaking of lands for those bands.

In testimony whereof, the said William P. Dole and Clark W. Thompson, on behalf of the United States, and Henry M. Rice and the undersigned chiefs and headmen, on behalf of the Indians, parties to this treaty, have hereunto set their hands and affixed their seals this eleventh day of March, A.D. one thousand eight hundred and sixty-three.

Wm. P. Dole, Commissioner of Indian Affairs. [SEAL.]
Clark W. Thompson, superintendent of Indian Affairs for the northern superintendency. [SEAL.]
Henry M. Rice. [SEAL.]

Gull Lake Band:
Qui-we-shen-shish, or Bad Boy, his x mark. [SEAL.]
Wa-bo-geeg, or White Fisher, his x mark. [SEAL.]
J. Johnson, **Rabbit Lake band:** [SEAL.]
Me-jaw-ke-ke-shick, or Sky that Touches the Ground, his x mark. [SEAL.]
Ah-ah-jaw-wa-ke-shick, Crossing Sky, his x mark. [SEAL.]
Naw-gaw-ne-gaw-bow, or One Standing Ahead, his x mark. [SEAL.]

Sandy Lake and Rice Lake bands: [SEAL.]
Aw-aw-bedway-we-dung, or Returning Echo, his x mark, [SEAL.]

Po-ke-ga-ma band: [SEAL.]
Ma-ya-je-way-we-dung, or Chorister, his x mark. [SEAL.]

Mille Lac band:
Shob-osh-kunk, or Passes under Everything, his x mark. [SEAL.]
Me-no-min-e-ke-shen, or Ricemaker, his x mark. {SEAL.]
Pe-dud-ence, Rat's Liver, his x mark. [SEAL.]

Te-daw-kaw-mo-say, Walking to and fro, his x mark. [SEAL.]
Mose-o-man-nay, or Moose, his x mark. [SEAL.]
Way-sa-wa-gwon-aib, Yellow Feather, his x mark. [SEAL.]
Me-no-ke-shick, or Fine Day, his x mark. [SEAL.]

Pillager band of Leech Lake:
Be-she-kee, or Buffalo, his x mark. [SEAL.]
Naw-bon-e-aush, Young Man's Son, his x mark. [SEAL.]
O-ge-ma-way-che-waib, Chief of the Mountain, his x mark. [SEAL.]
Ke-me-wen-aush, Raining Wind, his x mark. [SEAL.]
Keh-beh-naw-gay, the Winner, his x mark. [SEAL.]

Winne-pe-go-shish band:
Kob-mub-bey, or North Star, his x mark. [SEAL.]
Mis-co-pe-nen-shey, Red Bird, his x mark. [SEAL.]

Cass Lake band:
Maw-je-ke-shick, Travelling Sky, his x mark. [SEAL.]
Ma-ne-to-ke-shick, Spirit of the Day, his x mark. [SEAL.]
O-Gee-tub, the Trader, his x mark. [SEAL.]

Executed in presence of –

E.A.C. Hatch,
Geo. C. Whiting,
A.S.H. White,
George Fuller,
James Whitehead,

D. Geo. Morrison,
Paul H. Beaulieu, United States interpreter,
Peter Roy, interpreter,
J.G. Morrison, interpreter,
James Thompson.

Treaty with the Chippewa, Mississippi, and Pillager and Lake Winnibigoshish Bands, 1864

Articles of agreement and convention made and concluded at the city of Washington this seventh day of May, A.D. 1864, between William P. Dole, Commissioner of Indian Affairs, and Clark W. Thompson, superintendent of Indian affairs for the northern superintendency, on the part of the United States, and the Chippewa chief Hole-in-the-Day, and Mis-qua-dace, for and on behalf of the Chippewas of the Mississippi, and Pillager and Lake Winnibigoshish bands of Chippewa Indians in Minnesota.

Article 1.

The reservations known as Gull Lake, Mille Lac, Sandy Lake, Rabbit Lake, Pokagomin Lake, and Rice Lake, as described in the second clause of the second article of the treaty with the Chippewas of the twenty-second of February, 1855, are hereby ceded to the United States, excepting one half section of land, including the mission buildings at Gull Lake, which is hereby granted in fee simple to the Reverend John Johnson, missionary, and one section of land, to be located by the Secretary of the Interior on the southeast side of Gull Lake, and which is hereby granted in fee simple to chief Hole-in-the-Day, and a section to chief Mis-qua-dace, at Sandy Lake, in like manner, and one section to chief Shaw-vosh-kung, at Mille Lac, in like manner.

Article 2.

In consideration of the foregoing cession, the United States agree to set apart, for the future home of the Chippewas of the Mississippi, all the lands embraced within the following-described boundaries, excepting the reservations made and described in the third clause of the second article of the said treaty of February 22d, 1855, for the

Pillager and Lake Winnibigoshish bands; that is to say, beginning at a point one mile south of the most southerly point of Leach Lake, and running thence in an easterly course to a point one mile south of the most southerly point of Goose Lake, thence due east to a point due south from the intersection of the Pokagomin reservation and the Mississippi River, thence on the dividing-line between Deer River and lakes and Mashkordens River and lakes, until a point is reached north of the first-named river and lakes; thence in a direct line northwesterly to the outlet of Two Routes Lake, then in a southwesterly direction to Turtle Lake, thence southwesterly to the head-water of Rice River, thence northwesterly along the line of the Red Lake reservation to the mouth of Thief River, thence down the centre of the main channel of Red Lake River to a point opposite the mouth of Black River, thence southeasterly in a direct line with the outlet of Rice Lake to a point due west from the place of beginning, thence to the place of beginning.

Article 3.

In consideration of the foregoing cession to the United States, and the valuable improvements thereon, the United States further agree, first, to extend the present annuities of the Indians, parties to this treaty, for ten years beyond the periods respectively named in existing treaties; second, and to pay towards the settlement of the claims for depredations committed by said Indians in 1862, the sum of twenty thousand dollars; third, to the chiefs of the Chippewas of the Mississippi, ten thousand dollars, to be paid upon the ratification of this treaty; and five thousand dollars to the chief Hole-in-the-Day, for depredations committed in burning his house and furniture in 1862.

Article 4.

The United States further agree to pay seven thousand five hundred ($7,500) dollars for clearing, stumping, grubbing, breaking, and planting, on the reservation hereby set apart for the Chippewas of the Mississippi, in lots of not less than ten acres each, at such point or points as the Secretary of the Interior may select, as follows, viz: For the Gull Lake band, seventy (70) acres; for the Mille Lac band, seventy (70) acres; for the Sandy Lake band, fifty (50) acres; for the Pokagomin band, fifty (50) acres; for the Rabbit Lake band, forty (40) acres; for the Rice Lake band, twenty (20) acres; and to expend five thousand dollars ($5,000) in building for the chiefs of said bands one house each, under the direction of the Secretary of the Interior.

Article 5.

The United States agree to furnish to said Indians, parties to this treaty, ten (10) yoke of good steady work oxen, and twenty log-chains annually for ten years, provided the Indians shall take proper care of and make proper use of the same; also for the same period annually two hundred (200) grubbing-hoes, ten (10) ploughs, ten (10) grindstones, one hundred (100) axes, handled, not to exceed in weight three and one-half pounds each, twenty (20) spades, and other farming implements, provided it shall not amount to more than fifteen hundred dollars in one year; also two carpenters, and two blacksmiths, and four farm-laborers, and one physician.

Article 6.

The United States further agree to pay annually one thousand dollars ($1,000) towards the support of a sawmill to be built for the common use of the Chippewas of the Mississippi and the Red Lake and Pembina bands of Chippewa Indians, so long as the President of the United States may deem it necessary; and to expend in building a road, bridges, &c., to their new agency seven thousand five hundred dollars ($7,5000); and to expend for new agency buildings, to be located by the Secretary of the Interior for the common use of the Chippewas of the Mississippi, Red Lake, and Pembina, and Pillager and Lake Winnigigoshish bands of Chippewa Indians, twenty-five thousand dollars ($25,000).

Article 7.

There shall be a board of visitors, to consist of not less than two nor more than five persons, to be selected from such Christian denomination or denominations as the chiefs in council may designate, whose duty it shall be to be present at all annuity payments to the Indians, whether of goods, moneys, provisions, or other articles, and to inspect the fields, buildings, mills, and other improvements made or to be made, and report annually thereon, on or before the first day of November; and also as to the qualifications and moral deportment of all persons residing upon the reservation under the sanction of law or regulation, and they shall receive for their services five dollars per day for the time actually employed, and ten cents per mile for traveling expenses; Provided, That no one shall be paid in any one year for more than twenty days' service, or for more than three hundred miles' travel.

Article 8.

No person shall be recognized as a chief whose band numbers less than fifty persons; and to encourage and aid the said chiefs in preserving order, and inducing by their example and advice, the members of their respective bands to adopt the pursuits of civilized life, there shall be paid to each of said chiefs annually out of the annuities of said bands, a sum not exceeding one hundred and fifty dollars, ($150,) to be determined by their agent according to their respective merits.

Article 9.

To improve the morals and industrial habits of said Indians, it is agreed that no agent, teacher, interpreter, trader, or other employees shall be employed, appointed, licensed, or permitted to reside within the reservations belonging to the Indians, parties to this treaty, missionaries excepted, who shall not have a family residing with them at their respective places of employment or trade within the agency, whose moral habits and fitness shall be reported upon annually by the board of visitors; and no person of full or mixed blood, educated or partially educated, whose fitness, morally or otherwise, is not conducive to the welfare of said Indians, shall receive any benefit from this or any former treaties, and may be expelled from the reservation.

Article 10.

All annuities under this or former treaties shall be paid as the chiefs in council may request, with the approval of the Secretary of the Interior, until otherwise altered or amended, which shall be done whenever the board of visitors, by the requests of the chiefs, may recommend it: Provided That no change shall take place oftener than one in two years.

Article 11.

Whenever the services of laborers are required upon the reservation, preference shall be given to full or mixed bloods, if they shall be found competent to perform them.

Article 12.

It shall not be obligatory upon the Indians, parties to this treaty, to remove from their present reservations until the United States shall have first complied with the stipulations of Articles IV and VI of this treaty, when the United States shall furnish them with all necessary transportation and subsistence to their new homes and subsistence for six months thereafter: Provided, That, owing to the heretofore good conduct of the Mille Lac Indians, they shall not be compelled to remove so long as they shall not in any way interfere with or in any manner molest the persons or property of the whites: Provided, That those of the tribe residing on the Sandy Lake reservation shall not be removed until the President shall so direct.

Article 13.

Female members of the family of any government employe[e] residing on the reservation, who shall teach Indian girls domestic economy, shall be allowed and paid a sum not exceeding ten dollars per month while so engaged: Provided, That not more than one thousand dollars shall be so expended during one year, and that the President of the United States may suspend or annul this article whenever he may deem it expedient to do so.

Article 14.

It is distinctly understood and agreed that the clearing and breaking of land for the Chippewas of the Mississippi, as provided for in the fourth article of this treaty, shall be in lieu of all former engagements of the United States as to the breaking of lands for those bands, and that this treaty is in lieu of the treaty made by the same tribes, approved March 11th, 1863.

In testimony whereof the said Wm. P. Dole and Clark W. Thompson, on behalf of the United States, and Chippewa chiefs, Hole-in-the-Day and Mis-qua-dace, on behalf of Indians parties to this treaty, have hereunto set their hands and affixed their seals this seventh day of May, A.D. one thousand eight hundred and sixty-four.

W.P. Dole, Commissioner of Indian Affairs. [SEAL.]
Clark W. Thompson, Superintendent Indian Affairs. [SEAL.]
Que-ze-zance, or Hole-in-the-Day, his x mark. [SEAL.]
Mis-qua-dace, or Turtle, his x mark. [SEAL.]
Signed in presence of –
Peter Roy, special interpreter.
Benjn. Thompson.

The Nelson Act

An Act for the Relief and Civilization of the Chippewa Indians in the State of Minnesota

The Statutes at Large of the United States of America from December, 1887, to March, 1889, and Recent Treaties, Postal Conventions, and Executive Proclamations. Vol. XXV, pp. 642-646.

CHAP 24.— *An act for the relief and civilization of the Chippewa Indians in the State of Minnesota.*

Chippewa Indians of Minnesota

Be it enacted by the Senate and House of Representatives of the United States of America in Congress assembled, That the President of the United States is hereby authorized and directed, within sixty days after the passage of this act, to designate and appoint three Commissioners, one of whom shall be a citizen of Minnesota,

Commissioners to negotiate for relinquishment of lands
To be appointed.

whose duty it shall be, as soon as practicable after their appointment, to negotiate with all the different bands or tribes of Chippewa Indians in the State of Minnesota for the complete cession and relinquishment in writing of all their title and interest in and to all the reservations of said Indians in the State of Minnesota,

Lands excepted.

except the White Earth and Red Lake Reservations, and to all and so much of these two reservations as in the judgment of said commission is not required to make and fill the allotments required by this and existing acts, and shall not have been reserved by the Commissioners for said purposes, for the purposes and upon the terms hereinafter stated; and such cession and relinquishment shall be deemed sufficient as to each of said reservations, except as to the Red Lake Reservation,

Assent of tribes.

if made and assented to in writing by two-thirds of the male adults over eighteen years of age of the band or tribe of Indians occupying and belonging to such reservations; and as to the Red Lake Reservation the cession and relinquishment shall be deemed sufficient if made and assented to in like manner by two-thirds of the male adults of all the Chippewa Indians in Minnesota; and provided that all agreements therefore shall be approved by the President of the United States before taking effect:

Proviso. Allottees not to be disturbed.

Provided further, That in any case where an allotment in severalty has heretofore been made to any Indian of land upon any of said reservations, he shall not be deprived thereof or disturbed therein except by his own individual consent separately and previously given, in such form and manner as may be prescribed by the Secretary of the Interior. And for the purpose of ascertaining whether the proper number of Indians yield and give their assent as aforesaid, and for the purpose of making the allotments and payments hereinafter mentioned, the said commissioners shall, while engaged in securing such cession and relinquishment as aforesaid and before completing the same,

Census to be taken.

make an accurate census of each tribe or band, classifying them into male and female adults, and male and female minors; and the minors into those who are orphans and those who are not orphans, giving the exact numbers of each class, and making such census in duplicate lists, one of which shall be filed with the Secretary of the Interior, and the other with the official head of the band or tribe;

Assent to extinguish Indian title.

and the acceptance and approval of such cession and relinquishment by the President of the United States shall, be deemed full and ample proof of the assent of the Indians, and shall operate as a complete extinguishment of the Indian title without any other or further act or ceremony whatsoever for the purposes and upon the terms in this act provided.

SEC 2. That the said commissioners shall, before entering upon the

Bond and oath of commissioners.

discharge of their duties, each give a bond to the United States in the sum of ten thousand dollars, with sufficient sureties, to be approved by the Secretary of the Interior, and conditioned for the faithful discharge of their duties under this act, and they shall also each take an oath to support the Constitution of the United States, and to faithfully discharge the duties of their office, which bonds and oaths shall be filed with the Secretary of the Interior.

Compensation.

Said commissioners shall be entitled to a compensation of ten dollars per day for each day actually employed in the discharge of their duties, and for their actual traveling expenses and board, not exceeding three dollars per day.

Interpreters.

Said commissioners shall also be authorized to employ a competent interpreter while engaged in the performance of their duties, at a compensation and allowance to be fixed by them, not in excess of that allowed to each of them under this act.

Removal of Indians to White Earth Reservation.

SEC. 3. That as soon as the census has been taken, and the cession and relinquishment has been obtained, approved, and ratified, as specified in section one of this act, all of said Chippewa Indians in the State of Minnesota, except those on the Red Lake Reservation, shall, under the direction of said commissioners, be removed to and take up their residence on the White Earth Reservation,

Allotment of lands on Red Lake Reservation.

and thereupon there shall, as soon as practicable, under the direction of said commissioners, be allotted lands in severalty to the Red Lake Indians on Red Lake Reservation, and to all the other of said Indians on White Earth Reservation, in conformity with the

Vol. 24, p.388

act of February eighth, eighteen hundred and eighty-seven, entitled "An act for the allotment of lands in severalty to Indians on the various reservations, and to extend the protection of the laws of the United States and the Territories over the Indians, and for other purposes"; and all allotments heretofore made to any of said Indians on the White Earth Reservation

Prior allotments confirmed

are hereby ratified and confirmed with the like tenure and condition prescribed for all allotments under this act:

Provisos.

Provided, however, That the amount heretofore allotted to any Indian on White Earth Reservation

Deductions.

shall be deducted from the amount of allotment to which he or she is entitled under this act:

Provided further, That any of the Indians residing on any of said reservations may,

Allotments on other reservations.

in his discretion, take allotments in severalty under this act on the reservation where he lives at the time of the removal herein provided for is effected, instead of being removed to and taking such allotment on White Earth Reservation.

Survey of ceded lands.

SEC. 4. That as soon as the cession and relinquishment of said Indian title has been obtained and approved as aforesaid, it shall be the duty of the Commissioners of the General Land Office to cause the lands so ceded to the United States to be surveyed in the manner provided by law for the survey of public lands, and as soon as practicable after such survey has been made, and the report, field-notes, and plats thereof filed in the General Land Office, and duly approved by the Commissioner thereof, the said Secretary of the Interior, upon notice of the completion of such survey shall appoint a sufficient number of competent and experienced examiners, in order that the work may be done within a reasonable time,

Subdivision into forty-acre lots.

who shall go upon said lands thus surveyed and personally make a careful, complete, and thorough examination of the same by forty-acre lots, for the purpose of ascertaining on which lots or tracts there is standing or growing pine timber,

"Pine lands."

which tracts on which pine timber is standing or growing for the purpose of this act shall be termed "pine lands," the minutes of such examination to be at the time entered in books provided for that purpose, showing with particularity the amount and quality of all pine timber standing or growing on any lot or tract, the amount of such pine timber to be estimated by feet in the manner usual in estimating such timber, which estimates and reports of all such examinations shall be filed with the Commissioner of the General Land Office as a part of the permanent records thereof, and thereupon that officer shall cause to be made a list of all such pine lands, describing each forty-acre lot or tract thereof separately,

Minimum Valuations

and opposite each such description he shall place the actual cash value of the same, according to his best judgment and information, but such valuation shall not be at a rate of less than three dollars per thousand feet, board measure of the pine timber thereon, and thereupon such lists of lands so appraised shall be transmitted to the Secretary of the Interior for approval, modification, or rejection, as he may deem proper.

New appraisals.

If the appraisals are rejected as a whole then the Secretary of the Interior shall substitute a new appraisal and the same or original list as approved or modified shall be filed with the Commissioner of the General Land Office as the appraisal of said lands, and as constituting the minimum price for which said lands may be sold, as hereinafter provided, but in no event shall said pine lands be appraised at a rate of less than three dollars per thousand feet board measure of the pine timber thereon.

Lists to be filed.

Duplicate lists of said lands as appraised, together with copies of the field-notes, surveys, and minutes of examinations shall be filed and kept in the office of the register of the land office of the district within which said lands may be situated, and copies of said lists with the appraisals shall be furnished to any person desiring the same upon application to the Commissioner of the General Land Office or to the register of said local land office.

Pay of examiners.

The compensation of the examiners so provided for in this section shall be fixed by the Secretary of the Interior, but in no event shall exceed the sum of six dollars per day for each person so employed, including all expenses.

Agricultural lands.

All other lands acquired from the said Indians on said reservations other than pine lands are for the purposes of this act termed "agricultural lands."

Sale of pine lands.

SEC. 5. That after the survey, examination, and appraisals of said pine lands has been fully completed they shall be proclaimed as in market and offered for sale in the following manner:

Advertisement

The Commissioner of the General Land Office shall cause notices to be inserted once in each week for four successive weeks in one newspaper of general circulation published in Minneapolis, Saint Paul, Duluth, and Crookston, Minnesota; Chicago,

Illinois; Milwaukee, Wisconsin; Detroit, Michigan; Philadelphia and Williamsport, Pennsylvania; and Boston, Massachusetts,

Auction sale.

of the sale of said lands at public auction to the highest bidder for cash at the local land office of the district within which said lands are located, said notice to state the time and place and terms of such sale. At such sale said lands shall be offered in forty-acre parcels, except in case of fractions containing either more or less than forty acres, which shall be sold entire. In no event shall any parcel be sold for a less than its appraised value.

Private sale.

The residue of such lands remaining unsold after such public offering shall thereafter be subject to private sale for cash at the appraised value of the same upon application at the local land office.

Sale of agricultural lands.

SEC.6. That when any of the agricultural lands on said reservation not allotted under this act nor reserved for the future use of said Indians have been surveyed, the Secretary of the Interior shall give thirty days' notice through at least one newspaper published at Saint Paul and Crookston, in the State of Minnesota, and,

To be sold under homestead law.

at the expiration of thirty days, the said agricultural lands so surveyed, shall be disposed of by the United States to actual settlers only under the provisions of the homestead law:

Provisos

Provided, That each settler under and in accordance with the provisions of said homestead laws

Prices, etc.

shall pay to the United States for the land so taken by him the sum of one dollar and twenty-five cents for each and every acre, in five equal annual payments, and shall be entitled to a patent therefor only at the expiration of five years from the date of entry, according to said homestead laws, and after the full payment of said one dollar and twenty-five cents per acre therefor, and due proof of occupancy for said period of five years; and any conveyance of said lands so taken as a homestead, or any contract touching the same, prior to the date of final entry, shall be null and void:

Prior entries not disturbed.

Provided, That nothing in this act shall be held to authorize the sale or other disposal under its provision of any tract upon which there is a subsisting, valid, pre-emption or homestead entry, but any such entry shall be proceeded with under the regulations and decisions in force at the date of its allowance, and if found regular and valid, patents shall issue thereon:

Second entries.

Provided, That any person who has not heretofore had the benefit of the homestead or pre-emption law, and who has failed from any cause to perfect the title to a tract of land heretofore entered by him under either of said laws may make a second homestead entry under the provisions of this act.

Funds to be deposited to credit of Chippewas.

SEC.7. That all money accruing from the disposal of said lands in conformity with the provisions of this act shall, after deducting all the expenses of making the census, of obtaining the cession and relinquishment, of making the removal and allotments, and of completing the surveys and appraisals, in this act provided, be placed in the Treasury of the United States to the credit of the Chippewa Indians in the State of Minnesota as a permanent fund, which shall

Interest.

draw interest at the rate of five per centum per annum, payable annually for the period of fifty years, after the allotments provided for in this act have been made, and which interest and permanent fund shall be expended for the benefit of said Indians in manner following:

Distribution of interest.

One-half of said interest shall, during the said period of fifty years, except in the cases hereinafter otherwise provided, be annually paid in cash in equal shares to the heads of the families and guardians of orphan minors for their use; and one-fourth of said interest shall, during the same period and with the like exception, be annually paid in cash in equal shares per capita to all other classes of said Indians; and the remaining one-fourth of said interest shall, during the said period of fifty years, under the direction of the Secretary of the Interior, be devoted exclusively to the establishment and

Schools.

maintenance of a system of free schools among said Indians, in their midst and for their benefits; and at the expiration of the said fifty years the said permanent fund shall be divided and paid to all said Chippewa Indians and their issue then living, in cash, in equal shares:

Proviso.

Provided, That Congress may, in its discretion, from time to time, during the said period of fifty years,

Advances, from principal.

appropriate, for the purpose promoting civilization and self-support among the said Indians, a portion of said principal sum, not exceeding five per centum thereof.

Anticipating interest.

The United States shall for the benefit of said Indians, advance to them as such interest as aforesaid the sum of ninety thousand dollars annually, counting from the time when the removal and allotments provided for in this act shall have been made, until such time as said permanent fund, exclusive of the deductions hereinbefore provided for, shall equal or exceed the sum of three million dollars, less any actual interest that may in the meantime accrue from accumulations of said permanent fund; the payments of such interest to be made yearly in advance, and in the discretion of the Secretary of the Interior, may, as to three-fourths thereof, during the first five years be expended in procuring live-stock, teams, farming implements, and seed for such of the Indians to the extent of their shares as are fit and desire to engage in farming, but as to the rest, in cash:

Re-imbursement.

and whenever said permanent fund shall exceed the sum of three million dollars the United States shall be fully reimbursed out of such excess, for all the advances of interest made as herein contemplated and other expenses hereunder.

Appropriation.

SEC.8, That the sum of one hundred and fifty thousand dollars is hereby appropriated, or so much thereof as may be necessary, out of any money in the Treasury not otherwise appropriated, to pay for procuring the cession and relinquishment, making the census, surveys, appraisals, removal, and allotments, and the first annual payment of interest herein contemplated and provided for, which money shall be expended under the direction of the Secretary of the Interior in conformity with the provisions of this act.

Statement to be made.

A detailed statement of which expenses, except the interest aforesaid, shall be reported to Congress when the expenditures shall be completed.

Approved, January 14, 1889.

No. 735

IN THE SUPREME COURT OF THE UNITED STATES

OCTOBER TERM, 1912

THE UNITED STATES,

Appellant,

—vs.—

THE MILLE LAC BAND OF CHIPPEWA INDIANS IN THE STATE OF MINNESOTA,

---

BRIEF FOR APPELLEE.

GEORGE B. EDGERTON,

Attorney for Appellee.

F.W. HOUGHTON,

HARVEY S. CLAPP,

DANIEL E. HENDERSON,

Of Counsel for Appellee.

SUBJECT INDEX

----o----

Page of Brief.

STATEMENT.

THE RECORD 1

FACTS SHOWN IN FINDINGS 2

FACTS NOT SHOWN IN FINDINGS 8

CONCLUSION ON FACTS 14

POINTS AND AUTHORITIES 15

ARGUMENT,

    I   – Under the act of February 15, 1909 (32 Stat. L., 619), which reads as follows:

That the Court of claims be, and it is hereby, given jurisdiction to hear and determine a suit or suits to be brought by and on behalf of the Mille Lac Band of Chippewa Indians, in the State of Minnesota, against the United States, on account of losses sustained by them, or the Chippewas of Minnesota, by reason of the opening of the Mille Lac Reservation in the State of Minnesota, *** to public settlement, under the general land laws of the United States; and from any final judgment or decree of the Court of Claims either party shall have the right to appeal to the Supreme Court of the United States, *** equity jurisdiction is not conferred upon the Court of Claims, and hence the finding of the Court of Claims determine all matters of fact precisely as the verdict of a jury 20

    II.   —The jurisdictional act was correctly interpreted by the Court of Claims 23

III. —The jurisdictional act gives to the Court of Claims jurisdiction to determine the losses suffered by the Mille Lac Band of Chippewa Indians in the State of Minnesota or the Chippewas of Minnesota, by reason of the opening of the Mille Lac Reservation in the State of Minnesota to public settlement under the general land laws of the United States 25

IV. — By each of the treaties, to wit: of March 11, 1863, and May 7, 1864, the Mille Lac Reservation was reserved to the Mille Lac band of Chippewas of the Mississippi, the appellee herein, as and for an Indian Reservation, to be occupied by them as such so long as they should not in any way interfere with or molest the persons or property of the whites..................... 27

V. –The Court will construe the treaties of March 11, 1863, and May 7, 1864, and the instrument by which the Mille Lac Band relinquished their right of occupancy on the Mille Lac Reservation as the Indians understood such treaties and such instrument.. 40

VI. By the very instrument of cession and relinquishment by the Mille Lacs to the United States on October 5, 1889, thereafter approved by President Harrison, the United States acknowledged and confirmed the Indian title of the Mille Lac Reservation to be then in the Mille Lac Band of Chippewas of Mississippi 47

VII. The relinquishment of the Mille Lac Reservation was obtained from the Mille Lacs with the understanding and belief on their part that such reservation would be classified into pine lands and agricultural lands, the pine lands estimated and sold, and, after allotments of the agricultural lands were made, the remaining agricultural lands would be sold, and the moneys received from both paid into the United States Treasury under and in accordance with the provisions of said act of January 14, 1889............ 59

VIII. Such session and relinquishment of the Chippewa Indians of Minnesota of their various reservations in Minnesota under the act of January 14, 1889, including the cession and relinquishment of the Mille Lac Band of Chippewas of Mississippi and its relinquishment of the Mille Lac Reservation was a cession and relinquishment of each of said reservations to the United States in trust, which trust is expressed in the provisions of the act of January 14, 1889 60

IX. The failure of the United States to carry out the provisions of the act of January 14, 1889; the passing of the joint resolution of December 19, 1893 (28 Stat. L., 576), confirming the large number of entries theretofore made upon the Mille Lac Reservations and confirming the title in such entrymen constitute such failure of duty on the part of the United

	States as gives the Mille Lac band a right of act against the United States for damages under the jurisdictional act 61
X.	The measure of damages for the opening up of such reservation to settlement under the public land laws is the reasonable value of the pine timber and agricultural lands on such reservation on December 19, 1893, with interest thereon at the rate of 5 per cent, from such date 68
XI.	The passage of the joint resolution of December 19, 1893 (28 Stat. L., 576), and the passage of the joint resolution of May 27, 1898 (30 Stat. L., 745), do not indicate any intention on the part of Congress to confiscate the Mille Lac Reservation, or that in the exercise of its plenary power Congress intended to take from the Chippewas of Minnesota the value of such reservation 71
XII.	Undoubtedly the Congress with the consent of all the Indians had the right to pool the interests of all the Chippewa Indians of Minnesota, classify and sell their lands and divide the proceeds among them as provided by the act of January 14, 1889 77
XIII.	The judgment of the Court of Claims should be affirmed 87

Exhibit "A." 90

III & IV

INDEX OF CASES CITED.

------o------

Page of Brief.

California & Oregon Land Co. v. Worden, 85 Fed. R. 94 .... 17, 34

California & Oregon Land Co. v. Rankin, 87 Fed. R. 532 .... 17, 34

Cherokee Intermarriage cases (*Red Bird v. U.S.*), 203 U.S. 76 17

Cherokee Nation v. Hitchcock, 187 U.S. 294 .... 20, 75

Choctaw Nation v. U.S., 119 U.S. 1 .... 17, 19, 64

Fond du Lac, 34, C. Cl. 426 .... 82, 84

Harvey v. U.S., 105 U.S.671 16

Jones v. Meehan, 175 U.S. 1 .... 17, 32, 41

La Abra Silver Mining Co. v. U.S., 175 U.S. 423 16

Leavenworth, etc., R.R. Co. vv. U.S., 92 U.S. 733 .... 16, 33

Lone Wolf v. Hitchcock, 187 U.S. 553 .... 17, 19, 20, 65, 73

McClure v. U.S., 116 U.S. 145 15

Minnesota v. Hitchcock, 185 U.S. 373 .... 17, 18

Mitchell v. U.S., 15 Pet. 52 16

Red Bird v. U.S. (Cherokee Intermarriage Cases), 203 U.S. 76 17

Spalding v. Chandler, 160 U.S. 394 .... 17, 19, 33

Stewart v. U.S., 206 U.S. 185 ....

Stone v. U.S., 164 U.S. 380 15

Tillson v. U.S., 100 U.S. 43 15

United States v. Blackfeather, 155 U.S. 180 .... 19, 62, 69

V

Page of Brief.

United States v. Carpenter, 111, U.S. 347 .... 19, 66

United States v. Cherokee Nation, 202 U.S. 101 19

United States v. Choctaw, etc., Nation, 179 U.S. 494 17

United States v. Old Settlers, 148 U.S. 427 .... 16, 19

United States v. Thomas, 151 U.S. 577 17

United States v. Winans, 198 U.S. 371 .... 17, 35, 40

White v. Wright, 83 Minn. 222 .... 18, 49

Worcester v. Georgia, 6 Pet. 515 .... 17, 17

----o----

INDEX TO ACTS, TREATIES, STATUTES AND RESOLUTIONS

Treaty of September 30, 1854, 10 Stat. 1109.

Treaty of February 22, 1855, 10 Stat. 1165.

Treaty of March 11, 1863, 12 Stat. 1249.

Treaty of May 7, 1864 (Proclaimed March 20, 1865), 13 Stat. 693.

Treaty of March 19, 1867, 16 Stat. 719.

Executive Order, October 19, 1873.

Act of July 4, 1884, 23 Stat. 98.

Act of May 15, 1886, 24 Stat. 44.

Act of January 14, 1889, 25 Stat. 642.

Act of July 22, 1890, 26 Stat. 290.

Joint Resolution, December 19, 1893, 28 Stat. 576.

Joint Resolution, May 27, 1898, 30 Stat. 745.

Act of May 27, 1902, 32 Stat. 268.

Act of June 27, 1902, 32 Stat. 401.

Act of Feb. 15, 1909, 35 Stat. L. 619.

VI

IN THE

SUPREME COURT of the UNITED STATES

----o----

The United States, Appellant,

vs.

The Mille Lac Band of Chippewa Indians in the State of Minnesota

No. 736.

----o----

APPEAL FROM THE COURT OF CLAIMS

----o----

BRIEF AND ARGUMENT ON BEHALF OF APPELLEE.

----o----

STATEMENT.

1

The Record.

The appellee, Mille Lac band of Chippewas in the State of Minnesota, under the jurisdictional act of February 15, 1909 (35 Stat. L., 619, Rec. p. 7), brought suit against the United States to recover their damages on account of the opening of the Mille Lac reservation to public settlement under the general land laws, which reservation was reserved to the Mille Lac band of Indians under the treaties of 1863 and 1864, and relinquished by it to the United States, under the act of January 14, 1889, to be sold as provided in such act, and the moneys paid into the United States Treasury for the benefit of the Chippewas of Minnesota as provided in such act.

The suit was tried and judgment rendered in the Court of Claims in favor of the claimants on the 29th of May, 1911, for the sum of $764,210.89. Thereafter a motion for new trial was made by appellant and a motion to correct the findings by the appellee, and after hearing had on the 6th day of May, 1912, the motion for new trial was denied, the motion to correct the findings by appellee was granted in part, and thereupon the Court of Claims made and filed its findings of fact and conclusion of law thereon and entered judgment in favor of the appellee and against the appellant for the sum of $827,580.72. Rec. p. 1-18.

This is an appeal from such judgment.

The jurisdictional act does not confer upon the Court of Claims special equity jurisdiction.

THE FACTS SHOWN IN FINDINGS

Inasmuch as counsel for appellant have not stated the facts as counsel for appellee understand them and as the Court of Claims have found the facts to be, we deem it necessary to make a statement of fact as follows:

The Chippewas of the Mississippi in 1855 were composed of six bands of Indians, known as the Gull Lake, Sandy Lake, Rabbit Lake, Pokagomin Lake, Rice Lake, and Mille Lac bands.

On February 22, 1855, the United States made a treaty with the Chippewas of the Mississippi, the Pillager and Lake Winnibigoshish bands of Indians.

By such treaty such Indians ceded to the United States all their lands in the State of Minnesota, which consisted of about ten million acres. In consideration for such cession the United States by such treaty reserved and set apart a sufficient quantity of land for the permanent homes of said Indians.

For the Pillager and Lake Winnibigoshish bands three separate tracts were reserved and set apart.

For the Chippewas of the Mississippi six distinct and separate reservations were reserved and set apart, one for each of the six bands.

It was apparently the purpose of the Government to have the members of each of said bands of Chippewas live together on one reservation. Accordingly, each of the six different bands remained upon the reservation bearing its name. So the Mille Lac band remained upon the Mille Lac Reservation.

Nevertheless, the six bands of Chippewas of the Mississippi had a joint interest in each of said reservations.

In 1862 such Mille Lac band was instrumental in preventing a general uprising of the Chippewas, incited by Chief Hole-in-the-Day, against the United States.

Such good conduct of the Mille Lac band was rewarded by the Government under the provisions of the treaties hereinafter mentioned.

On March 11, 1863, and May 7, 1864, respectively, the United States again entered into a treaty with the Chippewas of the Mississippi, the Pillager and Winnibigoshish bands of Indians.

By each of said Treaties, *all* the said six reservations so reserved and set apart for the Chippewas of the Mississippi under the treaty of 1855, *except the Mille Lac Reservation*, were ceded back to the United States.

By each of these two treaties the Gull Lake, Sandy Lake, Rabbit Lake, Pokagomin Lake and Rice Lake bands of Chippewa of the Mississippi, with the consent, and at the suggestion, of the United States, *in effect*, ceded all their right and interest in the Mille Lac Reservation to the Mille Lac band; such Mille Lac Reservation was by the terms of each of such treaties *reserved* to the Mille Lac band and made the separate and sole property of the Mille Lac band, to be occupied by such band as an Indian Reservation so long as the Mille Lac band of Indians in no way interfered with the persons or property of the whites.

In other words, the Mille Lacs by each of the treaties of 1863 and 1864 became possessed of the Indian title in and to the Mille Lac Reservation.

Such Mille Lac Reservation consisted of *four* fractional townships and three small islands in Mille Lac, and contained in the aggregate 61,028.14 acres of land.

In October, 1889, the six bands of Chippewas of the Mississippi numbered 3,002, of which 895 were Mille Lac Indians.

On October 5, 1889, the Mille Lac band of Indians was still in possession of such Mille Lac Reservation, claimed to be the sole owner thereof, was possessed of exclusive right of occupancy of such Reservation and had never done anything to forfeit any of the rights in such Reservation reserved to such band in each of the treaties of March 11, 1863, and May 7, 1864.

On January 14, 1889, Congress passed an "act for the relief and civilization of the Chippewa Indians in the State of Minnesota." (25 Stat. L., 642, Rec. p. 15)

Thereafter the president of the United States, pursuant to such act, appointed three Commissioners.

Such Commissioners at once qualified by giving a bond and taking the oath required by such act; the census of the several Indian tribes was taken, and negotiations were commenced, pursuant to the provisions of such act, to obtain the cession and relinquishment from all the Indians mentioned in such act of all their lands in the State of Minnesota, except the White Earth and Red Lake Reservations, and so much of each of those as was not needed for allotment as provided in such act.

COUNCIL AT MILLE LAC

On October 2, 3, 4 and 5, 1889, councils were had by said Commissioners with the Mille Lac band of Indians at Mille Lac, with the result, that, on October 5, 1889, the Mille Lacs ceded to the United States all their right, title and interest in and to so much of Red Lake and White Earth Reservations as should not be required for allotments, as in such act provided; all of the right, title and interest in and to the lands reserved to them in the first article of the treaty proclaimed April 18, 1867, also to the Executive Order addition thereto made and described in Executive Order dated October 19, 1873; and, *did forever relinquish to the United States their right of occupancy on the Mille Lac Reservation reserved to them by the treaty of March 11, 1863, and May 7, 1864,* on the condition and with the express promises on the part of the United States, through its Commissioners, that as soon as it could be reasonably done, the United States would, under the direction of the Interior Department, cause such lands of the Mille Lac Reservation to be examined in forty acre tracts, and those upon which pine timber should be found *classified as "pine lands"*, and all other lands of such Reservation *classified as "agricultural lands."*

The pine was then to be estimated on each of the forty acre tracts. Thereafter all of such pine lands, in accordance with the provisions of said act, were to be sold at public auction to the highest bidder in forty acre tracts at not less than three dollars per thousand feet, board measure, of the pine timber estimated to be upon each of said forties.

The moneys arising from the sale of such pine lands were to be paid into the United States Treasury; the principal sum to draw interest at five per cent per annum for 50 years, the interest to be paid annually, and at the expiration of the period of 50 years the principal sum to be distributed as provided in such act.

By the provisions of such act each of the Mille Lac Indians might, at his discretion, take allotment of the agricultural lands on the Mille Lac Reservation, or, in his discretion, take allotment on the White Earth Reservation.

It was also provided that when any of the agricultural lands on such reservation, not allotted under such act, nor reserved for the future use of said Indians, have been surveyed, the Secretary of the Interior shall give 30 days notice by publication, and at the expiration of 30 days the said agricultural lands so surveyed shall be disposed of by the United States to actual settlers *only* under the provisions of the homestead law; provided, that each settler, under and in accordance with the provisions of said homestead laws, shall pay to the United States for the land so taken by him the sum of $1.25 for each and every acre, in five equal annual payments, and shall be entitled to patent therefor only at the expiration of five years from the date of entry, according to the homestead laws, and after the full payment of said $1.25 per acre therefor and due proof of occupancy for said period of five years.

The moneys arising from the sale of the agricultural lands were to be paid into the United States Treasury, draw interest and be distributed the same as the moneys derived from the sale of pine lands.

Thereafter, in accordance with the provisions of said act of January 14, 1889, such cession and relinquishment was ratified by President Harrison, and was approved by him on the 4th day of March, 1890.

Notwithstanding the provisions of said act of January 14, 1889, and the promises and agreements of the United States, through its said Commissioners, the United States did not examine and classify such lands as "pine lands" and "agricultural lands"; did not make any estimate of the pine timber upon such lands; did not sell such pine lands or pine timber; the United States, through the Interior Department, refused to permit the Mille Lac Indians to take allotment on such Reservation; the entire reservation was opened to public settlement, such reservation was extinguished as an Indian Reservation; all the rights of the Mille Lacs in and to such Reservation were denied; their pine timber and pine lands were allowed to be taken by white settlers; and the Mille Lacs were deprived of their reservation for homestead and every other purpose whatsoever.

Between 1871 and the time of such relinquishment in October, 1889, fraudulent entries covering about 55,000 acres of land had been made upon the Mille Lac Reservation.

By the rulings of the Interior Department and legislation of Congress these entries had been declared fraudulent and held in suspense.

By subsequent legislation, hereinafter referred to, some of these entries were legalized, and finally the entire Reservation was thrown open to public entry under the general land laws of the United States.

At the time of the taking of such Reservation there were upon such Reservation large bodies of pine timber of great value, and many thousand acres of such Reservation were good agricultural land. Rec. pp. 7-18.

FACTS NOT SHOWN IN FINDINGS

Inasmuch as counsel for appellants have disregarded the *findings,* and in their brief have made many statements of facts not found in the Record, and have referred to various public documents and reports, and, as counsel for appellee believe, are in error in such statement of facts, we refer to the following facts not found in the findings, most of which facts, however, are found in H.R. Ex. Doc. 247, 51st Cong., 1st Sess., referred to by the Court of Claims in the Finding of Fact, VI, Rec. p. 11 and offered in evidence in the Court of Claims.

This document contains the act of January 14, 1889, in full, the minutes of the proceedings of the councils between the Commissioners and the Indians at the various reservations; the ten instruments by which the Indians ceded and relinquished to the United States the ten reservations, and the approval of President Harrison of each of such cessions and relinquishments; the letter of transmittal by the Commissioners to the Commissioner of Indian Affairs, accompanying the account of the proceedings; the letter of transmittal by the Commissioner of Indian Affairs to the Secretary of the Interior, the letter of transmittal by the Secretary of the Interior to the President of the United States, and the letter of the President to Congress.

We believe it is proper to refer to certain facts found in such document concerning which there can be no dispute.

On page 9 thereof there is given in tabulated form the census taken by such Commissioners, which shows the number of adults, minors and orphans found by the Commissioners upon each of said ten Chippewa Reservations in Minnesota.

Those given on the Mille Lac Reservation are as follows: Total 895; male adults, 213; female adults 289; male minors 180; female minors 204; male orphans 6; female orphans 3.

That there may be no mistake concerning this, we print the entire statement as found on page 9, except the recapitulation, and marked Exhibit "A".

In the letter of transmittal to the President by Secretary Noble, dated January 30, 1890, he says concerning the Mille Lac Indians:

> "The Indians at Mille Lac were found to be intelligent, cleanly, and well behaved, and of good reputation among the neighboring whites." H.R. Ex.
>
> Doc. 247, 51st Cong., 1st Sess., p. 5.

In the letter of transmittal by the Commissioners to the Secretary of the Interior, dated December 26, 1889, the Commissioners said the following:

"On the 2d of October we met the Mille Lac Indians, and were with them until the close of the 5th, and almost constantly in council.

"Contrary to the general opinion, we found them intelligent, cleanly, and well behaved. Their neighboring white settlers gave them a good name. Some who had been on these borders for many years said they had never been molested in person or property by them." Ib. 22.

At the beginning of page 28 in said document is the following printed statement:

"Schedule showing the number of acres in the Chippewa Reservations in the State of Minnesota.

"Bois Fort	107,509
Deer Creek	23,040
Fond du Lac	92,346
Grand Portage	51,840
Leech Lake	94,440
Mille Lac	61,014
Red Lake and Pembina bands	3,200,000
Vermillion Lake	1,080
White Earth	796,672
Winnebagoshish, Cass Lake and White Oak Point	329,000
Total	4,747,931"

In the report of the Commissioner of Indian Affairs for 1890 is a letter by John W. Noble, Secretary, bearing date March 5, 1890, which letter, after referring to the said act of January 14, 1889, and its various provisions, the proceedings of the Commissioners in obtaining the cession and relinquishment thereunder, and the approval thereof by President Harrison, concludes as follows:

"Therefore, this is to give notice that none of said land, whether "pine lands" or "agricultural lands", within the said reservations of said Chippewa Indians in Minnesota, viz: White Earth, Red Lake,

Leech Lake, Cass Lake, Lake Winnebogoshish, White Oak Point, Mille Lac, Fond du Lac, Boise Fort, Deer Creek, and Grand Portage, are open or will be open to sale or to settlement by citizens of the United States until advertisement to that effect, as required in said act, shall be given, and then only as provided in said act. All persons are, therefore, hereby warned not to go upon any of the lands within the limits of the reservations as heretofore existing for any purpose or with any intent whatsoever. No settlement or other rights can be secured upon said lands, and all persons found unlawfully thereon will be dealt with as trespassers and intruders."

(Report of Commissioners of Indian Affairs, 1890, pp. XLII, XLIII.)

On page 113 of the same Report is found a tabulated statement, showing the number of Indians located at each of the ten reservations so ceded under the act of January 14, 1889. In such statement is given the males, 18 years and upwards; females, 14 years and upwards; school age, 6 to 16; total number of males, total number of females, and total number located at each of said reservations.

The number given in such tabulated statement located at the Mille Lac Reservation is as follows:

Males, 18 years and upwards, 217; females, 14 years and upward, 317; school age, 6 to 16, 273; total number of males 407; total number of females, 481; total number of Mille Lacs located at Mille Lac, 888.

This number of Mille Lac Indians were located at the Mille Lac Reservation in the year 1890, as shown by this report.

We also refer to the Report of Commissioner of Indian Affairs for the year 1893, which report is dated September 16, 1893. On page 168 of such report is a tabulated statement similar in character to the one of 1890 just referred to.

The number of Mille Lacs located on the Mille Lac Reservation, according to that report, were males, 18 years old and upwards, 249; females, 14 years and upwards, 309; school age, 6 to 16 years and upwards, 285; total number of males, 470; total number of females. 520; total Mille Lacs, 900.

There is, however, the following immediately below such tabulated statement:

"Note, — Two hundred and twelve removals from Leech Lake to White Earth and 212 removals from Mille Lac Reservation are included in their original bands."

This note then fixes and determines the fact that in the year 1893 there were living on Mille Lac Reservation of the Mille Lac band of Chippewa Indians 990 less 212, or 788 Mille Lac Indians.

In the report of the Commissioner of Indian Affairs for the year 1902, dated September 26 of that year, on page 224 is found a tabulate statement of the total number of Indians remaining on the Mille Lac Reservation, which is given as 870.

In the report of Commissioner of Indian Affairs, dated September 4, 1903, page 187, the statement shows the number of Mille Lacs remaining on the Mille Lac Reservation to be 828.

And in the report for 1904, dated September 2, 1904, page 222, the number of Mille Lacs remaining on the Mille Lac Reservation at such time is shown to be 723.

OWNERS OF THE TEN CHIPPEWA RESERVATIONS IN MINNESOTA IN 1889

An examination of the 10 instruments of cession and relinquishment beginning on pages 28, 32, 35, 43, 49, 56, 59, 61, 64, respectively, of said Document 247, will show that the 10 Reservations belonging to the Chippewas of Minnesota prior to cession and relinquishment under the act of January 14, 1889, were owned as follows:

The Chippewas of the Mississippi were the exclusive owners of the White Earth Reservation under the Treaty of March 19, 1867, and were also joint owners with the other Chippewas of Minnesota of the Red Lake Reservation.

The Mille Lac band of Chippewas of the Mississippi was the exclusive owner of the Mille Lac Reservation.

The Red Lake band of Chippewas, residing on Red Lake Reservation, and the Pembina band of Chippewa Indians, were joint owners with the other Chippewas of Minnesota, including the Chippewas of the Mississippi, of the Red Lake Reservation.

The Pillager and Lake Winnibigoshish bands were the owners of Leech Lake, Cass Lake and Lake Winnibigoshish Reservations, and were joint owners with the other Chippewas of Minnesota of the Red Lake Reservation.

The Grand Portage band was the owner of the Grand Portage Reservation, and was a joint owner with the other Chippewas of Minnesota of Red Lake Reservation.

The Fond du Lac band was the owner of the Fond du Lac Reservation and joint owner with the other Chippewas of Minnesota of Red Lake Reservation.

Boise Fort and Deer Creek bands were the owners of Boise Fort and Deer Creek Reservations, and were joint owners with the other Chippewas of Minnesota of the Red Lake Reservation.

Finding VI of the Court of Claims concludes with the following statement:

> "The said Mille Lac Indians have, without exception, upon all occasions and in connection with all controversies relating to the title they possessed to the reservation set apart to them by the treaty of 1855, proclaimed and persisted in their claim of the right of occupancy to said reservation and have continually and openly occupied

said reservation from that time until subsequent to the passage of the act of January 14, 1889."

Rec. pp. 12,13.

CONCLUSION.

From the above statement of facts it conclusively appears that:

1. The Mille Lac band of Indians understood and believed that by the treaties of 1863 (12 Stat. L., 1249) and 1864 (13 Stat. L., 693) they were reserving to themselves the Mille Lac Reservation as a permanent home to be occupied by them so long as they should not molest the persons or property of the whites.

2. That the Mille Lac band of Chippewa Indians continued thereafter to occupy such Reservation, with such understanding and belief, and resided thereon, in spite of all opposition and attempted invasion and expulsion, without intermission, until October 5, 1889, and subsequent thereto.

3. On October 5, 1889, after meeting on the reservation daily for four successive days with the Commissioners appointed under the Nelson act, they ceded and relinquished their rights in the other reservations in Minnesota, and relinquished their right of occupancy in the Mille Lac Reservation, believing and understanding and having been informed, that such reservation came under the act of 1889, that it would be classified into "pine lands' and "agricultural lands' and disposed of in the same manner as the other reservations ceded and relinquished by the Chippewas of Minnesota under such act of January 14, 1889, and that the moneys received from such sales would be paid into the United States Treasury for the same purpose as the moneys obtained from the sale of the other reservations, and that they had the right of allotment upon the Mille Lac Reservation, if they should so elect.

-----o-----

POINTS AND AUTHORITIES.

I.

Under the Act of February 15, 1909 (35 Stat. L. 619), which reads as follows:

> "That the Court of Claims be, and it is hereby, given jurisdiction to hear and determine a suit or suits to be brought by and on behalf of the Mille Lac band of Chippewa Indians in the State of Minnesota against the United States on account of the losses sustained by them or the Chippewa Indians of Minnesota by reason of the opening of the Mille Lac Reservation in the State of Minnesota, * * * to public settlement under the general land laws of the United States; and from any final judgment or decree of the Court of Claims either party shall have the right to appeal to the Supreme Court of the United States."

Equity jurisdiction is not conferred upon the Court of Claims and hence the findings of the Court of Claims determine all matters of fact precisely as the verdict of a jury.

> *Stone v. United States*, 164 U.S. 380, 382, 383.
> *McClure v. United States*, 116 U.S. 145.
> *Tillson v. United States*, 100 U.S. 43.
> *Harvey v. United States*, 105 U.S. 671.
> *United States v. Old Settlers*, 148 U.S. 427.
> *LaAbra Silver Mining Co. v. United States*, 175 U.S. 423.

II

The jurisdictional act was correctly interpreted by the Court of Claims.

> Rec. pp. 22, 23.

III

The act gives to the Court of Claims jurisdiction to determine the losses suffered by the Mille Lac band of Chippewa Indians in the State of Minnesota or the Chippewas of Minnesota by reason of the opening of the Mille Lac Reservation in the State of Minnesota to public settlement under the general land laws of the United States.

See act of February 15, 1909. (35 Stat. L., 619)

IV

By each of the treaties, to-wit, of March 11, 1863, and May 7, 1864, the Mille Lac Reservation was reserved to the Mille Lac band of Chippewa Indians, the appellee herein, as and for an Indian Reservation, to be occupied by them as such so long as they should not in any way interfere with or in any manner molest the persons or property of the whites.

> *Worcester v. Georgia,* 6 Pet. 515.
> *Mitchell v. United States,* 15 Pet. 52.
> *Leavenworth, etc. R. v. United States,* 92 U.S. 733.
> *Spalding v. Chandler,* 160 U.S. 394.
> *Jones v. Meechan,* 175 U.S. 1.
> *United States v. Choctaw Nation,* 179 U.S. 494.
> *Lone Wolf v. Hitchcock,* 187 U.S. 553.
> *United States v. Winans,* 198 U.S. 371.
> *Cal. & Oreg. Land Co. v. Worden,* 85 Fed. R. 94.
> *Cal. & Oreg. Land Co. v. Rankin,* 87 Fed. R. 532.
> *United States v. Thomas,* 151 U.S. 577.
> *Minnesota v. Hitchcock,* 185 U.S. 373.
> Act of July 22, 1890 (26 Stat. Ch. 714, p. 290).

V.

The Court will construe the treaties of March 11, 1863, and May 7, 1864, and the instrument by which the Mille Lac band relinquished their right of occupancy of the Mille Lac Reservation in 1889 as the Indians understood such treaties and such instrument.

> *Worcester v. Georgia,* 6 Pet. 515.
> *United States v. Winans,* 198 U.S. 371-380.
> *Jones v. Meehan,* 175 U.S. 1, 11.
> *Lone Wolf v. Hitchcock,* 187 U.S. 553.
> *Cherokee Intermarriage Cases,* 203 U.S. 76, 88-90.
> *Choctaw Nation v. United States,* 119 U.S. 1.

VI.

By the very instrument of cession and relinquishment by the Mille Lacs to the United States on October 5, 1889, thereafter approved by President Harrison, the United States acknowledged the Indian title of the Mille Lac Reservation to be then in the Mille Lac band of Chippewas of Mississippi.

See instrument of cession and relinquishment, Finding IX, Rec. p. 15.

White v. Wright, 83 Minn. 222.
Act of July 22, 1890 (26 Stat. Ch. 714, p. 290).

VII.

The relinquishment of the Mille Lac Reservation was obtained from the Mille Lacs with the understanding and belief on their part that such reservation would be classified into pine lands and agricultural lands, the pine lands estimated and sold, and, after allotments of the agricultural land were made, the remaining agricultural lands would be sold to actual settlers and the moneys received from both paid into the United States Treasury under and in accordance with the provisions of said act of January 14, 1889.

Instrument of Cession, Finding IX, Rec. p. 15.
Finding IX, Rec. pp. 14-16.
Act of January 14, 1889.

VIII.

The cessions and relinquishments of the Chippewa Indians of Minnesota of their various reservations in Minnesota under the act of January 14, 1889, including the cession and relinquishment by the Mille Lac band of Chippewas and its relinquishment of the Mille Lac Reservation, was a cession and relinquishment of each of said Reservations to the United States in trust, which trust is expressed in the provisions of the act of January 14, 1889.

Minnesota v. Hitchcock, 185 U.S. 373, 394.

IX.

The failure of the United States to carry out the provisions of the act of January 14, 1889, and the adoption by Congress of the Joint Resolution of December 19, 1893, (28 Stat. L., 576), confirming certain entries made upon the Mille Lac Reservation mentioned in said resolution, constituted such a failure of duty on the part of the

United States as gives the Mille Lac band a right of action against the United States for damages under the jurisdictional act.

> *United States v. Blackfeather,* 155 U.S. 180.
> *Choctaw Nation v. United States,* 119 U.S. 1.
> *Lone Wolf v. Hitchcock,* 187 U.S. 553, 564, 567.
> *United States v. Carpenter,* 111 U.S. 347.
> *Spalding v. Chandler,* 160 U.S. 404.

X.

The measure of damages for the opening up of such reservation to settlement under the public land laws is the reasonable value of the pine timber and agricultural lands on such reservation on December 19, 1893, with interest thereon at the rate of five per cent. from such date.

> *United States v. Blackfeather,* 155 U.S. 180.
> *United States v. Old Settlers,* 148 U.S. 427.
> *United States v. Cherokee Nation,* 202 U.S. 101.
> Act of January 14, 1889 (25 Stat. L., 642)

XI.

The passage of the Joint Resolution of December 19, 1893, (28 Stat. L., 576), and the passage of the Joint Resolution of May 27, 1898 (30 Stat. L., 745), do not indicate any intention on the part of Congress to confiscate the Mille Lac Reservation, nor that in the exercise of its plenary power Congress intended to take from the Chippewas of Minnesota the value of such reservation.

> *Lone Wolf v. Hitchcock,* 187 U.S. 553).
> *Cherokee Nation v. Hitchcock,* 187 U.S. 294.
> Act of February 15, 1909 (35 Stat. L., 619).

XII.

Certainly Congress, with the consent of all the several bands of Indians, had the right to pool the interest of all the Chippewa Indians of Minnesota, classify and sell their lands and divide the proceeds among them as provided by the act of January 14, 1889.

XIII.

The judgment of the Court of Claims should be affirmed.

ARGUMENT.

The ultimate question on this appeal, in the opinion of counsel for appellee, is whether the findings of fact of the Court of Claims are sufficient to warrant the conclusion of law based thereon and the judgment following.

Nevertheless, in view of the contention of the appellant, the assignment of errors by counsel and the propositions in their brief, we submit the following propositions in reply.

I.

UNDER THE ACT OF FEBRUARY 15, 1909 (35 STAT. L., 619) WHICH READS AS FOLLOWS:

"THAT THE COURT OF CLAIMS BE, AND IT IS HEREBY GIVEN JURISDICTION TO HEAR AND DETERMINE A SUIT OR SUITS TO BE BROUGHT BY AND ON BEHALF OF THE MILLE LAC BAND OF CHIPPEWA INDIANS IN THE STATE OF MINNESOTA AGAINST THE UNITED STATES ON ACCOUNT OF THE LOSSES SUSTAINED BY THEM OR THE CHIPPEWAS OF MINNESOTA BY REASON OF THE OPENING OF THE MILLE LAC RESERVATION IN THE STATE OF MINNESOTA, * * * TO PUBLIC SETTLEMENT UNDER THE GENERAL LAND LAWS OF THE UNITED STATES; AND FROM ANY FINAL JUDGMENT OR DECREE OF THE COURT OF CLAIMS EITHER PARTY SHALL HAVE THE RIGHT TO APPEAL TO THE SUPREME COURT OF THE UNITED STATES."

EQUITY JURISDICTION IS NOT CONFERRED UPON THE COURT OF CLAIMS, AND HENCE THE FINDINGS OF THE COURT OF CLAIMS DETERMINE ALL MATTERS OF FACT PRECISELY AS THE VERDICT OF A JURY."

THE DISSENTING OPINIONS

The record contains the dissenting opinions of Chief Justice Peelie and Judge Howry. In their statement of facts counsel have frequently referred to the statement of facts given by Judge Howry in his opinion to contradict the Findings of the Court of Claims, and have done the same in their argument.

Counsel also have gone outside the Record in their statement of facts and have, in effect, asked this Court to make Findings upon such statement of facts by counsel.

We protest against such use of the dissenting opinions, and going outside the record.

The Findings of the Court of Claims determine all matters of fact precisely as the verdict of a jury, and we feel warranted in contending that counsel must confine themselves in their statement of facts to the Findings of the Court of Claims.

McClure v. United States, supra, was a motion to order up evidence from the Court of Claims accompanied by an alternative motion to order that Court to make specific findings of fact.

Such suit was brought in the Court of Claims under a special act of Congress passed February 24, 1874, which among other things provided: "That the claims of Daniel McClure, assistant paymaster general, for credits on differences in his account as paymaster, under his official bond, dated March 2, 1859, shall be and are hereby referred to the Court of Claims with jurisdiction to hear and determine said claims. And if the said Court shall be satisfied from the evidence that any of the moneys charged to him were in fact received by him, or that other just and equitable grounds exist for credits claimed by him, it shall make a decree setting forth the amount to which the said McClure shall be entitled to receive credit. * * * (18 Stat. 531.)"

Held, that such act of Congress conferred no equity jurisdiction upon the Court of Claims but only the ordinary jurisdiction of the subject as a court of law, subject to be proceeded with as in ordinary suits, and subject to the rule regulating appeals in ordinary judgments. Hence the motion to order up the evidence from the Court of Claims was denied.

To the same effect was *Tillson v. United States,* 100 U.S. 43:

"Where the court was authorized and directed to * * * ascertain, determine and adjudge the amounts equitably due said firm, if any, for such loss or damage' this court decided that the reference was made to the court as a court and not to the judges as arbitrators and that the word 'equitably' as there used meant no more than the rules of law applicable to the case should be construed liberally in favor of the claimants."

The other cases cited, except the 160 U.S., are examples of where this Court held that the special acts conferred equity jurisdiction upon the Court of Claims.

Counsel for appellee contend that, in this case, "the findings of the Court of Claims determine all matters of fact precisely as the verdict of a jury."

And as said by this Court in *Stone v. United States,* 164 U.S. 380,383, this Court "is not at liberty to refer to the opinion for the purpose of eking out, controlling or modifying the scope of the findings."

This was said in reference to the opinion of the Court; much more would it be true of dissenting opinions.

We shall endeavor to discuss and meet the assignment of errors by appellant and the propositions argued by counsel under the following propositions:

II.

THE JURISDICTIONAL ACT WAS CORRECTLY INTERPRETED BY THE COURT OF CLAIMS.

Judge Booth speaking for the Court of Claims on pages 22 and 23 of the Record said:

> "The jurisdictional statute refers a claim; it determines no rights other than the one to litigate; provides a forum with authority to ascertain, adjudicate, and enforce rights. The question of damages alleged to have been suffered by claimant Indians must be determined by the court upon the same legal principles as appertain to controversies between individuals, and while it defined the nature of the cause of action and recognizes the justice of determination, it extends no further as respects the merits of the issue (*Stewart v. United States,* 206 U.S., 185.)
>
> "The jurisdiction of the court is challenged by the defendants. The contention is the plenary authority of Congress over Indian tribes and tribal property. The question of Indian policy is a political one, immune from the action of the courts: (*Cherokee Nation v. Hitchcock,* 187 U.S., 294; *Lone Wolf v. Hitchcock,* 187 U.S., 553:) The court recognizes the force of the decisions cited, and if this case came within them would dismiss it immediately. We are not dealing with acts regulating the administration of Indian property and Indian funds in the sense of their validity or invalidity. The question at issue rests upon the construction of treaties and acts of Congress and rights acquired thereunder. The authority of Congress in the premises is not questioned. The jurisdiction conferred extends to an inquiry as to what if any damages the claimants suffered by reason of an alleged taking of their property acquired under treaties which failed of execution because of acts of Congress. It is a warrant of authority to adjudicate results and not determine the means employed to bring about the same. In *Cherokee Nation v. Hitchcock, supra,* the court said: 'There is no question involved in this case as to the taking of property; the authority which it is proposed to exercise, by virtue of the act of 1898, has relation merely to the control and development of the tribal property, which still remains subject to the administrative control of the Government, even though the members of the tribe have been invested with the status of citizenship under recent legislation.' Lone Wolf vs. Hitchcock, followed the Cherokee case, *supra,* and the court therein was dealing with

administrative measures designed to control Indian property, a mere change in the form of investment of Indian tribal property."

We can not believe that such holding of the Court of Claims was error.

It can not be that Congress would have passed the jurisdictional act if such act was meaningless. Certainly Congress had some object and purpose in passing the act. And counsel for the appellee believe that this act, taken in connection with the Joint Resolution of December 19, 1893, and the Joint Resolution of 1898, negatives any intention on the part of Congress in such resolutions to take from the Indians of Minnesota the value of the Mille Lac Reservation.

III.

THE JURISDICTIOAL ACT GIVES TO THE COURT OF CLAIMS JURISDICTION TO DETERMINE THE LOSSES SUFFERED BY THE MILLE LAC BAND OF CHIPPEWA INDIANS IN THE STATE OF MINNESOTA OR OF THE CHIPPEWAS OF MINNESOTA, BY REASON OF THE OPENING OF THE MILLE LAC RESERVATION TO PUBLIC SETTLEMENT UNDER THE GENERAL LAND LAWS OF THE UNITED STATES.

The contention of the appellee is:

The Mille Lac band, the claimant, had a reservation, the Mille Lac Reservation; that claimant relinquished such reservation to the United States in trust under the Nelson act; by the terms of the Nelson act, as explained and interpreted to the claimant by the Commissioners, and as understood by the claimant, such reservation was to be classified into pine and agricultural lands; the pine lands estimated and sold, the agricultural lands allotted, and the remainder, if any, of the agricultural land, after the allotments were made, sold, or, in case of no allotments, all the agricultural lands to be sold to actual settlers as provided in the act, and the moneys disposed of as provided therein.

That the United states failed in executing the trust; that, recognizing such failure on the part of the Government, Congress passed the jurisdictional act giving the Court of Claims authority to determine the losses suffered on account of the failure of the trust.

Appellant contends: That claimant had no reservation; or if so, it had been abandoned; that there was no trust agreement; or if so, it had been executed; that there were no losses ; or if so they have been paid; therefore, there was no claim, or at most a claim to determine the value of the naked right of occupancy.

This is a strange contention.

Suppose Congress had opened up any other of the nine Chippewa Reservations of which a cession and relinquishment were obtained under the Nelson act, and had passed a statute precisely like the jurisdictional act in the instant case. Would counsel then contend, that since Congress in the exercise of its plenary power had opened up such reservation to public settlement under the general land laws, therefore the intention of Congress was to confiscate such reservation?

That is what such contention ultimately means.

In the case of *United States v. Choctaw Nation,* cited to sustain contention of counsel, to the jurisdictional act therein was attached the following proviso:

"And provided further, that nothing in this act shall be accepted or considered as a confession that the United States admits that the Choctaw and Chickasaw Nations have any claim to, or interest in, said lands or any part thereof."

There is no proviso in the act of February 15, 1909. But this Court will interpret for itself the jurisdictional act in view of the conditions and circumstances which led to its passage.

IV.

BY EACH OF THE TREATIES, TO-WIT, OF MARCH 11, 1863, AND MAY 7, 1864, THE MILLE LAC RESERVATION WAS RESERVED TO THE MILLE LAC BAND OF CHIPPEWAS OF THE MISSISSIPPI, THE APPELLEE HEREIN, AS AND FOR AN INDIAN RESERVATION, TO BE OCCUPIED BY THEM AS SUCH AS LONG AS THEY SHOULD NOT IN ANY WAY INTERFERE WITH OR MOLEST THE PERSONS OR PROPERTY OF THE WHITES.

Counsel for appellant say:

> "The Mille Lac Reservation was ceded to the United States by the treaties of 1863 and 1864, and became public land opened to settlement. The Mille Lac band acquired no title thereto, but was permitted to remain thereon temporarily."

Brief of Appellant, p. 33.

> "On February 22, 1855, the United States entered into a treaty with the Gull Lake, Mille Lac, Sandy Lake, Pokagomin Lake, Rabbit Lake and Rice Lake bands of Indians known as the Chippewas of the Mississippi, and the Pillager and Lake Winnibigoshish bands of Chippewas. This treaty secured to the United States a cession of all the lands belonging to the various bands of Indians mentioned in the State of Minnesota, and set apart for them specific reservations mentioned in the treaty. The Mille Lac Reservation was set apart for the Mille Lac band of Chippewas." (Finding II, Rec. p. 8.)

Prior to August, 1862, the Mille Lac band of Chippewas had rendered a great service to the United States in preventing an uprising of the Chippewas of Minnesota and their joining with the hostile Sioux in an outbreak against the United States." (Finding III, Rec. pp. 8 and 9.)

> "In March, 1863, Commissioner Dole, in company with the headmen and chiefs of the Chippewa bands, came to Washington, D.C., and on March 11, 1863, procured their assent to another treaty." (Finding IV, Rec. p. 9.)

This treaty between the Chippewas of the Mississippi and the United States provided in terms for the cession to the United States of the Reservations set apart to them under the treaty of 1855 with certain exceptions, and the following proviso in article 12 of such treaty:

> "It shall not be obligatory upon the Indians parties to this treaty to remove from their present reservations until the United States shall have first complied with the stipulations of articles 4 and 6 of this treaty, when the United States shall furnish them with all necessary transportation and subsistence to their new homes, and subsistence for six months thereafter: Provided, That owing to the heretofore good conduct of the Mille Lac Indians, they shall not be compelled to remove so long as they shall not in any way interfere with or in any manner molest the persons or property of the whites." (Finding IV, Rec. pp. 9, 10.)

On the 7th day of May, 1864, the United States entered into another treaty with the bands of Indians (13 Stat. L., 693), which treaty was substantially the same as the treaty of March 11, 1863, before mentioned.

Article 12 of the treaty of 1864 was exactly the same as article 12 of the treaty of 1863 with the additional proviso as follows:

> "That those of the tribe residing on the Sandy Lake Reservation shall not be removed until the President shall so direct."

The Mille Lac Band were at the time residing upon and occupying the Mille Lac Reservation, which under the treaty of February 22, 1855, had been reserved to the Chippewas of the Mississippi with the five other reservations for the permanent homes of such Chippewas.

And in entering into the treaty of 1863 as well as the treaty of 1864, it was the intention and understanding of the Mille Lac band of Indians that they were only releasing and *ceding* their interest in the other five reservations reserved by the United States to the Mississippi Chippewas in 1855, and that their own reservation, the Mille

Lac Reservation was by the terms of such treaty reserved to them forever as a permanent home, or so long as they did not interfere with the persons or property of the whites.

For some reason the treaty making power, acting on behalf of the United States, was very willing that the Mille Lac band of Indians should not be compelled to remove to the new reservation to which the United States evidently intended to remove all the other Chippewas of the Mississippi.

There had been a recent uprising of the Indians; there might be another. The Government could more easily guard and control, and so prevent, a second uprising by segregating these Indians on one reservation.

The Government had no fear of the Mille Lac Indians, they had given conclusive evidence of their loyalty to the United States, and had prevented one uprising.

What more natural then than that the United States should leave these Indian friends on a reservation nearer to the center of population and segregate all the other Chippewa Indians on a reservation much farther removed? By doing this the Mille Lac Indians would act as scouts for the United States.

If history can be relied upon, that was the real intent of the United States in leaving the Mille Lacs upon their reservation.

But the United States realized that the Mille Lacs were *Indians*; so the proviso which gave them the right to remain in the occupancy of the Mille Lac Reservation was conditioned upon their continued loyalty to the United States expressed in the terms "so long as they shall not in any way interfere with or in any manner molest the persons or property of the whites."

Counsel for appellant suggest that if the United States had intended by this proviso that such occupancy was to be anything more than a mere license, the commissioners would have expressed it in a different manner, and instances the case of the Commissioners who made the treaty reserving a section to one of the chiefs, and says: "An express exception excludes all others."

Would counsel contend that the Indians were supposed to understand such technical rules of law and that they would probably be able to apply these rules as counsel does here?

This strikes us as being altogether too technical to consider in construing the treaty made with the Indians.

Again, counsel say, the privilege is merely, "not to be compelled to remove."

That means what? Simply that they may occupy.

They were in the occupation of a reservation reserved to them for a permanent home.

A tenant is in the occupation of a house. The landlord writes to him, "you shall not be compelled to remove for ten years." Is that an extension of the lease? Does that mean the tenant can only occupy a part of the house, one or two rooms?

A tenant is in the occupation of a farm consisting of ten thousand acres, the landlord writes him, "you shall not be compelled to remove from the farm for the next ten years, if you will not allow mustard to grow on the west thousand acres of the farm." Would that be an extension of the lease of the farm? Would that continue the tenant in the exclusive occupancy of the farm so long as he observed the conditions?

These Mille Lac Indians, according to the Findings of the Court of Claims, had been in exclusive occupation of the Mille Lac Reservation from the year 1855.

Giving the natural meaning to the language used as the Indians would understand it, what would the words mean?

"Not be compelled to remove." From where? From the Mille Lac Reservation. The other five reservations had been ceded to the United States, and not one of them is ever heard of as a reservation thereafter. But the Mille Lac Reservation in all public documents, in all reports, even in the Document 247, is referred to as the Mille Lac Reservation." Counsel for appellant on page 20 of their brief unconsciously have referred to it as a "reservation." For, they say: "the quantity of land in all of the Chippewa Reservations in said state aggregating 4,747,931 acres."

Those figures include the Mille Lac Reservation, which, as we have seen in our statement of facts, found on page 28 of Executive Document 247, under the heading:

> "Schedule showing the number of acres in the Chippewa Reservation in the State of Minnesota," is found among such reservations. The sixth in the schedule is "Mille Lac, 61,014 acres."

As we have seen, the Court of Claims have found what the understanding and belief of the Mille Lac Indians was in reference to the reservation.

> "At the time of the execution of the treaty of 1863 and 1864, by the Mille Lac Indians, the said band of Indians understood and believed that they were reserving to themselves the right to occupy the Mille Lac Reservation set apart to them by the treaty of 1855."
>
> (Finding VI, Rec. p. 11.)

The Court of Claims had all the various documents and records at their disposal, they examined and weighed the evidence and that is their finding.

We say that finding determines the fact precisely as the verdict of a jury.

But counsel contend this was only a "right of occupancy." We say that "the right of occupancy" was the only title to land that such Indians have held within the domain of the United States since the beginning of the Nation.

In the case of *Jones v. Meehan,* 175 U.S., 1, Mr. Justice Gray speaking for the Court, on page 8, said:

"Undoubtedly, the right of the Indian nations or tribes as to their lands within the United States was a right of possession or occupancy only; the ultimate title in fee in those lands was in the United States; and the Indian title could not be conveyed by the Indians to anyone but the United States without the consent of the United States."

In Leavenworth, *L. & G. R. Co. v. United States,* 92 U.S., 733, the late Mr. Justice Davis speaking for the Court, on page 742, said:

"As long ago as the *Cherokee Nation v. Georgia,* 5 Pet. 1, this court said, that the Indians are acknowledged to have the unquestionable right to the lands they occupy, until it shall be extinguished by a voluntary cession to the Government; and recently in *United States v. Cook,* 19 Wall., 591, that right was declared to be as sacred as the title of the United States in fee."

In the case of *Spalding v. Chandler,* 160 U.S., 394, Mr. Justice White, now Chief Justice White, speaking for the court on page 402, said:

"It has been settled by repeated adjudications of this court that the fee of the lands in this country in the original occupation of the Indian tribes was from the time of the formation of this government vested in the United States. The Indian title as against the United States was merely a title and right to the perpetual occupancy of the land with the privilege of using it in such mode as they saw fit until such right of occupation had been surrendered to the Government. When the Indian reservations were created, either by treaty or Executive order, the Indians held the land by the same character of title, to-wit, the right to possess and occupy the lands for the uses and purposes designated."

To the same effect are all the cases from this court.

The case of *Cal. & Oreg. Land Co. v. Worden,* 85 Fed. R. 94, is almost on all fours with the case at bar. In that case, we quote from the syllabi:

"Alternate sections were granted by the United States to aid in the construction of a military road, the route of which lay through Indian country. Afterwards, by treaty, the Indians ceded to the Government a large region described by metes and bounds. Following the words of cession was a proviso that 'the following described tract, within the country ceded by this treaty', shall, until otherwise directed by the President of the United States, be set apart as a residence for said Indians, and held and regarded as an Indian reservation.

"*Held*, that this was not a cession and recession of the reserved lands, but a mere reservation to the Indians of the same title and right that they originally had, and hence that the military road grantees acquired no better right in sections falling within the reservation than they had before; so that a subsequent allotment of lands in severalty to certain of the Indians, pursuant to the treaty, was no infringement of its rights."

This case was subsequently affirmed on a motion for rehearing before the Circuit Court. See *Cal. & Oreg. Land Co. v. Rankin*, 87 Fed. R., 532.

So in the instant case, while, to be sure, the Mille Lac band did not, under the treaty of 1855, separately own the Mille Lac reservation they had in common to such reservation and to five other reservations ceded under the treaty of 1855 with the other five bands of the Chippewas of the Mississippi.

But all the six bands of the Chippewas of the Mississippi did own the Mille Lac reservation, and the five other reservations. And the six bands of the Chippewas of the Mississippi were all parties to the treaties of 1863 and 1864, and so it may truly be said that the proviso to article 12 was a reservation by all the six bands of the Mississippi to the Mille Lac band alone of the right of occupancy, as held in the case cited.

In the case of *United States v. Winans*, 198 U.S., 371, Mr. Justice McKenna, speaking for the Court, on Page 381, said:

> "The right to resort to the fishing places in controversy was a part of larger rights possessed by the Indians, upon the exercise of which there was not a shadow of impediment, and which were not much less necessary to the existence of the Indians than the atmosphere they breathed. New conditions came into existence to which those rights had to be accommodated. Only a limitation of them, however, was necessary and intended, not a taking away. In other words, the treaty was not a grant of rights to the Indians, but a grant of rights from them, — a reservation of those not granted. And the form of the instrument and its language was adapted to that purpose."

How true of the instant case. The Chippewas of the Mississippi owned six reservations. They ceded to the United States five of them absolutely. By proviso to article 12 the Chippewas of the Mississippi reserved to the Mille Lac band, with the consent of the United States, the Indian title to such reservation so long as they should not interfere with the persons or property of the whites. The consideration for the consent of the United States to this reservation was two-fold. First, it was the "heretofore good conduct" of the Mille Lacs, viz.,that of preventing an uprising of the Chippewas and their joining with the Sioux and thus causing an Indian war, and, Second, the continuance of this good conduct by not interfering with the persons or property of the whites.

The Mille Lacs have not violated the second condition. They had not violated it at the time of the cession and relinquishment on October 5, 1889. Surely, the Indian title to the Mille Lac reservation was in them, remained in them until they parted with it by cession and relinquishment.

So we say, the treaties of 1863 and 1864 can not be construed as the granting of a right by the United States to the Mille Lac band of Indians. On the contrary, a proper construction of each treaty is the granting of certain rights by the Mille Lac band and the other five bands of the Chippewas of the Mississippi to the United States, reserving, however, to the Mille Lac band, with the consent of the United States, the right of occupancy of the Mille Lac reservation. That this is true is seen by the very instrument of cession in 1889 which was prepared by the United States Government itself and furnished to the commissioners under the direction of the Secretary of the Interior.

Turning to the instrument of cession, Finding IX., Re. p. 15, we read:

"And we do also hereby forever relinquish to the United States the right of occupancy on the Mille Lac Reservation, *reserved* to us by the 12th article of the treaty of May 7, 1864."

Presumably, as a matter of fact, this instrument of cession and relinquishment was prepared by the United States Government, not by the Mille Lacs.

By the very terms then of this instrument it is conceded that this reservation was reserved to the Mille Lac band by the 12th article of the treaty of May 7th.

Again, attention is called to the beginning of the instrument, viz.:

"We, the undersigned, being male adult Indians over 18 years of age, of the Mille Lac Band of Chippewas of the Mississippi, *occupying and belonging to the Mille Lac Reservation under and by virtue of a clause in the Twelfth Article of the treaty of May 7, 1864* (13 Stat., p. 693), do hereby certify and declare that we have heard, read, interpreted, and thoroughly explained to our understanding the act of Congress approved January 14, 1889, entitled *'An act for the relief and civilization of the Chippewa Indians in the State of Minnesota.'*"

So it is seen that in the very instrument prepared by United States Commissioners these Indians were admitted to be occupying and belonging to the Mille Lac Reservation reserved to them under and by virtue of a clause in the 12th article of the treaty of May 7, 1864.

Can there be any doubt that by the treaties of 1863 and 1864 the Mille Lac Reservation was reserved as an Indian Reservation to the Mille Lac Band of Chippewas of the Mississippi so long as they should not in any way interfere with or molest the persons or property of the whites? They had not forfeited such right of possession at the time they made the cession and relinquishment.

Counsel argue, in effect, that there was not a sufficient consideration passed to the United States for reserving to the Mille Lacs of the Mille Lac Reservation.

But the United States in 1863 and 1864 thought differently. The Commissioners who framed the treaty probably understood better the conditions and the value of the service than counsel do today. Such consideration was deemed sufficient and was declared in the treaty to be the consideration for the proviso, in connection with the continuation of the same kind of conduct.

Now, much is attempted to be made out of the question who were "the whites" referred to in the proviso. The Court of Claims in their opinion have discussed that phrase of the subject very thoroughly (Rec. pp. 25-27), and we adopt the argument expressed by Judge Booth in the opinion of the Court as our own.

Counsel suggest that there were two objects to be accomplished by the treaties of 1863 and 1864:

1. The benefit to the Indians, and

2. The opening up of the lands to public settlement for the benefit of the whites.

The treaties of 1863 and 1864 were real treaties.
The Indians were persuaded to make those treaties with the Government, and understood that they were parties to the treaties.

We presume the first proposition was for the Government to get the land. Suppose we look simply to that part of the treaty which pertains to the lands of the Mississippi Chippewas.

The Mississippi Chippewas had at that time reserved to them six reservations for permanent homes.

The United States proposed that the Indians cede these back in consideration of a new reservation upon which all of the bands of Chippewas of the Mississippi could live together in one compact body.

The Indians were perfectly willing to cede five of the reservations, but when it came to ceding the Mille Lac Reservation, presumably the Mille Lacs objected. There was a halt in the proceedings. It may be that all six bands objected to moving. Apparently the Commissioners were deaf to the entreaties of the five other bands, but when it came to the Mille Lac band they looked at it from a different point of view. The Mille Lacs had performed a loyal service for the Government in preventing an Indian war. On this account the Government were willing to allow the Mille Lac band to remain in occupation of the Mille Lac Reservation so long as they should continue such loyalty to the United States, and so by each of said treaties of 1863 and 1864, as said in our statement of facts, all, of said six reservations, so reserved and set apart for the Chippewas of the Mississippi under the treaty of 1855, except the Mille Lac Reservation, were ceded back to the United States.

By each of these two treaties, the Gull Lake, Sandy Lake, Rabbit Lake, Pokagomin Lake and Rice Lake bands of Chippewas of Mississippi, with the consent, and at the suggestion, of the United States, in effect, ceded all their right and interest in the Mille Lac Reservation to the Mille Lac band. Such Mille Lac Reservation was, therefore, by the terms of each of said treaties, *reserved* to the Mille Lac band and made the separate and sole property of the Mille Lac band, to be occupied by such band as an Indian Reservation so long as the Mille Lac band of Indians in no way interfered with the persons or property of the whites.

We think then it clearly appears that the second proposition of the appellants (appellants' brief, p. 33) and the 2nd, 3rd and 5th errors assigned are at least answered in part.

V.

THE COURT WILL CONSTRUE THE TREATIES OF MARCH 11, 1863, AND MAY 7, 1864, AND THE INSTRUMENT BY WHICH THE MILLE LAC BAND RELINQUISHED THEIR RIGHT OF OCCUPANCY OF THE MILLE LAC RESERVATION AS THE INDIANS UNDERSTOOD SUCH TREATIES AND SUCH INSTRUMENT.

As said in reference to the preceding proposition, we again say here:

> "At the time of the execution of the treaty of 1863 and 1864 by the Mille Lac Indians the said band of Indians understood and believed that they were reserving to themselves the right to occupy the Mille Lac Reservation set apart to them by the treaty of 1855."
>
> (Finding VI, Rec. p. 11.)

In the case of *United States v. Winans,* 198 U.S., 370. on page 380, Mr. Justice McKenna, speaking for the Court, said:

> "And we have said we will construe a treaty with the Indians as 'that unlettered people' understood it, and 'as justice and reason demand, in all cases where power is exerted by the strong over those to whom they owe care and protection' and counterpoise the inequality by the superior justice, which looks only to the substance of the right without regard to technical rules. (*Choctaw Nation v. United States,* 119 U.S., 1) (*Jones v. Meehan,* 175 U.S. 1.) How the treaty in question was understood may be gathered from the circumstances."

In *Jones v. Meehan,* 175 U.S., 1, Mr. Justice Gray, speaking for the Court on pages 10 and 11, said:

> "In construing any treaty between the United States and an Indian tribe, it must always *** be borne in mind that the negotiations for the treaty are conducted, on the part of the United States, an enlightened and powerful nation, by representatives skilled in diplomacy, masters of the written language, understanding the modes and forms of creating the various technical estates known to their law, and assisted by an interpreter employed by themselves; that the treaty is drawn up by them and in their own language; that the Indians, on the other hand, are a weak and dependent people, who have no written language, and are wholly unfamiliar with all the forms of legal expression, and whose only knowledge of the terms in which the treaty is framed is that imparted to them by the interpreter employed by the United States; and that the treaty must therefore be construed, not according to the technical meaning of its words to learned lawyers, but in the sense in which they would naturally be understood by the Indians."

The Instrument of relinquishment by which the Mille Lac band relinquished to the United States their right of occupancy to the Mille Lac Reservation is found in Finding IX, Rec. pp. 15,16.

The Court of Claims in Finding VI, found:

> "On October 2, 1889, a council of the Mille Lac Indians assembled on the reservation set apart to them by the treaty of 1855, was addressed by Senator Henry M. Rice, one of the commissioners who participated in the procurement and execution of the treaty of 1863, who told the Indians that he knew that it was understood by them that they were reserving their reservation, that he so understood the meaning of the treaty and assisted in its negotiations with that intent. At the same time and place the chief and headmen of the Mille Lac Indians insisted and openly proclaimed that such was their intention in the execution of said treaty."
>
> Rec. p. 11.

And in Finding IX, the Court of Claims found (referencing to the act of January 14, 1889):

> "This act further provided for the appointment of commissioners to negotiate with the Chippewa Indians in Minnesota for the cession of their reservations, and in compliance therewith the commissioners so appointed held councils with the Mille Lac Indians on their reservation, occupied by them since the treaty of 1855, represented

to them that they came within the terms of the act of 1889, and by virtue of said representation secured their assent and a written relinquishment of their reservation as contemplated by the act."

Rec. p. 15.

The Court of Claims, speaking through Judge Booth, Rec. p. 24, said:

> "In construing Indian treaties ambiguities and doubtful clauses should be construed in favor of the Indians. This rule is ancient and elementary. It is predicated upon the disparity in intelligence between the contracting parties, the lack of a comprehensive written language for the Indian, and the innumerable and manifest opportunities to misinterpret the meaning of treaty stipulations. The intention and understanding of the Indian tribe of the rights secured to them by conventions of this character is of paramount importance and councils at which they were ratified and confirmed are admissible in evidence to this end. They are not to be construed according to the technical meaning of the words employed, but in that generous and comprehensive manner which justice exacts in dealings between a strong and intelligent party on the one side and an illiterate and inferior party on the other. (*Worcester v. Georgia*, 6 Pet., 515; *Choctaw Nation v. United States*, 119 U.S., 1; *Jones v. Meehan, supra, United States v. Winans, supra*)."

The very instrument of cession and relinquishment begins as follows:

> We, the undersigned, being male adult Indians over 18 years of age of the Mille Lac band of Chippewa of the Mississippi, occupying and belonging to the Mille Lac Reservation under and by virtue of a clause in the 12th article of the treaty of May 7, 1864, etc."

Rec. p. 15.

It will be admitted that this instrument was prepared by the United States Government through the Interior Department and the Commissioners.

Then the United States by the very instrument by which it obtained the relinquishment of the right of occupation of the Mille Lac Reservation, admits that the instrument was executed by the 189 adult Mille Lacs who signed it as Mille Lacs who belonged to and occupied the Mille Lac Reservation.

Under the proposition we are now discussing we shall also discuss the contention of appellant found on page 43, where counsel say:

> "The lands on the Mille Lac tracts were not, therefore, to be sold under the Nelson Act. According to the terms of section 4, it was only lands which were *ceded* to the United States which were to be surveyed and sold. This land was not ceded nor was there any need for its cession."

Peelle, Ch. J., and Howey, J., in their dissenting opinions each made the same contention. Referring to this contention the Court of Claims, speaking through Judge Booth, say on page 34, Rec.:

> "The technical language used in the written instrument subsequent to claimants' assent to the act of January 14, 1889, is cited as indicating a difference in title as to claimant Indians. The use of the word 'relinquish' when speaking of the Mille Lac Reservation as distinguished from the word 'cede' when referring to the White Earth and Red Lake Reservations, can hardly be relied upon in the determination of Indian title. The words are frequently used in Indian treaties conjunctively, and insofar as they affect the conveyance of Indian title the employment of either word would effectively divest the Indians of their right of occupancy. It is quite true that to the trained lawyer they have a distinct technical significance, but are so nearly synonymous that even they employ them carelessly. In construing Indian treaties their technical significance vanishes."

> "In *Worcester v. United States* (6 Pet., 236), Chief Justice Marshall, in language so directly applicable to this case that we cite it in full, said: 'It is reasonable to suppose that the Indians, who could not write, and most probably could not read, who certainly were not critical judges of our language, should distinguish the word "allotted" from the words "Marked out". The actual subject of contract was the dividing line between the two nations, and their attention may very well be supposed to have been confirmed to that subject. When in fact they were ceding lands to the United States and describing the extent of their cession, it may very well be supposed that they might not understand the term employed as indicating that instead of granting they were receiving lands. If the term would admit of no other signification, which is not conceded, its being misunderstood is so apparent, results so necessarily from the whole transaction that it must, we think, be taken in the sense in which it was most obviously used.' The rule established by this case has been followed by the Supreme Court in construing Indian treaties ever since."

The Century Dictionary gives the following definition of "Relinquish":

1. – To give up the possession or occupancy of; withdraw from; leave; abandon; quit.
2. – To cease from; give up pursuit or practice of; desist from.
3. – To renounce a claim to; resign.

Synonyms: Abandon, desert, let go, yield, cede, surrender, give up, lay down.
The same author defines "Cede" as follows:

1. – To yield; give away, submit. To pass; to be transferred.
2. – To yield or formally resign and surrender to another; relinquish, transfer; give up; make over.

It is thus seen that there is no difference primarily in the meaning of the two words, and it is idle to claim that Congress, through its commissioners, intended to take advantage of this illiterate band of Indians by using two terms like "relinquish" and "cede" in a technical way, and in accordance with the technical use of those words interpret a statute to those Indians.

The free use of the word "relinquish" for the word "cede" is illustrated in the dissenting opinion of Judge Howry, where, on page 51, he says:

"Stipulation permitting the small number of Mille Lacs to remain on lands (which for consideration the band had just *relinquished* to the United States) was not a recession of such title as the band had before."

What the distinguished jurist meant was that, speaking technically, "the band had just *ceded* to the United States."

The Indians understood by the treaties of 1863 and 1864 that they were reserving to themselves the Mille Lac Reservation to be occupied by them so long as they should not interfere with the persons or property of the whites. In other words, they understood that the Mille Lac Reservation was to be their permanent home so long as they did not commit acts of violence against the persons or property of the neighboring whites.

VI.

BY THE VERY INSTRUMENT OF CESSION AND RELINQUISHMENT BY THE MILLE LACS TO THE UNITED STATES ON OCTOBER 5, 1889, AND THEREAFTER APPROVED BY PRESIDENT HARRISON, THE UNITED STATES ACKNOWLEDGED AND CONFIRMED THE INDIAN TITLE OF THE MILLE LAC RESERVARTION TO BE THEN IN THE MILLE LAC BAND OF CHIPPEWA OF THE MISSISSIPPI.

The instrument of cession, as we have previously stated, is found in Finding IX, Rec. p. 15, and we quote the following part thereof, which is sufficient for our purpose:

> "We, the undersigned, being male adult Indians over 18 years of age, of the Mille Lac band of Chippewas of the Mississippi, occupying and belonging to the Mille Lac Reservation under and by virtue of a clause in the 12th article of the treaty of May 7, 1864 (13 Stat., 693), do hereby certify and declare that we have heard read, interpreted, and thoroughly explained to our understanding the act of Congress approved January 14, 1889. Entitled 'an act for the relief and civilization of the Chippewa Indians in the state of Minnesota * * *' which said act is embodied in the foregoing instrument, and after such explanation and understanding have consented and agreed to said act, and have accepted and ratified the same, and do hereby accept and consent to and ratify the said act and each and all of the provisions thereof, and do hereby grant, cede, relinquish and convey to the United States all our right, title and interest in and to all and so much of the White Earth Reservation * * * for the purposes and upon the terms stated in said act; and we do also hereby cede and relinquish to the United States all our right, title and interest in and to all and so much of the Red Lake Reservation * * * and we do also hereby forever relinquish to the United States the right of occupancy on the Mille Lac Reservation, reserved to us by the 12th article of the treaty of May 7, 1864, (13 Stat. p. 693.)

"Witness our hands and seals hereto subscribed and affixed at Mille Lac in the state of Minnesota, this 5th day of October, 1889.

Henry M. Rice,
Joseph R. Whiting,
Commissioners."

> "Then follow the signatures of 189 adult Indians. Said agreement was approved by President Harrison on March 4, 1890."

Rec. pp. 15, 16.

The Court of Claims found as follows:

> "At the time of the execution of the treaty of 1863 and 1864, by the Mille Lac Indians the said band of Indians understood and believed that they were reserving to themselves the right to occupy the Mille Lac Reservation set apart to them by the treaty if 1855."

(Finding VI. Rec. p. 11☺

"That the said Mille Lac Indians have, without exception, upon all occasions and in connection with all controversies relating to the title they possessed to the reservation set apart to them by the treaty of 1855, proclaimed and persisted in their claim of the right of occupancy to said reservation and have continually and openly occupied said reservation from that time until subsequent to the passage of the act of January 14, 1889."

(Finding VI. Rec. pp. 12, 13.)

"On January 14, 1889, Congress passed an act (25 Stat. L., 642), providing for the classification of lands belonging to the Chippewas of Minnesota, into pine lands and agricultural lands and for their sale for the benefit of all Indians in the state of Minnesota, the proceeds arising therefrom to constitute a permanent fund from which annuities would accrue to said Indians for a period of 50 years.

"This act further provided for the appointment of commissioners to negotiate with the Chippewa Indians in Minnesota for the cession of their reservations, and in compliance therewith, the commissioners so appointed held councils with the Mille Lac Indians on their reservation, occupied by them since the treaty of 1855, represented to them that they came within the terms of the act of 1889, and by virtue of said representation secured their assent and a written relinquishment of their reservation as contemplated by the act."

(Finding IX. Rec. p. 15.)

The case of *White v. Wright 83 Minn.*, 22, involved the construction of the act of January 14, 1889. Mr. Justice Collins delivered the opinion of the Court and on page 225 speaking for the court, referring to the Nelson Act he said:

"Its terms were accepted by the Indians and thereupon the President approved the cession and the Indians' title became extinguished. The special provision was made in the law itself for the disposition of the land at public auction under certain restrictions. The proceeds of the sales to be devoted to the use of the Indians. This specified disposition of the lands and of the proceeds amounted to an agreement between the government and its ward and an inhibition upon the sale or disposition of the lands in any other manner. It operated to forbid a disposal of the lands therein mentioned, except in the precise way pointed out by the act. * * * This construction of the Nelson Law is unavoidable, if we are to pay the least attention to its avowed purpose, or to the necessity of keeping faith with the Indians."

The Court of Claims in its opinion, speaking through Judge Booth, said:

> "The Department of the Interior, the commissioners appointed by the President to procure the assent of the Indians to the act of January 14, 1889, all treated the Mille Lac Indians as coming within the purview of its provisions. A council extending over several days was held on the Mille Lac Reservation to secure their approval thereto; they were positively and repeatedly assured by the representatives of the Government that they were within its terms; and their written relinquishment of their title to the same, executed by a majority of the tribe residing on the reservation, was secured upon the faith of said representations. Absolutely no doubt existed then as to the scope of the law or its applicability to claimant Indians. The fact of allowance of homestead entries to the chief of the band and his son argues little. We need not cite authorities to sustain the proposition that the Interior Department is entirely without authority to issue valid patents to Indian lands. (*United States v. Carpenter*, 111 U.S., 347.) If these patents are at all valid they must rest upon treaty rights or statutory law.
>
> "The Mille Lac Indians were the only band mentioned in the treaties of 1863 and 1864 subsequently asked to relinquish their reservation under the act of January 14, 1889. Surely their status was something different from that of their ancient allies.
>
> "The Congress as late as July 22, 1890, treated the Mille Lac Reservation as Indian lands, for on that date an act was approved granting a railway company a right of way and other privileges through and upon the reservation, expressly reserving to the Mille Lacs in their tribal capacity the damages incident thereto." (26 Stat. L., 290) Rec. p. 33.

In section 2 of said act of July 22, 1890, referred to by the Court of Claims, *supra*, among other things, it is provided:

> "The amount of damage resulting to the Mille Lac Indians in their tribal capacity, by reason of the construction of said railroad, through such lands of the reservation as are not occupied in severalty, shall be ascertained in such manner as the Secretary of the Interior may direct, and be subject to his final approval; but no right

of any kind shall vest in said Railway Company in or to any part of the right of way herein provided for until plats thereof, made upon actual survey for the definite location of such railroad, and including grounds for station, buildings, depots, machine shops, etc. * * * shall have been approved by the Secretary of the Interior, and until the compensation aforesaid shall have been fixed and paid and the consent of the Indians on said reservation to said right of way and as to the amount of compensation shall have been first obtained in a manner as the President may prescribe."

"Provided, that no part of the said lands herein authorized to be taken shall be leased or sold by the company, and they shall not be used except in such manner and for such purposes only as shall be necessary for the construction and convenient operation of said railway, telegraph and telephone lines, and when any portion thereof shall cease to be used such portion shall revert to the nation or tribe of Indians from which the same shall have been taken."

(26 Stat. Ch. 714, p. 290.)

In view of these facts and in view of the further fact that the instrument of cession and relinquishment was prepared by the United States and presented to these Indians for their signature with the knowledge, presumably on the part of the Government, through its commissioners, that it was the understanding and belief of the Mille Lac band when they made the cession and relinquishment of October 5, 1889, to the United States:

1. That all the lands on such reservation would be classified into "pine lands" and "agricultural lands."

2. That the pine timber would be estimated on the pine lands in forty-acre tracts.

3. That after such estimate, the pine lands would be sold, on due notice by publication, at public auction, to the highest bidder, at not less than three dollars per thousand feet, board measure, of the pine timber estimated to be on such forty-acre tract.

(This was amended later so that the price of white pine was five dollars and Norway pine four dollars a thousand feet.)

4. That the moneys received from such sale of pine lands would be paid into the United States treasury for the benefit of the Mille Lac band, the principal to be held in trust for 50 years, interest to be paid on such principal annually at

the rate of 5 per cent per annum, at the end of 50 years the principal to be distributed as provided in such act.

5. That any of the Mille Lacs so desiring would be allotted agricultural lands on such Mille Lac Reservation or the White Earth Reservation, at the election of such Indian.

6. The agricultural lands remaining on such Mille Lac Reservation, after the allotments were completed, to be sold under the homestead laws at not less than a dollar and a quarter an acre. The moneys arising from such sales of agricultural lands to be disposed of in the same way as the money from the sale of the pine lands.

We say it clearly appears that by the very instrument of cession and relinquishment the United States acknowledged and confirmed the Indian title of the Mille Lac Reservation to be then in the Mille Lac band of Chippewas of Mississippi. And such relinquishment was obtained upon such representations of the Government.

But the appellants claim that the second proviso to section VI. of such act of January 14, 1889, excluded from the act the Mille Lac Reservation. The provisos are as follows:

"Provided, that nothing in this act shall be held to authorize the sale or other disposal under its provisions of any tract upon which there is subsisting, valid pre-emption or homestead entry, but any such entry shall be proceeded with under the regulations and decisions in force at the date of its allowance, and if found regular and valid, patents shall issue thereon; provided, that any person who has not heretofore had the benefit of the homestead or pre-emption law, and who has failed from any cause to perfect the title to a tract of land heretofore entered by him under either of said laws, may make a second homestead entry under the provisions of this act."

There were no subsisting, valid pre-emption or homestead entries at the time this cession and relinquishment was made.

The Government itself admitted, through its commissioners, and in the instrument of cession itself, that the Mille Lacs had done nothing at the time to forfeit their right of occupancy of the Mille Lac Reservation. If that were true, then they had the right of occupancy at the time this cession and relinquishment was made.

The Mille Lacs say that they had been told by the commissioners just before signing that the reservation was theirs. That the lands would be sold under the act of January 14, 1889, that they would receive the benefit, that they could have allotments there.

They had the title, as much as Indians hold within the United States, to the Mille Lac Reservation at the time of such cession and relinquishment.

If that is true, then the action of the Interior Department, or of the officers of the Government, in permitting entries to be made by the use of various kinds of scrip upon these lands in no way affected the rights of the Indians under the treaty of 1863 and 1864.

It does not appear that these provisions were brought to the attention of the Mille Lac Indians.

It will hardly be claimed that this illiterate band of Indians ought to have been of sufficient understanding to have read, with the critical understanding of lawyers, this act of 1889, disregarding the assurance of the commissioners, and have discovered that there had some way crept into this act these provisos which might defeat their right.

Will it be claimed that the Government in face of the title of this "act for the relief and civilization of the Chippewas of Minnesota" would be guilty of deceiving this illiterate band of Indians by putting in such a proviso, which their understanding would not grasp, with the intent to defeat the very provisions of the act itself? That the Government would do this to the band of Indians who had befriended it during the Civil War, that the reservation presented to them by the Government in good faith for their loyalty would be taken from them in such a way and in such a manner seems hardly conceivable.

The purpose and intent of Congress was too lofty and noble to admit that. Though these provisos were in the bill for the purpose of furnishing the lumbermen the means to get hold of this pine timber on this reservation, they would in no way affect the right of the Mille Lacs to the reasonable value of such timber.

We say it does not seem possible that such a contention will obtain in this court.

Further, by the very provisions of such Nelson act the lands were to be classified into "pine lands" and "agricultural lands".

> Section 1 of such act relates to the appointment of the commissioners and the method to obtain the cession and relinquishment.
>
> Section 2 relates to the qualifications of the commissioners.
>
> Section 3 relates to the removal of the Indians to White Earth Reservation, the allotments of lands to the Indians.
>
> Section 4 relates to the examination and classification of lands into pine and agricultural lands.
>
> Section 5 relates to the sale of the pine lands.
>
> Section 6 relates to the sale of the agricultural lands.

These provisos are found under section 6 and must therefore relate to agricultural lands. But these entries, as found by the Court of Claims, were made on pine lands and not agricultural lands, and, therefore, these provisos did not relate to pine lands in any manner.

The Court of Claims in the opinion rendered by Judge Booth discuss this proviso very fully, and we have adopted the views there expressed as our own,

See Rec., pp. 30, 31, 32.

On page 33 the Court of Claims say:

> "It is hard to believe that the Government of the United States would by express treaty stipulations grant a right to peaceable, loyal, well-behaved Indians, a right doubly sacred to them, and then in not to exceed seven years from the date of said grant, countenance their ejectment from the lands so granted by a series of fraudulent entries under the general land laws. If the Government intended the Mille Lac Indian Reservation to be open to entry and settlement under the general land laws, it would have so announced, removing all doubt, and doing as is usually done under similar circumstances."
>
> Rec., p. 33.

APPELANTS CONTENTION.

Counsel for appellant approach the construction of the Nelson Act from a different viewpoint and one not warranted by the facts.

On page 41 of their brief under Proposition IV they say:

> "At the time the Mille Lac band were in this situation, the large majority of them had already removed to White Earth, but a remnant still lived in primitive Indian fashion on or near the old Mille Lac Reservation."

We have seen that counsel are in error in this statement. On page 42 of their brief counsel for the appellant say:

> "In this situation the United States, by the Nelson Act, offered that if all the Indians would remove, some to the White Earth Reservation and the others to the Red Lake Reservation, and would cede to the United States all their lands, such ceded lands would be sold and the proceeds applied to the use of the Indians, and that each Indian would be given an allotment in severalty on White Earth or Red Lake."

Now, that is only a part of the truth, for section 3 of the Nelson Act, which provided for the removal of the Indians to White Earth and Red Lake Reservations concluded with the following proviso, viz.:

> "Provided, further that any of the Indians residing on any of said reservations may, in his discretion, take his allotment in severalty under this act on the reservation where he lives at the time of removal herein provided for is effected, instead of being removed to and taking such allotment on White Earth Reservation."

Continuing on page 42 appellant says:

> "This offer was accepted by all the Indians and each band made deeds expressing the acceptance of the provisions of the act, and ceding to the United States the specific reservations which they owned."

> "The Mille Lac Band with the others accepted the act, and thereby agreed that the remnant of their band still remaining on or near the old reservation should remove to White Earth."

And here again counsel for appellant are in error. As we have conclusively shown, 895 of the Mille Lac Band of Chippewas resided upon and occupied the Mille Lac Reservation when they relinquished their right of occupancy to the United States under the Nelson Act on October 5, 1889.

They accepted such act as it had been interpreted and explained to them.

Counsel for appellee contend that it is wholly immaterial how soon after the relinquishment of this Mille Lac Reservation the Mille Lac Indians moved away from it, except as to their right of election to take allotments thereon.

After the relinquishment of the right of occupancy of the Mille Lacs in this Reservation they could take their allotments there, so far as the agricultural land would go, or they could take their allotments on White Earth Reservation or the other Chippewa reservations in the State of Minnesota.

Suppose the Mille Lacs had elected at once upon their relinquishment of their right of occupancy to take their allotments severally on White Earth Reservation? Would such moving away have released the United States from their obligation to carry out the trust agreement, viz., to classify the lands into pine lands and agricultural lands and sell them as provided in such act?

Why, by the very provisions of the act the Indians were expected to move away, unless they chose to exercise their privilege under the proviso 3 of such act.

If this is true, then what is the force or value of the argument of counsel that the Mille Lacs had abandoned their reservation subsequent to the act of 1889?

But, we contend that even as late as 1904 the major number of the Mille Lac band still resided on the Mille Lac Reservation. See page 222, Report of the Commission of Indian Affairs for the year 1904, dated September 2, 1904, already referred to in the statement of facts.

VII.

THE RELINQISHMENT OF THE MILLE LAC RESERVATION WAS OBTAINEED FROM THE MILLE LACS WITH THE UNDERSTANDING AND

BELIEF ON THEIR PART THAT SUCH RESERVATION WOULD BE CLASSIFIED INTO PINE LANDS AND AGRICULTURAL LANDS, THE PINE LANDS ESTIMATED AND SOLD, AND, AFTER ALLOTMENT OF THE AGRICULTURAL LANDS, THE REMAINING AGRICULTURAL LANDS WOULD BE SOLD, AND THE MONEYS RECEIVED FROM BOTH PAID INTO THE UNITED STATES TREASURY UNDER AND IN ACCORDANCE WITH THE SAID ACT OF JANUARY 14, 1889.

> This follows as a corollary to the preceding proposition and the arguments made sustaining such proposition.

VIII.

SUCH CESSION AND RELINQUISHMENT OF THE CHIPPEWA INDIANS OF MINNESOTA OF THEIR VARIOUS RESERVATIONS IN MINNESOTA UNDER THE ACT OF JANUARY 14, 1889 INCLUDING THE CESSION AND RELINQUISHMENT BY THE MILLE LAC BAND OF CHIPPEWAS OF MISSISSIPPI AND ITS RELINQUISHMENT OF THE MILLE LAC RESERVATION WAS A CESSION AND RELINQUISHMENT OF EACH OF SAID RESERVATIONS TO THE UNITED STATES IN TRUST, WHICH TRUST IS EXPRESSED IN THE PROVISIONS OF THE ACT OF JANUARY 14, 1889.

The case of *Minnesota v. Hitchcock,* 185 U.S., 373, which was a dispute concerning school lands conveyed by the United States to Minnesota, and which lands were within the Red Lake Reservation, called for a construction on the part of this Court for the provisions of the act of January 14, 1889, and on page 394 of that case this Court, speaking through the late Mr. Justice Brewer, said:

> "The act of January 14, 1889, provided for a commission to negotiate for the cession and relinquishment of 'all and so much of

the White Earth and Red Lake reservations as in the judgment of the commission should not be required to satisfy the allotments required by the existing acts, the cession to be 'for the purposes and upon the terms hereinafter stated.'***. The ceded lands were to be divided into two classes; one appraised and sold at auction and the other disposed of to actual settlers at $1.25 per acre. The proceeds of these sales were to be placed in the Treasury of the United States as a permanent fund to the credit of the Indians, drawing interest at five per centum for fifty years, the interest to be expended, three-fourths paid in cash to the Indians severally and the remaining one-fourth devoted, under the direction of the Secretary of the Interior, 'exclusively to the establishment and maintenance of a system of free schools among said Indians in their midst and for their benefit.' *The cession was not to the United States absolutely, but in trust.* It was a cession of all of the unallotted lands. The trust was to be executed by the sale of the ceded lands and a deposit of the proceeds in the Treasury of the United States to the credit of the Indians, such sum to draw interest at five per cent, and one-fourth of the interest to be devoted exclusively to the maintenance of free schools among the Indians and for their benefit."

(The italics are our own.)

It can not be believed that the Mille Lacs alone, the ones who were so loyal to the United States during the civil war, were singled out by the United States as the one band who would not be offered the advantages of the act of 1889, and that their reservation, given to them as a present by the United States, would alone be held as not coming within the purview of the act of January 14, 1889.

Therefore, appellee contends that the Mille Lac reservation was relinquished to the United States in trust.

IX.

THE FAILURE OF THE UNITED STATES TO CARRY OUT THE PROVISIONS OF THE ACT OF JANUARY 14, 1889, THE PASSAGE OF THE JOINT RESOLUTION OF DECEMBER 19, 1893 (28 STAT. L., 576), CONFIRMING A LARGE NUMBER OF ENTRIES THERETOFORE MADE UPON THE MILLE LAC RESERVATION, AND CONFIRMING TITLE IN SUCH ENTRYMEN, CONSTITUTE SUCH A FAILURE OF DUTY ON THE PART OF THE UNITED STATES AS GIVES THE MILLE LAC BAND A RIGHT OF ACTION AGAINST THE UNITED STATES FOR DAMAGES UNDER THE JURISIDICTIONAL ACT.

The case of *United States v. Blackfeather,* 155 U.S., 180, is a case in some respects similar to the instant case.

The second and principal assignment of error before this Court in that case arose from an allowance of the sum of $260,999.24 based upon a treaty made August 8, 1831, * * * with a branch of the Shawnees residing in Ohio, under which they ceded to the United States their lands in Ohio, the Government agreeing to give in exchange certain lands upon the western side of the Mississippi.

The seventh article of the treaty provided as follows:

> "The United States will expose to public sale to the highest bidder, in the manner of selling the public lands, the tracts of land herein ceded by the Shawnees, and after deducting from the proceeds of such sale the sum of seventy cents per acre, exclusive of the cost of surveying, the cost of the gristmill, sawmill, and blacksmith shop and the aforesaid sum of thirteen thousand dollars, to be advanced in lieu of improvements; it is agreed that any balance, which may remain of the avails of the lands, after sale as aforesaid, shall constitute a fund for future necessities of the tribe, parties to this compact, on which the United States agree to pay to the chiefs, for the use and general benefit of their people, annually, five per centum on the amount of said balance, as an annuity. Said fund to be continued during the pleasure of Congress, unless the chiefs of the said tribe, or band, by and with the consent of their people, in general council assembled, should desire that the fund thus to be created, should be dissolved and paid over to them; in which case the President shall cause the same to be so paid, if in his discretion he shall believe the happiness and prosperity of said tribe would be promoted thereby.
>
> "The court found the total amount ceded under this treaty to have been 96,051.48 acres, and of this amount 9,841.27 acres were sold at public sale to the highest bidder for $20,543.65, or at the rate of $2.08 ¾ an acre.
>
> "The remainder of the land so ceded was sold at private sale at the rate of $1.35 per acre."

This court speaking through Mr. Justice Brown, on page 190, referring to this matter said:

> "If it had appeared that the government had 'exposed' these lands to public sale, to the highest bidder, and failing to find a bidder above the statutory price of $1.25 per acre, had then sold them at private sale at that price, its obligation would have been com-

pletely discharged. But as there is no evidence that they were ever exposed to public sale, we incline to the view expressed by the Court below that, as between the government and the Indians, there was a failure on the part of the former to observe the stipulation of the treaty and a violation of its trust. The obligation being expressed to expose them to public sale, it was incumbent upon the government to show, either that it had done so and failed to find a bidder, or for some reason it had been released from the provisions of the treaty. The privilege of selling the lands, 'in the manner of selling public lands,' does not nullify the obligation to expose them at public sale, which still remained; but it required them to be sold subject to the conditions and in the manner prescribed by the act of 1820."

It can not be denied that under their plenary power Congress had the right to prescribe the terms and conditions upon which the Commissioners might obtain from the Chippewas of Minnesota the cession and relinquishment of their lands. This includes the right on the part of Congress of incorporating in the statute an agreement on the part of the United States that they would receive such lands in trust and the method and manner of the execution of such trust. In other words, the manner in which the lands should be dealt with after such cession and relinquishment, their classification, the allotments, the estimate, the sale and the distribution of the money. Congress has done this. It has provided in specific terms how the cession and relinquishment should be obtained and what should be done with the lands so relinquished and ceded.

The agreement was made on the part of the Government through three able commissioners appointed by the President. The Indians were represented by their chiefs and headmen.

In the case of *Choctaw Nation v. United States,* 119 U.S. 1, on page 28, this Court, speaking through the late Mr. Justice Matthews, said:

> "The recognized relation between the parties to this controversy, therefore, is that between a superior and an inferior, whereby the latter is placed under the care and control of the former, and which, while it authorizes the adoption on the part of the United States of such policy as their own public interests may dictate, recognizes on the other hand, such an interpretation of their acts and promises as justice and reason demand in all cases where power is exerted by the strong over those to whom they owe care and protection. The parties are not on an equal footing, and that inequality is to be made good by the superior justice which looks only to the substance of the right, without regard to technical rules framed under the system of

municipal jurisprudence, formulating the rights and obligations of private persons, equally subject to the same laws.

"The rules to be applied in the present case are those which govern public treaties, which, even in case of controversies between nations equally independent, are not to be read as rigidly as documents between private persons governed by a system of technical law, but in the light of that larger reason which constitutes the spirit of the law of nations."

In the case of *Lone Wolf v. Hitchcock*, 187 U.S., 553, this Court, speaking through then Mr. Justice, now Chief Justice White, on page 565, said:

"But the right which the Indians held was only that of occupancy. The fee was in the United States, subject to that right, and could be transferred by them whenever they chose. The grantee, it is true, would take only the naked fee, and could not disturb the occupancy of the Indians: that occupancy could not be interfered with or determined by the United States. It is presumed that in this matter the United States would be governed by such considerations of justice as would control a Christian people in their treatment of an ignorant and dependent race. Be that as it may, the propriety or justice of their action towards the Indians with respect to their lands is a question of governmental policy, and is not a matter open to discussion in a controversy between third parties, neither of whom derives title from the Indians.

"Plenary authority over the tribal relations of the Indians has been exercised by Congress from the beginning, and the power has always been deemed a political one, not subject to be controlled by the judicial department of the government. Until the year 1871 the policy was pursued of dealing with the Indian tribes, and, of course, a moral obligation rested upon Congress to act in good faith in performing the stipulations entered into on its behalf. * * *"

In *United States v. Carpenter*, 111 U.S., 347, it was held:

"The location of land scrip upon lands reserved for Indians under the provisions of a treaty with an Indian tribe, and the issue of a patent therefor, are void."

From 1855 until their relinquishment to the United States on the 5th of October, 1889, the Mille Lac band of Chippewas had occupied the Mille Lac reservation under the treaties of 1855, 1863 and 1864.

> "The reservation thus created stood precisely in the same category as other Indian reservations, whether made by the direct authority of Congress in the ratification of a treaty or indirectly through the medium of a duly authorized executive officer."

Spalding v. Chandler, 160 U.S., 404.
Again:

> "Private rights could not, without the authority of congress, be acquired in the tract during the occupancy of the reservation under the treaty, for the lands in question lost their character as public lands in being set apart or occupied under the treaty, and became exempt from sale and preemption."

Ib., 405, citing *Mo. Kans. Tex. Ry. V. Roberts.* 152 U.S., 114, 116, 118.
In *U.S. vs. Carpenter, supra,* it is said:

> "The purposes of the treaty could not be defeated by the action of executive officers of the government."

This last is also cited with approval on page 405 of *Spalding v. Chandler, supra.*

Further, there is nothing in the joint resolution of December 19, 1893, that would warrant the Court in holding that by such resolution Congress, in the exercise of its plenary power, intended to confiscate the Mille Lac Reservation. But, on the contrary, in view of the confusion brought about by the varying decisions of the Interior department, there might be a few individuals who had in good faith filed upon some of the agricultural lands in the Mille Lac reservation, and that to protect them Congress would pass such resolution, knowing that it was within its power to compensate the Mille Lac band for any damages which might result to it because of such entries.

In short, nothing but an express declaration by Congress would justify a court in holding that Congress had exercised its plenary power over the property of Indians to the extent of confiscation.

Nevertheless, by the passage of the joint resolution of December 19, 1893, Congress placed it beyond its power to execute its trust in reference to the Mille Lac reservation as provided by the act of January 14, 1889, and hence there was a failure of duty in that regard. Because of that we feel warranted in saying that there was at once a right of action against the United States for damages which only awaited the action of Congress to give its ward authority to sue the United States for such failure of duty.

X.

THE MEASURE OF DAMAGES FOR THE OPENING OF SUCH RESERVATION TO SETTLEMENT UNDER THE PUBLIC LAND LAWS IS THE REASONABLE VALUE OF THE PINE TIMBER AND AGRICULTURAL LANDS ON SUCH RESERVATION ON DECEMBER 19TH, 1893, WITH INTEREST THEREON AT THE RATE OF FIVE PER CENT FROM SUCH DATE.

This was virtually admitted by the United States in the Court of Claims, and ought not to be questioned here.

If the pine lands and agricultural lands were to be sold, of course as soon as the Congress put it beyond the power of the Government to execute the trust the cause of action arose, and was only in abeyance until the Indians were authorized by special act to bring suit against the United States.

The value of the pine lands and agricultural lands obtained, the sales would be held to be as of that date, to-wit: December 19th, 1893.

Since the moneys realized from the sales of the pine and agricultural lands were to be paid into the United States Treasury and draw interest at the rate of five per cent per annum, as provided in such act, the Indians would be entitled to interest at that rate from such date on such value.

This is in accordance with the cases cited to this proposition.

In the case of the *United States v. Blackfeather, supra*, it was held the United States, having undertaken, by article 7 of the treaty of August 8th, 1831, with the Shawnees, "to expose to public sale to the highest bidder" the lands ceded to them by the Shawnees, and having disposed of a large part of the same at private sale, were thereby guilty of a violation of trust; under the provisions of said treaty the Shawnees were entitled to interest on such damages as annuity.

And on page 182 of such case this court, speaking through Mr. Justice Brown, said:

> "Are the Indians entitled to interest upon this amount? By Rev. Stat. Par. 1091: 'No interest shall be allowed upon any claim up to the time of the rendition of judgment thereon by the Court of Claims, unless upon a contract expressly stipulating for the payment of interest.' The real question here is whether there was a contract expressly stipulating for the payment of interest, or is this a mere claim for unliquidated damages?
>
> "By the seventh article of the treaty, it was agreed that the proceeds of the lands, after making the several deductions, 'should constitute a fund for the future necessities of said tribe, parties to this compact, on which the United States agree to pay to the chiefs, for the use

and general benefit of their people, annually, five per centum on the amount of said balance, as an annuity. Said fund to be continued during the pleasure of Congress, unless the chiefs of the said tribes or band, by and with the consent of their people, in general council assembled, should desire that the fund thus to be created should be dissolved and paid over to them.' While this is not literally an agreement to pay interest, it has substantially that effect. It is true it is called an annuity, but the amount of the annuity is measured by the interest paid upon funds held in trust by the United States (Rev. Stat., Par. 3659) upon investments for Indians (Par. 2096), as well as by the interest paid upon an affirmance by this court of judgments of the Court of Claims." (Par. 1090.)

Now, in the instant case, section 7 of the act of January 14th, 1889, provides:

"That all moneys accruing from the disposal of said lands in conformity with the provisions of this act shall * * * be placed in the treasury of the United States to the credit of all the Chippewa Indians in the State of Minnesota as a permanent fund, which shall draw interest at the rate of five per centum per annum, payable annually for the period of 50 years.

So, there can be no doubt that the money was to draw interest, and it was to draw interest for 50 years. Inasmuch as this land was obtained from the Mille Lacs under the act of January 14, 1889, it is not too much to say that the Government agreed to pay interest at the rate of five per cent.

The other cases cited are to the same effect as the Blackfeather case.

XI.

THE PASSAGE OF THE JOINT RESOLUTION OF DECEMBER 19TH, 1893 (28 STAT. L., 576), AND THE PASSAGE OF THE JOINT RESOLUTION OF MAY 27TH, 1898 (30 STAT. L., 745), DO NOT INDICATE ANY INTENTION ON THE PART OF CONGRESS TO CONFISCATE THE MILLE LAC RESERVATION, OR THAT IN THE EXERCISE OF ITS PLENARY POWER CONGRESS INTENDED TO TAKE FROM THE CHIPPEWAS OF MINNESOTA THE VALUE OF SUCH RESERVATION.

The joint resolution of December 19th, 1893, provides:

"That all bona fide pre-emption or homestead filings or entries allowed for lands within the Mille Lac Indian Reservation, in the State of Minnesota, between the ninth day of January, eighteen hundred and ninety-one, the date of the decision of the Secretary of the Interior holding that the lands within said reservation were subject to disposal as other public lands under the general land laws, and the date of the receipt at the district land office at Taylor's Falls, in that State, of the letter from the Commissioner of the General Land Office communicating to them the decision of the Secretary of the Interior of April twenty-second, eighteen hundred and ninety-two, in which it was definitely determined that said lands were not subject to disposal, but could only be disposed of according to the provisions of the special act of January fourteenth, eighteen hundred and eighty-nine (25 Stat., 642), be, and the same are hereby, confirmed where regular in other respects, and patent shall issue to the claimants for the lands embraced therein, as in other cases, on a satisfactory showing of a bona fide compliance on their part with the requirements of the laws under which said filings and entries were respectively allowed."

The joint resolution of March 27th, 1898, provides:

"That all public lands formerly within the Mille Lac Indian Reservation, in the State of Minnesota, be, and the same are hereby, declared to be subject to entry by any bona fide qualified settler under the public land laws of the United States; and all preemption filings heretofore made prior to the repeal of the pre-emption law by the act of March third, eighteen hundred and ninety-one, and all homestead entries or applications to make entry under the homestead laws, shall be received and treated in all respects as if made upon any of the public lands of the United States subject to pre-emption or homestead entry."

Referring again to what we have said under proposition IX, we once again affirm:
The court would not be warranted in holding that, by the passage of such two joint resolutions, it was the intention of Congress, in the exercise of its plenary power, to confiscate such Mille Lac Reservation.

It would be, indeed, too violent an assumption for the court to make unless in such resolutions Congress had so expressed itself in specific terms.

The proper assumption would rather be that Congress was exercising its plenary power, because of the many varying rulings of the land department, to treat the settlers fairly and also to treat the Indians in good faith. In other words, that finally, as was done, Congress would pass a law authorizing the Indians to bring a suit against the United States for its failure to execute the trust in reference to the Mille Lac Reservation.

This court has never yet held that the Congress, in the exercise of its plenary power, has the absolute right of confiscation of Indian property.

If Congress by such two joint resolutions intended to confiscate the Mille Lac Resolution, why did Congress pass the jurisdictional act of February 15th, 1909, the statute under which this suit is brought?

Would Congress submit to the Court of Claims for its determination the proposition, "Has Congress in the exercise of its plenary power, the right to confiscate Indian property?"

That is all there would be left for the Court of Claims to determine.

Counsel contended in the court below that the passage of these two joint resolutions simply nullified any agreement to execute the trust as provided by the act of January 14th, 1889, and still so contend.

In *Lone Wolf v. Hitchcock.* 187 U.S., 553, on page 564, the then Mr. Justice, now Chief Justice, White, speaking for the Court, said:

> "Now, it is true that in decisions of this court the Indian right of occupancy of tribal lands, whether declared in a treaty or otherwise created, has been stated to be sacred, or, as sometimes expressed, as sacred as the fee of the United states in the same lands.

Johnson v. McIntosh (1823), 8 Wheat., 543, 574; *Cherokee Nation v. Georgia* (1831), Pet., 1, 48; *Worcester v. Georgia* (1832), 6 Pet., 515, 581; *United States v. Cook* (1873), 19 Wall., 591, 592; *Leavenworth, etc. R.R. Co. vs. United States* (1875), 92 U.S., 733, 755; *Beecher v. Wetherby* (1877), 95 U.S., 517, 525. But in none of these cases was there involved a controversy between Indians and the Government respecting the power of Congress to administer the property of the Indians. The questions considered in the cases referred to, which either directly or indirectly had relation to the nature of the property rights of the Indians, concerned the character and extent of such rights as respected States or individuals. In one of the cited cases it was clearly pointed out that Congress possessed a paramount power over the property of the Indians, by reason of its exercise of guardianship over their interests, and that such authority might be implied, even though opposed to the strict letter of a treaty with the Indians. Thus, in *Beecher v. Wetherby,* 95 U.S., 517, discussing the claim that there had been a prior reservation of land by treaty to the use of a certain tribe of Indians, the court said (p. 525):

> "'But the right which the Indians held was only that of occupancy. The fee was in the United States, subject to that right, and could be transferred by them whenever they chose. The grantee, it is true, would take only the naked fee, and could not disturb the occu-

pancy of the Indians; that occupancy could only be interfered with or determined by the United States. It is to be presumed that in this matter the United States would be governed by such considerations of justice as would control a Christian people in their treatment of an ignorant and dependent race. Be that as it may, the propriety or justice of their action toward the Indians with respect to their lands is a question of governmental policy, and is not a matter open to discussion in a controversy between third parties, neither of whom derives title from the Indians.'"

In the case of *Cherokee Nation v. Hitchcock*, 187 U.S., 294, "there was involved the question of the power of Congress to provide a method for determining membership in the five civilized tribes, and for ascertaining the citizenship thereof preliminary to a division of the property of the tribe among its members, and whether Congress was vested with authority to adopt measures to make the tribal property productive, and secure therefrom an income for the benefit of the tribe."

The then Mr. Justice, now Chief Justice, White rendered the opinion in that case, and on page 307 of the opinion, speaking for the Court, said:

"There is no question involved in this case as to the *taking* of property; the authority which it is proposed to exercise, by virtue of the act of 1898, has relation merely to the *control and development* of the tribal property, which still remains subject to the administrative control of the government, even though the members of the tribe have been invested with the status of citizenship under recent legislation.

"We are not concerned in this case with the question whether the act of June 28, 1898, and the proposed action thereunder, which is complained of, is or is not wise, and calculated to operate beneficially to the interests of the Cherokees. The power existing in Congress to administer upon and guard the tribal property, and the power being political and administrative in its nature, the manner of its exercise is a question within the province of the legislative branch to determine, and is not one for the courts."

(Italics ours.)

Now, in neither of these cases does this court go to the extreme of saying that Congress has the power to confiscate Indian property.

But granted, for the sake of argument, that Congress has such power; it is a power of such arbitrary character that, unless expressed in terms absolutely specific in their meaning, no Court would be warranted in holding that Congress had exercised such power.

In the instant case it seems most reasonable to appellee that this Court, construing the two joint resolutions with the jurisdictional act, must say that Congress never intended to confiscate the Mille Lac Reservation, that Congress never intended that the Chippewa Indians of Minnesota should suffer damage on account of the failure of the Government to execute the trust as provided in the act of January 14th, 1889, in reference to the Mille Lac Reservation.

Therefore, we contend that the passage of the joint resolution of December 19th, 1893, and the passage of the joint resolution of May 27th, 1898, do not indicate any intention on the part of Congress to confiscate the Mille Lac Reservation, or that in the exercise of its plenary power Congress intended to take from the Chippewas of Minnesota the value of such reservation.

XII.

UNDOUBTEDLY CONGRESS, WITH THE CONSENT OF THE INDIANS, HAD THE RIGHT TO POOL THE INTERESTS OF ALL THE CHIPPEWAS OF MINNESOTA, CLASSIFY AND SELL THEIR LANDS AND DIVIDE THE PROCEEDS AMONG THEM AS PROVIDED BY THE ACT OF JANUARY 14, 1889.

By section 7 of that act it is provided,

> "That all money accruing from the disposal of said lands in conformity with the provisions of this act shall, after deducting all the expenses of taking the census, of obtaining the cession and relinquishment, of making the removal and allotments, and completing the surveys and appraisals in this act provided, be placed in the treasury of the United States to the credit of all the Chippewa Indians in the State of Minnesota as a permanent fund, which shall draw interest at the rate of five per centum payable annually, for the period of 50 years.*** and at the expiration of said 50 years, the said permanent fund shall be divided and paid to all of said Chippewa and their issue then living, in cash, in equal shares."

At the time of the passage of the act of January 14, 1889, there were ten Indian reservations in the State of Minnesota belonging to the Chippewa Indians of that State.

As we have seen, at the time of the cession and relinquishment of the ten Chippewa Reservations to the United States under the Nelson Act there were 8,304 Chippewa Indians in the State of Minnesota; 3,002 were Chippewas of the Mississippi, 895 of the Chippewas of the Mississippi were Mille Lac Indians or members of the Mille Lac band. The Mille Lac band, therefore, comprised about one-third of the Chippewas of Mississippi and nearly one-ninth of the entire Chippewa Indians of Minnesota.

As appears from such act of January 14, 1889, the plan and scheme of the United States was to get these several bands of Chippewas of the state of Minnesota and the Chippewas of the Mississippi to live together, as far as possible upon two reservations, viz., the White Earth Reservation and the Red Lake Reservation. Hence, the peculiar provisions of the act of January 14, 1889.

But the United States did not intend to compel obedience to their scheme or plan, and so, accordingly, in section 3 of the act of January 14, 1889, as we have before stated, it was provided:

> "That any of the Indians residing on any of said Reservations may, in his discretion, take his allotment in severalty under this act on the reservation where he lives at the time of the removal herein provided for is affected, instead of being removed to and taking such allotment on White Earth Reservation."

POOLING OF INTERESTS

It was also the understanding and agreement of the United States and these several bands of Chippewas of Minnesota, including the Chippewas of the Mississippi, that each and every of the ten reservations ceded and relinquished to the United States, was ceded and relinquished in accordance with the provisions of the act of January 14, 1889, and that the provisions of that act and all of them applied to each and every one of those reservations.

As already suggested, section 1 of the act of January 14, 1889, concludes as follows:

> "And the acceptance and approval of such cession and relinquishment by the President of the United States shall be deemed full and ample proof of the assent of the Indians, and shall operate as a complete extinguishment of the Indian title without any other or further act or ceremony whatsoever *for the purpose and upon the terms in this act provided.*"

Reading the entire act, with section 7, of which part has already been quoted, it thus plainly appears, that in accordance with the agreements the several bands were each and all to pool their interests. But there were ten separate instruments of cession and relinquishment.

Referring to that point in his letter to President Harrison, under date of January 30, 1889, Secretary Noble says:

"I invite attention to the fact that the instruments presented by the Commission as the result of the negotiations, and as the evidence that the Chippewa Indians in Minnesota have given their consent in writing to the cession and relinquishment of their title and interest in and to the lands as therein set forth, comprise ten parts, marked separately as A, B, C, D, E, F, and H, G, I, K and L. These, however, in fact constitute as a whole one instrument, and the part marked C, entitled 'Signature Roll Mississippi Chippewa Indians, White Earth Reservation, Minnesota,' should be placed and considered as the first part for the reason that it is the only part that embraces the text of the act under and for the purposes of which the commission was appointed.

"This is considered necessary, in view of the fact that the act is not recited in the other parts of the instrument, but is referred to therein as follows:

"'Which said act is embraced in the foregoing instrument,' meaning evidently that part marked C, etc., as above stated.

"With this as explanation, and as a matter of record for proper understanding of the instruments, I think it would nevertheless be well for the approval of the President to be endorsed upon each of the separate parts of said instrument." (Ex. Doc., 247, pp. 11, 12.)

Accordingly, President Harrison approved each one of the ten agreements separately; but, as was well said by the Secretary of the Interior, the ten cessions and relinquishments together constitute but one agreement.

Therefore, to change any part of any of the ten agreements would be to change the entire agreement.

All the parties have consented to the pooling of their several and joint interests, why should counsel be heard to raise some objection, which some one of the parties might have raised at the outset, but which none of the parties did raise?

We have cited no authorities to sustain our contention, but we believe that Congress, in the exercise of its plenary power, made these provisions, and it is not within the power of counsel for appellant by argument only, to destroy the provisions of the act of 1889.

Inasmuch as each of the dissenting opinions makes reference to the Fond du Lac Indian case, 34 C. Cls., 426 (Rec. pp. 43, 55,), we offer the following suggestions in reference to that case.

The Fond du Lac case arose out of the following facts:

On September 30, 1854, the United States made a Treaty with the Chippewa Indians of Lake Superior and the Mississippi.

By the terms of that Treaty to the Fond du Lac band was ceded a reservation by metes and bounds, which was to contain not less than 100,000 acres of land, and which was also to include the principal settlements and buildings of the Fond du Lac band.

In 1858 a survey was made of such proposed Fond du Lac Reservation, and it was found to contain 125,294 acres.

However, after such survey of the proposed reservation was made, it was found that such reservation did not extend on the south to within several miles of the principal settlements and buildings of such Indians.

In 1859, by order of the President, another survey was made of a second reservation.

This new survey included the principal settlements and buildings of the Indians.

In the later survey the southern boundary of the reservation was extended five miles and five chains further south than in the former survey, thereby adding 41,280 acres of land on the south.

However, in the latter survey there was taken off from the west side of the former survey a strip of land containing 66,453 acres.

The land added on the south in the new survey was rolling, arable land, and very productive; while the land taken off from the west of the former survey by the new survey was low and swampy and unfit for agriculture.

The 41,280 acres of land added on the south in the later survey were equal in value to the 66,453 acres taken off on the west.

Hence, the Fond du Lac Indians lost nothing by the exchange.

At the time the later survey was made the Indians seemed satisfied.

The 66,453 acres taken off on the west by the second survey were opened to public settlement and sold.

The officers of the government understood that the Indians were satisfied with the new reservation.

From 1859 until 1880 a period of thirty years, the Fond du Lac Indians were content and occupied only the later survey.

During all this period of thirty years, the Fond du Lac Indians made no claim to the 66,453 acres taken off on the west or any part thereof.

However, when the commissioners appointed under the Act of January 14, 1889, were negotiating with the Fond du Lac band for the Fond du Lac Reservation the Fond du Lac Indians called the attention of the commissioners to the decrease in the acreage of their reservation by the later survey, and the commissioners promised to bring the same to the attention of the United States.

Accordingly, when the commissioners made their report they called the attention of the United States to the difference in area between the former and the later survey.

The result was that on June 7, 1897, Congress passes an Act authorizing the Fond du Lac band to bring a suit against the United States, in the Court of Claims, which Court was given jurisdiction:

I. To find the difference in area between the former and later survey.

II. And whether or not there had been, since such later survey, any equitable adjustment made to the Fond du Lac Indians for such difference in area, and such Act further provided that the Court in so determining: "shall also take into consideration, and make due allowance for, the fact that said Indians were given a share in the proceeds of the lands sold and disposed of under and pursuant to the provisions of the Act of January 14, 1889.

The suit was brought, and the Court of claims found, in effect, that the second reservation was equal in value to the first reservation, that is to say, that the tract of 41,280 acres added on the south was equal in value to the tract of 66,453 acres taken off on the west.

Hence, there was no equity in the claim of the Indians.

The Court of Claims also found that the Fond du Lac Indians were also permitted to participate in the proceeds of the sale of the lands of all the reservations, etc., which was also an equitable adjustment, taking into account the small area of the Fond du Lac Reservation in comparison to the west area put into the pool.

However, this last point was by no means essential to the decision. For, if the value of the tract added on the south was equal to the value of the tract taken off on the west there was no damage, and hence no equity.

On page 434 of the decision in the Fond du Lac case, Mr. Chief Justice Peelle, speaking for the Court, said:

> "The findings show that the difference 'between the area of the reservation actually set apart to said Indians and that provided to be set apart in said treaty is 25,173 acres.'
>
> "That being established, it only remains for the court, in the language of the act, 'to take into consideration and determine whether, since the date of said treaty, there has been any equitable adjustment made to said Indians, in whole or in part, for the alleged difference in area,' and in the determination of that question the act provides that 'the court shall also take into consideration and make due allowance for the fact that said Indians were given a share in the proceeds of the lands sold and disposed of under and pursuant to the provisions' of the act of January 14, 1889."
>
> "Although the original reservation was diminished 25,173 acres, it is quite evident from the findings of fact that the lands on the west,

excluded by the last survey, were of no greater value than the lands added on the south, so that in respect of the value of the original and diminished reservations there was little, if any difference."

And, on page 436, Mr. Chief Justice Peelle, speaking for the Court, said:

"It is true that such benefit results to them by reason of the mutual action of their brethren in the cession of their reservation as aforesaid, but the Congress, by the language of the act of our jurisdiction, commends us by the imperative shall, 'to take into consideration and determine whether since the date of said treaty there has been any equitable adjustment to said Indians in whole or in part for the alleged difference in area,' and further that 'the court shall also take into consideration and make due allowance for the fact that the said Indians were given a share in the proceeds of the lands sold and disposed of under and pursuant to the provisions of the Act entitled 'An act for the relief and civilization of the Chippewa Indians in the State of Minnesota,' approved January 14, 1889.

"Hence, taking into consideration the character of the lands added on the south and those excluded on the west of the original survey, by the new or Forbes survey, the court is of the opinion that there was little, if any, difference in the value of the two areas occasioned thereby."

So, after all, the real ground of the decision in the Fond du Lac case was that the difference in value between the original and diminished reservations was nothing. In other words, there was no equity in the claim of the Fond du Lac Indians.

The Fond du Lac Reservation, however, was sold and the proceeds of the sale went into the general fund for distribution. As already remarked the Mille Lac Reservation was not sold; hence, the Minnesota Indians have been deprived of the value of the Mille Lac Reservation.

We have already suggested that while there were ten instruments of cession and relinquishment, each of which was separately approved by President Harrison; yet, as stated by the Secretary of the Interior in his letter of transmittal to the President heretofore quoted from, there was only one agreement.

That one agreement was that the Chippewa Indians of Minnesota on the one part ceded and relinquished to the United States of the other part ten reservations in trust, as provided by the Nelson Act. The United States accepted the trust, and agreed to dispose of the ten reservations as provided by the Nelson Act.

That agreement required that the United States should dispose of all ten of the reservations and pay the proceeds of the sales of such reservations into the United States Treasury for distribution as provided in such act.

The agreement is not fulfilled by allowing, as suggested by counsel, the Mille Lac Indians to participate in the general distribution.

The Mille Lacs, as joint owners, with the other Chippewas of the Mississippi, of the White Earth Reservation, and, as joint owners, with the other Minnesota Chippewas, of the Red Lake Reservation, were, independently of the Mille Lac Reservation, as much entitled to participate in the general distribution as any one of the other five bands of the Chippewas of the Mississippi, or as any band of the Minnesota Chippewas. And to say now that they were paid for the relinquishment of their right of occupancy to the Mille Lac Reservation by being allowed to participate in such distribution is to say that that right of occupancy was of no value whatever. More, it is to say that in order that the Mille Lacs Indians may enjoy equal rights with the other five bands of the Chippewas of the Mississippi, they shall be required to give a bonus, viz., their rights in the Mille Lac Reservation, the *present* given to them for loyalty by the United States in 1863.

So that instead of being paid for the Mille Lac Reservation they have as yet been paid nothing, nor have the Minnesota Indians.

XIII.

THE JUDGMEN OF THE COURT OF CLAIMS SHOULD BE AFFIRMED.

Finally, the questions involved in this suit do not seem complicated, but clear and simple.

The appellee was not served with the brief of the appellant in this case until Friday morning, April 4th. Hence, we have, perhaps, repeated ourselves somewhat in our discussions and not always expressed ourselves as tersely as we should. However, we have tried, in the propositions discussed to meet all the arguments of appellant.

Counsel have in some instances stated that certain facts are conceded. We make no concession whatever outside of the facts that we have stated; and, excepting what we have admitted in our discussion, we do not in any way concede the legal proposition of appellant.

We do not think that any of the cases cited by counsel for appellant are in conflict with the contention of appellee.

On February 22, 1855, the United States entered into a treaty with the Gull Lake, Mille Lac, Sandy Lake, Pokagomin Lake, Rabbit Lake and Rice Lake bands of Indians known as the Chippewas of the Mississippi. This treaty secured to the United States a cession of all the lands belonging to the various bands of Indians mentioned in the State of Minnesota, and set apart for them specific reservations mentioned in the treaty for permanent homes. The reservations set apart for the Mille Lac Indians embraced 61,028.14 acres and was known as the Mille Lac Reservation.

During the year 1862 the Mille Lac band of Chippewas of the Mississippi rendered a great service to the United States by preventing the uprising of the other bands of the Chippewas of the Mississippi and their joining with the Sioux in an Indian war for the massacre of the white people in Minnesota.

On March 11, 1863, the United States persuaded the Chippewas of the Mississippi to enter into another treaty, and by the terms of that treaty five of the reservations which were ceded to the Chippewas of the Mississippi by the treaty of 1855 were ceded back to the United States and there was reserved by the Chippewas of the Mississippi, the United States consenting, the Mille Lac Reservation to the Mille Lac band of Indians to be occupied by them so long as they should not in any manner interfere with the persons or property of the whites.

This reserving of the Mille Lac Reservation to the Mille Lacs was in a proviso to article 12 of such treaty, and the United States allowed or consented to such reservation in consideration of the patriotic conduct of the Mille Lac band in so preventing an Indian war, and the further condition that they should continue loyal to the Government by not interfering with the persons or property of the whites.

The Mille Lac band of Indians understood and believed that the proviso to article 12 secured to them the Mille Lac Reservation for a permanent home, and they continued to occupy such reservation in that belief, giving notice to the whole world that they were the owners of such reservation, until the act of January 14, 1889, was passed. Then the commissioners appointed by the President to secure the cession and relinquishment of all the reservations of the Chippewas of Minnesota went to their reservation, and, after several meetings in council with the head men and members of the Mille Lac band, the Mille Lac band finally relinquished to the United States the Mille Lac Reservation, as they believed and understood, and as they were informed by the commissioners under and in accordance with the provisions of the act of January 14, 1889.

The United States accepted such relinquishment under such act; and the cession and relinquishment of the Mille Lac band was approved by President Harrison.

By the act of January 14, 1889, these various Indian Reservations were ceded and relinquished to the United States in trust, according to the provisions of the act of January 14, 1889.

In reference to the Mille Lac Reservation the Government failed to execute the trust and finally placed itself in a condition where it was impossible to fulfill the trust, and, thereafter and on February 15, 1909, Congress passed the jurisdictional act giving to the Court of Claims jurisdiction to hear and determine a suit or suits to be brought by and on behalf of the Mille Lac band of Chippewa Indians of the state of Minnesota against the United States on account of losses sustained by them or the Chippewas of Minnesota by reason of the opening of the Mille Lac Reservation in the state of Minnesota, embracing about 61,000 acres of land, to public settlement under the general land laws of the United States.

After due consideration the Court of Claims have rendered the judgment in this case, and, we believe because of the premises, that judgment of the Court of Claims should be affirmed.

Respectfully submitted.

>GEORGE B. EDGERTON,
>*Attorney for Appellee.*
>F.W.HOUGHTON,
>HARVEY S. CLAPP,
>DANIEL B. HENDERSON,
>*Of Counsel for Appellee.*

EXHIBIT "A."

RED LAKE AND PEMBINA BANDS

	TOTAL	ADULTS		MINORS		ORPHANS	
		MALE	FEMALE	MALE	FEMALE	MALE	FEMALE
Red Lake	1168	303	359	237	247	15	7
Pembina	218	83	63	38	33	0	1
Total	1386	386	422	275	280	1	8

MISSISSIPPI BANDS

	TOTAL	ADULTS		MINORS		ORPHANS	
		MALE	FEMALE	MALE	FEMALE	MALE	FEMALE
White Earth	1169	284	279	300	292	9	5
Gull lake and scattering	277	61	75	49	89	1	2
White Oak Point	661	176	211	129	114	15	16
Mille Lac	895	213	289	180	204	6	3
Total	3002	734	854	658	699	31	26

PILLAGER AND LAKE WINNIBIGOSHISH BANDS

	TOTAL	ADULTS		MINORS		ORPHANS	
		MALE	FEMALE	MALE	FEMALE	MALE	FEMALE
Leech Lake	1141	324	348	239	215	8	7
Otter Lake	657	164	180	154	158	1	
Cass Lake	241	67	71	53	43	1	6
Lake Winnibigoshish	169	45	50	34	33	3	4
Total	2208	600	649	480	449	12	18

GRAND PORTAGE, BOISE FORTE AND FOND DU LAC BANDS

	TOTAL	ADULTS		MINORS		ORPHANS	
		MALE	FEMALE	MALE	FEMALE	MALE	FEMALE
Grand Portage	294	73	85	60	71	2	3
Bois Forte	743	228	224	153	132	3	3
Fond du Lac	671	157	187	168	140	9	10
Total	1708	458	496	381	343	14	16

Supreme Court of the United States

OCTOBER TERM 1912

No. 736

THE UNITED STATES, Appellant

vs.

THE MILLE LACS BAND OF CHIPPEWA INDIANS

IN THE STATE OF MINNESOTA

———————————

Appeal from the Court of Claims

BRIEF OF C.F. RICHARDSON

For the Respondents

The Jurisdictional Act

The Act conferring jurisdiction upon the courts "to hear and determine" this cause, if it did not indeed "create a claim," was at least a recognition of the existence of a cause. The language of the statute was similar to that employed in numbers of related instances where Congress, appreciating its lack of facilities for hearing a case on its merits, delegated its powers to the judiciary, and vested the courts with all necessary authority to perform this duty and to pronounce final judgment. Where the Court of Claims has validated claims under like authority, we find no record of the denial of this power.

The Indian Affairs Committee of the House of Representatives, in its very comprehensive report upon the bill (H.R. 24054) which was afterward enacted into the statute in question, said:

> "This bill is for the purpose of allowing the Mille Lac Indians in Minnesota to procure from the Court of Claims a decision as to their rights and equities in and to the Mille Lac Reservation, or to indemnify for losses sustained by them on account of the opening of the Mille Lac Reservation to public settlement under the general land laws of the United States.
>
> The evidence in support of the bill seems to show that the Mille Lac Reservation has been added to the public domain and entered under the homestead laws, but fails to show in terms that any adequate compensation has been given or agreed upon for property so taken, notwithstanding the equitable doctrine which forbids a guardian or trustee to take a profit from the ward or beneficiary.
>
> The committee believe that an opportunity should be given these Indians to show what rights, if any, remain to them under treaties and agreements heretofore made with the Government, and therefore recommend the passage of the said bill without amendment."

This report was agreed to only after a long and careful consideration of the matter by the committee, which included a hearing at which several Mille Lac chiefs related their grievances.

COURTS MAY REVIEW

It is contended by the opposing counsel that the courts have no jurisdiction to review the exercise of the plenary power of Congress in dealing with the tribal property of tribal Indians. This was true of the cases cited by counsel; but in this case

Congress has directed that its plenary power shall be reviewed. Congress has paused and considered, and has admitted that it may have violated the treaties and abused its own plenary power. Congress has virtually said "if we were guilty of an injustice to the Mille Lac Indians when we ratified the unauthorized acts of the land department in accepting filings on the reservation, we want to make amends." What Congress did was to refer the matter to the judiciary, with full legal and equitable jurisdiction to investigate and say what rights the Mille Lac Indians had under the treaties, what rights had been impaired and what these rights were worth. And Congress went still further when it directed the courts to remedy the error found, by rendering a final judgment therefor. The question of jurisdiction is amply provided for in the Act of February 15, 1909, by direction of which this cause was initiated, and the statute speaks for itself.

THE TREATIES AND AGREEMENTS.

The laws and treaties to be considered in this case are but four — three treaties and one statute, the latter of which was agreed to by the Indians and was given the appearance of a treaty. These have been made to appear very formidable, and have been misconstrued and tortured into the very opposite of their intent. The treaty of February 22, 1855 (10 S.L. 1165) ceded to the Government millions of acres, reserving, among other reservations, the Mille Lac Reservation now at bar. The treaty of March 11, 1863 (12 S.L. 1249) divested the other Indians, the Chippewas of Minnesota, of their common share in the ownership of the Mille Lac Reservation, but did not change the status of those for whom it was originally reserved, the Mille Lac Indians. The treaty of May 7, 1864 (13 S.L. 693) practically reiterated the preceding treaty. The Act of January 14, 1889 (25 S.L. 642) provided for the opening and sale of various Chippewa Reservations in Minnesota, and the Mille Lac Indians joined in it because of their common interest in all the tribal lands of said Chippewas in general, but upon the understanding that their consent to this Act should not invalidate any rights which they had in and to the Mille Lac Reservation.

C. E. RICHARDSON,
Of Counsel for Respondents.

No. 736

In the Supreme Court of the United States
October Term, 1912

The United States, Appellant

Vs.

The Mille Lac Band of Chippewa Indians in the State of Minnesota

APPEAL FROM THE COURT OF CLAIMS

BRIEF FOR THE UNITED STATES

INDEX.

	Pages
STATEMENT	1–26
Jurisdictional Act, Feb. 15, 1909 (35 Stat., 619)	1
THE QUESTIONS INVOLVED	2–3
THE TREATIES—	
Of July 29, 1837 (7 Stat., 536)	4
Of Sept. 30, 1854 (10 Stat., 1109)	4
Of Feb. 22, 1855 (10 Stat., 1165)	4
Of March 11, 1863 (12 Stat., 1249)	5
Of May 7, 1864 (13 Stat., 693)	5–6
Of March 19, 1867 (16 Stat., 719)	7
THE GOOD CONDUCT OF THE INDIANS	8–9
REMOVAL OF THE INDIANS FROM MILLE LAC	9–10
DEPARTMENTAL DECISIONS AND ACTS OF CONGRESS	10–26
Lands opened to settlement in 1871	10–11–37
Secretary Chandler's decision, appeal of Folsom, March 1, 1877 (Appendix A)	11–12–37
Secretary Schurz's decision, cancelling entries	13–38
Secretary Teller's decision, May 10, 1882, reinstating entries (Appendix C)	13–38
Secretary Teller's decision, August 7, 1882	13
Appropriation Act, July 4, 1884 (23 Stat., 78)	14
5 Land Decision, 541 (Robert Lowe)	14
5 Land Decision, 102 (State of Minnesota)	15
Appropriation act, May 15, 1886 (24 Stat., 44)	15
Secretary Lamar's decision, Oct. 23, 1886, (Appendix D)	16
Nelson Act of January 14, 1889 (25 Stat., 642)	16
Amendment of June 27, 1902 (32 Stat., 400)	16–19
Cession to United States by Mille Lac Band of all title, etc. to four townships of White Earth Reservation, etc.	21

8 Land Decision, 409, treating act of July 4, 1884, as yet in force 21

10 Land Decision, 3, recalling above decision... 21–22

12 Land Decision, 52 (Secretary Noble holding that act of 1889 was
    further legislation required by act of 1884 22

Secretary Noble further held, right given any Indian by sec. 3,

act of 1889, to make allotment on reservation on which he resided
    did not apply to Mille Lac 23

Secretary Noble, Jan. 21, 1891, reaffirms his decision holding lands
    should be disposed of as other public lands (Appendix E) 24

Secretary Noble, Sept. 3, 1891 (13 Land Decision, 230) held that
    railroad company was not authorized prior to act of 1889 to make
    lieu selections on Mille Lac Reservation 24

Secretary Noble, April 22, 1892 (14 L.D. 497), wrote Commissioner
    of General Land Office, decision in *Northern Pacific R.R. Co. v. Walters*
    was to be followed 24

Secretary's first ruling adopted as correct by Congress, act of
    Dec. 19, 1893 (28 Stat., 576) 24–25

Resolution, May 27, 1898 (30 Stat., 745).. 25–26

Indian appropriation act, May 27, 1902 (32 Stat., 268), providing
    for payment to Indians of $40,000 for improvements made by
    them on Mille Lac Reservation, etc... 26

Agreement, Aug. 30, 1902, by which Mille Lac Indians still residing
    on former Mille Lac Reservation were to remove to White Earth
    Reservation, etc. 27

ASSIGNMENT OF ERRORS 28–29

ARGUMENT 30–54

I. The jurisdictional act creates no liability, but simply furnishes a forum for the adjudication of the claim.

Stewart v. United States, 206 U.S. 185, 194 30

The Sac & Fox Indians, 220 U.S. 481, 489 30

Court of Claims in error in holding in effect act of 1909, is a
    legislative decision that something is due Indians..................................... 30

Jurisdictional act not intended to strip Government of all legal
    and equitable defenses 30

(a) Congress has plenary power and control over Indians 30
   Cherokee Nation v. Hitchcock, 187 U.S. 294 30
   Lone Wolf v. Hitchcock, 187 U.S. 565 30
   Congress did not intend by act of 1909 to authorize courts to inquire into justice and fairness of dealings with Indians...... 30–31
   United States v. Choctaw and Chickasaw Nations, 179 U.S., 494, 531–535 31
   United States v. Old Settlers, 148 U.S., 427, 466 31
   Congress subsequent to 1870 (when land was first opened to settlement) ratified all prior entries and opened unoccupied land to settlement 32
   Joint resolution, Dec. 19, 1893 (28 Stat., 576), confirmed all entries made on Mille Lac in 1891 and 1892 32
   Joint resolution, May 27, 1898 (30 Stat., 745), declares land within Mille Lac Reservation subject to entry, confirming all entries theretofore made 32

(b) If legislation, above mentioned, be not conclusive, then question before court is whether United States by opening Mille Lac tract, infringed legal rights of Indians 32

II. **Mille Lac Reservation was ceded to United States by entries of 1863 and 1864, and became public land open to settlement. Mille Lac Band acquired no title thereto; simply permitted to remain thereon temporarily 33**

   Claim of Indians is based upon proviso of article 12 of treaty, and correctness of above proposition depends upon proper construction of that proviso 33
   By treaty of 1855, nine tracts, under supervision of one agent, had been set apart for Indians; and settlers were approaching from south.. 33
   Commissioner of Indian Affairs, Dole, Sept. 14, 1862, by letter to Gov. Ramsey, of Minnesota, shows need for Indians' removal 33
   Report, Secty. of Interior, 1862, pp. 227, 228 34
   Objects of treaty are apparent from its provisions 4
   Six reservations occupied by Mississippi Bands were ceded to United States (art. 1), for which larger reservation was created near those occupied by Pillager and Lake Winnibigoshish Bands (art. 2); and large payments

were made to Indians and annuities were extended (art. 3); United States agreed to prepare new lands for cultivation, etc. (art. 4); large sums were to be expended for implements and animals (art. 5); sawmill to be built, roads established, etc. (art. 6) 34–35

Absolute cession of land to United States and intention to remove Mille Lac Band to new reservation, not destroyed by proviso 35

Construction contended for by claimants would defeat objects of treaty... 36

Treaty was a purchase from Indians of title to six ceded reservations; land so purchased became public land open to settlement 36

Reservation was so regarded by officers of Interior Department 37

Land surveyed in 1870 and settlements began in 1871; shortly thereafter the then Secty. of Interior suspended further entries.. 37

Secty. Chandler's decision on appeal of Folsom in 1877, sustaining Government's contention 37

Reinstatement of all entries by Secty. Teller in 1882............................ 38

Congress suspends, in 1884, all entries pending further legislation ... 38

Erroneous statements in majority opinion, relative to decisions of secretaries Schurz and Teller... 38, 39

Decision of Secty. Lamar in 1866 39

Construction given to treaty by Interior Dept. will be given great weight by courts, and evidently was recognized by majority of Indians, etc. 9

Upon full consideration of the foregoing, follows that rights of Indians were not infringed.. 40

III. The Mille Lac Band abandoned any claim to reservation by voluntary removal therefrom.

Prior to 1899, majority of Mille Lac Band had voluntarily removed to White Earth Reservation; thereby claim of whole band to reservation was abandoned 40

United States deals with tribes, not individual Indians...................... 40

Blackfeather v. United States, 190 U.S., 368, 377................................ 40

IV. By accepting conditions and benefits of acts of 1889 and 1902, Indians abandoned all claim to Mille Lac tract.. 41

 (a) Nelson Act of 1889 was final settlement with all Minnesota Chippewas. Mille Lac Band accepted its terms, agreeing to move to White Earth, and thereby ended all right of occupancy of Mille Lac tract..41

  Situation of Mille Lac Band and of other Indians at the time of the passage of the Nelson Act, and offer of the United States to the Indians under such act 41–42

  Acceptance of such offer by Mille Lac Band and other Indians 42

  When Indians voluntarily agreed to remove and accept benefits of Nelson Act , proviso of article 12 was at an end and there arose a compulsion to remove 42

  Therefore there was no necessity for cession of of the old reservation, etc... 43

  Lands on Mille Lac tract were not to be sold under Nelson Act; only lands which were *ceded* to United States were to be sold..... 43

  14 Land Decision, 497 43

  Congress by resolutions of 1893 and 1898 declared that entries made on this land were valid and land was open to settlement... 44

  Report of Committee on Indian Affairs of House of Representatives on resolution of Dec. 19, 1893 44

  Cong. Rec. vol. 26, pt. 1, pp. 35, 36: 53d Cong., 2d sess.................. 44

  United States v. Binns, 194 U.S. 486 44

  Report of Secty. of Interior, on resolution of May 27, 1898, from which appears Congress did not recognize any rights of Mille Lac Indians in old reservation 44

  Cong. Rec., vol. 31, pt. 5, p. 4781; 55th Cong., 2d sess..................... 45

  Therefore, rights of Indians were not violated by opening of Mille Lac tract to settlement, and there can be no recovery......... 45

  No injustice done Indians under this construction............................ 45

  Result of census taken under act 45

  Quantity of land ceded to Government, etc....................................... 46

  Result to Chippewas of agreements under act 46

  Remarkable result of judgment of Court of Claims........................... 46

  Government derived no pecuniary benefit from Cession and settlement of Mille Lac Reservation 46–47

(b) *The act of 1902.*

Indians abandoned last vestige of claim to any part of Mille Lac tract by accepting conditions and benefits of act of May, 1902 (32 Stat., 268). 47–48

V. **If Mille Lac Reservation be considered one of the reservations ceded by Indians under Nelson Act of 1889, their measure of damages is found in that statute. Section 6 excludes from sale under that act every tract on which there was a subsisting valid preemption or homestead entry. Such subsisting entries covered over 55,000 acres of Mille Lac tract; only remaining 5,000 acres could therefore be sold under Nelson Act.**

Assuming that Mille Lac tract should be treated as a reservation under Nelson Act, judgment of Court of Claims overlooks fact that 55,000 acres had been filed upon and that land, under provision of sec. 6, can not be sold for benefit of Indians.. 49–50

12 Land Decision, 54 50

United States v. Schurz, 102 U.S., 378 50

Will be contended for Indians that Mille Lac tract was an Indian reservation on which, under the law, entries could not be made, etc. 50

Sec. 2257, R.S., U.S 50

But such contention goes too far, for it nullifies the entire proviso 50

American Security & Trust Co. v. D.C., U.S., 491 51

United States v. Hartwell, 6 Wall., 396 51

Congress by this proviso recognized and preserved all subsisting entries, etc. 51

These entries were known both to Congress and to the Indians 51

Same conclusion reached by another line of argument 51

Meaning of term allowance as here used 51

Under regulations and decisions in force in Department of Interior, all entries made in 1871 and 1872, and between 1977 and 1884, were valid subsisting entries at the time of passage of Nelson Act 52

Such was conclusion of Secretary Noble in the Walters case (12 L.D., 52) 52

Follows that rights of Indians were not infringed by perfection of entries subsisting in 1889; their damages are therefore confined to value of lands not then entered upon 53

If such construction be correct, case must be remanded with directions to ascertain value of portion of reservation which should have been sold under Nelson Act 53

VI. If the Nelson Act be inapplicable, the loss sustained by the Indians is merely the value of their right of occupancy, and not the fee-simple value of the land.

Under the treaty of 1864, Mille Lac Band had mere right of occupancy during good behavior, etc............................. 53

Was an uncertain tenure, subject to determination upon violation of the condition, and did not give Indians right to cut timber, except for domestic use, etc............. 54

Act Feb. 16, 1889 (25 Stat., 673; 3 Fed. Stat. Ann., 377) 54

United States v. Cook, 19 Wall., 591 54

CONCLUSION 54
Judgment should be reversed, with directions to dismiss petition 54

APPENDICES 55–69

MISCELLANEOUS REPORTS, HOUSE DOCUMENTS, ETC.

13 Stat., 541, 543, 560, 561 9

14 Stat., 273, 496 9

15 Stat., 202 9

16 Stat., 19, 339, 549 9

17 Stat., 169, 443 9

24 Stat., 44 10

H.R. Doc. 1388. 60th Cong., 1st sess., pp. 6-8-12-13 10-11-12

H.R. Doc. No. 287, 51st Cong., 1st sess. 10

H.R. 48th Cong., vol. 199; Cong. Rec., vol. 15, pt. 6, p. 5800 14

H.R. Doc. 247, 51st Cong., 1st sess., pp. 9, 15, 27 20

Report of Commissioners, Senate Ex. Doc. 115, 49th Cong., 2d sess., p. 19 ... 10

Reports of Secty. Of Interior for 1862 and 1863, vol. , pp. 223 to 231 9

Heard's History of the Sioux War and Massacres, p. 239 9

In the Supreme Court of the United States

October Term, 1912

The United States, Appellant.

v.

*The Mille Lac Band of Chippewa Indians
In the State of Minnesota*

No. 736

Appeal from the Court of Claims

BRIEF FOR THE UNITED STATES

STATEMENT.

This appeal is from a judgment of the Court of Claims rendered in favor of the Chippewa Indians of Minnesota for $827,580.72.

Jurisdiction was conferred on the Court of Claims by the act of February 15, 1909 (35 Stat., 619) which provides:

That the court of Claims be, and it is hereby, given jurisdiction to hear and determine a suit or suits to be brought by and on behalf of the Mille Lac Band of Chippewa Indians in the State of Minnesota against the United States on account of losses sustained by them or the Chippewas of Minnesota by reason of the opening of the Mille Lac Reservation in the State of Minnesota, embracing about sixty-one thousand acres of land, to public settlement under the general land laws of the United States; and from any final judgment or decree of the Court of Claims either party shall have the right to appeal to the Supreme court of the United States.

While the judgment in this case is in favor of the Minnesota Chippewas, the petition was filed and the claim is asserted by only the Mille Lac Band of those Indians. In their petition it is alleged that by virtue of certain treaties between the United States and the Indians, the Mille Lac Band in 1864 became vested with the Indian title to a tract of land in Minnesota called the Mille Lac Reservation, and that thereafter the United States, in violation of the rights of the Indians, opened the tract to settlement as public land, whereby the Indians suffered great damage. The United States contended that the Indians had no such title, and that the land had been opened in strict conformity to law. The court took the view advanced by the Indians, and entered judgment in the amount stated. The decision was by a bare majority of the court, and separate dissenting opinions were filed by the Chief Justice (R., 41) and Judge Howry (R., 45).

THE QUESTIONS INVOLVED.

The case involves the title of the Indians to the Mille Lac Reservation, which was created by treaty of 1855.

By the treaties of 1863 and 1864 the Indians ceded the reservation to the United States, and a new reservation was provided for their occupancy; these treaties contained a proviso (in article 12) that the Mille Lac Indians should not be compelled to remove — so long as they shall not in any way interfere with or in any manner molest the persons or property of the whites.

The Mille Lac Reservation was opened to settlement as public land in 1871, and by 1889 nine-tenths of it had been entered; by joint resolutions of 1893 and 1898 these entries were confirmed and the entire tract was declared open to settlement.

The Nelson Act of 1889, and a subsequent act of 1902, offered gratuities to the Indians if they would remove to the other reservation, and the provisions of both acts were accepted by the Indians.

On these facts, more fully stated hereafter, the questions are –

Did the Indians by the proviso above quoted acquire any such title to the Mille Lac Reservation as prevented its settlement as public lands?

If so, did they surrender that title by voluntary removal, or by accepting the benefits of the Nelson Act or the act of 1902?

May the court go behind the confirmatory resolutions of 1893 and 1898?

If any right of the Indians was violated, what losses did they suffer?

THE TREATIES.

The Mille Lac Reservation, as appears from the map attached to this brief, covered three fractional townships on the southern border of Mille Lac Lake, as well as several islands therein. This land was ceded to the United States by treaty of July 29, 1837 (7 Stat., 536), with the Chippewa Indians, who at that time occupied the northern part of Minnesota.

By treaty of September 30, 1854 (10 Stat., 1109), the Chippewa Indians of Lake Superior, and of Mississippi, partitioned the lands theretofore occupied in common, and the Lake Superiors ceded to the United States the lands bordering Lake Superior, except certain tracts which were reserved for occupancy by the several bands. These tracts subsequently became known as reservations and are shown on the map as the Grand Portage, Fond du Lac, Bois Forte, and Deer Creek Reservations.

By treaty of February 22, 1855 (10 Stat., 1165), the Mississippi, Pillager and Lake Winnibigoshish Bands of Chippewa Indians, then occupying the land west of that ceded by the Lake Superior Chippewas, ceded their lands to the United States.

By article 2 of the treaty there was reserved and set apart a sufficient quantity of land for the permanent homes of the Indians. For the Mississippi Bands there were set apart six tracts which subsequently became known as the Mille Lac, Rabbit Lake, Gull Lake, Pokagomin Lake, Sandy Lake, and Rice Lake Reservations.

The Mille Lac tract, as before stated, was set apart out of lands ceded in 1837; the other five tracts were in the southern portion of the land ceded by the present treaty. All six tracts are shown in red on the map. For the Pillager and Lake Winnibigoshish Bands three other tracts were reserved, and these are in the center of the ceded land and shown on the map (in red) as adjoining Leech Lake, Cass Lake, and Winnibigoshish Lake.

It is to be noted that in the case of this treaty, the title to the reserved tracts was held in common, while in the treaty with the Lake Superiors each band had a separate title to its reservation.

The other provisions of the treaty clearly show that Congress intended the Indians to settle upon the reserved tracts and turn to agricultural pursuits. For instance, in article 4, the Government promised to have plowed and prepared for cultivation suitable fields on each reservation. Large sums of money in cash, as well as in annuities for twenty years, were to be paid by the United States in full compensation for the ceded land.

Upon the execution of this treaty the bands signing it were settled upon nine small and widely separated tracts, with but one agent to care for them. The arrangement evidently was not satisfactory, and on March 11, 1863 (12 Stat., 1249), a new treaty was signed by the same bands. This treaty was superseded by another signed May 7, 1864 (13 Stat., 693), which, except in matters unimportant here, is in substance the same. The treaty of 1864 will be the one discussed in the brief.

By article 1 of this treaty the Mississippi Bands ceded absolutely to the United States the six tracts theretofore set apart for them.

In consideration of this cession the United States agreed to set apart for the future home of the Mississippi Chippewas one single reservation, which is described by boundaries and contains a much greater area than the six ceded tracts, and which adjoins and surrounds the three reservations of the Pillager and Lake Winnibigoshish Bands, and to this new reservation all the Indians were to remove.

By article 3 the United States extended the present annuities of the Indians for a period of 10 years, and made large cash payments to them.

By article 4 the United States agreed to make clearings on the new tract for each band and to build a house for each chief; for the Mille Lac Band 70 acres were to be cleared.

By article 5 the United States was to furnish the Indians oxen and agricultural implements and to provide carpenters, farm laborers, and a physician.

By article 6 the United States was to build a sawmill and to contribute $1,000 annually towards its support; to build a road to the new agency, and to expend $25,000 for agency buildings on the new reservation for the common use of the parties to the treaty and of the Red Lake and Pembina Bands.

By article 12 it was provided that it should not be obligatory upon the Indians to remove from their present reservations until the United States had first complied with the provisions of articles 4 and 6, at which time the United States was to furnish them with transportation and subsistence at their new homes and subsistence for six months thereafter. This article concluded with the following proviso (and upon this the present claim of the Indians is based):

That, owing to the heretofore good conduct of the Mille Lac Indians they shall not be compelled to remove so long as they shall not in any way interfere with or in any manner molest the persons or property of the whites. (13 Stat., 695.)

By article 14 it was distinctly understood that the clearing and breaking of land for the Chippewas of the Mississippi provided in the fourth article of the treaty should be in lieu of all former obligations for breaking lands for these bands, and that the treaty was in lieu of the aforesaid treaty of 1863.

In the Senate, article 12 was, at the instance of the Indians, amended to provide that the members of the tribe residing on Sandy Lake Reservation should not be removed until the President should so direct. (Ib., 696.)

It is conceded in this case that the United States complied with articles 4 and 6 of this treaty.

On March 19, 1867, there was concluded another treaty between the United States and the Chippewa Indians of the Mississippi (16 Stat., 719), the preamble of which recited that a part of the reservation created by the treaty of 1864 was not adapted for agricultural purposes; therefore the Indians ceded to the United States all of said reservation, except the tract therein described by boundaries, and which is shown (in yellow) on the map.

In order to provide a suitable farming region for the Indians, by article 2 there was set apart an additional tract of land to be located in a form as nearly square as possible, which was to include White Earth Lake and Rice Lake and to contain 36 townships of land and to one or the other of these reservations the Indians were to remove. This reservation was subsequently called the White Earth Reservation, and is so marked and shown in yellow on the map.

In further consideration of the cession, the United States agreed to appropriate $46,500 for schools and the erection of houses for the Indians who should move to the new reservation, and for the purchase of stock, provisions, agricultural implements, medicine, clothing, etc.

THE GOOD CONDUCT OF THE INDIANS.

The claim of the Indians is that the proviso of article 12 of the treaty of 1864 gave them the absolute title to the Mille Lac Reservation.

They lay great stress upon the "heretofore good conduct" which they assert was the consideration for the grant to them. The Court of Claims in Finding 3, after calling attention to an uprising of the Sioux in 1862, and the fact that certain of the Chippewa Bands desired to join in the outbreak, finds that the Mille Lac Band went to the assistance of the United States forts, and by demonstrations of loyalty to the Government prevented the other members of the Chippewa Bands from joining in the uprising, and this the court said was the good conduct mentioned in the treaty.

While the question is probably not of any great importance, the Government contends that the real reason which prevented the Chippewas joining the uprising was the hereditary enmity between them and the Sioux and the promises of the Commissioner of Indian Affairs to have their wrongs inquired into. This contention is established by the reports of the Secretary of the Interior for 1862 and 1863, volume 2, pages 223 to 231, and by Heard's History of the Sioux War and Massacres, page 239, which documents are open to this court for consideration.

Judge Howry, in his dissenting opinion (R., p. 48), states the substance of the Secretary's report.

In determining the true construction of the proviso relied upon, considerable weight will be given to the subsequent acts of the Government officers and of the Indians.

REMOVAL FROM MILLE LAC.

Appropriations were made annually for removal and subsistence of the Mississippi Chippewas from 1865 to 1873. (13 Stat., 541, 543, 460, 561: 14 Stat., 273, 496; 15 Stat., 202; 15 Stat., 19, 339, 549; 17 Stat., 169, 443).

Before 1872, twenty-five members of the Mille Lac Band had removed to the White Earth Reservation, and by May 10, 1882, about 500 Indians remained on Mille Lac (H.R. Doc. 1388, 60th Cong., 1st sess., p. 8; Rec., 53, Appendix c).

According to the report of the commissioners appointed under the act of May 18, 1886 (24 Stat., 44), to negotiate with the Chippewa Indians for the modification of existing treaties and changes of reservations, there were on December 1, 1886, not more than 200 Indians remaining on the Mille Lac tract; few of them were actually living on that reservation, but the majority were scattered throughout the country south of it; and with the exception of three or four shanties, there was not a house on the reservation; these remnants of the bands were living, summer and winter, in birch-bark wigwams, and the children and women were in a state of barbarism. (R., 49, 53; Report of Commissioners, Senate Executive Doc. 115, 49th Cong., 2d sess., p. 19.)

A census taken in the summer of 1889 showed but 895 Mille Lac Indians, and while that census does not show where they were located, evidently most of them were on the White Earth Reservation. (H.R. Doc. No. 247, 51st Cong., 1st sess., 9 R. 50.)

DEPARTMENTAL DECISIONS AND ACTS OF CONGRESS

Between 1879 and 1884 nine-tenths of the Mille Lac Reservation was settled upon or preempted by the whites.

The public surveys of this reservation were completed in 1870. (H.R. Rep. 1388, p. 6.) Between May and August, 1871, preemption entries aggregating 11,026.42 acres were located on the former Mille Lac Reservation, and during the same months 117 declaratory statements were filed covering several thousand additional acres. (Finding VIII, R. 13.)

On August 22, 1871, the Commissioner of Indian Affairs, learning of this fact, wrote the Secretary of the Interior that in his opinion it would be improper to permit white settlers to go upon the reservation while the Indians remained. Thereupon on September 1, 1871, the General Land Office instructed the local land officers at Taylors Falls, Minn., in which district the reservation lay, to give public notice that settlements on the reservation were illegal, and would not be recognized. (H.R. Rep. 1388, 60th Cong., 1st sess., pp. 6 — 12.)

By letter of January 24, 1872, of the General Land Office, all such entries on land in said reservation were declared cancelled, and the local land officers directed to make proper entry on their records, and to notify the proper parties thereof. (Ib., p. 12, Rec., p. 14.)

Subsequently, one Frank W. Folsom appealed to the Secretary of the Interior from the decision rejecting his application. Secretary Chandler on March 1, 1877, held that the proviso to Article XII of the treaty of 1864 did not exclude the lands of Mille Lac Reservation from sale and disposal by the United States under the General Land Office, but because there was no appropriation available for the immediate removal of the Mille Lac Indians, and solely as a matter of expediency, directed that the execution of his decision be suspended and that no filings of entries upon said lands be allowed until the close of the next session of Congress. (H.R. Rep. 1388, p. 13, and Rec., p. 14.) The Secretary's decision is Appendix A to this brief.

Instructions in accordance with this decision were issued to the local land officers at Taylors Falls on March 15, 1877. (H.R. Rep. 1388, p. 13.)

The session of Congress in question adjourned about June 20, 1878. Secretary Schurz, who had succeeded Mr. Chandler, on June 21, directed, in a letter to the Land Office, that all claims on any of said lands subject to entry should remain in *statu quo*, and ordered the local land officers to allow no entries upon any of said land until the result of the action of Congress in relation to the right of the Indians to occupy the reservation was determined. Copies of this letter were sent to the district land officers on June 28, 1878. (Ib., 13.)

The last session of the Forty-ninth Congress adjourned in March, 1879, without passing pending bills relating to these Indians. In the meantime 285 soldiers' homestead entries, embracing over 23,000 acres in area, had accumulated at the local land office. The officers there assumed that the instructions for the suspension of these entries terminated with the expiration of Congress, and on March 12, 1879, allowed the applications, some of which had been pending nearly four years. (H.R. Rep. 1388, pp. 13, 14.)

On May 21, 1879, Secretary Schurz (whose letter is filed herewith as Appendix B) directed that these entries be cancelled because made in violation of departmental instructions.

May 10, 1882, Secretary Teller, who had succeeded Mr. Schurz, wrote to the Commissioner of Indian Affairs, adopting the views of Mr. Chandler, and holding that the so-called Mille Lac Reservation was public land open to homestead and preemption claims. Copy of this opinion is attached hereto as Appendix "C." (R., 14.)

On August 7, 1882, the Commissioner of the Land Office wrote the Secretary of the Interior asking for specific instructions upon the cancelled entries, and on the same day Secretary Teller replied:

I want all the entries heretofore canceled in the so-called Mille Lac Reservation reinstated for an examination as to their *bona fide* character, for if made in good faith the canceling of such entries was without authority of law, and in derogation of the rights of the parties making such entries. It is necessary, to save the rights of such persons and prevent a conflict with others, to reinstate such entries, and, therefore, this ought to be done at once. (H.R. 1388, p. 15.)

In the last-mentioned report is an abstract of another letter of Secretary Teller, dated February 13, 1883, to the Commissioner of the Land Office, stating that he had previously held that there was no reservation, and that the Mille Lac land was public land (ib., p. 15).

The cancelled entries were reinstated by order of the Land Office, and in accordance with the principle of the ruling on which that order was based the local land officers thereafter permitted the filing of new claims, so that by March 31, 1884, out of 61,028.14 acres contained in the reservation, 55,976.42 acres had been filed upon under the general land laws of the United States, of which 7,792.16 acres had gone patent, leaving only 5,051.72 acres open at that time to settlement. (Rec., p. 14; Appendix C; 12 Land Dec. 54, Walters et al.)

At this juncture the following paragraph was included in the Indian appropriation act of July 4, 1884 (23 Stat., 78):

That the lands acquired from the White Oak Point and Mille Lac Bands of Chippewa Indians on the White Earth Reservation, in Minnesota, by the treaty proclaimed March twentieth, eighteen hundred and sixty-five, shall not be patented or disposed of in any manner until further legislation by Congress.

The words "on the White Earth Reservation" are repugnant, and the act should be read with them eliminated. (5 Land Dec., 541.) This paragraph originally contained an appropriation for the removal of the White Point and Mille Lac Indians "on the White Earth Reservation," and these words were inadvertently left in the paragraph as passed. (H.R., 48th Cong., vol. 15, pt. 6, p. 5800.)

As said by Judge Howry, the appropriation was no doubt omitted for the reason that the great majority of the Indians had already removed to the White Earth Reservation. (R., 50.)

On August 21, 1886, the State of Minnesota having appealed from a decision of the Commissioner of the Land Office rejecting the claim of the State under the swamp land grant to certain lands in the Mille Lac Reservation, Secretary Lamar affirmed the decision on the ground that the department had no authority to dispose of the lands because of the prohibition of the act of July 4, 1884. (5 Land Dec., 102.)

The Indian appropriation act of May 15, 1886 (24 Stats., 44), authorized the Secretary of the Interior to negotiate with the several tribes and bands of Chippewa

Indians in Minnesota relative to such modifications of their treaties and such change of their reservations as might be deemed desirable, and as to what sum should be an equitable liquidation of all claims which any of said tribes then had against the Government.

At this time all but 200 of the Mille Lac Indians had removed to the White Earth Reservation. Most of these 200 were scattered throughout the country south of Mille Lac tract, principally on Snake River. Messrs. Wright, Whipple, and Larrabee, commissioners appointed under the act, met in council with these for the purpose of securing their removal to the White Earth Reservation, but the negotiations were unsuccessful.

During these negotiations the commissioners read to the Indians a communication from Secretary Lamar, of October 23, 1886, in which he said the President had heard with great surprise and disappointment of their refusal to consent to remove to the White Earth Reservation, where they would be beyond the reach of avaricious white men and have good homes with peace and plenty; and if they persisted in remaining on their old reservation they would do so at their own risk; that "it is the desire of the President that the commissioners explain fully to these Indians the condition of affairs; that they have ceded the lands of the Mille Lac Reservation to the United States, and are permitted to remain there only so long as they shall not in any way interfere with or molest the persons or property of the whites. The President desired that the commissioners shall make another effort to induce these Indians to remove to White Earth, where all the Chippewas will be united in one happy and prosperous family." (Appendix D.)

The act of January 14, 1889, entitled "An act for the relief and civilization of the Chippewa Indians in the State of Minnesota" (25 Stat., 642), and commonly known as the Nelson Act, is, next to the treaty of 1864, of decisive importance in this case.

By section 1 of this act the appointment of three commissioners was authorized "to negotiate with all the different bands or tribes of Chippewa Indians in the State of Minnesota for the complete cession and relinquishment in writing of all their title and interest in and to the reservations of said Indians in the State of Minnesota, except the White Earth and Red Lake Reservations," and on those two reservations it provided for the cession of all surplus lands after the necessary allotments in severalty had been made to all of the Chippewa Indians in Minnesota. Where allotments had been made in severalty to any Indian upon any of said reservations he should not be disturbed without his consent; that for the purposes of the cession and making allotments and payments the commissioners should make an accurate census of each tribe or band before securing the cessions and relinquishments of their reservations; that the acceptance and approval of the cessions and relinquishments by the President should be deemed full and ample proof of the assent of the Indians, and should operate as a complete extinguishment of the Indian title without any other or further act or ceremony whatsoever for the purposes and upon the terms in said act provided.

By section 3 it was provided that as soon as a census had been taken and the cession and relinquishment approved and ratified, all of the said Chippewas in the State of Minnesota, except those on the Red Lake Reservation, under the direction of said commissioners, should be removed to and take up their residence on the White Earth Reservation, and as soon as practicable, under the direction of said commissioners, should be allotted lands in severalty to the Red Lake Indians on the Red Lake Reservation, and to all other of said Indians on the White Earth Reservation; and all allotments theretofore made on the White Earth Reservation were ratified and confirmed, to be held in accordance with the conditions prescribed for allotments under this act.

This section contained a proviso that any of the Indians residing on any of said reservations might in his discretion take his allotment on the reservation where he lived.

Section 4 provided that upon the cession and relinquishment of the Indian title, the ceded lands should be surveyed by the Commissioner of the General Land Office as public lands and divided up into 40-acre tracts and a thorough and careful examination made and notes taken showing the quantity and quality of the pine growing thereon and classified as "pine lands"; and a list giving the description of each 40-acre tract should be made, and opposite each description the cash value of the same, such valuation to be of a rate of not less than $3 per 1,000 feet board measure. If the appraisals should be rejected the Secretary of the Interior should substitute new appraisals, etc., and the same or original list as approved and modified should be filed with the Commissioner of the General Land Office.

Section 5 provided for the sale of the pine lands by advertisement, auction, and private sale.

Section 6 provided for the sale of agricultural lands as public lands under the homestead laws, and that each settler should pay in accordance with the provisions of said laws for the allotment so taken by him the sum of $1.25 for each and every acre in five equal annual payments, and should be entitled to a patent at the expiration of five years from the date of entry, and after the full payment of said $1.25 per acre therefor, and proof of occupancy for said period of five years, etc., with a proviso:

That nothing in this act shall be held to authorize the sale or other disposal under its provision of any tract upon which there is a subsisting valid preemption or homestead entry, but any such entry shall be proceeded with under the regulations and decisions in force at the date of its allowance, and if found regular and valid, patents shall issue thereon.

Section 7 provided that of the moneys accruing from the sales of these lands, after deducting the expenses of census, cessions and relinquishments, removals and allotments, surveys and appraisals, the balance should be placed in the Treasury of the

United States to the credit of all the Chippewa Indians in the State of Minnesota as a permanent fund, which should draw interest at the rate of five per cent per annum, payable annually for a period of 50 years after the allotments provided for in this act have been made. The section then provides for the distribution of the funds.

Sections 4 and 5 of the act were amended by the act of June 27, 1902 (32 Stat., 400), so as to permit the sale of the pine timber and the pine lands separately, and authorized the Forester of the Agricultural department to set apart a forest reserve and supervise the cutting of timber thereon, and fixed the minimum price of Norway and white pine at four and five dollars per thousand feet on the stump, respectively.

In pursuance of the act of January 14, 1889, the President of the United States on February 26, 1889, appointed three commissioners, who, after having qualified as required by the act, took a census of the Chippewa Indians of Minnesota, and the Mille Lacs were registered to the number of 895, the total number of Chippewa Indians in Minnesota aggregating 8,304, and the quantity of land in all of the Chippewa reservations in said State aggregating 4,747,931 acres, of which the Mississippi Chippewas were interested in but 796,672 acres (H.R. Doc. 247, 51st Cong., 1st sess., pp. 9, 15, 27), and thereafter, on different dates, by different agreements with the different bands, secured the cession and relinquishment to the United States of the Grand Portage Reservation, Fond du Lac Reservation, Boise or Wood Forte Reservation, and Deer Creek Reservation, and the surplus lands of the White Earth and Red Lake Reservations not required for allotment in severalty to said Indians, parties to said treaties, and the right of occupancy of the former Mille Lac Reservation under article 12 of the treaty of May 7, 1864, was relinquished by the Mille Lac Band. Each separate agreement made with each of the bands of the Chippewas in Minnesota was separately approved, in accordance with the act of January 14, 1889, by President Benjamin Harrison.

On March 4, 1890, the report of the commissioners and the agreements with the different bands were transmitted by President Harrison to Congress and were printed as House of Representatives Executive Document No. 247, Fifty-first Congress, first session.

On October 5, 1889, the Mille Lac Band, under the provisions of the act of January 14, 1889, *supra,* ceded, relinquished, and conveyed to the United States all of their right, title, and interest in and to four townships of the White Earth Reservation; reserved by article 2 of the treaty of April 18, 1867, *supra,* and the lands reserved by article 1 of said treaty not embraced in the White Earth Reservation; they also ceded and relinquished all their right, title, and interest in and to the Red Lake Reservation, and *relinquished* their right of occupancy of the Mille Lac Reservation, reserved by article 12 of the treaty of May 7, 1864, *supra.* (Rec., pp. 15, 16.)

April 10, 1889 (8 L.D., 409), Secretary Noble, apparently overlooking this act of January 14, 1889, treated the act of July 4, 1884, as still in force and held that it prohibited action on an entry made prior to its passage.

January 8, 1890 (10 L.D., 3), this decision was recalled, but the Secretary held that he was still without power to dispose of the entry, because he thought the cession by the Indians of their remaining interest in the lands was a condition precedent to action by him under the proviso of section 6 on entries theretofore made on said land.

A year later, January 9, 1891, in the case of Amanda J. Walters (12 L.D., 52), the negotiations with the Indians under the act of January 14, 1889, having in the meantime been concluded, Secretary Noble held that the act of 1889 was the further legislation required by the act of 1884, and that therefore all pending entries, if found regular and valid in other particulars, should proceed to patent, and, because of the long delay, he directed that they all be made special. In his opinion the Secretary called attention to the facts already stated, that the pending claims covered almost the entire Mille Lac Reservation; that these entries were valid under the decisions of Secretary Chandler and Secretary Teller, and that the right of the department under the act of 1889 to allow the entries to proceed to patent seemed clear aside from any question of relinquishment of claims by the Mille Lac Indians. He continued:

Nevertheless it is also true, and adds greatly to the force of the argument, that the Mille Lac Indians joined in the agreement under the act of 1889, whereby the Indian lands save in the reservations therein mentioned were ceded to the United States. By this any possible interest the Mille Lacs may have had was transferred to the United States. I think the language of the statute of 1889 that the lands upon which the Mille Lacs have enjoyed the favor of residence so long as they should not interfere with the whites is equivalent to a declaration that this favor or license did not amount in effect to a "reservation" of these lands upon which the Mille Lacs could take allotments, because it was upon these lands *alone* that subsisting valid preemption of homestead entries existed or were claimed under the regulations and decisions in force at the dates that they were severally allowed and which this statute declares shall now proceed to patent.

It is to be remembered also that another reservation was thereby made (the White Earth), to which the Mille Lacs could remove. There was thus provided, on the one hand, legislation for the perfection of the entries of the white men, and on the other, a place of abode for the Indians.

He then held that the right given by section 3 of the act of 1889 to any Indian to make his allotment on the reservation on which he resided did not, for the reason stated, apply to the Mille Lac Reservation. He said:

Suffice it to say that the land in question was not a reservation within the meaning of the act. It was ceded in 1863; it had been declared open to entry by successive decisions of the Land Office, and was the very land referred to and intended to be covered by the proviso to section 6.

On January 21, 1891, Secretary Noble wrote to the Commissioner of the Land Office reaffirming his last decision, and holding that the Mille Lac lands should be disposed of as other public lands under the general laws, and consequently would not be surveyed under the act of 1889. (See Appendix E.)

On September 3, 1891, in the case of *Northern Pacific Railroad Company v. Walters* (13 L.D., 230), Secretary Noble held that the railroad company was not authorized prior to the act of 1889 to make lieu selections on the Mile Lac Reservation. He also expressed the view, apparently unnecessarily, that the Mille Lac lands not disposed of were to be sold as pine or agricultural lands under the act of January 14, 1889.

In 1892 the Commissioner of the General Land Office wrote to the Secretary asking which of his decisions should govern, and on April 22, 1892 (14 L.D., 497), the Secretary curtly replied that the decision in *Northern Pacific Railroad Co. v. Walters* was the later expression of the department, and was rendered in a case where the status of the Mille Lac lands was the specific question, and it was therefore to be followed.

Evidently a large number of entries on the lands within the Mille Lac Reservation had been made between the Secretary's first ruling and his reversal thereof. The matter was taken to Congress, with the result that the Secretary's first ruling was adopted as correct, by the act of December 19, 1893 (28 Stat., 576), which provides:

That all bona fide preemption or homestead filings or entries allowed for lands within the Mille Lac Indian Reservation, in the state of Minnesota, between the ninth day of January, eighteen hundred and ninety-one, the date of the decision of the Secretary of the Interior holding that the lands within said reservation were subject to disposal as other public lands under the general land laws, and the date of the receipt at the district land office at Taylors Falls, in that state, of the letter from the Commissioner of the General Land Office communicating to them the decision of the Secretary of the Interior of April twenty-second, eighteen hundred and ninety-two, in which it was definitely determined that said lands were not so subject to disposal, but could only be disposed of according to the provisions of the special act of January fourteenth, eighteen hundred and eighty-nine (25 Stat., 642), be, and the same are hereby, confirmed where regular in other respects, and patent shall issue to the claimants for the lands embraced therein, as in other cases, on a satisfactory showing of a bona fide compliance on their part with the requirements of the laws under which said filings and entries were respectively allowed.

On May 27, 1898 (30 Stat., 745), Congress passed a joint resolution declaring:

> That all public lands formerly within the Mille Lac Reservation, in the State of Minnesota, be, and the same are hereby, declared to be subject to entry by any bona fide qualified settler under the public land laws of the United States; and all preemption filings heretofore made prior to the repeal of the preemption law by the act of March third, eighteen hundred and ninety-one, and all homestead entries or applications to make entry under the homestead laws, shall be

received and treated in all respects as if made upon any of the public lands of the United States subject to preemption or homestead entry.

In the Indian appropriation act of May 27, 1902 (32 Stat., 268), there was inserted the following provision:

> For payment to the Indians occupying the Mille Lac Reservation, in the State of Minnesota, the sum of forty thousand dollars, or so much of thereof as may be necessary, to pay said Indians for improvements made by them, or any of them, upon lands occupied by them on said Mille Lac reservation, said payment to be made upon investigation, examination, and appraisement by the Secretary of the Interior, upon condition of said Indian removing from said Mille Lac Reservation: *provided,* that any Indian who has leased or purchased any Government subdivision of land within said Mille Lac Reservation from or through a person having title to said land from the Government of the United States shall not be required to move from said reservation, but shall be entitled to the benefits of said appropriation to all intents and purposes as though they had removed from said reservation: *And provided further,* That this appropriation shall be paid only after said Indians shall, by proper council proceedings, have accepted the provisions hereof and declared the manner in which they wish the money disbursed; and said Indians upon removing from said Mille Lac Reservation shall be permitted to take up their residence and obtain allotments in severalty either on the White Earth Reservation or on any of the ceded Indian reservations in the State of Minnesota on which allotments are made to Indians.

In pursuance of the provisions of the above act an agreement was entered into on August 30, 1902, between the United States and the Mille Lac Indians still residing on the former Mille Lac Reservation, by which they agreed to remove to White Earth Reservation on the payment of $40,000 appropriated by the act of May 17, 1902, for their improvements, and the agreement was signed by 74 adults. These improvements at the time of their appraisement were practically of no value, the objet in view being the possible removal of the Indians to White Earth Reservation. The clause contained in the agreement (Appendix F) that nothing therein should be construed to deprive said Indians of any benefits to which they might be entitled under existing treaties or agreements not inconsistent with the agreement then entered into of the act of May

27, 1902, is the identical provision which has been inserted in every agreement made with the Indians since 1896. (Rec., pp. 12, 17, 35, 36, 43, 54.)

ASSIGNMENT OF ERRORS

The Court of Claims erred:

1. In holding that the act of 1909 did anything more than furnish a forum for the adjudication of the claim.
2. In holding that the joint resolutions of 1893 and 1898 were not an exercise by Congress of the plenary power over the lands.
3. In holding that any right of the Indians was violated by the opening of the Mille Lac Reservation to public settlement under the general land laws of the United States.
4. In holding that the Indians sustained any losses by reason of such opening of said reservation to public settlement.
5. In holding that the Mille Lac Band of Indians had such title to said reservation as excluded the same from settlement as public land.
6. In not holding that the Mille lac Band had abandoned all claim to said reservation by voluntary removal therefrom prior to 1889.
7. In not holding that the acceptance by the Mille Lac Band of the benefits of the Nelson Act of 1889 was a final settlement of their claims to the Mille Lac Reservation.
8. In not holding that the acceptance of the provision of the act of 1902 was a settlement of the Indians claims.
9. In disregarding section 6 of the Nelson Act, and in holding that the Indians were entitled to the value of the entire Mille Lac Reservation, including the nine-tenths thereof upon which valid entries were subsisting at the passage of the act.
10. In holding that the Indians were entitled to the sale value of the land.

ARGUMENT.

I.

The jurisdictional act creates no liability, but simply furnishes a forum for the adjudication of the claim.

This is the rule laid down by this court. (*Stewart v. U.S.,* 206 U.S., 185, 194; *The Sac and Fox Indians,* 220 U.S., 481, 489.)

The Court of Claims, therefore, was in error in holding in effect that the act of 1909, referring the claim to that court, is a legislative decision that something is due the Indians.

It was not intended by the jurisdictional act to strip the Government of all legal and equitable defenses and submit to the court the single question of the amount of losses. If the only question open were the extent of damages, that is a simple question of fact; while this court is primarily concerned with the law; the right of appeal, therefore, would be useless. It follows that the question of liability was left open for the decision by the courts.

(a) Congress has plenary power and control over the Indian tribes. (*Cherokee Nation v. Hitchcock,* 187 U.S., 294; *Lone Wolf v. Hitchcock,* 187 U.S., 565.)

> Congress did not intend by the act of 1909 to authorize the courts to inquire into the justice and fairness of its dealings with the Indians, and to throw open the propriety of the legislation with reference to the Mille Lac Band. The question presented to the court is whether, taking all the treaties and statutes together, any right of the Indians was violated by the opening of the Mille Lac Reservation to settlement. And, of course, in deciding this question, if there be a conflict between an earlier treaty and a later statute, the provisions of the statute will apply. And there can be no imputation of unfairness to Congress; nor can the court go behind a treaty or statute on the ground that it was obtained by duress or fraud.

These principles are settled by this court in cases of *United States v. Old Settlers,* 148 U.S., 427, 466; *United States v. Choctaw and Chickasaw Nations,* 179 U.S., 494, 531-535.

These cases are particularly pertinent because they, like the present, were referred by special acts to the Court of Claims for adjudication. In *United States v. Choctaw Nation* this court said at page 535:

It is thus clear that the Court of Claims is without authority to determine the rights of parties upon the ground of mere justice or fairness, much less, under the guise of interpretation, to depart from the plain import of the words of the treaty. Its duty was to ascertain the intent of the parties according to the established rules for the interpretation of treaties

* * * * * * * * *

If the treaty of 1866, according to its tenor and obvious import, did injustice to the Choctaws and Chickasaws, the remedy is with the political department of the Government (p. 535).

In the present case the land involved was first thrown open to settlement in 1870, and by 1884 claims were filed upon nine-tenths of it. We show hereafter that the land was public land and that its settlement was in strict accordance with the law, but passing for future discussion that question as well as questions arising under the Nelson Act of 1889, by subsequent legislation Congress clearly exercised its plenary power over this land, ratified all prior entries and opened the unoccupied land to settlement.

The joint resolution of December 19, 1893 (28 Stat., 576), confirmed all entries made on the Mille Lac land in 1891 and 1892, and authorized patents to issue.

The joint resolution of May 27, 1898 (30 Stat., 745), declares that all lands within the Mille Lac Reservation were subject to entry, and confirmed all entries theretofore made.

This legislation effectually disposed of all doubts upon the matter, and opened these lands to settlement. Congress acted within its plenary power, and there was therefore no injury to the Indians.

> (b) If the legislation just mentioned be not conclusive, the question then before the court is whether the United States by opening the Mille Lac tract to settlement as public land infringed any legal rights of the Indians acquired by them under the treaties of 1863 and 1864, and which were not relinquished, either voluntarily, or by accepting the terms of the Nelson Act and the act of 1902.

II.

The Mille Lac Reservation was ceded to the United States by the treaties of 1863 and 1864, and became public land open to settlement. The Mille Lac Band acquired no title thereto, but was permitted to remain thereon temporarily.

If this be true, the right of the Indians was not violated by the opening of the land to settlement, and they have suffered no damages.

The claim of the Indians is based upon the proviso of article 12 of the treaty, and the correctness of the foregoing proposition depends upon the proper construction of that provision.

In determining this question the court will consider the conditions leading up to the treaty, the objects sought to be accomplished, as well as the language used, and the practical construction given to the treaty by the parties.

By the treaty of 1855 there had been set apart for the Indians nine widely separated tracts or reservations under the supervision of a single agent; and the settlers were gradually approaching from the South.

Need for the removal of the Indians is shown by a letter, dated September 14, 1862, from Mr. Dole, Commissioner of Indian Affairs (who signed both the treaties of 1863 and 1864), to Governor Ramsey, of Minnesota, in which it is said:

> In my council with the Mille Lac Indians I promised them that their due proportion of the goods and moneys due them this fall should be paid to them at their reservation, without subjecting them to a payment of any portion of the damages for depredations committed by the Chippewas within the last four weeks. I trust you will not find it necessary to make any change in this arrangement.
>
> If it could be arranged to remove these Indians further north toward Red Lake and Red River, I have no doubt that both the Indians and the white man would be benefited, and that it would be approved by the Government; and you are authorized to negotiate with them to this effect, subject to the usual confirmation by the Senate. (Report of Secretary of Interior, 1862, pp. 227, 228.)

There were thus two objects of the treaty. One, for the benefit of the Indians, to collect them all upon one compact reservation where they would be within easy supervision, their children would have access to schools, and they might engage in agricultural pursuits; and the other, to open the desired lands to settlement by the whites.

These objects are apparent from the provisions of the treaty.

The six reservations occupied by the Mississippi Bands were absolutely ceded to the United States (article 1), in compensation for which a new and larger reservation was created in the immediate neighborhood of the three reservations occupied by the Pillager and Lake Winnibigoshish Bands (article 2); in further consideration large cash payments were made to the Indians, and their annuities under the treaty of 1855 were extended for a period of ten years (article 3); the United States also agreed to prepare lands on the new reservation for cultivation and to build houses for the chiefs; 70 acres were to be cleared especially for the Mille Lac Band (article 4); large sums were to be expended for farming implements and animals, and farmers were to be employed to teach the Indians (article 5); a sawmill was to be built and maintained, roads established, and new agency buildings erected (article 6). By article 14 it is expressly stipulated that the clearing and breaking of land as provided for in the fourth article of the treaty shall be in lieu of all former engagements of the United States for breaking land for these bands. Appropriations were made for the removal of the Indians from the ceded to their new reservation and subsistence thereon, in accordance with the provisions of the treaty, from 1865 to 1873.

The absolute cession of the lands to the United States and the unmistakable intention to remove the Mille Lac Band to the new reservation are not destroyed by the proviso. The language used is not susceptible of that construction.

In the first place, if it had been intended to give the land to the Indians, a cession would not have been made to the United States, but there would have been a reservation or exception to the Mille Lac band alone. The framers of the treaty knew how to do this, for by article 1 they did except one section at Mille Lac, which was granted in fee simple to Chief Shaw-vosh-kung. An expressed exception excludes all others.

Again, the language of the proviso is not appropriate to convey the Indian title or establish or continue a reservation. The Indian title is not conditioned on good conduct.

The language used has not in its ordinary acceptation the meaning contended for by the Indians. The privilege is merely *not to be compelled to remove* from a certain large tract of land. This is not a right to exclusively occupy the entire tract and to prevent settlement by the whites. The Indians did not in fact, as appears in the case, need or use the entire tract. It is a misuse of language to say that such a privilege confers the right to exclude all others. On the contrary, the language not to interfere with nor molest the whites recognizes and implies the very right of the latter to come and settle upon the lands, for as yet no whites were there.

On the claimants' construction the United States is placed in the attitude of being both grantor and grantee in the same instrument.

The construction contended for would defeat the very objects of the treaty, for it would, as said by Judge Howry (R., 51) destroy the manifest intention of the Government to provide homesteads for white settlers and the manifest intention of the Mille Lac Band to adjust themselves to that expectation.

The treaty was in fact a purchase from the Indians of all their title to the six ceded reservations, and ample consideration was paid therefor, both in land and in money. The land so purchased therefore became public land open to settlement.

The reservation was so regarded by the officers of the Interior Department, in their practical administration of the land laws.

The land was surveyed as public land in 1870 and settlements began in 1871, and within four months thereafter entries were filed covering perhaps one-fourth of the land (R., 13, 14, Finding VIII). Thereupon, the Commissioner of Indian Affairs persuaded the then Secretary of the Interior that it would be unwise to permit white settlers on the tract while any of the Indians remained, and the Secretary suspended further entries upon the reservation.

In 1877, on the appeal of Folsom, Secretary Chandler delivered an elaborate opinion construing the statute in accordance with the Government's contention.

He said:

All of the conditions of said treaties having been complied with by the United States, the title to said lands now rests absolutely in the United States.

* * * *

Under this proviso it is true that, so long as said Indians do not interfere with the persons or property of the whites, they cannot be *compelled* to remove; but it by no means gives them an exclusive right to the lands, nor does it, in my judgment, exclude said lands from sale and disposal by the United States.

It was anticipated, evidently, that these lands would be settled upon by white persons; that they would take with them their property and effects, and it was provided that so long as the Indians did not interfere with such white persons or their property, they might remain, not because they had any right to the lands but simply as a matter of favor.

In this view of the case, I am satisfied that this is the proper construction of said proviso, said lands are now, and were at the time Folsom offered to file his declaratory statement, subject to preemption filing and entry. (Appendix A.)

There had been appropriations for moving the Indians, but they had not all left Mille Lac. For this reason, therefore, Secretary Chandler directed that further entries be suspended until appropriation be made or until the Indians should voluntarily remove. This direction was continued by Secretary Schurz, and certain entries were cancelled by him because made in violation of his order. Thereafter, in 1882, Secretary Teller, upon a full consideration of the entire question, adopted Mr. Chandler's construction of the statute and reinstated all entries. The Secretary held that there was no reservation; that the Mille Lac tract was public land, and the cancelling of entries made in good faith was without authority of law and in derogation of the rights of the entrymen.

And this decision was in force in 1884, when Congress suspended all entries until further legislation.

Attention should be called to several erroneous statements in the majority opinion with reference to the decisions of Secretaries Schurz and Teller.

It is said (R., 14, 20) that Secretary Schurz held all the land entries invalid and reversed the decisions of his predecessor.

The fact is that Secretary Chandler, while holding the land to be public and open to settlement, ordered that entries be suspended merely as a matter of expediency;

Schurz adopted and repeated this order; and his opinion referred to on page 14 merely held invalid those entries which he thought had been permitted in violation of his instructions. (Appendix B.)

Again, it is said (R., 14) that Secretary Teller suspended the question of the validity of the land entries until Congress should legislate concerning the rights of the Indians. On the contrary, Secretary Teller expressly held that the reservation was public land open to homestead and preemption claims. (Op. of May 10, 1882, Appendix C.) In this opinion he also said that it was not claimed that it was necessary to exclude white settlers from the reservation in order to keep in good faith the treaty with the Indians.

These decisions of Secretaries Chandler and Teller were followed by Secretary Lamar in 1886, who held that the land was public and open to settlement.

This practical construction given to the treaty by the executive department charged with its enforcement (and which will be given great weight by the courts, *Brown v. U.S.,* 113 U.S., 568) was evidently recognized by the great majority of the Indians, who voluntarily abandoned the reservation and removed to White Earth, where they accepted allotments.

Upon this full consideration, therefore, of the language of the treaty; the considerations under which it was made; and the subsequent action of the Government officials, as well as of the Indians, it is submitted that the Indians had no title to the Mille Lac tract, but that it was public land. It necessarily follows that the rights of the Indians were not infringed in opening this land to settlement.

III.

The Mille Lac Band abandoned any claim to the reservation by voluntary removal therefrom.

It has already been shown, the majority of the Mille Lac Band prior to 1889 had voluntarily removed to the White Earth Reservation. Thereby the claim of the whole band to the reservation was abandoned.

The United States deals with tribes and not with individual Indians. (*Blackfeather v. United States,* 190 U.S., 368, 377.)

So, in the present case, the agreement was with the band and not with individual members thereof. Therefore, any Indian title which might have existed to the Mille Lac Reservation was in the band itself, and when the majority of them voluntarily removed that title was gone. The contrary argument, followed to its logical conclusion, means that a single Indian remaining on the reservation could hold title to it.

IV.

By accepting the conditions and benefits of the acts of 1889 and 1902, the Indians abandoned all claim to the Mille Lac tract.

A. The Nelson Act of 1889 was a final settlement with all the Minnesota Chippewas. The Mille Lac band accepted its terms, agreeing to remove to White Earth, and thereby ended all right of occupancy of the Mille Lac tract.

At the time of the passage of this act the Chippewas were widely scattered throughout northern Minnesota. The Lake Superiors occupied the four reservations — Grand Portage, Fond du Lac, Bois Forte, and Deer Creek — already mentioned; the Mississippi bands were upon two reservations, White Earth and the one just north of Leech Lake, while the Red Lake and Pembina bands still occupied an unceded tract in northern Minnesota.

It was the desire of the United States to gather these numerous bands of Indians upon one or two reservations and open to settlement the vast tracts then occupied by the Indians.

At this time the Mille Lac Band were in this situation: The large majority of them had already removed to White Earth, but a remnant still lived in primitive Indian fashion on or near the old Mille Lac Reservation; three Secretaries of the Interior had ruled that the Mille Lac tract was public land open to settlement, and by virtue of homestead and preemption claims nine-tenths of the Mille Lac tract was then occupied and claimed by the whites, and at least one-tenth of the tract had actually been patented. There was left for the occupancy of the remnant of the Mille Lac Indians but as little over 5,000 acres of land.

In this situation the United States, by the Nelson Act, offered that if all Indians would remove, some to the White Earth Reservation and the others to the Red Lake Reservation, and would cede to the United States all their lands, such ceded lands would be sold and proceeds applied to the use of the Indians, and that each Indian would be given an allotment in severalty on White Earth or Red Lake.

This offer was accepted by all the Indians, and each band made deeds expressing the acceptance of the provisions of the act, and ceding to the United States the specific reservations which they owned.

The Mille Lac Band with the others accepted the act, and thereby agreed that the remnant of their band still remaining on or near the old reservation would remove to White Earth.

The proviso of article 12 of the treaty of 1864, under which these Indians based their claim of title, simply provided that they *should not be compelled to remove.* The moment, therefore, they voluntarily removed, all claim of title would vanish. So, when they voluntarily agreed to remove and to accept the benefits of the Nelson Act, the proviso was at an end, for there then arose a compulsion to remove.

There was therefore no necessity for the cession of the old reservation, and while the Mille Lac Band were asked to and did sign deeds ceding all their interest in those portions of White Earth and Red Lake Reservations desired for settlement, when it came to the Mille Lac tract, their deed omitted the word cede and used only the word relinquish. The relinquishment, of course, was no more than a quitclaim, and even it was simply a precautionary measure, for the tract had long since been ceded to the United States, and all claims of occupancy ceased by the agreement to remove and without a cession.

The lands on the Mille Lac tract were not, therefore, to be sold under the Nelson Act. According to the terms of section 4, it was only lands which were *ceded* to the United States which were to be surveyed and sold. This land was not ceded nor was there any need for its cession. Nor, for the same reason, was the tract a reservation within the meaning of the proviso of section 3 of the Nelson Act authorizing an allotment in severalty on the particular reservation on which the Indian lived.

And this was the legislative construction given by subsequent acts of Congress to the Nelson Act.

It will be remembered that the Secretary of the Interior, after first taking this view of the Nelson Act, reversed himself and held that the Mille Lac tract should be disposed of under that act. (14 Land Dec., 497.)

In the meantime a large number of entries had been made upon the land. So, by the resolutions of 1893 and 1898, Congress declared that these and all other entries made on this land were valid and that the land was open to settlement, and thus expressly adopted and confirmed the construction theretofore given to the treaties and statutes by the several Secretaries of the Interior.

These legislative constructions are entitled to great weight.

The Committee on Indian Affairs of the House of Representatives, in its report on the resolution of December 19, 1893, which we use on the authority of *United States v. Binns* (194 U.S., 486), started out with the statement that "The Mille Lac Indian Reservation (owned by the Chippewas) was ceded to the United States in 1863 and had been declared open to entry by successive decisions by the Department of the Interior." (Cong. Rec., vol. 26, pt. 1, pp. 35, 36; 53d Cong., 2d sess.)

From the following extract from the report of the Secretary of the Interior, adopted as the report of the Committee on Public Lands on the resolution of May 27, 1898, it clearly appears that Congress did not recognize any rights of the Mille Lac Indians in the old Mille Lac Reservation:

> From the facts in the case, as disclosed by the reports of the Commissioner of Indian Affairs, it appears that by the treaties in 1863-4 these Indians ceded all their lands in this reservation to the Government, taking other lands in lieu thereof: ***
>
> *It would appear, therefore, that the Indians, after due consideration and in the most formal manner, have, by treaty and agreement duly executed, parted with all their rights to the lands in this reservation.* That being true, it is not apparent why the equities of settlers who

have in good faith gone upon these lands under the belief that they were vacant public lands of the United States and made valuable improvements on them, should not be recognized by the passage of some law that would permit said settlers to perfect their title to said lands. *Such an act would be no infringement upon the rights of the Indians, for the reasons above stated.*

(Cong. Rec., vol. 31, pt. 5, p. 4781; 55th Cong., 2d sess. Italics ours.)

It necessarily follows that the rights of the Indians were in no way violated by the opening of the Mille Lac tract to settlement, and there can, for that reason, be no recovery in this case.

No injustice was done to the Indians under this construction, for under the Nelson Act they were given the right to participate in the proceeds of a vast tract of land to which they in reality had no claim.

The census taken under the act showed 8,304 Chippewa Indians; of those 3,002 were Mississippi Chippewas, including the Mille Lac Band, which numbered 895.

The total quantity of land ceded to the Government (less that necessary to give each Indian an allotment in severalty of 160 acres) was 4,407,931 acres. Of this the Mississippi Chippewas had owned 796,692 acres embraced in White Earth and the reservation north of Leech Lake, the remaining land belonging to the Red Lake and Pembina Bands.

As a result of the agreements under the act, the Mississippi Chippewas, including the Mille Lacs, numbering 3,002, secured the right to participate in the sale and allotments of 3,951,259 acres, in which they had no interest prior thereto. In return for this, the 5,301 other Chippewa secured the right to participate in only 796,672 acres, in which they had no interest prior thereto.

Apparently the Mille Lac Band were well paid for what they surrendered.

The judgment of the Court of Claims has this remarkable result — it not only amounts to double compensation to the Indians for their cession of this land in 1864, but the right of occupancy which is claimed to have been given to the small band of Indians as a reward for their good conduct in 1862, becomes an occupation for the benefit of the very Indians engaged in the outbreak against the whites and whom the Mille Lacs were rewarded for refusing to join.

The Government derived no pecuniary benefit from the cession and settlement of the Mille Lac Reservation, expended large sums of money on the appellees at different times as a consideration for the cession of the Mille Lac Reservation. A very small part of the reservation was sold at $1.25 an acre under the general land laws as public lands.

Nearly all of the reservation was entered upon with soldiers' additional scrip, Chippewa half-breed scrip, and agricultural college scrip, from which the Government received no compensation. Not over 5,000 acres were sold to settlers at $1.25 an acre after joint resolution of May 27, 1898, aggregating about $6,250, as against the great sums paid to or expended upon the Mille Lac and other Mississippi Chippewas.

B. The act of 1902

The Indians by accepting the conditions and benefits of the act of May, 1902 (32 Stat., 268), abandoned the last vestige of claim to any part of the Mille Lac tract.

As already appears, all of the Indians had agreed to remove to White Earth when they accepted the provisions of the Nelson Act; however, some few of them remained on or near the old reservation. Therefore, the act of 1902, which was in reality a mere gratuity in order to secure the peaceful removal of this remnant, offered to pay not exceeding the sum of $40.000 "upon condition of said Indians removing from said Mille Lac Reservation."

It is noticeable that this act provides "for the payment to the Indians occupying, etc."; there is no reference to the Mille Lac Band as a band, but merely to the few scattered Indians who are remaining upon the reservation without right. When, therefore, the Indians accepted this statute, there could be no further claim to the Mille Lac Band.

The mere fact that the agreement which the Indians signed contained a proviso "that nothing therein shall be construed to deprive them of any benefits to which they might be entitled under existing treaties and agreements not inconsistent with the treaty of 1902," is immaterial; they can not make any conditions, except those mentioned in the statute, to the acceptance of its provisions.

And as said by Judge Howry (R., 54), this is the mere general provision which has been inserted in every agreement made with the Indians since 1896, and no special significance is to be attached to it.

V.

If the Mille Lac Reservation be considered one of the reservations ceded by the Indians under the Nelson Act of 1889, their measure of damages is found in that statute. Section 6 excludes from sale under that act every tract on which there was a subsisting valid preemption or homestead entry. Such subsisting entries covered over 55,000 acres of the Mille Lac tract; only the remaining 5,000 acres could therefore be sold under the Nelson Act.

The judgement of the court below proceeds on the assumption that the Mille Lac Reservation was a reservation ceded to the United States by the Chippewas within the meaning of the provisions of the Nelson Act, and that, with slight exceptions, the entire tract should have been sold as pine or agricultural land under that act; that the opening of the land to settlement under the public-land laws was a violation of the terms of the act, and that the Indians were entitled to the full value of the entire tract, even including the more than 7,000 acres which had already been patented. The judgment accordingly estimates the value of 34,480.89 acres of pine land and 25,000 acres of agricultural land (R., 18, 40).

Assuming, for the purpose of argument, that the Mille Lac tract should be treated as a reservation under the Nelson Act, the judgment below entirely overlooks the fact that 55,000 acres had been filed upon, and that under section 6 of the act such land can not be sold for the benefit of the Indians.

The proviso to this section is as follows:

> *Provided,* That nothing in this act shall be held to authorize the sale or other disposal under its provision of any tract upon which there is a subsisting, valid, preemption or homestead entry, but any such entry shall be proceeded with under the regulations and decisions in force at the date of its allowance, and if found regular and valid, patents shall issue thereon: *Provided,* That any person who has not heretofore had the benefit of the homestead or preemption law and who has failed from any cause to perfect the title to a tract of land heretofore entered by him under either of said laws may make a second homestead entry under the provisions of this act.

By March 31, 1884, 55,976.42 acres of the total acreage of 61,028.14 had been filed upon as open to settlement, and 7,792.16 acres had been patented. (R., 14, 20; 12 Land Dec., 54.)

It is difficult to understand how the court below avoids this proviso of said section 6. Certainly, those lands which had gone to patent were not to be sold for the benefit of the Indians. The United States did not undertake to engage in litigation; it simply promised to sell land which the Indians should cede; the title to the patented land had gone from the United States, and could not again be sold — (it is immaterial that the patents had not been delivered; *United States v. Schurz,* 102 U.S., 378) — nor did the Nelson Act commit the United States to make any payments for such lands; the Government was simply to make sale of the lands and apply the proceeds to the benefit of the Indians.

It will be contended for the Indians that the Mille Lac tract was an Indian reservation on which, under the law, entries could not be made, and that therefore there were no valid entries upon that tract. (See sec. 2257, R.S. U.S.)

But this contention goes too far, for it nullifies the entire proviso. The Nelson Act contemplated only the cession to the United States of Indian lands, and if there could be no valid entries on such lands the proviso was a foolish and useless thing. A statute will, if possible, be construed to have some effect. (*U.S. v. Hartwell,* 6 Wall., 396; *A,. Sec & Trust Co. v. D.C.,* 224 U.S., 491.)

The truth is that Congress by this provision recognized and preserved all subsisting entries, and directed that they be treated as if made on public lands, and patents issued if the claims were valid in all other respects; but all objections that the lands were not open to settlement were removed from the consideration of the land officers. This conclusion is inevitable from the subsequent language of the proviso: "Any such entry shall be proceeded with under the regulations and decisions in force at the date of its allowance, and if found regular and valid patents shall issue thereon." And it is strengthened by the further provision of the section that if the entrant had failed to perfect his title he might make a second homestead entry.

These entries were known both to Congress and to the Indians. Congress was making a liberal and beneficial settlement with the Indians, and this provision for prosecuting the pending entries to patent was an agreement that all land claimed under such entries should be excluded from sale.

The same conclusion is reached by another line of argument. As already stated, every subsisting entry was to be proceeded with under the regulations and decisions in force at the date of its allowance.

The term allowance here does not mean the issuance of the patent, but the receipt of the claim at the local land office and its acceptance for filing.

It already appears that all of the entries upon the 55,000 acres involved here were made at dates when the head of the Department of the Interior held the Mille Lac tract public land open to settlement. They were made in 1871 and 1872, and between Secretary Chandler's decision in 1877 and the act of 1884; it is true that some of these entries were cancelled, but in 1882 they were all reinstated by Secretary Teller, and directed to be proceeded with. So that, under the regulations and decisions in force in the Department of the Interior, all of these entries were valid subsisting entries at the time of the passage of the Nelson Act.

Such was the conclusion of Secretary Noble in the Waters case, 12 Land Decisions, 52. Here, after describing the entries on the Mille Lac tract, the Secretary said:

> It is impossible for me to conclude, in view of these facts, that the provision of the act of January 14, 1889, was not intended to control the action of this department in the further consideration of the claims above mentioned pending in the General Land Office. It is to my mind clear that this is the "further legislation" required by the act of July 4, 1884, and that the words "subsisting valid preemption or homestead entries" embrace the entries upon which it is now asked by the petitioners patent may be issued. It is required that these shall be proceeded with under the regulations and decisions in force at the date of the allowance of these entries.
>
> These regulations and decisions exist in relation to these entries, the decisions being those of Secretary Chandler, dated March 1, 1877, and Secretary Teller, dated May 10, 1882, and the regulations being those set forth in the letter of Commissioner McFarland,

dated April 25, 1884, and there will be no further difficulty in following them.

It necessarily follows, therefore, that under any proper construction of the Nelson Act the rights of the Indians were not infringed by the perfection of the entries subsisting in 1889. Their damages are therefore confined under the most favorable aspect of the statute to the value of the lands not then entered upon.

If this construction of the law be correct, the case must be remanded with directions to ascertain the value of the small portion of the reservation which should have been sold under the Nelson Act.

VI.

If the Nelson Act be inapplicable, the loss sustained by the Indians is merely the value of their right of occupancy, and not the fee-simple value of the land.

Under the most favorable construction to them of the treaty of 1864, the Mille Lac Band had a mere right of occupancy during good behavior. This was not intended as a fee simple — for Article I of the treaty of 1864 used other and appropriate language to create fee-simple estates; nor did the language used create the ordinary Indian title, for that was never conditioned on good conduct.

It was a feeble and uncertain tenure, subject to determination upon violation of the condition. This did not give the Indians the right to cut the timber, except for their domestic use or for improving the land. *United States v. Cook,* 19 Wall., 591; act Feb. 16, 1889 (25 Stat., 673; 3 Fed. Stat. Ann., 377). By far the larger part of the present judgment consists in the value of the timber. The judgment should therefore be reduced to the value to the remnant of the band left on the reservation to occupy it in Indian fashion.

CONCLUSION.

The judgment should be reversed, with directions to dismiss the petition.

JESSE C. ADKINS
Assistant Attorney General.

GEORGE M. ANDERSON
Attorney.

APPENDIX A.

DEPARTMENT OF THE INTERIOR

Washington, D.C., 1st March, 1877

Sir: I have considered the appeal of Frank W. Folsom from your decision of May 27th, 1876, affirming the action of the register and receiver in rejecting his D.S. dated May 1st, 1876, for the S.E. ¼ of N.W. ¼ and lots 1, 2 & 3 of sec. 6, T. 43, R. 27, Taylors Falls land district, Minnesota.

Your decision is based on the ground that the tracts mentioned were within the Mille Lac Indian Reservation.

This reservation was created by a treaty entered into by and between the United States and the Mississippi bands of Chippewa Indians (including the Mille Lac), dated February 22d, 1855 (10 Stats., 1165) and included the following fractional townships, viz, 42 N., R. 25 W., 42 N., R. 26 W., and 42 & 43 N., R. 27 W., and also three islands in the southern part of Mille Lac in the then Territory, now State, of Minnesota.

On the 11th of March, 1863, another treaty was entered into by and between the United States and said bands of Indians, by which all of the tracts included in said reservation were ceded to the United States. (12 Stats., 1249.)

In consideration of the cession so made the United States agreed, among other things, to set apart, and did set apart, for the future homes of the Chippewas of the Mississippi other lands described in said treaty; to extend the annuities of said bands ten years beyond the periods mentioned in existing treaties; to pay certain sums of money for the purposes therein mentioned; to clear, stump, grub, and break, upon the reservation set apart for said Chippewas, a certain number of acres for each of said bands; to build houses for their chiefs, and to furnish them with teams and farming utensils, &c., for the period of ten years.

On the 7th of May, 1864, another treaty was entered into by and between the United States and the Chippewas of the Mississippi and Minnesota, by which, in consideration of the cession aforesaid, other and additional lands were set apart as a reservation for said lands, and the sums of money to be expended by the United States for the objects therein mentioned were particularly stated.

The sums of money required by said treaty have been appropriated by Congress from time to time, and a full compliance with its terms has been made or tendered by the United States. A part of said band has been removed to White Earth Reservation and a part still remains at Mille Lac, although they have been repeatedly solicited to remove, and ample preparations were long since made on the former reservation for their permanent location thereon.

All of the conditions of said treaties having been complied with by the United States, the title to said lands now rests absolutely in the United States.

In your communication of the 30th ultimo, you state that "the reason said lands have been suspended from sale or other disposition is that, on the 22d of August, 1871, a request was made by the Indian Office that no part of said reservation be considered as subject to entry or sale as public lands until notification to the General Land Office by the Indian Office that the lands comprising the reservation were no longer needed for Indian purposes."

This request of the Indian Office, from the communication of the Commissioner of Indian Affairs of the 29th ultimo, appears to have been made upon a construction given to the proviso to the 12th article of the treaty aforesaid, which is as follows: "That owing to the heretofore good conduct of the Mille Lac Indians, they shall not be compelled to remove so long as they shall not in any way interfere with or in any manner molest the persons or property of the whites,"

Under this proviso it is true that, so long as said Indians do not interfere with the persons or property of the whites, they can not be *compelled* to remove; but it by no means gives them an exclusive right to the lands, nor does it, in my judgment, exclude said lands from sale and disposal by the United States.

It was anticipated evidently, that these lands would be settled upon by white persons, that they would take with them their property and effects, and it was provided that so long as the Indians did not interfere with such white persons or their property, they might remain, not because they had any right to the lands, but simply as a matter of favor.

In this view of the case, and I am satisfied that this is the proper construction of said proviso, said lands are now, and were at the time Folsom offered to file his D.S., subject to preemption filing and entry.

But in view of the fact that there is now a part of said band of Indians upon said tracts of lands, and also that there is no appropriation available for their immediate removal to the White Earth Reservation, you are hereby instructed to suspend the execution of this decision and to direct the local officers to allow no filings or entries upon any of said lands included in the Mille Lac Reservation until the close of the next regular session of Congress, unless said Indians shall voluntarily remove therefrom prior to that date, and I further direct that, in the meantime, all existing claims or any of said lands, if any there be, remain *in statu quo.*

For the reasons herein stated, your decision is reversed, and the papers transmitted with your letter "G" of October 31st, 1876, are herewith returned.

Very respectfully,

Z. CHANDLER,
Secretary.
The Comr. of the Genl. Land Office.

APPENDIX B.

DEPARTMENT OF THE INTERIOR

Washington, D.C., 19th May, 1879.

Sir: I have received your letter of the 17th instant, inclosing the returns of the register of the U.S. land office at Taylors Falls, Minnesota, for the month of March, 1879, showing the number of entries made during that month on what is known as Mille Lac Indian Reservation, in said State, in violation of the instructions of this department and of your office, and stating that said entries "are invalid, and if it meets the Secretary's approval they will be at once cancelled by this office, and the parties advised."

I concur in your opinion, and you will please cancel said entries and notify the parties accordingly.

The papers transmitted are herewith returned.

Very respectfully,

C. SCHURZ,
Secretary.
The Comr. of the Genl. Land Office.

APPENDIX C.

DEPARTMENT OF THE INTERIOR

Washington, May 10, 1882.

Sir: I have the honor to acknowledge the receipt of your letter of the 26th of April concerning the Mille Lac Reservation in the State of Minnesota. I have carefully considered the same, and after an examination of the statutes cited and the action of my predecessor, Hon. Z. Chandler and Hon. Carl Schurz, I feel constrained to substantially adhere to the decision made by Mr. Chandler. I do not think there can be any controversy as to the status of the Indians on that reservation. The twelfth article of the treaty of 1863 provides as follows:

"It shall not be obligatory upon the Indians, parties to this treaty, to remove from their present reservations until the United States shall have first complied with the stipulations of articles 4 and 6 of this treaty, when the United States shall furnish them with all necessary transportation and subsistence to their new homes, and subsistence for six months thereafter: *Provided,* That owing to the heretofore good conduct of the Mille Lac Indians they shall not be compelled to remove so long as they shall not in any way interfere with or in any manner molest the persons or property of the whites."

This proviso gave to this band of Indians the right to remain on the reservation until they should voluntarily remove therefrom. At the time of the making of the treaty there was a large number of other Indians who either resided on the reservation or had the right to do so, who were to be removed; but, owing to the good conduct of these Indians, they were not compelled like their brothers to go to the White Earth Reservation. It has been insisted that the proviso allowing the Mille Lac Indians to remain gave them the exclusive permission to occupy the entire reservation to the exclusion of white settlers.

By the treaty of February 22, 1855, it was provided in article 2 that the President might at any time he considered it advisable assign to each head of a family, or singly, 80 acres of land for his or their separate use. It does not appear that this was done, and it is to be presumed that whatever portion of the Mille Lac Reservation was occupied by the Mille Lac Indians at the time of the making of the treaty of 1863 was occupied in common and not held in severalty. Whatever title they had passes by this treaty to the United States, nothing remained in the Indians; but the Government saw fit to say that they need not remove therefrom until they were ready to do so. It was undoubtedly understood by the Government and the Indians that the Indians would ultimately remove therefrom to White Earth, as provided in the treaty, but they have refused to do so, and still refuse.

The interests of the Indians undoubtedly require their removal; but this can not be done by the department, except with their consent, unless the Indians by disturbing the whites have forfeited their right to remain. It is alleged that they have forfeited their right; this, however, has been denied. No provision is made in the treaty for determining a controversy on this point, and it ought not to be adjudged against the Indians except on the clearest proof. This does not appear to exist, and therefore it must be presumed that the Indians are rightfully on the reservation and entitled to the protection of the Government in all that was given them by the proviso in article 12.

The question is whether they may occupy the whole reservation or only the part that is necessary to make good the promise of the proviso of section 12. It is not claimed that they originally occupied the entire reservation or that it is now necessary to exclude white settlers therefrom to keep in good faith the treaty with them. I conclude that whatever they actually occupied in 1863 they are entitled now to occupy; if they have increased the area of their occupation they are entitled to that, if such occupation was prior to the occupancy by white people.

The reservation was public land open to homestead and preemption claims, subject only to the rights of the Indians to reside thereon and not to remove therefrom until they wish so to do. Good faith required the Government to reserve for them as much land as they needed. This could not be more fairly determined than by conceding to them all they had previously occupied. I understand the number of Indians on that reservation is about five hundred, while the reservation contains seven townships and three small islands. You will therefor ascertain as soon as practicable the quantity of land heretofore occupied by the Indians, as well as the quantity necessary for their support (if the quantity now occupied is insufficient), and report the same to this office, in order that such land may be reserved from the operation of the homestead and preemption laws, so that the remainder of the reservation may be occupied by the settlers who have in good faith attempted settlement thereon.

If you think it desirable, I will send an inspector there to examine and report on the area now occupied by the Indians, or you may ascertain the fact through your own agencies, as you prefer.

Very respectfully,

H.M. TELLER
Secretary.
Hon. Hiram Price,
Commissioner of Indian Affairs.

APPENDIX D.

OPINION OF SECRETARY LAMAR OF OCTOBER 23, 1886.

The following communication was telegraphed on October 23, 1886, by the Secretary of the Interior to the commissioners appointed under the act of May 15, 1886 (24 Stat., 44), while they were in council with the Mille Lac Indians endeavoring to secure a peaceable removal of about 200 of said band who still remained on the former Mille Lac Reservation (Sen. Ex. Doc. No. 115, 49 Cong., 2d sess., pp. 18 & 21):

ACTING COMMISSIONER OF INDIAN AFFAIRS:

In view of all the facts connected with the Mille Lac Indians and their reservation, the President hears with great surprise and disappointment that they have refused to give their consent to remove to the White Earth Reservation, where they would be beyond the reach of avaricious white men, and where they would have good homes with peace and plenty. If they persist in remaining on their old reservation, they must do so at their own risk and with disapprobation of the Government. It is the desire of the President that the commissioners explain fully to these Indians the condition of affairs; that they have ceded the lands of the Mille Lac Reservation to the United States, and are permitted to remain there only so long as they shall not in any way interfere with or molest the persons or property of the whites. The President desires that the commissioners shall make another effort to induce these Indians to remove to White Earth, where all the Chippewas will be united in one happy and prosperous family. The commission should say to them that it is the earnest desire of the President that they remove to White Earth, and that their interests, and that only, prompts the Government in urging them to take this step. The Indians should give the matter the most careful consideration, as the future welfare and happiness of themselves and children depends upon their their decision in this matter.

L. Q. C. LAMAR
Secretary.

APPENDIX E.

DEPARTMENT OF THE INTERIOR

Washington, January 21, 1891.

COMMISSIONER OF THE GENERAL LAND OFFICE.

Sir: I acknowledge the receipt of your communication of 20th instant in reply to department reference letter of Honorable S.G. Comstock, House of Representatives, requesting an estimate of cost of completing the necessary surveys within the Chippewa Indian reservations in Minnesota, under the provisions of the act of January 14, 1889, wherein you refer to department decision of 9th instant regarding the Mille Lac lands and suggest a doubt as to whether the lands in said reservation are to be disposed of under the provisions of the act of January 14th, 1889, or as other public lands under the general laws, and ask to be specifically instructed in reference to this point.

In reply you are informed that as department decision of 9th instant held "that the lands upon which the Mille Lacs have enjoyed the favor of residence, so long as they should not interfere with the whites, is equivalent to a declaration that this favor or license did not amount in effect to a reservation of these lands upon which the Mille Lacs could take allotments," etc., the Mille Lac lands should be disposed of as other public lands under the general laws, and consequently will not be surveyed under the act of January 14, 1889.

In transmitting your estimate to Mr. Comstock, I have called his attention to this matter.

Very respectfully,

JOHN W. NOBLE,
Secretary.
G.C.

APPENDIX F.

This agreement made and entered into this thirtieth day of August, nineteen hundred and two, by and between James McLaughlin, U.S. Indian inspector, and Simon Michelet, U.S. Indian agent, on the part of the United States, party of the first part, and the Mille Lac Chippewa Indians residing on the former Mille Lac Reservation, in the State of Minnesota, parties of the second part, witnesseth:

That whereas by act of Congress of the United States approved May 27, 1902, there was appropriated the sum of forty thousand dollars ($40,000), or so much thereof as might be necessary, for payment to the Indians occupying the Mille Lac Indian Reservation, said payment to be made upon investigation, examination, and appraisement by the Secretary of the Interior, upon condition of said Indians removing from said Mille Lac Reservation.

And whereas the improvements above referred to have been appraised by said James McLaughlin, U.S. Indian inspector, and said Simon Michelet, U.S. Indian agent, under direction of the Secretary of the Interior, at the aggregate sum of forty thousand dollars ($40,000), as per itemized list of appraisements hereto attached and made a part hereof:

Therefore the said party of the first part covenants and agrees to pay to the said parties of the second part the said sum of forty thousand dollars ($40,000) said payment to be made on the former Mille Lac Indian Reservation, in the manner set forth in the annexed council proceedings as soon as practicable after the approval of this agreement by the Secretary of the Interior.

Now, therefore, in consideration of the covenants and agreements of the party of the first part herein contained, the said Mille Lac Indians occupying the former Mille Lac Indian Reservation, parties of the second part, hereby accept the appraisement made by James McLaughlin, U.S. Indian inspector, and Simon Michelet, U.S. Indian agent, of even date herewith, aggregating forty thousand dollars ($40,000), as full compensation for improvements made by them, on said Mille Lac Reservation, and also accept the terms and conditions of said act of Congress and agree to remove from said Mille Lac Indian Reservation (except the excepted classes provided for in said act of Congress) upon payment to them of the said appraised sum of forty thousand dollars ($40,000), in the manner provided in the annexed council proceedings, as soon thereafter as notified by the proper authorities that the necessary arrangements have been made for them upon the White Earth Reservation or any of the ceded Indian reservations in the state of Minnesota on which allotments are made to Indians, said Indians to notify the disbursing officer when said payment is being made to them as to the reservation they elect to take allotments upon.

It is understood that nothing in this agreement shall be construed to deprive the said Mille Lac Indians of any benefits to which they may be entitled under existing treaties or agreements not inconsistent with the provisions of this agreement or the act of Congress relating to said Indians approved May 27, 1902.

In witness whereof the said James McLaughlin, U.S. Indian inspector, and the said Simon Michelet, U.S. Indian agent, on the part of the United States, and the male adult Indians occupying the former Mille Lac Indian Reservation in the State of Minnesota, have hereunto set their hands and seals at Lawrence, Mille Lacs County, Minnesota, this thirtieth day of August, A.D. nineteen hundred and two.

JAMES MCLAUGHLIN
U.S. Indian Inspector.
SIMON MICHELET,
U.S. Indian Agent.

Note to reader: Brief also includes maps of involved area not reproduced here.

U.S. Supreme Court

U S v. MILLE LAC BAND OF CHIPPEWA INDIANS, **U.S. 498 (1913)**

229 U.S. 498

UNITED STATES, Appt.,

v.

MILLE LAC BAND OF CHIPPEWA INDIANS

in the State of Minnesota

No. 736

Argued April 8 and 9, 1913

Decided June 9, 1913

Assistant Attorney General Adkins and Mr. George M. Anderson for appellant. [229 U.S. 498, 499]

Messrs. George B. Edgerton, F.W. Houghton, C.E. Richardson, Harvey S. Clapp, and Daniel B. Henderson for appellees.

Mr. Justice Van Devanter delivered the opinion of the court:

This suit was begun under the act of February 15, 1909 (35 Stat. at L. 619, chap. 126), which authorized the court of claims 'to hear and determine a suit or suits to be brought by and on behalf of the Mille Lac band of Chippewa Indians in the state of Minnesota against the United States, on account of losses sustained by them or the Chippewas of Minnesota by reason of the opening of the Mille Lac Reservation ... to public settlement under the general land laws of the United States.'

The lands to which the act and the suit relate are four fractional townships bordering on the Mille Lac in Minnesota, and three islands in that lake, comprising in all a little more than 61,000 acres. The suit was begun in the name of the Mille Lac band, and the court of claims, two judges dissenting, gave judgment against the United States in the sum of $827,580.72, with a direction, in substance, that the amount recovered be credited to the Chippewas of Minnesota and distributed among them under the provisions of 7 of the act of January 14, 1889 (25 Stat. at L. 642, chap. 24), 47 Ct. Cl. 415. The case is here upon the appeal of the United States.

The judgment was sought and was rendered on the theory that the lands were set apart and reserved for the occupancy and use of the Mille Lac band by treaties of February 22, 1855 (10 Stat. at L. 1165), March 11, 1863 (12 Stat. at L. 1249), and May 7, 1864 (13 Stat. at L. 693), and were subsequently relinquished to the United States pursuant to the act of January 14, 1889, supra, upon certain trusts therein named, and that in violation of those treaties and [229 U.S. 498, 500] that act they were opened to settlement and disposal under the general land laws of the United States and were disposed of thereunder, to the great loss and damage of the Mille Lac band or the Chippewas of Minnesota.

The arguments at the bar and the briefs are addressed to these questions: 1. The scope of the jurisdictional act. 2. The rights of the Indians in the lands under the treaties of 1863 and 1864. 3. The effect to be given to the act of 1889 and its acceptance by the Indians. 4. Whether the disposal of the lands, or any of them, under the general land laws, was violative of the rights of the Indians.

The jurisdictional act makes no admission of liability, or of any ground of liability, on the part of the government, but merely provides a forum for the adjudication of the claims according to applicable legal principles. Nor does it contemplate that recovery may be founded upon any merely moral obligation, not expressed in pertinent treaties or statutes, or upon any interpretation of either that fails to give effect to their plain import, because of any supposed injustice to the Indians. *United States v. Old Settlers,* 148 U.S. 427, 469, 37 S.L. ed. 509, 524, 13 Sup. Ct. Rep. 650; *United States v. Choctaw Nation,* 179 U.S. 494, 535, 45 S.L. ed. 291, 307, 21 Sup. Ct. Rep. 149; *Sac and f. Indians v. Sac & F. Indians,* 220 U.S. 481, 489, 55 S.L. ed. 552, 556, 31 Sup. Ct. Rep. 473.

Under the treaty of 1855, supra, there were reserved for the occupancy and use of the Mississippi bands of Chippewas, of which the Mille Lac band was one, six separate tracts of land in Minnesota. One of these embraced the townships and islands before mentioned, and came to be separately occupied by the Mille Lacs, Although all the reservations were claimed in common by all the bands. By the treaty of 1863, supra, the lands in the six reservations, the one occupied by the Mille Lacs being in terms included, were expressly ceded to the United States (art. 1), and one large tract of other lands in Minnesota reserved for the future home of all the bands, including [229 U.S. 498, 501] the Mille Lacs (art. 2). Provision was made (art. 4) for clearing and breaking a limited area in the new reservation for each of the bands, the Mille Lacs being in terms included, and (art. 6) for removing the agency and sawmill from one of the ceded reservations to the new. Article 12 of this treaty was as follows, -special importance being now attached to its proviso:

> 'It shall not be obligatory upon the Indians, parties to this treaty, to remove from their present reservations until the United States shall have first complied with the stipulations of article 4 and 6 of this treaty, when the United States shall furnish them with all necessary transportation and subsistence to their new homes, and subsistence for six months thereafter:
>
> Provided, That, owing to the heretofore good conduct of the Mille Lac Indians, they shall not be compelled to remove so long as they shall not in any way interfere with or in any manner molest the persons or property of the whites.'

The treaty of 1864, supra, superseded that of 1863, and in so far as their provisions are material here they were identical, so we shall speak only of the later one. In addition to the creation of the single large reservation, provision was made for the payment of large annuities to the Indians in consideration for the cession of the six original reservations, and it is not questioned that these annuities were duly paid to all the bands, including the Mille Lacs, nor that there was a full compliance with articles 4 and 6.

A treaty negotiated in 1867 (16 Stat. at L. 719) eliminated a considerable portion of the large tract reserved by article 2 of the treaty of 1864 and substituted a new tract, consisting of thirty-six townships, which came to be known as the White Earth Reservation. This treaty is not important here, save as it explains subsequent references to the White Earth Reservation.

A controversy soon arose over the meaning and effect [229 U.S. 498, 502] of the proviso to article 12 of the treaty of 1864, declaring, 'that, owing to the heretofore good conduct of the Mille Lac Indians, they shall not be compelled to remove [from the old reservation to the new one] so long as they shall not in any way interfere with or in any manner molest the persons or property of the whites.' On the part of the executive and administrative officers it was insisted-not, however, without some differences among themselves-that the proviso did not invest the Mille Lacs with any right in the old reservation expressly ceded by article 1 of the treaty, but merely permitted them to remain thereon as a matter of favor; that one purpose of the cession was to enable the government to survey the lands and open them to settlement, and that it was not intended that the permission to remain should interfere with this. But the Mille Lacs maintained that the proviso operated to reserve the lands for their occupancy and use indefinitely, and that the lands could not be opened to settlement while they remained and conducted themselves properly towards the whites in that vicinity. The survey was made, the lands were declared open to settlement and entry, and entries in considerable numbers were allowed from time to time; but the Mille Lacs persisted in their claim and refused to move, although repeatedly entreated to do so. This continued to be the situation until the act of 1889 was passed by Congress and accepted by the Mille Lacs and other Chippewas of Minnesota. In the meantime an order was issued by one Secretary of the Interior, suspending the allowance of further entries, as also further action upon those already allowed, and this order was recalled by a succeeding Secretary. Congress then passed the act of July 4, 1884 (23 Stat. at L. 76, 89, chap. 180), directing that the lands should not 'be patented or disposed of in any manner until further legislation.' The entries allowed up to that time covered about 55,000 acres, or approximately nine-tenths of the lands, and some were under [229 U.S. 498, 503] investigation upon charges that they were fraudulent. After the passage of the act of 1884, all further action was suspended awaiting further legislation.

That legislation came in the act of 1889. It provided for a commission to negotiate with all the bands of Chippewa in Minnesota for the cession and relinquishment of all their reservations, excepting the White Earth and Red Lake Reservations, and for the cession and relinquishment of so much of them as should not be required for allotments. It further provided that the cession and relinquishment should be obtained as to each reservation, other than the Red Lake, through the assent in writing of two thirds of the male adults of the band 'occupying and belonging to' it, and, as to the Red Lake Reservation, through a like assent of two thirds of the male adults of all the

Chippewas in the state; that the cession and relinquishment as to each reservation should be subject to the approval of the President, and when approved should operate as a complete extinguishment of the Indian title 'for the purposes and upon the terms' stated in the act; that thereupon all the Chippewas in the state, excepting those on Red Lake Reservation, should be removed to and take up their residence on the White Earth Reservation, and receive allotments in severalty therein, and allotment to those on the Red Lake Reservation should be made in that reservation; that any Indian residing on any of said reservations might, in his discretion, take his allotment 'on the reservation where he lives ... instead of being removed;' that the ceded lands not so allotted should be classified as 'pine lands' and as 'agricultural lands,' and be disposed of in the manner and at the prices stated in the act; and (7) that all moneys accruing from their disposal, after deducting expenses, should be placed in the treasury of the United States to the credit of all the Chippewas of Minnesota as a trust fund, drawing interest at 5 per cent per annum, the interest to be used [229 U.S. 498, 504] for their benefit and the principal to be distributed among them at the end of fifty years. In 6 there was a proviso, deemed important here, declaring 'that nothing in this act shall be held to authorize the sale or other disposal under its provisions of any tract upon which there is a subsisting, valid pre-emption or homestead entry, but any such entry shall be proceeded with under the regulations and decisions in force at the date of it allowance, and if found regular and valid, patents shall issue thereon.'

Through negotiations conducted under the authority of that act, the commissioners secured agreements with the Indians embodying the contemplated cessions and relinquishments, and these, upon submission to the President, were approved by him March 4, 1890. The agreement with the Mille Lacs, in addition to embodying a cession and relinquishment of the lands in the White Earth and Red Lake Reservations not required for allotments, contained an express assent to all the provisions of the act of 1889, and an express relinquishment of the lands in the Mille Lac Reservation, as is shown by the following excerpt from the agreement:

> 'We, the undersigned, being male adult Indians over eighteen years of age, of the Mille Lac band of Chippewas of the Mississippi, occupying and belonging to the Mille Lac Reservation under and by virtue of a clause in the twelfth article of the treaty of May 7, 1864 (13 Stat. at L. p. 693), do hereby certify and declare that we have heard read, interpreted, and thoroughly explained to our understanding the act of Congress, approved January 14, 1889, entitled, 'An Act for the Relief and Civilization of the Chippewa Indians, in the State of Minnesota' (Public, No. 13), which said act is embodied in the foregoing instrument, and after such explanation and understanding, have consented and agreed to said act, and have accepted and ratified the same, and do hereby accept and consent to and

ratify the said act, and each and all the provisions [229 U.S. 498, 505] thereof, ... and we do also hereby forever relinquish to the United States the right of occupancy on the Mille Lac Reservation, reserved to us by the twelfth article of the treaty of May 7, 1864.'

This agreement was negotiated at a council of the Mille Lacs, wherein they reiterated their claim under article 12, and at first declined to assent to the act of 1889, but upon further consideration assented and then signed the agreement. The commission, in reporting the result of its labors, gave a tabulated statement of the reservations, with the area of each, covered by the relinquishments, and included the Mille Lac Reservation, with an area of 61,014 acres, in the statement. In submitting the agreements, including that with the Mille Lacs, to the President, with the recommendation that each be separately approved, as was done, the Secretary of the Interior referred to the prolonged controversy with the Mille Lacs and said: 'The rights of the Indians upon this reservation have been a vexed question, full of difficulties and embarrassments; but it is hoped that this agreement will furnish a basis for its early and final solution.' Upon approving the agreements (they were sometimes spoken of as constituting in the aggregate a single document), the President transmitted a copy of them and of the accompanying papers to Congress for its information, and in the letter of transmittal said: 'Being satisfied from an examination of the papers submitted that the cession and relinquishment by said Chippewa Indians of their title and interest in the lands specified and described in the agreement with the different bands or tribes of Chippewa Indians in the state of Minnesota was obtained in the manner prescribed in the 1st section of said act, and that more than the requisite number have signed said agreement, I have as provided by said act, approved the said instruments in writing constituting the agreement entered into by the commissioners with the Indians.' Shortly [229 U.S. 498, 506] thereafter, and before the Mille Lacs removed from the old reservation, Congress passed the act of July 22, 1890 (26 Stat at L. 290, chap. 714), whereby a railroad right of way, including station grounds, was granted through that reservation upon condition that compensation therefor be paid to the United States for the use of the Indians, and that a failure to use the right of way and station grounds for railroad purposes would inure to the benefit of the Indians, thereby recognizing that the Indians had then come to have an interest in the disposal of the lands.

After the Mille Lacs gave their assent to the act of 1889 the entries theretofore allowed were examined and passed upon by the Land Department in regular course, and such as were found to be regular and bona fide were passed to patent. The remaining lands in the reservation were subsequently disposed of, not under the act of 1889, but under the general land laws, in pursuance of directions contained in the joint resolutions of December 19, 1893 (28 Stat. at L. 576) and May 27, 1898 (30 Stat. at L. 745).

Whatever might be said of its merits, it is apparent that there was a real controversy between the Mille Lacs and the government in respect of the rights of the former under article 12 of the treaty of 1864, and that the controversy was still subsisting when the act of 1889 was passed by Congress and assented to by the Indians. And we think it also is apparent that this controversy was intended to be and was thereby adjusted and composed. A manifest purpose of the act was to bring about the removal to the White Earth Reservation of all the scattered bands residing elsewhere than on the Red Lake Reservation, the Mille Lacs as well as the others; and this was to be accomplished, not through the exertion of the plenary power of Congress, but through negotiations with and the assent of the Indians. The provision in 6 for perfecting subsisting pre-emption and homestead entries, if found regular and valid, pointed most persuasively to a [229 U.S. 498, 507] purpose to extend the negotiations to the Mille Lac Reservation. The commission, the Secretary of the Interior, and the President, in seeking, obtaining, and approving the relinquishment of that reservation, all treated it as within the purview of the act, and the Mille Lacs did the same. Then, too, Congress recognized by the act of 1890, shortly following the approval of the agreement, that the Indians had come to have an interest in the disposal of the lands in that reservation.

But while the government thus waived its earlier position respecting the status of the reservation, and consented to recognize the contention of the Indians, this was done upon the express condition, stated in the proviso to 6, 'that nothing in this act shall be held to authorize the sale or other disposal under its provision of any tract upon which there is a subsisting, valid pre-emption or homestead entry, but any such entry shall be proceeded with under the regulations and decisions in force at the time of its allowance, and if found regular and valid, patents shall issue thereon.' In other words, the controversy was intended to be and was adjusted and composed by concessions on both sides, whereby the lands in the Mille Lac Reservation were put in the same category, and were to be disposed of for the benefit of the Indians in the same manner, as the lands in the other reservations relinquished under the act, but subject to the condition and qualification that all subsisting bona fide pre-emption and homestead entries should be carried to completion and patent under the regulations and decisions in force at the time of their allowance.

True, it is said on behalf of the Indians that they did not so understand that existing entries could be thus carried to patent. But of this it is enough to observe that the language of the proviso to 6 is plain and unambiguous; that the agreement recites that the Mille Lacs 'do hereby accept and consent to and [229 U.S. 498, 508] ratify the said act, and each and all of the provisions thereof;' and that the Indians, no less than the United States, are bound by the plain import of the language of the act and agreement. Not only so, but the act conferred upon the Mille Lacs many very substantial advantages which doubtless constituted the inducement to the adjustment and composition to which they assented. Among other advantages, it enabled them to share in the proceeds of the disposal of a vast acreage of lands in which they otherwise would have had no interest.

On behalf of the Indians it also is said that the proviso was limited to 'regular and valid' pre-emption and homestead entries, and that no entry of lands within an Indians reservation could come within that limitation. But this assumes the existence of the Mille Lac Reservation at the time of the entries, which was the very matter in dispute. Besides, the interpretation suggested could not be accepted without wholly rejecting the proviso, for if it was inapplicable to entries in the Mille Lac tract, it was equally inapplicable to any of the other tracts relinquished under the act. In saying this we do not indicate that there were other entries, for the reports of the Land and Indian Offices, which were before Congress when the act of 1889 was passed, disclosed the entries in the Mille Lac tract and did not show any others. Of course, the proviso cannot be rejected. It had an office to perform and must be given effect. It meant, as its terms plainly show, that entries made in accordance with existing regulations and decisions could, if bona fide, be carried to completion and patent in the usual way; and the phrase 'if found regular and valid' was evidently used with special reference to the charge that some of the entries were fraudulent, and with the purpose of eliminating such as were of that character.

We are accordingly of opinion that the act of 1889, to which the Indians fully assented, contemplated and [229 U.S. 498, 509] authorized the completion, and the issuing of patents on, all existing pre-emption and homestead entries in the Mille Lac tract which, in the course of the proceedings in the Land Department, should be found to be within the terms of the proviso of 6, and therefore that no rights of the Indians were infringed in so disposing of lands embraced in such entries. And we think the evident purpose of the proviso requires that it be held to include entries of that class theretofore passed to patent, of which there were some instances during the early period of the controversy.

As respects other lands in that tract, that is, such as were not within the terms of the proviso, we are of opinion that they came within the general provisions of the act, and were to be disposed of thereunder for the benefit of the Indians, in like manner as were the ceded lands in the other reservations, of which it was said in *Minnesota v. Hitchcock*, 185 U.S. 373, 394, 46 S.L. 3e. 954, 965, 22 Sup. Ct. Rep. 650: 'The cession was not to the United States absolutely, but in trust. It was a cession of all of the unallotted lands. The trust was to be executed by the sale of the ceded lands and a deposit of the proceeds in the Treasury of the United States, to the credit of the Indians, such sum to draw interest at 5 per cent.'

As before stated, the lands not within the proviso were disposed of, not under the act of 1889, but under the general land laws; not for the benefit of the Indians, but in disregard of their rights. This was clearly in violation of the trust before described, and the Indians are entitled to recover for the resulting loss. In principle it is as if the lands had been disposed of conformably to the act of 1889, and the net proceeds placed in the trust fund created by 7, and the government then had used the money, not for the benefit of the Indians, but for some wholly different purpose. That the wrongful disposal was in obedience to directions given in two resolutions of Congress does not make it any the less a violation of the trust. The resolutions [229 U.S. 498, 510], unlike the legislation sustained in *Cherokee Nation v. Hitchcock,* 187 U.S. 294, 307, 47 S.L. ed. 183, 190, 23 Sup. Ct. Rep. 115, and *Lone Wolf v. Hitchcock,* 187 U.S. 553, 564, 568 S., 47 L. ed. 299, 305, 307, 23 Sup. Ct. Rep. 216, were not adopted in the exercise of the administrative power of Congress over the property and affairs of dependent Indian wards, but were intended to assert, and did assert, an unqualified power of disposal over the lands as the absolute property of the government. Doubtless this was because there was a misapprehension of the true relation of the government to the lands, but that does not alter the result.

The court of claims gave no effect to the proviso to 6, and the findings afford no basis for separating the damages rightly recoverable from those erroneously assessed on account of lands disposed of under pre-emption and homestead entries allowed prior to the act of 1889. The case must be remanded for a reassessment of the damages.

By reason of a contention advanced in the briefs, it is well to observe that the damages should be assessed on the basis of the prices which would have been controlling had the act of 1889 been rightly applied.

The judgment is reversed, and the case is remanded for further proceedings in conformity with this opinion.

REVERSED.

Mr. Justice McKenna and Mr. Justice Day dissent.

United States Department of the Interior
Office of Indian Affairs

Mar 18, 1937

Hon. Elmer Thomas,
  Chairman, Committee on Indian Affairs,
  United States Senate.

My dear Mr. Chairman:

I have your letter of March 12 requesting seven sets of documents relating to the Indian Reorganization Act. Herewith and under separate cover, I am sending you the following:

1) List of Indian tribes under the Indian Reorganization Act.
2) List of Indian tribes who have adopted constitutions and by-laws in accordance with the Indian Reorganization Act.
3) List of Indian tribes who have adopted charters of incorporation in accordance with the Indian Reorganization Act.
4) Copy of the "Law and Order Regulations" approved by the Secretary of the Interior, November 27, 1935.
5) Copy of the "Code of Ordinances of the Gila River Pima-Maricopa Indian Community".
6) Printed copies of seventeen charters of incorporation and fifty constitutions and by-laws.

We are unable to send you copies of the following:

1) Five charters of incorporation and nine constitutions and by-laws which have been adopted.
2) Copies of several constitutions and charters which have been submitted for election, or which are in the process of being submitted.
3) Copies of law and order codes which have been adopted by certain tribes.

It would place a very excessive demand upon our stenographic force, to supply you with copies of the above. They are, however, available for inspection at this Office.

Sincerely yours,
Signed.   John Collier
Commissioner.

INDIAN TRIBES UNDER THE I.R.A.

STATE	AGENCY OR SCHOOL	RESERVATION OR RANCHERIA	TRIBE	TOTAL POPULATION (ESTIMATED)
Arizona	Colorado River	Colorado River	Chemeheuvi	705
			Mojave	
		Fort Mojave	Mojave	432
		Cocapah		32
		Fort Apache	Apache	2,718
	Paiute (Utah)	Kaibab	Paiute	93
	Phoenix	Camp Verde	Pavapai-Apache	451
	Pima	Fort McDowell	Mohave-Apache	205
		Gila River	Pima-Maricopa	4,659
		Salt River	Pima	1,049
		Ak Chin		179
	San Carlos	San Carlos	Apache	2,843
	Sells	Gila Bend	Papago	228
		San Xavier	Papago	525
		Papago	Papago	5,146
	Truxton Canon	Havasupai	Havasupai	201
		Truxton Canon		431
	Hopi	Hopi	Hopi	2,538
California	Hoopa Valley	Trinidad	Trinidad	4
		Cresent City		16
		Blue Lake	Blue Lake	
	Colorado River (Ariz.)	Fort Young	Apache	519
	Mission	Capitan Grande	Capitan Grande	160
		Inc. Barona	Barona	
		Cuyapaipe	Cuyapaipe	
		Laguna		3
		La Posta	La Posta	3
		Meazanita		67
	San Pascual			9

STATE	AGENCY OR SCHOOL	RESERVATION OR RANCHERIA	TRIBE	TOTAL POPULATION (ESTIMATED)
		Santa Ynez		90
	Sacramento	Alexander Valley		28
		Alturas		25
		Big Bend		
		Big Valley		92
		Cache Creek		30
		Buena Vista		4
		Cedarville (No residents)		
		Cloverdale		40
		Colusa		72
		Colfax (No residents)		
		Cortina		40
		Coyote Valley		16
		East Lake (Robinson)		46
		Fort Bidwell		180
		Guideville		54
		Grindstone		50
		Hopland		112
		Jackson		3
		Likely		50
		Lookout		24
		Lytton (No residents)		
		Manchester		92
		Middletown		25
		Millerton (No residents)		
		Montgomery Creek		14

STATE	AGENCY OR SCHOOL	RESERVATION OR RANCHERIA	TRIBE	TOTAL POPULATION (ESTIMATED)
		Nevada City		36
		Paskenta		52
		Pinoleville		102
		Potter Valley		52
		Redwood Valley		36
		Rumsay		22
		Santa Rose		
		Sebastopal (No residents)		
		Sheep Ranch		1
		Stewart's Point		140
		Sulphur Banks		40
		Susanville		18
		Strathmore (No residents)		
		Taylorville		4
		Tuolumne		80
		Tule River		188
		Upper Lake		72
		Wilton		28
		Round Valley	Covelo	827
Colorado	Con. Ute	Southern Ute	Ute	389
		Ute Mountain	Ute	445
Florida	Seminole	Seminole	Seminole	580
Idaho	Coeur d'Alene	Kalispel	Kalispel Cree	88
	Fort Hall	Fort Hall	Shoshone-Hannock	1,839
Iowa	Sac and Fox	Sac and Fox	Sac and Fox	419
Kansas	Potawatomi	Potawatomi	Potawatomi	955
		Sac and Fox	Sac and Fox	99
		Kickapoo	Kickapoo	308

STATE	AGENCY OR SCHOOL	RESERVATION OR RANCHERIA	TRIBE	TOTAL POPULATION (ESTIMATED)
		Iowa	Iowa	498
Minnesota	Con. Chippewa	White Earth	Chippewa (Minn.)	8,059
		Leech Lake	"	2,076
		Fon du Lac	"	1,298
		Bois Fort	"	627
		Grand Portage	"	377
	Red Lake	Red Lake		1,968
	Pipestone		Lower Sioux)	
		Pipestone	Granite Falls)	552
			Prairie Island)	
Michigan	Great Lakes (Wis.)	L'Anse		1,116
		Bay Milles		190
		Isabella		848
		Hannahville		108
		Ontanagon		
Mississippi	Choctaw	Choctaw	Choctaw)	1,792
		Chetimaha (La.)	Chetimaha)	70
Montana	Blackfeet	Blackfeet	Blackfeet	3,962
	Flathead	Flathead	Conf. Salish & Kootenai	2,964
	Fort Belknap	Fort Belknap	Assiniboine Cros Ventre	1,367
	Rocky Boy's	Rocky Boy's	Chippewa Cree	676
	Tongue River	Tongue River	Cheyenne	1,562
Nebraska	Winnebago	Winnebago	Winnebago	1,187
		Ponca	Ponca	392
		Omaha	Omaha	1,642
		Santee	Santee	1,277
Nevada	Carson	Fort McDermitt		273
		Pyramid Lake		549

STATE	AGENCY OR SCHOOL	RESERVATION OR RANCHERIA	TRIBE	TOTAL POPULATION (ESTIMATED)
		Summit Lake		64
		Reno-Sparks		190
		Dresslerville	Waahoe	150
		Lovelocke		90
		Winnemucca		50
		Battle Mountain		30
		Elko		80
		Ely		70
		Indian Ranch		20
		Walker River		492
		Yerington	Paiute	102
	Paiute (Utah)	Moapa River		158
		Las Vegas Tract		40
	West Soshone	Duck Valley	Shoshone-Paiute	516
New Mexico	Mescalero	Mescalero	Apache	722
	Jicarilla	Jicarilla	Apache	703
	United Pueblos	Nambe	Pueblo	128
		Picuris	"	117
		Pojoaque	"	9
		San Ildefonso	"	126
		Santa Clara	"	400
		San Juan	"	561
		Taos	"	745
		Tesuque	"	123
		Acomo	"	1,125
		Cochiti	"	305
		Isleta	"	1,103
		Laguna	"	2,271
		Sandia	"	129
		San Felipe	"	596

STATE	AGENCY OR SCHOOL	RESERVATION OR RANCHERIA	TRIBE	TOTAL POPULATION (ESTIMATED)
		Santa Ana	"	241
		Santa Domingo	"	366
		Sia	"	189
		Zuni	"	2,051
New York	New York	Cornplanter (Penn.)		80
North Carolina	Cherokee	Cherokee	Eastern Cherokee	3,254
North Dakota	Fort Berthold	Fort Berthold	Arikara)	
			Gros Ventre)	1,569
			Mandan)	
	Standing Rock	Standing Rock	Sioux	3,775
Oregon	Salem	Grand Ronde	Grand Ronde	356
	Warm Springs	Warm Springs		992
	"	Burns		134
South Dakota	Cheyenne River	Cheyenne River	Sioux	3,288
	Crow Creek	Lower Brule	Sioux	603
	Flandreau	Flandreau	Santee Sioux	503
	Pine Ridge	Pine Ridge	Oglala Sioux	8,370
	Rosebud	Rosebud	Sioux	6,362
	Rosebud	Yankton	Sioux	2,018
Texas	Kiowa (Okla.)	Ala. & Coushatta		300
Utah	Paiute	Goshute	Goshute	155
	"	Cedar City	Paiute	28
	"	Gandy	Paiute	6
	"	Konosh	Paiute & Ute	24
	"	Keosharen	Ute	30
	"	Las Vega		40
	"	Paiute	Paiute	19
	"	Shivwitz	Shivwitz	79
	"	Skull Valley	Goshute	41
	Uintah & Curay	Uintah & Curay	Ute	1,251

STATE	AGENCY OR SCHOOL	RESERVATION OR RANCHERIA	TRIBE	TOTAL POPULATION (ESTIMATED)
	Fort Hall (Idaho)	Washakie		137
Washington	Taholah	Makah		403
		Nisqually		63
		Ozette		2
		Quinaielt		1,729
		Hoh		4
		Quileute		242
		Skokomish		189
		Squaxin Island	Squaxin	39
	Tulalip	Muckleshoot	Muckleshoot	200
		Fort Madison	Suquamish	171
		Puyallup	Puyallup	328
		Swinomish	Swinomish	373
		Tulalip	Tulalip	663
		Clallam	Clallam	738
		Nooksak		235
		Skagit-Suiattle		205
Wisconsin	Great Lakes	Bad River	Chippewa	1,211
		Lac Courte Oreille	"	1,559
		Red Cliff	"	506
		Potawatomi	"	388
		Lac du Flambeau	Lac du Flambeau	853
	Keshena	Menominee	Menominee	2,077
		Oneida		3,128
		Stockbridge		500

March 18, 1937

Honorable John Collier
Commissioner
Office of Indian Affairs
Washington, D.C.

Dear Mr. Collier:

This will acknowledge receipt of the data sent me by messenger, relative to the Indian Reorganization Act.

Thanking you for this favor, I am

Yours very cordially,

Elmer Thomas

Index

A

Aay-gwon-ay-be, 151
Abbott, Dr. Wm., 194
Ada-we-ge-shik, 265
Adkins, Assistant Attorney General Jesse C., 397, 410
Ah-ah-jaw-wa-ke-shick, 279
Ah-nah-me-ance (ALSO Ah-nank-me-ance), 226, 227
Aish-ke-bo-ge-koshe (ALSO Aish-ke-bug-e-koshe), 265, 267, 273
Aitkin County, 30, 242
Aitkin, William A., 19, 20, 30, 31, 41, 242, 264
Ak Chin, 419
Allen, E. A., 196
Allotment Act, 126, 157, 161, 235
Allotments, 111, 127, 131, 135, 136, 138, 144, 145, 147, 148, 150, 157, 160-167, 176, 177, 182-184, 187, 188, 191, 192, 195-198, 201, 202, 205, 207, 208, 212-222, 232, 235, 236, 242, 285-288, 291, 292, 295, 302, 311, 316, 334, 335, 337, 339, 341, 349, 378-381, 383, 390, 393, 406, 408, 412, 413
Allottees, 127, 188, 196-198, 217-219, 222, 223, 286
American Dream, 126
American Eagle, 52
American Fur Company, 29-32, 229
American Indian Citizenship, 251
American Indian Movement, 236
American Security & Trust Co. v. D.C., 368
Anderson, George M., 397, 410
Anderson, William, 227
Appropriation Act, 363, 364, 377, 383
Arrowood, John, 200-201
Arthur, President Chester A., 110, 111
Ashman, Edward, 274
Astor, John Jacob, 29
Atcheson, Indian Agent George, 100, 249
Austin, Minnesota Governor, 102, 104, 250
Aw-aw-bedway-we-dung, 279
Ay-dah-wah-ne-kway-be-naos, 152
Ayer, Harry D., 189, 203, 227, 228
Ayer, Jeannette O., 228

B

Bailey, Goddard, 32
Baker, Howard, 64, 65
Baker, J. H., 105
Baldwin, Melvin R., 215
Battle of Wounded Knee, 128
Be-dud-dunce, 101
Be-she-kee (ALSO Be-sheck-kee,), 267, 279
Beaulieu, Charles N., 125, 151, 274
Beaulieu, Claude, 21
Beaulieu, Frank D., 185
Beaulieu, Gustav H., 135, 136, 176, 178-180, 181, 185, 186
Beaulieu, John H., 135, 136
Beaulieu, N., 125, 251
Beaulieu, P. H., 151
Beaulieu, Paul H., 43, 47, 55, 62, 132, 185, 186, 274, 279
Beaver Creek, 69
Bedausky, Billy, 205
Bede, Congressman, 176
Beecher v. Wetherby, 347, 348
Bemidji, 184
Benjn, 284
Bennett, William J., 246
Berg, Nils B., 184
Berghold, Alexander, 64, 65, 69
Berry, George A., 185
Besheck-kee, 273
Bieulieu, 125

427

Big Cloud, 265
Big Drum, 26
Big Fork River, 267
Big Frenchman, 265
Big Mouth, 265
Big Woods, 64
Birch Coulee, 69, 75
Black River, 268, 281
Blackfeather, 297, 312, 340, 344, 345, 366, 390
Blake, Peter W., 226
Blatchford, Frank, 153
Bois Fort (ALSO Boise Forte, Boise Forte, Bois Forte), 136, 185, 195, 198, 206, 208, 209, 210, 231, 242, 243, 305, 306, 307, 358, 372, 391, 422
Bois Forts Reservation, 152, 153
Bolsheviks, 235
Bonga, Stephen (ALSO Steven), 35, 266
Booth, John Wilkes, 33
Booth, Judge, 315, 324, 327, 328, 332, 336
Borup, Dr. Charles, 30, 31
Brainerd, 19
Breck, James Lloyd, 81
Breckenridge, 74
Bresbois, Bernard, 31
Broken Tooth, 17, 18
Brower, Attorney, 181
Brown Wing, 64
Brown v. U.S., 390
Browning, Commissioner of Indian Affairs, 215
Bruce White, 246
Brunson, Missionary Alfred, 16, 17, 21
Buck More Dam, 246
Buffalo River, 268
Buffalo, 14, 44, 45, 53, 75, 82, 265, 267, 268, 273, 279
Bull Run, 70, 76
Burke Act, 155, 216
Burke, Commissioner of Indian Affairs Chas. H., 193, 195, 200, 201, 222
Burns, Consolidated Chippewa Agency Superintendent M.L., 203, 206-210
Bush, Joe, 205
Bushnell, Daniel P., 40, 264, 266

C

California, 27, 108, 419
California & Oregon Land Co. v. Rankin, 297, 310, 322
California & Oregon Land Co. v. Worden, 297, 310, 321
Camp Ripley, 80
Campbell, Chippewa Commission Chairman, 214
Campbell, Francis M., 226
Campbell, Indian Agent William M., 212
Campbell, Scott, 35, 266
Campbell, William M., 214, 215
Canadian Indians, 113
Canarsie Indians, 8
Capitan Grande, 419
Carcieri v. Salazar, 210
Carlson, John M., 227
Cass Lake Agency, 193, 194
Cass Lake Reservation, 185
Cass Lake, 46, 93, 136, 139, 141, 142, 185, 193-195, 197-200, 203, 208, 222, 252, 253, 255, 269, 271, 279, 305-307, 358, 372
Cass, Lewis, 17, 18, 34
Caw-caug-e-we-goon (ALSO Cawcang-e-we-gwan), 267, 273, 274
Chandler, Secretary of Interior Zachariah, 106, 119, 122, 250, 400, 402
Chapman, U.S. Indian Inspector George M., 122, 123, 125, 176
Charette, Joseph, 135
Che-a-na-quos, 265
Cherokee Intermarriage Cases, 297, 310
Cherokee Nation, 173, 274, 297, 298, 312, 315, 321, 347, 348, 365, 385, 417
Cherokee Nation v. Georgia, 321, 347
Cherokee Nation v. Hitchcock, 312, 315, 348, 365, 385, 417
Cherokees, 349
Chicago, 33, 289
Chickasaw Nations, 317, 365, 385
Chickasaws, 386
Chien, 18, 19, 29, 31
Childs, W. H., 78
Chippewa Agency, 86, 100, 117, 189-192, 195, 196, 198-200, 203, 205-209, 222-224, 242, 249
Chippewa Commission, 212-216
Chippewa Fund, 230
Chippewa Indians of Lake Superior, 352, 372
Chippewa Indians of Minnesota, viii, 131, 184-187, 190, 209, 241, 285, 295, 296, 309, 311, 312, 338, 349, 350, 355, 371, 380
Chippewa Indians of Minnesota v. United States, 209
Chippewa Outfit, 31
Chippewa Treaty Rights, 246
Chippewas of Minnesota of Red Lake Reservation, 307
Chippewas of Mississippi, 295, 311, 325, 334, 338, 350
Choctaw Nation, 310, 312, 317, 325, 327, 341, 385, 411
Choctaw Nation v. U.S., 297, 310, 312, 325, 327, 341
Chorister, 267, 273, 279
Chouteau Company, 30, 31
Christian Chiefs, 75
Christian Sioux, 70
City of Sherrill v. Oneida Indian Nation of New York, 6, 243
Civil War, 33, 70, 72, 73, 76, 95, 98, 126, 130, 139, 147, 156, 243, 335, 339

Clapp Act (ALSO Clapp Acts), 155, 190, 218-220, 222
Clapp, Minnesota Senator Harvey S., 177, 293, 357, 410
Clark, Commissioner of Indian Affairs William, 18
Clearwater County, 194
Cleland, Charles E., 22, 30, 31, 246, 247, 249
Cleveland, 108, 111, 126, 128, 130, 131
Cleveland, President Grover, 111, 126, 128, 130, 131
Cloquet, 2, 194, 199
Cloyd, J. C., 188
Club Women of Minnesota, 193
Clum, Commissioner of Indian Affairs H.R., 104, 105, 250
Cobmubbi (ALSO Cobnubby), 44, 87
Coffey, James I., 184, 186
Coleman, John, 142
College Park, 255
Collier, Commissioner of Indian Affairs John, xii, 206, 207, 209, 233-237, 242, 243, 255, 256, 418, 426
Columbus, 7, 8, 250
Columbus, Christopher, 7
Coming Home Following, 43
Commissioner of General Land Office, 250, 364
Company B, 69
Confederates, 73
Congrefs, 106, 107
Consolidated Chippewa Indian Agency, 195, 196, 198-200, 202, 203, 205-209, 222-224, 242
Constant, Susan, 8
Continental Congress, 3, 27
Cooper, Eugene A., 227
Coriell, Wm. W., 266
Cormorant Point, 10
Cowen, Secretary of Interior B.R., 104

Cox, Hank H., 75, 247
Cragg, R. L., 188
Crooked Creek, 188
Crooks, 30, 31
Crookston, 289, 290
Croping Sky, 43
Cross-in-the-Sky, 88
Crossing Sky, 80, 267, 273, 279
Crossing, Chief, 80
Crow Feather, 267, 274
Crow Wing River, 268
Crow Wing, 19, 23-26, 89, 263, 268, 271
Crowfeathers, 43
Cuba, 243, 244
Curly Head, 17, 18
Curtis, W. W., 250
Cut Ear, 265

D

Dahlgren Brothers, 205
Daiker, Fred, 209
Dakota Dawn, 74, 247
Dakota Territory, 77
Dakota, 1-4, 9-11, 14, 16-24, 26, 29, 74, 75, 77, 128, 247, 424
Dakotas, 19, 23, 75, 93
Danbury, Wis., 204, 210
Dawes Land Allotment Act, 108, 111, 126-128, 130, 131, 133, 135, 143, 144, 154, 157, 211, 216, 226, 235, 236, 240
Dawes, Senator Henry L., 126, 127
Day, Justice, 171, 417
Declaration of Independence, 3, 4, 129
Declaration of Policy, 220
Deer Creek Reservation, 198, 380
Deer Creek, 136, 153, 305-307, 372, 391
Deer River, 276, 281
Delano, Secretary of Interior Columbus, 250
Denmark, 30
Dennis, Fred, 161
Department of Interior, 368

Department of Justice, 218, 221, 222
Department of War, 34
Detroit Lakes, 213
Detroit, 213, 215, 229, 290
Dinwiddie, 145, 148, 195
Director of Lands, 208, 242, 243
District Attorney of Minnesota, 104
District Court, 227
District of Minnesota, 176
Doctrine of Discovery, xi, 5-8, 28, 245, 246
Dodge, Governor Henry, 34-41, 99, 238, 246, 263, 265
DOI, 251-255
Dole, Commissioner of Indian Affairs William P., 24, 25, 81, 82, 83, 85, 86, 88, 89, 91-93, 95-97, 99, 127, 129, 158, 175, 230, 239, 275, 278, 279, 280, 283, 284, 318, 365
Domit of Danbury, 204
Douglas, Indian Agent, 117
Dousman, Hercules L, 30, 31, 41, 264, 266
Dowling, John, 274
Dresslerville, 423
Drummond, Commissioner Willis, 104, 105, 110, 115, 250
Drunken Indians, 124
Du Lhut, Seiur, 9
Dubay, Jean Baptiste, 35, 266
Duck Valley, 423
Dufauld, Michael, 154
Duluth, 2, 9, 289
Dutch East India Company, 8
DVM, i

E

East Savannah River, 267
East Swan River, 267
Eastman, 47
Eastside Township, 209
Edgerton, George B., 170, 293, 357, 410

Edwards, Secretary of Interior John H., 195
Elko Theatre, 184
Elko, 184, 423
Emerson, J., 266
Emigrants, 58, 100
Emmegahbowh, 80-82
Episcopalian Bishop of Minnesota, 6
Episcopate, 247, 248
Era of Dredd Scott, 251
Ewing, Thomas, 31
Executive Order, 96, 108, 150, 298, 302, 321
Executive Proclamations, 285

F

Falls of St. Anthony, 21
FDR, 234
Fifth Minnesota Infantry, 69
Fifth Regiment Infantry, 266
Fifty-first Congress, 380
Fine Day, 279
Firewater, 62, 63
First National Bank of Cass Lake, 197
First Seated Feather, 81
Fishing Rights, 246
Flambeau, 35, 263, 265, 425
Flandreau, 424
Flat Mouth, Pillager Chief, (ALSO Flatmouth), 17, 35, 36, 38, 44-47, 51, 52, 60, 61, 63, 139, 141, 142, 265, 267, 273
Flat Mouth, Ruth, 139, 141, 142
Fletcher, J. E., 274
Flint, Indian Agent, 213
FOIA, v
Folsom, Frank W., 106, 110, 119, 376, 398
Fond-du-lac, 210
Forbes, Wm. H., 266
Forest City, 72
Fort Abercrombie, 75
Fort Apache, 419
Fort Atkinson, 229
Fort Belknap, 422
Fort Berthold, 424
Fort Bidwell, 420
Fort Hall, 421, 425

Fort Madison, 425
Fort McDermitt, 422
Fort McDowell, 419
Fort Mojave, 419
Fort Ridgely, 64, 67, 69-75, 80
Fort Ripley, 24, 25, 70, 79-83, 89-92, 99, 129
Fort Snelling, 17-21, 29, 35, 66, 70, 73, 83, 229
Fort Young, 419
Forty-ninth Congress, 376
Fox Indians, 364, 385
France, 27, 28
Franklin, Benjamin, viii, 11
Frazer, Jac, 73
Fuller, George, 279

G

Gag, Anton, 68
Galbraith, Indian Agent, 67, 70
Garden City, 73
Gardner, Indian Inspector, 125
Garfield, President James A., 109
Garretson, O. E., 102
Garrison, D. E., 124
Garvey, Lewis, 204
General Allotment Act, 126, 157
General Land Commissioner, 102
General Land Office, 28, 104-106, 110, 114, 119, 120, 195, 250, 288, 289, 346, 364, 376, 379, 382, 396, 399, 406
Geo, D., 279
Georgia, 298, 310, 321, 327, 347
Gere, Lt. Thomas, 70
Ghost Dance, 128
Gilfillin, Joseph A., 72, 176
Gingioncumigoke, 30
Ginsberg, Justice Ruth B., 6
Godspeed, 8
Goose Lake, 275, 281
Goumean, Francois, 266
Grand Marias, 152, 193
Grand Medicine Lodge, 80

Grand Portage Chippewa, 152
Grand Portage Reservation, 152, 195, 307, 380
Grand Portage, 136, 152, 193-195, 198, 199, 203, 205, 206, 208-210, 222, 231, 242, 243, 305-307, 358, 372, 380, 391, 422
Grand Rapids, 143
Granite Falls, 422
Grant, Hiram P. 75
Grant, Ulysses S., 98
Great Britain, 3, 28, 51
Great Council, 50, 55, 133
Great Father, 21, 22, 25, 37, 38, 49, 52, 55, 84, 86, 87, 90, 91, 93, 97, 100, 114, 140, 142, 164, 165, 231, 244
Great Lakes, 247, 422, 425
Great Miami River, 12
Great Spirit, 37, 43, 66, 101, 144
Greysolon, Daniel, 9
Grindstone, 420
Grove City, 64
Guiteau, Charles, 109
Gull Lake Band, 91, 93, 276, 279, 281
Gull Lake Indians, 89, 135, 138
Gull Lake Ojibwe, 21
Gull Lake Reservation, 112, 277
Gull Lake, 19, 21-24, 35, 36, 63, 79, 80, 82, 84, 87-93, 101, 112, 127, 135, 138, 169, 170, 225, 265, 268, 275-277, 279-281, 300, 301, 317, 325, 356, 358, 372

H

Ha-tau-wa, 265
Hall, Darwin, 211, 212, 213, 214, 216
Hancock, General, 101
Harriman, Indian Agent, 145
Harrison, Minneapolis Attorney Alexander M., 178, 180

Harrison, President Benjamin, 126, 128, 131, 149, 152, 154, 164, 170, 211, 295, 303-305, 311, 329, 330, 351, 355, 357, 380
Hart, Mark, 176
Harvey v. U.S., 297, 309
Hatch, E. A. C., 279
Hauke, C. F., 190
Haverstock, 209, 210, 228
Haverstock, Catherine B., 228
Haverstock, Henry W., 228
Hayes, President Rutherford B., 106-108, 250
He That Passes Under Everything, 63, 267
Heard, Isaac V. D., 76
Henderson, Daniel B., 357, 410
Henderson, Daniel E., 293
Hennepin, Father, 9
Herriman, David J., 43
Herriman, Indian Agent D.B., 61, 62, 274
Hicks, Dr. Frank, 193
Hill, James J., 230
Hill, Tom, 190
Hitchcock, Secretary of Interior Ethan, 173, 174, 177, 209, 297, 310-312, 315, 339, 342, 347, 348, 365, 385, 416, 417
Ho Chunk, 20, 21
Hole-in-the-Day, Gull Lake Chief (ALSO Hole-in-the-day, Holein-the-day), xi, 15-26, 36, 39, 41-51, 53-55, 57-63, 79-83, 85, 91-96, 99, 101, 109, 113, 126, 127, 129, 157, 158, 166, 211, 225, 239, 248, 265, 267, 269, 280, 281, 283, 284, 301
Homeless Mille Lacs, 187
Hook, Land Field Agent A. L., 210
Hoopa Valley, 419
Hopkins, S. G., 187
Hopkins, Secretary of Interior S.G., 187, 188
Houghton, F. W., 293, 357, 410

House, Dr. Z. E., 194
Howard-Wheeler Act, 206
Howard, General, 102
Howard, J. R., 179
Howard, Nebraska Congressman Edgar, 235
Howry, Judge, 171, 313, 329, 371, 375, 377, 388, 394
Hoxie, Frederick E., 251
Hudson River, 8
Hudson, Henry, 8

I

I-ta-tso-yi-jig, 177
In-zahn, 151
India, 7, 8
Indian Affairs Committee, 126, 127, 130, 360
Indian Affairs, i, v, vii, 17, 18, 24, 25, 27, 28, 31, 34, 40, 42, 68, 81-83, 85, 89, 93, 95, 96, 98, 99, 103-106, 109-111, 117, 121, 126-130, 133, 148, 158, 162, 175-178, 182, 184, 187-190, 195, 200, 205-210, 213, 215, 220-222, 230, 237, 241-243, 249-251, 264, 270-272, 275, 277, 279, 280, 284, 304-307, 338, 360, 365, 367, 374-376, 387, 388, 392, 399, 404, 405, 418, 426
Indian Child Welfare Act, 237
Indian Reorganization Act, viii, 205-207, 210, 236, 237, 241-243, 418, 426
Indian Territory, 217
Indian Tribes Under the I. R. A., 206, 256, 419, 426
Indian Trust Fund, 29, 32
Intercourse Acts, 246
Iowa Territory, 229
IRA, 105, 114, 194, 236
Iron Sky Woman, 80
Iroquois, 1
Isanti County, 101
Island of La Pointe, 1
Isle Royale, 30
Izatys, 10

J

Jackpot Junction Casino, 67
Jackson County, 74
James, Edwin, 12, 246
Jamestown, 4, 8
Japan, 7
Jefferson, Thomas, 156, 157
Jekey, John, 200, 201
Johnson, President Andrew, 225
Johnson, Reverend John, 25, 80, 137, 138, 275, 279, 280
Johnson v. M'Intosh, 6, 347
Jones, Commissioner of Indian Affairs, 158, 176
Jones, George W., 34
Jones, Robinson, 64
Jones v. Meechan, 310
Jones v. Meehan, 297, 321, 325, 326
Jones v. Meehan, supra, 327
Jourdan, Interpreter Allen R., 151
Jurisdictional Act, 171, 294-296, 300, 309, 312, 315-317, 347, 349, 357, 359, 360, 363, 364, 385, 410

K

Ka-be-ma-be, 265
Ka-cheu, 227
Ka-ka-quap, 265
Ka-nan-da-wa-win-zo, 265
Kalamazoo, 229
Kandiyohi County, 72
Kansas, 421
Kaom-de-i-ye-ye-dan, 64
Karaim, Reed, 245
Karbekaun, 276
Kathio, 195
Kaw-be-mub-bee, 267, 274
Kay-gwa-daush, 267, 273
Kay-ke-now-aus-e-kung, 141, 142
Ke-che-wa-me-te-go, 265
Ke-me-wen-aush, 279
Keh-beh-naw-gay, 279
Keith, Charles, 227
Kentucky River, 12
Kentucky, 12, 15

Keys, Riley, 274
Killing Ghost, 64
King George, 3, 237
Kirkwood, Secretary of Interior Samuel J., 109, 111
Kis-ke-ta-wak, 265
Knutson, Congressman Harold, 189
Ko de Quah, 166
Kob-mub-bey, 279
Kootenai, 422
Kropotkin, Peter, 234

L

L. & G. R. Co. v. United States, 321
La Abra Silver Mining Co., 297, 309
La Point, 2, 30
La Pointe Agency, 153
La Pointe, 1, 2, 16, 20, 30, 31, 35, 147, 153, 265, 276
La Posta, 419
La Trappe, 265
LaAbra Silver Mining Co., 309
Lac Courte Oreilles, 35
Lac De Flambeau, 265
Lake Calhoun, 20
Lake Courteoville, 265
Lake De Flambeau, 263
Lake Hassler, 269
Lake Huron, 1
Lake Mille Lac (ALSO Lake Mille Lacs), vii, 9, 35, 93, 127, 144, 167, 170, 177, 194, 208, 225, 275, 280, 317, 356
Lake Shetek, 71, 72
Lake Shore Mille Lacs, 183
Lake St. Croix, 263
Lake Superior Chippewa, 35, 97, 153
Lake Superior Mining Company, 30
Lake Superior Ojibwe, 23
Lake Superior, 1, 2, 13, 16, 23, 30, 35, 57, 95, 97, 153, 158, 263, 265, 266, 352, 372

Lake Winnebagoshish (ALSO Winnebogoshish, Winnibigoshish, Winnigigoshish), XII, 46, 136, 139, 142, 225, 247, 249, 256, 267, 269-276, 280, 282, 300, 301, 306, 307, 317, 358, 365, 372, 373, 387
Lake Winnibigoshish Bands, xii, 256, 267, 269, 270, 272-276, 280, 300, 301, 307, 317, 358, 365, 372, 373, 387
Lake Winnibigoshish Reservations, 307
Lakota Sioux, 128
Land Acquisition Program, 255
LaPointe, 96
Larrabee, 378
Las Vega, 424
Latrappe, 36, 37
Le Brocheux, 265
Leach Lake (ALSO Leech Lake), 16, 17, 19, 24-26, 35, 36, 38, 46, 84, 85, 93, 135, 138, 139, 142, 143, 145, 185, 194, 195, 198, 199, 203, 205, 206, 208-210, 222, 232, 242, 243, 265, 266, 269, 271, 272, 275, 277, 279, 280, 281, 305-307, 358, 372, 391, 393, 422
Leaf River, 268
Leahy, Captain M. A., 153
Leavenworth, Lt. Colonel Henry, 17, 297, 310, 321, 347
Leavenworth, etc., R.R. Co. v. U.S., 297, 310, 347
Leech Lake Band, 93, 139, 143
Leech Lake Indians, 84, 85, 194
Leech Lake Pillagers, 139
Leech Lake Reservation, 26, 185, 195, 198
Leon Houde, 109
LeSeuer County, 73
Leslie, Frank, 78
Lincoln, Mary Todd, 76

Lincoln, President Abraham, 32, 33, 76, 109, 130
Lindbergh, Charles A., 186, 187
Litchfield, 64
Little Boy River, 269
Little Crow, 20, 24, 25, 65-67, 69, 71, 72, 75, 79, 80
Little Crow, Chief, 20, 24, 25, 65-67, 69, 71, 72, 75, 79, 80
Little Falls, 21, 72, 100, 109, 249
Little Frenchman, 266
Little Hill (ALSO Litle Hill), 267, 273
Little Rice River, 268
Little Six, 39, 265
Lockwood, E., 266
Lone Man, 265
Lone Wolf, 174, 297, 310, 312, 315, 342, 347, 365, 385, 417
Lone Wolf v. Hitchcock, 174, 297, 310, 312, 315, 342, 347, 365, 385, 417
Long Lake Portage, 268
Long Prairie, 19, 47
Long-Knife, 55
Loons Foot, 266
Louisiana Purchase, 27, 156
Lowe, Robert, 363
Lower Sioux Agency, 67
Lower Sioux Indian Community, 67
Loyalists, 3
Lund, Thomas, 246
Luse, Indian Agent, 125, 176
Lytton, 420

M

Ma-cou-da, 265
Ma-ghe-ga-bo, 265
Ma-ne-to-ke-shick, 279
Ma-ya-je-way-we-dung, 279
Mackinac, 29
Madeline Island, 1, 2, 16, 30
Magejabo, 44
Magizzy, 44

Index • 433

Mah-eeng-annce (ALSO Mah-eng-aunce), 151, 232
Mah-ge-gah-bow (ALSO Maug-e-gaw-bow), 140, 267, 274
Mah-ge-ke-wis, 151
Mah-yah-ge-way-we-durg, 267, 273
Mahnomen, 194
Maine Prairie, 72
Maine, 32, 72
Malone, Charles, 33, 179, 181
Mang-go-sit, 266
Manhattan Island, 8
Manhattan, 8
Manifest Destiny, xi, 5, 245
Manitowab, Isaac, 81
Mankato, Chief, 73-75, 77, 78
Manney, Reverend, 24
Manypenny, Commissioner of Indian Affairs Colonel George W., 23, 42-51, 55-60, 62, 126, 161, 239, 267, 273
Manypenny, Louis, 161
Markville, 202
Marsh, Captain John, 70
Marshall, Chief Justice John, 6, 156, 157, 328
Marty, Bishop Martin, 131, 133-135, 137, 141, 152-154
Maryland, 8
Mashkorden, 276
Mashkordens River, 281
Massachusetts, 8, 126, 130, 290
Massacres, 72, 369, 375
Maw-je-ke-shick, 279
May-dway-aush, 152
May-dway-gon-on-ind, Chief, 133, 134
Mayflower, 8
Mayo, Dr. William, 74
McCarty, Ellen, 26
McClellan, General, 76
McClellan, Reuben F., 226
McClure, Daniel, 314
McClure v. U.S., 297, 309
McClurken, James M., 246

McFarland, Commissioner, 110, 397
McKechnie, Dr. Wilfred, 194
McKenna, Justice, 171, 322, 325, 418
McKinley, President, 157
McLaughlin, Inspector James ,161, 165, 167, 407, 408
Mdewakanton Dakota Sioux (ALSO Mdewankonton Dakota), 9, 29, 65, 66
Me-ge-zee, Mille Lac Chief, 182, 188, 189, 192
Me-jaw-ke-ke-shick, 279
Me-no-ke-shick, 279
Me-no-min-e-ke-shen, 279
Me-zee-gun, 151
Me-zhake-ge-shig, 136
Medicine Bottle, 68
Meeker County, 64
Mendota, 29, 35
Menomenies, 138, 139
Menomenkeshin, 63
Menominee, 20, 425
Merchants National Bank of St Cloud, 179
Meritt, Assistant Commissioner of Indian Affairs E. B., 188, 190
Mezian, Wesley R. , 195
Mi-gi-di (ALSO Mi-gi-si), 177, 267, 274
Michelet, Indian Agent Simon, 158, 161, 164, 167, 176-180, 407, 408
Michigan Chippewa, 96
Michigan State University, 247
Michigan, 31, 32, 65, 96, 229, 247, 290, 422
Michno, Gregory F., 74, 247
Middle Creek, 69
Middletown, 420
Migizi, Chief, 81
Mile Lac Reservation, 382
Mille Lac Band Brief, xii, 304
Mille Lac Lake, 111, 181, 182, 194, 198, 202, 204, 238, 372
Mille Lac Non-Removal Indians, 204
Mille Lac Removal Indians, 176

Mille Lac Resolution, 347
Mille Lacs Council, 150
Mille Lacs County Courthouse, 228, 255
Mille Lacs County, i, vii, viii, 98, 99, 110, 131, 157, 195, 228, 237, 238, 241, 243, 255, 408
Mille Lacs Day School, 193
Mille Lacs District, 209
Mille Lacs Indian Trading Post, 204
Mille Lacs Lake Indian Reservation, 260, 261
Mille Lacs Reservation Boundary, 247
Mille Lacs Reserve, 105
Millerton, 420
Milwaukee, 290
Minneapolis, 124, 178, 199, 205, 251, 289
Minnesota Chippewa Indian Tribe, 59, 99, 127, 154, 199, 205, 208-211, 227, 228, 231, 242, 243, 285, 355, 367, 371, 391
Minnesota Consolidated, 242, 243
Minnesota Fund, 187, 188
Minnesota Historical Society, 46, 228
Minnesota Indians, 238, 355
Minnesota Regiment, 74
Minnesota River Valley, 75
Minnesota River, 69, 75
Minnesota Sioux, 83
Minnesota State Legislature, 23
Minnesota Territory, 230
Minnesota v. Hitchcock, 173, 209, 297, 310, 311, 339, 416
Minot, 18
Mis-co-pe-nen-shey, 279
Mis-qua-dace, Sandy Lake Chief, 93, 94, 127, 158, 225, 280, 283, 284
Mississippi Band of Chippewa, 19, 23, 26, 35, 42, 45, 47, 53, 56, 57, 59, 63, 83, 85, 87-89, 95, 96, 118, 153, 184, 208, 213, 225, 238, 239, 267-269,

271, 272, 274, 351,358, 365, 372, 373, 387, 391, 398, 411
Mississippi Railroad Company, 158
Mississippi River, 9, 21, 29, 267-269, 276, 281
Mississippi Valley, 31
Mitchell v. U.S., 297, 310
MN Historical Society, 249
Mo. Kans. Tex. Ry. v. Roberts, 343
Mo-so-ma-na, 124
Mo-so-ma-ni Point, 190
Mo-zo-eno-nay, 101
Mo-zo-eno-nay, Chief, 101
Moapa River, 423
Molassel, 200
Mon-o-min-a-ga-shee, 85
Monks, J.S., 242
Monroe Skinaway, 210
Mont-so-mo, 266
Montana, 235, 422
Montevideo, 75
Montreal, 1
Moore, Judith, 246
Moose, 2, 14, 279
Mooze-o-mah-nay, 151
Morgan, Commissioner of Indian Affairs T. J., i, 128, 148, 241
Morison, U. S. Indian Agt, G. A., 151
Morrill, Ashley, 25
Morrison County Petition, 250
Morrison County, 109, 118, 226, 250
Morrison, Donald S., 161
Morrison, White Earth Field Clerk John G., 185, 186, 203,-204, 253, 279
Mose-o-man-nay, 279
Muh-eng-aunce, Chief, 145-147
Mun-o-min-e-kay-shein, 267
Murdering Yell, 266
Murray County, 71
Muskrat, 13, 36, 63

N

Na-qua-na-bie, 265
Na-ta-me-ga-bo, 265
Na-wa-ge-wa, 265
Naba, 44
Nadoueciouz, 10
Nagi-wi-cak-te, 64
Nah-bah-nay-aush, 151
Nah-gah-nup, 153, 154
Nah-gua-na-be, 124
Nah-gus-na-be, 124
NAID, i, 251-255
NAKC, i, 251-255
Narragansett Bay, 8
National Anthropological Archives, 22
National Archives, v, 255
National Bank of St. Cloud, 178, 179
Native American Graves, 1
Naudin, 265
Naw-bon-e-aush, 279
Naw-gaw-ne-gaw-bow, 279
Nay-bun-a-caush, 267, 273
Nay-she-kay-we-gaj-bow, 185
Nay-tow-aush, Chief, 136
Nay-tum-gwon-a, 177
Naytahwash (ALSO Naytahwaush), 194, 199
Ne-be-da-gonce, 226
Ne-gaun-ah-quod, Chief, 132
Ne-gon-e-binase, Mille Lac Chief, 182
Neb-a-wash, 87
Negroes, 33, 157
Nelson Act, ix, xi, xii, 16, 126-131, 133, 135-140, 142, 144, 152-154, 158, 160, 161, 163, 164, 168, 169, 171, 175-177, 205, 208-212, 216, 218, 226, 230-233, 236, 240-242, 251, 253, 255, 285, 308, 316, 317, 328, 331, 335-337, 350, 355, 363, 367-369, 372, 378, 384, 386, 391-397
Nelson Law, 332
Nelson, Knute, 114, 125, 127, 130, 133 230, 251
Netherlands, 8
Nett Lake Indians, 194
Nett Lake, 194, 195, 198, 199, 203, 205, 208, 209, 222
New Amsterdam, 8
New Deal, 234
New Netherlands, 8
New Ulm, 67, 68, 71-74
New York City, 235
New York, 1, 6, 33, 59, 97, 235, 424
Nicholas V, Catholic Pope, 5
Nichols, David A., 32, 247-249
Nichols, John D., 246
Nicolay, John, 81, 82, 90
Nicollet County, 74
Nicollet, N., 266
Niigaanigwaneb, 81
Nisqually, 425
Nixon, 236
Noble, Secretary of Interior John W., i, 305, 406
Non-removable Mille Lacs Band, 210
Non-Removal Mille Lac Chippewa, 184
Non-removal Mille Lacs Indians, 182, 183, 187, 188
Non-Removal Mille Lacs, viii, xi, xii, 174-176, 181-185, 187-189, 193-195, 198, 203-205, 208, 241, 242, 251
North Star, 53, 267, 274, 279
Northern Fur Company, 31
Northern Indians, 59
Northern Outfit, 30, 31
Northern Pacific R.R. Co. (ALSO Northern Pacific Railroad Co., Northern Pacific Railroad Company, Northern Pacific Railway), 158, 364, 382
Northern Pacific R.R. Co. v. Walters, 364, 382
Northwest Commission, 137
Northwest Ordinance, 27, 129, 248
Northwest Territory, 27
Norway, 200, 334, 380

Index • 435

O

O-be-gwa-dans, 265
O-ge-ma-ga, 265
O-ge-ma-way-che-waib, 279
O-ge-mah-woub, 144
O-ge-mah, Chief, 140, 141
O-Gee-tub, 279
Obama, President Barrac, 243
Ocha-sua-sepe, 263
Office of Indian Affairs, i, 28, 31, 162, 190, 221, 242, 418, 426
Ogechie Lake, 9-11, 246
Ogechie, 9-11, 246
Ohio River, 12
Ohio, 12, 31, 32, 340
Ojibway, 4, 10, 13, 30, 245, 246
Ojibwe, 1-4, 10, 11, 16-26, 30, 79-82, 210, 246
Old Northwest, 30
Old Settlers vs. United States, 298, 309, 312, 365, 385, 411
Onamia, 184, 190, 194, 203, 204, 205
One Standing Ahead, 279
One Who Knows, 43
Oneida County, 6
Oneida Indian Nation of New York, 6, 243
Oneida, 6, 243, 425
Oneida County v. Oneida Indian Nation, 6
Onigum, 194, 199
Ontanagon, 422
Oregon Land Co., 297
Otherday, John, 70
Ottawa Indian, 80
Otter Lake, 358
Otter Tail Lake, 46
Otter Tail Pillager, 141
Ottertail City, 24

P

Pa-ga-we-we-wetung, 265
Pa-goo-na-kee-zhig (ALSO Pagoonakeezhig), 36, 265
Pa-qua-a-mo, 265
Pa-se-quam-jis, 265
Pa-zo-i-yo-pa, 64

Parker, Commissioner of Indian Affairs Ely S., 98, 100, 101-104, 249, 250
Passes Under Everything (ALSO Passeth Under Everything), 63, 225, 267, 274, 279
Patents-in-fee, 196, 223
Pay-ajik, 265
Payment Point, 142, 143
Pe-dud-ence, 279
Pe-zhe-ke, 265
Pe-zhe-kins, 265
Pe-zhe-kr, 265
Pedudense, 63
Peelie, Chief Justice Stanton J., 313
Peelle, Chief Justice Stanton J., 171, 328, 353, 354
Peltier, Charles, 100, 249
Pembina Chippewa Bands, 134, 136, 282, 305, 307, 358, 373, 391, 393
Penn, William, 8
Pennsylvania, 8, 20, 290
Pequette, F. H., 188
Petaga Point Archeological Site, 9, 246
Petaga Point, 9, 246
Petud-dunce, 267, 273
Philadelphia, 11, 290
Philp, Kenneth R., 235, 255
Pierce, Ira H., 105, 114
Pierce, President Franklin, 42, 60
Pierre Chouteau Company of St. Louis, 30, 31
Pilgrims, 8
Pillager Chippewa, 35, 42
Pillager Ojibwe, 23
Pillager, xii, 23, 35, 42, 44, 46, 51, 52, 57, 59, 60, 83, 87, 139, 141, 142, 169, 225, 238, 247, 249, 256, 267, 269, 270, 272-276, 279, 280, 282, 300, 301, 307, 317, 358, 365, 372, 373, 387
Pin-de-ga-ge-Shie, 226
Pindr Ga, 227
Pine County, 168, 177, 187-189, 202, 205
Pine Point, 139, 141

Pine Ridge, 424
Pinta, 7
Pioneer Press, 125
Pipestone, 422
Pish-ka-ga-ghe, 265
Plover Portage, 263
Plymouth Rock, 8
Po-ke-ga-ma, 279
Pojoaque, 423
Pokagomin Lake (ALSO Pokagomon Lake), 93, 127, 169, 170, 225, 268, 275, 280, 300, 301, 317, 325, 356, 372
Pokagomin, 93, 127, 169, 170, 225, 275, 276, 280, 281, 300, 301, 317, 325, 356, 372
Polk, President, 22
Pope, General John, 76, 77
Porter, Frank, 176
Potawatomi, 421, 425
Potter Valley, 421
Potter, William, 185
Poughkagemie, 88, 91
Powell, Justice, 6
Prairie Island, 422
Preemption Act, 64
Prescott, Philander, 67, 68
Price, Commissioner of Indian Affairs Hiram, 109-111, 121, 123, 125, 251, 404
Price, David, 4
Princeton, 98, 100, 101, 115, 227, 249
Proposition IV, 336
Public Lands, 106, 114, 288, 340, 341, 343, 346, 347, 364, 372, 379, 381-383, 392-394, 396, 399, 406
Public Law, 1
Pug-gwon-ay-ge-shig, 151
Pug-o-na-ke-shick, 267, 269
Puritans, 8
Pyramid Lake, 422

Q

Quay, 226
Que-we-sans-ish, 267, 273
Que-ze-zance, 284
Qui-we-shen-shish, 279

Quileute, 425
Quinaielt, 425
Quinn, Patrick, 35
Quinn, Peter, 266

R

R-che-o-sau-ya, 265
Rabbit Lake, 24, 80, 87, 93, 127, 143, 169, 170, 225, 268, 275, 276, 279-281, 300, 301, 317, 325, 356, 372
Rabbit River, 268
Rainey Lake (ALSO Rainy Lake), 13, 85, 267
Raining Wind, 279
Rainy Lake River, 267
Rait, James M., 187
Raiter, Dr. Franklin S., 194
Ralette, Joseph, 29
Ramsey Crooks, 30, 31
Ramsey, Governor Alexander, 23, 25, 31-33, 72-74, 76, 77, 387
Range, N., 114
Rats Liver, 265
Raw-be-mow, 83
Red Bird, 279
Red Bird v. U.S., 297
Red Blanket Woman, 29
Red Cedar Lake, 266
Red Cliff, 425
Red Lake Chippewa, 83, 132, 134, 175
Red Lake Ojibwe, 16
Red Lake Reservation, 131, 150, 164, 172, 199, 214, 259, 281, 286, 287, 307, 330, 337, 339, 350, 355, 379, 380, 391, 412, 413,
Red Lake River, 281
Red Lake, 16, 46, 83, 99, 100, 122, 131, 132, 134-138, 150, 158, 163, 164, 172, 175, 199, 202, 205, 208, 209, 211, 214-216, 240, 242, 259, 266, 281, 282, 285-287, 302, 305, 307, 328, 330, 337, 339, 350, 355, 358, 373, 378-380, 387, 391-393, 412, 422

Red Lakers, 137
Red Middle Voice, 64, 65, 67, 75, 79, 80
Red River Valley, 30, 74
Red River, 13, 30, 74, 75, 268, 387
Redwood Agency, 67
Redwood Valley, 421
Redwood, 67, 70, 421
Regiment of Minnesota Volunteers, 73
Rejeke, 44
Removal Mille Lac (ALSO Removal Mille Lacs), 176, 180, 184, 189, 193-195, 198, 209, 241
Removal of Indians, 28, 42, 287
Removal of the Indians From Mille Lac, 363
Reno-Sparks, 423
Renville Rangers, 70, 71
Renville Sr., Joseph, 19
Repatriation Act, 1
Report of Commissioner of Indian Affairs, 306, 307
Report of Secretary of Interior, 387
Republican Party, 126
Resting Feather, 22
Returning Echo, 279
Revolutionary War, 17, 35, 129, 237
Rhode Island, 8
Rice Creek, 65
Rice Lake Reservations, 93, 225, 372
Rice Lake, 87, 88, 93, 127, 169, 170, 225, 268, 275, 276, 279-281, 300, 301, 317, 325, 356, 372, 374
Rice Maker (ALSO Ricemaker), 63, 273, 279
Rice River, 268, 281
Rice Treaty, 163
Rice, Henry Mower, xii, 25, 31, 53, 56, 59, 63, 77, 93, 131, 133, 135-137, 138-140, 143, 144-147, 148, 151-154, 157, 164, 166, 168, 175, 211, 212, 213, 216, 229-233, 238-240,
249, 255, 275, 278, 279, 326, 330
Rice, Senator Henry M., 32, 57, 63, 92, 93, 157, 175, 230, 326
Rice, Susan, 243
Richardson, C. E., 361, 410
Richardson, Nathan, 109, 226
Riggs, Reverend Stephen (ALSO Stephan), 70, 76
Roadman, Dr. Ira M., 194
Roadman, Dr. O. M., 184
Robbins, D. H., 124, 184, 188
Roberts, Joseph, 100, 108, 249, 250
Roberts, Ry. V., 343
Rodwell, Dr. Thomas F., 194
Roosevelt, President Theodore, 157, 236
Ross, P., 274
Roy, Peter, 44, 274, 279, 284
Ruffee, Indian Agent for the Chippewas C. A., 118
Rule of Warfare, 3
Rum River, 9-11, 246, 270
Runs Against Something When Crawling, 64
Russell, William H., 32

S

Sa-ga-ta-gun, 265
Sac and f. Indians v. Sac & F. Indians, 364, 385, 411, 421
Sacred Heart Creek, 69
Saint Paul, 289, 290
Salazar, 210
Salem, 424
Salish, 422
San Antonio, 233
Sandstone, 177
Sandy Lake Band of Ojibwe, 210
Sandy Lake Indian Reservation, 210, 283, 318, 374
Sandy Lake Indians, 143
Sandy Lake River, 268
Sandy Lake, 16-19, 25, 30, 35, 61, 84, 85, 87, 88, 90, 91, 93-96, 127, 143, 158,

169, 170, 210, 225, 265, 268, 275, 276, 279-281, 283, 300, 301, 317, 318, 325, 356, 372, 374
Sandy Lakers, 17, 19, 93
Sandy Lakes, 84
Santa Maria, 7
Santee Sioux, 32, 424
Satterlee, Marion P., 74
Satz, Ronald N., 246
Sauk Center, 72
Sault St. Marie, 1
Sault Ste, 17, 18, 29, 229
Savages, xi, 3, 4, 43, 44, 157, 245
Scalping, 3, 4
Scalps, 3, 80
Schall, Congressman Thomas D., 189
Schultz, Duane, 67, 69
Schurz, Secretary of Interior Carl, 108, 109, 250, 402
Scott, Dredd (ALSO Dred Scott), 33, 129, 156, 25
Scott, Martin, 266
Sec & Trust Co. v. D.C., 396
Second Battle of Bull Run, 76
Second Continental Congress, 3
Sells, Commissioner of Indian Affairs Cato, 182, 189, 220
Senate Indian Affairs Committee, 126, 127, 130
Senate Indian Affairs, 126, 127, 130
Seneca Indian, 98
Sha-bosh-chung, Mille Lac Chief (ALSO Shaboshkung, Shah-baush-kung, Shaw-bah-skung, Shaw-bosh-Kung, Shaw-bus-com, Shaw-bus-cum, Shaw-vosh-Kung, Shob-aush-Kung, Shob-osh-kunk), 82, 85, 86, 87, 88, 90, 92, 93, 94, 101, 110, 124, 127, 145, 147, 148, 151, 225-228, 239, 255, 279, 280, 388
Sha-go-bai, 265
Sha-wa-ghe-zhig, 266

Shakopee, Chief, 65, 75
Shar-Vash-King, 110
Shaw-ne-yaw, 101
Shaw, Chief, 99, 157, 232
Shawnee Indian, 13
Shawnees, 340, 344
Sheehan, Lt., 71
Sherman, John, 32
Sherrill, City of, 6
Shields, Assistant Attorney General George H., 213
Shing-go-be, 266
Shipstead, Senator Henrick, 199, 200
Sho-bos-cum, 83
Sho-ne-a, 266
Show-baush-king, 267, 274
Shuler, Indian Agent B.P., 132, 135, 142, 144, 146, 147, 212
Sibley, Colonel, 73, 74
Sibley, Henry Hastings, 29, 30-32, 72, 230
Simmons, J., 109
Sioux Indians, 9, 67, 76, 78
Sioux Nation, 9
Sioux Uprising, xi, 25, 63, 64, 72, 79, 83, 85, 98, 247
Sioux War, 369, 375
Sissetons, 70
Six Nations of New York, 1
Skinaway, 210
Slattery, Dr. Peter A., 194
Slaughter Slough, 72
Slavery, 42, 130, 156
Slayton, 71
Smallpox, 29
Smith Creek, 69
Smith, Caleb B., 32
Smith, Captain John, 8
Smith, Commissioner of Indian Affairs John Q., 102, 106, 250
Smith, E. P., 117
Smith, General W. R., 35
Smith, Henry, 4
Smith, Indian Agent, 102-105, 114, 117
Smith, P., 101, 117, 250
Smithsonian Institute, 22

Snake River, 35, 39, 95, 122, 124, 136, 168, 176, 241, 265, 267, 378
Snelling, Colonel Josiah, 17
Soldiers Lodge, 64, 65
Songa-ko-mig, 265
Sounding Sky, 266
South Bend, 74
Spalding v. Chandler, 297, 310, 312, 321, 343
Spalding v. Chandler, supra, 343
Squaw Lake, 199
St Croix, 19, 20, 35, 263, 265
St. Cloud, 72, 178-181
St. Croix Ojibwe, 19
St. Croix River, 35, 263, 265
St. Croix, 19, 20, 35, 263, 265
St. Joseph, 72
St. Lawrence River, 1
St. Louis River, 267
St. Mary, 1
St. Paul Daily, 200
St. Paul, 24, 26, 30, 31, 62, 76, 79, 82, 85, 100, 101, 104, 105, 108, 115, 199, 200, 205, 230, 233, 249, 250
St. Peter Sibley, 73
St. Peter, 29, 70, 71, 73, 74
St. Peters Agency, 35
St. Peters, 35, 41, 263, 265, 266
Stambaugh, S. C., 266
Steele, General James, 29
Steele, Sarah Jane, 29
Steenerson Act, 216
Stepping Ahead, 267, 274
Stewart, J. M., 208, 242
Stewart v. U.S., 297, 385, 315, 364
Stock, J. F., 105, 115
Stone v. United States, 314
Stowe, Harriet Beecher, 245
Striped Cloud, 30
Stone v. U.S., 297, 309
Strong Ground, 265
Strout, Richard, 75
Sturgeon Man, 143
Sturgis, 70, 73
Stuyvesant, Peter, 8

Sugar Point, 16
Sungigodan, 64
Supreme Court, ix, xii, 33, 129, 156, 171, 175, 191, 202, 210, 238, 241, 243, 256, 293, 294, 299, 309, 313, 328, 329, 358, 359, 362, 369-371, 409
Swamp Lake, 242
Swamp Lands, 104, 105, 114
Swan Lake, 35

T

Ta-qua-ga-na, 265
Taliaferro, Indian Agent Major Lawrence, 17-20, 266
Taney, Chief Justice Roger, 33, 156
Tanner, Acting Commissioner of Indian Affairs A.C., 177
Tanner, Helen, 246
Tanner, John, xi, 12, 13, 15, 80, 246
Taos Pueblo, 235
Taos, 235, 423
Tay-bway-wain-dung, 153
Taylor Falls Land Office, 105
Taylor, President Zachary, 96
Taylors Falls Office, 103, 104
Taylors Falls, 103, 104, 250, 376, 382, 398, 401
Te-daw-kaw-mo-say, 279
Teller, DOI Secretary, 251
Teller, Henry, 111, 251
Territorial Legislature, 57
Territory of Minnesota, 57, 267, 268
Territory of Wisconsin, 41, 263, 265
The Assassination of Hole-in-the-Day, 16
The Ethnohistory, 247
The Homeless Non-Removal Mille Lacs, viii, xi, xii, 174, 175, 182, 183, 187, 188, 205, 241, 242, 251
The Mille Lac Reservation, 101, 104, 107, 114, 115, 118-120, 122, 123, 126, 127, 130, 134, 149-151, 157, 159, 162-164, 166, 167, 169-173, 175, 177, 191, 198, 208, 212, 231, 232, 239-241, 243, 294-296, 300-304, 306-313, 316-320, 322-332, 334, 335, 337-340, 343, 344, 346, 347, 349, 355-357, 360, 361, 371, 372, 374, 375, 377, 378, 380-386, 390, 393, 394, 400, 402, 405, 410, 414-416
The Sioux, viii, xi, 9, 10, 13, 14, 21, 25, 31, 32, 34, 63-65, 67-77, 79-81, 83-85, 89, 93, 98, 99, 129, 138, 144, 230, 238, 246, 247, 263, 323, 356, 369, 374, 375
The United States, Appellant v. The Mille Lac Band of Chippewa Indians, 370
Thief River, 281
Thomas, Senator Elmer, xii, 195, 206, 242, 256, 418, 426
Thompson, Agency Superintendent Clark W., 24, 89, 90, 127, 275, 278-280, 283, 284
Thompson, James, 279
Tillson v. U.S., 297, 309, 314
Time O Day Store, 204
Timms Creek, 69
Traveling Hail, 66
Travelling Sky, 279
Treuer, Anton, 16, 17, 20, 21, 23, 79, 82, 96, 245, 247-249
Tribal Law, 243
Trout Lake, 143
Tug-o-na-ke-shick, 273
Turtle Lake, 268, 281
Turtle River, 269
Two Lodges Meeting, 265
Two Routes Lake (ALSO Two-Routes Lake), 276, 281

U

U. S. Army, 266
U. S. Indian Agent Chippewa Agency, 249
U. S. Indian Agent, 161, 167, 176, 249, 407, 408
U. S. Indian Inspector, 161, 165, 167, 176, 407, 408
U. S. Interpreter, 43, 153, 266
U. S. Military Academy, 76
U. S. Sub-Indian Agent, 266
U. S. Supreme Court Decision, xii
U. S. Supreme Court, xii, 33, 156, 409
Uncle Tom, 245
United States Army, 229
United States Brief, xii
United States Commissioners, 323
United States Congress, 230
United States Constitution, 237, 243, 244
United States Court of Claims, ix, 169
United States District Attorney, 191
United States Government, viii, 83, 170, 216, 230-232, 323, 327
United States of America, 3, 5, 8, 130, 183, 263, 285
United States Senate, 82, 125, 230, 418
United States Supreme Court, ix, 33, 129, 171, 175, 202, 210, 241, 243, 256
United States Treasury, 132, 230, 295, 300, 302, 303, 308, 311, 334, 338, 344, 355
United States v. Binns, 367, 392
United States v. Blackfeather, 297, 312, 340
United States v. Blackfeather, supra, 344
United States v. Carpenter, 298, 312, 332, 343
United States vs. Carpenter, supra, 343
United States v. Cherokee Nation, 298, 312
United States v. Choctaw and Chickasaw Nations, 365, 385

Index • 439

United States v. Choctaw Nation, 310, 317. 411
United States v. Cook, 321, 347, 368
United States v. Hartwell, 368, 396
United States v. Choctaw, etc., Nation, 298
United States v. Mille Lacs Band of Chippewa Indians, 185, 409
United States v. Minnesota, 209
United States v. Mille Lac Band, 209
United States v. Old Settlers, 298, 309, 312, 365, 385, 411
United States v. Thomas, 298
United States v. Winans, 298
United States v. Schurz, 368, 395
United States v. Thomas, 310
United States v. Winans, 310, 322, 325
United States v. Winans, supra, 327
United States, Appt., v. Mille Lac Band of Chippewa Indians in the State of Minnesota, 409
University of Minnesota Law Center, 251
Upper Mississippi Outfit, 31
Upper Mississippi Valley, 31
Upper Peninsula of Michigan, 96
Uran, Jack, 205
Usher, John Palmer, 84
Usher, Secretary of Interior John P., 84

V

Van Antwerp, Harman, 266
Van Antwerp, Ver Planck (Also Verplanck), 35, 266
Van Buren, President, 34
Venison, 109
Vermillion Lake, 305
Vermillion River, 267
Vermillion, 152, 199, 267, 305

Vermont, 229
Vespucci, Amerigo, 7
Vigilante Justice, 245
Vineland Lodge, 204
Vineland, 99, 184, 188, 189, 191, 193-195, 203, 205, 210
Vineyard, Miles M., 40, 264, 266
Virginia Company of London, 8
Virginia, 8, 12

W

Wa Boose, 227
Wa-be-ne-me, 265
Wa-bo-geeg, 279
Wa-boo-jig, 265
Wa-bose, 265
Wa-me-te-go-zhins, 266
Wa-shask-ko-kone, 265
Wa-zau-ko-ni-a, 266
Waahoe, 423
Wabasha, 75
Wadena, Chief, 190, 191, 200, 201
Wadsworth, P. R., 189, 190, 193-195
Wah-de-nah, Chief, 138
Wah-tap, 263
Wah-we-yay-cumig, 151, 197
Wah-we-yay-cumig, Chief, 197
Wah-we-yea-cumig, Chief, 176
Wahkon, v, 161, 184
Wahpetons, 70
Walker, Indian Agent Lucius C., 24, 25, 82, 423
Wall Street, 8, 157
Wallblom, Charles, 226, 227
Wallblom, Mathilda, 227
Walleyes, 238
Walters, 364, 368, 377, 381, 382
Walters, Amanda J., 381
Wand-e-kaw, 267
War Department, 28
War Powers, 243
Warren, Annie C., 226
Warren, Eugene J., 185

Warren, Henry W., 185
Warren, Lyman M., 30, 36, 41, 264, 266
Warren, T. A., 274
Warren, William W., 2, 4, 10, 245, 246
Washakie, 425
Washaskkoone, Mille Lacs Chief, 36
Washington Office of Indian Affairs, 190
Washington, President George, 27, 59, 129
Waud-e-kaw, 273
Way-ke-ge-ke-shie, 226
Way-me-tig-ozhence, 143
Way-sa-wa-gwon-aib, 279
Way-she-ge-skie-go-gua (ASLO Way-She-ye-Shic-go-gua), 226
Way-we-yay-cumig, 145
We-we-shan-shis, 265
Weide, Millie M., 228
Weisner, Louis, 104
Wen-ghe-ge-she-guk, 265
West Savannah River, 268
Western Outfit, 29, 30
Westwood, Assistant Solicitor Charlotte T., 208
Wet Month, 265
Wetherby, 347, 348
Wheeler-Howard Act (ALSO Howard-Wheeler Act, Wheeler-Howard Bill, Wheeler-Howard Law) 206, 207, 235
Wheeler, George A., 100, 249
Wheeler, Montana Senator Burton, 235, 236
Whipple, Bishop George, 102, 123, 124, 130, 250
Whipple, Bishop Henry Benjamin, 6, 25, 27, 28, 33, 74, 80, 82, 97, 99, 100, 247, 248
White Cloud, Chief, 135, 137, 138
White Crow, 265
White Earth Agency, i, 178, 179, 184, 189, 218, 220-222

White Earth Band, 137, 143, 242
White Earth Boarding School, 222
White Earth Chippewas, 223
White Earth Indian School, 183
White Earth Lake, 374
White Earth Land Suit Settlement Cases, 221
White Earth Reservations, 131, 214, 302
White Earth School, 182
White Earth Superintendent, 193
White Fisher, 265, 279
White Oak Point Indians, 142, 143
White Oak Point Reservation, 118, 143, 198
White Oak Point, 118, 135, 136, 142, 143, 185, 198, 305, 306, 358, 377
White Point, 377
White Rice, 232
White Thunder, 265
White, Chief Justice Edward Douglas, 321, 342, 347, 348
White, S. H., 279
Whitehead, James, 279
Whites, 13, 20, 24-26, 43-49, 51-58, 62, 64, 65, 67, 69, 70, 75, 79, 82, 84, 85, 87-89, 91-93, 99, 101, 106, 112, 113, 115-119, 122, 123, 126, 133, 135, 141, 145-149, 165, 170, 278, 283, 295, 301, 304, 308, 310, 317-319, 322-325, 329, 356, 371, 373, 375, 378, 381, 387-389, 391, 393, 399, 402, 403, 405, 406, 411, 412
White v. Wright, 298, 311, 331
Whiting, 131, 132, 135, 142-144, 151-154, 211, 231, 232, 279, 330

Whiting, Commissioner C., 132, 135, 142-144, 152, 153, 231, 232, 279
Whiting, Joseph B., 131, 151, 154
Whiting, Joseph R., 330
Whitney, Joel Emmons, 46, 65
Wigwam Bay, 195
Wild Rice River, 268
Wild Rice, 1, 41, 122, 138, 143, 146, 200, 218, 242, 246, 264, 268
Wilkinson, 32, 82
Wilkinson, Minnesota Senator Morton S., 82
Wilkinson, Senator Morton, 32
Williams, Roger, 8
Williamson, Dr. Thomas, 70
Williamson, J. A., 250
Williamsport, 290
Wilson, Woodrow, 220
Winans, 298, 310, 322, 325, 327
Winne-pe-go-shish, 279
Winnebago (ALSO Winnebagoes, Winnebagos), 20, 30, 31, 34, 61, 74, 83, 230, 422
Winnebagoshish (ALSO Winnebegoshish, Winnebigoshish), 51, 93, 136, 139, 142, 225, 247, 249, 305
Winner, 279
Winneshiek, 52, 53
Winnibegoshish Ojibwe, 23
Winnibegoshish Reservation, 185
Winnibigoshish Lake, 372
Winnibigoshish (ALSO Winnibegoshish), xii, 23, 44, 46, 87, 169, 185, 256, 267, 269-276, 280, 300, 301, 307, 317, 358, 365, 372, 373, 387

Wisconsin Indians, 20, 35, 36, 238
Wisconsin Territory, 34, 238
Wisconsin, 16, 20, 21, 23, 29, 34-36, 41, 65, 96, 138, 153, 204, 238, 263, 265, 276, 290, 425
Wood Forte Reservation, 380
Wood Lake, 75
Wood Pecker, 265
Wooster, Dr., 197, 201
Worcester, 298, 310, 327, 328, 347
Worcester v. Georgia, 298, 310, 327, 347
Worcester v. United States, 328
Worden, 297, 310, 321
World War I, 220
Wright, John, 125
Wright, Reverend Charles, 137
Wright, Special Agent John A., 123

Y

Ya-banse, 265
Yellow Feather, 279
Yellow Medicine Agency, 70
Yellow Medicine, 67, 70
Yellow Robe, 266
Yerington, 423
Young Buck, 265
Young Buffalo, 265
Young John, 12, 13
Young Man, 13, 15, 16, 18, 19, 64, 66, 80, 196, 267, 273, 279
Young-man, 44

Z

Zimmerman, Assistant Commissioner of Indian Affairs William, 206

www.ingramcontent.com/pod-product-compliance
Lightning Source LLC
Chambersburg PA
CBHW022210090526
44584CB00012BA/366